FROM BLACK GOLD TO
FROZEN GAS

CENTER ON GLOBAL ENERGY POLICY SERIES

CENTER ON GLOBAL ENERGY POLICY SERIES

Jason Bordoff, series editor

Making smart energy policy choices requires approaching energy as a complex
and multifaceted system in which decision makers must balance economic,
security, and environmental priorities. Too often, the public debate is dominated
by platitudes and polarization. Columbia University's Center on Global Energy
Policy at SIPA seeks to enrich the quality of energy dialogue and policy by
providing an independent and nonpartisan platform for timely analysis and
recommendations to address today's most pressing energy challenges. The Center
on Global Energy Policy Series extends that mission by offering readers
accessible, policy-relevant books that have as their foundation the academic rigor
of one of the world's great research universities.

FROM BLACK GOLD TO FROZEN GAS

How Qatar Became an Energy Superpower

Michael D. Tusiani

with

Anne-Marie Johnson

Columbia University Press

New York

Columbia University Press
Publishers Since 1893
New York   Chichester, West Sussex
cup.columbia.edu

Library of Congress Cataloging-in-Publication Data
Names: Tusiani, Michael D., author. | Johnson, Anne-Marie (Journalist), author.
Title: From black gold to frozen gas : how Qatar became an energy superpower /
    Michael D. Tusiani with Anne-Marie Johnson.
Description: New York : Columbia University Press, [2023] | Includes bibliographical
    references and index.
Identifiers: LCCN 2023003149 (print) | LCCN 2023003150 (ebook) |
    ISBN 9780231210867 (hardback) | ISBN 9780231558624 (ebook)
Subjects: LCSH: Petroleum industry and trade—Qatar. | Energy industries—Qatar.
Classification: LCC HD9578.Q37 T87 2023 (print) | LCC HD9578.Q37 (ebook) |
    DDC 338.2/7280095363—dc23/eng/20230418
LC record available at https://lccn.loc.gov/2023003149
LC ebook record available at https://lccn.loc.gov/2023003150

Cover design: Milenda Nan Ok Lee
Cover photo: GagliardiPhotography © Shutterstock

This book is dedicated to the memory of my brother, Joseph, who a month before he passed away in 2020 at age 96 read through the entire draft of this manuscript despite having had a stroke and poor eyesight. He found numerous misspellings and incorrect grammar and made valuable suggestions for improvement. Joseph guided me through life.

—Michael D. Tusiani

To Ian Seymour, who as the highly respected editor in chief of the *Middle East Economic Survey* chronicled the golden age of OPEC and every major oil and gas event in the region during the tumultuous years of the 1960s, 1970s, 1980s, and 1990s. I am forever grateful to Ian for his mentorship during my time at *MEES*.

And to Rowan and Molly, the loves of my life.

—Anne-Marie Johnson

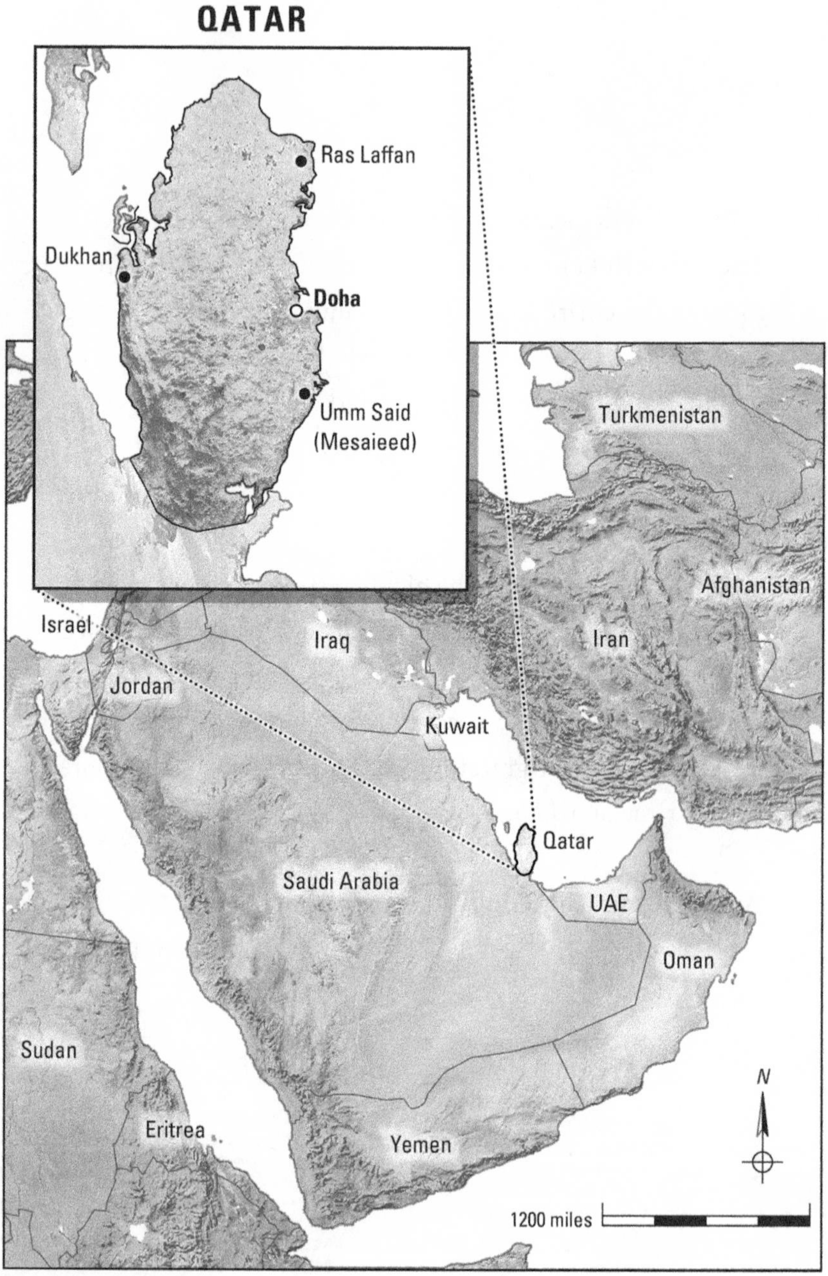

QATAR

Ras Laffan

Dukhan

Doha

Umm Said
(Mesaieed)

Israel

Jordan

Iraq

Iran

Turkmenistan

Afghanistan

Kuwait

Qatar

Saudi Arabia

UAE

Oman

Sudan

Eritrea

Yemen

N

1200 miles

0.1 Map of Qatar.

Drawn by Ron Weickart.

Contents

Foreword

LUCIO A. NOTO

Former vice chairman, ExxonMobil, and former chairman and CEO, Mobil Corporation

QatarEnergy plans to become the world's leading exporter of liquefied natural gas (LNG) and dominate LNG trade for decades to come. On February 8, 2021, the company announced it was proceeding with an almost $30 billion investment to expand its North field LNG production capacity by nearly 45 percent, to 110 million tons per year—an impressive expansion which QatarEnergy called "the largest LNG capacity addition ever." But this announcement was important for reasons beyond scale. It culminated in the resumption of Qatar's LNG development, which began in 2017 after more than a decade during which North field work was suspended, motivated primarily for political reasons. At the time, QatarEnergy stated it had concerns about damaging the gas-producing reservoir with excessive drilling and extraction. As is common in Qatar, however, there were backstories involving the country's relations with its larger neighbors. The North field extends across Qatar's maritime border with Iran, where it is known as South Pars. In 2005 South Pars remained largely undeveloped, and suspending North field work may have eased Iranian worries about "drainage"—migration of gas in the subsurface from undrilled, non-producing areas to wells in producing parts of the field—and gave the Islamic Republic time to catch up. For oil and gas projects in the region, diplomacy influences decision-making as much as geology and engineering studies.

From Black Gold to Frozen Gas: How Qatar Became an Energy Superpower probes the decision-making of several generations of leaders in Qatar and the companies and governments doing business with them, tracing the advances and reversals of a poor, desert sheikhdom, reliant on outsiders, as it developed its hydrocarbon resources and eventually became the world's wealthiest country. The book illuminates the complexity of forces shaping the projects that would make Qatar, first, a producer and exporter of crude oil and, later and more importantly, a leading producer and exporter of LNG, natural gas liquids, fertilizer, and petrochemicals. Those forces included geopolitical pressures on Qatar from expansionist neighbors and global superpowers, economic stresses from oil and gas market gyrations and mechanical setbacks, competitive maneuvering among expatriate companies, and internal strains from royal family rivalries. I can attest that this was the mercurial context for every business decision made during Qatar's emergence as an energy superpower. I experienced it while helping to guide Mobil Corporation into Qatar's emerging LNG industry in the early 1990s as the company's chairman and CEO. Michael Tusiani, a close friend and adviser, was the one who urged me to believe in Qatar and invest in its gas potential. He knew Qatar well as CEO of Poten & Partners, which had been active in the nation since 1974 as a gas and shipping consultant. In retrospect, investing in Qatar was Mobil's best decision. A strong position in Qatar's LNG industry has become ExxonMobil's prize asset. And Tusiani, with his background and access to people and information, is more qualified than anyone I know to chronicle Qatar's fascinating energy history.

Rich as its past, it is a history with more future than past. Qatar is a relatively young country, having become an independent state in 1971. And it only recently brought its ambitions into full view. In 2018, a year after disclosing its intention to revive the development of its North field, QatarEnergy raised its LNG export capacity target to 110 million tons per year. It also jolted the oil-producing world with an announcement that underscored its priorities—the following year it would leave the Organization of Petroleum Exporting Countries (OPEC), to which it had belonged since OPEC's second meeting in 1962. A midlevel oil producer at best, Qatar was aligning its future with its dazzling endowment of natural gas. Furthermore, it was serving notice that it would again become the world's largest exporter of LNG, surpassing both the United States and Australia. Plans do not end there. In a second phase Qatar intends to further expand LNG capacity to 126 million tons per year and has said it is "evaluating further LNG capacity expansions beyond that amount."

As impressively comprehensive about Qatar's past as *From Black Gold to Frozen Gas* is, it also brings the reader to the start of a future promising to be even more interesting. It is a future in which I have full confidence. I have seen Qatar through setbacks and disruptions. I have seen the country wield influence beyond its size with a spirit of determined independence. And I look forward to watching as its gas-based destiny unfolds. For anyone wanting to understand an energy super-power committed to managing its affairs its own way, the information and insights in this book are indispensable.

Preface

MICHAEL D. TUSIANI

My introduction to Qatar came on March 9, 1977, when I first met Dr. Ali Al Kuwari, then the marketing director of the Qatar General Petroleum Co., the country's national oil company, at a liquefied petroleum gas, or LPG, conference I moderated in Saint-Paul-de-Vence, France. He was responsible for the sale of LPG from a newly constructed export facility expected to be completed later that year. Dr. Al Kuwari and I hit it off, and we agreed to meet in Doha the following month to discuss a potential purchase on behalf of a client.

When I arrived at Dr. Al Kuwari's office a month later, he greeted me at the door and said: "Sorry, you've traveled all the way from New York for nothing—there's no LPG to buy, the plant exploded and is gone." My reaction was disbelief. Sadly, it was true. The accident had happened on April 3. While a huge setback for Qatar, the incident nonetheless led to my career-long involvement in the country.

I met many interesting people in Doha and learned a great deal about Qatar's unique way of doing business. There was always intrigue and confusion. It felt as though "wheels within wheels were spinning" in both the public and private sectors. What amazed me the most during those early days was that no one understood, or wanted to understand, the concept of "conflict of interest." Government officials, regardless of rank or position, were allowed to have their own private businesses. They engaged in transactions directly or via family members or friends, even in areas where they had decision-making authority or influence. The politics behind this soon became apparent. I learned the key to success in Qatar, as in other countries in the region, was to identify the primary decision maker on any project and then the individual(s) in his inner circle who could influence the outcome.

Over a span of fifty years, I've had the pleasure to deal with many high- and medium-level Qatari government officials and local businesspeople. The experiences were eye opening and diverse. I witnessed former U.S. vice-president Dan Quayle telephone his counterpart, the Crown Prince, to provide my client, Newport News, a chance to be considered to build ships for Qatargas, the country's first liquefied natural gas, or LNG, export project and entry into a global industry in which Qatar became a leader. This highly qualified shipbuilder had not been invited to bid because of a technicality that was deliberately included in the tender document to eliminate any possible U.S. participation in this Japanese-dominated project. I was delighted when Mobil Oil followed my advice and guidance about entering Qatar's fledgling LNG sector. It was a great achievement for Mobil and continues to be an even bigger success for ExxonMobil.

Given the emphasis on the environment and climate change, natural gas in the form of LNG will continue to serve as the transitional fuel substituting for coal in power generation and supporting the increasing use of renewables. Natural gas emits much less CO_2 than coal and petroleum products, and it complements the intermittency of renewables rather than competing with them. This will be the case until large, utility-scale battery technology is developed that proves to be economical. Worldwide LNG demand has grown from just 2 million tons per year in 1970 to 103 annually in 2000 and 357 million tons in 2020, when—absent the COVID-19 pandemic—it would have reached 375 million. Demand is projected to surpass 535 million tons per year by 2030 and 575 million tons annually by 2035. Currently among the world's top three LNG exporters, Qatar is preparing to supply over 25 percent of global supply—an amazing amount given that Saudi Arabia accounts for about 15 percent of global oil exports.

Keeping everyone constantly guessing and pitting one person or company against the other to create uncertainty rather than clarity seems to be the country's modus operandi on all levels—political and commercial. For many years Qatar was seen as a small and rather insignificant nation. The insecurity this generated forced the country to forge its own identity apart from its larger and often more powerful neighbors. In the process, Qatar's leaders made what many considered to be unconventional and controversial political decisions. Sitting on top of one of the world's largest gas reserves was no doubt luck, but Qatar learned how to leverage this largesse to its best advantage. With a vision for future generations, it invested heavily in education and human capital. There will continue to be bumps in the road, but more success will undoubtedly follow. Qatar—home to only 3 million people, barely more than 10 percent of whom are nationals—knows it doesn't need enemies even if it has repeatedly demonstrated that it is not afraid to chart an independent path if its self-interests dictate. With determined independence and global ambition, it has indeed found its identity, its place in the region, and its destiny in the world.

Abbreviations

ADMA	Abu Dhabi Marine Areas Limited
API	American Petroleum Institute gravity
Aramco	Arabian American Oil Company
Btu	British thermal unit
CDF-Chimie	Charbonnages de France-Chimie
CFP	Compagnie française des pétroles
CNOOC	China National Offshore Oil Corporation
Conoco	Continental Oil
CPC	China Petroleum Corporation
E&GSynd	Eastern & General Syndicate
Enel	Ente nazionale per l'energia elettrica
Eni	Ente nazionale idrocarburi
GCC	Gulf Cooperation Council
GTL	gas-to-liquids
HBJ	Hamad Ibn Jassim Ibn Jabir Al Thani
ICC	International Chamber of Commerce
ICJ	International Court of Justice
IMF	International Monetary Fund
IOL	International Octane Ltd.
IPC	Iraq Petroleum Company
LIBOR	London Inter-Bank Offered Rate
LNG	liquefied natural gas
LPG	liquid petroleum gas
MTBE	methyl tertiary-butyl ether
NEDC	Near East Development Corporation

NGL	natural gas liquid
NGL-1	1977–1980 project
NGL-2	second NGL project
NNG	Northern Natural Gas Company
NODCO	National Oil Distribution Company
OPEC	Organization of Petroleum Exporting Countries
PCL	Petroleum Concessions Limited
PDQ	Petroleum Development (Qatar) Limited
QAFCO	Qatar Fertilizer Company
QAPCO	Qatar Petrochemical Company
QASCO	Qatar Steel Company
QDR	Qatar-Dubai riyal
QE	QatarEnergy
QGC	Qatar Gas Company Limited
QGPC	Qatar General Petroleum Corporation
QNB	Qatar National Bank
QNPC	Qatar National Petroleum Company
QP	Qatar Petroleum
QPC	Qatar Petroleum Company
QPPA	Qatar Petroleum Producing Authority
QVC	Qatar Vinyl Company
RAF	Royal Air Force
SIPM	Shell internationale petroleum maatschappij B.V.
Socal	Standard Oil of California
Socony	Standard Oil of New York
Sohio	Standard Oil Company of Ohio
TPC	Turkish Petroleum Company
UAE	United Arab Emirates

Introduction

"They don't like our independence. They see it as a threat." That was the blunt assessment of Qatari amir Tamim Ibn Hamad Al Thani in a 2017 interview as he summed up the reasoning behind the air, land, and sea embargo imposed on his nation by the United Arab Emirates (UAE), Saudi Arabia, Bahrain, and Egypt on June 5 of that year.[1] Today the sun-scorched peninsula of barren hills that one Victorian adventurer described as bleak, monotonous, and dreary is a fabulously wealthy petrostate and elite gas supplier with the highest per capita income in the world, gleaming cityscapes of glass and steel, and an independent streak that has annoyed its larger neighbors to the south and east for years.[2] Riyadh and Abu Dhabi—as well as their allies in Manama and Cairo—accused Doha of crimes ranging from supporting Egypt's banned Muslim Brotherhood and other Islamist groups to financing terrorism, harboring dissidents, and cozying up to Saudi Arabia's regional archrival Iran. Not to mention its support of Al Jazeera, the Arabic television and media empire launched in 1996 by the amir's father, Sheikh Hamad Ibn Khalifa Al Thani. Al Jazeera's critical coverage of events has been a constant irritant to Qatar's neighbors, even if it has been more circumspect in its reporting at home than it has abroad.

The 2017 attempt to chasten Qatar was not the first blockade or embargo the emirate has suffered through, although it proved to be the most ineffectual, given the country's nearly infinite ability to buy its way out of any supply disruptions or discomfort to its citizenry. The embargo—which Al Jazeera dubbed the "Game of Thobes" in punning reference to the television series and ankle-length garments worn by men in the Arabian Peninsula—was finally lifted on January 5, 2021. There were no concessions from Qatar, and it emerged from the

0.2 Sheikh Tamim Ibn Hamad Al Thani, r. 2013–present.
Source: Government Communication Office, State of Qatar, https://www.gco.gov.qa/wp-content
/uploads/2021/01/hh-1-360x488.png.

forty-three-month blockade with an arguably stronger economy and an even
more independent foreign policy. There are echoes of the past in this resilience:
The Ottoman Turks blockaded Doha from sea and land in 1893, only to be van-
quished by Jassim Ibn Mohammad Al Thani, the sheikh widely regarded as the
father of modern Qatar. Bahrain imposed an even more bruising trade and
travel embargo on then dirt-poor Qatar in 1937 following a skirmish over the
contested town of Zubara in northwest Qatar, only lifting it in 1944 after a
British-brokered truce restored the status quo at Zubara without resolving its
sovereignty. Qatar's first oil discovery at Dukhan was still three years away when
that blockade was imposed, while commercial production wouldn't begin for

more than a decade. The peninsula had long been dependent on more prosperous Bahrain for its imports, making it vulnerable to economic attack.

Saudi Arabia had chafed at the go-it-alone approach Qatar carved out even before Sheikh Hamad, then the crown prince (now known as the Father Amir) overthrew his father in a bloodless coup in 1995. Qatar's foreign policy started to diverge from its Arab neighbor in the late 1980s as it strove to avoid antagonizing Iran over a giant offshore gas field lying between the two countries. The Saudis privately blamed Sheikh Hamad for a violent border clash in 1992, and Riyadh was irritated again in 1994 when he pursued a controversial Qatari gas sale to Israel to enhance the Middle East peace process. This culminated in an economic cooperation agreement with the Jewish state and the opening of an Israeli trade office in the capital city Doha. The embryonic relationship withered soon after Benjamin Netanyahu of Israel's right-wing Likud party was elected prime minister for the first time in 1996. Sheikh Hamad also invited the Americans in, first signing a defense pact with Washington in 1992 and then hosting a major U.S. air base at Al Udeid after the U.S. Air Force vacated its former Saudi Arabian hub in 2003. Al Udeid now houses about ten thousand U.S. military personnel and is the regional headquarters of the U.S. Air Force. Relations with Washington continue to strengthen, with President Joe Biden designating Qatar a major non-NATO ally in January 2022 in recognition of the deepening "strategic partnership" between the two countries.[3] Qatar joins seventeen other countries the United States considers its most reliable partners, a list that includes Japan, Israel, and Australia.[4]

Qatar's perceived transgressions—most recently its support of the Arab Spring uprisings in 2011, its self-anointed role as peacemaker in disputes both near and far, and its enormously elevated profile on the world stage—have annoyed its Arab neighbors. But Doha has its own grievances to nurse, which go back a long way. In 1922 Abdul Aziz Ibn Abdul Rahman Ibn Saud, then amir of Nejd and future king of Saudi Arabia, made a bold-faced attempt to include the whole of the Qatar peninsula in his first oil concession. He was warned off by Sir Percy Cox, the powerful British high commissioner, but Saudi Arabia's designs on Qatar continued. Ibn Saud recognized just a small coastal strip around Doha as Al Thani territory in the lead-up to the 1934 Anglo-Saudi frontier negotiations. It was only after the British agreed to extend their maritime protection guarantee to include attack by land—and by marauding Bedouin tribes who maintained their allegiance to Ibn Saud—that Qatar's ruler, Sheikh Abdullah Ibn Jassim Al Thani, awarded his own oil license to a British company rather than the American one favored by the Saudis. Even then, Ibn Saud threatened to terminate any oil drilling until the question of Qatar's southern border was settled.

Saudi Arabia would later lay claim to the Jebel Dukhan range running down the peninsula's west coast. This was where oil was first discovered in 1939 and the site of Qatar's largest oil field for most of its petroleum history. The claim was vigorously contested by Sheikh Abdullah. After World War II Ibn Saud eventually conceded the hills to Qatar under British pressure. The two countries finally signed a boundary agreement in 1965, but the territorial dispute flared up again in 1992. It was not until 2001 that they finalized their sixty-one-kilometer land border. Nearly one year after Saudi Arabia and the three other blockading states imposed their embargo on Qatar, reports surfaced that Riyadh was fielding offers from at least five bidders to dig a 660-foot-wide canal covering the full length of the border, effectively cutting Qatar off from its only land crossing. Dubbed the Salwa Channel, this navigable waterway would cost about $750 million, split between investors from Saudi Arabia and the UAE. Qatar itself studiously ignored the threat to turn it into an island nation, and the canal ended up being a propaganda ploy.

The development of Qatar's prodigious oil and gas resources—especially its North field, the largest single gas accumulation in the world—has transformed this tiny peninsula of just 11,586 square kilometers into an energy powerhouse, funded its outsized global ambitions, and allowed it to forge a separate identity from its much bigger neighbors. But the road to riches was by no means smooth or speedy. This book chronicles that bumpy journey, from the twists and turns of Qatar's first oil concession to the decades it took to develop the gigantic North field following its unheralded discovery in 1971. It is a story of rivalries, both within the large and unruly Al Thani clan and between international oil companies keen—or not so keen, as was sometimes the case—to cash in on Qatar's natural resources. It is also a story of wily leaders like Sheikh Abdullah, who shrewdly used colonial Britain's obsessive insistence on keeping the Americans out of Qatar to extract the best terms for his oil, and his grandson, Sheikh Khalifa Ibn Hamad Al Thani, whose success in turning largely wasted resources into exportable products like gas liquids, fertilizers, and petrochemicals was overshadowed by the spectacular achievements of his son, Sheikh Hamad.

This story includes the often-fraught process of finding, developing, and producing Qatar's onshore and offshore fields over the sixty-odd years following the first oil discovery at Dukhan. Yet it was not primarily oil that created the wealth evident in the country today. Qatar has never been a large oil producer. Its all-time peak of nearly 900,000 barrels per day was eclipsed many times over by Saudi Arabia and the other big OPEC members. It was North field gas that finally put Qatar on the energy map in the 1990s and in the next decade turned it into the world's largest exporter of the super-chilled gas known as liquefied natural gas, or LNG. That saga is replete with missteps and lost opportunities, personal rivalries, and the near fatal defection of one international oil company following the ouster of another. Even after Doha found a reliable partner in Mobil Corporation, which provided the technical expertise and financial heft to launch Qatar's LNG industry, there were shareholder battles to fight and marketing challenges to overcome before the first multibillion-dollar projects were finally realized.

Amid these struggles, Qatar nearly went bankrupt, hawking its oil production forward to pay its share of expenses for the North field and scrambling to raise funds for other high-profile industrial projects. This became even more difficult after 1995, when Sheikh Hamad overthrew his father and the deposed amir absconded with billions of dollars of state funds. An unsuccessful countercoup, mounted by Sheikh Khalifa's emissaries the following year, soured relations with Saudi Arabia and the UAE still further, as they had tacitly supported the father's attempt to reclaim the throne. Sheikh Hamad's government eventually reached a settlement with the former amir resulting in the return of a large share of the pilfered funds to the treasury in 1997, and father and son ultimately reconciled. The new amir expanded Qatar's already expansive gas development plans despite plunging oil prices and empty coffers, tapping global bond markets for the first time, borrowing from the country's international partners, piling on bank debt, and taking on much more risk than his famously penurious father had allowed. His gamble proved highly successful. Qatar's gross domestic product rose nearly twenty-five-fold between the 1995 coup and 2013, when Sheikh Hamad abdicated in favor of his fourth son, Tamim.

When I started in the energy industry in 1970, Qatar was probably the least interesting of the Gulf countries and the one least likely to become a significant force in the region and the world. It is now an energy behemoth exporting vast amounts of gas, condensates, refined products, petrochemicals, and fertilizers. Qatar also produces steel, iron, and aluminum and is the second-largest supplier of helium in the world. It has expanded its footprint abroad, acquiring oil and gas assets in the Middle East, Africa, the Mediterranean, Latin America, and Canada. With local oil production declining, state-owned Qatar Petroleum (renamed QatarEnergy in 2021) has acquired stakes in emerging exploration acreage in Brazil's pre-salt blocks, unconventional shale resources in Argentina, and sparsely explored basins off Mozambique and deep-sea Southern Africa, working with the likes of ExxonMobil, Shell, Total (now TotalEnergies) and Italy's Eni S.p.A. Qatar has extended its LNG reach into the United States, announcing plans with ExxonMobil to start exporting in 2024 from its majority-owned Golden Pass project in Texas. That deal is likely to lead to further investments in the United States and elsewhere. Qatar is also investing heavily at home, with plans to hike its LNG production capacity to 126 million tons per year from the current 78 million tons per year by 2027. With Washington's European allies scrambling to reduce their dependence on gas imports from Russia in the wake of Moscow's invasion of Ukraine, Qatari officials have said as much as half of this extra output could go to Europe.[5]

What follows is a dedicated history of Qatar's oil and gas development. It traces this tiny country's route from black gold to frozen gas, concentrating on the eight decades from the first exploratory interest by British and American oil companies in the 1920s to the launch of the multibillion-dollar projects that turned Qatar into the largest exporter of LNG in the world shortly after the turn of the century. It is this foundation, painstakingly laid over a span of some eighty years, that would ultimately lead to the energy superpower and tenaciously independent state that is now modern Qatar.

CHAPTER 1

Qatar Before Oil

A Historical Perspective

To have an idea of [Q]atar, my readers must figure to themselves miles on miles of low barren hills, bleak and sun-scorched, with hardly a single tree to vary their dry monotonous outline: below these a muddy beach extends for a quarter of a mile seawards in slimy quicksands, bordered by a rim of sludge and seaweed. If we look landwards beyond the hills, we see what by extreme courtesy may be called pasture land, dreary downs with twenty pebbles for every blade of grass; and over this melancholy ground scene, but few and far between, little cluster of wretched, most wretched, earth cottages and palm-leaf huts, narrow, ugly, and low; these are the villages, or rather the "towns" (for so the inhabitants style them), of [Q]atar.

—William Gifford Palgrave

As the twentieth century dawned, settled life on the Qatar peninsula was no different from what the English adventurer William Palgrave witnessed in 1863 upon entering Bedaa', the principal town of Qatar in what is now modern-day Doha. In 1907 Qatar amounted to a string of poor villages scattered along the coast. Its population of twenty-seven thousand was largely concentrated on the west coast in Doha and Wakrah.[1] Qatar's barren landscape almost completely ruled out agriculture, although there was some limited date palm production as well as camel breeding. The sea, especially pearl-fishing, provided a livelihood for most of the adult male population. The nearby pearl banks were, remarked Palgrave, the most copious in the Persian Gulf and provided "an abundance almost beyond belief of whatever other gifts the sea can offer or bring."[2]

When Palgrave visited Qatar, Mohammed Al Thani was the governor of Bedaa' and the acknowledged head of the province. This notwithstanding, he exerted very little control over the other villages and had no authority whatsoever in the interior, where the Bedouin tribes of the Manaseer and Al Morrah roamed freely, from the frontiers of Al Hasa in modern-day Saudi Arabia to Sharjah in what is now part of the United Arab Emirates. Palgrave noted that Al Thani's principal occupation was extracting the annual tribute from the pearl fisheries. "We are all from the highest to the lowest slaves of one master, Pearl," Al Thani told the Englishman, who observed that the governor seemed more like a businesslike pearl-merchant than an Arab ruler.[3]

The bulk of the collected tribute went to Bahrain's ruling Al Khalifa family, who controlled the port of Zubara on the peninsula's northwest coast and expected yearly payments from Doha. But Bahrain's hold over Qatar was tenuous, particularly after the British replaced Sheikh Mohammed Ibn Khalifa Al Khalifa with his brother Ali following the former's 1867 maritime attack on Qatar.[4] The Bahraini force of seven hundred men and twenty-four boats was joined by two thousand men and seventy boats belonging to Sheikh Zayed Ibn Khalifa of Abu Dhabi, and they utterly destroyed Doha and Wakrah.[5] Great Britain, the predominant maritime power in the Persian Gulf, had paid little attention to Qatar until this attack, dismissing the peninsula as a dependency of Bahrain bound by earlier treaties between the Al Khalifas and the British. When the tribes of Qatar retaliated against Bahrain one year later, Britain's position as peacekeeper in the Gulf was threatened and it was forced to intervene in the dispute.

In 1868, after deposing the Bahraini sheikh in favor of his brother and forcing the Al Khalifas to pay reparations to Qatar, the British political resident in the Persian Gulf, Col. Lewis Pelly, brokered a deal in Wakrah with Mohammed Al Thani. While the agreement was not a formal treaty, Al Thani promised to desist from maritime warfare and refer future tribute disputes to the political resident as the leading British official in the Gulf. He also promised not to ally himself with Bahrain's deposed Mohammed Ibn Khalifa and return to Doha from Khor Hassan in northern Qatar, where he had fled after 1867. Britain did not formally recognize Qatar's independence; in fact, the deal codified its subservience to Bahrain by regulating the tribute paid to the Al Khalifas by the peninsula's various tribes. But the 1868 agreement was significant in that it represented the first British recognition of both Qatar and the leadership of Mohammad Al Thani as the signatory sheikh.

When Mohammed Al Thani died in 1878, his son Jassim was already courting the Ottoman Turks, who controlled the Hijaz and occupied Al Hasa in nearby Nejd in 1871 after pushing out Qatar's Wahabi allies. The younger Al Thani accepted limited Ottoman sovereignty after the Turks established themselves in Al Hasa, probably as a counterweight to the Al Khalifas as the fall of the Wahabis in Al Hasa left Qatar exposed to renewed attack from Bahrain. For the next forty years, Jassim played the Ottomans off against the British while simultaneously keeping the Bahrainis at bay. For its part, Britain never officially acknowledged Ottoman claims to sovereignty over Qatar. But British policy at the time was to preserve the balance of power in Europe, and that meant maintaining the territorial integrity of the Ottoman Empire. Jassim himself was probably unaware of the wider complexities of Anglo-Ottoman relations but undoubtedly recognized the value of pitting the two powers against each other. "His actions often had him walking a tightrope," one historian writes, "but he finally emerged in a far more powerful position than the one he had inherited from his father."[6]

Relations between Jassim and the Ottoman Turks were often strained. In 1893 matters came to a head. An Ottoman force led by the *wali* (governor) of Basra took Jassim's brother Ahmad hostage, blockaded Doha by land and sea, and marched on Wajbah where Jassim had taken refuge. Jassim, by then in his late sixties, rallied his troops and after a fierce fight forced the Ottomans to retreat to a fort in Doha protected by a gunboat. When Jassim cut off the Turks' water supply, they had no alternative but to concede. In exchange for safe passage to Al Hasa for the Ottoman cavalry, Jassim secured his brother Ahmad's release and a full pardon for himself. This defeat is considered a landmark in the history of modern Qatar, solidifying Jassim's authority and prestige, and is still celebrated today.

After 1893 Jassim left his brother Ahmad to rule Doha and his son Abdul Rahman to govern Wakrah. Despite subsequent challenges from Ahmad and his own semiretirement in the oasis of Bu Hasa some twenty kilometers inland from Lusail, Jassim effectively remained the undisputed ruler of Qatar until his death.[7] Reflecting on his first visit to the peninsula to meet Jassim in 1905, the political agent in Bahrain commented that the elderly sheikh, by then in his early eighties and sporting a long gray beard, nonetheless looked much younger than his age. The impression was reinforced when the old man proudly showed off his six-year-old son to the Englishman.[8] Jassim continued to maintain control through family members. When Ahmad was murdered by his servant in 1905, leaving Doha without a leader, Jassim's fourth son, Abdullah, reluctantly agreed to govern the town at his father's insistence.

By the time Jassim died in July 1913, the resurgent Wahabis under the leadership of Abdul Aziz Ibn Abdul Rahman Ibn Saud, the future king of Saudi Arabia, had driven the Turks from Al Hasa. The same month, the Ottoman Empire renounced all rights to Qatar and Bahrain in the Anglo-Turkish Convention, which formally ended Turkish occupation of the peninsula. When the sheikh of Bahrain tried to reassert his claim to tribute from Qatar just two days later, citing the terms of the 1868 agreement, he was informed by the British government that article 10 of the convention had explicitly barred Bahrain from collecting Qatari tribute.[9] Abdullah succeeded Jassim as ruler of the Qatar peninsula, including the fortified settlement of Zubara destroyed by Jassim and his allies in 1878 that would remain the focus of repeated Bahraini claims. He also inherited the family disputes stemming from his ten often dissident brothers as well as those of his cousins, the sons of Ahmad.

The provisions of the Anglo-Turkish Convention were not enacted on the Qatari peninsula until 1915, when the last of the Ottoman troops fled Doha following the arrival of British warships. By this time Britain and Turkey were at war following the outbreak of World War I. The following year Qatar became the ninth and final of the Trucial States, as the littoral sheikhdoms on the southeastern side of the Persian Gulf were then known, to conclude a treaty of protection with Britain. This was signed of November 3, 1916, by Sheikh Abdullah and Maj. Percy Cox, the British political resident and the highest-ranking British official in the Persian Gulf. Doha thus became the capital of the British Protectorate of Qatar.

DAWN OF THE PERSIAN GULF OIL ERA

Such were the conditions on the Qatar peninsula at the dawn of the oil era in the Persian Gulf. This essentially began in 1901, when British entrepreneur William Knox D'Arcy agreed with the shah of Persia to take over "certain existing seepages, worked privately at Shustar, Qasr-i-Shirin and Dalaki."[10] In addition to these named tracts, the sixty-year concession covered the entire Persian Empire except for five northern provinces. Seven years of disappointments later, D'Arcy's team struck commercial oil at Masjid-i-Suleiman in southwest Persia on May 26,

1908. The No. 1 well was drilled to a depth of 1,180 feet and gushed oil that "rose intermittently 75 feet above the level of the ground," according to Britain's chargé d'affaires in Tehran.[11] Less than a year later, D'Arcy and the Glasgow-based Burmah Oil (which provided nearly all the initial capital) formed the Anglo-Persian Oil Company to develop the concession. At the instigation of the Admiralty, eager to ensure fuel for the Royal Navy, which had converted its ships from coal to oil, the British government purchased 51 percent of Anglo-Persian for £2.2 million in 1914.

Because of Britain's power in the Persian Gulf, Anglo-Persian was able to move directly to "examining" Bahrain, Kuwait, the territories of Ibn Saud (then the amir of Nejd) and the Trucial States in what is now the United Arab Emirates.[12] At first there was no attempt by the company to obtain preliminary prospecting licenses from the ruling sheikhs. With the Americans showing interest in oil from Iraq after World War I, however, Anglo-Persian decided it might be prudent to line up such undertakings. Following the Cairo Conference, convened by Colonial Office in 1921 to decide how Britain would control its territories in the Middle East, the company demanded that the British authorities intervene on its behalf.[13] Anglo-Persian asked that the political resident in the Persian Gulf, the highest-ranking British officer in the region, be instructed to personally approach the rulers of the coastal sheikhdoms for exclusive prospecting licenses.[14] In particular, it specified "the Sultan of Muscat, the Trucial Chiefs, the Shaikh of Bahrain, the Amir of Nejd and the Shaikh of Kuwait."[15] But the company did not offer to pay for these prospecting rights, declaring "no payment would become due to the Chiefs in respect of these prospecting licenses."[16]

By early 1923 political resident Lt. Col. Arthur Trevor had lined up "undertakings regarding oil" for Anglo-Persian with the rulers of Ras Al Khaimah, Sharjah, Dubai, Muscat, Abu Dhabi, and Umm Al Quwain along the Trucial coast. These fell short of exploration licenses, however. Two years later only Muscat had a survey agreement in place with the oil company. This was signed on May 26, 1925, with the D'Arcy Exploration Co., a wholly owned prospecting subsidiary of Anglo-Persian set up in 1914. Anglo-Persian and the political officers of the British Raj were less successful in Bahrain, the amir of Nejd's Al Hasa coast, and Kuwait.[17] There Anglo-Persian ran up against the formidable New Zealander Maj. Frank Holmes and his London-based Eastern & General Syndicate, or E&GSynd. Eventually they also encountered the Americans: Standard Oil of California, or Socal, and Gulf Oil Corporation, which acquired the syndicate's concessionary interests and went on to develop the vast oil fields of Saudi Arabia and Kuwait.

In its first directors' report, E&GSynd reported that Holmes and a colleague had "proceeded to Arabia to look into several propositions that had been suggested."[18] Indeed, Holmes had mapped out a string of possibilities along the Arabian coast from Kuwait to Qatar. At a 1923 meeting with Lieutenant Colonel Trevor, the British political resident, Holmes revealed that Qatar's Sheikh Abdullah Ibn Jassim Al Thani had sent him a personal letter and several special messengers imploring Holmes to negotiate a prospecting license. Holmes claimed he was unable to act on the sheikh's request because he had been warned off by the

1.1 Sheikh Abdullah Ibn Jassim Al Thani, r. 1913–1949.

Source: Official site of the Amiri Diwan of the State of Qatar, https://www.diwan.gov.qa/about-qatar /qatars-rulers/sheikh-abdullah-bin-jassim-al-thani.

1.2 Maj. Frank Holmes.

Source: Tatweer Petroleum, "Bahrain Oil Field," (Chevron Archive) http://tatweerpetroleum.com /bahrain-oil-field/.

Colonial Office, whose instructions he was "loyally obeying."[19] In fact, E&GSynd had applied for a concession in Qatar the previous year but had been turned down by the British government, as indeed had Anglo-Persian despite initial support from the political resident. The Colonial Office decreed that any oil negotiations with Sheikh Abdullah and the other Trucial coast sheikhdoms were politically unsuitable because of the "backwardness" of these states.

Despite the Colonial Office's dictum, Holmes began visiting Qatar to pursue a personal friendship with Sheikh Abdullah. During one such visit, the New Zealander supposedly impressed the ruler, who loved to hunt, with his knowledge of hunting dogs. According to this story, when Holmes laid eyes on one of the sheikh's prized salukis he remarked, "I know this dog. Her mother is Hoja." Much impressed, Sheikh Abdullah, turning to the other hunters, said: "If this man can identify one dog among so many, surely he can identify where our oil is hidden."[20] He then proceeded to express his desire to award Qatar's oil concession to Holmes. The dog had been a gift from Sheikh Hamad Ibn Isa Al Khalifa of Bahrain, but what the Qatari ruler did not know (and Holmes chose not to enlighten him about) was that the New Zealander had presented the dog's mother, Hoja, to the Bahraini leader himself.

1922 UQAIR CONFERENCE: IBN SAUD EYES QATAR FOR AL HASA CONCESSION

Around this time the British noticed what one official dryly called "the apparent inclination of His Highness Ibn Sa'ud to absorb the Qatar principality."[21] Indeed, Qatar was very nearly included in the Al Hasa concession negotiated by Major Holmes with Ibn Saud in 1922. This covered a large tract of Nejd territory later secured by Socal, territory that would eventually make history with Socal's huge Dammam discovery on March 4, 1938. It was only the decisive intervention of Sir Percy Cox, the powerful British high commissioner to Iraq, that kept the Qatar peninsula from being included in the Al Hasa concession. The setting was the Uqair conference of 1922, convened by Britain with the then amir of Nejd to settle the borders of the lands controlled by Ibn Saud, Iraq and Kuwait. To the surprise of Sir Percy and the other British officials, Holmes attended the conference at Ibn Saud's invitation.

Just before the five-day meeting ended, the future king of Saudi Arabia presented Sir Percy with a map on which he had marked in blue pencil the concession he proposed to grant E&GSynd. The British high commissioner was taken aback: The area "included the whole of the Hasa province and the Qatar peninsula—the south western and southern boundary of the concession being marked on the map by a line drawn down the Wadi Faruq as far as Jaw al Dukhan and then turning east from there to Khor Ad Dhuwaihin on the sea."[22] Annoyed with this "barefaced" attempt on the part of Holmes and Ibn Saud to "bluff" him, Sir Percy immediately drew a line in red pencil from Jaw al Dukhan to Dohat al Salwa, thereby excluding the Qatar peninsula from the Al Hasa concession. Sir Percy then reminded Ibn Saud that according to the terms of his 1915 treaty with Britain, "he had nothing to do with Qatar except to respect it."[23]

Several years after being rebuffed by the Colonial Office, Anglo-Persian turned its attention back to Qatar. In 1925 the company asked acting political resident Lt. Col. C. G. Crosthwaite to help its geologist, George M. Lees, examine the Qatar peninsula as well as the islands along the Trucial coast—and to provide transport on a British naval vessel. "The immediate object of this examination is not so much to ascertain whether or not we desire to apply for a concession in Qatar," wrote Anglo-Persian's Sir Arnold Wilson, "as to correlate the geology on the southern side of the Gulf with the known facts as to the geological conditions on the Persian side."[24] While the company did not intend to pay Sheikh Abdullah or the other Trucial coast rulers for surveying their territory, it offered to make an application in the "usual way" should the result of these investigations "warrant the expenditure of money on prospecting or in sinking wells."[25] The political resident replied that a proper concession involving an exploration license was necessary before Lees could enter Qatar or the other Trucial sheikhdoms "because, when all is said and done, the travelling of your geologist through that territory in reality and technically amounts to exploration."[26]

In response, Anglo-Persian argued that a "cursory and superficial" examination by a geologist was no different from earlier reconnaissance exercises carried out in Bahrain and Kuwait before and after World War I. "Unless we can ascertain what, if any, prima facie prospects there are of suitable geological formations existing, it will scarcely be worth our while to endeavor to obtain separate concessions from each and all of the chiefs concerned," the company wrote.[27] Anglo-Persian also pointed out that other parties (presumably Holmes and the

Americans) might not be as reluctant to apply for such licenses as a way of challenging the legality of restrictions imposed by the 1916 treaty of protection between Britain and Sheikh Abdullah of Qatar. As with other treaties signed with the Trucial sheikhdoms in 1892, Kuwait in 1913, and Bahrain in 1914, this agreement contained a clause constraining the sheikh's ability to grant concessions without the consent of the high British government.[28]

CHANGE OF HEART AT THE COLONIAL OFFICE

The Colonial Office had resisted earlier attempts by Anglo-Persian and E&GSynd to gain footholds in the area but now agreed there was no longer any prima facie reason for discouraging oil development in Qatar and the sheikhdoms of the Trucial coast. Permission was given to Lees and his party to survey the Qatar peninsula, although the political resident, Lt. Col. F. B. Prideaux, left it up to the geologist to explain the purpose of their visit: "I did not think it opportune on my recent visit to Bidaa' [Doha] to say anything to Sheikh Abdullah bin Jassim [Qasim] about oil development," Prideaux informed the company.[29] He also confided to Anglo-Persian that E&GSynd might still be in the dark about the government's change of heart. "I don't think the Eastern & General Syndicate have heard yet the Colonial Office's recent dictum about Qatar."[30]

Lees arrived in Qatar on March 1, 1926, accompanied by William Richard "Hajji" Williamson, a British born Muslim convert and Anglo-Persian employee, as well as a British army captain named Smith. They made only "minor expeditions" by car from Doha during their stay, certainly not the east to west peninsular reconnaissance the company planned. "As a result, I have not been able to decide if the oil prospects of Qatar justify negotiation for a formal concession," Lees explained in a handwritten account of the trip.[31] The geologist did come away with a letter from Sheikh Abdullah dated March 9, 1926, in which the ruler gave Anglo-Persian's exploration subsidiary exclusive rights for eighteen months to negotiate an oil concession in his territory.

It took another six years for the company to act, however. By this time it was optimistically referring to the sheikh's letter as an "exclusive exploration license." In 1932, saying it might shortly turn its attention to Sheikh Abdullah's territories, Anglo-Persian informed the political resident it was sending its senior officer, Charles Clark Mylles, to Doha to "confirm and extend" this long-lapsed

1.3 First Geological Survey Party in Qatar. In February 1933 E. W. Shaw (Iraq Petroleum Company) and P. T. Cox (Anglo-Persian Oil Company) landed in Doha by a small steamer to begin a detailed geological survey of Qatar. They brought with them a light truck and a Chevrolet car, which, apart from a Buick limousine that the ruler possessed, were the first motor vehicles ever to land in Qatar. In Doha they were met by William Richard "Hajji" Williamson, who acted as their interpreter.

Source: QatarEnergy website, https://www.qatarenergy.qa/PublishingImages/QP%20History/photo-exibition%202_NEW.jpg.

agreement with the sheikh. While Mylles did secure two years of sole exploration rights for Anglo-Persian (until August 6, 1934) as well an exclusive option within that period to submit an offer for an oil concession, he later complained to the British political agent in Bahrain that he had to pay far more than he had foreseen: 1,500 rupees per month over the two years.[32]

No longer stalling, Anglo-Persian immediately began making arrangements to send a geological survey party to Qatar on board the company's vessel, SS *Khuzistan*. Pressure to act quickly came from the Foreign Office in London, who told the Colonial Office that "it is important that any rights in regard to oil exploration and exploitation which may be granted in respect of the Arab Principalities of the Persian Gulf should not be merely of a blocking nature."[33] Anglo-Persian's local representative reported in early 1933 that the survey led by its two geologists, E. W.

Shaw and P. T. Cox, was proceeding well. Apart from Sheikh Abdullah's Buick limousine, the light truck and Chevrolet car the geologists had brought with them were the first motor vehicles to land in Qatar.[34] The ruler, however, refused to allow the survey party to use its wireless radio transceiver set. By May of that year Anglo-Persian's regional office in the Iranian city of Abadan had requested permission from the political resident to send a negotiator to Qatar to commence discussions with Sheikh Abdullah regarding an oil concession.

CHAPTER 2

Qatar's First Oil Concession

Twists and Turns

The negotiator chosen for the job of haggling terms of an oil concession with the hereditary ruler of a British protectorate lacking settled borders and governmental structures was A. C. Sampson, on loan to Anglo-Persian from the Iraq Petroleum Company, or IPC. Anglo-Persian itself was barred by a "group agreement" from entering oil concessions independently of IPC in any area of the former Ottoman Empire (excluding Kuwait). At an interdepartmental meeting held at the Colonial Office in London in May 1933, AngloPersian explained to officials from the Foreign Office, the Admiralty, and the India Office that it was "only acting as agents of IPC in this matter. The Qatar area came within the agreement made between the various constituent groups of the Iraq Petroleum Company and by that agreement each group had undertaken not to seek concessions individually in certain areas which included Qatar."[1] With IPC's agreement, Anglo-Persian proposed to obtain the concession in its name and then assign it to a subsidiary of IPC created for the purpose. The fact that the IPC wasn't a thoroughly British affair did not please the assembled bureaucrats, although the Admiralty conceded that the international consortium's partial British composition was at least preferable to the American interests working with Major Holmes.

IPC's self-denial provisions dated from 1912, when its forerunner the Turkish Petroleum Company, or TPC, was formed to group mainly German, British, and Dutch interests. After World War I the German share in TPC was transferred to the French. Entry was later provided under pressure to five American oil companies through a syndicate known as the Near East Development Corporation, or NEDC. This was formalized in 1927, when the U.S. State Department finally withdrew its legal objections to the TPC concession. The following year TPC signed the Red Line Agreement, so-called because the area to which the self-denial provisions applied was mapped in red. By the time TPC was renamed the Iraq Petroleum Company in 1929, the consortium was held in blocks of 23.75 percent each by Anglo-Persian, Royal Dutch Shell, Compagnie française des pétroles, and the NEDC syndicate (grouping Standard Oil of New Jersey, Standard Oil of New York [Socony], Gulf Oil, Atlantic Richfield, and the Pan-American Petroleum and Transport Company). The remaining 5 percent went to Calouste Gulbenkian, a Turkish-born Armenian who was the driving force behind TPC and later referred to as "Mr. Five Percent."

Anglo-Persian was anxious to get the sheikh to commit, particularly since Holmes and his associates were still sniffing around. "You will be interested to learn that we have every reason to believe Holmes has made definite overtures to the Ruler of Qatar direct, and has received a reply granting him permission to proceed to Qatar when he is able to do so. There is therefore no time to be lost. . . . I must get Sampson into Qatar before he [Holmes] appears on the scene again," Anglo-Persian's manager in Abadan wrote to the political resident in June 1933.[2] Thus alerted to potential American competition through Holmes, the political resident decided it was a good time for the British government to exert some pressure of its own on the Qatari ruler. He therefore directed the political agent to remind Sheikh Abdullah of his treaty obligations not to grant any concessions without the consent of the British government, a missive the sheikh indignantly and correctly interpreted as arm-twisting on behalf of Anglo-Persian.

It would not be the last time the British government intervened in Qatar on Anglo-Persian's behalf. The British were now seriously worried about American encroachment. Standard Oil of California (Socal) had already acquired an oil concession on the neighboring island of Bahrain from Holmes and his syndicate, a transfer the Colonial Office had grudgingly approved when Anglo-Persian showed no interest on IPC's behalf. Anglo-Persian had in fact allowed an earlier option covering Bahrain to expire in 1925. "At one time Anglo-Persian were interested, but it is understood that their geologists have condemned practically the whole of the main land of Arabia," the Petroleum Department wrote in 1930.[3] That decision was now very much regretted. The Admiralty, in particular, went into a tailspin. It warned that if Holmes and his syndicate obtained the Qatar concession, "the Bahrain concession may gradually be merged into a much larger undertaking, the whole of which will be under the control of American interests . . . no step should be neglected which might enable the Anglo-Persian Oil Company to bring Qatar into their sphere of control."[4]

As Anglo-Persian's representative, Sampson made two trips to Qatar to discuss the oil concession with Sheikh Abdullah in June and July 1933 before the
Qatari ruler was urgently summoned to Riyadh for talks with Ibn Saud, by then
the king of Saudi Arabia. Ibn Saud was more than a little unhappy with Anglo-
Persian's efforts to negotiate an oil concession in Qatar. He much preferred Socal,
who several months earlier had been granted the Al Hasa concession after
E&GSynd's agreement foundered on a lack of funds and the king's military cam-
paigns in eastern Arabia. "News received on 28th August that Shaikh of Qatar
left for Riyadh two or three days ago at urgent summons of King who is said to
be enraged at the grant of oil concession to Anglo-Persian Oil Company," the
political agent in Bahrain reported excitedly.[5] No agreement had in fact been
granted yet, although Anglo-Persian described its discussions with the Qatari
sheikh as "very full and amicable." Negotiations with Sheikh Abdullah resumed
in October on his return from Saudi Arabia, despite Anglo-Persian's concerns
that Ibn Saud's present of "motor cars, slaves, rifles and ammunition" had hard-
ened the sheikh's position.[6]

BRITAIN PUSHES FOR POLITICAL SAFEGUARDS
IN CONCESSION

The British may have been resigned to the fact that Anglo-Persian would turn
the Qatar concession over to IPC or one of its subsidiaries, but they were still
keen to insert certain "safeguards" to prevent further assignment to non-British
companies and ensure a level of British control similar to that existing in Bahrain. To gain approval from the British government for the reassignment of the
Bahrain concession, Socal had to register its Bahrain venture in Great Britain or
Canada, appoint a British citizen to head this new company, submit its chief local
representative to the British government for approval, and employ as many British citizens or subjects of Bahrain as possible. In addition, the American firm was
required to build a refinery in Bahrain once oil flows reached commercial levels
and had to allow preemption of oil by the British navy in wartime.

Anglo-Persian hinted at possible difficulties with its foreign partners in IPC
over these pro-British safeguards. It predicted that the Compagnie française des
pétroles, or CFP, the French firm that had assumed the government's shareholding in IPC upon its establishment in 1924, would balk at the provision for wartime

preemption of oil by the Royal Navy. Afraid of scaring off IPC, the Admiralty conceded it might be prudent not to press for this specific condition at such a sensitive stage in the negotiations. "American interests have already secured Hasa and Bahrein and may also secure Koweit, and we are therefore anxious to avoid still further American penetration and do not wish to frighten the Iraq Petroleum Company out of Qatar," the Admiralty wrote to the India Office in September 1933.[7]

Britain also arbitrarily decided expediency called for separating the commercial aspects of the concessions from the issue of safeguards, which could be handled under parallel political agreements between the companies and the British government. This policy would be pursued both in Qatar and in Kuwait, where Anglo-Persian was partnered with the U.S. company Gulf Oil Corporation for the concession first negotiated by Holmes and his syndicate. "It has been decided in each case that the commercial side of the proposed concessions should be embodied in an agreement between the Company and the Sheikh concerned, which would not come into force until parallel agreements between His Majesty's Government and the Company concerned have been concluded. The safeguards of British interests which we require will be embodied in these Government agreements," the India Office ruled.[8]

Both Sheikh Ahmad Ibn Jabir Al Sabah in Kuwait and Sheikh Abdullah in Qatar were deliberately kept in the dark about the deliberations over safeguards within Britain's colonial apparatus as well as about the India Office's ultimate ruling. Sheikh Ahmad wasn't even given a copy of the political agreement between the British government and the Kuwait Oil Company until five weeks after it was signed. His own concession with the Anglo-American joint venture was made permanently subordinate to this arrangement—over Sheikh Ahmad's strong objections.[9]

ANGLO-PERSIAN'S OPTIMISM WANES

Anglo-Persian's optimism regarding an early settlement with Sheikh Abdullah had waned by December 1933. Archibald Chisholm, Sampson's replacement as negotiator, reported that the sheikh did not like the terms the company was offering; the ruler thought he'd wait until the two-year exclusivity period expired to see what might be available from "other parties." This was clearly a reference to Socal, as Chisholm said he had been shown a letter from the U.S. firm's chief representative in the Al Hasa city of Hofuf seeking to start negotiations with Sheikh Abdullah. "Anglo-Persian Oil Company have temporarily broken off negotiations with Shaikh of Qatar, who, having been approached by American group at Hasa, is making exorbitant demands," reported the political agent.[10] Anglo-Persian had no intention of losing Qatar to the Americans. Meeting in London with officials from the Foreign Office, the Petroleum Department, the Admiralty, and the India Office, the company's deputy chair assured the British government that the financial terms under the concession would not be "ungenerous" to the sheikh. Indeed, they would have to be rather too generous from Anglo-Persian's perspective given what Socal had paid in Al Hasa.

Britain now recognized it could help secure the concession for Anglo-Persian by expanding the protections guaranteed under the 1916 treaty. The British government had agreed in this treaty to protect Qatar from aggression by sea but had only promised its "good offices" if the peninsula should be attacked by land. In 1921, when Sheikh Abdullah asked for protection from Wahabi attacks emanating from Ibn Saud's territory, particularly one with internal support from his dissident brothers, Britain said it would lend only diplomatic assistance.[11] With his unruly relatives running directly to Ibn Saud every time a dispute arose, Sheikh Abdullah tried again in 1930. He pointedly asked the political agent if the British government would prevent Ibn Saud from meddling in Qatar's internal affairs should his relatives appeal to the Saudi ruler for help. Again, the British demurred.[12] In 1932 Sheikh Abdullah made a third attempt to obtain protection by land, this time offering to give the Royal Air Force an emergency landing ground near Doha in exchange for securing his inland border. Britain only agreed to protect Doha and the areas along the coast, and the talks broke down in acrimony.[13]

By early 1934 official British resistance to extending its treaty obligations was crumbling with the arrival of American oil interests in nearby Al Hasa and their competition with Anglo-Persian in Qatar. "I would, therefore, suggest that we consider offering Shaikh 'Abdullah bin Qasim [Jassim] al Thani protection of all his territory (at any rate up to the Salwa-Anbak-Dhuwaihin line) provided that he gives the concession to the Anglo-Persian Oil Company," the political agent advised his superiors.[14] The British were convinced that Ibn Saud was behind Socal's attempt to penetrate Qatar, which they saw as part of a general policy by the Saudi king to absorb the Arab sheikhdoms. Sheikh Abdullah's authority was essentially confined to the coastal areas of the Qatar peninsula, leaving him especially vulnerable in the interior to migratory Bedouin tribes from Saudi Arabia.

Since the interior was presumably where oil operations would be carried out, British officials fretted that Ibn Saud would gain a definite foothold in Qatar should the Americans win the concession. "The only way for His Majesty's Government to repel this combined American oil interest-Bin Saud offensive is to take their stand on Article V of the Qatar 1916 Treaty and inform Shaikh that they will not permit him to grant concession to any company which is not at least partly British," the political resident cabled the secretary of state for India in London. "As incentive to Shaikh to fall in with our views he might be informed that should he give concession to the Anglo-Persian Oil Company, which will naturally increase His Majesty's Government's interests in his area, latter will guarantee him the protection he previously asked for."[15] The oil company was also prodding the British government to offer Sheikh Abdullah protection from Ibn Saud and marauding Bedouin on his borders.[16]

It does seem Ibn Saud was making another attempt at annexing Qatar despite Sir Percy Cox's 1922 warning. British officials reported that the Saudi king had told Sheikh Abdullah during the Qatari ruler's visit to Riyadh that he viewed Al Thani authority as extending only to Doha and the surrounding coastal villages, while also expressing his displeasure toward Anglo-Persian. "Certainly all the Bedouins of Hasa look upon the Qatar desert (Bar al Qatr) as belonging to Bin Saud," wrote the British political agent in Kuwait, Lt. Col. Harold Dickson.[17] Dickson argued that Sheikh Abdullah would never give the concession to Anglo-Persian unless Britain assured him it would defend Qatar's landward frontier through "any and every quarrel that Bin Saud may choose to pick with him in the future."[18] Anglo-Persian weighed in as well, warning that "if Bin Thani is allowed to give the oil concession to the Americans, it will be tantamount to acknowledging Bin Saud's definite suzerainty over Qatar."[19]

It was then that Sir Samuel Hoare, Britain's secretary of state for India, proposed that he authorize the political resident Lt. Col. Trenchard Fowle to promise full protection against aggression by land, as Sheikh Abdullah had requested in 1932. This protection, however, would only occur "in the event of his granting the concession to Anglo-Persian," a precondition that Sir Samuel suggested should be conveyed to Sheikh Abdullah personally by Fowle.[20] The sheikh would also have to surrender jurisdiction over foreigners living in Qatar and allow three dormant articles of the 1916 treaty to come into force. Under these articles, Sheikh Abdullah would have to let British citizens reside in his country and protect their lives and property, accept the appointment of a British political agent resident in Qatar, and allow the establishment of British post and telegraph facilities.[21]

Only the Foreign Office in London expressed reservations about Sir Samuel's proposal to join the promise of enhanced protection with the award of the oil concession to Anglo-Persian and eventually to the IPC consortium. It predicted that bringing pressure to bear on the sheikh to grant the concession to IPC would not be compatible with the Open Door Policy pursued by the United States, which maintained that U.S. commercial interests should have the same rights and privileges as those from other countries. This policy had been adopted by President Woodrow Wilson after the 1920 San Remo conference essentially kept American companies out of the oil fields of the Middle East. It allowed the State Department to vigorously oppose any government that discriminated against U.S. firms competing for access to new markets and raw materials. The Foreign Office, however, was hardly strenuous in its objections, and Foreign Secretary Sir John Simon ultimately concluded that "it should be possible to base a reasonably good answer to the United States Government upon the peculiar political situation in Qatar and upon the fact that the Iraq Petroleum Company is a company of international composition with United States participation."[22]

THE VEXED PROBLEM OF QATAR'S SOUTHERN BORDER

From London's perspective, there was only one obstacle to defending Qatar's interior: its undefined southern border. Some British officials, notably Dickson, argued that Qatar's southern boundary ran southeast from the foot of the Dohat al Salwa bay on the western side of the peninsula to Anbak (also known as Mabak) in the desert, and then to Khor al Dhuwaihin on the eastern coast. This proved unacceptable to the government of India, which was unwilling to set the border as far south into the interior as Anbak without Ibn Saud's formal concurrence. It preferred a line running from Dohat al Salwa to the water wells of Sakak, as given in John Lorimer's *Gazetteer of the Persian Gulf*. Lorimer's *Gazetteer* was published in secret in 1908 by the British government in India.

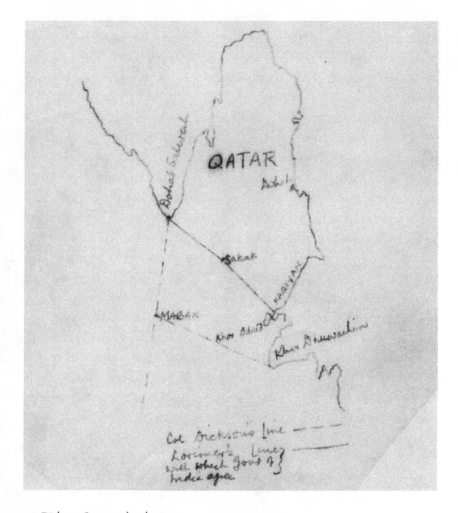

2.1 Dickson *Gazetteer* sketch map.

Source: "Dickson/Gazetteer Sketch of Qatar," fol. 212r, image 1/2, British Library: India Office Records and Private Papers, IOR/R/15/2/412, in Qatar Digital Library, https://www.qdl.qa/archive/81055/vdc _100023550521.0x000035.

This map kept the border much further north than Anbak, and away from Ibn Saud's influence. Nor was the government of India pleased with Dickson's line from the Sakak water wells to Khor al Dhuwaihin on the eastern side of the peninsula. This included the inlet of Khor al Odaid and territory further south along the coast that Britain had already given to the Trucial sheikh of Abu Dhabi. It therefore decreed: "In view of this, Colonel Dickson's suggestion appears unacceptable and the Government of India are of the opinion that from Sakak wells

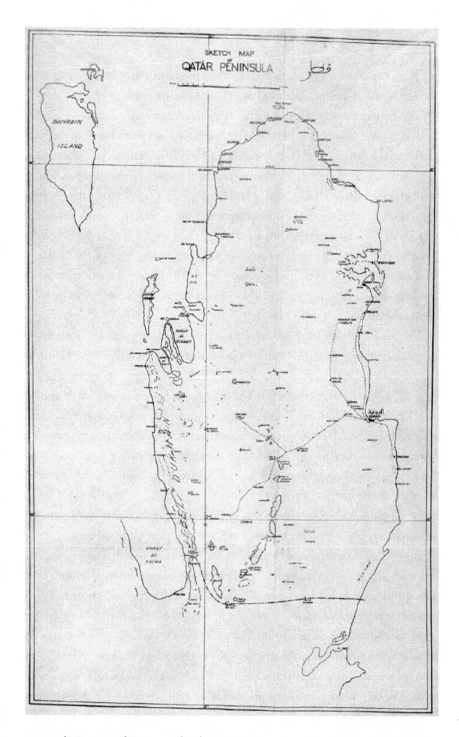

2.2 Anglo-Persian Oil Company sketch map.

Source: "SKETCH MAP OF QATAR PENINSULA, fol. 5r, image 1/2, British Library: India Office Records and Private Papers, IOR/R/15/2/416, f 5, in Qatar Digital Library, https://www.qdl.qa/archive /81055/vdc_100024084949.0x000019.

the line runs eastward by south to the southern end of the Nikyan sandhills on the north side of the entrance to Khor al Odaid as described in the Gazetteer."[23]

This boundary was more compatible with the sketch map compiled by Anglo-Persian during its survey in early 1933. It originated at a point north of the head of Dohat al Salwa, turned sharply southeast from Jabul Nakhsh to Qalat ali Bin Said near Sakak, and then headed due east to the sea and the Nikyan sandhills some eight miles north of Khor al Odaid (see fig. 2.2). Anglo-Persian also claimed the southern boundary shown on its map was "indicated by the Sheikh himself."[24] The India Office seemed inclined to accept the company's map with a slight modification bringing the line twelve miles south to the head of the Dohat al Salwa. Saudi Arabia would later lay claim to Jebel Nakhsh at the southern end of Jebel Dukhan, a move resisted by Britain on Qatar's behalf because of its location within the oil concession.[25]

The Saudi claim to Jebel Nakhsh lapsed after World War II, possibly because rumors of oil deposits in this southern border area proved unfounded.[26] Khor al Odaid, however, remained a bone of contention. While the inlet went to Qatar in its 1965 boundary agreement with Saudi Arabia, Britain continued to uphold Abu Dhabi's claim to Khor al Odaid until 1974. At that point, the recently constituted federation of the United Arab Emirates finally gave in to Saudi pressure for an outlet to the Persian Gulf south of the Qatar peninsula, giving Saudi Arabia a twenty-five-kilometer stretch of coastline running from Khor al Odaid to Sabkhat Mattie in Abu Dhabi.[27]

While the British government was now prepared to give Sheikh Abdullah a guarantee against aggression by land in return for granting the oil concession to Anglo-Persian, Britain wanted to confine its protection to major acts of aggression such as an unprovoked attack by a neighboring state or a large Bedouin raid. The sheikh was on his own when it came to minor fights or self-provoked skirmishes. Britain also decided it might not be wise to commit itself to a definitive territorial boundary, preferring instead to consider the line laid down merely as an arbitrary limit of the oil concession and the area guaranteed protection. This strategy was suggested by Britain's minister in Jeddah, Sir Andrew Ryan, who wanted to keep his options open prior to talks with Ibn Saud. The British were bracing for tough negotiations. Indeed, Ibn Saud's opening gambit in June 1934, prior to the commencement of the Anglo-Saudi frontier negotiations, recognized only a small coastal strip around Doha as belonging to the Al Thani state.[28]

This discussion of protection guarantees and boundary limits was being conducted wholly within Britain's far-flung colonial apparatus. Sheikh Abdullah himself was kept completely in the dark about the impending offer. When Fowle finally went to Qatar in March 1934 to personally outline Britain's mix of demands and inducements to the sheikh and his advisers, the Arab ruler seemed singularly unimpressed. The political resident found Sheikh Abdullah quite out of sorts with Anglo-Persian and particularly with Archibald Chisholm, with whom the sheikh said he had reached agreement the previous December, only to have the company later change its position and offer new terms he considered unacceptable. When Fowle told the ruler that the British government would not agree to the oil concession being granted to a company that was not at least partly British, Sheikh Abdullah objected strenuously, citing both Kuwait and Bahrain as examples where concessions were under discussion or had already been awarded to foreign firms.

Shown Article V of the 1916 treaty, under which Sheikh Abdullah had agreed not to award any concession without the approval of the British government, the sheikh insisted he had every right to negotiate a prospecting license with another company—a reference, Fowle assumed, to the dreaded Standard Oil—when Anglo-Persian's exclusivity period expired on August 6, 1934. After this prospecting license was over, assuming he reached terms on a concession with the company concerned, the sheikh told the political resident that he would then submit this concessionary agreement to Britain for approval according to his treaty obligations. Fowle was somewhat taken aback by this nuanced approach. He commented in his meeting notes that it was clear Sheikh Abdullah and his advisers had been "carefully and cleverly tutored," presumably by Ibn Saud and the U.S. oil company.[29] The political resident was convinced the sheikh's astute countermove had been their idea.

The British official noticed a marked change in attitude the following day when he revealed plans to extend the guarantee of protection to include attack by land as well as by sea. "I told you yesterday that there is something else which I wanted to tell you. In the past the Government promised to protect you by sea and give their good offices (i.e., words) in the event of an attack on you by land," Fowle told Sheikh Abdullah. "Now the Government are prepared to protect you against an attack by land with the necessary force in case of an attack upon you. That is to protect the whole of Qatar."[30] The ruler then agreed to "discuss matters urgently" with Anglo-Persian in the remaining months before its exclusivity expired. He also asked the resident to keep the matter secret, probably to prevent word of the offer reaching Ibn Saud. Sheikh Abdullah admitted having an "arrangement" with the Saudi king according to which "no one ventures to encroach on my territory." Sheikh Abdullah refused point-blank to explain this arrangement further, although the British surmised he might be referring to the one hundred thousand rupees a year the sheikh had earlier admitted to be secretly paying Ibn Saud.[31] The officials guessed this sum varied with the rise and fall of the Saudi king's prestige and power.

Fowle left to give Sheikh Abdullah time to mull his offer, promising to return to Qatar shortly. After learning of the ruler's threat to award a prospecting license to another company following the expiration of Anglo-Persian's exclusivity period, the Foreign Office recommended that Sheikh Abdullah be informed immediately that the British government was of the opinion that a "right of survey" in Qatar was part and parcel of a concession and therefore could not be granted by the sheikh without its permission. Sheikh Abdullah was also instructed that he had broken the terms of the 1916 treaty, specifically Article IV, in which the sheikh promised not have relations or correspond with any other power, and that whatever "arrangement" he had come to with Ibn Saud over his southern boundary could not be permitted to continue. To reinforce this message, the political resident suggested that a show of British force—specifically air reconnaissance by the Royal Air Force accompanied by a Navy sloop—might have a "salutary effect" on the sheikh.

On his return to Qatar in early April, Fowle finally brought up the issue of boundaries with Sheikh Abdullah, who confirmed that his southern border followed Anglo-Persian's map. He also told the political resident that Ibn Saud had in recent years claimed the area from Khor al Odaid to Sabkhat Mattie and begun collecting zakat (annual tribute) from the tribes in this region. Sheikh Abdullah intimated that he would be in danger if he did not continue his own still-unspecified arrangement with the Saudi king. This led both Fowle and the political agent, Lt. Col. Gordon Loch, to conclude that the sheikh was "dominated by fear" of Ibn Saud and his Bedouin allies.[32] Meanwhile, Socal kept up its pressure on Sheikh Abdullah. Its Al Hasa representative had written to the ruler to inform him that his company was prepared to offer better terms than Anglo-Persian; the British heard from a "reliable" source that the U.S. firm was willing to pay 10 percent more than any British concern.[33]

BRITISH STAKE OUT SPHERE OF INFLUENCE
EAST OF BLUE LINE

By April 1934 the Royal Air Force had ordered a reconnaissance of the Qatar peninsula from Dohat al Salwa to Khor al Odaid, with the Royal Navy to station a sloop near Odaid during the operation. "This action would serve as a warning to the Americans as well as to Bin Saud and should make it definitively clear to Shaikh of Qatar that we mean business," political agent Lieutenant Colonel Loch wrote to Fowle.[34] That same month Sir Andrew Ryan informed Ibn Saud that Britain regarded the Blue Line defined in the Anglo-Turkish Convention of 1913 as the eastern boundary of Saudi Arabia. This ran directly south from the bay opposite Zakhnuniyah island on the Persian Gulf to the Rub al Khali, where it met the demarcation between Turkish Arabia and Aden at parallel 20 degrees north. Wary of Ibn Saud's reaction, Fowle urged the Royal Air Force and Royal Navy to commence aerial reconnaissance of the Qatar peninsula as soon as possible. The HMS *Shoreham* moved into place off Qatar on May 7, and a detachment of Flying Boats carried out the mission on May 9, taking "studious care" not to fly over Zakhnuniyah island or cross into Saudi territory.

The following day Loch personally delivered a message to Sheikh Abdullah, who had decamped to Umm Al Quhaib, where he was living in Bedouin style. The British made sure the Qatari ruler was aware of the contents of the note Sir Andrew had handed to Ibn Saud on April 28. Sheikh Abdullah was also told that the "intermediate area" to the east of the Blue Line and up to Anglo-Persian's line was within Britain's sphere of influence. Socal was also warned off and informed through the U.S. Embassy in London that the British government would not allow it to operate east of the Blue Line. "Sheikh Abdullah appeared to me to be impressed by the message regarding Bin Saud's eastern boundary and the British Sphere, but I had the feeling it was not entirely fresh news to him," Loch informed the political resident.[35]

Privately, the British conceded that the prime objective of the Blue Line communication to Ibn Saud was to prevent any encroachment by Socal east of the Blue Line and to serve as a starting point in Anglo-Saudi frontier negotiations. The Admiralty realized that it would be impossible, or at least extremely costly and difficult, for the British government to prevent Ibn Saud from extending his jurisdiction if diplomatic persuasions failed. Other officials argued that "spheres

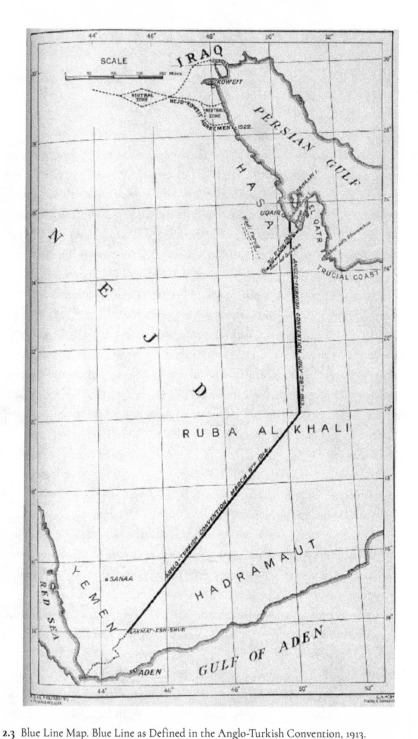

2.3 Blue Line Map. Blue Line as Defined in the Anglo-Turkish Convention, 1913.

Source: "File 10/3 V Qatar Oil Concession," fol. 187r, image 390/527, British Library: India Office Records and Private Papers, IOR/R/15/2/414, in *Qatar Digital Library*, https://www.qdl.qa/archive/81055/vdc _100031220649.0x0000bf.

of interest" meant nothing in international law. The tribes within the self-described British sphere east of the Blue Line continued to pay zakat to Ibn Saud's bands of armed men. No one dared interfere with the Arab king's authority. But the British officials wanted to avoid any question of compromise with Saudi Arabia over the 1913 Convention line until the Qatari oil concession was decided. "Any eventual compromise should if possible be staved off until *after* Shaikh has given oil concession to Anglo-Persian Oil Company," the political resident advised London.[36]

Loch felt it was the opportune time for Anglo-Persian to return to Qatar, as Sheikh Abdullah now appeared more favorably disposed toward it. The company sent its Bahrain-based agent, Hajji Yusuf Ibn Ahmad Kanoo, who thought an agreement could be reached with the sheikh if Anglo-Persian increased its offer. He also said Sheikh Abdullah might agree to extend the existing exploration license by six months if the firm paid a higher monthly amount during that period. Anglo-Persian wasn't keen, suggesting instead that the existing arrangement be allowed to lapse and the matter taken up again in the winter at the company's convenience. "A few months without money coming in, might, in view of his greedy nature, make the Sheikh more tractable," it wrote to the political agent on June 17, 1934.[37] But the British government was not willing to give Socal an opening by letting the arrangement with Anglo-Persian expire. It pushed instead for an extension to give the two sides more time to negotiate a concession.

MYLLES EXTENDS ANGLO-PERSIAN'S EXPLORATION LICENSE

That same month, the Bahrain Petroleum Company exported its inaugural cargo, the first ever from the Arabian side of the Persian Gulf. The tanker *El Segundo* left Bahrain for Japan on June 7, 1934, with 3,300 tons of crude oil. Four weeks later, Charles Mylles passed through Bahrain on his way to Qatar with instructions from Anglo-Persian to seek an extension of the exploration license. He came away from his meeting with Sheikh Abdullah with an eight-month extension, for which the sheikh would be paid 2,500 rupees per month.[38] While this was less than the 3,000 rupees Anglo-Persian had authorized him to offer, Mylles found the sheikh and his advisers armed with copies of the Bahraini, Persian, Iraqi, and Hasa concessions as well as the exact details of the Kuwait agreement. "Mylles is

of the opinion that the Shaikh will eventually agree to terms similar to those of
the Kuwait concession but will not under any circumstances be prepared to accept
less," the political agent reported.[39]

Hajji Williamson, who accompanied Mylles to Qatar, noted that Sheikh Abdullah's attitude had improved since the company's last visit. British officials speculated hopefully that Ibn Saud's standing had dropped with Sheikh Abdullah and
the other rulers along the Trucial coast and Kuwait because of the 1934 Saudi-
Yemeni war. Ibn Saud's troops had apparently retreated from Hodaida and the
Yemen littoral without the payment of any subsidy by Iman Yahya, the king at
the time. According to the British political resident, the 1934 border conflict "was
not regarded by the Arabs of the Gulf as by any means too successful from Bin
Saud's point of view."[40]

In addition to bringing direct pressure to bear on Sheikh Abdullah to award
the oil concession to Anglo-Persian, the British used indirect means to achieve
their objectives. "It is desired to influence the people of Qatar, so that they may
in their turn influence the Shaikh," noted one official. "Qataris coming to Bahrain are to be asked about the discontent, which is understood to be rife in Qatar,
at Shaikh Abdullah refusing to grant the concession and so keeping money out
of the poor people's pockets and also out of the pockets of his family."[41] The passport clerk in Bahrain was instructed to delay entry for all citizens of Qatar, sending them to the agency for special passes with the aim of reminding Sheikh
Abdullah that the British could disrupt the free movement of his subjects. Anglo-
Persian lent a hand in this effort too. It directed Yusuf Kanoo to explain to the
sheikh's relatives that only his obstinacy kept the Al Thani family from reaping
the benefits of the oil concession. Kanoo was also told to say that Sheikh Abdullah could not give the concession to another company—which even the British
admitted was not strictly correct.

In October 1934, several months after the extension with Anglo-Persian was
signed, Sheikh Abdullah visited Bahrain and toured its oil field with the Bahraini
ruler, Sheikh Hamad Ibn Isa Al Khalifa. The Qatari sheikh seized the opportunity to complain to the British political agent. "He evidently disliked the pin pricks
of air reconnaissance and the insistence on passes and felt not only that his dig-
nity had been lowered but thought that Government were trying to help the
Anglo-Persian Oil Company to get cheap terms."[42] Believing their message had
penetrated, the political resident ordered the special procedures regarding passes
to be relaxed. With Anglo-Persian now set to resume concession negotiations with

Sheikh Abdullah, there was some discussion between the company and the British authorities as to the most suitable time to introduce the political agreement enumerating all the safeguards the British demanded. It was decided that, as in Kuwait, there was no need to tell Sheikh Abdullah this agreement had in fact already been negotiated.

The following month, Charles Mylles went back to Qatar for a quick visit but was unable to resume commercial negotiations with Sheikh Abdullah. Anglo-Persian suspected the sheikh had purposely moved to an inconvenient spot in the desert to await word from Kuwait on the terms of its concession. "We have every reason to believe that he is closely informed of every step there, and that he has no intention of any serious negotiations pending the completion of the Kuwait negotiations," the company admitted.[43] Sheikh Abdullah did give Anglo-Persian permission to install a wireless station in Doha so that Mylles could communicate with the company's Abadan offices, although this was not allowed to operate until talks formally resumed in early 1935.

Mylles then drove into the interior, where the company's survey crew reported that Ibn Saud and the California Arabian Standard Oil Company (the Hasa affiliate set up by Socal) had been trying hard to get Sheikh Abdullah to admit that the Jebel Dukhan range running down the west coast of Qatar to a point just north of Salwa was outside his territory. Anglo-Persian's geologists had not yet fully surveyed these low-lying hills, which were just two hundred feet high but extended thirty-one miles along the coast and three miles inland. Mylles noted that the range was similar to the identically named Jebel Dukhan in Bahrain, the site of the Bahrain Petroleum Company's producing oil field. He advised the political agent that, "in view of the proved structure in Bahrain and the probable structure in Qatar, the neighboring hills on the mainland should be regarded as potential oil country until the contrary is proven by examination."[44]

Jebel Dukhan had already been the focus of correspondence between Ibn Saud and Sheikh Abdullah. The Saudi king had first claimed that the border should run from a point east of Jebel Dukhan to Khor al Odaid, leaving the land to the north of this line to Qatar and Jebel Dukhan and the territory to the south to Saudi Arabia. Sheikh Abdullah contested Ibn Saud's claim. He argued that the line should run from Dohat al Salwa to Odaid, thereby including Jebel Dukhan in Qatar. Claims went back and forth, but the political agent reported that Sheikh Abdullah's last letter from Ibn Saud on the subject conceded the Jebel Dukhan hills to Qatar.[45] Ibn Saud also said he considered the boundaries of the two states to be the same, thereby implicitly rejecting Britain's sphere of influence to the east of the Blue Line and the Blue Line itself. The Saudi king had already explicitly rejected both British-backed concepts in the lead-up to the Anglo-Saudi frontier negotiations.

Mylles returned to Qatar in late January, taking the slow mail boat from Iraq to Bahrain and then a launch to Doha. In mid-February he reported that talks with Sheikh Abdullah were going slowly but not unfavorably. Mylles also said that Maj. Frank Holmes had written to the sheikh again, guaranteeing better terms than "anything we put up" and mentioning plans to visit Qatar. This prompted a flurry of telegrams between the political agents in Kuwait and Bahrain to determine the whereabouts of a "certain individual" whose movements, as Loch in Bahrain put it, "may affect the show next door to me."[46] Holmes, it was reported, was in England and wasn't expected back in Kuwait until early March. Upon his arrival, Holmes told the visiting political resident, Fowle, that he had secured 100 percent British backing for a potential concession from Sheikh Abdullah. But he also said he had informed his investors that there was "nothing doing" in Qatar until the option with Anglo-Persian expired. Mylles himself departed Qatar with a redraft of the concession approved by the sheikh and a further one-month extension of the option to May 4, 1935.

HOLMES KEEPS UP THE PRESSURE ON ANGLO-PERSIAN

With the concession tantalizingly close, Anglo-Persian remained deeply suspicious of Holmes. It told the India Office that the sheikh's comments on the redraft were in modern Egyptian Arabic rather than the local dialect, containing words and phrases unknown in Qatar. "You are doubtless aware that Holmes has all his translations and printing done in Cairo through a man named Hammond," Anglo-Persian wrote ominously.[47] The British were steadfast in their support of Anglo-Persian despite mounting evidence that Socal was no longer backing Holmes. The secretary of state for India directed the political resident to "leave nothing undone to encourage Shaikh to clinch with Anglo-Persian Oil Company as against negotiating with Holmes and his friends."[48] Finalization was still some way off. The redraft had only contained Sheikh Abdullah's views on the concession's general terms, and it did not address financial details.

By early April Mylles was back in Qatar. The political resident followed on board the sloop HMS *Fowey* on April 16. Fowle's main mission was to reach agreement with Sheikh Abdullah on the resolution of disputes between foreign Anglo-Persian employees and the sheikh's subjects. The sheikh demanded that such disagreements be tried before his local Sharia (religious) court. This was unacceptable to Anglo-Persian and the British government. Fowle insisted that jurisdiction over the persons and property of British and British-protected subjects, as well as those of non-Muslim foreign powers, had to rest solely with Britain or his government would not approve the concession with Anglo-Persian or "whomsoever it may be." A compromise was finally reached by which most of these disputes were handled by a joint court in Doha, consisting of the sheikh and the nearest British officer (in this case the political agent in Bahrain) or their respective representatives.

As a condition of this compromise over jurisdiction, Sheikh Abdullah demanded that Britain recognize his second son, Hamad, as his heir apparent and consequently accord him full support after he became ruler. Fowle balked, as it was against British policy to recognize a particular heir of any Persian Gulf sheikh. The political resident was convinced that Hamad, whom he deemed "most unpopular" in Qatar, had orchestrated the demand himself.[49] As these matters were debated, Mylles made progress on the concession's commercial terms. On May 3, the day before the option expired, Anglo-Persian received what it described as a "vaguely worded" letter of acceptance of the concession terms from Sheikh Abdullah. The sheikh, however, wished to delay signature until the remaining political issues had been agreed with the British government and offered a further ten days to complete these negotiations. In the meantime, news reached Dickson, the political agent in Kuwait, that the California Arabian Standard Oil Company in Hasa was preparing to approach Sheikh Abdullah as soon as Anglo-Persian's option expired.

At this point the British officials relented and agreed to recognize Hamad as the heir apparent, provided Sheikh Abdullah implement the 1916 Treaty in full—including its dormant articles. They also acceded to the Qatari ruler's exclusive jurisdiction over the citizens of Kuwait, Bahrain, and the Trucial coast despite their status as British-protected subjects.[50] Since the 1916 Treaty was signed personally by Sheikh Abdullah and did not devolve to his heirs, it was converted into an "heirs and successors" agreement with Hamad promising to accept it upon his accession. In addition to expanding the sheikh's protection guarantee to include "serious and unprovoked attacks which may be made on your territory from outside your frontier," Britain promised to support Sheikh Abdullah and his successors internally if any difficulties arose from the oil company's operations.[51] This

2.4 Sheikh Abdullah Ibn Jassim Al Thani (*second from left*) with sons, Sheikh Hamad (*far left*) and Sheikh Ali (*second from right*).

Source: Photo included in the "virtual notebook" of John Lockerbie at *Catnaps.org*, http://catnaps.org /islamic/islamimages/shabdport01.jpg.

was less than the "full support in internal matters" the sheikh wanted for himself and Hamad, but it was all the British government was willing to give.

SHEIKH ABDULLAH SIGNS SEVENTY-FIVE-YEAR OIL CONCESSION

On May 17, 1935, following an exchange of letters with the British government, Sheikh Abdullah finally granted Anglo-Persian a seventy-five-year oil concession. This agreement gave the company the sole right to explore, prospect, extract, transport, refine, market, and export petroleum and natural gas throughout the principality of Qatar. A side letter obliged Anglo-Persian to drill free of charge two artesian water wells for the ruler and forbade employees of the company from displaying forbidden items such as "intoxicating liquors." Anglo-Persian also agreed to employ two "informed persons" selected by Sheikh Abdullah to represent him in matters related to the concession and to supply an annual amount of petrol and kerosene to the sheikh at no cost before and after the production of any crude oil.

Immediately after he signed the concession on behalf of Anglo-Persian, Mylles handed a letter to Sheikh Abdullah from the political resident reiterating that it was subject to the approval of the British government. Fowle had already shown a draft of the political agreement between Britain and Anglo-Persian to the ruler, but he reportedly took little interest in the document. Sheikh Abdullah may have thought it only concerned the two signatories, although it rendered his own concession with Anglo-Persian subordinate to the political agreement. Finalization of the political agreement followed the concession by less than three weeks and was signed in London on June 5.

Sheikh Abdullah, however, took a very active interest in his own agreement with the British authorities, and he used their almost obsessive desire to see the concession go to Anglo-Persian to extract the maximum political advantage for himself and his successors. The resulting government agreement included an enhanced protection guarantee, recognition of Hamad as heir apparent, changes to the 1916 Treaty, and several matters relating to jurisdiction. It was subject to several redrafts in the weeks after signature of the concession with Anglo-Persian, as the sheikh pushed his luck with the British. A last-minute attempt to add machine guns and armored cars to Sheikh Abdullah's annual import quota of five hundred rifles was rejected by London, despite strong support from the political resident, who argued that the sheikh of Kuwait had been allowed to purchase machine guns that he mounted on Ford Vanettes. "His Majesty's Government had Kuwait precedent before them but do not regard Qatar, in view of lightness of Shaikh's authority and backwardness of State, as comparable with Kuwait," the secretary of state for India decreed.[52]

Britain signed the government agreement with Sheikh Abdullah on June 6, after which Fowle, who had been biding his time off Doha on board the HMS *Bideford*, was finally allowed to affix his signature to the concession. In addition to the 400,000 rupees he received upfront from Anglo-Persian as a cash bonus,

Sheikh Abdullah was to get 150,000 rupees annually during the concession's first five years and 300,000 rupees per annum from years six to seventy-five. On the discovery of hydrocarbons, the Qatari ruler and his successors would receive a royalty of 3 rupees per ton of oil produced and 2 annas for every one thousand cubic feet of natural gas extracted and sold. These terms were broadly in line with the Kuwait Oil Company concession concluded with Sheikh Ahmad Al Sabah, a copy of which Sheikh Abdullah and his advisers had no doubt already obtained, with slight variations in annual payments and royalty rates. The Kuwait deal had been finalized on December 23, 1934, with Archibald Chisholm signing for Anglo-Persian and Frank Holmes representing Gulf Oil.

Two years in the making, Anglo-Persian's oil concession marked the starting point for Qatar's development as a political entity and, eventually, an energy superpower. Its signing, however, only stoked the regional, international, and commercial rivalries that sometimes threatened to derail negotiations.

CHAPTER 3

Eureka!

Oil Is Discovered at Qatar's Dukhan Field

News that Sheikh Abdullah had signed the oil concession with Anglo-Persian quickly reached Ibn Saud. He was predictably unhappy with this development and dispatched a special messenger to Doha with a letter of warning for the sheikh. Until the boundary issue was settled, Ibn Saud wrote, he'd be "compelled to protest and to stop operations and to prevent anything being done" if the company were to start drilling or other work.[1] The Saudi king also asked the Al Thani sheikh to postpone the concession until the border was determined, promising that once the boundary was fixed, Sheikh Abdullah would be "at liberty to do what he likes." Sheikh Abdullah was noncommittal in his response to Ibn Saud, saying only that the boundaries of Qatar were well known and that, as he had already granted the concession to Anglo-Persian, he could not go back on it. He then dispatched his secretary to Bahrain to tell the political agent about the king's letter. The Saudis delivered a similar message to Britain's minister in Jeddah, omitting their threat to halt Anglo-Persian's operations if it commenced work before the frontier was delimited.

It probably had not escaped Ibn Saud's notice that the Royal Air Force (RAF) had already started to implement the inland protection guarantee given to Sheikh Abdullah as part of the Anglo-Persian concession. While the Royal Navy secured Qatar's maritime borders under the 1916 Treaty, responsibility for protecting the interior from external aggression fell to the RAF. Its planes conducted low-flying reconnaissance to select an appropriate location for a landing ground in early July, just one month after the government agreement with Sheikh Abdullah was signed. By mid-August permanent markings were cemented at the chosen airfield site at

Nasraniyah north of Doha, and a small petrol store was constructed to fuel RAF planes. Sheikh Abdullah still pushed for armored cars to back up the planes, arguing that his forces needed such vehicles to police the southern border.

Anglo-Persian and its partners in the Iraq Petroleum Company (IPC) established a new subsidiary called Petroleum Concessions Limited (PCL) to seek "oil concessions in the territory known as the Neutral Zone, the unallotted part of Bahrein Island, the Trucial Coast, and possibly along the Pirate Coast to Muscat."[2] Registered in Great Britain on October 14, 1935, PCL was held by the same companies and in the same proportion as IPC. The composition of PCL's board was similar as well, although it had no Iraqi government director. Due notice was given to the British government that the concession granted by the ruler of Qatar would be transferred from Anglo-Persian, which by this stage had officially changed its name to the Anglo-Iranian Oil Company, to PCL "at the appropriate time."[3] Sheikh Abdullah himself was not consulted about the concession's transfer to PCL. He would later complain that, while Anglo-Iranian had been generous, the "new" company was treating him badly.[4]

Recent options obtained by Anglo-Iranian from the rulers of Ras Al Khaimah, Sharjah, and Dubai on the Trucial coast would henceforth be held by PCL as well. The British government was informed through the India Office that PCL planned to employ Maj. Frank Holmes—Anglo-Iranian's old nemesis—as its negotiator for all further concessions in the Persian Gulf. The terms offered to the sheikhs would be based on the Qatar royalty precedent of three rupees per ton of oil produced, with adjustments in the annual cash payments to reflect differing sizes of territory.

PCL formed a separate company called Petroleum Development (Qatar) Limited, or PDQ, to hold and operate the Qatar concession and assume Anglo-Iranian's responsibilities under its political agreement with the British government. PDQ was registered in London on August 21, 1936, with an initial share capital of £100,000.[5] Drilling two artesian water wells for Sheikh Abdullah was its first order of business; the company sent out two geologists to Qatar in November for this purpose. In a move that would later be a source of considerable friction with Doha, PCL set up its administrative headquarters for the whole Persian Gulf area, including the Qatar peninsula, in Bahrain. E. V. Packer, the company's first resident general manager in Bahrain, was also appointed chief local representative for Qatar. He resided in Bahrain and only visited Qatar when the need arose, much to the annoyance of Sheikh Abdullah and his advisers.

SHAKY START FOR AN OIL COMPANY

By the end of 1936 Sheikh Abdullah was threatening to halt PDQ's water-drilling operations over the salaries of the two advisers representing him, one of whom was the heir apparent. The scope of their duties was also in dispute. The sheikh argued that all invitations to tender for contracts should be issued through his oil representatives, who would also select contractors and control company recruitment. After PDQ threatened to withdraw its staff and suspend cash payments to Sheikh Abdullah if the water boring was halted, the political agent intervened to ensure that work continued while discussions on the remuneration and role of the sheikh's representatives were under way. Fearful of setting a precedent, the company was adamant in not increasing its offer, telling the political agent it would only "encourage obstruction on all possible occasions in the future."[6]

The first water well near the sheikh's garden in Doha was abandoned in January 1937 when the hole caved in at 85 feet. A second at his Riyan residence (some three to four miles west of Doha) was drilled to a depth of 605 feet before it too was abandoned. By the end of April PDQ had withdrawn its crew and ended its operations in Qatar for the October 1936–April 1937 season. The issue of the sheikh's two oil representatives and their salaries was still not settled, although the company reported in its summary of that season's work program that arbitration was not favored by the ruler. Two of the firm's geologists, T. E. Williamson and R. Pomeyrol, returned to Qatar the following November to map the peninsula and choose sites for more water wells and the initial oil wells.[7] In anticipation of serious oil drilling, PDQ started building its first camp on the peninsula's west coast, some two to three miles inland near the northern end of Jebel Dukhan.

The provision of guards for the Dukhan drilling camp and their pay quickly became another flash point between the ruler and PDQ. Protection was to be provided by Sheikh Abdullah at the company's expense. But it complained that the sheikh had "visions of maintaining quite a small army at the Company's expense with Shaikh Hamad the heir apparent possibly in command."[8] When Sheikh Abdullah and his advisers cited the dangers posed by the camp's isolation and its proximity to Saudi Arabia, PDQ responded that a normal state of security needed to be provided at the camp, not a state of war. Ten guards should be more than sufficient, the company told Sheikh Abdullah; in Saudi Arabia small camps of this nature had five guards only. The fact that twenty-five guards were employed at California Arabian Standard Oil Company's Al Khobar camp in Saudi Arabia was not mentioned. In the end, PDQ gave in to Sheikh Abdullah's insistence on a minimum of twenty guards at the Dukhan camp.

A new unloading base at Zekrit on the west coast was built to supply the Dukhan camp. Hired craft carrying company cargoes were required to pay harbor dues to the Qatar government. Customs duties were virtually the sole source of state revenue before the export of oil, so the oil company's jetty at Zekrit was an important source of income for government. Agreement was finally reached in January 1938 between PDQ and the ruler on the salaries for Sheikh Abdullah's two representatives, and this was made retroactive to the signature of the oil concession. Hamad, the heir apparent, received 1,000 rupees monthly as one of the two designated oil representatives while Saleh el Mana, the ruler's longtime secretary and general adviser, was paid 250 rupees per month as the second.

Heightened tensions between Qatar and Bahrain made it difficult for the ruler's representatives to collect his annual payments from PDQ, which were deposited each May into Sheikh Abdullah's account at the Bahrain branch of the British-owned Eastern Bank. Collection became impossible in late 1937 when Sheikh Hamad Ibn Isa Al Khalifah of Bahrain imposed a crushing embargo on all trade and travel with Qatar following another clash over the ownership of the town of Zubara. Since there were still no banks in Qatar, in 1938 the managing director of PCL instead personally delivered most of the 163,250 rupees due under the concession to Sheikh Abdullah.[9] In addition to the annual payment of 150,000 rupees, this amount included the cash equivalent of the sheikh's petrol and kerosene allotment.

Once the drilling camp was up and running in October 1938, the company was finally able to sink its first test well for oil. Drilling commenced in December, two and a half years after the concession had been signed. The following month Hugh Weightman, the new political agent, visited Dukhan. "I stayed in the PCL camp at Jebel Dukhan and found them all very cheerful," Weightman wrote to Fowle in Bushire on January 16, 1939. "They have built a very pleasant small camp and have nine or ten people there who seem to get on very well together and also with the Qatar coolies. They are down to 2,050 ft. and are setting casing to that depth this week. Afterwards they start drilling again into what may be the first oil horizon."[10] Weightman noted that relations between the company and the sheikh had improved. Sheikh Abdullah had approved a request from PDQ to build its own landing ground near Dukhan, a proposal supported by the political agent so that the RAF could use the airstrip for defense purposes. The India Office had no objection, although it ensured the facility lay outside the southwestern territory claimed by Ibn Saud (who by this time had laid claim to Jebel al Nakhsh).

FIRST TEST WELL AT DUKHAN HITS OIL

By July 1939 the first test well had reached a depth of 4,440 feet, with plans in place to drill to 6,500 feet and then abandon the well if there were still no sign of oil. On October 11 the political agent cautiously reported that "Petroleum Development Qatar have had a slight show of oil in the test well."[11] The company informed the India Office and the Petroleum Department in London of the promising development nine days later, reporting that oil had been struck at a depth of approximately 5,685 feet. It also cautioned that considerably more drilling was necessary to establish the presence of a commercial oil field. In January 1940 Weightman confirmed that further tests of the well had proved highly satisfactory. That same month PCL asked the political agent to write to Sheikh Abdullah congratulating him on the successful well test. This letter was duly sent, although the good news was overshadowed by the looming war in Europe. "It is most regrettable that the Company's operations are bound to be delayed by the war which has been forced on us by Hitler and the German Government," Weightman wrote (see fig. 3.2).[12]

After determining that oil similar in quality to that being produced in Bahrain existed at Dukhan, the company made immediate plans to drill ten miles south of the existing well to assess the size of the structure. If the results of this second well were favorable, PDQ told the sheikh it would then be possible to formulate a drilling policy for commercial exploitation. By May 1940 the company was prepared to build a second drilling rig for its Qatari operations as soon as possible—only for the British government to refuse to authorize the purchase of the steel it needed because this material was required for the war effort. A decision had already been made by the allied forces not to accelerate oil production from new sources in British-controlled territory. Areas where production equipment and marine loading facilities already existed, like Saudi Arabia and especially Bahrain, were prioritized instead.

Well No. 2 hit oil at six thousand feet by early 1941 and appeared capable of producing at least as high as its predecessor. A location for a third well one mile

3.1 The first well, Dukhan No.1.

Source: Qatar Petroleum website, https://www.qatarenergy.qa/PublishingImages/QP%20History/photo
-exibition%206_NEW.jpg.

north of Well No. 1 was selected, and further drilling was being considered to
establish the extent of the field at Dukhan. The company's plans called for a
pipeline to an export terminal on the opposite side of the peninsula, as the shallow waters and abundant coral reefs along the west coast ruled out a terminal
closer to the Dukhan field, and a survey party scoured the east coast of Qatar for
a suitable oil tanker anchorage. Soundings were taken at three possible sites: Ras
Laffan, forty miles north of Doha; a second location just south of Wakrah; and a
third alternative near the southern Nikyan sandhills but well north of Khor al
Odaid.

Relations with the ruler were still fraught, with the oil company lamenting
that Sheikh Abdullah and his entourage regarded PDQ as a "cow to be milked as
much and as often as possible."[13] The ruler taxed the pay of local employees, levy-
ing a form of income tax equivalent to about 10 percent through his adviser and
petroleum representative, Saleh el Mana.[14] Sheikh Abdullah regularly pressed
the company to create work for more men. "If the Shaikh and his son, Hamad,
could be brought to realize that interference in the conduct of the Company's

No. C/65 - 10/3

The 14th January 1940

To

Shaikh Abdullah bin Qasim
Al Thani, C.I.E.,
Ruler of Qatar.

After Compliments.

I hear that the Oil Company have had a very successful test of their well at Dukhan and I write to congratulate you most heartily on the discovery of oil in Qatar. I earnestly hope that future drilling which the Company will undertake will prove that Qatar possesses a valuable oil field.

2. It is most regrettable that the Company's operations are bound to be delayed by the war which has been forced on us by Hitler and the German Government. We must all hope that victory will be speedily achieved so that normal conditions may return to the whole world.

3. I trust that you are enjoying the best of health and that all is well on your side.

Usual Ending.

Political Agent, Bahrain.

3.2 Congratulatory letter on discovery from British political agent to Sheikh Abdullah Ibn Jassim Al Thani, 1940.

Source: "File 10/3 XI Qatar Oil Concession," fol. 243r, image 500/594, British Library: India Office Records and Private Papers, IOR/R/15/2/418, Qatar Digital Library, https://www.qdl.qa /archive/81055/vdc_100024164774 .0x000065.

operations, particularly the persistent attempt to control recruitment and extort money from employees, hinders progress, relations between the Co. and the Shaikh would be easier and the work would be proceed more smoothly," PDQ wrote to the political agent, Maj. R. G. Alban, in early 1941, while imploring him to put a stop to this "meddling in employment matters."[15]

WORLD WAR II HALTS OIL OPERATIONS IN QATAR

Operations had wound down considerably by the end of 1941 due to the war's absorption of both equipment and experienced drillers. After a visit to Qatar in November, the political resident Sir Rupert Hay noted that PDQ was working at very low strength, with no more than thirteen Europeans employed on the peninsula. While a third well was drilled, it was "off structure" and yielded only salt water. There was talk of a fourth well, but it would be nearly five years before it was drilled. On June 28, 1942, Sheikh Abdullah was notified by the British government that it was directing the oil company to suspend operations in his territory because of the war. One month later, all three wells were permanently plugged with cement as a denial measure against enemy invaders. Dukhan's one drilling rig was moved to storage facilities in India and its field equipment to Iraq, and orders were given not to leave anything behind of conceivable use to the enemy. By the end of 1942 the Dukhan camp had closed its wireless station and evacuated its foreign workers.

Negotiations for the temporary suspension of operations continued through 1943 but were finally concluded between Sheikh Abdullah and political agent Maj. Tom Hickinbotham in late November. PDQ would continue to pay Sheikh Abdullah the annual concession fee (which had risen to 300,000 rupees in 1941) for the duration of the suspension, meet the salaries of the sheikh's two representatives, and pay 13,250 rupees per year as compensation for the annual allotment of petrol and kerosene.[16] The company agreed to keep the customs director at Zekrit, the chief guide, the guard commander, and thirty-four other guards on its payroll. Monthly payments for these individuals were made directly to the sheikh, who paid the wages on to their intended recipients after "taxing" them. PDQ would continue to arrange sea transport between Bahrain and Zekrit to ferry the weekly mail, underwrite the cost of the camel train traveling between Doha and the company's camp at Dukhan twice a month, and pay for one of the sheikh's representatives to inspect the camp monthly.

Despite the oil company's settlement, Sheikh Abdullah had to mortgage his home to pay his debts. Qatar was hard-hit in the late 1930s by the crash in the pearl market following the introduction of cheaper cultured pearls from Japan, the Great Depression, and the Bahraini embargo imposed in 1937 after the flare-up over the contested town of Zubara. The embargo was only lifted in 1944 after a British-brokered truce that restored the status quo at Zubara but did not resolve its sovereignty. Sheikh Abdullah was further squeezed financially when whole villages led by his rebellious brothers and other dissident relatives refused to pay him tribute. Qataris found employment during the war years in relatively prosperous Bahrain and in the oil fields of Al Hasa in Saudi Arabia, often migrating as entire clans with families and retainers in tow. So many people left that the population fell dramatically, from twenty-seven thousand at the beginning of the century to sixteen thousand or possibly even lower by 1949.[17] Aerial photos taken in the 1940s show large swaths of ruined area. Most of Qatar's merchant class, never large compared to other Persian Gulf states, fell on hard times and migrated. But the Al Thani ruling family survived, and in fact benefited: the wartime exodus of the local trading community made the sheikhs the most important players in Qatar when commercial oil production finally commenced.[18]

Kuwait suffered a similar fate as Qatar, with its oil operations entirely shut down in early 1942. Its wells were also filled with cement and most of Kuwait Oil Company's materials and equipment moved overseas. Because it was already producing oil and kerosene for the war effort, existing operations in neighboring Bahrain continued with few restrictions. New drilling ceased in late 1940 for six years after the Italians bombed the island, but the Bahrain Petroleum Company maintained full production of crude oil and refined products. Operations in Saudi Arabia continued as well, supplying the Bahrain refinery with crude oil throughout the war. In mid-1943 the U.S. government, acting on the urgent need for petroleum products and worried about drawing too heavily on its own oil supplies, made rapid wartime development in Saudi Arabia a priority. Secretary of the Interior Harold L. Ickes even came up with a plan for the government to become a shareholder in California Arabian Standard Oil Company, although this was rejected by its parent companies.[19] The firm was renamed the Arabian American Oil Company, or Aramco, in January 1944.

There was talk of resuming oil field development in Qatar to assist the war effort in the Pacific and Indian Oceans as well as to meet the needs of formerly occupied areas of Europe. "Plans have already been formulated in America for development of oil fields there to highest capacity and it has now become matter of urgent necessity in face of change in war situation to consider as complementary measure opening up more crude oil production in Iraq, Persia and Persian Gulf," the secretary of state for India told the political resident in November 1943.[20] PCL put forward a proposal that included ordering three American rigs to enable continuous two-rig drilling in Qatar. This proposal and another from Kuwait Oil Company for resuming Kuwaiti development were approved by the Oil Control Board in January 1944 and submitted to Washington for a final decision. Oil companies in the Persian Gulf were by this time almost entirely dependent on the United States for oil field equipment and material; PCL's £500,000 budget for the resumption of Qatari drilling was in reality nearly all in American dollars.[21]

OIL OPERATIONS RESUME IN POSTWAR QATAR

Postwar operations in Kuwait were prioritized over Qatar, partly because of the Kuwait Oil Company's half American ownership and partly because of its more advanced stage of development. This resumption in work was ordered by the Allied Command in early 1945, and the 50–50 venture between Anglo-Iranian and Gulf Oil commenced production by mid-1946. Kuwait consequently took a high place as an oil supplier in the immediate postwar period.[22] Nothing came of PCL's proposal to the Oil Control Board on Qatar until September 1945, when the company finally informed Sheikh Abdullah that its local subsidiary PDQ had been authorized to reopen operations at Dukhan. PCL had envisioned output of twenty thousand barrels of crude oil per day, based on the geological data and tests from the two promising wells that had already been drilled at Dukhan, and it wanted to move speedily. But preparations at the Dukhan camp were not set to begin until early 1946, following a seismic survey of the field that winter. Drilling wouldn't commence until the fourth quarter of 1946, and the wartime authorities only approved one rig rather than the three sought by PCL.[23]

A request from Sheikh Abdullah for an advance of 500,000 rupees on future oil royalties was approved by PCL in 1945, a gesture designed to smooth any feathers ruffled by the drilling delay. This interest-free sweetheart loan was provided by the company, recoverable through annual installments not greater than 20 percent of the advance and paid only in years when total royalties exceeded 300,000 rupees. Col. A. C. Galloway, the political agent, considered advising the sheikh to put some of this money toward improvements in national education and medical facilities. But he eventually concluded that such suggestions were imprudent, given the postponement in drilling. The monthly salaries of the sheikh's two representatives were also increased to 2,000 rupees, and the company agreed to pay Sheikh Abdullah an additional 2,500 rupees monthly to use its Zekrit jetty as well as the still-unconstructed east coast oil terminal. Sheikh Abdullah had complained in the past about the failure of PDQ to use Doha as a port of entry, depriving him of customs revenue; it was hoped the new payment would mollify him.

Sheikh Abdullah was opposed to Wakrah as a site for the east coast oil terminal, principally because a dissident branch of his family controlled customs and port access in that area. Attention subsequently shifted to another location further south along the Nikyan sandhills, about fifteen miles north of Khor al Odaid. The political agent assured the oil company that the site was comfortably within Qatari territory and that Saudi Arabia's claim extended only as far north as the Khor.[24] PDQ also announced plans to construct a new harbor on the west coast, at Al Hamlab some twenty-two miles south of Zekrit, to service a future permanent camp a few miles inland at Umm Bab. A road would be built from Umm Bab to Wakrah, with branches up to Doha and down to the export terminal, following the proposed pipeline as closely as possible.

PDQ extended its seismic work southward from Dukhan in the winter of 1947–1948, reaching the southern limit of its concession on the peninsula's west side. Since frontier negotiations with Ibn Saud were by this time in abeyance, the British decided against telling the Saudi king about the survey party, "on the assumption that it would be most unlikely that he should learn that it had operated in territory claimed by him."[25] This seismic work, which covered the whole of the western half of the concession right up to its southern boundary, was completed in early 1948 and PDQ's crew immediately withdrawn. Nor was there any early prospect of drilling in the concession's southwest corner, the company assured the Foreign Office. "The only continuing activity which we have in the area which you showed me as included in Ibn Saud's 1935 claimed line, is the extraction of gypsum which we have been taking for some time past from a point fairly far

3.3 Sheikh Abdullah inspects start of Dukhan Well No. 4, September 23, 1947.

Source: Qatar Petroleum website, https://www.qatarenergy.qa/PublishingImages/QP%20History/photo
-exibition%208_NEW.jpg.

south in the area shown in your map as Jebel Nakhsh: nobody seems to have raised
any objection to this," PCL wrote to the Foreign Office in early 1948.[26]

Three drilling rigs were habitually deployed at the Dukhan structure from 1947
onward. By early 1948 the company had two hundred British and American personnel working in Qatar with orders to start production as soon as possible. A
degassing plant for initial oil/gas separation was built at Khatiya on the north
end of Dukhan, and a pipeline was laid to the east coast. This line consisted of
eighteen miles of twelve-inch-diameter pipe and nearly fifty miles of fourteen-
inch pipe, both of which were constructed in 1949 by way of Umm Bab. A surface road was laid alongside the pipeline, as was a telegraph line. Qatar had no
paved roads, and the company road was unique. But it was not properly leveled,
nor was it surfaced with tar. Instead, crude oil was simply poured on to compact
the loose sand surface.[27] PDQ had also settled on a deep-water anchorage south
of Wakrah for its export terminal, and work was under way on the facility. This
came to be known as Umm Said, a name neither recorded nor marked on maps
before the oil company's arrival.

Sheikh Abdullah's relations in Wakrah, led by his nephew Saud Ibn Abdul Rahman Al Thani, caused a minor upset by repeatedly removing a navigational beacon that PDQ was trying to install on Jebel Wakrah to help ships traveling to Umm Said. After sending a sharply worded letter to the dissident nephew demanding that he cease disrupting oil company operations, the political resident decided it might be opportune if the naval sloop HMS *Wren* showed itself off Wakrah. When this did not have the desired effect, the HMS *Flamingo* was dispatched to Qatar with instructions to send a party ashore. "If practicable you might add that as a first step you would train your guns on his house and blow it up," the political resident suggested to the ship's commanding officer.[28] The so-called sheikh of Wakrah backed down, and the navigational aid went up without further incident.

SHEIKH ABDULLAH ABDICATES IN FAVOR OF SON

Sheikh Abdullah was gradually handing over his duties to Hamad, the heir apparent. By the early 1940s Hamad had become the virtual ruler, and by 1944 the political agent reported Hamad had the use of his father's seal. "It is interesting to note that Sheikh Hamad should have succeeded in so far gaining control as to have the custody of that most precious of all the Arab emblems of sovereignty, the signet ring," Major Hickinbotham wrote.[29] But Hamad suffered from a variety of ailments, including diabetes. He died on May 27, 1948. The following month, Sheikh Abdullah declared to an assembly of notables and members of the Al Thani family that his eldest son, Ali, would replace Hamad as his successor. While the attendees subsequently signed a letter agreeing to this, the whole affair was kept secret from the British authorities until November when the political resident visited Qatar. "It is rumored that Sheikh Abdullah has designated Khalifah, who is the third son of the late Hamad and a boy of 18, as the second successor to the Sheikhdom," Sir Rupert Hay wrote to the Foreign Office.[30] He added a prescient observation: "If this is true, the action is unfortunate and may lead to trouble later, as Ali has a large number of sons of his own."[31]

On August 20, 1949, Sheikh Abdullah abdicated at the age of eighty-four, and Ali became ruler. It was not a smooth transition. Abdullah demanded that his son direct the oil company's payment for customs dues and guards' wages to him.

3.4 Sheikh Ali Ibn Abdullah Al Thani, r. 1949–1960.

Source: Official site of the Amiri Diwan of the State of Qatar, https://www.diwan.gov.qa/-/media/Diwan-Amiri/Images/Qatar-Rulers/Sheikh-Ali-Bin-Abdullah-Al-Thani.ashx.

The British later forced Sheikh Ali to recover most of this money from Abdullah, who as part of the abdication settlement was already due a substantial stipend from the state. "The old Shaikh has handed over nothing to his son and successor," Hay confided to the Foreign Office. "He has sent most of his money out of the country, has retained all his cars and has given the beautiful launch he received from Petroleum Concessions Limited away to Abdulla Darwish."[32] Shortly before he abdicated, Sheikh Abdullah had come under intense pressure from his relatives, who threatened to rebel and burn down the bazaar if they did not get a share of the royalties from pending oil sales. The ensuing crisis convinced

Britain it needed a political officer in Qatar itself, rather than relying on visits from the political agent based in Bahrain. A. J. Wilton, the first political officer posted to Qatar, took up residence in Doha three days after the abdication. He immediately set about forming a properly armed and organized police force under a retired British officer named Ronald Cochrane, bolstering Sheikh Ali's standing in any further disputes with his father or his Al Thani rivals.

The new ruler's authority was further reinforced by an advance of 400,000 rupees from PDQ just seven days after the abdication. This money was quickly used to satisfy old debts, to buy cars, and to furnish the palace. By early September the British authorities had approached the firm to suggest a second advance for Sheikh Ali—this time one controlled by Wilton, Britain's political officer in Qatar.[33] PDQ readily agreed to advance Sheikh Ali a further 400,000 rupees, but it attached two conditions: that the political officer supervise the sum's expenditure and that it be fully repaid from oil royalties accruing in 1950. This offer was unacceptable to Sheikh Ali. Rather than relinquish total control to Wilton, he borrowed money from the powerful Darwish family. One of its three patriarchs, Abdullah Darwish, had been a close confidant and business partner of Sheikh Hamad, Sheikh Ali's younger brother and the heir apparent before his death in 1948. Darwish was now closely allied with Sheikh Ali, who had appointed him to replace Saleh el Mana as the ruler's petroleum representative after his accession in 1949.

Britain clearly intended to use royalties from pending oil sales to build a functioning government in Doha. This included paying the salary of a future British adviser to Sheikh Ali as well as that of Cochrane and underwriting a considerably augmented police force. Wilton was asked to draw up a rough budget that included these costs as well as that of a civil list appointed by Sheikh Ali and funds to satisfy his "rapacious relations."[34] Part of this brief included appointing suitable members of the ruling family to government posts since, the political agent explained in a letter to Wilton, "there seems to be no reason why some of them should not also work for a living."[35] However, the political officer would not have the direct financial control over the ruler that the British authorities desired. As the Foreign Office pointed out, "the sheikh will be receiving large royalties in the future and . . . the extent to which we can hope to control his finances will presumably be conditioned by his good will and by the influence which the Advisor, when appointed, can succeed in creating."[36]

QATAR'S FIRST OIL CARGO SHIPPED FROM UMM SAID

In the meantime, PDQ was preparing to ship crude oil from Umm Said. The first cargo was loaded on board the SS *President Manny*, which set sail for Europe on December 31, 1949. That same month the political officer noted that relations between Sheikh Ali and the company were not good. "This is partly due to the former's instability, and ingenuity in thinking up new ways of getting money and goods from the Company, and to his inability to control pilfering," Wilton reported. "A contributory cause has been the Company's attempt to achieve the impossible feat of conducting its relations with the Shaikh through a representative in Bahrain, of whose work Qatar forms only a part."[37] Under pressure from the British political authorities, PCL conceded that the early appointment of a chief local representative in Qatar was desirable, given the imminent commencement of commercial production by its subsidiary PDQ. But it sent this representative to live in Dukhan, on the other side of the peninsula from Doha, where Sheikh Ali was normally resident.

The company also agreed to advance Sheikh Ali 400,000 rupees, which, unlike the previous transaction, was billed not as a loan but as an early payment of royalties. No conditions would be attached to the payment this time. PCL felt compelled to act immediately in order to counter the rising influence of Superior Oil Company, a competitor from America that had only recently appeared on the scene in Qatar but was already making waves. PCL told the political agent that Superior was almost certainly ready to advance money to Sheikh Ali if PCL itself did not. The Los Angeles–based firm had obtained an offshore concession from Sheikh Abdullah in the final weeks of his reign. This was now the subject of a contentious and still undecided arbitration battle with PCL, who argued that Qatar's maritime waters were part and parcel of its own concession. On land, Superior was eyeing territory south of the original 1935 boundary line that might accrue to the state of Qatar after its frontier with Saudi Arabia was finally fixed, an area PCL also claimed.

At the request of Sir Rupert Hay, who felt the transaction had to be conducted through Britain's political officer in Qatar, PCL reluctantly delayed the early royalty payment from its subsidiary to the sheikh. Shortly afterward, it became unnecessary. By the end of January 1950, PDQ had shipped 96,000 tons of crude oil from Umm Said and paid Sheikh Ali nearly 300,000 rupees in royalties.[38]

CHAPTER 4

Choppy Waters

Qatar's First Marine Oil Concession

As exports began of Qatari crude produced onshore, attention turned to oil potential offshore. Discussions with Sheikh Abdullah on Qatar's first marine concession were headed by Sir Hugh Weightman, Britain's former Bahrain-based political agent from 1937 to 1940 who had since joined Central Mining & Investment Corporation, Superior Oil Company's British partner. Neither company was known on the Arab side of the Persian Gulf at the time, but Superior was already a veteran offshore operator in the Gulf of Mexico. Founded in 1921, it had constructed the first oil platform off the Louisiana coast in 1938 together with Pure Oil, another independent oil company in the United States. While Central Mining had no oil industry experience, it had been around since 1905, and its founders played an important part in developing South Africa's Witwatersrand gold field.

Weightman's arrival on the scene in 1948 surprised established oil players in Qatar and Saudi Arabia, where Aramco was under pressure from the Saudi government to surrender unexploited portions of its concession. It soon became apparent that Superior and Central Mining were interested in securing exploitation rights to the seabed outside Saudi Arabia's territorial waters, although Saudi officials were certainly not adverse to using Weightman to frighten Aramco's American owners.[1] PCL's subsidiary in Qatar also became increasingly agitated, arguing that its concession gave it the right to search for and exploit oil across the entire area ruled by Sheikh Abdullah, including the territorial waters belonging to the mainland as well as all islands, reefs, and pearling grounds.

Local rulers were beginning to take advantage of the interest in offshore oil. In mid-1949, all the heads of the Persian Gulf states (including Sheikh Abdullah) issued proclamations that the seabed and subsoil lying beneath the high seas of the Persian Gulf, contiguous to their territorial waters and extending seawards to boundaries yet to be determined, belonged to them and were subject to their absolute jurisdiction. After these declarations were made, PCL claimed its concessions covered the seabed and subsoil these rulers had annexed. Several of the disputes ended up in arbitration. In each case, it was decided that the original concessions covered only land above water and the subsoil of territorial waters. Rulers were free to grant separate concessions for the subsoil outside the limits of their territorial waters.

In Qatar the dispute with PCL was referred to arbitration in June 1949 under article 16 of the original 1935 concession signed with Anglo-Persian. But Sheikh Abdullah had no intentions of waiting until the arbitration proceedings were over. On August 5, just two weeks before his abdication, the aging ruler signed the agreement with Weightman, from whom he immediately received a signature bonus of 750,000 rupees, equivalent to about £56,300 at the time.[2] The concession referred only to the submarine area of the high seas under Sheikh Abdullah's jurisdiction, and no mention was made of territorial waters. Under the agreement, Sheikh Abdullah or his successor was to receive 25 percent of the market value of the crude oil produced in royalties or one million rupees per year, whichever sum was greater.[3]

To operate the concession, Superior and Central Mining formed a so-called Canadian 4K company named International Marine Oil Company Limited with a nominal capital of $500,000. Central Mining took a 12.5 percent interest in this subsidiary and Superior the remaining 87.5 percent. The Foreign Office was quite supportive of Superior's interest in Qatar and the other Persian Gulf sheikhdoms, saying a larger American stake in the area had certain political advantages. It also pointed out that a new concern might be more eager to actually develop the concession than PCL and the other subsidiaries of the Iraq Petroleum Company. These companies, the Foreign Office said, were "engaged in so many areas that it is difficult to be certain that they would be able actively to pursue any further commitments for the present."[4]

The arbitration hearings on Qatar's seabed rights were held in Doha over six days in February 1950. In its decision, the three-member arbitration panel ruled that Qatar's territorial waters and islands were included in the 1935 concession but not "the seabed or subsoil or any part thereof beneath the high seas of the Persian Gulf contiguous with such territorial waters."[5] Not surprisingly, PCL pushed back on the interpretation of territorial waters, which was not covered in the Qatar arbitration or others involving the Trucial coast sheikhdoms. Appealing to the Foreign Office, the company argued that in certain regions the limit for territorial waters was set at three miles, whereas in other areas it was six and even twelve miles.[6] PCL said a six-mile limit had been used, or claimed, in the Persian Gulf. It also passed on a rumor that Superior already had a drilling barge on its way out to Qatar and might start drilling four miles offshore, thereby suggesting what the company called a narrow rather than broad territorial water belt.[7]

London quickly put paid to the six-mile concept, telling PCL the territorial waters of Qatar should be calculated based on three nautical miles. As it turned out, PCL needn't have worried about Superior's immediate drilling plans. The marine concession called for Superior and its British partner to drill their first test well within two years from the date of signature, but in early 1951 this deadline was extended to August 5, 1952. In return for the extension, and after a considerable amount of haggling, Superior agreed to give Sheikh Ali three motor-launches and a Diamond T truck.[8] When two of the launches were delivered to Doha in April 1951, Sheikh Abdullah immediately claimed they were promised in the days of his rule and belonged therefore to him. The aging sheikh eventually backed down, and Sheikh Ali kept the launches, even giving one to his British adviser.

Since the seabed had not been fully delimited, the British government defined a provisional area to Superior in which it would be free to operate. Off the peninsula's west coast, this extended to the median line between Qatar and Bahrain fixed by Britain in 1947. Included in the area were the waters adjoining Dibal and Jaradeh, two shoals that had been given to Bahrain in 1947 but did not carry territorial waters. By the time Superior approached the British for permission to carry out a seismic survey over the whole of its concession, however, it had become apparent that the two shoals might indeed carry territorial waters under evolving international law. "Pending a decision on the territorial waters question involving Dibal and Jaradeh, we desire to include these waters in our exploratory work," Superior wrote to the political agent C. J. Pelley in November 1950. "We are, however, prepared to commit ourselves not to drill any well within the three-mile band of waters surrounding Dibal and Jaradeh, at least until our right to do so has been established."[9] Superior was given the go-ahead if none of its survey work had a permanent impact on the area around the shoals. But the Foreign Office also elected not to communicate this decision to the rulers of Qatar and Bahrain.

Qatar was not the only Persian Gulf sheikhdom to attract the U.S. company's interest. Superior was awarded a seabed concession by Abu Dhabi's Sheikh Shakh-but Ibn Sultan Al Nahyan in late 1950. This prompted PCL's local affiliate, Petroleum Development (Trucial Coast) Limited, to reopen arbitration proceedings against Sheikh Shakhbut. Superior even financed the sheikh's case. Once again, it was decided that the onshore concessionaire's rights extended to territorial waters only and did not include the seabed or subsoil outside those limits. The American firm also secured a marine concession from Dubai's Sheikh Said Ibn Maktum, whose separate arbitration with PCL returned basically the same result as in Qatar and Abu Dhabi. The terms of Superior's Dubai concession were a lot less favorable to the ruler, which the political agent put down to the amount of territory involved. Dubai's seacoast was only 40 miles long, compared with nearly 300 miles in Abu Dhabi and 250 miles in Qatar, while the sea off Dubai's coast contained few shoals and was of much greater average depth.

But it was not long before Superior's interest in the Persian Gulf, including Qatar, waned. "Mr. Lower of the Superior Oil Company called this morning to say that because of the very high cost of Marine operations in the Gulf and the ever increasing and, in his view, extremely unreasonable demands of the Sheikhs, the Superior Oil Co and its majority held subsidiary International Marine had decided to surrender all of their off-shore concessions in the Gulf," a Foreign Office official reported in early 1952.[10] The company also said it had been disturbed by the uncertainty of the sea boundaries in the area. Rumors pointed to financial difficulties at Superior as well, although the company would survive on its own until it was acquired by the Mobil Corporation in early 1984.

Central Mining, which had not been consulted about Superior's decision to withdraw from the Persian Gulf, officially informed the British government that its majority partner was about to surrender the marine concession in Qatar on March 14, 1952. While Superior notified Sheikh Ali Ibn Abdullah Al Thani that it was suspending its operations shortly afterward, it was nearly two months before its representatives told the ruler of the firm's decision to pull out of the country completely. Sheikh Ali had no time for Superior's explanation of high offshore costs, instead ascribing its withdrawal to its rumored financial difficulties. Superior was in no mood to hand over the annual concession payment of one million rupees, which was due on August 5, 1952. After the company refused to pay this amount to Sheikh Ali, the two sides ended up in arbitration of their own. The case was eventually decided in the ruler's favor.

Word quickly spread in London oil circles that Superior might relinquish its offshore acreage in Qatar, Abu Dhabi, and Dubai. The Royal Dutch Shell Group and Anglo-Iranian both wanted the seabed concession in Qatar, while Anglo-Iranian planned to independently pursue Superior's Abu Dhabi concession. Rumors circulated that Standard Oil of California might also be interested in Superior's Persian Gulf acreage, a prospect that drew immediate condemnation from Britain's Foreign Office. "We would not welcome an extension of Standard Oil in the Trucial Coast in view of their large holdings in Aramco, as this might give rise to charges of monopoly," it wrote in April 1952.[11]

Since Shell and Anglo-Iranian were both members of the Iraq Petroleum Company and therefore subject to the Red Line restrictions, they first had to ensure the consortium was not interested in acquiring these concessions. This would allow the individual partners in IPC to pursue the opportunity separately from the group. Permission was forthcoming toward the end of March, after the American and French members in IPC showed no interest in acquiring the Qatar concession. Anglo-Iranian felt it would be wise to let matters lie for a year or so, arguing that a little indifference in the Middle East would prevent local rulers from entertaining exaggerated ideas of their importance and of what they could extract from the oil companies in terms of remuneration. It proposed a "gentlemen's agreement" to its partners in IPC that they show no interest in the marine concession for the time being.[12]

Shell, undoubtedly influenced by the fact that it had no concessions of its own in the region, was not willing to wait. It quickly dispatched a team to Qatar to obtain a right of first refusal from Sheikh Ali. This option was granted in early May, and Shell almost immediately remitted the initial payment to the ruler in anticipation of a final deal. Anglo-Iranian was told by the Foreign Office that a separate approach to Sheikh Ali would be "most embarrassing" to Britain given Shell's fait accompli.[13] Its chair, Sir William Fraser, protested to the Foreign Office that Shell had "put over a fast one" in Qatar. Anglo-Iranian also pushed the British authorities to press for some form of joint interest in the concession.

It was clear, however, that Shell's participation had priority within the Foreign Office and the Ministry of Fuel and Power. Sir William was told he would have to accept a solution that left Qatar for Shell and Abu Dhabi for Anglo-Iranian.[14] The Iranian parliament had only just nationalized Anglo-Iranian's oil assets in that country. British officials therefore "felt serious concern at the prospect of an undignified scramble over Qatar, particularly at this time, when our overall policy is to assume indifference over Iran and to discourage exaggerated notions of the importance of Middle East oil generally."[15]

Shell signed an "entirely satisfactory" agreement with Sheikh Ali on May 19, 1952. The company told the British authorities it would follow the lead set by PCL, whose local subsidiary was negotiating with Sheikh Ali for 50–50 profit-sharing, and said it had secured a short preliminary period for exploration and survey during which fixed annual payments equivalent to Superior's would be made to the sheikh. Sir Donald Fergusson, who headed the Ministry of Fuel and Power, initially expressed dismay at the speed of Shell's approach, but he quickly backed down after the concession was signed. "There has never been any question of your acting regarding the Qatar Maritime Concession without the full knowledge and approval of this Ministry and the Foreign Office," Sir Donald assured Shell's Sir Francis Hopwood four days after the agreement. "What I was anxious to avoid was competitive bidding for this concession as I felt that this would be calculated to have undesirable effects on all Middle Eastern oil producing countries."[16]

While agreeing in principle that payments to Sheikh Ali after commercial oil production would reflect a 50–50 profit split, Shell wanted PCL's subsidiary in Qatar to implement the arrangement first. Therefore, it decided to replace its initial accord with a proper concession agreement once negotiations with the onshore operator ended. Shell initially offered Sheikh Ali 1,000,000 rupees as a signing bonus. Abdullah Darwish, the ruler's petroleum representative, convinced the sheikh to press for more, however, and Shell ended up agreeing to 3,500,000 rupees, or the equivalent of about £264,000 at the time.[17] Half the amount was paid in cash upon the agreement's signature. Britain's political officer in Qatar, M. S. Weir, noted that Shell's three-man team completed their business with remarkable dispatch, for which he credited the dominating force of Abdullah Darwish—although he also admitted the Shell representatives were openly eager to conclude an agreement speedily "at any price."[18]

There were conditions. Sheikh Ali insisted that Shell establish its local headquarters in Qatar, as he was much annoyed when Superior chose Bahrain for its subsidiary's main base. The company was informed that the boundary of the Qatar concession was provisional and that it must accept any modification the British government felt necessary. Shell had to acknowledge the safe zone for operations given earlier to Superior. This safe zone was within the area the Foreign Office considered the ruler of Qatar had a valid claim. The Foreign Office also reiterated that while the concession's western boundary was the line announced to the rulers of Qatar and Bahrain in October 1947, it had yet to make a firm decision on whether the shoals of Dibal and Jaradeh awarded to Bahrain carried territorial waters. It also pointed out that Qatar's northern, eastern, and southeastern seabed boundaries were still undetermined, and so instructed Shell to respect "the temporary limits which are defined."[19]

The seventy-five-year concession agreement with Shell Overseas Exploration Company Limited was signed on November 29, 1952. Financial terms closely followed the recently completed negotiations with PCL's local subsidiary. Shell's concession was defined as all the seabed and subsoil within Sheikh Ali's jurisdiction beyond the territorial waters of Qatar—some ten thousand square miles in total. But the agreement also explicitly acknowledged the uncertain nature of these boundaries. Article 1 of the concession read: "When the precise boundaries of this area shall hereafter be determined a map shall be prepared showing the agreed boundaries which shall be attached to this Agreement and shall be a part thereof."[20] Shell made a commitment to begin exploration activities within nine months of the signature of the concession, and to drill a test well within two years from that date extendable by another two years upon further payment. The work program outlined initial steps in an exploratory program that would lead to the discovery, two decades later, of the world's largest natural gas field.

CHAPTER 5

Qatar's Ruler Presses for Better Oil Terms

By 1950 drilling results had expanded knowledge about the geology of Qatar's first onshore oil field and raised production enough to elicit talk about a local refinery. Production from the Upper Jurassic Limestone of the Dukhan structure was obtained from twenty-five wells drilled to depths of around 6,000 feet. Initial output at a rate of about 1.5 million tons per year was sourced from eight wells drilled into the No. 3 Limestone horizon. A relatively rapid pressure drop following the beginning of production led PCL to target the slightly deeper No. 4 Limestone, where oil had been discovered in 1949. After 1950 all wells were drilled into this horizon, although a minor accumulation of oil was found in the Lower Jurassic Uwainat formation about 1,100 feet below the No. 4 Limestone in 1954. The No. 4 Limestone accounted for 75 percent of the Dukhan field's output by the end of 1951, which at that point had hit 2 million tons per year. Oil production reached an annual rate of 3.5 million tons (about 67,000 barrels per day) by the end of 1952 and continued to increase.

Commercial production at the Dukhan field triggered some discussion between the onshore operator and the Foreign Office at the end of 1950 about whether the time had come for the company to meet its refinery obligations under the 1935 political agreement. Article 9 of this agreement read: "The Company declare that it is their intention, should they consider that commercial conditions justify it, to erect a refinery in Qatar. If and when the Company is satisfied that commercial production is assured, the Company agrees to examine with His Majesty's Government the question of establishing a refinery in Qatar of suitable type and capacity." After briefly considering the matter, the Foreign Office decided to defer the question. PCL was informed that the British government saw no need to call upon the company's subsidiaries in Qatar or the Trucial coast to fulfill their refinery obligations.[1] No attempt was made to consult Sheikh Ali or his advisers, and the potential benefits of a refinery for the local economy do not seem to have been considered more than cursorily.

Sheikh Ali himself raised the matter a year later, telling Sir Rupert Hay that he considered the construction of a refinery in his state of utmost importance. This followed the cessation of petrol and kerosene imports from Iran's Abadan refinery, blockaded by British warships after the Iranian parliament nationalized Anglo-Iranian's local operations in March 1951. Replacement fuel supplies arranged through Bahrain were far from satisfactory. The idea of building a refinery in Qatar to provide bunker fuel for tankers and products for local consumption was discussed, as had already been done in Kuwait. PDQ drew up a new plan for a topping plant with an annual capacity of 100,000 tons, costing about £250,000.[2] The proposal was rejected once again by the British government, which said the 350 tons of steel required would be wasted on an unessential plant.

The refinery idea was floated again in late 1952 at Sheikh Ali's request and the oil company began working on plans for a considerably smaller topping plant. Local needs were assessed at just 9,500 tons per year, comprising 5,500 tons of gas oil, 3,500 tons of petrol, and 500 tons of kerosene. Qatar's annual crude oil production was approaching 4 million tons, and the refinery proposal finally gained some traction with the British. "Our view is that a small topping plant would mollify local susceptibilities and be useful for local supplies," the Ministry of Fuel and Power told a skeptical Foreign Office. "Qatar is the only oil producing state in the Middle East without some sort of refining plant."[3] The Foreign Office responded that it now considered it "worthwhile" to meet the ruler's request with a scaled down plant of this kind.

In early 1953 PCL's subsidiary in Qatar informed Sheikh Ali that it was proceeding with a topping plant at Umm Said designed to meet local consumption as well as the company's own needs. Average output per stream day would be as shown in table 5.1:

TABLE 5.1

Product	Average output per day (gallons)
Petrol	5,670
Kerosene	3,570
Gas Oil	4,200
Residue	7,560
Total	**21,000**

Source: PDQ, in letter to the Foreign Office, March 20, 1953; see POWE, *Qatar: Oil Concessions*, 1952–1961, 33/2094, National Archives, United Kingdom.

SHEIKH ALI SECURES ROYALTY ADJUSTMENT

Unhappy with the original royalty agreement, which, he joked, paid him less than if he exported water, Sheikh Ali moved to secure a rate increase in 1951. He got one, but PDQ's offer of ten rupees per ton was considerably lower than in other Persian Gulf countries including Kuwait. At the same time, the ruler fended off a request by PDQ to include "any territory which is, or may at any future time become, part of the dominions of the Sheikhdom of Qatar, including that part lying to the south of the line shown in the map attached to the concession."[4] This was obviously designed to thwart Superior Oil, who had earlier shown interest in territory south of the concession's boundary line. Sheikh Ali did agree in writing to open negotiations with PDQ once the country's southern frontier was demarcated, conceding that it would be "most undesirable" for another company to be granted a concession south of the current line. The ruler extracted two seven-seater Cadillac motorcars as the price of his signature on this assurance.

There was talk, Sheikh Ali's British adviser reported, of putting money into a reserve fund. The Foreign Office found this encouraging since it had been "difficult to induce [Sheikh Ali] to take a responsible view of the proportions in which his income from oil revenues should be divided between himself and his family on the one hand and the general requirements of the State on the other."[5] Sheikh Ali had reluctantly agreed earlier to make a distinction between private and public money by taking a set 25 percent of oil income and customs duties—the only two sources of revenue at the time—for himself. The remaining 75 percent went into an account the sheikh held jointly with his British adviser at the Eastern Bank. Its management was under orders to only honor checks signed by both men.

Allowances to other members of the ruling family, including Sheikh Abdullah's annual pension, came out of the state's share of the revenues.

But the system wasn't working satisfactorily. This was partly because Sheikh Ali's first British adviser, selected directly by the political resident with virtually no input from the ruler, was a former Royal Air Force officer who had no administrative experience. Group Captain P. L. Plant took up his post in early 1950 and was forced to resign just two years later.[6] It was also due to the avarice of the ruling family, with little left over to fund public works such as the country's first school, hospital, and law court as well as new roads, a jetty, and a warehouse. Plant's first provisional budget covered March 1950 to February 1951. It showed an estimated income of 6,500,000 rupees, or about £490,000. Of this, royalty and concession payments from PDQ came to 4,800,000 rupees, while Superior Oil's concession payment amounted to 1,000,000. Nearly half of this revenue was absorbed by Sheikh Ali, his father's pension, and other Al Thani family members. Another large chunk paid for the 130-strong regular police force, 50 Bedouin bodyguards, and the sheikh's personal security detail. It was impossible to save the target figure of 25 percent of the total state income in a reserve fund.

QATAR PREPARES ITS FIRST DEVELOPMENT PLAN

The revised royalty agreement with PDQ was quickly replaced with a 50–50 profit-sharing arrangement like the one imposed by Ibn Saud on Aramco in 1950. After learning Aramco had paid more in U.S. taxes than it had in royalties, the Saudi king first requested and then demanded an equal share of the petroleum income along the lines set in Venezuela and Iran. In Qatar the new agreement with PDQ was signed with Sheikh Ali on September 1, 1952. It provided for an income tax that, when added to all other taxes, duties, rents, and royalties, equaled 50 percent of the concessionaire's net income. For the first time all payments to the sheikh were made in sterling rather than Indian rupees. These were paid into the ruler's account at the Eastern Bank, which by this time had set up a Doha branch. PDQ followed the precedent set by Shell by undertaking to bear any losses incurred by Sheikh Ali in converting sterling into rupees, still the primary currency in the Persian Gulf.

In late 1952, with the new 50–50 profit-sharing arrangement in place and oil output rising, the British authorities forecast a rapid increase in Qatar's state oil revenues. These were reckoned to jump from £1.9 million in 1952 (based on annual crude oil production of 3 million tons) to £4.1 million in 1953 (assuming output of 3.8 million tons) and then to £6.6 million in 1954 (at 4.6 million tons per year or about 88,000 barrels per day). This, wrote one PCL manager rather pompously, represented "fantastic wealth by Qatari standards, posing moral as well as material problems to the population and their ruler."[7] The execution of a development plan now became a priority. A two-part Doha electricity scheme, a government hospital, and roads in and around Doha were seen as immediate requirements. This followed the completion of Qatar's first government primary school for boys in 1949 and a courthouse in 1951. Sheikh Ali and his British adviser, Plant, were also anxious to ensure a piped supply of drinking water to Doha. Police barracks, a prison, and a new customs house were planned as well. Qatar's first state hospital opened its doors in 1959.

The ruler moved to ban slavery in 1952, a long-standing practice within the Al Thani family and among wealthier merchants to which the British had, despite public condemnation, historically turned a blind eye. Even PDQ employed slaves in Qatar. In 1949, its first year of oil production, the company had 250 local slaves working for it, many at the personal request of a slaveholder. The government reimbursed the former slaveholders for their loss, with Sheikh Ali personally contributing 25 percent of this compensation money. According to Sir Rupert Hay, payments for 660 slaves emancipated in May 1952 peaked at a high of about 2,000 rupees for a slave girl but averaged 1,500 rupees.[8] The policy had the unintended consequence of spreading oil wealth to relatively poor villagers with only one or two slaves. It was, the political officer noted, "by far the widest distribution of wealth that has yet resulted from oil royalties."[9]

FRAYED RELATIONS WITH QATAR PETROLEUM COMPANY

In mid-1954 PCL's local subsidiary PDQ changed its name to the Qatar Petroleum Company, or QPC. Production had already reached over 4.5 million tons per year, up from just under 4 million tons in 1953. The company was actively exploring for oil outside of the Dukhan structure in western Qatar. QPC had drilled one well at Kharaib in the center of its concession, but deep drilling in early 1953 showed the No. 4 Limestone horizon in this location contained water and no oil. Talks with Abdullah Darwish, Sheikh Ali's petroleum representative, commenced on extending QPC's acreage to include the territory between the boundary line marked on the original concession map and Qatar's southern frontier with Saudi Arabia. However, the company did not rate the chances of finding additional fields outside of Dukhan particularly high.

Despite increased production from Dukhan and rising oil revenues, relations between Sheikh Ali's government and QPC remained tense. In mid-1954 Hay's replacement as political resident reported that the political standing of the oil company was not a happy one. "They have more arguments and disputes with the Qatar Government than all the other Oil Companies in the Gulf put together," Sir Bernard Burrows informed the Foreign Office.[10] Part of the problem (as the Foreign Office saw it) was that the company stood too rigidly on the letter of the law instead of responding favorably to more or less reasonable requests from Sheikh Ali and his representatives. Yet it wasn't clear whether QPC even wanted to solve the problem; IPC's managing director conceded to Burrows that the company's shareholders felt that Aramco had got into serious difficulty in Saudi Arabia by conceding to the Saudis too much and too quickly. They were determined not to make the same mistake in Qatar.

In late 1954 Saudi Arabia alleged that QPC had drilled a well south of the inlet of Khor al Odaid that the Saudis claimed as their territory. This was strongly denied by the company, which reported that its most southerly drilling on the east side of the peninsula had been 30-40 kilometers north of the Khor. It later emerged that QPC's geologists had indeed recommended drilling nearer to Khor al Odaid but had been overruled by the company's political experts. Talks with Sheikh Ali for additional territory in the disputed area were still ongoing in early 1956. The government's recently appointed oil consultant, himself a former QPC official, felt that the 250-square-mile area was probably not worth more than £250,000 given its poor oil prospects. But he had also suggested the company might pay more just to keep this southern territory out of American and Saudi hands. By the end of 1956, with QPC's offer of £200,000 rejected by the Qataris and the border question still unresolved, the matter of this southern frontier strip was temporarily shelved.

Meanwhile, QPC's topping plant at Umm Said proved woefully inadequate by the time it was brought online in June 1955, thus exacerbating the company's already frayed relations with Sheikh Ali and his son Ahmad. Its design capacity was just 680 barrels of crude oil per day. Gasoline output was very low octane, and this forced the country to keep importing better grades of fuel from

Bahrain at great expense. Local consumption outpaced the plant's supply capabilities from the outset. Having a proper refinery was a matter of prestige for Sheikh Ali, who described himself as a camel in the desert dying of thirst with a water tank on his back.[11] In 1955 QPC assured the sheikh that it would give a refinery project serious consideration. By mid-1958, however, it was clear that the company had not. Political officer J. S. R. Duncan conceded to Sir Bernard that QPC "have indeed rather led the Ruler up the garden path, the reason being that they have been unwilling to come out in the open and say that they do not want to put up their share of the money."[12]

A proper refinery, QPC estimated, would take three years to build and cost at least £500,000. The company did not want to foot the bill, having already spent £206,000 on the Umm Said topping plant. It suggested that the government of Qatar build and finance the refinery itself, rather than putting its money into securities in the United Kingdom. This type of local involvement in refining had already been tried in Iraq, and QPC cited it as precedent. QPC naively offered to lend its own "facilities and help" in the effort. This clearly annoyed both Sheikh Ahmad and the political resident, who noted that if Qatar did decide on a refinery of its own, it would prefer to find a firm other than QPC to build and operate the project. "It is most unfortunate how this company always seems to be getting into trouble," Sir Bernard complained to the Foreign Office in August 1958.[13]

SHELL STARTS OFFSHORE EXPLORATION

By early 1953 Shell had moved a specially equipped ship called *Shell Quest* to the waters off Qatar. "Exploration has now begun and the ship will facilitate the work by serving as a floating depot for men and equipment," London's *Financial Times* reported on April 9.[14] The vessel had been trading in West Africa, converted for its new purpose by Grayson Rollo and Clover Docks in the English town of Birkenhead. Shell acquired a barren stretch of shore on the outskirts of Doha for use as a staging area, land discovered by a "remarkable coincidence," as the political officer put it, to belong jointly to Abdullah Darwish and the ruler's eldest son, Sheikh Ahmad Ibn Ali Al Thani.[15] A new subsidiary called Shell Company of Qatar was formed to hold the concession on October 3, 1953. "The figure of £1,000,000 as the initial share capital has been adjudged suitable since a

5.1 *Shell Quest*, used for marine survey work off the coast of Qatar in 1953–1955.

Source: In Michael Quentin Morton, "The Petroleum Gulf," *GEOExPro*, December 1, 2016, https://geoexpro.com/the-petroleum-gulf.

PETROLEUM COMPANY'S UNDERSEA ENTERPRISE

19 OCT 1954

5.2 Shell's first drilling platform, circa 1954.

Source: Glasgow Herald, October 19, 1954, NA-UK.

substantial capital is desirable in the interests of local prestige and relationships with the Sheikh of Qatar," Shell informed British treasury officials.[16]

Shell Company of Qatar formally took over the concession from Shell Overseas Exploration on August 17, 1954. The same year, Shell moved what the *Glasgow Herald* dubbed a "1,200-ton moveable island of steel, with many features unique to the relatively new science of drilling for oil at sea," to a drilling site immediately outside territorial waters off the northeast coast of Qatar.[17] Built at a cost of £500,000, the 140-foot-long, 90-foot-wide drilling platform had been completed in just over nine months. But Shell's first well, called Matbakh 1, proved dry and was abandoned at 6,706 feet. A second hole targeting the Idd el-Shargi structure much further east was also unsuccessful. At the end of 1955 the company approached the Foreign Office about drilling another well in the northern part of its concession, on the edge of the so-called safe zone in which it was permitted to drill.

Shell also pressed for a decision on whether the Dibal and Jaradeh shoals awarded to Bahrain in Britain's 1947 decision carried territorial waters, a question the British government was still dithering over. "In the circumstances, it would seem that it might be advantageous to all concerned if the boundary could be more precisely defined before such operations are started, which may be within the next six weeks or two months," Shell wrote to the Foreign Office.[18] The British now appeared to have flip-flopped on whether the two shoals carried territorial waters. Because the only features uncovered at high tide were artificial, the Foreign Office told the political agent, its present thinking would lead to the conclusion that Dibal and Jaradeh did not carry territorial waters. But the Foreign Office was still not ready to issue a definitive opinion on the matter.

The urgency to define the seabed boundary between Qatar and Bahrain dissipated after Shell decided to drill again in the east. This well, drilled to a depth of nearly twelve thousand feet, did not find oil in commercial quantities. Shell drilled through only three or four feet of oil-bearing rock in No. 1 Limestone. A heavy, tarry substance deemed useless by the company was present in No. 2 Limestone, while No. 3 Limestone found only traces of oil and the fourth was reportedly water-bearing. By July 1956 Shell was pondering whether to move the drilling platform to the center of the Idd el-Shargi structure or to the northeast of its concession area. "While they think they may find oil if they move to the centre of the structure, they doubt whether any oil-field which could exist there would be large enough to make production profitable," F. B. Richards reported from the political residency.[19] Two months later it seemed the company would try again in the northeast but was not particularly hopeful of finding oil. "If they have no luck there they may or may not drill one more hole before pulling out altogether."[20]

Shell's senior technical experts in the Netherlands were by this point arguing against another exploration well, saying there was only a slight chance of finding oil, and it would only waste more money. The company had already spent $21 million in Qatar on fruitless underwater exploration. R. P. R. McGlashan, the firm's local manager, campaigned strenuously to continue drilling during visits to Shell's headquarters in London and The Hague in late 1956. While conceding the chances of finding oil were negligible, he argued that, if oil was found, it would be in large quantities and that the company's reputation would be tarnished if Shell withdrew without drilling another well after leading Sheikh Ali to believe it would sink more wells. Management acquiesced and McGlashan returned to Qatar with a mandate to drill again, probably in the northern part of its concession.[21]

OFFSHORE DRILLING PLATFORM SINKS IN FREAK STORM

Then disaster struck. Shell's mobile drilling platform sank during a freak storm on the night of December 27, 1956, with the loss of twenty-one lives. Two 1,800-ton pontoons had been towed out to the offshore drilling site and positioned under the platform in anticipation of moving the facility to Doha for modifications. "We were about to start raising the spud legs and start the tow when suddenly a low long interval swell started in from the North East," McGlashan reported. "This swell, on meeting with the swell from the Northwest, built up suddenly at intervals of a minute or so a series of high peaks and this coupled with a confused turmoil of water caused the cross sections holding the two pontoons to break."[22] The tugboats worked frantically and unsuccessfully to pull the pontoons free. With the platform in danger of disintegrating, the order was given to abandon it. Both pontoons sank, the platform's helicopter pad disappeared, one side of the lower deck collapsed with the loss of much heavy equipment, and the spud legs were badly damaged. During all this a fire broke out and burned into the next morning.

Following the disaster, McGlashan informed Sheikh Ali's representative for oil affairs—his son and heir, Ahmad—that Shell would probably abandon the sub-sea concession altogether without drilling another well. After finding that the cost of the wrecked platform was covered by insurance and convincing the sheikh to ease some of his concession terms, the company nonetheless opted to proceed. Shell told Sheikh Ahmad it would make a final drilling attempt in the north but that it would be forced to surrender its concession if this hole was also dry.[23] Even so, the firm reckoned drilling was unlikely to resume before early 1959 given the need to build a replacement platform. Shell placed its operations in Qatar on a "care and maintenance basis" in the interim, dispersing most of its European staff and considerably reducing its local workforce.

A new mobile drilling rig capable of withstanding one-hundred-mile winds and thirty-foot waves was ordered from Holland's N.V. Werf Gusto.[24] Dubbed the *Sea Shell*, the rig arrived in Qatar from Rotterdam in November 1959, and Shell resumed drilling in the eastern part of its concession the following month. This new location was chosen after a seismic survey south of the Dibal and Jaradeh shoals, claimed by both Qatar and Bahrain, proved disappointing. Additional permission had been obtained for this survey, as it was conducted outside the safe zone where Shell could operate without further reference to the British government (see fig. 5.3). But drilling on the eastern seabed still raised complications related to Qatar's unresolved maritime border with Abu Dhabi. With no land boundary between the two sheikhdoms, there was no prospect of a maritime frontier, and agreement on a dry border was still blocked by Abu Dhabi's claim to a large slice of Qatari territory far to the north of the Khor al Odaid. Also complicating a final settlement on the seabed boundary was Saudi Arabia's overlapping claim to the Khor al Odaid and to most of the Abu Dhabi coast.

Abu Dhabi's Sheikh Shakhbut protested "in the strongest terms" the presence of the Shell rig nine miles from the contested island of Halul.[25] However, the *Sea Shell* was determined to be well within the safe area. This had been defined in 1952 by the British for Shell's seabed concession and in 1953 for the oil company operating on the Abu Dhabi side of the approximate median line. "Shakhbut's latest complaint seems totally unreasonable and lends colour to the complaint of the Qatar Shaikhs that he is suffering from a kind of "folie de grandeur" which drives him to make evermore fantastic claims encroaching on their long-recognized rights," the political agent J. C. Moberly reported in mid-December 1959.[26] This was the first time Abu Dhabi's ruler had formally complained about Shell's

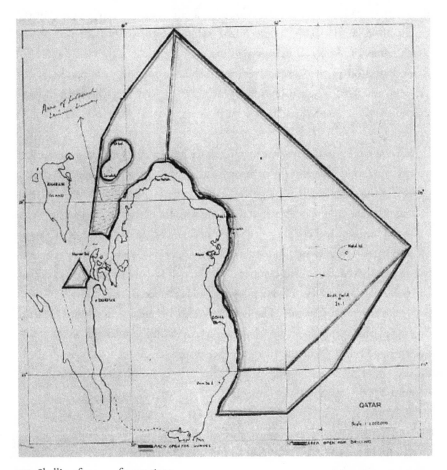

5.3 Shell's safe zone of operations.

Source: FO, *Oil Industry in Qatar,* 1959, ref. 371/140233, code BA file 1538, NA-UK, https://www.agda.ae/en/catalogue/tna/fo/371/140233/n/20.

exploration activities. No protest had been made in 1955 and 1956 when the rig destroyed in the storm had drilled at a location on Idd el-Shargi to the south of the *Sea Shell's* present site.

In May 1960, five months after the *Sea Shell* began drilling, Shell finally found encouraging quantities of oil on the northern dome of the Idd el-Shargi structure. These were discovered in the Upper Jurassic Limestone No. 3 and 4 formations, the Middle Jurassic Araej, and in the deeper Uwainat at depths between 4,600 and 8,500 feet. Shell immediately informed the ruler's nephew Sheikh Khalifa Ibn Hamad of the find, and exaggerated rumors of the extent of the discovery spread rapidly. The well flowed at a rate of 3,000 barrels a day, but the extent of the find was only determined after a third well was drilled on the north dome. In March 1961 the fourth Idd el-Shargi well on the field's southern dome found oil in the Lower Cretaceous Shuaiba formation but none of the other strata. This was a disappointment, as it showed that the field did not extend from the north dome to the south dome and was therefore smaller than expected.

Idd el-Shargi produced nearly 1.2 million tons from eight wells in 1964, its first year of operation. Initially the company used a permanently moored oil tanker called *Zenatia* as a floating storage and export terminal at Idd el-Shargi. After a second offshore oil field at Maydan Mahzam was discovered in 1963 some twelve miles northeast of Idd el-Shargi, however, permanent export facilities to handle 150,000 barrels per day (or about 5.5 million tons per year) were urgently required. While Maydan Mahzam was comparable in size to Idd el-Shargi, Shell expected the new field to produce at a much higher flow rate because of its larger proportion of recoverable reserves. The company also brought in a second floating drilling platform called the *Sidewinder* for Maydan Mahzam, as the *Sea Shell* was not equipped to drill in the field's deeper waters. Shell set its sights on using nearby Halul island as an operational base; a 1961 British decision giving the island to Qatar paved the way for its use.

CONTESTED HALUL LSLAND GOES TO QATAR

Claimed by both Qatar and Abu Dhabi, Halul island had long been considered by Britain as belonging to Abu Dhabi. But its sovereignty did not become a vital issue until the award of the seabed concessions in the two sheikhdoms in the early 1950s. After reviewing the evidence pertaining to the dispute, the Foreign Office concluded in 1955 that Qatar's claim to the island could not be rejected out of hand. For the next three years the British collected evidence with a view to referring the dispute to arbitration, efforts frustrated by the recalcitrance of the two rulers who refused to present proof of their ownership. Sheikh Shakhbut of Abu Dhabi even insisted on treating the Halul sovereignty issue as part of his more ambitious claim to the southeast coast of Qatar above Khor al Odaid, a claim that extended as far north as Umm Said.[27]

The Foreign Office ultimately put the matter aside in 1958, opting to consider Halul island as neutral territory for the time being—although without informing either of the two sheikhs of this decision. After Shell struck oil at Idd el-Shargi, however, neutrality over Halul island was no longer an option. The island, just over one mile long and about one-half mile wide, lay significantly closer to mainland Qatar than Abu Dhabi. In fact, Halul was situated well within the safe zone first articulated by Britain in 1950 to Superior. In 1961 Britain ruled in favor of Qatar after the Gault-Anderson legal opinion concluded its claims to Halul and another island called Bustarriyah were justified. The British also upheld Abu Dhabi's claims to the islands of Kafai, Machasib, Dayyinah, and Qarnein. Ownership of two other islands, Lasahat and Shara'iwah, was left undecided given the insufficient evidence.

Britain's decision freed Shell to begin constructing export facilities on Halul, although first it had to negotiate an exclusivity agreement with the government for which it paid £50,000.[28] A further complication arose in 1964, when the Qataris inadvertently included the island in a concession awarded to Continental Oil of the United States. This was eventually resolved, and Shell's terminal on Halul became operational in late 1965. Idd el-Shargi and Maydan Mahzam were linked to the island's oil installations by (respectively) twelve-inch, thirteen-mile and fourteen-inch, ten-mile submarine pipelines. Shell initially built four storage tanks on Halul totaling 172,000 tons and added a fifth 43,000-ton tank a few years later. Production from the two fields reached 4.7 million tons by 1966, the first full year of operations on Halul island.

Eight years after the Gault-Andersen opinion, Qatar's claim to Halul island was confirmed in an agreement signed between the rulers of Qatar and Abu Dhabi on March 20, 1969. In addition to determining the fate of Lasahat and Shara'iwah—which went to Qatar—the two rulers demarcated the border separating their offshore areas and provided for equal sharing of the offshore Bunduq field. Bunduq had been discovered in 1965 by Abu Dhabi Marine Areas Limited, or ADMA, the company created by Anglo-Iranian successor British Petroleum and France's Compagnie française des pétroles in 1954 to operate Abu Dhabi's seabed concession. The dispute over Bunduq was resolved by slightly offsetting terminal point B on the maritime boundary from the true equidistance line between the Qatar and Abu Dhabi coasts to coincide directly with the oil field.[29] For practical purposes, it was decided to let ADMA continue to operate the site, with all royalties, profits, and other fees equally divided between the governments of Qatar and Abu Dhabi when the field was eventually developed.

The 1969 offshore settlement with Abu Dhabi also resulted in the definition of the eastern boundary of Shell's concession and added around 1,300 square kilometers to its operating area. One particularly promising prospect in the new territory was the Bul Hanine structure some eight miles southeast of Maydan Mahzam, on which Abu Dhabi's offshore concessionaire ADMA had drilled a successful wildcat well in 1965. Through exploration and negotiation, Qatar's marine geology and geography were now coming into useful focus.

CHAPTER 6

Labor Strikes, Another Abdication, and an Industrial Project

As was common in the oil-producing Middle East, the profit-sharing arrangement with Qatar's onshore operator was amended on several occasions. Sheikh Ali and his son Ahmad encouraged labor unrest as a way of exerting pressure on QPC during these negotiations. In one such instance in August 1955, drivers at Dukhan went on strike and were soon joined by local employees at Umm Said. A clash ensued when the police intervened to recover company cars taken by the striking workers. The police force did not come out favorably, British staff were thrown out of their offices, and the strikers cut off electricity and water to QPC's headquarters. Alarmed at this turn of events, Britain sent a naval vessel to Umm Said and threatened to intervene if Sheikh Ali did not ensure the safety of the oil company's installations. Still, the ruler got QPC to introduce an incentive discount for incremental production above rated levels along the lines of those negotiated in Iran, Iraq, and Kuwait as well as an increase in the royalty rate.[1]

QPC continued to prove remarkably inept at labor relations through much of the 1950s. Problems were usually centered around the housing and food it provided its workers, and typically ended after mediation by Sheikh Ahmad with minor concessions from QPC. One time the company triggered a strike by forgetting to issue coffee rations to its local workers for several weeks. In another instance QPC tried to force men to work on Eid al-Fitr, the major holiday marking the end of the Muslim holy month of Ramadan, because of a calendar mix-up.[2] When the ruler's blind prayer-caller was mowed down by a company car in 1955, QPC cited its contractual right to handle matters of personnel and refused to fire the driver. "Qatar Petroleum Company is, I consider, fundamentally wrong in the way in which it appears to handle its relations with its labour, particularly its Qatari labour," the political resident reported to the Foreign Office that year.[3]

Sheikh Ali or, increasingly, Ahmad would often step in to arbitrate these disputes because QPC would usually fire whomever the strikers had nominated to negotiate on their behalf.[4] By 1957 Sheikh Ali started taking a harder line, and labor unrest became less frequent. Disputes continued. In late 1959 the company considered shutting down production altogether when Ahmad awarded strike pay to disgruntled workers, although it ultimately determined this could threaten the validity of the concession. Eventually a more formal mediation process was established, with labor legislation and a labor board for oil industry workers. The first labor law was introduced in 1962, requiring that hiring preference be given to Qataris and then other Arabs. This was followed by more protective nationality laws. In response QPC began making expatiates redundant and dramatically reduced its workforce. By early 1965 the company had 1,600 employees. In January 1960 it had boasted 4,000.

QPC had written to Sheikh Ali in 1953 agreeing to increase oil production to a maximum of 8 million tons per year.[5] The company, however, said it would take until 1957 to reach this level given the need for expanded installations, including a third degassing station, a new thirty-five-mile pipeline from Umm Bab to Umm Said, and another marine loading berth at the export terminal. "It is hoped that the first big increase in production will be to 5,250,000 tons in 1955," QPC informed the sheikh.[6] By early 1956 production was running at 6 million tons per year, and QPC estimated it would take another "two to three years" to meet the promised annual output rate of 8 million tons. This infuriated the ruler, who threatened to cancel the incentive discount system put in place in late 1955 to encourage the company's customers to buy more Qatari oil. Sheikh Ali insisted that he planned to put the surplus revenue from the production hike straight into a reserve fund, although members of the ruling family were pressuring him for an increase in their allowances of no less than 150 percent at the time.[7]

In its defense, QPC pointed to several recent disappointments. These included exploration wells at Juh and a second Kharaib well further north as well as into the deeper Uwainat horizon at the Dukhan field. Despite these setbacks, QPC told the sheikh the company hoped to produce at a rate of 6.2 million tons per year by the end of 1956. It also put the number of recoverable reserves in Dukhan at 180 million tons and assured Sheikh Ali that its depletion rate in Qatar was as high as any other Middle East country. "I must remark here that it becomes increasingly difficult for us to speak freely about our forecasts or estimates if they are to be interpreted as constituting commitments or obligations," the company's chief representative admonished the ruler's adviser in May 1956.[8] Just a few months later QPC informed Sheikh Ali that it would after all be able to reach an annual production rate of 8 million tons (about 150,000 barrels per day) in 1957. The reason: unforeseen problems in expanding export capacity for its parent company's production in Iraq, temporarily necessitating more oil from other sources, including Qatar.

Sheikh Ali increasingly favored his own son Ahmad over Khalifa, Hamad's son who had been named heir apparent when Sheikh Abdullah abdicated in 1949. Ahmad served as deputy ruler, and he assumed more responsibility for oil matters, particularly after Abdullah Darwish was ousted as the ruler's petroleum representative in late 1956 following a dispute with one of Sheikh Ali's other sons.[9] While Sheikh Ali did not openly back Ahmad as his successor until his father's death in 1957, tensions between Ahmad and his cousin Khalifa were never far below the surface.[10] During the 1950s prominent members of the ruling family began to move into high- and mid-level bureaucratic posts as the government took shape. This supplemented the civil list, under which outright monetary grants were given to over 150 adult male Al Thanis. The civil list also grew as the ruling family expanded and its demands increased with the rise in oil revenues. By the late 1950s every male Al Thani child received an allowance of £3,000 per annum from birth, with this amount increasing with age.

Family members began joining leading merchants to form companies to compete for oil company contracts and import deals. The Jaidah merchant family got its start in the 1950s by partnering with members of the Ahmad faction, as did the Al Attiyah clan.[11] The Al Mannai family, whose patriarch moved to Qatar from Bahrain in the 1940s, also became one of the largest merchant groups through ties with the sheikhs. In 1960 the authorities decreed that all goods ordered from foreign companies or manufacturers had to be placed through local agents chosen among the members of the merchant community. Qatari merchants had complained vigorously about being confined to the position of subagents for main agencies appointed in other countries, and such complaints resonated with their Al Thani partners.

The Qatar Armed Forces was formally established in 1959 under Mohamad Ibn Abdullah Al Attiyah, who eventually rose to the rank of brigadier general.

At its formation, the Qatar Armed Forces consisted of just twelve soldiers, two cars, and four motorcycles.

SHEIKH ALI ABDICATES IN FAVOR OF AHMAD

Revenues fell sharply in 1959 after the incentive discount scheme was suspended and output temporarily dipped. This forced Sheikh Ali to reduce allowances to members of the ruling family, which precipitated a political crisis. The following year, Khalifa's disgruntled brother, Nasir Ibn Hamad Al Thani, fired five bullets into Sheikh Ali's parked car at his holiday residence in the Lebanese mountain resort of Aley.[12] Nasir was angry over the allowance cut, and the ruler decided it was time to abdicate. Discontent with Ali's rule was widespread even before this purported assassination attempt, and his personal financial excesses (often committed abroad) meant spending on development projects had lagged considerably. On October 24, 1960, after a reign of just eleven years, Sheikh Ali abdicated in favor of his son Ahmad. Hamad's son Khalifa was officially named heir apparent and deputy ruler in deference to Sheikh Abdullah's 1949 promise.

Sheikh Khalifa assumed charge of all financial and petroleum matters, and he was the driving force behind the formulation and promulgation of many laws and decrees issued in his cousin Ahmad's name.[13] The deputy ruler was instrumental, for example, in the 1962 law that gave preference to Qataris in hiring decisions. There were no cabinets or ministries in the early 1960s, but several important departments related to agriculture, customs, immigration, labor and social affairs, and land registration had been created with the help of Egyptian and British advisers. In the late 1960s the Ministry of Finance was established with Sheikh Khalifa as its first minister, as well as departments covering petroleum and legal and administrative affairs. The supervision of the Department of Petroleum Affairs was entrusted to the Ministry of Finance in 1967.

Contrary to expectations by QPC in 1956 that the Dukhan field was unlikely to ever exceed 8 million tons per year, its output continued to rise. It hit 8.1 million tons in 1958, fell back slightly in 1959 to 7.9 million tons, and then regained momentum in 1960 when production once again reached 8.1 million tons as QPC loaded an average of one tanker a day from the Umm Said export terminal. In early 1961, at Sheikh Ahmad's invitation, the Saudi government sent two experts to Qatar to investigate development possibilities in QPC's

6.1 Sheikh Ahmad Ibn Ali Al Thani, r. 1960–1972.

Source: Official site of the Amiri Diwan of the State of Qatar, https://www.diwan.gov.qa/-/media/Diwan
-Amiri/Images/Qatar-Rulers/Sheikh-Ahmed-Bin-Ali-Al-Thani.ashx.

concession area. They concluded that more wells needed to be drilled in the
No. 3 Limestone in order to complete development of this reservoir. Production
from the No. 3 Limestone had been suspended in 1959 following a rapid pressure
decline in the field's Khatiya area. Altogether, only eight producing wells had
been drilled into the No. 3 Limestone, and they were all shut in. The experts also
recommended further development of the deeper Uwainat reservoir since its one
well was insufficient. Stepped-up exploration efforts outside of Dukhan were
additionally encouraged, particularly on two substructures east of the Hawar
Islands and west of Doha.

The Saudi study demonstrated just how dependent QPC was on the main No. 4 Limestone formation, which since 1958 had been producing from thirty-eight wells at a reasonably constant rate of 7.6–8.0 million tons per annum. While the experts determined the No. 4 Limestone was better developed than the No. 3 Limestone, they injected a note of caution. "It is quite probable that the pressure-production behavior, coupled with other factors such as excessive salt production, will indicate the necessity for the reduction of the rate of withdrawal in the near future."[14] Cumulative production from the No. 4 Limestone at the end of 1960 was estimated at 50.6 million tons, while the No. 3 Limestone was reckoned to have produced a total of 6.9 million tons before operations at this horizon level were suspended in 1959. Overall output from the Uwainat was estimated at just 100,934 tons since production from this reservoir commenced in 1955, and the study determined that an appreciative addition to overall flows could be realized with full development of this deeper horizon.

Output grew steadily, if unspectacularly, through the first half of the 1960s but did not really rise until early 1964, when the first flows materialized from Shell's marine concession. QPC produced nearly 8.7 million tons in 1962, up from 8.1 million tons in 1960. This rose to 9 million tons in 1963, the last year before the marine flows entered the picture, and essentially stayed at this level through the remainder of the decade. Total production countrywide touched 10 million tons in 1964, when Shell's Idd el-Shargi offshore field came online and stepped up to 10.8 million tons in 1965 after the second offshore field at Maydan Mahzam was brought into production. By 1968 crude oil production had reached 16.3 million tons (about 300,000 barrels per day), with QPC contributing 9.1 million tons of this total from Dukhan and Shell producing the remaining 7.2 million tons from Idd el-Shargi and Maydan Mahzam. Nearly all this output was exported, except for the 30,000 tons used annually in the Umm Said topping plant.

Unlike some of its neighbors, Qatar did not have a sudden and dramatic oil boom. Development projects started out on a small scale, and it was not until the 1960s that major construction efforts commenced. A new fifty-four-mile highway across the peninsula from Dukhan to Doha was built in 1965, paid in part by a £150,000 contribution from QPC. The Doha airport and new harbors were also constructed. Qatar National Cement Company, a public–private concern, was established in 1965 to build and operate a 100,000-ton-per-year cement plant at Umm Bab, where large quantities of limestone and clay were accessible. Gas to supply the cement plant's 3.3 megawatt power station was sourced from QPC's

Jaleha degassing station five miles to the north. In late 1967 Sheikh Khalifa hired a British consultant to study the feasibility of a nitrogenous fertilizer plant based on flared gas produced together with oil at the Dukhan field. The following year the government bought QPC's topping plant at Umm Said, taking over operations on October 1, 1968. By this time the refinery was meeting just one-quarter of the country's requirements of gasoline, kerosene, and diesel oil, with the remainder imported mainly from Bahrain and Saudi Arabia. All aviation fuels, lubricants, and bitumen were also being imported.

FIRST MAJOR INDUSTRIAL PROJECT GAINS MOMENTUM

After Gibb-Ewbank Industrial Consultants, the British consultant hired by Sheikh Khalifa, determined that there were sufficient quantities of associated gas being flared at the Dukhan field to support a fertilizer plant, the government began talks with the British firms PowerGas Corporation (a Davy-Ashmore subsidiary) and Hambros Bank on the estimated £26 million ammonia-urea complex.[15] A new company, called Qatar Fertilizer Company, or QAFCO, was established to own and operate the facility, and in December 1968 Sheikh Khalifa signed the main £19 million construction contract with PowerGas. The plant was to be built at Umm Said and designed to produce 990 tons daily of ammonia, of which 600 tons would be used to make 1,1000 tons daily of bagged and bulk urea for Asian and East African markets. Infrastructure, including a pipeline to carry the gas from the Dukhan field to Umm Said plus a deep export jetty, would be funded by the government. The gas would be provided by QPC free of charge, but the government charged QAFCO for its delivery in order to cover the pipeline costs.

PowerGas took a 7 percent share in QAFCO while Hambros Bank originally acquired 10 percent and arranged a £14.5 million loan to help finance the construction of the fertilizer plant. This loan was provided by a syndicate of six British banks led by Hambros, with the credit facilities guaranteed by Britain's government Export Credit Guarantee Department. Norway's Norsk Hydro-Elektrisk (now Norsk Hydro) formally joined the venture in 1969, eventually taking a 25 percent interest in QAFCO and agreeing to provide staff and supervisors to manage and operate the company as well as to market its production overseas. While PowerGas kept its stake unchanged, Hambros gave up half of its interest to Norsk Hydro-Elektrisk, thereby reducing its shareholding to 5 percent. The remaining 63 percent in the fertilizer complex was taken up by the Qatar government, although initially private investors had also been expected to participate in the shareholding.

Work on the Umm Said site commenced in 1970, and the project was completed by the end of 1973. It included 120 miles of pipeline, mainly twenty-four-inch and eighteen-inch in diameter, carrying up to 200 million cubic feet per day of gas from Dukhan to QAFCO's fertilizer plant at Umm Said and other gas users in Doha. The QAFCO plant itself was expected to use 55 million cubic feet daily of this throughput, but the pipeline network also included a spur line to transport associated gas to a power station, a water distillation plant, and other facilities in Doha operated by the government. This pipeline network was completed in late 1971, two years before the fertilizer plant began operation.

QATAR JOINS FOUNDING FIVE IN OPEC CARTEL

With oil revenue funding national development and associated natural gas spawning an industry, Qatar joined a collaboration of petrostates that would soon redefine participation terms for expatriate oil companies and eventually reshape the oil market. At a meeting in Baghdad in September 1960, representatives of Iraq, Kuwait, Saudi Arabia, Iran, and Venezuela had established the Organization of Petroleum Exporting Countries, or OPEC. Its original mission was to shore up posted or reference prices, which the major oil companies were trying to force down following the introduction of new crude oil supplies. The oil companies, including QPC, had first cut their posted prices for Venezuelan and Middle East crudes by 10 percent in early 1959, thus angering the producing countries. When these companies again reduced posted prices for Middle East supplies in August 1960, the Baghdad conference was convened, and OPEC was born. Qatar attended this inaugural meeting as an observer; it did not formally join the organization until its second meeting, in 1961. OPEC initially set up its headquarters in Geneva, Switzerland, but moved in 1965 to the Austrian capital, Vienna, after Switzerland refused to extend diplomatic privileges to its representatives. Ali Mohammad Jaidah, who worked in the Petroleum Affairs Department under Sheikh Khalifa, was appointed as Qatar's first representative on the OPEC Board of Governors.

One of OPEC's first achievements was to stabilize the posted prices of oil and check the unilateral price reductions imposed by the oil companies. From the posted prices, which were usually lower than actual selling prices, the companies would deduct production and selling costs, after which the governments would be paid 50 percent of the net profits under the typical 50-50 profit split. OPEC negotiated supplemental agreements with the oil companies to treat royalties as an expense rather than a credit against income tax liability. It then gradually eliminated the 6.5 percent allowance off posted prices given when this royalty expensing settlement was negotiated.[16] OPEC also reduced the marketing allowance deducted by the companies as a cost at the production stage from 1 percent of the posted price to one-half cent per barrel. In 1968 the organization estimated that this measure had increased the revenues of member countries by over $500 million per year. By this time OPEC included nine members: Indonesia and Libya joined OPEC in 1962 and Abu Dhabi in 1967.

The Qatari government entered negotiations with QPC in 1967 over the elimination of the discount allowance off posted prices permitted for tax calculation purposes under the OPEC royalty expensing agreement. Its delegation included representatives from the OPEC secretariat general as well as other member countries. Removal of the discount allowance resulted in large monetary gains for the organization's members at the time. The secretariat general estimated an increase in income of $54 million for Saudi Arabia, followed by $48 million for both Iran and Libya, and about $8 million for Qatar, one of the smallest producers.[17] The government eventually settled on a schedule that would see the 6.5 percent allowance eliminated by 1972. A separate allowance related to the American Petroleum Institute gravity (API)—a measure of how light or heavy a petroleum liquid is compared to water—of Qatari crude was cut gradually over the next two years. Abu Dhabi, whose light crude oil was comparable in quality to Qatar's Dukhan's 41° API on the institute's gravity scale, secured a similar arrangement.

NEW PLAYERS TAKE RELINQUISHED ACREAGE

Monetary gains resulting from OPEC's burgeoning influence gave Qatar and other members the incentive to press operating companies to increase production or surrender undeveloped acreage. Mandatory relinquishment was not a feature of the early Middle East concessions. The concept was first introduced in Saudi Arabia in 1948, when Aramco agreed on a program for the staged relinquishment of portions of its concession area. But the idea did not really take hold until December 11, 1961, when Iraq issued its famous Law Number 80 depriving IPC and two other companies operating in the country of 99.5 percent of their concession areas. This limited their operations to the 1,934 square kilometers of the producing oil fields. Oil companies operating in the Middle East ultimately acquiesced to relinquishment after Iraq's decisive action. QPC, however, spent most of 1961 trying to avoid giving up acreage in Qatar. Hoping to postpone the inevitable, it offered to increase its production by half a million tons to 8.5 million tons in 1962 through additional drilling. If this program failed, the company promised, the territory would be relinquished. Deputy Ruler Sheikh Khalifa rejected QPC's offer. "Shaikh Khalifah has said to me that the extra income derived from so small an increase would not compensate for the demands from the family for extra money should it become known that the Ruler had accepted increased production," Britain's political agent in Doha reported in mid-1961.[18]

Toward the end of 1961, the ruler asked QPC to add a second drilling rig at its existing structures to boost annual production to 10 million tons and to press ahead with exploration in areas outside of the Dukhan field—or to surrender all territory where the company was not already operating so that the government could try to improve its position with other parties. That December, its back against the wall, QPC made its first relinquishment of 1,737 square miles in the northern part of its concession (see fig. 6.2). The relinquished territory included an area around its earlier Kharaib 2 exploration well that QPC had tried but failed to retain for potential exploitation. At the same time, the company reluctantly agreed to hike output from the No. 4 Limestone to 8.5 million tons per year by adding another rig at Dukhan, and to potentially take it as high as 9 million tons by the end of 1962 through further exploitation of the deeper Uwainat reservoir.[19]

Oil reserves in the Uwainat were comparatively small and occupied a narrow band around a large gas cap. This, QPC cautioned, made directing the drill into the Uwainat difficult. Care was needed to ensure that the new wells did not produce an excessive amount of gas or water along with oil. QPC also said it would proceed with a program of miscible gas injection at the No. 3 Limestone to resume output from this horizon. But the company gave no assurances that this

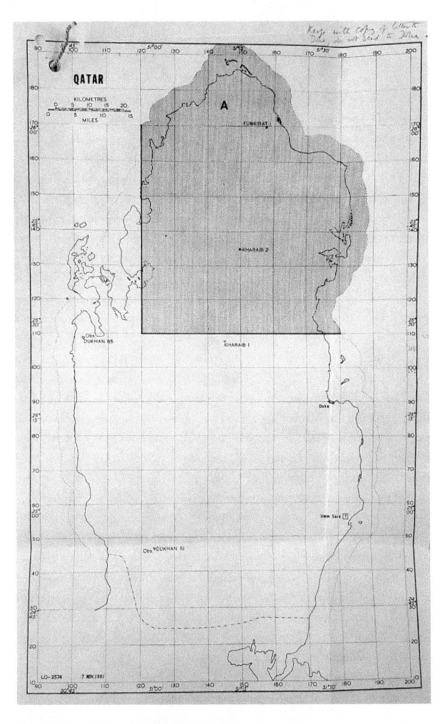

6.2 Map of QPC's first relinquished territory, December 1961.

Source: FO, Oil, 1962, ref. 371/162998, NA-UK.

method of secondary recovery, only recently introduced in the United States, would succeed in Qatar. It would require the installation of a special compression plant, and QPC explained that the application of the "miscible slug" drive on the scale proposed for Qatar had not previously been attempted anywhere in the world. "There is no certainty that injections of gas by this method will have the desired result. The experiment will be an expensive one and the Company can only hope that it will succeed," the political agent reported.[20]

QPC's initial relinquishment in 1961 was followed in July 1963 by another 1,237 square miles east of Dukhan and two years later by a further 1,104 square miles along the southeast coast. These relinquishments continued until the onshore operator's concession was ultimately reduced to just 1,000 square miles by 1970. The territory retained by QPC centered on the north-south trending Dukhan field and was about 50 miles long and 3 miles wide.

Offshore, Shell made its first relinquishment amounting to 2,300 square miles in 1963. This was roughly equivalent to about 25 percent of its seabed concession. The territory was located off the north coast where Shell had previously drilled four dry holes targeting the Umm Al Irshan and Umm Al Garse structures—wells that elicited howls of protest from Bahrain despite their location in the safe zone of operations defined by the British in 1952. Drilling by Shell at Structure Z, another location north of Halul island, was also negative, as was a well between the outer limits of the safe operating zone and Qatar's Persian Gulf median line with Iran. These two areas were not relinquished in 1963 as Shell planned to conduct further seismic surveys in both locations the following year.

The marine territory relinquished by Shell in 1963, together with the onshore acreage surrendered by QPC in 1961 and 1963, was soon acquired by Continental Oil (see fig. 6.3). Known as Conoco, the U.S. firm was the fifth largest of the American independents and was also active in Libya through its shareholding in Oasis Petroleum. Several other companies showed initial interest in the relinquished territory, including Italy's Ente nazionale idrocarburi, or Eni, and American Overseas Petroleum Limited, an exploration company owned by Standard Oil of California and Texaco. But it is not clear how serious these contenders were, and the British subsequently reported that Qatar had difficulty finding a company to take up the "unpromising" relinquished area that Conoco eventually obtained on September 15, 1963.[21] Pure Oil, a subsidiary of fellow independent Union Oil Company of California, subsequently joined Conoco with a half share in the Qatari concession in 1966.

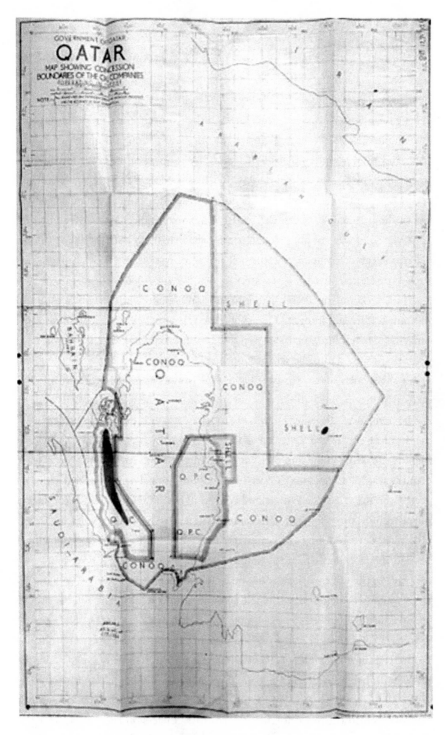

6.3 Map of Qatar concessions, 1964; Shell, QPC, and Conoco.

Source: FO, Oil, 1964, ref. 371/174662, NA-UK.

Conoco also signed up for the open territory to the south of QPC's boundary line, which the existing onshore operator had been eyeing for decades but formally chose not to pursue in 1961. While Sheikh Ahmad, the Qatari ruler, was still negotiating with Riyadh on the demarcation of his frontier with Saudi Arabia, the two countries would eventually reach a settlement in 1965—although without a clear and final boundary, this issue would flare up again in 1992. This border uncertainty obviously did not deter Conoco as it had QPC. The new concession was unique in that it did not, at Sheikh Ahmad's insistence, include a separate political agreement between the British government and Conoco. For the first time, the ruler was not obligated to consult the British authorities when he negotiated with an oil company, although he did agree to take their advice on matters such as operations in disputed waters.

The U.S. company already had a concession offshore Dubai, while another in Bahrain waters adjoining its Qatari acreage was concluded in September 1965. Since the seabed boundaries between Qatar and Bahrain were still contested, operating limits had to be set for Continental. Britain now had serious qualms about the legality of its 1947 award and had given its approval for the dispute to go to arbitration. But Bahrain was not prepared to include the Hawar Islands or the Jaradeh and Dibal shoals in this arbitration, agreeing only to discuss the 1947 median line set by the British. For its part, Qatar was equally determined to include the island chain and the two shoals in any arbitration. However, neither country wanted to hold up Conoco's drilling program. The two sides decided to accept the 1947 line as the division between Bahrain and Qatar for exploration purposes only, provided that both countries agreed to hold off exploitation of any oil discoveries straddling this boundary. This extended Conoco's operating limit beyond the so-called safe area given to Shell in 1952, which had been more prescriptive in the waters off western and northwestern Qatar.

In 1966 Continental moved the *Glomar Tasman* to Qatar from Dubai, where its subsidiary, Dubai Petroleum Company, had discovered the Fateh field. Rumors soon circulated that the company had made a substantial discovery at an exploration well some five miles off Ras Umm Hasa on Qatar's northeast coast. These proved unsubstantiated, and Conoco shifted its focus onshore. Its land-based wildcat at Al Karanah was also disappointing, and in 1967 Conoco drilled another offshore well in the most northerly part of its concession right up against the median line provisionally agreed with Iran. An asphalt-like deposit was found but no liquid oil, apparently matching findings on the Iranian side of the line. Yet another well off Ras Umm Hasa, drilled to 6,500 feet, proved dry; geophysical work in the southeast near the still uncertain maritime boundary with Abu Dhabi also was unpromising. A final unsuccessful well off the west coast was drilled to 10,000 feet in early 1968, close to the 1947 line between Qatar and Bahrain.

After spending $15 million on exploration, including four wildcats at sea and one on land, Conoco left Qatar in June 1968. The U.S. firm also relinquished its Bahrain concession following a dry well southwest of the Hawar Islands that reached 7,860 feet. Just one year later its offshore acreage in Qatar was included in a 7,300 square kilometer tract located off the east and southeast of the peninsula awarded to the Qatar Oil Company Limited (Japan), a special-purpose company formed to operate the concession and consisting of four Japanese firms— Tokyo Electric Power Company, Kansai Electric Power Company, Fuji Oil, and Kansai Oil. The fact that the area had already been relinquished twice by other companies did not deter the Japanese. "Oil companies and consumer governments with inadequate crude sources of their own are still prepared to pay a high price for even relinquished acreage in the Arabian Gulf area," the *Middle East Economic Survey* reported.[22]

The government of Qatar secured the right to participate in the Japanese venture as a 50 percent equity partner upon the discovery of commercial oil. Terms were described at the time as "OPEC plus" and included a 50 percent tax on posted prices and a sliding scale expensed royalty starting at 12.5 percent and rising to 14 percent for output above 100,000 barrels per day as well as 50 percent participation for the government.[23] A heavy expenditure commitment was also secured from the Japanese partners, who agreed to spend a minimum of $24 million during the first eight years of the thirty-five-year contract. The government of Qatar could expect average net income of around $1.03 per barrel of crude oil produced by the Japanese venture, equating to a profit split of 64-36 in favor of Qatar based on posted prices and roughly 89-11 based on actual realized prices.[24] Two months after securing its original concession, the Japanese group added another 1,200-kilometer block, boosting its aggregate total to 8,500 square kilometers.

Award of this offshore concession was followed in May 1969 by Qatar's first formal upstream bidding round, in which the government invited bids for three open areas totaling 22,400 square kilometers relinquished by QPC and Shell. Area No. 1 comprised 12,000 square kilometers and covered all the Qatar peninsula with the exception of a strip in the west representing the Dukhan field with QPC's existing operations; Area No. 2 consisted of 9,000 square kilometers mostly off the northeast coast but extending to the northwest; and Area No. 3 comprised 1,400 square kilometers in two separate locations off the west coast of Qatar (see fig. 6.4). Ali Jaidah, who in addition to his role as Qatar's OPEC delegate was instrumental in the Petroleum Affairs Department, told the *Middle East Economic*

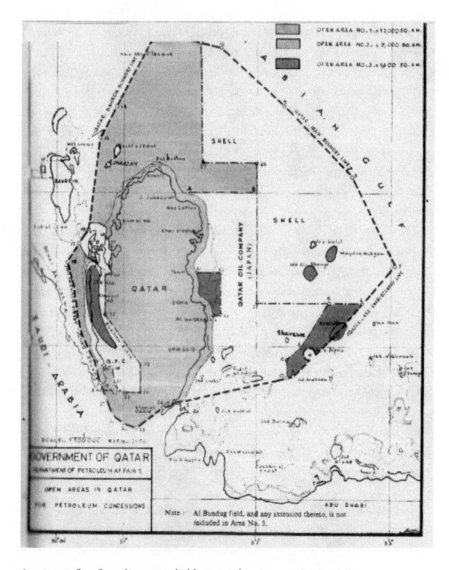

6.4 Qatar's first formal upstream bidding round, 1969.

Source: "Oil Developments in Qatar," *MEES* 13, no. 13 (January 23, 1970).

Survey that the government favored the joint-venture approach embodied by the Japanese deal for all future Qatari oil concessions.[25]

GOVERNMENT MULLS NATIONAL OIL COMPANY

With oil revenues reaching $118 million annually, Deputy Ruler Sheikh Khalifa was thinking expansively at the close of the 1960s.[26] He went public with plans to establish a national oil company that could handle all aspects of the petroleum industry, as well as a new government department devoted to the industrialization of Qatar. "Khalifa has a glint in his eye and intends to transform the whole future of Qatar and cover the ground with smelters, fertilizers, petroleum chemical factories and the like," the British political agent in Doha reported in January 1970. "Practical difficulties may slow him up considerably, but I would expect to see some fairly wild schemes considered in the next few months."[27] QAFCO's fertilizer plant, well into the construction phase by this time, represented the first fruit of Sheikh Khalifa's embryonic plans for industrializing Umm Said.

In 1969 the government had set up the National Oil Distribution Company, or NODCO, following the purchase of QPC's topping plant at Umm Said the previous year. This plant, which produced 680 barrels per day, was seen as the possible nucleus for a national oil company that would include subsidiaries for local product distribution and joint ventures in oil production, fertilizer output, and petrochemicals. Headed by Ali Jaidah, NODCO took over the local distribution and marketing of petroleum products (including the Umm Said output). The government-owned company imported most of its refined products from Shell's trading subsidiaries. NODCO's plan was to expand refining capacity by 5,000 barrels per day and reduce these costly fuel imports.

Sheikh Khalifa was particularly anxious to use the surplus production of natural gas from Qatar's oil fields, most of which was vanishing into the atmosphere through flaring. The government was pressing QPC hard for an export-oriented gas plant to recover natural gas liquids—primarily propane and butane—from Dukhan's associated gas. A resistant QPC argued that the recovery scheme was not cost-effective as the gas plant would cost at least £20 million. As a result, the company could only offer the government unfavorable terms for the project. But it was also aware that Shell, as a member of the QPC consortium, was anxious not to refuse Sheikh Khalifa's request because of its other commercial interests in Qatar. QPC therefore told the British authorities that it was "likely to look for ways in which they might be forthcoming over this issue."[28]

The oil producers viewed Khalifa's plans for a national oil company with mild trepidation rather than real concern. Operations were going well at Dukhan, with QPC engaged in a water injection scheme to raise output to 10 million tons, or over 200,000 barrels per day, from the average annual plateau of 9 million tons it had reached some years earlier. The company was doing reasonably well with its government relations despite the sometimes-fraught negotiations for the use of associated gas, even "rather uncharacteristically" contributing £300,000 toward a new government road between Doha and Umm Said.[29] However, both QPC and Shell were often roundly criticized by the government for their lack of interest in training programs for Qataris. The dearth of qualified local personnel to staff a national oil company was seen as a major impediment to its establishment.

Production at Shell's two offshore fields averaged 160,000 barrels per day in 1969—of which 45,000 barrels came from Idd el-Shargi and 115,000 barrels from Maydan Mahzam. By the end of 1970 Shell was on track to complete a water-flooding project at Maydan Mahzam to increase output by 55,000 barrels daily; a model of the project had attracted considerable interest at the Arab Petroleum Congress held in Kuwait earlier that year.[30] Shell had high hopes for the additional acreage secured as a result of Qatar's 1969 offshore boundary settlement with Abu Dhabi. It had carried out a seismic survey of this area and planned to drill at least two appraisal wells at the Bul Hanine structure in 1970. Shell had also signed a special long-term purchase arrangement with Eni in 1967, under which 20 percent of the output from its offshore fields in Qatar would go to the Italian firm in return for investment in exploration and production.

The results of Shell's first Bul Hanine well twenty-four miles southeast of its export terminal on Halul island were encouraging. "On short test, oil flowed at the rate of 3,050 barrels per day with the gravity of 36° API," the Anglo-Dutch company's local subsidiary announced from Doha on June 6, 1970.[31] Shell gave no indication of the size of the find and cautioned in its press release that further drilling was necessary to determine whether the structure contained oil in commercial quantities. But the British political agent reported the following day that he had reason to believe that Bul Hanine would fall between Idd el-Shargi and Maydan Mahzam in actual area.[32] The decision to go ahead with the development of Bul Hanine and expand Shell's export facilities on Halul island was made later that year.

Qatar Oil Company Limited (Japan) was also optimistic about its new offshore concession, hiring Western Geophysical Corporation to carry out a new seismic survey. In June 1970 the Japanese group announced it had awarded a drilling contract to the U.S. firm Southeastern Drilling Company. Its first well, one of three planned in the initial exploration program, was spudded six months later in January 1971. By this point no less than twenty-six other Japanese companies had joined Tokyo Electric Power Company, Kansai Electric Power, Company, Fuji Oil, and Kansai Oil in the concession. In addition to oil firms and power utilities, the consortium now included metallurgical, chemical, and shipbuilding companies as well as other industrial fuel consumers. While it depended mainly on American subcontractors for its survey and drilling work, the consortium had mobilized a twelve-man team in Qatar that included a former karate champion of Japan.[33]

Qatar's first upstream bidding round bore fruit in early 1970 with the award of the nine-thousand-square-kilometer offshore Area No. 2 to the U.S. independent Southeast Oil and Gas Company, a Houston-based firm with just four employees whose only oil and gas asset appeared to be a concession off the coast of Indonesia. Terms under this deal were even more favorable to the government than the earlier Japanese concession, including larger bonus payments, a higher royalty rate, and a slightly shorter contract duration (thirty years). It was negotiated by Ali Jaidah, the newly appointed acting head of the Petroleum Affairs Department, and signed by Sheikh Khalifa in his capacity as the minister of finance. The coordinates on the concession map conformed to the 1947 median line around the Hawar Islands and between Bahrain and Qatar. This led British officials to conclude with obvious relief that the Qataris were not "poaching" on Bahraini waters.

By July the deal with Southeast Oil and Gas looked even more questionable. The company had asked for a delay of two months on its first down payment of $100,000.[34] Since the concession had been negotiated directly by Ali Jaidah, it did not have the support of other influential local players. These included Mohamed Said Mishal, head of the technical side of the Petroleum Affairs Department, and Dr. Hassan Kamel, an Egyptian adviser who had replaced Ali Jaidah as head of Qatar's OPEC delegation. Neither of the two men had been consulted on the concession by Ali Jaidah and would not be unhappy if it failed. That seemed entirely possible: A Dun & Bradstreet report on Southeast Asia Oil and Gas obtained by the British Embassy in Washington showed that the firm had a gross income in 1968 of just $500,000.[35] The firm's principal partners had withheld all financial information in the past, and this made it difficult for outside parties to estimate its assets or liabilities.

Publication of the Qatar government's map showing the open areas caused a stir in Bahrain by giving the impression that the Jaradeh and Dibal shoals were part and parcel of Area No. 2. The concession's western boundary was in accordance with the 1947 line between Qatar and Bahrain, and its northern boundary defined by the 1969 line between Qatar and Iran. But when Britain's political agent asked for clarification on how Qatar had addressed the two shoals with Southeast Oil and Gas, Ali Jaidah said the status of Jaradeh and Dibal was deliberately left undefined by the concession: they were neither included nor specifically excluded.[36] The British decided not to press the matter. Southeast Oil and Gas had already failed to meet its financial obligations under the concession and seemed likely to miss its six-month deadline for commencing exploration work as well.

SHEIKH AHMAD GOES ABROAD AMID RISING DISCONTENT

One of Sheikh Ahmad's first acts as ruler was to divide oil revenues between his family and the state, taking 25 percent himself, giving leading Al Thani sheikhs another 25 percent, and leaving the remaining 50 percent for the government. He later put some restraints on the Al Thani family allowances, including his own, by forgoing his quarter of Shell's offshore oil revenues. "The Ruler passed the whole of the revenues from Shell in the first quarter of this year to the Government, and since he himself did not take a cut, is in a stronger position to resist his family's demands for higher allowances," the British political agent reported in 1964 after Shell brought its first field into production.[37] In 1968 Ahmad announced that Al Thani family members would henceforth be subject to ordinary law in disputes with commoners and would pay their debts like ordinary citizens. After a general strike in 1963, precipitated when one of Sheikh Ahmad's nephews fired his gun into a group of demonstrators, killing one, several workers' committees were formed to settle disputes.[38] In 1964 a law was passed giving low-income Qataris land and loans.

Discontent continued to grow, however. Sheikh Ahmad, who never displayed much desire to rule, began spending more and more time in Europe and Asia.

Khalifa stayed home, by the late 1960s essentially becoming the de facto ruler in all but name.[39] Matters came to the forefront in January 1968 after the shock announcement by Britain's Labor government that it would end all British defense commitments east of Suez by the end of 1971, effectively terminating the old treaties of protection with Qatar and the Trucial States. Some of the sheikhdoms offered to pay for the British military presence to remain, which would have cost about £12 million per year to cover six thousand ground troops plus air support units.[40] This option was strongly opposed by the government of Prime Minister Harold Wilson, which flatly ruled out British troops becoming "mercenaries" for hire.

Instead Britain actively encouraged efforts by the Persian Gulf sheikhdoms to form a federation. The first signs of union occurred just one month after its withdrawal announcement, when Abu Dhabi and Dubai announced they were forming a federation and uniting their foreign relations, defense, and internal security as well as citizenship and immigration affairs. In the February 18, 1968, announcement, Abu Dhabi's Sheikh Zayid Ibn Sultan Al Nahyan and Dubai's Shaikh Rashid Ibn Said al-Maktum invited the rulers of the other five Trucial coast sheikhdoms—Sharjah, Ajman, Umm Al Quwain, Ras Al Khaimah, and Fujairah—to join them in this federation and thereafter to invite the rulers of Qatar and Bahrain to participate. Later that same month, the nine sheikhs met in Dubai to consider a proposal from Qatar's Sheikh Ahmad for the creation of a federation, with a higher council made up of the nine rulers supported by an administrative federal council that would help formulate policies.

Ahmad's proposal was accepted, and the nine states issued a declaration of union. Khalifa, the deputy ruler of Qatar, was elected chair of the temporary federal council in July 1968, following agreement on the provisional organization of the new federation. But divisions quickly surfaced within the proposed nine-member union, and its actual creation proved an impossible feat. Two opposing blocs emerged among the four most powerful sheikhdoms, with Bahrain and Abu Dhabi on one side and Qatar and Dubai on the other. Abu Dhabi, which had sparred over the years with both Dubai and Qatar, was naturally aligned to Bahrain, while Doha had strong trading links with Dubai dating back to the 1930s. The two countries shared family ties (Sheikh Ahmad had married the daughter of Dubai's Sheikh Rashid) and even had a common currency. The Qatar-Dubai riyal, or QDR, had replaced the Gulf rupee in 1966 after it was devalued against the Indian rupee by the Indian government.[41]

The rulers of the nine Persian Gulf sheikhdoms in the proposed union met together as a group only four times. Their last meeting was in October 1969, when Abu Dhabi's Sheikh Zayid was elected the first president of the federation and Qatar's Sheikh Khalifa the first prime minister. The lower-level federal council continued to meet for quite some time, while Britain tried gallantly to keep the federation alive through near constant shuttle diplomacy between capitals. Saudi Arabia and Kuwait also lent their support to the union, although the Saudis were decidedly unhelpful at times to the consternation of both Britain and the United States.

After the Shah of Iran revived a long-standing claim to Bahrain, it looked increasingly likely that the number of states in the federation would be reduced to eight. Sheikh Zayid reportedly told the British that he could no longer risk alienating Qatar and Dubai, although he said the door would not be closed to Bahrain joining the federation later. Britain continued to press the Persian Gulf sheikhdoms for more time to settle Iran's claim to Bahrain. By early 1970, however, the Bahrainis themselves were disillusioned with the federation, and it seemed distinctly likely, as one U.S. diplomat put it, that a divorce could be arranged with feelings of relief on both sides.[42] When Iran suddenly dropped its claim to Bahrain in May, accepting a report from the secretary-general of the United Nations that the majority of Bahrainis wanted an independent state, it was clear Bahrain would opt for independence over inclusion in the federation. And Qatar, newly empowered by oil wealth and its affiliation with OPEC, faced a decision that would divide the royal family.

CHAPTER 7

Independence, First Gas Liquids Project, and a Bloodless Coup

While Sheikh Ahmad was a strong proponent of the proposed federation of Persian Gulf sheikhdoms, Sheikh Khalifa wanted Qatar to forge alone as an independent state. Disagreements between the cousins led to confusion, with Qatar putting forward "debilitating" proposals to the federation.[1] The enactment of a provisional constitution on April 2, 1970, further muddied the waters as it simultaneously proclaimed Qatar an independent sovereign state and a federation member. Qatar's constitution was the first of its kind among the nine sheikhdoms, establishing a Council of Ministers to assist a head of state (the latter would always be a member of the Al Thani family). The deputy ruler took the newly created role of prime minister, while ten ministries were set up within ninety days of the promulgation of the constitution. These were finance and petroleum; education and culture; justice; interior; public health; public works; labor and social affairs; industry and agriculture; communications and transport; and electricity and water. The thirty-three existing government departments were allocated across the newly created ministries. A Ministry of Economics and Commerce was added the next month.

A review of the UK government's 1968 military withdrawal was initiated in 1970 after the Conservatives came to power under Edward Heath. Sir William Luce, Britain's special representative for the Persian Gulf, concluded in his policy review that the four major sheikhdoms were determined to be fully independent by the end of 1971, either as separate states or in a federation. As a result, the Heath government decided there should be no attempt to prolong Britain's treaty arrangements with these sheikhdoms beyond the December 31, 1971, deadline for military withdrawal. It did offer the rulers new treaties of friendship providing for consultations in the event of any security threat, but without the specific commitment of active military assistance (although the use of force was not ruled out). Britain would continue its involvement in military supply and training while remaining a major weapons seller as well. London was clear: it intended to stay active in the region.

After a weeklong meeting in Dubai, six of the seven Trucial coast sheikhdoms announced on July 18, 1971, that they planned to conclude their federation by the end of the year when Britain withdrew from its treaty arrangements. The United Arab Emirates, or UAE, was officially created on December 2, 1971, without Bahrain or Qatar, both of which had already declared their independence. The Trucial coast emirate of Ras Al Khaimah initially opted out of the federation as well after disagreements over representation in the new legislature. But it became the seventh emirate in the UAE in early 1972 after its deputy ruler, Sheikh Khalid Ibn Saqr al-Qasimi, failed to broker a solo deal with the United States.

Bahrain formally declared independence on August 14, 1971. Qatar followed suit the next month. On September 3, 1971, Qatar's deputy ruler, Sheikh Khalifa, announced the promulgation of the constitution and the termination of the existing British treaties. A new ten-year treaty of friendship and cooperation with the United Kingdom was negotiated by Sheikh Khalifa and signed in Geneva on September 3 by the vacationing Sheikh Ahmad and Sir Geoffrey Arthur, the British political resident in the Gulf. In a speech delivered on national television, Sheikh Khalifa said Bahrain's proclamation of independence had left Qatar "with no alternative but to pursue the path of independence. It was the only way to maintain and consolidate the entity of our country."[2] Sheikh Ahmad did not return to Qatar for the independence celebrations.

Qatar joined the Arab League within days of its independence proclamation, and this was followed on September 21, 1971, by Qatar's admittance into the United Nations. The government in newly independent Qatar had a familiar composition. Of the original ten-member cabinet, seven were leading members of the Al Thani family. Only three portfolios went to nonfamily ministers: public works; labor and social affairs; and communications and transport. In addition to being deputy ruler, prime minister, and the minister of finance and petroleum affairs, Sheikh Khalifa became Qatar's first minister of foreign affairs on September 4, 1971, one day after the declaration of independence. The previous Department of Foreign Affairs was transferred to the new Ministry of Foreign Affairs. Sheikh Ahmad's son Abdul Aziz Ibn Ahmad Al Thani was named minister of public health.

When it declared independence in September 1971, Qatar had a population of around 111,000 and was almost entirely dependent on revenues from oil production. In the 1970 census about 45,000 residents were identified as Qatari. This compares to a total population of about 2.9 million today, of which just over 310,000 are thought to be citizens. Oil revenues represented 91 percent of the government's total income and were up 62 percent in 1971 to £82.5 million (see table 7.1). Of this amount, payments from QPC totaled £44.6 million, Shell contributed £37.9 million, and annual rents from the Qatar Oil Company Limited (Japan) for its offshore concession composed a nominal £40,000.[3] The revenue rise followed several measures by OPEC in 1970 and 1971, including the adoption of uniform posted price increases by member countries and a new accord establishing 55 percent as the minimum government tax on profits. In Qatar this higher profit share was achieved through supplemental agreements signed in 1970 with QPC and Shell.

Qatar had about £100 million in its investment fund at the end of 1971, hitting the target set by Deputy Ruler Sheikh Khalifa.[4] Its proved oil reserves stood at 6 billion barrels, up from 4.3 billion barrels on December 28, 1970, and its associated gas deposits were estimated at 8 trillion cubic feet.[5] The significant increase in oil reserves year-on-year was attributed to Shell's Bul Hanine discovery as well as the successful implementation of secondary recovery methods at Qatar's onshore and offshore fields. Crude oil output averaged 430,000 barrels

TABLE 7.1 State revenue from oil since 1965

Year	Millions pound sterling	% Increase
1965*	24.7	8.3
1966	32.4	31.2
1967	38.1	17.6
1968	46.6	22.3
1969	49.0	5.2
1970	51.0	4.1
1971	82.5	61.8
1972	132.0	47.9**

Source: FCO, From Petroleum Division of UK's DTI, "The Oil Industry in Qatar," dated early 1973, ref. 8/2086, NA-UK.
* First full year of production from Shell's offshore fields.
** Provisional.

per day that year, of which QPC contributed 222,000 barrels daily from the onshore Dukhan field, and Shell produced 207,000 barrels per day from the two offshore fields of Idd el-Shargi and Maydan Mahzam.[6] Dukhan's 1971 production represented a rise of nearly 17 percent from 1970.

QPC AGREES TO BUILD NATURAL GAS LIQUIDS PLANT

As Qatar's oil revenues increased, a related source of income was coming into view. The members of the Iraq Petroleum Company had met in London in July 1970 to discuss the question of associated gas from QPC's Dukhan oil field. Among the six IPC partners, only Shell expressed interest in the natural gas liquids, or NGLs, that could be recovered from this associated gas.[7] Shell offered to market and export the entire output of liquid petroleum gas—primarily propane and butane—from the plant, although any formal agreement for the project would have to be between QPC as the prospective infrastructure owner and the government of Qatar. While there were concerns about the cost of the proposed NGL plant, IPC acknowledged that local pressure made reaching an agreement very desirable. Qatar was understandably "unwilling to see its natural resources going to waste when the gas was simply flared," the Foreign Office reported.[8]

After the July meeting, Shell confirmed it was studying the export of QPC-produced gas with a view to financing the NGL plant itself. The company was optimistic that the project would be a commercial proposition and therefore hoped to contract out the construction of the plant toward the end of 1970. "It will be a great aid to QPC's always rather dodgy position here with the Government if this comes off," the British political agent in Doha commented hopefully.[9] In October a fiscal agreement under which the liquid petroleum gas from the plant would be produced and sold was signed with the Qatari government. The agreement was contingent on the project being found commercial, and the political agent cautioned that it could be six months before this was determined.[10]

QPC announced on March 11, 1971—almost exactly six months later—that it would proceed with a NGL plant at Umm Said based on associated gas from Dukhan.[11] The estimated £25 million project was to produce eight hundred thousand tons per year of propane, butane and plant condensate as well as an undisclosed quantity of ethane.[12] Although the plant itself would be owned and managed by QPC, Shell Petroleum Company Limited agreed to finance 95 percent of its construction. Partex, the company created by Calouste Gulbenkian to hold his interest in IPC and its affiliated companies, agreed to fund the remaining 5 percent. Principal construction contracts were awarded in May 1972. Shell internationale petroleum maatschappij B.V., or SIPM, was also appointed as technical consultant for the design, construction, maintenance, and operation of the plant under two separate contracts. Britain's PowerGas was hired as the main contractor, while Whessoe Limited would build the storage tanks to SIPM's specifications.

The project, which was supposed to take three years but ended up taking over five, involved the daily collection and compression of up to 340 million cubic feet of associated gas from Dukhan's three existing separation, or degassing, stations at Khatiya, Fahahil, and Jaleha. After passing through dehydration units to remove water, the gas was directed to a central stripping plant at Fahahil for further compression and refrigeration to temperatures between minus 20 and minus 50 degrees Fahrenheit. The heavier components of the gas were condensed out as raw liquid during this cooling process, while the lighter components remained as gas. Following heat exchange, the condensed raw liquid was pumped through a new fifty-five-mile twelve-inch pipeline to a fractionation plant built at Umm Said. The residue gas from the first cooling stage was directed into the government's existing gas gathering system and used for electricity generation, water distillation, and other industrial purposes.

At the Umm Said fractionation plant, the raw liquid was separated by a process of fractional distillation into a light gas fraction containing mostly ethane as well as up to 400,000 tons annually of propane, 250,000 tons of butane, and 150,000 tons of plant condensate. After refrigeration, the liquid gas products went to cold storage for loading. Six storage tanks were constructed—two propane tanks of 260,000 barrels each, two butane tanks of 158,000 barrels, and two floating roof tanks each of 295,000 barrels for the plant condensate. From the storage tanks the products were pumped to a 400-meter-long jetty that could handle vessels up to 120,000 cubic meters. Following treatment to remove water and sulfur, some of the light gas fraction was used as fuel in the fractionation plant. The remaining surplus gas would be supplied free of charge to QAFCO's nearby fertilizer plant, the State Electricity Department in Doha, and the Qatar National Cement plant at Umm Bab.

Japan was seen as the main export destination for the 650,000 tons per year of propane and butane the NGL plant was expected to produce when it reached full capacity. By late 1972 Shell had signed initial sales contracts with Japan's government-sponsored Kyodo Sekiyu group and its own Japanese subsidiary, Shell Sekiyu. These covered the full first-stage output of 345,000 tons per year of LPG, split roughly equally between the two buyers.[13] To handle the transportation, a 75,000 cubic meter LPG carrier was built in Japan by the Kawasaki group and chartered by Kyodo Sekiyu, with plans to build and charter a second ship around the same size for delivery in late 1975 in order to transport the Qatari plant's second phase of output.

NEW PLAYERS STRUGGLE FOR EXPLORATION SUCCESS

While an NGL export industry based on associated gas from Qatar's onshore oil production was being developed, exploration for new oil supply offshore continued. Qatar Oil Company Limited (Japan) became the second offshore operator after Shell to strike oil when the group's first exploration well found deposits in the Jurassic Araej formation at around ten thousand feet in May 1971. But this yielded only two thousand barrels per day on test, too low to be commercially viable. A second wildcat drilled on the same structure, known as the A-Structure, later in the year reported a higher flow rate of five thousand barrels per day. This second well was located a few kilometers east of Shara'iwah island, which the company was eyeing for the construction of potential export facilities but at the time was little more than a sandbar some seventy-five kilometers offshore.[14] Despite initial optimism over the find, a third well drilled on A-Structure proved dry, and the Japanese explorer moved to another part of the concession in 1972.

A little-known and ultimately questionable firm called the Belgian Oil Corporation—incorrectly identified initially by the press as Belgium's dominant oil company, Petrofina—was awarded the twelve-thousand-square-kilometer Area No. 1. The thirty-year concession was signed on August 12, 1971, by the company's two managing directors and by Sheikh Khalifa, whose office had handled all the negotiations. It covered the entire Qatar peninsula and its territorial waters except for QPC's existing Dukhan operations. The terms of the deal were very similar to the earlier agreement with the Japanese group. It included a bonus payment of $1.5 million due within ninety days of the effective date of the concession as well as a deadline of six months to begin exploration work.[15]

Like Southeast Oil and Gas, Belgian Oil failed to meet the obligations of its concession, and in March 1972 the government notified the two companies by telegram that it had terminated their agreements. "In both cases the decision was taken because the overseas parties concerned failed to take up their concessions within the time scales laid down in their agreements," the British Embassy, as the political agency in Doha had been renamed upon Qatar's independence, reported.[16] Belgian Oil itself remained a mystery. Both the Belgian Oil Federation and the Ministry of Foreign Affairs in Brussels denied any knowledge of the firm. The authorities later said it consisted solely of two businessmen with no oil experience; it may never have been legally established.

Meanwhile, Qatar's state-owned National Oil Distribution Company finally decided to go ahead with a new refinery at Umm Said to supplement the aging 680-barrel-per-day topping plant. In January 1972 NODCO awarded a twenty-month contract for the construction of a 6,200 barrel-per-day refinery to Hudson Engineering, an affiliate of McDermott International. Output would be directed into the local market, where consumption of refined petroleum products was running around 3,000 barrels per day.[17] Imports were meeting most of this demand, including approximately 2,000 barrels per day shipped in from Iran's Abadan refinery alone. The new Umm Said refinery was expected to cost $8 million and represented Qatar's first full-scale refining facility, hopefully allowing the country to supply all its own needs while exporting surplus production as well.[18]

SHEIKH KHALIFA OVERTHROWS HIS COUSIN IN BLOODLESS COUP

With the industry responsible for Qatar's wealth expanding, the newly independent emirate now faced grumbling from a discontented population and a rupture in the royal family over succession. The provisional constitution enacted on April 2, 1970, had called for the creation of an Advisory Council to make recommendations to the head of state. It was to be composed of twenty of the forty elected members representing Qatar's ten electoral districts, the Council of Ministers, and three personal appointees of the ruler. Sheikh Ahmad was supposed to play an important part in its composition: as ruler he was required to choose the twenty electoral members as well as his three personal appointees. By early 1972 he had still not moved to form the Advisory Council. Sheikh Ahmad's extravagant lifestyle, fueled by the one-quarter share of Qatar's oil revenues received for his personal use, also came in for criticism, as did his penchant for spending up to six months a year outside the country on various holiday excursions. He was a ruler "incapable of conforming to the new demands of his position," and his failure to do so left him vulnerable.[19] But it was Ahmad's efforts to install his son Abdul Aziz as heir apparent—contravening, yet again, Sheikh Abdullah's 1949 promise—that was the immediate factor behind Khalifa's decision to replace his cousin in early 1972.

As minister of public health, Abdul Aziz doled out both his father's money and government funds at a reckless rate, including sending thousands of his supporters to London, Cairo, and Beirut for luxurious and often unnecessary medical treatment. The situation was becoming tense, with Abdul Aziz adding to his personal retinue of armed Bedouin at an alarming pace and Sheikh Khalifa following suit with his own guards. British ambassador Edward Henderson reported that armed Bedouin could be found in large numbers outside the passages to Sheikh Khalifa's office, in the foyer of Government House, and even reclining while sipping coffee on the steps of the main building. "The feeling in Doha is a little tense and a stranger to Qatar might even think that violence is about to break out," the ambassador reported presciently the day before the coup.[20]

Sheikh Ahmad was away falconing in southern Iran when Khalifa made his move. On the evening of February 22, 1972, the first public acknowledgment of the coup was broadcast on Doha radio and television, announcing that thirty-seven-year-old Sheikh Khalifa had assumed the position of head of state and amir of Qatar with the support of the Al Thani family, the armed forces, and the public. Telephone and telex links had been cut off that morning, and the Doha airport closed. This severing of outside communications and air transportation prevented the deposed ruler from returning immediately to Qatar or marshaling his would-be supporters. No casualties were reported, and by nightfall Doha was quiet and normal, apart from enhanced military presences at Government House and some of the royal palaces.

> Sheikh Khalifah Bin Hamad Al Thani assumed power this morning as the Emir of Qatar amongst manifestations of unanimous support from the ruling Al Thani family, the armed forces, and the people.

In his first public statement, broadcast over Qatar radio and TV this evening 0600 p.m. local time, his Highness Sheikh Khalifah said that his assumption of power was aimed at correction of conditions in the country, and to remove elements that tried to hinder the country's progress and modernisation.

He added that since his appointment as Heir Apparent and Prime Minister he tried in vain to dissuade by advice and council these irresponsible elements, who had been indulging in profiteering, and accumulation of fortune at the expense of the people.

He said that to keep silent in the face of this deterioration of conditions, was tantamount to betrayal of our heritage and abandonment of my responsibilities towards my people.

Sheikh Khalifah, who had earlier in the day issued three decrees aimed at raising the standards of the people of Qatar, explained that all his previous efforts were met with deaf ears by those elements' self-indulgence and disrespect for public interest.

The country, he said, revolved in a vicious circle, and "our hopes and high aspirations for Qatar after independence withered away and were lost."

Sheikh Khalifah pledged that the new era would be one of enlightened rule, social justice and stability.

The statement emphasised the new ruler's resolution to take more steps and procedures to modernise the newly independent state and establish a sense of cooperation and fraternity between the authorities and the people.

Sheikh Khalifah extended his gratitude to the ruling family, the Qatari armed forces and the people for their immediate support to his assumption of power as the new Emir.[21]

Sheikh Ahmad's son Abdul Aziz, the only real immediate threat to Khalifa, was escorted to the Saudi border by police and helicopters, and measures were put in place to prevent his return to Qatar. Rumors of an assassination plot targeting Sheikh Khalifa were buttressed by the discovery of large arms caches at two of Abdul Aziz's palaces. The heir apparent had taken advantage of the permission granted to senior Al Thani family members to bring anything they liked into the country without customs inspection. His imports included automatic rifles, submachine guns, heavy machine guns, antitank bazookas, and sixteen gun-mounted vehicles, with the whole consignment equaling or exceeding the total

7.1 Sheikh Khalifa Ibn Hamad Al Thani, r. 1972–1995.

Source: Official site of the Amiri Diwan of the State of Qatar, https://www.diwan.gov.qa/-/media/Diwan
-Amiri/Images/Qatar-Rulers/Sheikh_Khalifa.ashx.

armament of Qatar's security forces.[22] "The implication of this is that either Shaikh
Ahmad knew that these armaments existed, in which case he connived at a plot
to overthrow his cousin in his own absence, or that . . . Ahmad had no control of
any kind over Abdul Aziz," Ambassador Henderson reported.[23]

The new ruler assured the British ambassador on the day of the coup that all
six hundred members of the Al Thani family had accepted him in the traditional manner at a meeting that morning. Another of Sheikh Ahmad's sons—a

police officer—had sworn allegiance to him publicly. Two of Ahmad's brothers also formally accepted Khalifa as the new amir. Shrewdly, Sheikh Khalifa announced an immediate 20 percent pay increase for all state employees, including members of the armed forces and police, while government loans to Qatari citizens for house purchases were forgiven and treated as gifts. These moves, commented Ambassador Henderson, "should do something to remove the reputation Khalifa has for stinginess which is probably his main weakness in the public eye."[24] Communications to Bahrain and London were restored within twenty-four hours of the coup and the airport reopened.

Lebanon was the first country to recognize the new regime. Its president and prime minister sent congratulatory messages to Sheikh Khalifa on February 24. This was followed the next day by telegrams from the heads of state of Iran, Bahrain, Oman, Somalia, and the Japanese ambassador in Kuwait. Britain, having put off early recognition to preempt suggestions that it had "some foreknowledge of the coup," fell into line on February 26.[25] The Saudis did not immediately react publicly to the coup, but they demonstrated their support with a show of armed force at the border and an article criticizing Sheikh Ahmad and lauding Sheikh Khalifa in the pro-government *Al Madina* newspaper. "The Kingdom of Saudi Arabia hopes only for the continued security and stability of sisterly Qatar, and that her ruling family will remain united and speak in one voice so that the country may flourish," the foreign ministry was quoted as saying.[26]

Sheikh Ahmad flew from Iran to Dubai three days after the coup, where the deposed ruler was joined by Abdul Aziz on February 28. The majority of the three-hundred-man entourage that had accompanied Ahmad on his hunting trip returned home to Qatar. Sheikh Rashid, Ahmad's father-in-law and the ruler of Dubai, initially wanted to oppose Khalifa's assumption of power. But he was overruled by Abu Dhabi and several of the smaller members of the United Arab Emirates, who viewed the change of leadership in Qatar as an internal family matter. For their part, the British were keen to see both Sheikh Ahmad and his son decamp to the former amir's villa in Geneva to avoid fanning tensions between Qatar and the fledgling UAE. "I can imagine that it is only natural for Rashid to harbour his son-in-law but he is hardly a penniless waif with no other palaces to lay his head in, and the sooner he is in Geneva the better for the Gulf including, and especially Dubai," Ambassador Henderson cabled fretfully to the Foreign and Commonwealth Office.[27] Despite pressure, Sheikh Ahmad continued to live in exile in Dubai. He died on November 25, 1977, at age sixty, unreconciled with the cousin who had deposed him.

Sheikh Ahmad had refused to staff the foreign ministry with undersecretaries and diplomats, but one of Sheikh Khalifa's first moves was to appoint his half brother and ally, Suhaym Ibn Hamad Al Thani, to replace him as minister of foreign affairs. Two other Al Thani family members were named ambassadors extraordinary and plenipotentiary and eventually took up ambassadorial positions in Britain and Egypt. The new amir also appointed his son Hamad Ibn Khalifa, a graduate of the prestigious British military academy at Sandhurst, as commander-in-chief of the armed forces with the rank of major-general. A nephew, Hamad Ibn Jassim Al Thani, was made commandant of police. They replaced two British subjects, including the retired army officer Ronald Cochrane (now known as Mohammed Mahdi after his conversion to Islam) who had set up Qatar's first organized police force in 1950 under Sheikh Ahmad's father, Sheikh Ali. Both British men were given new positions as military and security advisers, which ensured their continued loyalty.

Under Sheikh Khalifa's direction, the Council of Ministers transferred the one-quarter of Qatar's oil revenues reserved for Sheikh Ahmad's personal use to the government treasury. Sheikh Ahmad had received £20-£25 million in 1971 from this share, but Sheikh Khalifa turned down the money from the start.[28] In an interview conducted five days after the coup, the new ruler told the *Times* of London that one of the cornerstones of his reform program would be to curb the extravagances of the royal family.[29] Until this point, allowances paid to the ruling family had risen as oil revenues increased, with the family and the amir between them taking about half of the total. Sheikh Ahmad had been poised to increase allowances to his relatives. Sheikh Khalifa shelved this plan and reduced entitlements in a major break from his predecessor's policy. The newly added government funds went to pay raises for state employees and supported popular measures like a 30 percent increase in social aid and a 25 percent increase in retirement pensions.

A new faction of the Al Thani family took over government offices. Two months after the coup, the amir appointed his son Abdul Aziz Ibn Khalifa to replace him as minister of finance and petroleum, while Sheikh Khalifa's elder brother, Khalid Ibn Hamad, became minister of the interior (and thus in charge of the internal police services). Sheikh Khalifa opted to retain the post of prime minister himself. He also finally set up the Advisory Council, officially appointing twenty individuals to it on May 1, 1972. These were mainly non–Al Thani notables. In 1975 Khalifa increased the council's membership to thirty, with the constitution amended to raise the advisory body's term of office from three to six years. Its most important role was approving draft laws put forward by the Al Thani-dominated Council of Ministers. But its powers were limited since article 68 of the constitution allowed the ruler to dissolve the Advisory Council when the higher interests of the state were at stake.[30]

Relations between Qatar and Dubai remained strained after the coup. On May 19, 1973, Sheikh Khalifa introduced a new currency to replace the QDR: the Qatar riyal, or QR. It was agreed with the International Monetary Fund that the new currency would have the same par value as the QDR. Equating to 0.18662 grams of pure gold, this was also the same rate as the Gulf rupee before it was devalued by the Indian government in 1966. Sheikh Khalifa announced the establishment of a Qatar Currency Board to issue currency and manage the state's monetary affairs as well as oversee the twelve foreign banks operating in Qatar. Another of the amir's proposals—a common market in the Gulf with a unified currency—was less successful, although Qatar did take part in several joint projects set up in the area during 1973 and 1974. These included Bahrain's Arab Shipbuilding and Repair Yard Company, the Arab Maritime Petroleum Transport Company, and the Arab Petroleum Pipeline Company, which operates the SUMED oil pipeline linking the Gulf of Suez to the Mediterranean Sea.

OIL COMPANY RELATIONS IMPROVE AHEAD OF PARTICIPATION TALKS

Government relations with Shell and QPC on the eve of the coup were arguably better than they had been in years. In QPC's case, the improved atmosphere was directly related to the agreement, made the previous year, to proceed with the plant to recover natural gas liquids from associated gas produced at the Dukhan field. Not content with just harnessing these onshore gas reserves, Sheikh Khalifa had turned his attention to the associated gas from Shell's offshore oil fields, which he wanted to pipe to Umm Said for industrial use and possible export. Like QPC before them, the experts at Shell dismissed the concept as uneconomic, an opinion echoed by the government's own electric power consultants. Sheikh Khalifa had heard it all before, though. "Shell would be well advised to be fairly cautious as to how they set about dissuading him, because much of QPC's bad relations was due to the extent to which they poured cold water on all Khalifah's pet schemes," Ambassador Henderson warned in early 1972.[31]

QPC and Shell both received letters from Abdullah Jaidah, the director of labor and social affairs, shortly after the coup ordering them to increase the pay for their workers (including expatriates) by 20 percent, in line with Sheikh Khalifa's earlier directive on the salaries of government employees. The oil companies were also told to waive the remainder of loan payments on home ownership schemes. This caused some consternation, as the inflationary effect of the new measure threatened to cancel out any benefit government workers derived from the previous pay increase. It soon became apparent that Sheikh Khalifa had not authorized the directive, which was sent by Minister of Labor and Social Affairs Ali Al Ansari to all heads and directors of public companies and firms in Qatar. Worried that opposing the pay hikes would precipitate a strike, QPC and Shell moved to comply. Sheikh Khalifa intervened, and the companies ended up negotiating a more modest salary increase for local staff. The government also took over the repayment of the home ownership schemes sponsored by the two firms.

It was just as well that relations between the government and the oil companies were on a solid footing because difficult talks over the issue of participation had just commenced as 1972 began. OPEC had been agitating for the partial ownership by its members of the oil resources within their own borders for years and finally unveiled a blueprint of its demands on participation in upstream operations at a meeting in Beirut on September 22, 1971. Within OPEC, Qatar belonged to a more moderate Saudi Arabia-led group that originally also included Iran, Iraq, Kuwait, and Abu Dhabi. While the goal of all the participant states was to acquire a majority 51 percent holding in major concessions, the six-member Gulf group's modus operandi was to first achieve a minimum 20 percent participation and then eventually work up to this optimum level. Saudi Arabia's oil minister, Sheikh Ahmad Zaki Yamani, was appointed chair of the Gulf group's negotiating team. Qatar was represented by Dr. Hassan Kamel, who by this time was also Qatar's ambassador to the United Nations. Discussions with the oil companies commenced in Geneva on January 15, 1972.

The twelve oil companies represented at the Geneva talks grudgingly accepted the principle of participation. It was clear compensation was the greatest stumbling block, the two sides being far apart on the price the host governments would pay for their 20 percent share. "The Gulf states wanted to compensate the oil companies on the basis of net book value of above-ground assets, while the oil companies felt their compensation should include proved oil reserves as well as discounted future profits from the sales of those reserves," explains one OPEC historian.[32] Another major issue centered on the marketing and pricing of the government's participatory crude oil, which the foreign oil companies were supposed to buy back from the member states and sell through their existing sales channels.

QATAR ESTABLISHES NATIONAL OIL COMPANY

Doha was expected to take a balanced approach to participation. "I think we can safely regard the Qatar Government as being likely to take the most sensible attitude in regard to oil companies, but they will inevitably be carried along by fellow OPEC members and dare not be seen to be less progressive than they are," British ambassador Edward Henderson informed the Foreign and Commonwealth Office.[33] The government's ownership stake in QPC and Shell's local assets was to be held by Qatar's new national oil company, Qatar National Petroleum Company, or QNPC, which was formally established by Amiri decree on April 22, 1972, with an initial capital of QDR 100 million (about £8.7 million). QNPC was structured around NODCO, the state-owned petroleum product distribution firm. Like NODCO and the Petroleum Affairs Department, the new oil company would be led by Ali Jaidah.

QNPC's responsibilities extended to all matters affecting the production, refining, distribution and export of oil and associated products (including natural gas). Its assets initially included the topping plant at Umm Said as well as the refinery under construction by NODCO at the east coast port. QNPC would also administer the government's majority interest in the fertilizer company QAFCO as well as in its 50 percent share in the offshore concession operated by Qatar Oil Company Limited (Japan). In the immediate lead-up to the establishment of the national oil company, Ali Jaidah affirmed in a radio interview that QNPC would in due course seek a majority 51 percent stake in foreign oil companies operating in Qatar[34]—leaving no one in any doubt as to where the government stood with respect to the OPEC-sponsored participation talks led by Saudi Arabia's oil minister, Sheikh Yamani.

Sheikh Yamani initially concentrated his negotiating efforts on the American partners in Aramco, believing that the major British and French oil companies had already resigned themselves to state participation. When Aramco's first offer was rejected out of hand, King Faisal of Saudi Arabia warned of unilateral action should the U.S. companies not move forward at an acceptable pace in the participation talks. Just before an extraordinary OPEC meeting convened by Sheikh Yamani on March 10, 1972, Aramco capitulated and accepted an initial 20 percent state participation in its concession. Aramco's lead was immediately followed by IPC in Iraq as well as its affiliates in Qatar and Abu Dhabi and the British and U.S. partners in the Kuwait Oil Company. Despite this apparent cooperation, further negotiations revealed a wide divide between what host governments would pay to acquire the assets, the buy-back price for their share of the oil production and the schedule for reaching 51 percent participation.

The number of countries in OPEC's Gulf negotiating group dropped to five in June 1972 after Iran decided to go it alone in the participation talks (eventually securing a full government takeover of its oil consortium). Iraq nationalized IPC's remaining assets in its territory that same month, a decision OPEC fully endorsed and called "a lawful act of sovereignty to safeguard its legitimate interests."[35] After Saudi Arabia hinted at some form of government takeover of the Aramco concession, Qatar issued an official state radio announcement backing its neighbor and threatening to take similar measures. "Qatar fully supports the Saudi warning to the foreign oil companies about their procrastination and delay in the joint negotiations. Qatar will cooperate with the other oil exporting countries by adopting suitable measures to achieve their legitimate rights."[36] The implicit threat wasn't lost on the oil companies.

On October 5, 1972, Sheikh Yamani finally signed a comprehensive agreement with the oil industry in New York. The General Agreement on Participation called for an initial 25 percent participation by the host governments after the conclusion of specific agreements with their respective concessionaires, which was to rise in increments to 51 percent by January 1, 1983. Yamani had wanted to reach this level by 1979, and the oil companies agreed to boost the initial percentage from 20 percent to 25 percent in order to extend the transition period. The companies also took "updated" book value—written-down book value adjusted for inflation according to an agreed Middle East construction price index—for their net fixed assets, with nothing for oil and gas reserves still in the ground or the loss of future profits.[37] And they agreed to buy the host governments' shares of so-called bridging crude oil at prevailing market prices, and "phase-in" volumes at slightly less than market price.[38] The average buy-back price was set at $2.50 per barrel for the host government's share of production during the first 25 percent participation phase.

Saudi Arabia, Kuwait, Qatar, and Abu Dhabi signed the agreement, with Iraq abstaining as it objected to paying the updated book value for IPC's recently nationalized assets. Kuwait's free-spirited National Assembly also refused to ratify the agreement, opting instead to fast-track its majority share. Even the signatories didn't abide by the agreement for long. By the end of 1973 the goal of 51 percent participation was declared insufficient. The four countries escalated their demands to 60 percent, which was eventually extended to the full takeover of all oil company assets between 1975 and 1977.[39]

SHELL INAUGURATES QATAR'S THIRD OFFSHORE FIELD

It was against this backdrop of fundamentally changing relationships between OPEC members and the oil companies they hosted that oil started flowing from Shell's offshore Bul Hanine field in mid-1972. The initial daily rate of thirty thousand barrels was expected to hit one hundred thousand barrels by year's end. Shell built a second deep-water, single-point mooring buoy about one and a half miles off Halul to handle the increase in offshore oil production, linking it to existing export facilities at Halul island. It was still resisting government efforts to force the use of associated gas from its offshore fields, arguing that laying a pipeline from Halul to the mainland was prohibitively expensive, and it was not commercially sound to spend the enormous amount of money needed to extract, treat, and transport this gas. Sheikh Khalifa dismissed these concerns, saying that if Shell was not prepared to exploit the offshore gas itself, then it should allow another company to do so. "[The amir] maintains that even if it takes him 20 or 30 years to get his money back, it will be still worth piping the gas ashore because in the interim he will be able to set up diversified industries, and he is prepared to wait for his return on the capital outlay," the British ambassador reported after a meeting with Sheikh Khalifa.[40]

Shell was also showing new interest in "further investigation" of the area around the disputed Dibal and Jaradeh shoals off the northwest tip of the Qatar peninsula, where a preliminary seismic survey had earlier indicated the presence of a possible oil structure. Shell decided it might be wise to take the matter up with the Foreign and Commonwealth Office in London before approaching the Qatari government regarding a concession in the sensitive area. The Bahrain Petroleum Company, or BAPCO, had recently confirmed its interest in the two shoals as well, and a nervous British government directed Shell to proceed cautiously. Given the competing claims, the United Kingdom's Department of Trade and Industry fretted "that a major row might ensue between Qatar and Bahrain if Shell, BAPCO or some third company ... attempted to carry out any exploration in the disputed area."[41]

Sheikh Khalifa was pushing hard to exploit the offshore Bunduq field Qatar shared with Abu Dhabi against resistance from both Abu Dhabi Marine Areas Limited and the Abu Dhabi government, neither of whom was particularly interested in developing the structure since it would be expensive to pipe the oil to ADMA's export terminal on Das Island. Abu Dhabi had plenty of other options for increasing production at its huge offshore fields, and Bunduq was not a priority. By the end of 1972, however, ADMA had given in to the Qataris and confirmed a £10 million plan to develop the field within a period of thirty months. In a letter to the minister of finance and petroleum, Abdul Aziz Ibn Khalifa, Qatar's successful pressure tactics were very much in evidence: "We note Your Excellency's concern that the field should be developed as soon as possible and Your Excellency's advice that you will take such action as you consider necessary if the field has not been brought onstream within 30 months."[42] A provisional peak production rate of thirty thousand barrels per day was proposed under Bunduq's development plan. Oil would be piped to Das Island to be "fiscalized" before storage with ADMA's other crude streams for subsequent export. British Petroleum had sold a one-third share in Bunduq to a group of Japanese companies in 1970, reducing its interest in the field in line with the stake held by CFP of France. The three partners formed the El Bunduq Company, each with a one-third share. Roughly 90 percent of the investment, however, was Japanese.

While the news was favorable at Bul Hanine and Bunduq, other developments offshore were not so rosy. Despite its earlier enthusiasm, in late 1972 the Japanese group at Qatar's offshore Area No. 3 was still waffling on whether to go ahead with commercial development at its concession after completing its seventh exploration well. Qatar Oil Company Limited (Japan) would go on to drill two more holes on its 8,500 square kilometers before turning all rights back to the government on April 10, 1974. The Japanese firm spent some $36 million on exploration in the five years it held the acreage—substantially more than the $24 million that it had originally committed to spend. Of the nine wells, only two found small quantities of oil, although the seventh was also rumored to have yielded an unexciting result.

OFFSHORE NORTH WEST DOME GAS DISCOVERY GOES
VIRTUALLY UNNOTICED

Like many oil producers in the Middle East, Qatar raised oil flows—and revenue—faster than it found ways to use the less profitable associated natural gas. A consequently low gas use rate made non-associated gas discoveries easy to dismiss and their potential easy to overlook. The associated gas produced in the Dukhan region was originally used only in field operations or flared off into the atmosphere. Associated gas began to be used in electric power generation in 1963, when a fifty-mile-long gas pipeline was built across the peninsula to deliver up to 25 million cubic feet daily from Dukhan's Khatiya gas-separation station to the new 30-megawatt Ras Abu Aboud power station in Doha's industrial district. Ras Abu Aboud also boasted a desalination plant capable of producing 1.5 million gallons of fresh water daily. The power station started off with two steam generators, doubled its capacity to 60 megawatts in 1970, and added another 50 megawatts in 1972 and 1973. After a fifth stage was completed in 1976, the station's total capacity was 210 megawatts.

Of the estimated 373 million cubic feet of associated gas produced daily at Qatar's onshore and offshore fields in 1969, less than 30 percent was used in oil operations, power generation, and other applications.[43] Oil field operations accounted for the bulk of this usage. QPC directed just 11.5 million cubic feet per day by pipeline to Doha for use in power generation and seawater distillation in 1969, while the cement plant at Umm Bab consumed another 2 million cubic feet daily.[44] By 1971 this use rate had fallen to 22 percent as output rose to 435 million cubic feet per day on higher oil flows from both Dukhan and Shell's marine concession.[45] The QAFCO fertilizer plant was the first industrial user at Umm Said, but it did not start processing associated gas, sea water, and air to make liquid ammonia (the base material of the fertilizer industry) until late 1973.

QPC first discovered non-associated gas in the Permian Khuff formation underneath Dukhan's oil producing layers in 1959 at a depth of about 10,100 feet. With no use for this dry gas and no evidence of new oil horizons, the well was shut in at 13,261 feet. Over a decade later, in November 1971, the Shell Company of Qatar discovered non-associated gas offshore in the Khuff formation at a depth of about 8,071 feet. This discovery, which attracted absolutely no fanfare at the time, would turn out to be the largest non-associated gas accumulation in the world. Known for many years as the North West Dome gas field due to its location in relatively shallow waters ninety-five kilometers north west of Shell's Halul island oil operations hub, it was later called the North Dome field and is now commonly referred to as the North field.

With so much associated gas being flared, the discovery was hardly worth celebrating. Of the 190 million cubic feet per day of associated gas that Shell produced from its offshore oil fields in 1971, the year the North West Dome was discovered, all but 11 million cubic feet (less than 6 percent) was flared into the atmosphere.[46] At the amir's insistence, Shell carried out an analysis in 1972 in which it tentatively concluded that it would take over $1 billion to develop both associated gas from its offshore oil fields and non-associated gas from the North West Dome.[47] "Keep it in the ground a few more years," was the company's mantra. For their part, the Qataris wanted to exploit the two sources of gas together in these early days. The amir's advisers argued that exploitation of associated gas by itself was risky: it would be expensive, and its production directly related to continuing crude oil output.[48]

Shell did say it would not object to an outside company carrying out a feasibility analysis with the government to determine the economic viability of a natural gas liquids plant based on associated gas production from its three offshore oil fields. If this study proved positive, Shell hinted, it might undertake a second NGL project at Umm Said. But Shell wasn't prepared to relinquish its concessionary rights to a third party, nor would it allow another company to exploit the associated gas as drilling could endanger its oil operations. British officials were worried the company wasn't taking local sentiment against gas flaring into account. "The emotional feeling, which Shell have always underestimated, springs from the fact that the Qataris know that the associated gas is being flared off at sea in tremendous quantities every minute of the day," Ambassador Henderson fretted.[49]

The tussle with the Qataris over offshore gas use had tarnished Shell's standing in the country, as had a spate of work stoppages and strikes at the firm's offshore platforms in the late 1960s and early 1970s. During labor disputes in 1968 and 1973, including one where a striking worker commandeered a company boat that was on its way to an offshore well, Sheikh Khalifa had to personally order Shell's employees back to work. In contrast, QPC's star had risen with the amir and his advisers following the onshore operator's 1971 decision to proceed with the first NGL project at Umm Said based on associated gas produced from Dukhan. Its industrial relations had improved as well, with no recent labor problems and enhanced efforts by QPC management to train Qataris to take jobs in the company.

Gas use was higher onshore, although hardly spectacular in the years preceding the 1975 completion of the first NGL plant. QPC produced nearly 250 million cubic feet of associated gas from Dukhan in 1971, some 29 percent of which was utilized. Onshore usage rose to 34 percent in 1972, when 96 million cubic feet of associated gas was consumed daily, including the 32 million cubic feet supplied to the government for electricity and water desalination.[50] The onshore operator drilled a second well into Dukhan's Khuff formation in 1972, encountering a quantity of dry gas at 11,450 feet.[51] But this was also shut in. Development of Dukhan's non-associated gas resources would not begin until 1976, and production only commenced in 1978. It was an even longer wait offshore.

CHAPTER 8

The Early Khalifa Years

1970s Resource Nationalism

Details of oil company participation in Qatar's oil and gas resource development fell into place just months before events that would crystallize OPEC's influence over the oil market and reopen the issue. The principal agreement for QNPC, Qatar's state-owned oil company, to take a 25 percent stake in Shell Company of Qatar rising to 51 percent by the end of 1982 was signed on January 4, 1973, and was followed by a similar deal with QPC on January 10.[1] The government paid a total of $71 million for this participation, presumably representing the updated book value of the assets—book value adjusted for inflation according to the Middle East construction price index negotiated by Saudi Arabia's Sheikh Yamani. Of this amount, Shell received $40 million and QPC was paid $31 million. QPC also made a $3 million side payment to the government, which the British attributed to Qatari error in calculating the relative value of Dukhan crude oil versus the premium Murban crude produced in Abu Dhabi. "Had agreement not been achieved I think we should have had a long and tiresome tussle for QPC which would have led possibly to a complete impasse and possibly even legislation," Ambassador Edward Henderson reported. "It is worth $3 million to have saved them [QPC] that."[2]

Qatar's entire government share of participation crude oil—reportedly 16 million barrels of Dukhan onshore output and 19 million barrels of offshore crude through 1975—was sold to the U.S. independent company Koch Oil in mid-1973. Initial pricing was set at $3.15 per barrel for the 40° API Dukhan crude and $3.05 per barrel for the 36° API Qatar Marine crude, subject to quarterly renegotiation.[3] This purchase was tied to Koch's upstream interests, as the American company secured a concession for all of Qatar's uncommitted onshore acreage on its own and took a 35 percent interest in a second concession operated by

West Germany's Wintershall offshore. The first concession spanned the whole of Qatar's onshore territory excluding QPC's operations, while the offshore concession covered marine acreage not already controlled by Shell and Qatar Oil Company Limited (Japan).

In addition to Wintershall and Koch, the new offshore consortium included West Germany's Veba Oel and Deutsche Schachtbau and Canada's Gulfstream Resources. The concession covered the acreage formerly held by Southeast Oil and Gas in the northwest, including the disputed Dibal and Jaradeh shoals, as well as open territory in the southwest. Gulfstream Resources was headed by the former Shell official Adolf Lundin, who formed the company expressly for its share in the Qatari concession. Through his close associations in Qatar, Lundin was also pivotal in assembling the Wintershall-operated consortium, initially securing a 5 percent working interest in the concession for Gulfstream with an option on a further 5 percent carried interest. Equity in the concession was divided between Koch Industries (35 percent), followed by Wintershall (32.5 percent), Veba Oel (12 percent), Deutsche Schachtbau (10.5 percent) and Gulfstream (10 percent).

The ink was barely dry on the participation agreements when the Qataris initiated talks with Shell and QPC partner British Petroleum in London about the possibility of renegotiating both the equity deals and crude oil pricing under OPEC's 1971 Tehran settlement, which by mid-1973 had proven woefully inadequate in the face of world inflation. The fact that Qatar had sold Koch its participation oil at sums higher than posted prices was inducement enough to increase the state's 25 percent share in QPC and the Shell Company of Qatar. Kuwait's decision in early 1973 to go for a majority stake in its producing venture right off the bat, rather than start out at 25 percent and move gradually to 51 percent, further emboldened the Qatari government.

By August 1973 Sheikh Yamani was warning that some organization members wanted OPEC to scrap all pricing agreements with the oil companies and simply set prices on its own. This was followed by unilateral price increases imposed by OPEC after its Vienna meeting on October 8, two days after the start of the 1973 Arab–Israeli war. As tensions mounted leading up to the war, Sheikh Khalifa told the UK's *Daily Express* that he did not wish to mix trade and politics and would use his influence to keep the more extreme Arab countries from using oil in the fight against Israel. But the ruler also said he would not oppose the wishes of the Arab League or those of his compatriots within OPEC. Qatar ultimately participated in the cutbacks imposed on the United States and other Western countries for their support of Israel.

On October 19 Qatar's minister of finance and petroleum, Abdul Aziz Ibn Khalifa, said his government would reduce output by 10 percent immediately.[4] Qatar cut off oil exports to the United States entirely two days later, and on October 24 this blanket embargo was extended to Holland, destination of about one-third of the producer's exports. While the United States received just 3,000 barrels per day on average from Qatar in the first half of 1973, this had jumped to 26,000 barrels daily in September following the Koch deal on participation oil. By early November the Qataris had announced reductions totaling 150,000 barrels per day, equating to 25 percent of the country's prewar daily output of 600,000 barrels.[5] Altogether, between September and November the Arab members of OPEC removed 4.5 million barrels per day from the market, and further reductions were threatened at a monthly rate of 5 percent.

The result of the supply cutbacks was spiraling prices in the spot oil market, into which individual OPEC countries sought to sell tranches of their own participation crude. Iran, for example, in mid-December garnered $17.04 a barrel for the nearly half a million barrels per day it auctioned off to oil company buyers.[6] By early 1974 Qatar's deal with Koch for participation crude oil over the 1973–1975 period had fallen through, principally because the U.S. company's customers were resisting the high prices Koch was having to charge them after the oil price shock. In February Qatar invited bids from refiners for 68,000 barrels per day of Dukhan and Qatar Marine crude oil grades over periods ranging from six months to three years. The *Middle East Economic Survey* reported that opening offers from companies were in the range of $11 to $12 a barrel but that the Qataris were holding out for several dollars more.[7]

When the government of Kuwait secured a 60 percent equity position in Kuwait Oil Company from British Petroleum and Gulf Oil in January 1974, with compensation based on net book value with no adjustment for inflation, Qatar quickly followed suit. On February 20, long before the Kuwaiti model was ratified by its National Assembly, the government signed new agreements with QPC and Shell Company of Qatar that provided for an immediate 60 percent state participation in these companies.[8] This made Qatar the first among the Gulf states to actually ratify its 60/40 participation agreements, which reportedly pleased Sheikh Khalifa.[9] QPC received $27.5 million from the government under the new deal, while in Shell's case the amount of compensation was $11.2 million.[10] Both were considerably less than the companies got just one year earlier for smaller stakes. The agreements closely followed the Kuwaiti model, including giving the Qatar government full ownership rights to any surplus natural gas not already being used either in oil field operations or to meet existing commitments.

The volume of participation crude the government would sell back to QPC and Shell was also set at a minimum of 60 percent of the government's 60 percent share of output, usually equivalent to slightly over a third of total production. The average price per barrel bought back by the companies would be 93 percent of the posted price, subject to review every quarter after the first six months.[11] This deal to purchase the state's output share was significant: it was the first time a representative group of major companies had agreed to pay the equivalent of 93 percent of postings for buy-back oil and was expected to be replicated in Saudi Arabia, Kuwait, and Abu Dhabi.[12] The state retained the remaining 40 percent of its share of production, equal to just under a quarter of total output, for independent sale on the world market. However, QPC and Shell agreed to buy all or part of this tranche if the Qataris couldn't dispose of it themselves. Both companies were nervous about the government selling too much oil to small independents who may not be reliable about lifting their cargoes or renege altogether.[13]

Shell and QPC ended up lifting 100 percent of the government's participation oil in the first quarter of 1974—equating to about 340,000 barrels per day (see table 8.1). By early April 1974, however, the Ministry of Finance and Petroleum had awarded 98,000 barrels per day of its participation oil to U.S. companies Amerada Hess and Charter Oil and West Germany's Union Rheinischer, all at 93 percent of the posted price. This worked out to $11.55 per barrel for Dukhan

TABLE 8.1 Buy-back volumes in barrels per day

Distribution	Qatar Petroleum Company	Shell Company of Qatar	Total distributions
Companies' disposal (76%)	186,200	320,000	565,000
Equity share (40%)	98,000	128,000	226,000
Buy back (36%)	88,200	115,200	203,400
Government disposal (24%)	58,800	76,800	135,600
Total output	245,000	320,000	565,000

Source: MEES 17, no. 26 (April 19, 1974).

and $11.17 per barrel for Qatar Marine. These sales stretched from two to three years depending on the deal and represented a sizable portion of the 135,600 barrels per day available for direct sale by the government. Despite the output cutbacks, the sharp rise in world oil prices—at the end of 1974 Qatar's posted prices were about five times what they were in October 1973 on the eve of the Arab-Israel war—allowed the government to realize an estimated budget surplus of $3 billion, all of which was on short-term deposit with banks.[14]

NEW NATIONAL OIL COMPANY FORMED TO REPLACE QNPC

On July 4, 1974, Sheikh Khalifa formally dissolved QNPC and replaced it with a new national oil company, establishing the Qatar General Petroleum Corporation, or QGPC, with Amiri Decree No. 10 of 1974. Capitalized at QR 1,000 million (about $252 million), QGPC took over the government's 60 percent stake in QPC and Shell Company of Qatar as well as the ownership of the National Oil Distribution Company and the state's interest in the various pan-Arab marine transportation, pipeline, and ship repair firms in which Qatar participated. QGPC's functions covered all aspects of the oil industry in the country and abroad, including the exploration and drilling of oil, natural gas, and other hydrocarbon substances as well as their production, refining, transport, storage, handling, distribution, sale, and export.

Abdul Aziz Ibn Khalifa, the minister of finance and petroleum, was appointed chair of QGPC's board of directors. The six other board members were Dr. Hassan Kamel, adviser to the government of Qatar, who also became the corporation's deputy chair; Issa Al Kawari, the information minister as well as the amir's chef de cabinet; Ali Jaidah, the director of the Petroleum Affairs Department; Abdullah Sallat, the deputy director of the Petroleum Affairs Department; Dr. Taher Abdel Razak Al Hadidi, senior expert of petroleum affairs in the Ministry of Finance and Petroleum; and Mohamed Said Mishal, the director of administration at the Industrial Development Technical Center. QGPC almost immediately started recruiting staff, advertising widely in Egypt for engineers.

To no one's surprise, the government soon signaled that it would acquire the remaining 40 percent equity in the country's oil operations that it did not already own. This followed Saudi Arabia's decision to move forward with a full state takeover of Aramco. The new British ambassador to Qatar, David Crawford, noted that QPC and Shell seemed resigned to this eventuality. "I detected an air of resigned acceptance that QPC and Shell would become no more than consultants and technical managers for the two operations even as early as next year," he informed London in November 1974.[15] Qatar's minister of finance and petroleum made it official the following month: "In the same way that natural gas has become the right of the state, the oil will also be state-owned in accordance with this decision. Thus, the state will hold ownership of all its oil and gas wealth in its entirety," Abdul Aziz Ibn Khalifa announced on local radio.[16] Preliminary talks with the two operators commenced in Doha the following month, with QPC taking the lead and Shell sending just one official from London to observe the proceedings.

By this time Shell had finally agreed to participate in Sheikh Khalifa's plans to use associated gas from Qatar's offshore oil fields through a second natural gas liquids plant to be built at Umm Said as well as other potential projects. Plans for a joint gas company, the Qatar Gas Company Limited, or QGC, were announced in September 1974. This was followed by Amiri Decree No. 133 on December 15, 1974, establishing the company with a capital of QR 400 ($96.4 million). Qatar took a controlling 70 percent share in QGC, while Shell set up a subsidiary called Shell Gas B.V. to own the remaining 30 percent. The NGL project, which Shell initially estimated would cost $330 million, was to be managed by Shell on behalf of QGC.[17] Shell would also serve as construction consultant, with its manufacturing division in The Hague drawing up specifications for the plant and equipment and managing the tendering process.

Planners initially estimated the NGL plant's projected start up as early 1978, which was then delayed to late 1979. The plant ultimately began operations in late 1980. Three gas-gathering platforms were built offshore and connected to land by twin submarine pipelines—one large line to transport associated gas and another smaller one to move gas liquids separated offshore on the platforms. Each pipeline stretched for about ninety kilometers. Two overland pipelines, each about twenty-eight kilometers long, connected to these offshore lines at the landfall point at Wakrah and ran to the plant at Umm Said, which would produce nine hundred thousand tons per year of propane, butane, and plant condensate. The processing facilities at Umm Said included a stripping plant, fractionations units, degassing stations, refrigeration units, and compressors. Storage tanks for the resulting products were built at Umm Said harbor, and the loading jetty used by QPC's existing NGL plant was extended to accommodate the new project.

Reporting on the long-awaited gas utilization deal with Shell, the U.S. Embassy in Doha commented that the increasing value of NGLs—which it figured would exceed those for oil by about $2 per ton—as well as fuel requirements for industrial projects in Qatar had prompted the government's decision to use gas currently being flared. "The plant will provide feedstock for the French petrochemical complex scheduled for construction in Umm Said and fuel for the Japanese steel mill," the embassy reported after the formation of the gas company with Shell was announced.[18] These two projects had been unveiled earlier in 1974: a joint venture with the French state chemical company Charbonnages de France-Chimie, or CDF-Chimie, for a petrochemical complex in July and a deal with Japan's Kobe Steel and Tokyo Boeki for a steel mill. The government of Qatar had taken a majority interest in each of the companies formed to carry out these projects.

The joint venture with CDF-Chimie, in which the government of Qatar ultimately held an 84 percent stake, involved a $530 million petrochemical complex projected to produce 300,000 tons annually of ethylene, of which 100,000 tons would be exported and the remainder processed on-site into 140,000 tons of low-density polyethylene and 50,000 tons annually of high-density polyethylene. Ethane-rich gas fractions from QPC's NGL plant at Umm Said would be used as feedstock, as would those from Shell's second NGL plant. A related agreement was signed with the French shipowner and trader Gazocean for the transportation of petrochemicals and other products, with the Qataris taking a 60 percent stake in the venture. The steel mill with the Japanese was expected to produce 300,000 tons per year of iron and steel in its initial stage, mainly in the form of iron rods for reinforced concrete. About 75,000 tons per annum was to be used locally and the remainder exported. The government took a 70 percent share in this project, while Kobe Steel signed up for 20 percent and Tokyo Boeki 10 percent. Kobe Steel assumed responsibility for operating the plant, and Tokyo Boeki agreed to market the iron and steel abroad.

Significantly, the petrochemical deal with CDF-Chimie included a foreign component, representing the first time the Qataris had participated directly in a petroleum-related project overseas. In April 1975 it was announced that Qatar's state-owned oil company, QGPC, was taking a 40 percent stake in a $300 million petrochemical plant being built at Dunkirk in northern France, leaving CDF-Chimie with the remaining 60 percent equity. QGPC replaced the Dutch firm

Akzo N.V. via a new joint company known as Copenor. The Dunkirk project was to process 450,000 tons per year of the ethylene and polyethylene produced in Qatar at the Umm Said plant. QGPC's initial capital of QR 1,000 million was increased by 40 million French francs ($9.6 million) to cover its new share in the Dunkirk plant, which was scheduled for completion in early 1978.

And there were plans for further industrialization at home based on natural gas. At the end of 1974 QAFCO announced that it would double its daily output to 1,800 tons of ammonia and 2,000 tons of urea. The initial phase of the fertilizer plant ended up costing £32 million, including the gas pipeline from the Dukhan field and a new loading facility. Norway's Norsk Hydro, which already managed the plant and marketed its output, was appointed to supervise the $250 million expansion project. Shortly afterward, the United Kingdom's Credits Guarantee Department guaranteed a £1.3 million loan from the Royal Bank of Scotland to help finance two desalination plants for QAFCO at Umm Said. This coincided with the signature of an economic cooperation agreement between Qatar and the United Kingdom designed to strengthen commercial ties, including the setting up of joint commissions to encourage British participation in Qatar's development projects. The export credit agency guaranteed a further £12.8 million loan arranged by Hambros Bank of London in 1976 to help finance a contract supplying capital goods and services to the QAFCO expansion.

OIL FLOWS DIP AFTER OIL PRICE SHOCKS OF 1973–1974

Ominously, for a country using petrodollars to fund gas-based industrialization, the world oil market was showing signs of surplus. Conservation policies adopted by industrialized countries in the wake of OPEC's unilateral price hikes in 1973 and 1974 had reduced demand. Production cutbacks ensued, although at this point OPEC had yet to develop a formal mechanism of supply management, so reductions were introduced voluntarily by the individual states. Kuwait, for example, simply decided to shut in half a million barrels per day in 1974 when it was unable to sell its equity oil at the same price it had negotiated with its ex-concessionaires. In early 1975 Sheikh Khalifa publicly denied that Qatar's decision to reduce output was related to the fall in oil demand in the industrialized world, instead blaming it on the inability of his country to absorb high oil revenues. The ruler said that keeping the oil in the ground, rather than producing it, would yield a higher return for his country. This was because its value would increase several times over what could be realized from the investment of current oil revenues.[19]

Qatar's total daily crude oil output dropped to 518,400 barrels in 1974, down from 571,000 barrels daily in 1973. In 1975 it fell further to a daily average of 437,800 barrels. Flows started to rebound by the end of 1975. Buy-back arrangements were still in place, although they lapsed briefly in mid-1975 when the companies failed to agree with the government on prices and therefore stopped lifting the government's buy-back oil. The volume of onshore participation oil bought back from the government by four of the five major foreign shareholders in QPC—confined to British Petroleum, Shell, CFP, and Mobil after Exxon dropped out—was set at 80,000 barrels per day for the fourth quarter of 1975, while Shell agreed to buy back 106,000 barrels per day of Qatar Marine. These companies paid the government's direct sales price for this buy-back oil, subject to automatic application of future OPEC price decisions, although the price still worked out to 93 percent of postings: $11.85 for Dukhan and $11.66 for Qatar Marine on a per barrel basis.[20]

Evidence that Qatar was again flush with cash came in early 1976, when the government's annual budget was announced. The main sectors of the economy were allocated QR 3,942 million ($991 million) for the Hijri year 1396 (January 3–December 22, 1976, in the Gregorian calendar). This represented a rise of 118 percent over the previous year. The highest allocation went to heavy industry, which received QR 1,495 million ($376 million), up from just QR 305 million in the previous year. The economic services sector, which included transport, communications, agriculture, and light industry, received QR 1,062 million ($267 million).[21] These allocations reversed a trend that emphasized social services like housing, electricity, water, and ports over industry.

In March 1976 the capital of the national oil company QGPC was doubled to QR 2,000 million ($512.8 million) via funds drawn from the state reserve. By this time the cabinet had formally approved the transfer of more assets to QGPC. These included the fertilizer company QAFCO as well as the government's stake in the Qatar Petrochemical Company (QAPCO, the joint venture with CDF-Chimie) and the Qatar Gas Company (the joint venture with Shell). Recruitment had lagged, however, and very few of the vacancies on QGPC's management team had been filled, including the post of managing director.

GAS SHORTAGES MAKE FOR BUMPY START
AT UMM SAID NGL PLANT

Qatar's sagging oil production spelled trouble for industries reliant on associated natural gas. The first shipment of liquid petroleum gas from QPC's natural gas liquids plant at Umm Said—which ended up costing over $57 million—left for Japan on January 4, 1975. "There should be one or two shipments a month from now on," the British Embassy reported optimistically following this inaugural cargo.[22] Startup of the NGL plant raised issues for managing QPC's crude output, however, as Dukhan oil production significantly below 200,000 barrels per day meant the project would not have enough associated gas to operate effectively. Output at the onshore field had averaged just over this level the previous year and officials were concerned that a further drop in production could negatively impact operations at the new NGL plant, the QAFCO fertilizer plant and other industrial projects that used QPC's associated gas as a feedstock or fuel. Their concerns were well founded.

After averaging about 223,000 barrels daily in the final months of 1974, daily production from Dukhan dipped to just 185,000 barrels in February 1975.[23] The problems were mostly ascribed to France's CFP, which had refused to take its share of government participation oil since late January due to Qatar's high OPEC-driven posted prices. The falloff in onshore oil output brought with it a decline in the amount of associated gas needed to operate the newly opened NGL plant. QPC was forced to shut down production at the Umm Said plant temporarily in March, just two months after exporting its first LPG cargo, embarrassing the government, and delaying plans by Sheikh Khalifa to officially open the high-profile project.

British Petroleum, Shell, and the American partners in QPC had generally maintained their monthly oil off-takes in the face of Dukhan's price increases. But these other companies soon followed their French counterpart in scaling back on the government's buyback allotment. By May total onshore liftings had fallen to just 160,000 barrels per day. This drop in Dukhan output once again threatened to shut down the NGL plant just as final preparations were under way for its official inauguration ceremony on May 13, 1975. While the opening itself went without a hitch, by the end of the month the plant had closed again because of a shortage of associated gas stemming from a further drop in QPC's oil production to just 100,000 barrels per day. The closure followed inconclusive negotiations between the government and the two oil operators over the lifting price of oil and the 100 percent equity takeover.

Liftings from Shell's offshore fields remained unaffected at 300,000 barrels per day partly due to the lower price of Qatar Marine. By the middle of 1975, however, even Shell was having problems moving its oil. The company told the minister of finance and petroleum that it would have to cut offshore output in half unless prices were reduced.[24] While offshore production remained steady at 294,000 barrels per day through May, it dropped to 226,000 barrels per day in June and 150,000 barrels per day in July, when Shell stopped lifting the government's buy-back oil entirely after failing to reach agreement on third quarter pricing. QPC had already canceled its buy-back contract on similar concerns, lifting only its 40 percent equity entitlement from June when Dukhan production averaged 104,000 barrels per day.[25] Onshore output climbed slightly in July but at 122,500 barrels per day was still well off the government's daily ceiling of 223,000 barrels.

The Qataris were initially confident they could sell their 60 percent participation oil to third parties, but buyers like Amerada Hess and Charter Oil warned that they would not renew their purchase contracts beyond June 30 unless posted prices were cut. Efforts by Abdul Aziz Ibn Khalifa to sell cargoes on the open market weren't successful either, with the Qatari navy forced to impound two tankers laden with crude oil at Halul island after shady deals turned sour.[26] Amid widespread price cutting elsewhere in OPEC, by the fourth quarter of 1975 the Qataris finally relented and proposed more competitive prices to Shell and QPC for the government's buy-back oil. These were quickly accepted, although Qatar's insistence on an embargo clause banning oil sales to Israel or apartheid-era South Africa created a headache for Mobil (one of the two U.S. partners in QPC), as New York law prohibited American companies from accepting restrictions of this kind.

These newly competitive prices allowed QPC to increase oil production to its previous government-imposed limit of 223,000 barrels per day from the beginning of 1976. This, in turn, for the first time gave the NGL plant at Umm Said enough associated gas to function economically. Shell's maximum allowable production from its offshore fields was scaled back to 245,000 barrels per day from January 1, 1976, to compensate for the onshore rise. However, both producers were given permission to exceed these limits in the fourth quarter of 1975 to make up for the summer shortfalls. Shell therefore increased its offshore output to 320,000 barrels per day through the end of the year while QPC maximized its production from Dukhan as well.[27]

Income from oil and associated gas products was still expected to reach £800 million during 1975, of which just £400 million was needed for capital projects, military commitments, recurring government expenditures, and aid obligations to international and regional organizations.[28] The director of finance, Abdul Qader al Qadi, figured about half of Qatar's annual income would therefore be available for overseas investments.[29] This could rise to $500 million or even $600 million if local projects were delayed by inefficiency or chronic labor shortages. A new Qatar investment office was set up in London in a leased five-story building off Queen Victoria Street, charged with making recommendations to the Qatar Investment Board in Doha and executing its decisions. Sheikh Khalifa also purchased a Boeing 707 for his personal use, replacing an airliner chartered from Gulf Air.

With sufficient extra cash, Qatar was under pressure to contribute to the temporary facilities set up by the International Monetary Fund to finance oil deficits in importing countries after the price shocks of 1973 and 1974. Qatar had agreed to lend $100 million to the second of these funds, which was known as Witteveen II after the IMF's managing director, Johannes Witteveen. Sheikh Khalifa was also urged to provide grants and soft loans to developing countries as well as commercial rate loans to nationalized industries in the United Kingdom. The amir first made these latter loans contingent on higher offtake from the partners in QPC. He then put them off entirely after the output drop. "When I called on the Amir yesterday morning he said he wanted to invest his money in Britain, including loans to our public corporations, but only after his present problems with Shell and QPC had been settled," the British ambassador explained.[30]

PROSPECTS FOR LIQUEFYING NON-ASSOCIATED GAS RAISED

Despite hiccups with the first natural gas liquids plant, the recently formed Qatar Gas Company was proceeding full steam ahead with a second NGL project based on associated gas produced at Shell's offshore concession. NGL-2 was being managed by Shell internationale petroleum maatschappij, or SIPM, which now expected it to cost $350 million. Italy's Saipem was awarded a $23 million contract for the 290-kilometer offshore pipeline network, and most of the other work connected with getting the gas to shore had also been contracted out by SIPM. The Shell affiliate planned to issue tenders for the main process plant by the end of 1975, and annual production of 600,000 tons of liquid petroleum gas and 300,000 tons of plant condensate was still expected to commence in 1978.

The prospect of liquefying non-associated gas from Shell's North West Dome discovery was raised for the first time. "Shell is also investigating the size of a large unassociated gas field off the Northeast coast which could form the basis of a future liquified natural gas export industry. Initial measurements indicate that the field is a very large one," Britain's Department of Energy reported in mid-1975.[31] In this process, dry methane gas is superchilled into a liquid that takes up a tiny fraction of its space compared to its gaseous form. It can then be transported on specially built ships. The news reached the trade press nearly a year later, when the *Middle East Economic Survey* reported the size of the project was in the 1.2 billion cubic feet per day range. "The as yet unnamed non-associated gas field—which was discovered some time ago but has only recently surfaced in the news—is located northnortheast off the tip of the Qatar peninsula in the area bounded by the Iran-Qatar median line to the north and the dividing line between the Shell and Wintershall concessions to the west."[32]

Shell had already drilled three exploration and appraisal wells at the North West Dome, while a fourth was undertaken in late 1976. These confirmed the presence of a major gas accumulation in the massive limestone and dolomite rock formation, with each well producing more than 40 million cubic feet per day of gas from four separate Khuff reservoirs during testing. Shell, which had discovered gas in Iranian waters in 1966, suggested the North West Dome might extend across the maritime border into Iran. This prompted Sheikh Khalifa to order that all official maps be drawn to show the discovery located entirely in Qatar—resulting in an odd visual where the huge gas field essentially ended at the border without tapering off as would normally be depicted.

The interest in the North West Dome's non-associated gas reserves followed deep drilling to assess prospects in the Khuff and pre-Khuff strata underlying Shell's productive offshore oil fields. These included what the company described as a "very expensive" exploration well known as Bul Hanine 18, drilled to a depth of 14,307 feet in early 1974. This was nearly 2,200 feet deeper than any other well that had been drilled in Qatar, and one of the deepest wells in the Gulf up to that point.[33] The well, which resulted in a gas discovery in the Khuff formation, was drilled by the rig *Sea Shell*, which had been used for the exploratory and development drilling of all three of Shell's offshore oil fields.

GOVERNMENT MOVES SLOWLY IN 100 PERCENT TAKEOVER TALKS

Meanwhile, the takeover talks with QPC and Shell Company of Qatar that had begun soon after formation of QGPC in 1974 centered on the amount the national oil company would pay for the remaining 40 percent equity, the methods whereby the producers would manage and operate oil output in the country after full nationalization, and the rights of the two companies to acquire and sell crude oil. But Sheikh Khalifa was also eager to study the advantages of combining the onshore and offshore companies under one roof. "If the study showed that one company made sense (and there could be a lot of technical problems) from the point of view of economy and simplified administration he might request it in several years' time," commented the British ambassador on the amir's plans. "His immediate intention remained however to make separate management agreements with QPC and Shell."[34] The Qataris were monitoring Saudi Arabia's takeover negotiations with Aramco, in full swing by the end of 1975, and they wanted to wait until these were resolved before settling with their own operators.

The main outline of a deal became apparent by mid-1976. Qatar planned to adopt features of Kuwait's December 1975 takeover agreement with Gulf Oil and British Petroleum and aspects of the arrangement proposed in Saudi Arabia, with some tailoring to suit its own needs.[35] The government of Qatar would put up all future investment requirements, as had been agreed in Kuwait. Like Aramco in Saudi Arabia but unlike in Kuwait, QPC and Shell would continue to manage operations on behalf of the Qatari government under contract. This reflected Saudi arrangements under which Aramco ran operations for a fee of fifteen cents per barrel produced. The Saudi government still had to provide all the investment to support production operations whereas the foreign partners in Aramco only risked capital for exploration. This latter option wasn't necessary in Qatar's onshore sector; QPC had already relinquished all but a limited area of operations.

On the issue of compensation, the Qatari team made it clear that the equity still held by QPC and Shell would be calculated on the basis of net book value. It also insisted the government takeover be retroactively dated to December 22, 1974, when the decision to assume full ownership of Qatar's oil reserves was publicly announced by the minister of finance and petroleum.[36] This would be an expensive proposition for the oil companies because they would have to repay the difference between the cost of their equity oil and the government buy-back price since that date. During a June 1976 negotiating session, Qatar formally floated Sheikh Khalifa's idea for merging the two existing operators into a single integrated unit.[37] The companies rejected it as impractical.

In addition to negotiations with the two oil operators, the Qataris announced plans to amend the agreement with the Wintershall consortium to guarantee full state ownership of any oil or natural gas discovered in its offshore concession. An exploration- and production-sharing agreement replacing the original 1973 concession was signed with the German-led consortium on April 10, 1976. This type of contract was more flexible than the 100 percent participation model applied to Qatar's existing producers, giving the consortium an agreed portion of crude at a price that took into consideration its investment, exploration, and production costs.

The shareholders in QPC were to operate under a different participation model, essentially earning a fee for services performed. They initially proposed a fee of thirty-five cents per barrel on all production in return for the technical and managerial services provided in running the onshore operation, while the Qataris held out for fifteen cents on the barrels lifted by these companies.[38] This would mean just nine cents on all barrels produced, assuming the foreign partners continued to lift about 60 percent of Dukhan's total output. In September 1976 the two sides agreed on fifteen cents per barrel on all oil produced.[39] The fee was indexed to the movement of crude oil prices so that it remained a constant percentage of 1.266 percent of the government's official selling price.[40] This was the first application of an escalating fee for operational, technical, and management services in the Gulf. It differed from the Kuwaiti model, where a fixed fifteen-cent-per-barrel fee applied only to production lifted by the companies with no provision for escalation as oil prices increased (or decreased).

The government also agreed to pay £18 million for QPC's remaining assets.[41] This amount represented a slight premium over net book value. Liftings would be at the official government sales price, with the foreign shareholders in QPC agreeing to buy 130,000 barrels per day of Dukhan crude under a five-year contract. This was equivalent to 58 percent of QPC's allowable output of 225,000 barrels per day. With that, the Qataris withdrew their earlier insistence on ret-roactivity. The 100 percent takeover became effective in December 1976.

Responsibility for operating the QPC venture, as well as all its assets and lia-bilities, was assumed by a new wholly owned subsidiary of QGPC called the Qatar Petroleum Producing Authority, or QPPA. Sayyid Abdullah Sallat, a senior official at the Ministry of Finance and Petroleum, was named chair of QPPA; Issa Al Kawari, the minister of information and the amir's chef de cabinet, became its vice chair. The foreign firms in QPC agreed to form a service company called the Dukhan Service Company. It would work on behalf of and for the account of QPPA "to provide or procure the provision of services and undertake to manage and conduct the operations in conformity with good oil field practice and inter-national standards in the petroleum industry."[42] The service company was to be owned entirely by the foreign partners in QPC, incorporated in Qatar, and sub-ject to Qatari income tax at a maximum rate of 50 percent. It would also have the right to transfer all earnings overseas after payment of taxes.

The deal with QPC provided for the full takeover of the NGL plant at Umm Said, with the new service company managing the venture for a basic service fee of fifteen cents per barrel on all natural gas liquids produced. A similar approach was followed with Shell at Qatar Gas Company as the government assumed the 30 percent stake in QGC held by Shell Gas B.V., "an arrangement which suits the company well enough since it is reluctant to put up any share of the investment under the joint-venture pattern."[43] This reluctance stemmed from the govern-ment's refusal to guarantee Shell a 20 percent return on total investment, after which the company requested that the project be split into offshore and onshore components. Shell proposed to invest only in the onshore—and considerably more profitable—segment, which included the NGL plant. This proposal was also rejected, hastening Shell's amicable exit. The company continued "to func-tion as financial advisor/consultant on project," according to the U.S. Embassy.[44]

On the offshore oil side, takeover discussions with Shell Company of Qatar were more protracted. While the government insisted on paying the same esca-lated fee agreed with the foreign shareholders in QPC, Shell contended that the operational complexity of its offshore fields merited higher service charges.[45] It eventually capitulated, and a deal was reached on February 9, 1977, that was back-dated to the end of 1976. The basic 15-cents-per-barrel fee for management and operational services had by this time risen to 16.7 cents for Qatar Marine, fol-lowing an OPEC price increase at the beginning of 1977. Shell received £14 million (about $24 million), in compensation for its remaining 40 percent stake in the offshore venture.[46] It also agreed to a five-year contract to purchase 145,000 barrels daily of Qatar Marine at the government sales price. This represented 60 percent of the 245,000 barrels produced daily from Idd el-Shargi, Maydan Mahzam, and Bul Hanine.

Shell established the Qatar Shell Service Company to provide operational and management services to QPPA, mirroring the Dukhan Service Company set up by the international partners in QPC. Unlike the onshore-focused firm, Shell's new service company got an additional fee for oil and gas exploration and development outside the three offshore oil fields already in production. These operations included "a several-well exploration program together with an appraisal program for the huge gas field discovered in the northwestern part of the concession area, plus some additional technology required for offshore . . . production," the *Middle East Economic Survey* reported in February 1977.[47] The "huge gas field" was obviously a reference to the North West Dome.

The Ministry of Finance and Petroleum had at this point put the size of the North West Dome gas field at 80 trillion cubic feet, much larger than initial estimates suggested.[48] Shell and the government were still pondering the feasibility of a 1.2-billion-cubic-feet-per-day liquefied natural gas, or LNG, plant based on these massive gas reserves, the cost of which in 1976 was preliminarily estimated at $5 billion. Unlike the NGL-2 project at Umm Said, which was taken over completely by the government and would henceforth be operated by Shell's service company on a fee basis, Shell continued to retain a 30 percent stake in this embryonic LNG plan for developing non-associated gas from the North West Dome field.

OIL EXPLORATION FOCUS REMAINS OFFSHORE

Although Qatar's average annual crude oil output of 487,000 barrels per day in 1976 was up from its level a year earlier, it remained considerably below the emirate's daily capacity of 650,000 barrels. This placed the country at the bottom of OPEC's Middle East members in terms of overall production ranking. Even so, the reduced output rate brought in an estimated $2 billion in oil revenue in 1976, with government expenditures not even reaching half of this amount.[49] About 50 percent of Qatar's production in 1976 came from its offshore fields. These now included the shared Bunduq field on the maritime boundary between Qatar and Abu Dhabi, officially inaugurated on February 3, 1976. Bunduq production was initially held at 20,000 barrels per day due to high storage tank levels at Abu Dhabi's Das Island terminal where the crude was piped, and the field averaged just over 20,000 barrels daily in 1976. Output fell slightly in 1977 because of technical issues in the latter part of the year.

The Wintershall consortium was still searching for oil at its offshore concession. In mid-1976 one of the consortium's smaller partners announced that oil, natural gas, and condensate had been detected in various formations at the Qatar Marine B-1 well but that the size of the producing area could not be determined until more test wells were drilled. Finds included a well that flowed up to 40 million cubic feet of gas daily from a forty-foot perforated interval in the Permian Khuff formation as well as 7.4 million cubic feet a day from another thirty-foot interval.[50] Oil flowed less robustly by comparison at 1,395 barrels a day from the Arab formation (formerly known as the Limestone) overlying the Khuff. Gulfstream Resources also announced plans for further drilling in the so-called B structure in the hope of finding more oil.

Elsewhere offshore, a small American firm called Holcar Oil Company signed a separate exploration- and production-sharing contract with the Qatari government on January 1, 1976. Holcar's maritime concession covered the same eastern waters relinquished in 1974 by the Qatar Oil Company Limited (Japan). It was granted after several other U.S. companies, including Standard Oil of Indiana (renamed Amoco in 1985) and Mobil, had refused to take the acreage under production-sharing terms. The 8,700-kilometer area was bounded to the north by the Shell and Wintershall concessions, to the west by the continental shelf, and to the south by the Qatar–Abu Dhabi border. Holcar initially focused on the two structures discovered by the Japanese group in 1971, investigating their possible development via offshore field storage and a single buoy mooring export operation.

As exploration continued offshore, industrial expansion was making slow progress at Umm Said. After inaugurating its new 6,200-barrel-per-day domestic refinery in May 1975, the government almost immediately unveiled plans to boost the Umm Said plant's capacity to meet local fuel requirements. Kellogg International was hired to study this expansion proposal, and it was eventually decided to build a new 50,000-barrel-per-day refinery adjacent to the existing plant, which was itself expanded to produce 10,000 barrels daily in the interim. QGPC also pursued the construction of an export-oriented refinery with a capacity of up to 150,000 barrels daily, finally deciding to finance the project itself in 1974 after failing to convince British Petroleum, Shell, and Burmah Oil to join the proposed venture. In early 1976 the state-owned firm hired UOP Management Services to carry out a further market survey and feasibility analysis for this export refinery, but it wouldn't gain traction for many years.

Other industrial projects at Umm Said were also moving slowly forward. After lengthy delays caused by its 16 percent partner CDF-Chimie's protracted financial negotiations with the government, the petrochemical company QAPCO finally awarded the main construction contracts for its $531 million petrochemical complex in early 1977. These included a $225 million contract with the French engineering firm Technip to build a 280,000-ton-per-year ethylene steam cracker, a $112 million contract with Belgium's Coppee-Rust for a 140,000-ton-per-year low-density polyethylene plant, and a $81 million contract with the Japan Gasoline Company for the construction of ancillary facilities including sea water intakes, a feed gas supply system, a nitrogen production and air supply unit, a three-kilometer gas pipeline, and storage tanks. A $27 million contract with Italy's Turbotechnical for a dedicated fifty-megawatt power plant was also subsequently awarded.

By this point delays had pushed the petrochemical complex's start date from early 1979 into late 1980, and in the end QAPCO wouldn't begin production until early 1981. The government was already having second thoughts in 1977 about building a high-density polyethylene plant of fifty thousand tons per annum at QAPCO's Umm Said plant site, although this was the original plan and CDF-Chimie's preference. A French consultancy firm was hired to consider how (or if) surplus ethylene from the plant could be economically converted into products such as more low-density polyethylene as well as to give other recommendations.

The Qataris approached the European debt market for the first time to help fund QAPCO's petrochemical plants and other state projects. This came after active debate at the highest levels of government—the amir himself was well known for his reluctance to borrow money—on whether to seek debt financing for major projects or continue to fund them from Qatar's own substantial financial reserves. In early 1977, after cautiously testing the market for over a year, a $350 million state-guaranteed loan was syndicated among a small group of international banks led by Chase Manhattan.[51] This loan carried an interest rate of LIBOR (or London Inter-Bank Offered Rate) plus one hundred basis points repayable over seven years, although it was fully prepaid in January 1980. In addition to QAPCO, the borrowers included the fertilizer firm QAFCO, the Qatar Steel Company (the joint venture with Kobe Steel and Tokyo Boeki), and the national oil company QGPC. The first three of these entities borrowed $100 million each, while QGPC received $50 million to help fund its NGL-2 natural gas liquids project. Following the loan to QAPCO, the contractors began mobilizing and Japan Gasoline Company's equipment arrived at Umm Said in October.

Sheikh Khalifa inaugurated Qatar's second major power and water desalination complex at Ras Abu Fontas south of Doha in early 1977. Its initial stage included two gas turbines with a capacity of 100 megawatts and two desalination plants. A second phase ready for implementation in 1978 entailed four more gas turbines of 224 megawatts and another four desalination units, while a further six gas turbines totaling 288 megawatts and two additional desalination plants were to be added in the third and final phase scheduled for 1979. Upon completion, Ras Abu Fontas would have a daily capacity of 612 megawatts and 32 million gallons of fresh water.

Despite project delays and limits on the availability of associated gas during the lull in crude oil production, Qatar's industrialization effort advanced during this period. It was not long before it encountered a fateful setback.

CHAPTER 9

Explosion Destroys Qatar's First NGL Plant

I n a disaster with far-reaching consequences for Qatar's development efforts, the natural gas liquids plant at Umm Said formerly owned by QPC was severely damaged by a series of explosions and fires that broke out on the evening of April 3, 1977, and continued to rage throughout the next day. Six people were reportedly killed, including two of QGPC's employees and a Dutch secondee from Shell. A further thirteen were injured. According to local press reports some of the injured were villagers living over a mile away from the site. QPPA had taken over ownership of the facility at the beginning of the year. Now it halted production at the Dukhan field and shut down the gas line feeding the plant, eventually containing the blaze. Initial reports suggested all the tank farm's storage tanks had been destroyed, as had most of the process equipment. Only the export jetty was left relatively intact. Had the accident occurred during the regular day shift, when the full contingent of several hundred workers was present, the casualty figures would have been much higher.

Eyewitness reports suggested that the explosion occurred after propane escaped from a refrigerated storage tank, one of six situated only one hundred yards from the NGL processing plant. A wave of propane, which is gaseous when not pressurized but heavier than air, had swept over the containment dikes into the process area before igniting. The fire and the ensuing explosion engulfed three other loaded tanks as well as the nearby processing equipment. Two remaining tanks were empty at the time of the accident as their British builder, Whessoe Limited, was still testing its steel plate welds. Firefighters were able to control the fire, but only after forty-eight hours. It wasn't fully extinguished for another six days. On May 2, almost exactly one month later, a second fire broke out at the Umm Said refinery, destroying one storage tank. While favorable winds kept the fire from spreading, it burned out of control until the next morning and raised renewed concerns about on-site safety procedures.

At first British ambassador David Crawford reported that the "immediate and instinctive" conclusion of the commandant of the police, Sheikh Hamad Ibn Jassim Ibn Hamad Al Thani, was that the explosion at the NGL plant was caused by sabotage. This conclusion does not seem to have been based on any evidence, however, and Crawford did not refer to it again. Shortly after the incident, the U.S. Embassy also reported suspicions of industrial sabotage. But it also said that, after a thorough investigation, the Qatari security authorities had ruled this option out completely. U.S. ambassador Robert Paganelli pointed instead to a ruptured storage tank and the ignition of leaking product as the cause of the conflagration. "We are told that the NGL plant, which was inaugurated in May 1975, is almost total loss," he reported.[1] This was confirmed by Toplis & Harding of London, the first insurance adjuster to reach the scene.

Associated gas production had been running around 460 million cubic feet per day before the accident. However, Qatar's maritime sector accounted for over 40 percent of this output; almost all the offshore gas was still being flared, save a small amount used in oil field operations. Most of the onshore gas production of about 272 million cubic feet per day in 1976 was going to the power industry and other public utilities. The rest was directed to the NGL plant, which was operating well below its capacity of 340 million cubic feet per day. Even so, the revenue loss from the accident was expected to be substantial. Most of the liquids production from the plant was being sold to buyers in Japan, earning the government about $20 million in 1976. It was estimated the plant could generate about $100 million annually at full capacity. The two to three years it would take to replace the facility meant the government would lose significant income.

A hastily arranged session of the amir's cabinet on April 6 was devoted to financial cutbacks to compensate for the NGL plant loss. At QR 6.301 billion (about $1.6 billion), Qatar's development budget for 1977 was the highest ever, representing an increase of nearly 45 percent from the previous year.[2] By October the government had overspent its budget for the first three quarters, forcing it to face a looming liquidity crisis. Local businesspeople reported frequent underpayments on government contracts. There was a general slowdown in purchases of goods and services and delays in the start dates for existing supply contracts. Projects in preparation were decreased in size to lower costs while contractors were told to reduce their bids. At least one major project, the international airport outside Doha, appeared to be firmly on the back burner.

Of course, the explosion at the NGL plant wasn't the only reason for the liquidity crisis. Other visible areas of overspending included the vast sums expended for "medical treatment" in London and the royal family's draining government allowances. Aid to so-called confrontation states, mainly Egypt, Jordan, and Syria, consumed another $400 million, about one-fifth of Qatar's total oil income. There was also laxity in project management, stemming in large part from a lack of control by Minister of Finance and Petroleum Abdul Aziz Ibn Khalifa, who was frequently out of the country at OPEC meetings or vacationing in Europe. World inflation was a factor, having skyrocketed after the oil price rises of the early 1970s, as were what the U.S. Embassy euphemistically referred to as "high fees and commissions."[3] The amir himself told the ambassador that the cost of the steel mill under construction at Umm Said had ballooned from QR 500 million to QR 1.6 billion (about $400 million).

Meeting with a visiting U.S. trade mission, Sheikh Khalifa's technical adviser, Hisham Qaddumi, said the government would not initiate new projects during 1978 outside the four vital areas of housing, medical services, schools, and utilities.[4] Light industrial projects approved by the Industrial Development Technical Center and funded by private investors were also excluded from the freeze. The 1978 development budget was set at QR 5.165 billion (about $1.3 billion), representing an 18 percent decrease from the previous year. Given Qatar's high inflation rate, which reportedly peaked at 35 percent in mid-1977, this budget represented a severe belt-tightening by the government.[5] The U.S. Embassy noted approvingly that the Qatari government's policy of deliberately cooling its overheated economy seemed sound.[6] In further response to the fragile state of the world economy and sluggish demand for oil in industrialized countries, Qatar joined Saudi Arabia, Iran, the UAE, and Kuwait in calling for an OPEC price freeze in 1978.

Despite rising project costs, the steel company QASCO inaugurated its mill at the Umm Said industrial area ahead of schedule on April 26, 1978. The project was coordinated by the Industrial Development Technical Center, and its timely completion bolstered the reputation of this already powerful government agency, whose director general, Mohamad Said Mishal, also served as QASCO's chair. With annual production capacity of 300,000 metric tons of reinforcing rods and 100,000 tons of steel billets, QASCO was the first integrated steel plant in the Gulf. Its initial output was somewhat constrained as the sixty megawatts it required represented a fairly large demand on power generation, and the government had other priorities. Ironically, several months later workers digging a septic tank at QASCO's housing area struck oil at 4.5 meters. They had to scramble out of the pit as it rapidly filled with bubbling oil.

About one-third of the reinforcing rods were intended for local consumption, with the balance marketed by Kobe Steel and Tokyo Boeki in the Gulf area, particularly to Saudi Arabia and the UAE. The steel billets were to be processed by Kobe in Japan. Saudi Arabia's construction market was viewed as the main customer for QASCO's direct reduction steel rod plant. In December 1978, responding to weak domestic sales and with the steel company struggling to make interest payments on its loans, Qatar instituted a temporary six-month customs tariff of 20 percent on imports of reinforcing rods and steel billets.[7] This compared to a standard customs duty of 2.5 percent on other imports. Despite indefinitely extending this higher duty, local demand continued to lag against projections. It accounted for just 9 percent of sales in 1980.[8]

GOVERNMENT OPTS TO REPLACE DAMAGED
GAS LIQUIDS PLANT

NGL-2 was already well advanced in early 1977 when the former QPC-owned plant was destroyed and thus was not immediately impacted by the retrenchment. The project's main $70 million construction contract was awarded to Mitsubishi Corporation and Chiyoda Chemical Engineering and Construction Company in October 1976, while two months later Mitsubishi Heavy Industries won a $169 million contract from QGPC for the offshore gas-gathering and transmission facilities. After the accident the government considered expanding NGL-2 rather than rebuilding the original site. Shell, the consultant on NGL-2, and officials from Qatar's Industrial Development Technical Center even negotiated with contractor Mitsubishi–Chiyoda concerning this option.

Ultimately, however, it was decided to simply rebuild the destroyed plant rather than expand NGL-2. The tendering for the replacement of what would now be formally known as NGL-1 was in progress under Shell's consultancy by the end of 1977. Shell was eventually paid $12 million in fees for its work rebuilding NGL-1. QGPC awarded a $35 million design, engineering, and construction supervision contract for the plant to Japan's JGC Corporation the following year and commenced work at the site in February 1979. Scheduled for completion in 1980, the replacement plant at Umm Said would be able to produce 1 million tons a year of propane, butane, and plant condensate—more than its pre-accident capacity of 800,000 tons a year.

Interim solutions to allow Qatar to continue to export high-value natural gas liquids while the plant was rebuilt were raised. One of these came from the Northern Natural Gas Company (NNG), a U.S. firm based in Omaha, Nebraska. NNG approached QGPC in late 1977 with the idea of a floating NGL plant off Umm Said. According to NNG, the equipment for this floating plant already existed from other projects.[9] This equipment could be moved to Qatar and installed on a barge, from which it could be tied into storage facilities on land. The floating alternative would allow some production of NGLs during the reconstruction process, although not nearly as much as the destroyed plant. Nothing seems to have materialized from this proposal, possibly because of its lower output and the costs of the thirty to forty employees that NNG estimated it would have to move to Qatar to implement the project.

In August 1978 a Lloyds-led consortium of the NGL plant's insurers demanded that the government sue all third parties involved in the design and construction of the original project for the recovery of replacement costs. These third parties included Shell internationale petroleum maajschappij, Davy Powergas, and Whessoe. In the end, the Ministry of Finance and Petroleum hired four different teams of technical advisers from the University of Manchester, the Massachusetts Institute of Technology, Lloyds Industrial Services, and an unspecified French outfit to investigate the accident. Shell and Whessoe were allowed to conduct their own separate accident investigations, while Toplis & Harding sent investigators representing the insurers.

SHEIKH KHALIFA APPOINTS HAMAD AS CROWN PRINCE

By the late 1970s Sheikh Khalifa had solidified his power base by purging his cousin's side of the family and installing his own faction in government. With the unruly Al Thani family now under better control, the ruler issued an amiri decree appointing his son Hamad Ibn Khalifa, already at twenty-five years old the commander-in-chief of the armed forces, as crown prince on May 31, 1977. At the same time,

Sheikh Khalifa established a new Ministry of Defense and appointed the crown prince as its chief. The appointment of Hamad as heir apparent went over badly with some members of the Al Thani family, notably Sheikh Ahmad's side, who continued to claim that it had been agreed back in 1960 that succession should alternate between the heirs of Sheikh Abdullah's sons Hamad and Ali.[10]

The appointment was also opposed by Sheikh Khalifa's younger half brother, Suhaym Ibn Hamad, the foreign minister since the 1972 coup. Suhaym maintained he had been promised the role of crown prince or prime minister in exchange for his support. Efforts by Suhaym to get Saudi Arabia to back him in the family squabble were largely unsuccessful. In an interview with the Qatari daily Al Arab just one month before Sheikh Khalifa's amiri decree appointing his son as his chosen successor, Saudi crown prince Fahd Ibn Abdul Aziz Al Saud noted that the question of succession and of a crown prince in Qatar was strictly a Qatari problem, one that the amir was quite capable of deciding on his own.[11] Sheikh Khalifa's son Abdul Aziz chimed in too, contending that his father had also promised to make him crown prince.

After Sheikh Hamad's installation as crown prince, Sheikh Suhaym pointedly boycotted cabinet meetings in opposition. Rather than fire his half brother as foreign minister, Sheikh Khalifa created a parallel Ministry of State for Foreign Affairs. He also refused to appoint Sheikh Suhaym as prime minister, keeping the post himself instead. Divisions deepened further, as U.S. ambassador Andrew Killgore noticed in 1978. "Suhaym does not receive foreign ambassadors, attend diplomatic receptions (with the exception of the Saudi national day) and his movements and activities are not chronicled in the Qatari media."[12] When Suhaym visited West Germany in 1979, Sheikh Khalifa formally notified the West German ambassador that his half brother, while technically the foreign minister, had no authority to speak for the amir or for Qatar.

Suhaym was not without his admirers inside and outside the royal family. "A strikingly handsome man, he embodies all the ideals of the desert aristocrat: hunting with falcons, holding more or less constant open house, and spending with open-handed generosity," the U.S. ambassador wrote in 1979 when yet another rumor of a plot by Suhaym to overthrow Sheikh Khalifa proved baseless. "While Suhaym has many admirers, our assessment is that he is essentially a romantic with no stomach for power and probably with little ability to exercise it should fate ever throw the mantle across his shoulders."[13] The dispute between Khalifa and Suhaym still made for compelling drama, and stories of Suhaym's plots against his half brother would provide grist for the rumor mill until his 1985 death from a heart attack.

By late 1977 Sheikh Khalifa was able to leave the crown prince in charge while he vacationed abroad. This confidence was noted by British ambassador David Crawford, who wrote that the amir had "now demonstrated to his family that Hamad bin Khalifa has the power—if not the intellectual ability—to take charge for brief periods while he is away. Indeed, his absence could have been well timed since in recent weeks he has closed the tap severely on Al Thani stipends and handouts in order to demonstrate who runs the country. Perhaps the message had got through to members of the ruling family that less criticism means more money."[14]

Sheikh Khalifa moved toward détente with the Ahmad faction as well that year, unfreezing the former amir's assets when Ahmad died so that his heirs could receive their inheritance. The ruler also launched a much-publicized anticorruption campaign, resulting in the return of land plundered by minor officials to the Ibn Ali branch of the Al Thani family. Sheikh Khalifa even ordered a state funeral for the former ruler, inviting members of the Ibn Ali family still living abroad to return to Qatar—although the U.S. ambassador noted that this invitation did not include Ahmad's "apparently psychopathic" son Abdul Aziz, the former minister of public health.[15]

There were other personal and political strains within the ruling family. Some Al Thani members resented the amir's modernization drive. While Sheikh Khalifa remained committed to an ambitious program of modernization and industrial growth, oil revenue had not kept pace with inflation, and existing industry was not yet making a significant contribution to Qatar's income. Regional instability weighed on the amir as well. "He is also worried about the high cost of industrial diversification and the financial consequences for Qatar of instability in the Middle East," Britain's Foreign Office reported in December 1977. "But the Amir told our ambassador on 12 December of his firm intention to strengthen and modernize his Government."[16]

GOVERNMENT ANNOUNCES DIRECT CRUDE OIL SALES

Shortly after the 100 percent takeover agreements with Qatar's onshore and offshore producers were finalized in late 1976 and early 1977, the Qatar Petroleum

Producing Authority, or QPPA, announced the sale of 25,000 barrels per day to Japan's Sumitomo Shoji Kaisha Company. While buyers in Japan had purchased Qatari crude in the past, usually through Shell, this represented the first direct sales agreement between the two countries. It was widely seen as an attempt by the government of Japan to diversify its petroleum supplies and reduce its dependence on major oil companies. The sale to Sumitomo was divided equally between the Dukhan onshore stream and Qatar Marine, with prices set at the official rate: $13.19 a barrel for Dukhan and $13.00 per barrel for Qatar Marine.[17] Another direct sale was announced at the end of 1977 to Shell Oil of the United States, for 25,000 barrels per day of Dukhan crude at the official selling price subject to OPEC escalation.[18]

Of the nearly 477,000 barrels per day of sales lined up by QPPA's sales department for 1978, some 202,000 was sold to companies outside the former QPC and the participants in Shell Company of Qatar.[19] In addition to Sumitomo and Shell Oil of the United States, direct buyers included Japan Oil Company, Belgium's Petrofina, Union Rheinische of West Germany, and the American companies Charter Oil and Gulf Oil. The U.S. firm Amerada Hess, which lifted 25,000 barrels per day in 1977, had terminated its contract. As provided under the 100 percent takeover deals, the six partners in QPC—British Petroleum, CFP, Shell, Mobil, Exxon, and Partex—agreed to buy 130,000 barrels per day among them while the participants in Shell Company of Qatar—Shell and Eni—were to lift 145,000 barrels per day in 1978. Oil production had averaged 435,000 barrels per day in 1977, down about 11 percent from 1976 (see table 9.1). The sales figure for 1978 suggested that this downward trend would be reversed.

TABLE 9.1 Qatar' oil output and exports, 1977

Field	Output amount (thousands of barrels)	Terminal	Exports amounts (thousands of barrels)
Dukhan	73,100	Umm Said	70,524
Bul Hanine	45,772	Halul Island	82,915
Maydan Mahzam	36,096	–	–
Idd el-Shargi	3,860	–	–
Total	158,828	Total	153,439
Daily Average	435	Daily Average	420

Source: Data from the Ministry of Finance & Petroleum, Doha, cited in the Qatar section, *Middle East Economic Digest* May 29, 1978.

It wasn't all smooth sailing for QPPA. Intermediate and junior staff at its off-shore division, which was still managed by Shell, went on strike for a week in January 1978 over salaries and cost of living increases. Because the strikers were Qatari, deportation—the usual government response to labor unrest—was not an option. Ironically, the strike was not immediately noticed because of the high absentee rate. "On the third day someone noticed that all mid and junior level Qataris were missing," one U.S. diplomat reported wryly. "This may be indication of why they are still mid and junior level."[20] The strikers nonetheless easily secured government concessions. Shell reported that the offshore sector's monthly production total was unaffected by the labor unrest.[21]

Still in its infancy, QPPA was grappling with its future management structure. QPPA's chair, Sayyid Abdullah Sallat, took over as the amir's senior Qatari oil official following Ali Jaidah's appointment as OPEC's secretary general in December 1976. Sallat was pressing for the appointment of a general manager for onshore and offshore production, under whom managers for Dukhan (onshore oil and gas production), Halul (offshore oil and gas production), and Umm Said (gas liquids plus oil exporting and refining) would work. The thinking was that there might even be a need, at some future date, to appoint a fourth manager responsible for exploitation and production in the North West Dome non-associated gas field.[22]

The two designated producing authorities that emerged from the takeover of the former QPC and Shell interests in December 1976 each had their own staffing arrangements, terms of service, and operating procedures. QPPA Onshore and QPPA Offshore were brigaded as separate but equal entities under the Qatar General Petroleum Corporation, the holding company for all the oil and gas extraction operations in the country. Administratively, it made sense to eventually merge the two authorities under a unified chain of command, homogenous staff terms, and operating conditions. A committee headed by Issa Al Kawari, the vice chair of QPPA and the amir's chef de cabinet, was charged with drawing up the necessary administrative recommendations. These were duly approved by Abdul Aziz Ibn Khalifa, the minister of finance and petroleum, and announced to the media on May 1, 1978.[23]

However, the new terms were quickly withdrawn after it emerged that neither QGPC (which was working on its own terms of reference for amalgamating the two producing authorities) nor the Council of Ministers had approved the committee's recommendations. The objection to the plan was the inclusion of staff allowances, particularly relating to housing, that would have led to an increase in costs at a time when the amir was trying to rein in expenses. "Because of this, not only would the scale of allowances have cost the Government more than before in absolute terms . . . but also the senior staff of other Government entities, scenting fresh governmental bounties, came running with hands outstretched to claim the same privileges," the new British ambassador Colin Brant reported.[24]

A few months later, the amir put the whole idea of integration on hold following strong lobbying from Shell, which objected to merging its previous operations with those of the former QPC. Ostensibly, the dispute related to the provision of seconded staff for the combined operation. This was done through the Dukhan Service Company for the onshore operations and the Qatar Shell Service Company for the offshore. Under the terms of the 1976 takeover agreements, personnel from each entity were restricted to working in their respective enclaves. Shell argued that it had assumed certain technical responsibilities, upon which the continued satisfactory production of oil from the offshore fields depended, in its five-year contract with QPPA Offshore, and that integration could prevent it from discharging these obligations. The head of QPPA Onshore, himself a secondee from QPC's former parent company, Iraq Petroleum Company, told the British ambassador that the real reason for Shell's opposition to integration stemmed from the likelihood that it would "lose a profitable trade in secondments, supplies and services, as well as the current 22 cents per barrel which they were paid for providing them."[25]

It was hardly surprising that the Qataris wavered in the face of Shell's opposition. At least half of the country's revenues now came from offshore oil production. Because of this, the amir was loath to rock the boat by upsetting Shell and its many secondees in QPPA Offshore, where they made up a majority of the staff. With Qatar still losing money on its fertilizer and steel plants, there was strong and sustained pressure on Shell to produce more oil from the offshore fields. For his part, Brant expressed concern that Shell's tough stance on integration could come back to haunt it, or even threaten its influence with the government. The British ambassador warned that "if [Shell] push their point of view with the Qataris too hard, they might risk losing their very promising position here as the consultants for all Qatar's gas, and particularly the rich offshore field of the North West Dome."[26]

By early 1979 the Qatar General Petroleum Corporation was again looking to streamline the organizational structure at its main office and that of its five subsidiaries: Qatar Petroleum Authority Onshore and QPPA Offshore, the national oil distribution firm NODCO, the fertilizer company QAFCO, and the petrochemical venture QAPCO. The aim was to centralize duplicated functions. The U.S. Embassy reported that QGPC was seeking consulting assistance to carry out a one-year organizational study covering approximately seven hundred job descriptions and a labor force of four thousand.[27]

QATAR CANCELS HOLCAR OIL CONCESSION

By late 1977 the exploration- and production-sharing agreement with Holcar, negotiated by Ali Jaidah in 1975, appeared decidedly shaky. Holcar (which was registered in the Cayman Islands but owned by two U.S. citizens, including a retired Georgia state senator later convicted of bank fraud) had not met its initial twenty-four-month commitments. These included working over five old wells in its offshore concession and drilling three new ones into the Arab zones, one of which had to penetrate the deeper Khuff formation. The concession had been awarded despite the objections of Sayyid Abdullah Sallat, who had since taken over as the Petroleum Affairs Department's acting director when Ali Jaidah began his two-year stint as OPEC secretary general on January 1, 1977.

Holcar's concession was officially terminated by the minister of finance and petroleum on March 25, 1978. The U.S. Department of Justice had already begun investigating Holcar's activities, including claims the firm paid a senior Qatari official for favorable consideration of its concession application. This was reported after one of Holcar's principal partners told the ambassador and the embassy's commercial officer that the company secured the concession after depositing $1.5 million into the Geneva bank account of Ali Jaidah's brother, who managed the Jaidah family's commercial interests.[28] Ali Jaidah categorically denied any financial involvement with Holcar, claiming the firm's false allegations stemmed from an attempt to cover up its own failure to carry out basic commitments under the concession. But he did not resume his duties at the Petroleum Affairs Department upon his return to Doha from OPEC, instead becoming the managing director of the Qatar General Petroleum Corporation in early 1979.

Elsewhere offshore, production at the Bunduq field shared between Qatar and Abu Dhabi was shut down by the two governments in April 1978 after an alarming rise in the gas to oil ratio. Permission was finally given to Japan's United Petroleum Development, the field's operator and the principal investor in its initial £26 million development, to resume production three months later at a reduced rate of 10,000 barrels per day.[29] Despite installed capacity of 30,000 barrels per day, Bunduq had only achieved peak output of around 20,000 barrels per day in both 1976 and 1977. The two governments were pressuring the Japanese firm to come up with a secondary recovery and pressure maintenance program by means of water injection.[30] Bunduq was closed again in mid-1979 while United Petroleum Development debated with Qatar and Abu Dhabi over the terms of this $400 million scheme.

Despite the setback at Bunduq, Qatar's crude oil production rose steadily in 1978 to average 484,000 barrels per day. The production boost was particularly notable in the second half of the year, after the amir pressed QPPA Offshore to hike output to bring in extra cash.[31] Total flows hit a five-year high of 583,000 barrels per day in December, comprising daily output of 269,000 barrels from QPPA Onshore's Dukhan field and 314,000 barrels from the country's three producing offshore fields. This confirmed statements from the Ministry of Finance and Petroleum that Qatar's oil industry was operating at essentially full capacity. Production capacity was on track to increase further in 1979 after QPPA Offshore announced plans to raise output at Bul Hanine by 30,000 to around 163,000 barrels per day in 1979 and 1980 by drilling three wells in the main Arab IV reservoir.[32]

Higher oil prices allowed the government to hike development expenditures in its annual budget for 1979 to QR 5,934 million ($1,545 million), an increase of nearly 15 percent. The allocation to industry and agriculture of QR 2,067 ($538 million) included QR 1,802 million ($469 million) for a number of oil-related projects—an even more impressive rise of 21 percent.[33] A decree increasing the capital of the Qatar General Petroleum Corporation to QR 3,000 million ($782 million) was issued by Crown Prince Hamad on January 14, 1979, and represented QGPC's second capital infusion since its establishment.[34] That March Ali Jaidah was appointed managing director of the state-owned firm, and Rashid Ibn Awaidah Al Thani was made QGPC's deputy general manager. Sayyid Abdullah Sallat, who had been running the Department of Petroleum Affairs at the Ministry of Finance and Petroleum, was officially appointed as its director. Nasir Mubarak Al Ali was appointed deputy director.

NEW INDUSTRIES REQUIRE NEW SOURCES OF GAS

Finding gas for new industries had become a major topic. An exploratory deep drilling program was under way at the Dukhan field, but it was still uncertain how much additional non-associated Khuff gas would be found onshore. "At the worst—viz. if no further Khuff gas were found—new sources [of gas] for industry, electricity and water would have to be brought onstream within three years," the British ambassador reported in late 1977. "At the moment the Qataris are gambling on finding more Khuff gas in the Dukhan area or south of it."[35] Using associated gas for water desalination and electricity production without first removing valuable liquids like propane, butane, and plant condensate was wasteful. Finding more non-associated Khuff gas onshore for use in industry, power generation, and water desalination would allow the Qataris to avoid this unpalatable option.

Development of the offshore North West Dome field was only seen as a long-term and potentially prohibitively expensive solution for the country's gas supply needs. While a document distributed during the sixth session of Qatar's Advisory Council on November 29, 1977, noted that a liquefied natural gas project was being established for the North West Dome field, the proposal was still under study.[36] The previous year, Shell had estimated the cost of this LNG project at $5 billion, reflecting the horrendously high—at least in comparison to oil—capital investment costs of gathering, liquefying, and transporting LNG to market. The retrenchment imposed in the 1978 development budget implied that the Qataris did not have that kind of capital to spare. "The only factor that might impel the Qataris to step up activity in the North West Dome area would be if they find themselves short of unassociated gas for the industries," British ambassador Crawford reported in December 1977.[37]

Exploratory gas drilling in the southern end of the Dukhan field proved successful in early 1978 when a well drilled by the U.S. contractor Southeastern Drilling Company produced 65 million cubic feet per day of non-associated Khuff gas. "The latest find at the south end indicates that gas deposits in the Dukhan area are more extensive than previously believed," U.S. ambassador Killgore reported following the discovery.[38] Gas in the Khuff formation below Dukhan's oil horizons had been thought to be concentrated in the north end of the field. Estimates suggested Dukhan's non-associated gas deposits could be as high as 13 trillion cubic feet, double previous forecasts. In 1979 QPPA Onshore awarded a contract to the UK oil field production equipment specialists Black, Sivalls & Bryson for the construction and installation of four gas treatment plants, each sized to process 50 million cubic feet per day of non-associated Khuff gas from the Dukhan area.

Seismic evidence in late 1978 suggested that the North West Dome non-associated gas field extended into the Wintershall-led concession lying between the former Shell area now known as the QPPA Offshore area and the Qatari peninsula. There was even speculation that the gas-bearing Khuff layer could extend onto land, with seismic echoes indicating that the depth and thickness of this formation could be the same throughout the offshore and onshore areas. On November 5 Wintershall began drilling a well about thirty miles west of QPPA Offshore's western boundary in the so-called C structure. The German company had planned to drill down only to the zones overlying the Khuff formation but at the amir's urging agreed to drill into the Khuff. Two wells drilled in 1976 at the northeastern B structure had found oil in the Arab I and III zones as well as gas in the Khuff.[39] There was no evidence that the Khuff layer extended from the North West Dome to the well sites, however.

The government simultaneously announced plans to drill an onshore well at the north end of the Qatar peninsula to determine whether the North West Dome gas field extended into the peninsula itself. This onshore well was expected to be spudded in the summer of 1979. It was anticipated that Qatar would develop the non-associated gas in the onshore portion of its territory for use in domestic industry first—provided there was confirmation of both the government's onshore well and Wintershall's offshore well. "If both the wells are disappointing, the North West Dome would probably still be the largest gas field in the world," U.S. ambassador Killgore reported on November 8, 1978. "But if they both prove out the seismic evidence, the deposits would dwarf anything so far known about elsewhere."[40]

Neither Shell nor the Japanese, as likely buyers, were engaged in serious negotiations on the LNG project for the North West Dome, despite talks dating back to early 1976. In December 1978 two senior executives from Shell called on the amir with the bad news: Prospects for Qatar's LNG in the world market seemed distinctly limited at present.[41] The only real opening was in Japan, and then only in a fairly restricted window in the late 1980s when existing oil resources would start to be exhausted. That opportune period would close again when nuclear power entered the picture as a source of energy. Reflecting this pessimism, QGPC head Ali Jaidah said publicly that gas prices neither reflected the intrinsic value of the resource nor allowed a proper return on investment.[42] But QGPC and Shell still moved forward by agreeing to carry out a joint feasibility study on the North West Dome, expanding on Shell's 1976 report.[43]

Contractors working on the NGL-2 natural gas liquids plant were making headway on the project to harness QPPA Offshore's associated gas production. Bul Hanine was shut down for seven weeks in early 1979 to allow for the tie-in work necessary to connect the oil field to the liquids plant. A similar closure to join the Maydan Mahzam field commenced in mid-May, followed by Idd el-Shargi in June. While Bul Hanine produced a daily record of 237,000 barrels of crude oil on April 14, Qatar's three offshore fields were expected to average just 275,000 barrels per day in 1979 because of the shutdowns caused by this installation work.[44] On the marketing front, several of Japan's big trading companies sought natural gas liquids contracts with the Qataris. By early 1980 this resulted in the signature of three separate agreements with Mitsubishi, C. Itoh & Company, and Idemitsu Kosan. These contracts totaled 460,000 tons per year of liquid petroleum gas over five years beginning in 1981.[45]

IRANIAN REVOLUTION STIRS DEEP UNEASE IN DOHA

When revolution toppled Shah Mohammad Reza Pahlavi in Iran, disrupting global supply and lifting crude prices amid panic buying in the industrialized West, Qatar responded cautiously. OPEC increased both production and prices in the wake of the revolution. In the first seven months of 1979, the official posted price for Dukhan crude oil had risen from $14.03 per barrel to $21.42 per barrel. Senior oil officials still insisted Qatar was holding its prices at $2.00 per barrel below the OPEC authorized limit. The U.S. Embassy reported that Sheikh Khalifa had responded positively to a personal letter from President Jimmy Carter calling for price restraint. "The Amir said he agreed with the basic points made by President Carter," Ambassador Killgore reported. "He himself was convinced that sudden and sharp increases in oil prices would bring on world recession, damage the developing countries and endanger the prosperity of all, including the OPEC countries."[46]

Qatar also followed Saudi Arabia and other OPEC members in boosting production to compensate for the reduction from Iran. Daily flows were expected to average just over half a million barrels per day for 1979, after reaching significantly higher levels during the first half of the year. By September consensus was reached to reduce total output to an optimum daily level of around 450,000 barrels to maximize long-term production. Price increases throughout the year, together with Sheikh Khalifa's previous efforts to cool the economy, had ensured enough money for the country's needs at a lower production level. Although official posted prices were still below spot market levels, both Dukhan and Qatar Marine fetched over $27 per barrel by November 1979.[47]

But Qatar soon changed course, announcing it would keep production at around half a million barrels per day. It also signaled it would keep a lid on prices, which the U.S. ambassador put down to concerns about security in the Middle East region and a desire to stand with Saudi Arabia on oil policy. The Qatari change of heart came after a group of Iranian students stormed the U.S. Embassy in Tehran on November 4, taking over fifty diplomats and American citizens hostage and precipitating a 444-day crisis that ended in early 1981. Following the embassy takeover, Iran accused Qatar of raising its production to undermine Tehran's bargaining power with the United States. Doha emphatically denied the allegation, although flows did rise to 526,000 barrels per day in November. That same month QPPA stopped releasing its production figures to "avoid further misrepresentation of its oil policy."[48] Production averaged 506,000 barrels per day in 1979, nearly 5 percent higher than 1978.

While the shah of Iran was never popular in Qatar, he symbolized stability and legitimacy. The fact that the most powerful ruler in the region could be toppled stirred deep unease. At first it was thought that the Iranian revolution might prompt Khalifa to patch things up with his half brother Suhaym to foster family solidarity. The U.S. Embassy reported rumors of the imminent appointment of Suhaym as prime minister and the possible dismissal of the more incompetent members of the cabinet, including some from the Al Thani family.[49] But the only change was cosmetic: the appointment of Mohammad Ibn Hamad, another of the amir's brothers, as minister of education, culture, and youth. Qatar's first ambassador to the United Kingdom, Ahmad Ibn Saif Al Thani, became the minister of state for foreign affairs and the de facto foreign minister.

The Americans were unimpressed. "The Government of Qatar is inefficient and poorly run. Some Al Thani family ministers, including especially Minister of Finance and Petroleum Shaikh Abdul Aziz Bin Khalifa Al Thani, are doing a poor job," Ambassador Killgore informed U.S. secretary of state Cyrus Vance.[50]

The amir was also criticized. Killgore noted that Sheikh Khalifa had developed a profound distrust of practically everyone, was far less decisive than when he seized full power in 1972, and seemed unsure and privately dispirited. "At end of last year, the embassy thought Qatar was not far from administrative paralysis because the affairs of the country had burgeoned with increases in oil income," Killgore reported in late 1979. "The Amir then seemed almost overwhelmed and unable to cope with the sheer volume of decision-making required of him, he being the only one making decisions."[51] Sheikh Khalifa's serious disinclination to make decisions hurt Qatari businesspeople, who did not understand why more oil income was not being spent on internal development.

At an estimated $5 billion in 1979, Qatar's oil income was probably fifty times higher than it was in the late 1960s when it barely reached $100 million annually. Even adjusted for inflation, it was still thirty times greater. Yet the government's budget for 1980—corresponding to the 1400 Hijrah fiscal year, which began on November 20, 1979—was set at only QR 6,692 million (about $1.8 billion), up just 12.8 percent on the previous year's budget of QR 5,934 million. Only about 60 percent of the 1980 budget was spent, reflecting a trend of state underspending that marked subsequent annual budgets too. At the same time, Qatar's foreign assets were growing prodigiously. These were estimated at nearly $4.3 billion at the end of 1979, compared to just under $3 billion in 1978 and only $414 million in 1972.[52]

Revolutionary turmoil in Iran did increase dialog among the regional monarchies of Qatar, Bahrain, the UAE, Saudi Arabia, Kuwait, and Oman, resulting in enhanced intelligence exchange and a collective decision to strengthen their individual defense capabilities. This coordination eventually led to the formation of the six-member Gulf Cooperation Council on May 25, 1981, eight months after the outbreak of the Iran-Iraq war. The other consequence of the Iranian revolution was the growth of Qatar's fledgling military relationship with the United States as it began to assume responsibility for its own security. This included a formal request for a wish list of defensive weaponry comprising radar systems, advanced Hawk missiles, antiaircraft artillery, tanks, and fighter aircraft designed to intercept enemy planes.[53]

Ambassador Killgore recommended that the State Department look sympathetically on the arms request, noting that Qatar had no capability to defend its oil installations.[54] The giant North West Dome non-associated gas field was particularly vulnerable to attack, given its proximity to Iranian waters. Several options for exploiting the North West Dome were under study, including developing the field for local use only or in a combination of local use and lique-faction for export. Senior Qatari oil officials told the U.S. ambassador that the amir was unwilling to decide regarding either option until the Qatar Emiri Air Force and the Ministry of Finance and Petroleum could assure him that any investment could be defended. Since Qatar could obviously not buy everything on its weaponry wish list, the State Department sent a small military team to help Doha shortlist the armaments most appropriate to its defense needs.

The French scooped the vast majority of orders for defense equipment placed by Qatar in 1980, however. These included armored personnel carriers, jet train-ers, fighter aircraft, naval craft, and a full complement of surface-to-surface missiles for the ships, coastal defense, and a helicopter-borne maritime defense force. Britain supplied the helicopters for this force, and the country retained its supremacy in the provision of communications equipment. The United King-dom was also the main contender for a low-level air defense system; British Aerospace was well positioned to win this order with its Rapier system. "The chances of the Qataris heeding our advice on their defence arrangements are better now than in the past, because of the substantial fright administered to them by the Iranians in the early phase of the Iraq-Iran war, when the Iranian President threatened the destruction of the oil installations of any Arab State which materially aided Iraq," Britain's ambassador reported in early 1981.[55]

France's rapid emergence as the main weapons supplier to Qatar was a shock to its competitors, especially the United Kingdom.[56] By 1981 French weapons sales dwarfed all other bilateral trade between the two countries. The biggest reported contract, a $268 million deal for three two-hundred-ton Combattante-class ves-sels armed with thirty-five-mile range Exocet surface-to-surface missiles, together with another three mobile coastal defense batteries, also equipped with Exocets, followed a 1980 visit to Qatar by France's president, Valéry Giscard d'Estaing, and his defense minister, Yvon Bourges.[57] Another $200 million order included four-teen Mirage F-1 fighter aircraft. The ambitious military build-up illustrated Qatar's determination to defend not only its own borders but also other GCC states in the wake of the Iran–Iraq war.

The Qatar navy, known as the Sea Arm, already had one base in Ras Abu Aboud near Doha. Final designs for a second naval base near Zubara in the north-west were in progress at the end of 1981, and the government was expected to issue an invitation to tender for a harbor with repair facilities and housing by late 1982. Work was also under way to expand the existing base at Ras Abu Aboud.

At least two other Sea Arm bases were under consideration, one at Ras Laffan on the peninsula's northeast coast—the closest landfall point to North West Dome—and another on Halul island where Qatar's offshore oil operations were centered. The security of oil and gas installations was now a top priority for the government. The deputy commander-in-chief of the armed forces, the amir's third son, Abdullah Ibn Khalifa, flew to the North Sea to watch British troops conduct oil rig protection exercises in early 1982.[58]

CHAPTER 10

Crunch Time Looms for North West Dome Gas Field

S hell and the Qatar Petroleum Producing Authority were about to complete their updated feasibility study on the North West Dome's development possibilities in May or June 1980. The government planned to decide on the gas field's export option at that time. "This would enable the Government of Qatar to analyze the various proposals from interested companies (including Shell) and make a final decision on the subject by January 1981 so that actual construction could begin in late 1981," the U.S. Embassy reported optimistically.[1] An analysis by Colorado-based Scientific Software Corporation in November 1979 had estimated the size of the North West Dome at 260 trillion cubic feet of gas, making it the largest gas field in the world. U.S. officials were still cautious, noting that they had no way of confirming the accuracy of the reserve report.

But the embassy also lamented the lack of American interest in the North West Dome, saying the United States was the only major energy-consuming country that had not initiated serious high-level discussions with Qatar on the future of this immense resource.[2] This lack of interest had not gone unnoticed, as Dr. Taher Al Hadidi, a senior adviser at the Ministry of Finance and Petroleum, told the embassy's economic and commercial officer. "Hadidi frankly thought USG [U.S. government] had not really demonstrated any consistent interest in Dome development," U.S. ambassador Andrew Killgore reported.[3] He asked the State Department to alert other branches of the U.S. government and American businesses—particularly major oil and gas companies—to the potential of the huge gas field and also advised that high-level visits be paid to flatter the Qataris. This, the ambassador noted, "would impress the Qataris and facilitate profitable participation by U.S. interests."[4]

Wintershall was drilling a test well south of the main North West Dome structure just outside the QPPA Offshore area, and the results were expected to help
determine the field's exact boundaries. In March 1980 the West German company announced the discovery of "very significant" gas reserves in the Khuff
formation following tests of its Qatar Marine Dia exploration well.[5] These
showed four gas-bearing horizons at a depth of around ten thousand feet, leaving
no doubt that the North West Dome extended into its adjacent concession. Two
months later an evaluation by DeGolyer & MacNaughton indicated total gas
reserves in Wintershall's area of 65 trillion cubic feet, of which 37 trillion cubic
feet were deemed to be recoverable, and 1,200 million barrels of high-value field
condensate, of which 700 million barrels were listed as recoverable.[6]

The five-member Wintershall consortium, which also included Koch Industries, Veba Oel, Deutsche Schachtbau, and Gulfstream Resources, wasted no time
in proposing to QGPC an ambitious $4 billion liquefied natural gas project based
on these reserves. Its plan, unveiled shortly after the independent reserve evaluation by DeGolyer & MacNaughton, envisaged the production of about 12 billion cubic meters per year of natural gas starting toward the end of the 1980s. Of
this amount, some 8.8 billion cubic meters annually would be available for conversion to LNG and the rest supplied to the domestic sector for use in electricity
generation and industrial applications. Exports of LNG would be directed primarily to Western Europe, including markets controlled by West Germany's
BAFT Group, Wintershall's parent company.

Qatar was initially negative on the prospects for the early development of the
North West Dome, however. "We will exploit our gas resources only when we face
the need to decrease our crude oil production rates," Abdul Aziz Ibn Khalifa,
the minister of finance and petroleum, announced in April 1980.[7] While natural
gas was heavily underpriced on world markets relative to crude oil, the Qataris
recognized they would eventually need to develop their huge gas reserves, which
were now put at 200 to 300 trillion cubic feet. The tone quickly shifted as a
result. "Already, the Amir has ordered his officials to press on at full speed with
the development of this immense mineral wealth, not so much because he needs
the gas or the money now, but because production from the offshore oil fields is
expected to decline sharply in a decade or so, and because Qatar urgently
requires fuel for further electric power generation," the British ambassador
reported in January 1981.[8]

The newfound optimism was undoubtedly related to the feasibility study on the utilization of the North West Dome delivered by Shell and QPPA in late 1980, which included the potential for LNG exports from the field in addition to gas for local use. Several months later Ali Jaidah revealed that QGPC was negotiating possible joint ventures with international firms, which would be allowed a stake of about 20 percent in the planned LNG project, provided they shared in the cost of the plant.[9] The overall scheme would involve the delivery of gas for internal consumption first, followed by LNG exports within a year or two. The QGPC head said the immediate priority was to produce gas for local use at the Umm Said industrial zone and the power and desalination plants near Doha. Perhaps mindful of the petroleum minister's earlier comments, Jaidah was quick to stress that Qatar wanted to decrease its reliance on crude oil but did not intend to replace oil with gas as the country's main source of revenue at this initial stage of its gas development program.

Four of the six oil companies invited to participate in the North West Dome development responded by QGPC's deadline of January 7, 1981. Proposals were submitted by British Petroleum, CFP, Shell, and Wintershall. The two U.S. firms on the list, Exxon and Mobil, opted out. But the process soon bogged down in conflicts within the high-level government committee established to examine the exploitation of Qatar's gas resources. Some of its members wanted to develop the North West Dome field for domestic purposes only. In addition to QGPC head Ali Jaidah and QGPC board member Dr. Taher Al Hadadi, this committee included Mohamed Said Mishal, the director general of the Industrial Development Technical Center; Sayyid Abdullah Sallat, the director of petroleum affairs at the Ministry of Finance and Petroleum; Dr. Mohamed Orabi, the manager of refining, gas processing, and petrochemicals at QGPC; and Dr. Helmi Samara, an adviser on oil and gas to the petroleum minister. Frustrated with the often-emotional infighting, Said Mishal suggested approaching the World Bank for an outside opinion.[10]

The situation was further complicated when, two months later, four U.S. contractors—Fluor, Kellogg, Parsons, and Bechtel—submitted separate proposals. "No-one to whom we have spoken seems clear about the role which these contracting companies would be expected to fulfill: but it would be some kind of second-guessing on the engineering side, and possibly carrying out some of the major work such as pipe-laying etc., on the contracting side," the British

Ambassador reported.[11] BP explained the oil companies would be supervising the contractors, not the other way around, since the proposals submitted at the beginning of January covered the overall management of the two phases needed to exploit the North West Dome. It was keen to participate in a second liquefaction project in the region after completing the Middle East's first LNG plant on Das Island in Abu Dhabi in April 1977. BP was optimistic on its chances of winning the initial consultancy contract, particularly since neither Exxon nor Mobil had shown interest.

In the meantime, the gas field was growing after another Wintershall exploration well drilled some twelve kilometers offshore. "The Amir startled me when I saw him with the statement that recent drilling by Wintershall just off the N.E. coast of Qatar had found gas in sizeable quantities," the British ambassador wrote in early 1981. "So it looks as if the field is at least some sixty miles wide, and might well prove to contain the 300 TCF [trillion cubic feet] of gas which hitherto has been the upper estimate of the gas in place."[12] By this time the government had heeded Said Mishal's advice and asked the World Bank for help in deciding what to do with the Qatar's growing gas reserves. But the World Bank's involvement was restricted to evaluating the existing studies on the North West Dome. "The Bank staff have hinted to us that the reason for this is that the Qataris have already made up their minds how to proceed," the British Embassy in Washington (where the World Bank is headquartered) reported in May 1981.[13]

MARGARET THATCHER BACKS BP FOR NORTH WEST DOME

UK prime minister Margaret Thatcher made a hard pitch to the amir for BP's involvement in the North West Dome during her 1981 visit to Qatar, lauding BP's unique abilities while pointedly ignoring Shell, the other UK bidder vying for a role in the project.[14] The prime minister had been warned off Shell by her advisers, despite the firm's long history in Qatar, its leadership role in all the various feasibility studies that had been conducted on the gas field up to that point, and its implementation of a comprehensive 1980 study on the country's future energy needs. In a briefing in advance of her meeting with the amir, the UK Department of Trade told Thatcher that Shell had "blotted their record when the first natural gas liquids (NGL) plant at Umm Said (designed by Shell and Bechtel (UK) with Davy Powergas as main contractor) exploded in 1977."[15] The line taken by the prime minister with Sheikh Khalifa left no doubt that the United Kingdom had unofficially selected BP as its "chosen instrument" in staking a claim to the North West Dome project for British business interests. UK officials subsequently watered this label down to "our front interest" to avoid upsetting Shell.

Around this time a six-man gas coordination committee led by QGPC's deputy managing director, Rashid Ibn Awaidah Al Thani, was formed to evaluate the various North West Dome proposals. It included officials from QGPC, the Ministry of Finance and Petroleum, and the Department of Petroleum Affairs, mostly at the deputy director or department manager level, as well as familiar faces from the government's high-level gas exploitation committee.[16] The outline of the project was coming into focus, although its details and timing were still unclear. Production of some 2,000 million cubic feet per day of gas from the field was envisaged, of which around 800 million cubic feet would be used domestically in phase one and 1,200 million cubic feet used to manufacture an estimated 6 million tons per year of LNG for export in phase two. Other products would include 4,500 tons per day of gas liquids and 64,000 barrels per day of condensate. The overall cost of both phases of the project was tentatively put at $5.3 billion.

Ras Laffan, about sixty kilometers north of Doha, was identified as the probable location for the LNG plant. The amir had recently approved a major new 1,500-megawatt power plant and 48 million gallons per day desalination project there. Ras Laffan had been chosen because of its proximity to the field just forty-five miles offshore. It was almost entirely deserted in 1981, although it was linked by a desert track to the fishing village of Al Khor. Landowners had started claiming tracts of virgin land, and several leading businessmen were building beach villas in the area. Sheikh Khalifa himself broke ground on a palace near Al Khor in 1982. The Ministry of Municipal Affairs recommended that new towns should only be built in the context of a major program of industrialization, and Ras Laffan fit the bill. "It is the government's intention to build the LNG complex at Ras Laffan in order to develop an urban town there and not to concentrate solely on the industrial town of Umm Said south of Doha," Sheikh Rashid declared. "The government is planning to build a city with all facilities, including schools and hospitals for the families of people working there."[17]

In mid-1981 the first phase of the project involving offshore gas facilities and the pipelines to bring the gas ashore was envisaged as a wholly owned QGPC operation, although one carried out chiefly by foreign contractors. Sheikh Rashid's steering committee was considering the proposals submitted by Fluor, Kellogg, Parsons, and Bechtel, and there was speculation that QGPC might commission a conceptual design study from one of these four contractors. The LNG export plant was to be established in the project's second phase and would involve a 20 percent non-Qatar equity investment. This might be divided among two or three of the four oil companies that had put in proposals—British Petroleum, CFP, Shell, and Wintershall—in order to spread out risk and foster relations with the governments of the countries from which these firms hailed.

The North West Dome project nonetheless remained nebulous, its timing uncertain, and the demand for LNG in international markets unclear given the contemporary world surplus of hydrocarbons. Among the oil company contenders—which had expanded from four to six by the middle of 1981 after U.S. firms Texaco and Huffco expressed interest in being considered for the job—BP was apparently the only one to limit its equity interest to 10 percent. Shell, CFP, and Wintershall, the Qataris reported, appeared happy to accept the full equity amount of 20 percent originally set out by the government.[18] Qatari officials were concerned that BP might be dragging its feet, despite the British prime minister's representations to the amir on its behalf.[19] This impression was reinforced by the fact that the company had yet to receive permission from the local authorities to open its own office in Doha.

QATAR RESUMES NATURAL GAS LIQUIDS EXPORTS

After a hiatus of three and a half years, Qatar resumed exports in late 1980 from the reconstructed NGL-1 plant. One cargo of plant condensate was shipped out at the end of October and a second shipment in November. The new NGL-2 plant was brought online around the same time, about a year behind schedule, and exported a cargo of liquid petroleum gas to Japan in early November. But problems with the pipeline feeding NGL-2 meant that associated gas from the offshore fields was not reaching the plant. Except for a small amount used in oil field operations, all the offshore gas was still being flared. Instead, gas from the Dukhan field was diverted into NGL-2 to keep it ticking over, including about 85 million cubic feet per day of deep Khuff gas normally reserved for industrial users. "All together, some 50% of Qatar's gas was still shut in on the offshore fields because of the pipeline being unserviceable," Colin Brant, the British ambassador, reported in early January 1981.[20]

Tests found cracking at various points along the overland section of the pipeline, which ran from landfall at Wakrah to the NGL-2 plant site in Umm Said. Sections of the onshore pipe were sent for testing to the University of Manchester as well as to the British Institute of Welding, who reported that the inside of the pipeline was corroded and there was potentially dangerous cracking in the steel itself. Shell had used seawater to test the pipeline, and its critics argued that the seawater at Umm Said was both corrosive and high in sulfate-reducing bacteria that could damage steelwork. Experts from the University of Manchester advised against using the pipeline for transporting high-pressure gas; there was speculation that Shell's engineering team in the Netherlands had specified the wrong type of steel for the line.[21] The pipe was designed for dry gas operation, as the platforms were equipped with glycol treatment units to dry the gas before it passed through the line. Shell suggested it could have been contaminated by the wet sour gas produced offshore Qatar and instituted improved operating procedures for the glycol units.

There were also questions about the integrity of a smaller, parallel gas liquids line that carried the heavier hydrocarbon fractions separated offshore. This twelve-inch pipeline remained in service transporting gas liquids to NGL-2, although operators installed filters at the Umm Said plant to catch potential corrosion particles. Both lines stretched for 118 kilometers, of which 90 kilometers ran along the ocean bed and 28 kilometers over land. QGPC had already decided in December 1980 to replace another 500-meter pipeline from the receiver area, where the gas and gas liquid streams merged into one stream, to the plant. Tests carried out by QGPC Onshore revealed cracking on this small line, which could be particularly serious as it carried gas in liquid form and ran though the center of the plant. If exposed to atmospheric pressure, this gas would expand almost instantaneously, engulfing the plant in a volatile vapor cloud. Work to replace the 500-meter line was under way, and QGPC planned to demand that Shell pay for it.[22]

A joint investigation by the University of Manchester and Shell's Dutch technical team revealed that the land section of the gas pipeline was severely damaged by hydrogen-induced cracking, but they ruled out sulfate-reducing bacteria as the cause. Hydrogen-induced cracking—where hydrogen atoms produced through surface corrosion of the steel diffuse into it through microstructural defects, expanding and eventually cracking the steel—was a new phenomenon in the Gulf, and Shell maintained that no one had been aware of it when the pipeline was laid in 1976.[23] While insisting the gas pipeline was still usable, Shell nonetheless agreed in January 1981 to redesign and replace the thirty-kilometer onshore section running from Wakrah to Umm Said at its own expense. This would take up to a year, during which both NGL-1 and NGL-2 would operate at half capacity (see table 10.1). Likewise, Shell also agreed to replace the underwater sections of the gas pipeline if testing showed that it was not up to international standards.

By April 1981 QGPC estimated the financial loss to Qatar stemming from the delays and problems with NGL-2 and its associated pipelines had reached QR 1,000 million (about $275 million).[24] This represented the export value of the offshore gas that had been flared since September 1979, when the plant had originally been scheduled to come online. Shell and the other third parties involved in the construction of the first natural gas liquids plant destroyed in April 1977 were already at risk for compensation of around $52 million to the plant's insurers. "Apart from any liability accruing over the destruction of the plant itself, there is also a claim on the Qatar side of $160 million, possibly, representing the consequential loss of production and hence profits," the British ambassador reported. "This figure may increase to as much as $250 million according to assessments."[25]

Denis Thatcher, the prime minister's husband, had accompanied his wife on her recent trip to Qatar and visited the NGL complex at Umm Said. Briefed beforehand on Shell's pipeline problems, Mr. Thatcher was presented by the head of QGPC Onshore Operations with a small piece of corroded piping that had been cut out of the onshore line to the NGL-2 plant. This went on the prime

TABLE 10.1 Capacity of Qatar's natural gas liquids plants circa 1980

	Propane (tons per day)	Butane (tons per day)	Plant condensate/ natural gasoline (tons per day)	Methane gas (million cubic feet per day)	Ethane gas (million cubic feet per day)
NGL-1	740	470	310	140	24
NGL-2	220	730	73	110	28
Total	960	1,200	383	250	52

Source: Data from various December 1980 issues of *Middle East Economic Survey.*

minister's airplane for the return journey to London. Several weeks later Margaret Thatcher cornered a senior Shell executive at a social function, where she berated him for the company's dismal performance in Qatar. Embarrassed at being tackled by the prime minister at a semipublic occasion and concerned about its reputation, Shell's leadership hit back.

Sir Peter Baxendell, the chair of Shell's British arm, pinned the blame for the "one-sided" account the prime minister's group was given during its visit to Qatar on the ongoing rivalry between the onshore and offshore operators.[26] "Certainly we have had technical problems in Qatar," Sir Peter wrote in a letter to Prime Minister Thatcher. "However, we believe that these have not stemmed from any fundamental design defects, but rather from operational mishaps that were very regrettable but unfortunately can happen occasionally." He also lamented that the efforts Shell had made to "correct any deficiencies rapidly and effectively" had not been communicated to the prime minister.[27] In addition to agreeing to replace the land sections of the pipelines, these efforts included an offer to operate the lines for two years, after which QGPC would accept responsibility for their operation and indemnify Shell against any further liability. This offer, however, was turned down by QGPC's board of directors.

Thatcher responded that she was indeed somewhat concerned about the problematic gas pipelines in Qatar but assured Sir Peter that she was "never in any doubt" that Shell would remedy the situation.[28] By June, though, the Qataris had set up a formal commission of inquiry to look into the circumstances surrounding the failure of the pipelines. Headed by Ali Jaidah, the managing director of QGPC, this committee included senior government officials in the oil and gas business.[29] That same month Sir John Graham, an undersecretary at the Foreign and Commonwealth Office, met with Shell. The company continued to maintain that even in its corroded state the pipe was adequate for use and that the Qatari authorities were not being sensible in refusing to operate the pipeline.[30] But Shell also reiterated that it had offered to replace the land sections of the gas pipeline at its own expense.

The start-up of the two natural gas liquids plants finally allowed Qatar's first petrochemical complex to begin trial runs in December 1980. These were confined to the 280,000 ton per year ethylene cracker and the 140,000 ton per year low-density polyethylene unit, as the two partners in the Qatar Petrochemical Company, or QAPCO, had only just announced plans to go ahead with a 70,000-ton-per-year high-density polyethylene plant at their Umm Said site. The previous July nine international firms had been invited to bid for the contract to build this new unit, which was expected to cost $50 million. No announcement of the successful bidder had yet been made by QGPC and its minority partner in QAPCO, France's CDF-Chimie.

Both the ethylene cracker and the low-density polyethylene unit operated at very low capacity initially because of a lack of ethane feedstock from the problem-plagued NGL-2 plant. In 1981, QAPCO's first full year of operation, feedstock came exclusively from NGL-1 representing just half the petrochemical company's theoretical needs. The complex produced 63,000 tons of ethylene in the first half of 1981, less than 50 percent of its rated annual capacity. This had produced 55,000 tons of low-density polyethylene, of which 30,000 tons was exported. QAPCO was also designed to produce 50,000 tons per year of sulfur, and in 1981 it signed a three-year contract with Mitsui to market some 35,000 tons of this output annually. The Japanese trader took delivery of its first cargo of sulfur in September 1981.

Elsewhere at Umm Said, France's Technip won a contract worth QR 502.5 million ($138 million) in late 1980 to build the new 50,000-barrels-per-day refinery at Umm Said. This second refinery, which would be constructed adjacent to the existing 10,000-barrels-per-day refinery operated by NODCO, the national petroleum distribution company, was due for completion in early 1983. Imported petroleum products were costing the government QR 100 million ($27.5 million) annually, and the new refinery was intended to meet domestic demand for oil products until 1995. The government also reintroduced long-shelved plans to build an export refinery with capacity of 150,000 barrels per day. Announcing the estimated QR 1,500 million ($408 million) export project, the minister of industry and agriculture, Faisal Ibn Thani Al Thani, said the refinery was part of the country's efforts to diversify its industrial activities.[31]

QATAR REVAMPS SERVICE CONTRACTS WITH FORMER CONCESSIONAIRES

Meanwhile, the state-owned oil company continued to grow through another capital infusion and an important bureaucratic move. Qatar's Council of Ministers voted to increase the capital of the Qatar General Petroleum Corporation from QR 3,000 million to QR 4,000 million ($1.1 billion) on July 2, 1980. This represented the third capital increase since 1974 when QGPC was established and was funded from the state's general reserve.[32] Three weeks later, Sheikh Khalifa issued an amiri decree merging the Qatar Petroleum Producing Authority with QGPC. QPPA's holdings reverted to the state-owned firm in their entirety and the producing authority no longer functioned as a separate subsidiary. Two divisions were set up within QGPC to carry out the onshore and offshore operations formerly conducted by QPPA, comprising QGPC Onshore and QGPC Offshore. All the producing authority's personnel were transferred to QGPC without any change in their remuneration or benefits. The move gave QGPC and its managing director, Ali Jaidah, more control over the former concessionaires, who continued to provide technical services to the onshore and offshore sectors.

The original service contracts concluded with the foreign shareholders in the Qatar Petroleum Company as well as with Shell were due to expire in late 1981 and early 1982. In an interview on May 6, 1981, Jaidah said negotiations were under way with the onshore Dukhan Service Company and the offshore entity Qatar Shell Service Company to renew the various services contracts under different terms and conditions.[33] The basic service fee of fifteen cents per barrel on produced oil had escalated with official prices for Qatar's two crude grades, and this fee would have reached nearly fifty cents a barrel by 1981, given the market's sharp rise. But the escalation formula had been renegotiated in 1978, and the service fee on oil produced from both Dukhan and the three offshore fields linked to the Halul island terminal now stood at twenty-two cents per barrel. The service companies also got a fixed purchasing allocation. QGPC was widely expected to press for the elimination of the per barrel fee in favor of an annual lump sum payment.

BP had edged out its former partners in QPC by late 1981, negotiating independently to extend the management and operational service contact with the Dukhan Service Company. The British firm already had seventy employees deployed in the onshore operation, and this commitment worked in its favor. QGPC did not want to cut ties with the other ex-QPC companies and was expected to maintain links with CFP, Exxon, Mobil, and Partex for oil purchases. It seemed clear that the conceptual link between the new service contracts and the lifting arrangements was to be formally separated, and the crude oil transactions would be less favorable to the foreign firms in terms of both quantity and duration. This was confirmed in December, when the former shareholders in QPC agreed to lift 100,000 barrels per day with a three-month termination notice by either party.[34]

Since neither party had submitted the six-month notice required to cancel the service contract with the Dukhan Service Company, it remained in effect after the expiration date of December 2, 1981. Discussions between BP and QGPC Onshore principally centered on the deployment of BP's technical staff, as its ex-partners in QPC had formally voted not to compete with their old partner. Switching exclusively to BP meant losing wider international involvement in the onshore operation, however. Not everyone in Qatar was happy with this prospect. Dr. Hassan Kamel, the government adviser and deputy chair of QGPC, made a last, but ultimately unsuccessful, attempt to retain French and American participation in the service company. Qatar represented the last remaining operational commitment of the once-formidable Iraq Petroleum Company group, and it was assumed that its Cavendish Square office in London would be shut down if CFP, Exxon, Mobil, and Partex dropped out of the Dukhan Service Company.

Shell had more time to negotiate its renewal, as the contract with its offshore service company and the associated crude oil lifting agreement were not due to expire until March 31, 1982. Reports that Mobil was angling to take over from Shell in managing the offshore sector were officially denied by QGPC, although the Qataris undoubtedly welcomed the added pressure on Shell. "It was somewhat unlikely that the Qataris would want to dispense with Shell for the offshore operation and even more unlikely that Mobil would want to take on the heavy commitment involved," one UK official opined.[35] The Anglo-Dutch firm had up to 160 employees working in Qatar at any given time, and there was no obvious incentive for Mobil to take on the offshore servicing contract when it had access to large quantities of crude oil in Saudi Arabia at lower government posted prices.

But Shell was evidently not happy with where the discussions on the service contract were headed, given the separate but simultaneous negotiations on the much bigger North West Dome project. "The Qataris are masters at haggling and setting the oil companies at each other's throats," the new British ambassador Stephen Day reported in October 1981. "After dangling the prize of the LNG project, they instituted an intense competition among the companies for the service contracts. Shell are angry at what they consider un-brotherly conduct by BP who, to improve their chances for the big deal, produced bargain-basement offers on service and crude liftings that Shell were then told to mirror in their own proposals."[36] In the end the Qataris were in no hurry to settle new service terms. Shell's contract was allowed to continue after it expired in early 1982, although its lifting allowance was reduced to 75,000 barrels per day. This contract also included a three-month cancellation clause, declarable by either party.

Crude production averaged just 405,000 barrels per day in 1981, a decline of 14.4 percent. Offshore production bore the brunt of the fall, dropping 25 percent, while onshore output declined a more modest 8 percent.[37] Official government posted prices were higher, however, reaching nearly $36 per barrel for Dukhan and Qatar Marine by the end of 1981. Earnings from crude oil exports were expected to hit $5.13 billion for the year as opposed to $3.47 billion in 1980.[38] Nearly all of Qatar's major crude oil customers had attempted to get out of their lifting commitments because of the high prices. BP, for example, was taking only about half of its customary quantities, incurring a hefty penalty for underlifting in the process. The oil company had concluded that this penalty was worth paying for the potential long-term prospects in Qatar. But BP's decision to continue to lift even this reduced amount was not taken without considerable internal opposition.[39] While Japanese buyers renewed their oil supply contracts for 1982, this was only agreed after Mitsubishi, Sumitomo, Mitsui, and Idemitsu threatened to discontinue imports unless QGPC dropped stiff premiums over posted prices charged to buyers from Japan.

PLANS FOR NORTH FIELD DEVELOPMENT EVOLVE

Six months after initial proposals were submitted by the oil companies and the offshore contractors on the North field, as the North West Dome was now being called, Mohammed Said Mishal told the British ambassador that the Qataris were planning to offer one of Japan's big trading companies an equity partnership in the LNG plant to underscore the importance of the Japanese market. "The 20% available for foreign shareholders could be divided between that company and the oil company also selected, in any combination which would add up to a 20% stake," the British ambassador reported in June 1981.[40] Once these foreign participants were selected, a development company would be formed comprising QGPC, the oil company, and the marketing partner to carry out both phases of the project. This joint venture would then employ one or more of the four major contractors selected to bid for the actual development work.

Japan's involvement was subsequently reported by the *Middle East Economic Survey*, which noted that Mitsubishi, Mitsui, C. Itoh, Marubeni, and Nissho Iwai had joined Shell, BP, CFP, and Wintershall in submitting participation offers. "The project is apparently envisaged as a joint venture between QGPC and two foreign groups—one with LNG technological experience and the other with marketing expertise—on an 80-20 basis in favor of QGPC," it reported. "The marketing partner to be selected will probably be a Japanese firm since the project's output is to be directed mainly to the Japanese market."[41] But the Qataris were still keeping their options open on the equity split, with one member of the steering committee emphasizing that the marketing company wouldn't impact the extent of the principal partner's involvement in the project.[42] In the meantime, the five Japanese firms discussed forming a single negotiating group, a stance encouraged by Japan's powerful Ministry of International Trade & Industry.[43]

By July 1981 Rashid Ibn Awaidah Al Thani's evaluation team had completed its initial review of the offers submitted by the four oil companies at the beginning of the year as well as later expressions of interest from Texaco and Huffco. "As a result of this first review, we are now in a position to indicate the main nature, extent and terms of the participation which would be appropriate to our requirements," Sheikh Rashid informed the six oil firms. "We, therefore, invite your organization to formulate a revised, self-contained offer of participation in the light of the attached set of notes, to serve as the basis for further discussions between us."[44] The deadline for the submission of participation offers was August 22, 1981.

In its invitation, the committee explained that the development of the North field would be implemented in two separate but interdependent phases. The first phase, to be owned exclusively by QGPC, would cover the development of the field to produce 2.4 billion cubic feet per day including offshore drilling and gas-gathering platforms as well as a network of pipelines to bring this output ashore. A second phase would involve the construction, ownership, and operation of a 6 million ton per year LNG company. One of the four U.S. contractors invited to bid for the job—Fluor, Kellogg, Parsons, and Bechtel—was expected to assume the role of managing consultant and would, in the words of Sheikh Rashid, "look after the construction from A to Z."[45]

The selected Japanese companies, or *sogo shoshas*, as the five general trading houses were known in Japan, were separately invited to submit proposals for participating in the ordinary share capital of the proposed LNG company, dependent on their interest in the entire shipping and marketing aspects of the project and their capacity to arrange the financing of the LNG carriers.

Ownership of the LNG company would be along the following lines:

QGPC	80 percent
Foreign Partner (an international oil company)	10 to 15 percent
Foreign Partner (major Japanese firms)	5 to 10 percent

BP had by now opened its own office in Qatar, securing a floor in Doha's most prestigious office building, while its chair, Sir David Steele, visited the country in September 1981 in a show of support for BP's North field bid. The firm had decided not to take on a local commercial agent despite pressure from the British ambassador, who was unabashedly pushing BP to appoint Ahmad Mannai. This leading merchant already represented over one hundred UK firms on both the civil and defense sides, and Mannai's close association with the powerful minister of the interior, Khalid Ibn Hamad Al Thani, afforded him considerable influence.[46] The Mannai Trading Corporation—in which the minister of public works, Khaled Ibn Abdullah Al Attiyah, was also partner—was the largest and one of the best organized in Doha. "Experience has shown that he [Mannai] can apply considerable influence in commercial deals, especially in major capital projects in which his own rewards are likely to be substantial," a confidential UK government profile reads. "He displays little scruples in promoting the interests of the company he has chosen to represent, even at the expense of others who may also have appointed him as their agent."[47]

The choice of Rashid Ibn Awaidah, QGPC's deputy director and a personable American-educated young Al Thani, to lead the North field evaluation committee was widely seen as a rebuke to QGPC's managing director, Ali Jaidah.[48] His fall from grace (although momentary) was reckoned to be bad news for Shell, whose Qatari representative was Ali's brother Jassim. BP told UK officials that decisions on the North field couldn't be indefinitely delayed since gas from existing sources was declining and Qatar needed North field gas for its home market. Tender documents for the power and desalination complex at Ras Laffan were already being drawn up by West Germany's Fichtner Consulting Engineers and expected to be issued in the first half of 1982. This complex would need gas from the North field.

Several rounds of discussions were held with the oil companies that submitted revised offers. These numbered just five after Texaco dropped out. Rumors put Wintershall as the frontrunner on the strength of its operating stake in the adjoining concession, into which the gas field now definitively extended (see fig. 10.1). This was reinforced by a five-hour visit to Doha on October 4, 1981, by West Germany's foreign minister that included audiences with the amir and the crown prince.[49] The foreign minister was accompanied by the president of Wintershall, who stayed behind for talks with QGPC. But local pundits observed that each of the five contenders had been in the lead at one time or another, and there were still signs the Qataris would pick two companies rather than just one. The selection process was expected to be arduous, however, and it was assumed the Qataris would live up to their reputation of being among the hardest-headed negotiators in the region.

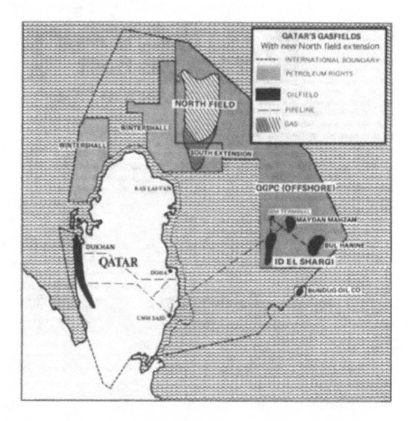

10.1 North Field Southern Extension.
Source: FCO, file note, ref. 96/1310, NA-UK.

It was evident that some form of accommodation had to be made with the Wintershall consortium regardless of whether the German firm was selected to participate in the North field project directly. This could be some form of financial compensation or the sale of gas from its adjacent concession into the overall system supplying the LNG plant. Among the five oil companies that put in proposals on the North field project, Wintershall was alone in still having a concession in Qatar. The company and its partners had already spent $60 million drilling four wells in their adjoining acreage since 1976, and a pooling of resources between the Wintershall group and QGPC made sense. Wintershall and its partners would presumably have the right to develop the portion of the North field that extended into their area even if the Qataris opted to delay development of the field's principal reserves.

DETERIORATING MARKET THREATENS TO DERAIL LNG PROJECT

More ominously, concerns were being raised about global demand for LNG. North field committee head Rashid Ibn Awaidah Al Thani admitted that the Japanese market was uncertain, and his pessimistic view was echoed by the Ministry of Finance and Petroleum.[50] Ideally, the entry of a Japanese marketing partner into the LNG consortium would help overcome this obstacle. The Qataris also saw Japanese participation as a way to secure cheap financing for the venture's shipping requirements. Ten tankers would be needed to transport 6 million tons per year of LNG, and there would be condensates, liquid petroleum gas, and sulfur to move to market as well. The government had made it obvious that it did not want to invest in transportation, which could involve as many as a dozen tankers. "Attractive financial arrangements for transportation, which the Japanese might be expected to offer, would be important to the Qataris," UK officials reported after a meeting with Shell.[51]

The various bidders visited Doha in October and November 1981 for further discussions with Sheikh Rashid's North field evaluation team. Committee members knew time was not on Qatar's side, as the market for LNG exports was weakening by the month. They therefore wanted to arrive at a recommendation that could be submitted to the ruler by the end of the year. But the Qatari team was having the "greatest difficulty" reconciling the different bids. It was trying, impossibly, to reduce each company's proposal into a single format in order to expedite the process. "In particular they are attempting to cost each set of proposals as if they were tenders for a construction project," Britain's ambassador Stephen Day reported.[52]

Storm clouds were gathering on the market side. "The Qataris are beginning to appreciate the marked deterioration (for them) in the world energy scene and the reduced appetite for gas especially in Japan but also Europe," Day wrote.[53] Widely viewed as an expensive and risky form of energy, LNG was particularly vulnerable in Europe to competition from lower-cost gas pipeline imports. Strenuous efforts by the administration of U.S. president Ronald Reagan to dissuade the Europeans, particularly France and West Germany, from signing major contracts with the Soviet Union for gas delivered via a proposed 3,700-mile pipeline from Western Siberia were unsuccessful. In addition to offering lower prices compared to oil, the Europeans were counting on the Soviet pipeline to trigger hefty orders from Moscow for heavy equipment and large-diameter steel pipe at a time of high unemployment and deepening recession in Western Europe.[54]

The outlook in Japan had soured as well, although its Ministry of International Trade & Industry still had the Qatari LNG project penciled in as a supply source beginning in "1987 or later."[55] Sheikh Rashid was struck by the change in attitude among the Japanese negotiators, who had adopted an increasingly hard tone since the summer. "The Japanese were a potential customer for the gas but had no wish to be too reliant on the Qataris for supplies and were publicly playing it cool," British officials reported.[56] The Qataris had so far paid little attention to negotiating the twenty-year supply contracts necessary to build the LNG plant or to obtain insulated tankers to transport the frozen gas to market. It was dawning on local decision makers that the project could not continue without such contracts being signed. Estimated costs were trending upward, now reaching $8 billion for the two phases of the overall North field development.[57] This would be a huge commitment, probably requiring Qatar to incur debt in excess of its total foreign assets.

Some of the ground rules laid down in the prospectus drawn up by Sheikh Rashid's evaluation committee the previous summer no longer seemed realistic either, particularly the small equity participation offered to the oil company partner and the exclusive marketing role that would be given to the selected Japanese player. In a visit to Qatar in late 1981, during which he had an audience with Crown Prince Hamad Ibn Khalifa, Sir Peter Baxendell of Shell Transport and

Trading set out his firm's requirements for participation in the LNG project. The Anglo-Dutch oil company would need at least 20 percent of the equity, a marketing role in Europe, and a say in the choice of the Japanese partner, which in Shell's case meant the selection of Mitsubishi, with whom it had a long-standing trading relationship. Shell would not object to a joint venture with BP, Sir Peter said, provided the equity distribution was sufficient. But it saw no advantage in dividing up the management role further.[58]

Word of foundation cracks at Abu Dhabi's Das Island LNG plant surfaced just as BP's negotiating team arrived in Doha for their next round of negotiations on December 9, 1981. BP had supervised the construction of the plant's first two process units, or trains, as they are better known in the LNG industry. Much of the concrete used in the foundation had been mixed using seawater, and rebar was not coated with polymer to protect against corrosion in the mid-1970s when the Das Island project was being built. The resulting corrosion caused the rebar to expand and led to concrete spalling. All the affected areas of the foundation had to be either replaced or shored up in a remedial program that became known as the Concrete Rehabilitation Project, resulting in at least one lawsuit against BP.

The British ambassador reported with evident relief in late December that news of the problems at Das Island had yet to reach QGPC.[59] But the setback was bound to get out, and British officials were concerned about the possible implications for BP's North field bid. In a meeting on December 31, 1981, Amir Khalifa told Day that a decision on the choice of the oil company partner for the LNG project would be made the following February.[60] This was met with considerable skepticism. "My own hunch is that the LNG scheme is still over the horizon and may never come to anything," Day predicted ominously. "A development of the field for local use, perhaps with sale of condensates is more likely."[61]

PARTIES AGREE TO ARBITRATION OVER DESTRUCTION OF NGL PLANT

The investigation into the accident that destroyed the first NGL plant was still underway in late 1981. QGPC had already commenced a High Court action in London jointly against Shell internationale petroleum maatschappij (SIPM) and Whessoe Limited, while simultaneously beginning separate arbitration proceedings before the International Chamber of Commerce, or ICC, in Paris. Although discussions had taken place in 1980 between QGPC, SIPM, and Whessoe about a tripartite arbitration, these talks had failed, and the Qatari company had not taken any further steps to pursue Whessoe via the High Court or the ICC. QGPC was claiming $536 million in damages from Shell through SIPM for the cost of the original plant and consequential losses.[62] There were also verbal, unspecified claims for lost profits.

QGPC Onshore considered its position to be a strong one: according to testimony from the onshore engineering manager, intergranular stress corrosion cracking of the propane storage tank was reported to Shell on April 23, 1976—nearly a year before the explosion.[63] The resulting vapor cloud, which reportedly traveled five hundred feet, fortunately did not ignite on that occasion. British Steel had supplied the steel plates for the tank farm and it tested samples after the problem was reported but determined that they complied with the design specifications Shell provided.[64] The tear was repaired by SIPM and the tank returned to service in October 1976—only to rupture again on April 3, 1977, with catastrophic results, underscoring Qatar's claims that the investigation into the original rupture by SIPM and Whessoe, and its subsequent repair, had been insufficient.

NGL-2 had still not been formally handed over to QGPC Onshore. The plant was shut down entirely from October through December 1981 because of what QGPC described as "excessive corrosion to the NGL-2 pipeline and plant."[65] SIPM was moving forward on replacing the onshore section of the twenty-four-inch pipeline bringing associated gas from the offshore fields to the gas liquids plant, although it continued to quibble with QGPC Onshore over who should pay for an additional five kilometers of pipe added to avoid a road. Shell claimed to have spent $35 million on replacing the pipeline and other repairs, work the company argued SIPM was not required to do and was only paying to "clear their name," according to British ambassador Day.[66]

The NGL plants and petrochemical producer QAPCO continued to operate at low levels due to a dearth of associated gas. This reduced output stemmed in part from lower crude oil production (cut by 25 percent to just 300,000 barrels per day in April 1982) and from ongoing problems with pipeline corrosion and blockage.[67] Only about 70 percent of the liquid petroleum gas contracted by the Japanese was being shipped. There were also price disputes. Mitsubishi, which had agreed to buy 160,000 tons of LPG annually over five years from 1981, had completely halted its purchases by mid-1982. Deals with Idemitsu Kosan for 200,000 tons annually and with C. Itoh for 100,000 per year were still active, and Iwatani signed up for 100,000 tons per year after Mitsubishi dropped out. But QGPC was still forced to drop its LPG prices to match those charged by Saudi Arabia and Kuwait.

QAPCO's general manager, Yves Michaux, estimated that deliveries of ethane-rich tail gas from the NGL plants met about 50 percent of requirements in 1982.[68] This mirrored the company's 1981 performance, when QAPCO received less than half the 2,000 tons per day necessary to make ethylene. All the ethylene produced, about 145,000 tons in 1982, was used to make 140,000 tons of low-density polyethylene. Had the steam cracker been running at its annual capacity of 280,000 tons, there would have been another 135,000 tons of ethylene ready for export. Long-running plans to use surplus ethylene on site were now frozen, despite the signature of a letter of intent in May 1981 with Japan's Mitsui Engineering & Shipbuilding for the construction of a 70,000 ton per year high-density polyethylene plant. "We are waiting until QGPC can guarantee feedstock to run ethylene production at 100 percent of capacity," Michaux told the *Middle East Economic Digest*.[69] The lack of surplus ethylene was having a real impact on QAPCO's cash flow, and it struggled to service loans taken out when the plant was first established.

Other gas users were hurting as well. The Qatar Fertilizer Company, or QAFCO, received its associated gas primarily from the Dukhan field, but it also secured supplies from the offshore oil fields. QAFCO estimated that because of gas shortages in 1981, it lost 107,000 tons of ammonia production and 49,000 tons of urea.[70] Its fortunes were also affected by the drop in world urea prices, which averaged just $150 per ton in 1982. Qatar Steel Company was faring better on the gas front, although it made a loss in 1982 because of low steel prices.[71] QASCO received its gas from the Khuff formation under the Dukhan field, and its water and electricity from the nearby Ras Abu Fontas power station, but the tight gas situation had still kept the steel company from expanding its direct reduction plant.

QGPC Onshore drew heavily on non-associated gas from Dukhan's deep Khuff reservoir, primarily for electricity generation at the Ras Abu Aboud and Ras Abu Fontas power stations and as a fuel for industrial users in Umm Said. The rapid depletion of these gas reserves—which had been developed in phases between 1978 and 1982, to include eight Khuff treatment plants—had people worried that the Dukhan Khuff would run out by 1986 or 1987, particularly in summer periods when consumption skyrocketed. Peak demand in the electric power and industrial sectors hit 372 million cubic feet per day in 1982, up from 347 million cubic feet in 1981, and over a third of that consumption was met by Khuff gas from Dukhan.[72]

Gas demand was poised yet again to increase substantially with the construction of Qatar's third major water and desalination complex at Wusail some twenty kilometers north of Doha. The 1,500-megawatt power and water desalination plant was originally due to be built at Ras Laffan, near its North field supply source, but the $1.1 billion project was shifted closer to the main load center of Doha in late 1982.[73] Given the uncertainty over the North field's development timetable, QGPC decided to link the Wusail complex to the Dukhan field, building two sixty-kilometer pipelines that would interconnect with the existing Dukhan-to-Umm Said oil and gas lines at Salwa. One thirty-inch pipeline would transport gas to Wusail, with a parallel ten-inch oil line as an emergency backup. Wusail's first phase, involving four 150-megawatt steam turbines and eight 5-million-gallons-per-day desalination units, was expected to be completed in the summer of 1985.[74]

ONSHORE GAS FIND RAISES PROSPECTS FOR NORTH FIELD DELAY

Results from a new onshore gas find at Ras Qirtas, on the northeast coast some fifteen kilometers north of Ras Laffan, promised to relieve Qatar's pressing gas shortage. Initial tests of the discovery, located at a depth of 11,800 feet, were surprisingly good. "The gas is sweet and is running at 40 million cubic feet a day through a one-inch choke," British ambassador Day informed London in August 1982. "If favourable results continue to emerge from these tests, it is possible that the North Field reservoir will be found to extend onshore in this area, in which case further onshore wells will be drilled."[75] While the Ras Qirtas discovery turned out to be an independent gas accumulation rather than an extension of the North field, QGPC was still hopeful that the more easily exploited onshore site had sufficient gas to supply local needs.

The implications of the new gas find for the North field LNG project were substantial. "Arguably, once internal needs are met, possibilities for delaying a decision on the LNG plant are infinite," Day observed.[76] Mirroring his observations, the *Middle East Economic Survey* said QGPC was proceeding with caution on the development of the North field in view of the heavy expenditure required and the disappointing world market for LNG.[77] Sheikh Rashid, the North field committee chair, was now talking about beginning construction on the liquefaction plant in the mid-1980s, with first production in the early 1990s.[78] While this was considered a realistic timetable, others were more cautious. "Proposals for North field development have been deferred to a point where Qatar has lost a market in the 80s and may not even find one in the 90s," Day warned.[79]

While little progress was made on the North field project, the list of oil companies bidding on the LNG scheme nonetheless increased from five to six with Exxon's late entry into the fray. The U.S. major acknowledged to the trade press that it was in "very preliminary" talks with the government of Qatar on the project.[80] QGPC was now looking to its oil company partner for help lining up LNG customers, suggesting the Japanese would not have an exclusive role in the marketing after all.[81] The five trading houses had by this point formed two consortia to compete for the North field business, with Mitsui, Mitsubishi, and C. Itoh forming one group and Marubeni and Nissho Iwai the other. Sheikh Rashid said publicly the equity slice given to the successful party would depend on what the consortium delivered in concrete sales commitments.[82]

With crude production down sharply, natural gas liquids exports severely constrained, and Qatar's industrial ventures strapped for feedstock and buffeted by low world prices for their fertilizer, steel, and petrochemical products, cash flow was tight, and it was expected to deteriorate further. Strains were beginning to appear in the Al Thani inner circle. Rumors swirled around possible alcohol and drug use by Abdul Aziz, the minister of finance and petroleum, and the amir himself was said to be drinking heavily. Sheikh Khalifa was certainly keeping a close eye on his troubled son, forcing him to work out of the amir's office under his guidance rather than at the ministry itself. There were mutterings in Qatari circles that Crown Prince Hamad Ibn Khalifa was heading toward a showdown with his father as difficulties mounted.[83]

Despite his proclivity for inaction, Sheikh Khalifa maintained an unremitting control over government decisions, particularly financial ones. According to the *Financial Times*, the money supply was so strictly and personally controlled by the amir that bankers could always tell when the ruler was on holiday.[84] Liquidity inevitably suffered if he was not at home, as Khalifa himself personally signed all government checks for more than QR 200,000 (about $55,000). This style of government, the British Foreign and Commonwealth Office wrote in a country assessment paper at the end of 1982, had fostered "slow development: when his attention is elsewhere, decisions are fudged and industrial development (of which the Qataris are unrealistically proud) has suffered from lack of foresight and poor management."[85] If the real price of oil continued to fall and oil production remained low, the paper warned, economic activity would slow and strains would grow within the royal family.[86]

On November 25, 1982, after more than a year of negotiations, the proposals for participation in the North field development project were finally put before the amir by the minister of finance and petroleum. Issa Al Kawari, Sheikh Khalifa's chef de cabinet, reported back to the British ambassador that the ruler clearly favored the offers submitted by BP and France's CFP.[87] Al Kawari intimated that Exxon's proposal was less attractive, and he suspected that Shell had no real enthusiasm for the scheme. Ambassador Day did not ask if the other bids had been discussed. Sheikh Khalifa, who at the best of times disliked making decisions, immediately departed for a week's hunting trip to Saudi Arabia, promising to make headway on the selection of partners for the project upon his return.[88]

For its part, the Wintershall consortium was now pressing hard for a much more limited gas development targeting its section of the North field. Its revised proposal, made in May 1982 and supported by Sayyid Abdullah Sallat, the director of the Department of Petroleum Affairs, involved making 400 million cubic feet per day from its contract area available to the government free of charge while marketing condensate and other gas liquids for its own profit.[89] This was seen as a potential solution to Qatar's looming gas shortage, given that further analysis of the Ras Qirtas onshore gas discovery north of Ras Laffan hadn't lived up to initial hopes. The timetable for when domestic gas demand would outstrip supply had now been pushed out to the summer of 1988, rather than 1986 or 1987, following revisions by QGPC.[90]

Wintershall's new proposal was not the only one being put forward to meet this gas challenge. QGPC's Ali Jaidah had instructed the company's onshore and offshore divisions to make provision in their 1983 budgets for preliminary studies to develop the North field for domestic consumption only.[91] Jaidah had long been critical of the way the North field development was being handled by Rashid Ibn Awaidah Al Thani's committee, particularly the second LNG export phase. His budget requests came as QGPC was forced to shut down Umm Said's NGL-1 natural gas liquids plant, closing it temporarily in early February as total oil production dropped to 200,000 barrels per day and supplies of associated gas plummeted. (It was reopened in late April as crude oil liftings improved.) NGL-2 continued to run, but it was transporting only 2,100 tons per day of liquids rather than its daily design capacity of 4,000 tons.

Under Ali Jaidah's scheme, QGPC's offshore division would be concerned with wells—a range of eight to twelve wells had been mentioned—together with initial processing platforms and a pipeline network to land the gas near Ras Laffan. Its onshore group would be responsible for the subsequent processing and piping of the gas to local users. The scheme allowed for a constant rate of production from the North field throughout the year by injecting excess quantities of gas into the Dukhan field's Khuff reservoir during the off-peak winter months, where it could be held in reserve. This would accommodate the wide seasonal swings between summer and winter demand.

SHELL THREATENS TO QUIT QATAR OVER LIABILITY CLAIMS

Shell's lack of enthusiasm for the North field project no doubt stemmed from the ongoing row over the natural gas liquids plants. In what was described as a "difficult" meeting with the amir just before he left on his hunting expedition, Shell executives insisted there would be no deal on Qatar's claims for contingent losses on the first NGL plant, which the Anglo-Dutch firm said exceeded the initial value of the production facility by a factor of ten.[92] While prepared to comply with its contractual commitments, Shell would not be forced into accepting liability or noncontractual damages. Headed by André Bénard, who would go on to lead the construction of the Channel Tunnel linking France to Britain as chair of Eurotunnel, the Shell team warned Sheikh Khalifa that the company would exit the country unless the government withdrew all litigation, including the ICC arbitration, and make certain personnel changes within QGPC.[93]

Qatar could ill afford to lose one of its largest crude oil lifters. The two sides agreed to continue their negotiations, although Shell had its doubts as to whether the amir would comply with its demands. While QGPC was now pursuing Shell mainly through the ICC tribunal in Paris, the Qatari firm's lawyers had also tried to bring a civil action in the United Kingdom.[94] Since the original agreements provided for ICC arbitration and this process was already under way, the British

High Court threw out the request. QGPC's legal representatives warned in response that Qatar would continue to pursue its claims in other courts, including by bringing legal action at home.[95]

Shell debated internally whether to withdraw the offer made in early 1981 for a new services agreement relating to the operation and management of Qatar's offshore oil fields.[96] From the company's perspective, there now seemed little incentive to keep the Qataris happy. The service arrangements had brought lots of headaches and little profit, while Shell and the other foreign company lifters viewed Qatari crude oil as overpriced in the present market glut. Shell claimed it was losing money on its liftings from Qatar since it paid the official price for oil it could obtain elsewhere at far lower prices.[97] Very little progress had been made on the North field LNG project since Shell first proposed it in 1975, seven years prior. BP was disillusioned for the same reasons, although it preferred not to withdraw its draft services agreement for the onshore Dukhan operations even if it—and the Qataris too, for that matter—had no intention of signing any contract in the immediate future.

The dispute regarding compensation for the NGL plant disaster came to a head on December 9, 1982. Shell's coordinator for the Middle East, Bill Bell, met with Abdul Aziz Ibn Khalifa for a quick, fifteen-minute meeting that ended up taking one and a half hours.[98] The minister of finance and petroleum then reported back to the amir and the Council of Ministers, who had been waiting patiently in the Diwan (the ruler's administrative offices) for an update. Subsequently, Issa Al Kawari, the ruler's chef de cabinet, informed Mr. Bell that he had insulted the amir and the state of Qatar with his very low offer and that, if Shell did not increase the amount substantially, it would be the end of the road for the company in Qatar. Moreover, Al Kawari continued, Qatar would see to it that Shell was driven out of the Gulf through coordinated Gulf Cooperation Council action.[99]

Sheikh Khalifa had taken umbrage at Shell's use of the term *token payment* in a letter from André Bénard delivered by Bill Bell in early December. The phrase had been interpreted by the amir as a bribe, and an insultingly small one at that.[100] Against Qatar's ICC tribunal claim of $536 million, representing the cost of the original natural gas liquids plant plus consequential losses, Shell offered to refund its design fee of $8 million and pay another $30 to $40 million toward the cost of the NGL plant. This "goodwill gesture" was contingent on the explosion being declared an act of God and the payment forming part of a total settlement for all outstanding claims, including those relating to the separate pipeline corrosion problems at the NGL-2 plant.[101]

Shell refused point-blank to pay consequential damages, arguing that the payment of these types of claims was contrary to the term of its contracts. In the case of the first NGL plant, these included agreements signed in 1971 and 1972 between Shell and the Qatar Petroleum Company, the facility's original owner, for the design and construction of the plant and its subsequent operation. These contained exemption clauses limiting Shell's legal liability to gross negligence or intentional default in the performance of its obligations, and they specified that Shell would under no circumstances be liable for consequential losses.[102] QGPC contended that the 1971–1972 agreements were forced on QPC by Shell because it was a major shareholder in the company and initially the only partner interested in the NGL plant. This, QGPC claimed, made Shell the de facto owner of the plant.[103]

The government's Council of Ministers, by this time composed of sixteen members, was convinced Shell would settle on Qatar's terms. "Arguments about the contractual liabilities and the limited nature of the Shell role post-nationalisation are brushed aside," Ambassador Day reported, while also suggesting the Qataris might nonetheless settle for an amount in the $250 to $300 million range.[104] For all their bluster, the diplomat wrote, the Qataris were deeply concerned about future oil sales and the mounting problems with their domestic gas grid. Shell's departure could damage Qatar badly by deferring work to resolve the gas supply shortage, which the ambassador estimated was only three years away from reaching crisis proportions.[105]

Lloyd's and the other insurers had already paid Qatar $70 million for the loss of the NGL plant.[106] This was on the understanding that QGPC would pursue SIPM and Whessoe for reimbursement. If Qatar were to withdraw from the ICC arbitration, it could incur a possible claim from the insurers for the return of this not-insubstantial insurance award. Furthermore, Shell had already started to reduce its crude oil dependence on Qatar. It was not clear how much losing this formerly influential lifter would hurt the government's coffers. The Anglo-Dutch firm had been gradually phasing out its oil purchases since the end of 1981 and was down to 60,000 barrels per day in the fourth quarter of 1982, but it was still Qatar's largest individual lifter.[107]

With the first round of arbitration talks set to commence in Washington, D.C., on January 17, 1983, Shell finally signaled some flexibility on the issue of consequential damages. The company informed the Qataris it would be willing to delay these proceedings if Qatar would consider Shell's proposals for a considerably reduced damages claim.[108] Shell also indicated that it wanted to renegotiate its offshore services agreement in parallel with the arbitration. Current events were in its favor. "The forthcoming OPEC meeting may bring home to the Amir the realities of the current oil market and persuade him of the need to keep friends with companies willing to buy his oil," the UK Foreign Office cabled its ambassador in Doha.[109]

PROJECTILE THEORY RAISED IN DISPUTE OVER NGL PLANT

It soon became apparent that the amir's intense aggravation with Shell wasn't due solely to the friction over the settlement of compensation claims. In their meeting with Abdul Aziz Ibn Khalifa, the Shell representatives had apparently referred to the so-called projectile theory to explain the rupture that caused the gas leak and explosion.[110] When Shell's inspectors finally gained access to the site one year after the fire, they found a hole in one of the propane storage tanks for which they claimed there was no satisfactory technical explanation. They had their own motives for pursuing this theory. "So there was speculation that it might have been caused by a 'projectile,' which would of course have absolved Shell from the responsibility for the fire and placed the matter firmly and embarrassingly in the laps of the Qatar authorities," the Foreign Office reported after a meeting with André Bénard and Bill Bell of Shell on December 16, 1982.[111]

Since Shell had not been given a copy of Qatar's own accident report, it hadn't been able to fully investigate the projectile theory. Nonetheless, the company was not above making the most of the theory in the arbitration talks.[112] The amir was incensed at Shell's apparent determination to use this line of argument, fearing it would raise embarrassing questions for Qatar's security authorities. Shell told UK officials that it wanted to keep the theory secret "unless or until" it decided to roll it out in the arbitration proceedings, which didn't stop the British from speculating on its plausibility. Ambassador Day reported from Doha that many of the ten thousand or so Yafais who had gone to Qatar from Aden, a British protectorate in the late 1960s and early 1970s, were skilled with rocket launchers and had reason to bear a grudge against the Al Thani leadership.[113]

The Yafais had fled the protectorate after the Upper and Lower Sultanates of Yafa were abolished in 1967 upon the founding of the Marxist-oriented People's Republic of South Yemen. Most of the Yafais had joined the Qatar Emiri Air Force or the police, but some had gravitated to Umm Said where they controlled lucrative stores. In the late 1970s their numbers had been cut sharply, allegedly because the Qataris had found the Yafais quarrelsome and too powerful. "Few people in the Middle East have more experience with rocket launchers than the Yafais," the ambassador reported. "A revenge attack for loss of lucrative jobs would be just their style and would certainly explain Qatar's sensitivity."[114]

Qatar was also pursuing Shell over the corrosion problems at NGL-2, threatening in early 1983 to initiate separate legal action against the company unless it paid up. QGPC was seeking $100 million for actual damages, plus an additional amount for consequential losses and written guarantees from Shell on all material and pipeline work for twenty years.[115] Shell claimed its efforts to satisfy the Qataris over NGL-2 had already cost it $35 million. This represented the $8 million already lost on its design fee—Shell had been paid $16 million in fees for its technical assistance in constructing the NGL-2 plant, whereas it claimed actual costs for this work of $24 million—plus the $27 million it was spending on replacing the thirty-kilometer onshore portion of the associated gas line as part of a deal reached with QGPC in January 1981.[116]

QGPC continued to insist that the parallel twelve-inch gas liquids line to NGL-2 also needed replacement, a move Shell was determined to resist. Unlike the larger gas pipeline, this smaller line had shown no sign of hydrogen-induced cracking. However, some pitting corrosion had been found. More worryingly, an unexplained "black dust" phenomenon had clogged the filters and reduced the gas liquids flow to a daily maximum of about two hundred tons, possibly creating corrosion.[117] The Qataris also claimed that some of the interfield lines offshore were inadequate and should be replaced, and they wanted Shell to replace the offshore section of the twenty-four-inch gas line in addition to the work it was already doing on the onshore portion. These claims were formally laid out in a strongly worded telex dated January 8, 1983, from Ali Jaidah to Shell's offices in The Hague.[118]

Shell insisted the pipelines were all operating satisfactorily and contended that any reduced flow stemmed from low offshore oil production rather than from safety concerns. Its view was that the replacement of the onshore section of the twenty-four-inch pipeline had almost certainly been unnecessary and had been done only as a gesture of goodwill to the Qataris. The company rejected suggestions that the pipeline problems had occurred because of incorrect material specifications and errors in pre-commissioning. If Shell was confident that the pipelines were in good working order, the Qataris responded, then it should supply them with an unconditional guarantee of performance for twenty years, plus agree to compensate Qatar for any loss of revenue should a pipeline fail during this period.[119] This request was unacceptable to Shell, who argued that it violated both the original construction services contract with SIPM and the supplemental agreement for the replacement of the onshore section of the gas pipeline.

BP MAKES HEADWAY ON ONSHORE SERVICES AGREEMENT

BP was at last making headway in taking over the operation and management of Qatar's onshore fields from the old Iraq Petroleum Company group. Its personnel and services agreement with QGPC had, for all intents and purposes, been negotiated, although BP was still pushing hard for an indemnity clause that would protect it from contingent liability.[120] The original 1976 services agreement with IPC's Dukhan Service Company had covered the provision of expatiate staff, a material ordering service, technical support services, and day-today operating advice and training. BP would now assume these responsibilities—which it was already providing, for the most part, as the most visible partner in the IPC subsidiary—on less advantageous terms than the service company had received.

The Qataris had asked BP to raise its crude oil liftings to twenty-four thousand barrels per day, but the oil company refused on commercial grounds. Like Qatar's other lifters, BP was losing five dollars per barrel or more at the government's posted prices.[121] It had already reduced its liftings to twelve thousand barrels per day by mid-1982, down from eighteen thousand barrels per day earlier in the year. With the services agreement for the Dukhan field now in sight, BP indicated that it might be able to hike liftings after all. The company offered to purchase between fifteen thousand and twenty-five thousand barrels per day under a separate arrangement, but only upon signature of the services agreement.[122] BP told QGPC that it wanted the two deals to take effect from the same date.

If BP's onshore services agreement was still under discussion, the same could not be said for Shell's offshore arrangement. The Anglo-Dutch firm's Doha representative confirmed there had been no progress on the management contract with QGPC since late 1981, and the two sides seemed content with the status quo for the time being.[123] With neither party issuing the six-month notice needed to cancel the arrangement, the original services agreement remained in effect. Qatar Shell Service Company was making a little more money from the existing terms than it would under the proposed agreement, while QGPC and the government were reluctant to rock the boat in any way that might affect crude oil liftings. Although Shell had reduced the amount of oil it had been taking earlier—fifty thousand barrels per day of Qatar Marine and twenty-five thousand barrels daily of Dukhan—its liftings were still within agreed limits.[124]

Despite BP's earlier hope of securing an exclusive onshore servicing agreement, it became apparent by the end of 1982 that the Qataris were not willing to rock the boat with the Dukhan Services Company either. Maintaining the status quo had obvious attractions for Qatar, as there were five partners in the service company with commitments to lift its crude. BP was equally philosophical. "BP for their part are content to let their earlier offer quietly expire, having proposed terms which are perhaps now less attractive to them than they were at the time, but see no need to create waves by specifically withdrawing their offer," the British embassy explained.[125]

Oil production, which had averaged 405,000 barrels per day in 1981, fell to a daily average of just 328,000 barrels in 1982. Output for the year still hit a peak of 381,000 barrels per day in October—well above Qatar's OPEC ceiling of 300,000 barrels a day—but weak oil prices eroded the government's spending power considerably. "Qatar has lost 30–40 percent of its revenue in real terms over the past year, at a time when Iraq and the other Arabs are pressing for a continuation of the massive subventions of 1981," the British Foreign and Commonwealth Office wrote in their 1982 country assessment paper, referring to the large grants of money Doha and other Gulf governments had extended to Saddam Hussain's Iraq in the wake of the Iran-Iraq war.[126]

The oil situation deteriorated further in early 1983. Lifting nominations equated to just 200,000 barrels per day in February, well short of QGPC's 300,000-barrel-per-day target.[127] Shell, traditionally Qatar's main lifter, requested just 45 percent of its expected requirements for the month. Nominations for March were even lower. "Production is now at such a low level that this could bring about the closure of Qatar's offshore gas gathering system and part, if not all, of the Umm Said industrial complex," officials fretted in early February.[128] Both Shell and BP continued to regard Qatar oil as overpriced, while Shell's ongoing legal travails hadn't exactly fostered goodwill on the lifting front. British diplomats speculated that Qatar's urgent need for revenue might induce it to break ranks with OPEC and cut prices unilaterally.[129]

Average oil output fell to just 171,000 barrels per day in March 1983, the lowest level since the late 1950s. Total liftings were about 32,000 barrels per day higher, however, as stocks were drawn down. The following month, the Persian Gulf's largest-ever oil spill reached the shores of Qatar. This oil had been gushing unchecked from a cluster of offshore wellhead blowouts in the Iran–Iraq war zone since early February, creating a slick that stretched some three hundred miles in length and up to fifteen miles in width.[130] Booms and other barriers were erected around Qatar's water desalination plants to protect them against contamination. With the slick threatening the country's water system, the price of bottled mineral water soared as Qataris bought up all available supplies. Water sold for up to $145 per barrel, and the government was forced to intervene to stop profiteering.

Shell effectively halved its contract liftings, notifying QGPC that it would lift just 10,000 barrels per day of Dukhan crude and 20,000 barrels per day of Qatar Marine from July 1, 1983. BP and CFP also revealed that they had been taking only 60 percent of their contract quantities since the beginning of the year. Oil production averaged about 290,000 barrels per day through the summer months, but it exceeded Qatar's 300,000-barrel-per-day OPEC ceiling in September and October and surpassed 400,000 barrels per day in November 1983. The output increases came as the Qataris found other outlets for their oil, including several barter deals with both civil and defense contractors working in Qatar. These arrangements attracted scrutiny at OPEC's ministerial meeting in Helsinki, Finland, in mid-July, but Qatar presented evidence that no incentives had been involved in their negotiation and they had been concluded based on official prices.[131]

Civil and military budgets were cut drastically in response to lower oil revenues and a projected deficit of QR 5 billion ($1.5 billion) for the fiscal year beginning April 1983.[132] The government defaulted on payments to contractors, and the capital budget for the Engineering Services Department, the division of the Ministry of Public Works responsible for most building and engineering work, was slashed from QR 3,500 to QR 623 million ($171 million). In what would turn out to be the first of several deferrals, the Ministry of Electricity and Water was forced to rebid the Wusail power and desalination plant. Local prices for petroleum products, hitherto heavily subsidized, went up as much as 260 percent to cut public expenditure.[133] Charges for health care, water, and electricity were introduced for expatriates. Departments were told to draw up lists of nonessential staff whose positions could be axed. A net total of 82,375 expatriates and their families left Qatar in 1983.[134] Abdul Aziz Ibn Khalifa told the press in November that Qatar was drawing down its financial reserves to meet the state's current obligations.[135]

Even so, cherished projects were still going ahead. These included the purchase of $1.5 million worth of bricks from Britain to pave the Doha corniche, part of a $28 million beautification program in preparation for the Gulf Cooperation Council summit on November 7–9, 1983. Shortly before the GCC meeting, the government announced that it had foiled a plot to blow up the Doha Sheraton during the summit. Arrests ensued, and members of the state security apparatus were detained. While some sources linked the plot to an Al Thani family dispute, others pointed to domestic opposition supported by Libya's revolutionary leader Muammar Al Gaddafi and the Libyan chargé d'affaires was forced to leave Qatar.[136] For their part, the British believed the plot was externally directed. They cited the discovery in Qatar of a large cache of smuggled arms two months before the GCC summit, believed to be intended for use against an unidentified visiting head of state.[137]

Barter arrangements were made for defense contracts and construction projects, and France agreed to buy all the crude oil its companies received in such deals. These included Alsthom Atlantique, which took payment in oil for four gas turbines installed at backup electricity stations near Doha. When it stopped making cash payments to Sumitomo Heavy Industries under a contract at the Ras Abu Fontas desalination plant, the Ministry of Water and Electricity fulfilled its commitments instead in crude oil. Sumitomo received a total of 2.8 million barrels to cover an outstanding ¥20 billion balance, with Marubeni Corporation acting as intermediary and handling the sale of the oil.[138] It was the first time that a Japanese company had received oil as payment for work abroad. South Korea's Daelim also took delivery of 1.6 million barrels of Dukhan crude oil as part payment for work at Ras Abu Fontas. A local firm, Midmac Contracting, was willing to take payment in oil for a QR 205 million ($56 million) contract to expand the Qatar University.[139]

Qatar arranged to pay South Korea's Hyundai Engineering & Construction in crude oil for a petroleum product export terminal at its new 50,000-barrel-per-day refinery in Umm Said as well as a multiproduct pipeline linking the refinery to Doha.[140] The refinery began trial runs in October 1983 prior to its official inauguration in early 1984. Completion allowed the country to stop importing petroleum products (mainly from Bahrain) to meet 40 percent of its consumption needs and saved the government about $100 million a year.[141] Estimated requirements for refined products in the local market had reached 14,000 barrels per day, leaving a surplus of about 48,000 barrels per day for export between the new refinery and the aging 12,000-barrel-per-day unit situated next door. The *Khaleej Times* reported that the new refining capacity was expected to meet demand in Qatar through the end of the century, with exports decreasing gradually in line with growing domestic requirements.[142]

By this time cash-strapped Qatar had broken ranks with OPEC and started undercutting its own prices. The media reported on an aid deal with Brazil's state-owned oil company Petrobras for 15,000 barrels per day over an unspecified period with 120-day credit terms, double the usual payment terms.[143] Certain Japanese customers negotiated 90-day payment terms. Production rose to an estimated 400,000 barrels per day in October 1983 as barter arrangements continued and QGPC offered other buyers discounts of about $1 per barrel below its own government-set prices. Under orders to produce every barrel possible, QGPC forecast shipments of 450,000 to 500,000 barrels per day in November 1983, some 60 percent over its OPEC quota. It ended up exporting 490,000 barrels per day that month.

Offshore, the secondary recovery project at the Bunduq field shared with Abu Dhabi was completed in late 1983. This allowed the Bunduq Oil Company to finally resume production, halted since mid-1979. The scheme involved the injection of 70,000 barrels per day of brine into the field to maintain the appropriate gas to oil ratio and aimed to more than double the field's recoverable reserves to 125 million barrels. Output from the main Arab IV reservoir restarted at just 10,000 barrels per day, but it was expected to rise to 15,000 barrels per day in 1984, 25,000 barrels per day in 1985, and reach up to 30,000 barrels per day in 1986. Japan's United Petroleum Development put up 97 percent of the $330 million required for the secondary recovery project; BP funded the remaining 3 percent. A separate $70 million project to get the Arab III reservoir producing 5,000 barrels per day by 1984 was also under way.

CHAPTER 11

Partners Selected for Major North Field Gas Project

On returning from hunting in the Saudi desert, the amir met with his ministers and other officials at the Diwan on December 4, 1982, to discuss foreign-company participation in North field development. Issa Al Kawari reported that Sheikh Khalifa would proceed with the full LNG project and was still inclined to invite BP and CFP to form a consortium with QGPC and a Japanese group. Shell, to no one's surprise, was not mentioned. The ruler instead instructed his chef de cabinet to seek clarification from the British government on whether BP had retained the services of a local agent in Qatar. "The future of Qatar depended on the success of the project, and he would not allow 'a Mannai or a Jaidah' to secure an open-ended slice of the revenue," Ambassador Stephen Day reported.[1] It was probably not a coincidence that Ahmad Mannai had lunched with BP chair Sir Peter Walters earlier in the month. Day assured Al Kawari that except for a longstanding relationship with a small local company marketing its lubricating oils, BP did not have an agent for its oil and gas operations. Al Kawari responded that he would call on Day's French counterpart to ask the same question regarding CFP. "He added with a smile that the French Ambassador might find it rather more difficult to give a direct answer."[2]

Sheikh Khalifa telephoned Abdul Aziz in Paris to suggest he initiate contacts with BP and CFP with a view to forming a consortium to develop the North field.[3] BP and CFP subsequently had one round of private talks in Paris in January 1983. Further discussions were scheduled for February, although the two oil companies had still not been officially notified of their selection to develop the North field gas reserves.[4] Despite this, the first meeting between QGPC and representatives from BP and CFP to discuss the details of the proposed joint venture was held on February 21, 1983. One week later the *Middle East Economic Survey* reported that QGPC had informed the two companies that their offers were acceptable from the technical and economic standpoints.[5]

The Qatari firm had proposed that BP and CFP each take a 7.5 percent share-holding in the new joint venture. There was no sign yet of a marketing partner, and BP indicated that a trading company would not be appointed until it was determined which of the Japanese contenders had made the best offer in terms of sales volume and financial arrangements. The marketing effort could take as much as two or three years. It would need to be finalized before work could begin on the LNG export phase, although the domestic part of the project might be implemented earlier.

BP and CFP immediately came under pressure to send technical staff to Qatar to begin work on easing the looming gas shortage. "They are talking in terms of a 50/60-man project team to be in place in Doha before the end of the year, but BP do not intend to post permanent staff until a preliminary agreement is signed," Ambassador Day reported in late March.[6] This memorandum of understanding was signed between the Qatar government, BP, and CFP on June 20, 1983. It set out the basic principles of the project and committed the parties to enter into a further agreement before the end of the year. But it soon became apparent that two major issues threatened to delay this main agreement—the question of liability and accountability of seconded staff from BP and CFP and what law would govern any disputes that might arise.[7]

The Qataris, no doubt mindful of the ongoing dispute with Shell over the natural gas liquids plants, sought a greater degree of liability from their two partners than was acceptable to either BP or CFP. Under instructions from the amir, the country had already started to impose tighter liability arrangements in new defense contracts and other major agreements. Following a round of talks in early August, the two sides were still far apart on the contentious issues of liability and governing law. Later that month, however, the amir met with Shaikh Rashid and the other members of the North field committee. He wanted to see visible progress, including the establishment of a project task force composed of personnel from both BP and CFP, before the end of 1983. Issa Al Kawari reported that the amir had instructed the committee not to allow the issue of liability to slow things down.[8]

SHELL ORDERED TO HAND OVER EVIDENCE OF
PROJECTILE THEORY

Despite Shell's last-minute attempts to delay the proceedings, the arbitration hearings over the NGL plant explosion went ahead on January 17, 1983. Acceding to the Qatari request for a full exchange of technical information, Shell was directed by the ICC tribunal to hand over all its evidence regarding its projectile theory. Stephen Day briefed Issa Kawari on the results of the Washington hearings in late January. "I stressed that it was the Qatari lawyers who had secured the tabling of this evidence before the tribunal and that Shell's attempts to keep the evidence under wraps had been rejected by the Qatari side," the ambassador reported.[9] With the lawyers taking over, prospects for a settlement were fast receding. It was the lawyers, including Qatar's London law firm, who were now the main beneficiaries of the dispute, senior QGPC officials acknowledged to British officials.

Shell had visually inspected the accident site in the wake of the explosion, but it was subsequently sealed off by the Qataris. It was only when the company's experts got back in and began clearing the rubble ahead of the reconstruction effort that the collapsed tank in question, which had been blown some four hundred feet from its base, was lifted up and the hole discovered in the roof of the tank.[10] The steel plate containing the hole was removed after teams from both Shell and QGPC photographed it in situ and checked for related evidence. Shell was not allowed to take a sample of the plate, which was subsequently taken away by QGPC. Since the hole had no obvious explanation, Shell initiated a series of tests in the Netherlands to determine how it could have been caused. The Dutch army was asked to fire various projectiles at similar pieces of plate.[11] QGPC personnel participated as observers in these early, though inconclusive, tests. The firm was also allowed to send a scientist from its main technical advisers at the University of Manchester.

The tank had been full of liquid propane at the time of the explosion and therefore would have been subject to low-temperature stresses. When these conditions were replicated at a subsequent round of Dutch army tests, the results were compatible with the hole found at the Umm Said site.[12] It is not clear whether the army concluded that the damage had been inflicted by a rocket launcher or a mortar. The Qataris were not present at this subsequent stage of testing. They

had settled their insurance claim in the interim, which had required them to institute legal proceedings against Shell and Whessoe; the two sides were no longer
cooperating. Of the four teams hired by the Qataris to determine the cause of
the explosion, only the one from the University of Manchester was asked to comment on the hole, and then only based on partial evidence. Shell claimed all four
teams had provided contradictory opinions.[13]

After meeting with Shell, the British ambassador sent a long missive to the
Foreign Office on the company's views on the projectile theory. "They are confident there is no technical consensus on any other cause of the explosion, though
they would not go so far as to say they are convinced a projectile did cause it,"
Day wrote.[14] SIPM's Middle East representative said Shell welcomed a full tabling
of the technical evidence as directed by the ICC tribunal. Sheikh Khalifa had earlier asked the Qatari armed forces whether the tank had been hit by a projectile,
and they had concluded it was impossible. In addition, the projectile theory did
not necessarily fit with the fact that the tank had already cracked once before
the explosion.

When the British ambassador met the amir several weeks after the arbitration
hearings, he found Sheikh Khalifa in a combative mood. The ruler emphatically
denied that the presentation of evidence supporting the projectile theory would
embarrass his government. "If there were evidence, he would blame it on Khomeini," Day reported, referring to Iran's supreme leader, Ayatollah Ruhollah Khomeini. "When I pointed out that Khomeini had not been in the Gulf at that time
[of the explosion], he observed that the Shah was as good a scapegoat or why not
the British who had so enjoyed firing off their missiles in the Falklands."[15] With
Qatar's claims for both NGL plants now surpassing a combined $700 million, the
ambassador noted that Sheikh Khalifa no longer seemed optimistic about reaching a compromise with Shell. "He said, with a laugh, that Shell had already offered
him a 'present' which he had rejected as absurd and even insulting."[16] This obviously referred to the offer (previously mentioned) that had caused so much
umbrage.

The British fretted that commercial pressures might now lead Shell into an
early departure from Qatar, allowing France's CFP or even an American firm to
move into the country's offshore oil sector. Another attempt by Qatar's lawyers
to take the dispute to the commercial court in London failed when Qatar lost its
appeal of the British High Court's original decision not to hear the case. But Shell
was no doubt taken aback by a statement toward the end of the London court

report in which the judge said the proper place for QGPC to sue Shell was in the Netherlands or, if Shell had a presence in the country, in Qatar itself.[17] Shell responded by sending a special emissary to Qatar to deliver a warning: any move to institute legal proceedings against the company in Qatar would seriously affect their existing relationship and put a stop to any further Shell participation in the country.[18]

QATARIS TAKE DISPUTE AGAINST SHELL TO LOCAL COURTS

This warning fell on deaf ears. In September 1983 two Shell employees in Qatar were served writs ordering them to appear before the country's justice, or non-Islamic, civil court. They included Shell's local representative and the head of a team from one of its subsidiaries under contract to SIPM to supervise the replacement of the onshore section of the twenty-four-inch gas pipeline to NGL-2. This pipe work was almost complete and ready to be connected to the plant during routine maintenance scheduled in February 1984.

The twenty-page writ demanded payment of QR 2.7 billion (about $730 million) for the loss of the original NGL plant, plus interest and legal costs.[19] Shell was accused of negligence and responsibility for the deaths of the six people killed in the explosion that destroyed the plant. The writ did not include specific claims related to the pipelines at NGL-2. "My impression, shared by the local Shell man, is that the writ is not the result of any new strategy by the Qatar government but an attempt by officials to break the log-jam and bring Shell back to the negotiating table," Ambassador Day informed the Foreign Office.[20]

Just two months earlier the University of Manchester had returned with the results of further tests on the onshore section of the twelve-inch gas liquids pipeline to NGL-2. These were not good. The general manager of QGPC Onshore reported that the line had a maximum life of five years but that perforation could occur in months.[21] If the high-pressure line leaked, the metal would become very cold and brittle and could easily break. The escaping gas liquids would turn to vapor, likely leading to an explosion. With the pipeline guarantees set to expire, QGPC debated whether to close the liquids line altogether while replacement pipes were being laid or place new ones alongside while the existing line was still in operation. It chose the latter option, and the liquids line continued to operate at half capacity. The Qataris had yet to follow through with their earlier written warnings of legal action against Shell on NGL-2, and British officials noted that continuing to operate the pipelines could undermine their legal position.[22]

QGPC head Ali Jaidah returned from a visit to London in early October with news that Shell was prepared to exit Qatar.[23] There had been no further settlement offer since late 1982 when Shell's proposal had caused such consternation. Its oil liftings, which had once reached 145,000 barrels per day, were now down to a daily level of just 30,000 barrels. Shell's supply managers were resisting lifting even this reduced amount. Hoping to avert a permanent rupture, Issa Al Kawari arranged a meeting at his beach house with Shell's local representative, Edwardes, and Day on October 6, 1983. The amir's chef de cabinet explained that if Shell would increase its liftings and offer $200 million to settle the dispute over the natural gas liquids plants—a figure he presented as a generous concession from Sheikh Khalifa—then Qatar would bury the past and bring Shell in as an equal partner on the LNG scheme.[24]

Edwardes, who had no authority to negotiate on Shell's behalf, promised to report back to his superiors but proffered his personal opinion that the Qatari offer was a nonstarter given that it was several times higher than the company's 1982 proposal. The British ambassador, not sanguine about the possibility of a compromise, noted that the only positive outcome from the meeting was the apparent bypassing of Abdul Aziz Ibn Khalifa, the minister of finance and petroleum.[25] Hanging over the talks was the issue of Qatar's local court action against Shell, which Day told Al Kawari had made an already difficult situation virtually impossible.

The ICC arbitrators met again in London on October 24-26, 1983, to consider the question of their jurisdiction over all the claims related to NGL-1. QGPC had argued that the principal claims should be excluded from the tribunal's jurisdiction since they arose from negligence and therefore were subject to Qatari law. Although the arbitrators put off a decision on the issue until the tribunal's next meeting in early 1984, they strongly warned the claimants against moving forward with Qatari court proceedings until the uncertainty over jurisdiction was resolved.[26]

Shell was cautiously pleased. It had steadfastly maintained that the Qatari courts had no jurisdiction over the dispute, agreeing only to abide by the ICC ruling. In a letter to the amir on the eve of the Doha court hearing on November 27, Shell's group managing director, Peter Holmes, stated that Shell would not be represented in the Qatari court but instead expressed a willingness to continue with the ICC arbitration proceedings.[27] During this hearing the local judge set aside the writs served on the two Shell employees, accepting the argument that neither individual represented SIPM.[28] QGPC's attorneys said they would issue a further summons to SIPM, and this was subsequently forwarded through the Ministry of Foreign Affairs. The judge set a new hearing for February 5, 1984; QGPC indicated it would seek a default judgment against SIPM in absentia if the company failed to appear.

The Qataris reduced their settlement offer down to $150 million shortly after the initial Doha court hearing in November 1983.[29] This figure was confined to the first NGL plant and did not include any compensation related to the pipeline corrosion problems at NGL-2. While the new offer was also seen as a nonstarter by Shell, Issa Al Kawari told the British ambassador in early December that the dispute had been discussed recently within the Al Thani inner circle, including with Hamad Ibn Khalifa, the crown prince, as well as Khalid Ibn Hamad, the minister of the interior and Sheikh Khalifa's brother.[30] It was hoped that Sheikh Hamad especially would be a moderating influence.

PARTIES AGREE TO TERMS OF NORTH FIELD JOINT VENTURE DEAL

On September 13, 1983, BP's chief negotiator, Michael Clegg, met with the amir to discuss progress on the North field LNG project. Clegg told Sheikh Khalifa that both his company and CFP were ready to begin preparatory work and had nominated staff for the task force who were prepared to fly to Doha immediately.[31] But he warned negotiations were still blocked by a failure to agree on liability and legal principles. "The Amir took note and summoned Sheikh Rashid, the head of the gas committee, the following day to tell him for the third time in a month to get a move on," according to the British ambassador, who attended the meeting.[32] Shell's local representative and the general manager of QGPC Onshore (a BP man) had earlier briefed Clegg and his team on Shell's legal problems in

Qatar. BP knew the critical importance of standing firm on the issues of liability and the choice of governing law.

After an arduous fortnight of negotiations in late November and early December 1983, the BP-CFP team still hadn't resolved these outstanding issues with the Qataris. It was agreed to extend the memorandum of understanding by three months, to March 30, 1984, in order to give the two sides more time. A slightly earlier target date of February 22, 1984, was set for concluding the basic joint venture agreement.[33]

Remarkably, BP, CFP, and QGPC reached agreement on the basic documents of association, including the joint venture agreement, by this target date. The amir met with Rashid Ibn Awaidah Al Thani, the chair of the North field evaluation committee, on February 26, 1984, to approve the broad outline of the texts.[34] They would, of course, need to be reviewed by Sheikh Khalifa's legal team and endorsed by the Council of Ministers and possibly also by the Advisory Council. But the plan was to initial the agreements in a few weeks, including provisions on liability and governing law acceptable to all parties. An official signing ceremony would follow on April 8.

At a press conference in Doha in February 1984, Ali Jaidah put the North field's probable reserves at 300 to 400 trillion cubic feet, of which 150 trillion cubic feet were considered recoverable.[35] This followed the completion of the deepest-ever test well at the field in October 1983, drilled to a record 16,192 feet. The test well, Matbakh 2, was located about thirteen kilometers offshore from the northeastern tip of the Qatar peninsula. As such, it was designed to investigate a southeasterly extension of the North field. The Qataris were still hoping the structure might extend to the peninsula itself, as the country was fast depleting its nonassociated gas reserves at the onshore Dukhan area. Matbakh 2 was the tenth well drilled at the mammoth gas field since its discovery in late 1971.

In its quarterly magazine *al-Misha'al*, QGPC noted that the Matbakh 2 well had indeed proved a southeastern extension of the North field, with the top of the Khuff formation "being found at exactly the depth predicted."[36] Hopes of finding gas in deeper formations following initial seismic indications of a larger structure below the Khuff were not realized. While QGPC concluded that the entire section had been gas-bearing at one time, the more porous sands now contained only water, and the less porous sands were too "tight," or impermeable, to yield the limited amounts of gas still trapped within them.[37]

QGPC's managing director had certainly not given up on plans to develop the North field for domestic consumption. In early 1984 just as Rashid Ibn Awaidah Al Thani was wrapping up negotiations with BP and CFP on their joint venture agreement, Ali Jaidah told Shell's head of exploration and production that the most likely North field development was the production of moderate quantities of gas for local use. This, he said, would involve the recovery and sale of associated liquids and the reinjection of excess amounts of dry gas, probably into Dukhan's onshore Khuff reservoir, for later use. Shell's view, presumably shared by Ali Jaidah, was that there would be no market for LNG from the North field before the late 1990s.[38]

Just how much Qatar's electric power, desalination, and industry were now dependent on Khuff gas supplies from the Dukhan field became evident with the release of the 1983 production figures. Output of non-associated gas from the Dukhan area jumped to 320 million cubic feet per day that year, with considerable swing between the high-demand summer air conditioning months and the low-demand winter season.[39] This compared to a daily rate of 240 million cubic feet of associated gas, including 155 million cubic feet from the onshore oil sector and 85 million cubic feet from offshore sources. Crude oil production in 1983 totaled 102 million barrels, or an average of 270,000 barrels per day, and Umm Said's two natural gas liquids plants produced 1.12 million tons of NGLs. This last figure included the equivalent of 419,000 tons of ethane-rich gas as well as 305,000 tons of propane, 216,000 tons of butane, and 184,000 tons of plant condensate.[40]

Fed up with the lack of ethane-rich tail gas from the Umm Said NGL plants, which had prevented the petrochemical producer from operating at normal capacity since its inception in late 1980, QAPCO awarded a QR 200 million ($55 million) contract to construct a turbo-expander ethane recovery unit at its Umm Said complex to CDF-Chimie in early 1984.[41] The new unit, the first of its kind in the Middle East, would process 150 million cubic feet per day of associated gas from the Fahahil section of the Dukhan field, separating it into plant condensate, propane, butane, ethane, and methane. QAPCO said the turbo-expander would increase the petrochemical complex's daily supply of ethane to 1,100 tons upon its completion in late 1985. Funds for the new project were sourced from a $100 million Euroloan guaranteed by the Ministry of Finance and Petroleum.

EVIDENCE OF PROJECTILE THEORY PRESENTED AT ARBITRATION HEARINGS

The ICC arbitration tribunal finally ruled on the question of jurisdiction in January 1984, ruling that it had exclusive jurisdiction over all disputes between QGPC and SIPM arising from the two failures of the propane tank and the subsequent destruction of the first natural gas liquids plant on April 3, 1977.[42] SIPM now formally presented its projectile theory to the tribunal, which was composed of three distinguished former judges from the United States, France, and Malaysia. Its lawyers pointed to physical evidence that an object traveling at high velocity penetrated the roof of the propane tank. Almost immediately, the repercussions of this assertion were felt back in Qatar. "The police are, I understand, holding a series of exercises around the Umm Said installations to demonstrate to witnesses that a projectile could not have been fired unobserved," the British ambassador reported on February 13, 1984.[43]

In response, statements from the Qatar police (reportedly drafted by QGPC's lawyers) were submitted to the tribunal in which it was argued that security measures at the time of the explosion ruled out any possibility of terrorist attack. The official in charge of Qatar's onshore operations, BP's most senior secondee in the QGPC organization, was summoned to Paris to rebut Shell's projectile theory.[44] His predecessor, who had ordered the steel plate with the hole removed after it was found by Shell during site clearing, had already appeared before the tribunal on QGPC's behalf.[45]

After the first hole was found in the roof of the tank and the site photographed, the steel plate was taken away under cover of darkness in a private vehicle owned by an engineer working for QGPC and stored in a locked cupboard at QGPC Onshore. Unbeknown to Shell, at least one more hole had been found in the tank. This was also removed by QGPC and stored with the first plate. The two samples were eventually sent for testing to Qatar's technical advisers at the University of Manchester. Results were inconclusive: one of the holes appeared to have been made from the outside in and the other from the inside out.[46] Even so, QGPC argued before the ICC tribunal that defective welding of the tank during construction created structural weakness, causing it to fail under normal operating conditions. It also alleged that SIPM was negligent in the investigation and repair of the tank after the original 1976 leak and in its insistence that it could be returned to service.[47]

The case had come up again in the Qatari court on February 5, 1984, and there was a further hearing on March 4. QPGC's lawyers continued to argue that the proceedings in Qatar were in addition to the ICC arbitration process. They also contended that the arbitration clauses in the original 1971–1972 agreements between Shell and Qatar Petroleum Company were entered into before the government takeover of the remaining 40 percent ownership in the NGL plant in October 1976 and thus not binding on QGPC. Shell steadfastly denied the local court's jurisdiction and once again did not appear. "If the process is not stopped, it seems almost inevitable that a judgment in absentia will be given," Ambassador Day predicted.[48] Fortunately for SIPM, this gloomy prediction was averted when QGPC's lawyers submitted a copy of the ICC arbitration tribunal's decision on jurisdiction to the Qatar Civil Court and requested an indefinite adjournment. After some discussion, the local judge postponed the proceedings until July 15, 1984.[49]

Shell's Peter Holmes met with the amir's chef de cabinet, Issa Al Kawari, twice in Geneva during February 1984, floating the idea of compensating Qatar by guaranteeing additional crude oil liftings over the following three to four years. He offered to hike liftings to 100,000 barrels per day, arguing that Shell did not require Qatari oil and stating that the current daily quantity of 30,000 barrels would have already been canceled if Shell had been acting on a strictly commercial basis.[50] The quid pro quo for the increase was the withdrawal of legal proceedings in Qatar and at the ICC in Paris. Al Kawari went through Shell's latest proposal carefully with the amir, who deemed that the offer was worth only $100 million and rejected it.[51] In any case, the two sides agreed to keep talking, and Al Kawari assured Holmes that he would not be arrested or embarrassed should he visit Qatar.

Meanwhile, the parallel dispute at the NGL-2 plant worsened. Further corrosion was found during the annual offshore maintenance shutdown in early 1984, and QGPC's lawyers traveled to Qatar to gather evidence.[52] Maintenance teams reported that they had to conduct their work and remove defective material during the shutdown in front of independent witnesses. The Qataris had at least postponed legal action while settlement talks with Shell on the first NGL plant were under way. On the technical level, they had agreed to replace the twelve-inch liquids line and the interplatform offshore lines. Who would pay for these replacements was still undecided. Shell took the view that the longer legal action on NGL-2 was deferred, the less convincing QGPC's case became, particularly since the guarantee periods under the initial construction services contracts expired without any move by the Qataris to close the lines.

The ICC hearing in Paris concluded in December 1984, and the arbitrators were expected to deliberate on liability by April 1985.[53] Their opinion would then have to go to the ICC Court for validation before it could be finalized. In the end the ICC Court decided to refer the conclusions of the three-man arbitration panel back to the arbitrators and not to ratify them. While this was a surprising and disappointing outcome for Shell, who had expected to be vindicated, the company told the Foreign Office it was unlikely that the ICC would ultimately find it liable on the major damages issues.[54] Shell speculated that a leak from the ICC indicating a pending judgment sympathetic to the oil company might have been behind a recent decision by QGPC to step up legal action in Qatar, despite an earlier understanding between the two sides to leave the issue to the ICC and accept its judgment.

After convening briefly on December 16, 1984, to discuss the matter, the local civil court adjourned the proceedings until March 17, 1985. Shell continued to warn the Qataris "verbally in very clear terms" that if a decision were reached in Qatar finding the company liable, it would almost certainly lead to Shell's full withdrawal from the country.[55] The Qataris seemed to totally ignore this warning. "They had unrealistic ideas about the importance of Qatar to Shell and the level of profits made," according to Stephen Day, who had now moved on to a posting at the Foreign Office's Middle East Department.[56]

SHELL PRESSED TO INCREASE OFFSHORE OIL SECTOR ACTIVITIES

At the same time the Qataris were seeking massive damages from Shell—the official claim related to the first NGL plant was still QR 2.7 billion, or approximately $730 million—they were agitating for an increase in the Anglo-Dutch company's involvement in their offshore oil sector, including the secondment of a larger number of technical staff than the 110 Shell employees currently there. A review of QGPC Offshore's future development program completed in early 1984 had revealed the need to exploit more difficult, and therefore more expensive, oil reserves. QGPC Offshore had been concentrating almost exclusively on the extraction of easily accessible oil, which cost an estimated $10 per barrel to produce.[57] Shell reckoned this easy oil would be exhausted by 1990 under present operating conditions, at which point Qatar would need to tap more difficult and considerably more costly reservoirs.

The Anglo-Dutch company estimated these reserves would cost about $25 per barrel to produce at 1984 prices. Shell's exploration and production experts had argued, and Ali Jaidah apparently agreed, that Qatar should immediately prepare to develop these reserves to produce an economic blend of cheap and expensive oil.[58] Despite a recently approved government budget based on minimizing recurring costs and maximizing revenue, the QGPC head was confident the money could be found for this development program. The problem was that more Shell secondees were needed to implement these new plans. The irony of asking for greater offshore oil assistance from Shell while simultaneously taking the firm to court for damages hadn't escaped the oil company's notice.

Qatar's oil output in January 1984 was estimated at 450,000 barrels per day, well over its quarterly OPEC quota of 300,000. This dropped precipitously to 250,000 barrels per day in February because of the annual shutdown of offshore oil operations. Production rebounded after maintenance was completed, reaching 500,000 barrels per day in May. By early June production was at 550,000 barrels.[59] The offshore fields contributed about half of this figure, close to the maximum capacity of their gas handling equipment. Officials warned that an increase in offshore output would lead to gas flaring, which required government approval. Higher crude oil production meant more associated gas for the NGL-1 and NGL-2 plants at Umm Said, where the output of natural gas liquids reached record levels in the first half of 1984. It also led to a short-term reversal of fortune for QAPCO, which was now able to run its ethylene unit at 90 percent capacity in May and June after receiving more ethane-rich gas feedstock.[60]

A considerable amount of Qatar's crude oil had been showing up on the spot market at discounted prices since late 1983. Some of this volume was undoubtedly linked to the so-called counter-purchase deals, when Qatar had essentially paid contractors in crude oil for construction projects, and the oil in question was then resold at whatever cost the market would accept. But there was also speculation that Qatar itself had been selling cargoes on a "deemed processing basis," whereby the oil price was netted back to the load port from market realizations on refined product prices in consuming countries, particularly Rotterdam in the Netherlands. The authoritative *Middle East Economic Survey* estimated that such netbacks probably worked out to sixty to seventy US cents per barrel below official selling prices.[61]

Slowing market demand and shipment deferrals by several lifters forced Qatar to cut oil output to just under 500,000 barrels per day in August 1984. Production continued to fall, hitting a daily average of 430,000 barrels in October. This rate was, of course, still over the country's OPEC ceiling of 300,000 barrels per day. Qatar's production quota was reduced even further to 280,000 barrels per day at the organization's ministerial meeting in Geneva in October 1984.[62] Qatar came under heavy pressure in Geneva from the other OPEC members, particularly Saudi Arabia, who demanded that it curtail illicit production and stick to OPEC rules. The authorities in Doha subsequently issued strict instructions to QGPC's onshore and offshore divisions that the new ceiling of 280,000 barrels per day should be adhered to in November.[63]

This was not difficult. The second-largest offshore production platform was already scheduled to close on November 1, 1984, for maintenance, removing 100,000 barrels per day from Qatar's total output for over a month. When this platform came back onstream on December 7, QGPC Offshore elected to take another platform out of production for maintenance, thereby allowing Qatar to hold down its overall output.[64] But this production discipline was not expected to extend into 1985, as the offshore fields were scheduled to be back producing at least 200,000 barrels per day by the end of December.

Oil production for 1984 ended up averaging 402,000 barrels per day, up from 270,000 barrels per day in 1983. Higher oil flows meant more associated gas for the two NGL plants at Umm Said, where output across the product spectrum was up 18 percent in 1984, to 1.43 million tons from 1.21 million tons in 1983.[65] This had a knock-on effect on QAPCO, whose production performance also improved. Despite continuing shortages of ethane-rich gas feedstock, the petrochemical producer managed to increase ethylene output to 204,000 tons in 1984, an increase of some 40,000 tons over 1983. Output of low-density polyethylene also rose by 5,000 tons to 150,000 tons in 1984, while sulfur production increased to 33,000 tons from 19,000 tons in 1983.[66] Despite this, QAPCO still failed to break even.

QATAR BUNGLES SIGNATURE OF JOINT VENTURE
AGREEMENT ON NORTH FIELD

With the joint venture agreement on the North field still set for signature on April 8, 1984, the Qataris announced the imminent deal to the press.[67] They spoke too soon. As the BP team was still in the air on its way to Doha from London for the official signing ceremony, committee chair Rashid Ibn Awaidah Al Thani indicated there would be a slight delay. Reports suggested Sheikh Rashid had omitted to obtain agreement to the deal from QGPC's board of directors.[68] As chair, Abdul Aziz Ibn Khalifa hastily called a board meeting for the morning of April 8. Signature of the joint venture agreement was postponed until the afternoon—after rather than before the scheduled celebratory lunch.

Just as the signatories and invited dignitaries were assembling to eat, they received word that the QGPC board had failed to approve the agreement. The signing was unceremoniously canceled, although the lunch proceeded amid dangerously rising tempers among the BP and CFP delegations. As one board member later explained, the board was presented with 250 pages of legal documents with just a few hours to review them and ask questions. This explanation was dismissed by the foreign partners, whose own boards had already signed off on the long-negotiated deal. BP and CFP warned the Qataris there was no question of further amendments to the agreement.[69] If QGPC wished to reopen negotiations on substantive issues, the three parties would have to restart the whole process.

This debacle occurred as the amir was preparing to set off for a state visit to the Far East, and the optics of the bungled signing ceremony were hardly propitious. "The Japanese were following the course of events with great care and the entire operation depended on the establishment of confidence in the project, no easy matter in the light of its history," Stephen Day explained to Issa Al Kawari later that same day.[70] The ambassador appealed personally to Al Kawari, hoping for signature the following morning. After all, Day pointed out, as minister of information, Al Kawari would have to face embarrassing press inquiries about what had happened.

Al Kawari was unable to sway the QGPC board, even after the amir's personal intervention. When the BP and CFP teams next saw the minister of finance and petroleum, they were told only that more time was needed to consider the agreement.[71] BP did succeed in obtaining a joint public statement in which the Qataris committed to sign the deal in about a month. The only encouraging development to come out of the episode, Day believed, was the close cooperation displayed by BP and CFP, who reiterated their strong opposition to any further changes to the documents.[72] Day also noted that the events underscored the amir's inability to make difficult decisions. "He is not the conscientious manager he once was. He is isolated, largely distracted by foreign affairs and surrounded by sycophants."[73] Faced with difficult decisions, the diplomat reported, Sheikh Khalifa would invariably fudge and defer.

NORTH FIELD AGREEMENT FINALLY SIGNED
WITH BRITISH AND FRENCH FIRMS

Sheikh Khalifa returned from his Far East tour encouraged by his talks in both Japan and South Korea. He had left his son Abdul Aziz behind in Tokyo to continue the discussions, setting up a joint committee of "experts" on gas and other issues proposed by Prime Minister Yasuhiro Nakasone. This was agreed after Sheikh Khalifa attempted to sound out the Japanese leader and other officials on the prospects for a market in Japan for Qatar's LNG project during face-to-face meetings. The Japanese team, which would be led by the country's ambassador to Qatar, did not expect the joint committee to hold its first meeting until late 1984 or early 1985.[74]

Senior Qatari officials insisted that prospects for signature of the North field joint venture agreement were still good. Even opponents of major aspects of the project like Ali Jaidah seemed resigned to the inevitable, although it was apparent that some face-saving changes to the agreement would be necessary before it could be finalized with BP and CFP. The Qatari side indicated that it only wanted to reopen certain legal issues pertaining to the joint venture agreement while the basic parameters of the scheme would be left unchanged. BP's initial reaction was very relaxed, asking the Qataris to put any counter proposals in writing.[75] These would have to be considered by its own board before any further negotiations.

BP and CFP reached agreement on the outstanding issues—the most important of which centered on applicable law—with the Qataris on June 15, 1984. The deal was finally initialed by the three partners in Paris on June 21, and this was followed by an official signing ceremony held in Doha on June 25. Local radio and press carried the story the following day.[76] Abdul Aziz Ibn Khalifa, the minister of finance and petroleum and the chair of the board of directors of QGPC, signed the agreement on behalf of the Qatari firm. Colin Webster, the managing director and chief executive officer of BP Gas International, signed for BP, while Bernard Madinier, the director of CFP's Middle East Division, represented the French firm. BP and CFP were each allocated 7.5 percent equity in the LNG phase of the project, leaving QGPC with 85 percent.

An accompanying statement specified that the first phase of the project, to supply 800 million cubic feet per day of gas for Qatar's domestic needs, was to be completed by 1987. This phase was to be fully controlled by QGPC, although BP and CFP could provide technical services and manpower on a contract basis to this portion of the project at the invitation of the Qataris. No date was given for commencement of the scheme's second phase, the manufacture and export of 6 million tons per year of LNG. This would depend on lining up markets for the gas and was therefore much more uncertain. But BP and CFP did agree to help secure long-term customers for the LNG, and a completion target of 1992 for this export phase was mooted in the press. The June agreement further stipulated that full ownership of other activities, including gas, field condensates, and liquid petroleum gas, would be retained by QGPC.[77]

The Qatar Liquefied Gas Company was established by amiri decree on November 1, 1984, as a Qatari shareholding company. It was capitalized at QR 500 million ($140 million). Interestingly, the decree establishing what would eventually become the country's first LNG producer was issued not by the ruler Sheikh Khalifa but by his son and heir, Hamad Ibn Khalifa Al Thani. At its founding, Qatar Liquefied Gas Company had a paid-up capital of QR 20 million, of which BP and CFP's proportion was QR 1.5 million each, in line with the 7.5 percent shareholding accorded to the two foreign partners in the June 25 agreement. The new company would manage the second phase of the North field project, as the first phase was wholly Qatari controlled.

Of the thirteen men on the new company's first board of directors, eleven were appointed by the Qataris. BP and CFP were each given one seat. The Qatari side consisted of the full nine-member board of QGPC, plus Dr. Helmi Samara, the senior petroleum adviser to the minister of finance and petroleum, and Nasir Mubarak Al Ali, the deputy director of the Petroleum Affairs Department. Colin Webster and Bernard Madinier represented BP and CFP (see table 11.1). The new

TABLE 11.1 Qatar Liquefied Gas Company

Initial board members

Board member	Affiliation
Sheikh Abdul Aziz Ibn Khalifa Al Thani	Minister of finance and petroleum
Dr. Hassan Kamel	Adviser to the State of Qatar
Issa Al Kawari	Minister of information, director of Amir's Office
Ali Mohamed Jaidah	Managing director of QGPC
Abdulla Sallat	Director of the Department of Petroleum Affairs
Dr Taher Abdel Razak Al Hadidi	Senior petroleum expert, Ministry of Finance and Petroleum (Egyptian)
Mohamad Said Mishal	Managing director of the Industrial Development Technical Center
Fuad Al Mahmoud	Assistant director, Office of Minister of Finance and Petroleum
Dr Helmi Samara	Senior petroleum adviser to the minister of finance and petroleum
Nasir Mubarak Al Ali	Deputy director of Petroleum Affairs Department
Colin Webster	Managing director, BP International Gas
Bernard Madinier	Director, Middle East Division, CFP

company's name was initially shortened to Qalingas, which within a few months was changed to Qatargas because the Arabic word *qalil*—variously meaning small, scarce, little, or slight—sounded far too similar to Qalingas.[78]

NORTH FIELD'S FIRST PHASE IMMEDIATELY MIRED IN CONFUSION

Almost immediately after signature of the long-awaited North field deal, the details of the project's first development phase became mired in confusion. The June 1984 agreement with BP and CFP allowed them to provide certain services for a QGPC-led development to bring gas ashore for local use. But efforts by the three partners to establish a project team proceeded at a snail's pace, and the committee headed by Rashid Ibn Awaidah Al Thani was still focused on testing the market for LNG, including holding talks with the two Japanese trading groups. "It is, of course, quite conceivable that QGPC will go ahead with this initial development without invoking the BP/CFP agreement," Ambassador Day commented, while also noting that a smallish development of the North field for internal consumption was probably within QGPC's existing resources.[79]

Ali Jaidah had instructed QGPC Offshore to press ahead with plans for a much bigger development. This would bring gas ashore for local use as well as allow a large quantity of high-value condensates to be stripped out for export.[80] Surplus dry gas not used domestically would be injected into the Dukhan reservoirs after condensate removal. While Jaidah envisaged QGPC carrying out this project entirely on its own, there was no question that such an ambitious undertaking would require international finance and a major increase in offshore activity. Initial estimates suggested that QGPC would have to increase the number of offshore drilling rigs from two to five and drill as many as fifty wells in three years.[81] But the QGPC head was characteristically persistent. He had already appointed Fluor to provide engineering and consulting services related to the project under a $7 million contract.[82] Fluor had been recommending this type of development scenario for several years and had carried out several preliminary studies of it.

QGPC's managing director had obviously not backed off his opposition to the BP-CFP scheme for LNG, and the condensate recovery project held some attraction. "The Amir has been interested in condensates for some time and sees such a route as a good deal less risky than LNG," the British ambassador reported.[83] Fluor had apparently assured the Qataris the investment could be repaid within eighteen months, which helped fuel this perception. In mid-July, following the first round of negotiations with CFP and Sheikh Rashid's committee, BP reported that the Qataris were in an uproar over Fluor's contract for the feasibility study as none of the six committee members had been consulted before it was awarded. "The contract is clearly inconsistent with the BP/CFP role," the British ambassador wrote. "However, once the task force has been set up there is provision for the appointment of an engineering consultant with the agreement of the three parties and Fluor is an obvious candidate."[84]

When the Fluor contract was finally signed just one day before signature of the North field joint venture agreement with BP and CFP, it was initially taken as confirmation of Ali Jaidah's reputation for deviousness. It certainly added to the confusion over Qatar's plans for the gas field. As it turned out, however, the amir had personally approved the contract with Fluor.[85] His reasoning was entirely in character, and thoroughly Qatari: Sheikh Khalifa did not want either BP or

CFP to think they had the North field project sewn up. As he had so often in the past, the amir proposed to divide and rule. "Frankly, while he [Sheikh Khalifa] is in charge of things, I despair of real progress on this project," Stephen Day wrote to his successor, Julian Walker, in early 1985.[86] This divide-and-conquer approach, used by the Qataris to keep companies on their toes and create both competition and confusion, was regularly employed to achieve the best results for the nation.

Meanwhile, BP was doing its utmost to build up its presence in Qatar. In July 1984, just weeks after the signature of the North field agreement, the British company signed on to purchase fuel oil from the new Umm Said refinery. Under the eighteen-month contract, BP agreed to buy 30,000 tons per month of fuel oil from October 1984 with volumes potentially increasing when the refinery reached full capacity of 50,000 barrels per day.[87] Transport would be undertaken by the state-owned Qatar National Navigation and Transport. Its subsidiary, Qatar National Bunker and Tankers, had earlier signed a five-year contract worth $450 million with QGPC to transport excess refined products to overseas markets. Press reports at the time of the BP deal put the output earmarked for export at 10,000 barrels per day of fuel oil and 2,000 barrels per day of gas oil.[88]

Qatar National Bunker and Tankers purchased the country's first products tanker, a secondhand vessel of 62,135 deadweight tons, to transport output from the refinery to the Umm Said jetty for export. While the shuttle service was meant as a temporary solution until pipelines linking the new refinery to the export jetty could be built, this infrastructure would not be completed for nearly four and a half years. The two pipelines—a sixteen-inch line for light refined products and a parallel twenty-inch line to carry heavy products—were not officially inaugurated until February 24, 1989. Work on a forty-two-kilometer products pipeline linking the Umm Said refinery to a new storage facility for motor gasoline, gas oil, and jet fuel at Abu Hamour west of Doha was also completed at the same time.

NEW STEERING COMMITTEE FORMED TO EXECUTE NORTH FIELD DEVELOPMENT

A new seven-member gas steering committee for the development of the North field was appointed on November 11, 1984, under the chairmanship of Abdul Aziz

Ibn Khalifa, the minister of finance and petroleum. His mandate was to execute the project by coordinating the operations of QGPC and the new Qatar Liquefied Gas Company. Ali Jaidah and Rashid Ibn Awaidah Al Thani were also members. While the steering committee was strongly controlled from the top by the minister of finance and petroleum, Sheikh Rashid continued in his role. Indeed, the structure was meant to facilitate Sheikh Rashid's progress within the executive committee and expedite the LNG phase of the North field project.[89]

The appointment of Ali Jaidah as the steering committee's deputy chair marked his official inclusion in the North field development. This was supposed to rein in his more maverick tendencies.[90] Several of Qatar's foreign advisers were appointed to the new committee as well, including Palestinian, Egyptian, and Iraqi experts. Also represented was Dr. Jabir Al Marri, a Qatari national and close confident of Crown Prince Hamad Ibn Khalifa. Sheikh Hamad and Ali Jaidah had often clashed, but the two men were reportedly trying to patch up their differences. Al Marri's presence on the committee meant the crown prince would be kept up to date on its progress.

With Ali Jaidah now firmly involved in the North field project, cooperation with BP and CFP was expected to improve as well. BP had begun to cultivate the Qatari official seriously in 1983, although the British government was still dubious whether Jaidah was enthusiastic about the LNG project. "We should be particularly interested to hear whether Ali Jaidah's attitude has changed now he is in a key role," Britain's Foreign Office wrote to Ambassador Walker in January 1985. "His criticisms of the scheme were always coherent and consistent and within the industry he towers above all other Qataris in terms of experience and intelligence."[91]

Fluor had already completed its initial contract and drawn up tenders for well drilling and platform jackets for the North field's first development phase. Although the bidding for these tenders was not necessarily expected to produce immediate orders, it would give the steering committee much-needed budgetary guidelines. The North field project was virtually budgetless, with an allocation of just $10 million through 1984, even though total expenditures were expected to reach $4 billion in 1984 dollars.[92] The first stage alone would require $1.5 billion, and the steering committee planned to approach international banks for this funding by the middle of 1985. The British ambassador predicted that "by 1986 expenditure on the project should reach 2 million dollars per day and then tail off, with final expenditure on phase 1 planned for 1989."[93]

Sheikh Abdul Aziz explained in early 1985 that the North field's initial development would be carried out in stages, with the first of them sized to handle 800 million cubic feet of non-associated gas per day as well as 40,000–50,000 barrels per day of condensates and other gas liquids. Offshore installations would include three wellhead platforms, a production complex, and pipelines for transporting gas and condensates to Umm Said. Gas treatment and fractionation facilities would be built onshore as well as gas liquids export facilities and a lean gas domestic distribution system. This lean gas system would include facilities for injecting up to 400 million cubic feet per day of surplus gas into the Dukhan reservoirs, where it could be stored for future use. Shell had told the minister there would be no difficulty injecting this excess gas, provided the injection platforms were placed well away from existing production equipment.

Qatar invited six short-listed international engineering groups—Fluor, Bechtel, Foster Wheeler, Technip, M. W. Kellogg with Lummus Crest, and Ralph M. Parsons with Worley Engineering—to submit offers for the basic engineering design for the first stage of development in early 1985. By August QGPC had initialed a $1.1 million, five-month contract with Bechtel for this work.[94] The six competitors were also asked to bid for a separate and much larger contract covering the management consultancy for the project. This consultant would carry out the detailed engineering design for the first stage development and assist QGPC in procurement as well as coordinate and supervise the fabrication, installation, construction, and commissioning of all facilities.

With plans for the North field under way, industrial users began jostling to be first in line for the promised gas supplies. The Qatar Fertilizer Company announced in late 1985 that its board of directors had approved the construction of a third ammonia plant with capacity of 1,500 tons per day to supplement its existing urea and ammonia units. QAFCO's chair, Mohamed Said Mishal, said the $200 million project was still awaiting approval from QPGC and Norway's Norsk Hydro, the company's two remaining shareholders after the exit of both PowerGas and Hambros Bank. Mishal explicitly linked the expansion to the gas field development, saying QAFCO wanted the ammonia plant to be "ready when the North field gas project goes ahead."[95]

The gas supply situation in Umm Said was also set to improve with the imminent completion of the new ethane recovery unit at the petrochemical complex operated by QAPCO. This so-called turbo-expander, commissioned in February 1986, essentially doubled the amount of ethane feedstock available for

QAPCO's ethylene plant to 1,100 tons per day. Processing 150 million cubic feet per day of associated gas from the Dukhan field, the unit was designed to produce 500 tons per day of pure ethane, 210 tons per day of propane, and 120 million cubic feet per day of dry methane gas.[96] This surplus dry gas was to be directed to QAFCO's fertilizer plant. Ethylene production at QAPCO rebounded with the completion of the new ethane recovery unit, hitting 253,000 tons in 1986 and 263,000 tons, or nearly 94 percent of design capacity, in 1987.

JAPAN'S MARUBENI AGREES TO JOIN NORTH FIELD LNG PROJECT

The gas steering committee had begun parallel negotiations with the two Japanese firms interested in taking equity in the LNG project. Marubeni seemed to be the keenest, despite the loss of former partner Nissho Iwai when it backed out to pursue a competing venture taking shape in Canada. After a visit by the director general of the Marubeni Group to Doha in early November 1984, the minister of finance and petroleum agreed to give the Japanese firm a 7.5 percent stake in the project in exchange for an undertaking from Marubeni that it would use its best endeavors to ensure the sale of LNG to electric power and gas utilities in Japan.[97] Both BP and CFP advised the Qataris not to rush into a commitment with Marubeni as the Japanese trader was relatively inexperienced in marketing gas.[98] But their advice was ignored.

Later that month the minister announced an agreement had been reached with Marubeni to exploit the North field's gas reserves and market Qatari LNG in Japan. In the letter of intent that Marubeni sent to the Qataris, the trading house promised to market 2 million (out of a total annual production of 6 million) tons per year of LNG by 1992 in exchange for a 7.5 percent slice in Qatargas. Although it was unhappy at being left with only 7.5 percent to divide among themselves, the rival consortium of Mitsui, Mitsubishi, and C. Itoh hadn't given up hope of participating in the project as well, perhaps with an increased stake.[99] BP and CFP were also hoping to hike their share to 10 percent each, which might be possible if the Japanese did not take the full amount of equity reserved for the marketing partners.[100]

On September 5, 1985, Marubeni signed a formal agreement with QGPC that entitled the Japanese company to take a 7.5 percent equity stake in Qatargas.[101]

The accord was signed by Abdul Aziz Ibn Khalifa and Marubeni's deputy president, Isao Hiroe, following a visit to Japan by a Qatargas delegation led by Rashid Ibn Awaidah Al Thani. This delegation, which included representatives from BP and CFP, met with an array of Japanese companies, including trading organizations, oil companies, and government officials. In early November the Qatargas delegation also toured Europe, where it met with prospective buyers like British Gas, Gaz de France, Italy's Snam, and West Germany's Ruhrgas. Sheikh Rashid announced that Qatargas would open a representative office in London the following month.[102]

GULF COOPERATION COUNCIL GAS GRID CONCEPT
GETS OFF TO SLOW START

At their summit meeting in Doha in November 1983, the heads of state of the six countries in the Gulf Cooperation Council had in principle approved a GCC gas grid to be supplied with up to 1.5 billion cubic feet per day of gas from Qatar and potentially the UAE as well. Conceptually, the project involved the development of the North field for piped gas to Bahrain, Kuwait, and Saudi Arabia, in addition to the reserves already slated for local consumption in Qatar and conversion to LNG for export. A second part of the project would link gas sources in the UAE to potential markets in the southeastern Gulf. The organization's secretariat general was directed to carry out a feasibility study on the Arabian Peninsula pipeline scheme.

When the six heads of state convened again in Geneva one year later, the concept of a regional gas grid was still low on the GCC secretariat's list of priorities. After some discussion these leaders announced that before engineering work could begin on the gas grid, the price for the gas would have to be agreed between the potential suppliers—Qatar and the UAE—and the potential buyers—Bahrain, Saudi Arabia, and Kuwait.[103] That wasn't going to be easy. The Bahrainis argued that the price should give Qatar a net return comparable to what the export of gas in liquefied form to Europe or Japan could provide. Because the capital cost of exported LNG would be far higher, explained Bahrain's minister of development and industry, Yusuf Shirawi, the delivered unit price to customers for piped gas in the region should be much lower.[104]

The Saudis were thought to need gas to keep their petrochemical plants running, given that much smaller quantities of associated gas were being produced in their own oil fields. This view was not widely shared, and some oil industry experts argued that demand in the kingdom could be more easily satisfied by the development of non-associated gas reserves in Saudi Arabia itself. Production of non-associated gas in the kingdom was already running at 1 billion cubic feet per day, and plans were in place to produce gas from the deep Khuff reservoir on the southeastern edge of the Ghawar oil field by 1986.[105] "If, as has been suggested, Saudi Arabia were to supply Kuwait with gas from this field then the GCC scheme for supplying Kuwait might be based on Saudi Arabian gas rather than Qatari gas," the British Embassy in Doha reported.[106]

Saudi Arabia's plans for developing non-associated gas reserves at the Ghawar field caused some concern in Doha, where planners at QGPC were now uncertain that a pipeline would ever be needed to supply gas to Bahrain and Kuwait. "The Saudi field does not of course rule out a northern pipeline from Qatar, it simply makes it a less attractive proposition," the British Embassy in Doha commented in September 1984.[107] This was one of the points BP and CFP were expected to address once their teams arrived in Doha to begin working on the North field. Qatar's plans for reinjecting surplus lean gas from the offshore field into the onshore Dukhan reservoirs for later use put the sale of piped gas to Bahrain and Kuwait even further in doubt.

Other pipeline schemes, including an ambitious project to pipe Qatari gas to Western Europe via Turkey, were also under discussion. Following Sheikh Khalifa's state visit to Turkey in early 1985, the two governments agreed to conduct a feasibility study on the transcontinental pipeline, which would pass through Saudi Arabia, Kuwait, Iraq, and Syria on its way to Turkey. Ankara was happy to host a gas pipeline from the GCC states as well as one from Iran to Western Europe, to wean Europeans from dependence on Russian gas and to align revolutionary Iran to the west.[108] Turkey, whose own gas consumption was rising steadily, also indicated it might buy a fair amount of the gas itself. Qatar made it clear, however, that it would not be economical for it to pipe gas only to Turkey, and that other European countries would need to come forward with firm purchase commitments to support the pipeline.[109]

The two export projects—pipeline gas and liquefied natural gas—were not necessarily seen by the Qataris to be in competition. "People are talking about exporting gas through pipelines to Turkey and further up to France," one Qatargas director explained in mid-1985. "If it is liquefied gas, the talks are about Japan, Europe, America and South Asia. We are approaching the markets in both directions, trying to promote our exports."[110] But the talks with Turkey achieved little progress, and in early 1986 the Turkish company Botas invited bids for the construction of an 840-kilometer pipeline bringing up to 6 billion cubic meters annually of Soviet natural gas from the Bulgarian border to Ankara. This followed a February 1986 gas supply agreement between the two countries.

NORTH FIELD DECISION PUTS SPOTLIGHT ON MEDIAN LINE WITH IRAN

Now that the authorities had decided to develop the North field, the issue of Qatar's median line with Iran assumed renewed importance. Qatar had assiduously kept its ties with Iran free of confrontation, in large part because the huge offshore gas deposits were likely to extend into Iranian waters. Despite Tehran's seeming respect for international law, Doha was worried that revolutionary Iran under Ayatollah Ruhollah Khomeini might challenge the 1969 median line agreement reached between Sheikh Khalifa, then the deputy amir, and the deposed shah of Iran. "Qatar's North field extends, according to Shaikh Hamad, a few miles on the Iranian side of this median line—so Iranian Qatari co-operation will be needed in the future to ensure its smooth development," British ambassador Julian Walker wrote in April 1985 after a meeting with Crown Prince Hamad Ibn Khalifa.[111]

The Foreign Office replied that, rather than any challenge to the 1969 agreement, it expected Qatar and Iran to negotiate a participation agreement that would take into account Iran's claims to gas reserves on its side of the boundary line.[112] While the offshore accord clearly defined the maritime border, it did not address how cross-border oil and gas reserves should be shared between Qatar and Iran. Petroleum drilling within 125 meters on either side of the median line was explicitly banned in the 1969 agreement, but this was the only restriction.[113]

There was also the issue of securing the North field from potential attack. "Incidentally, the Amir once told me quite clearly that he would never give the go-ahead for investment in the Field until he was confident the platforms would not be attacked by Iran," Stephen Day informed his successor in early 1985. "I doubt if he would be any more confident now than he was three years ago when he made that statement to me and certainly we could not offer reassurance—though we would gladly sell him a few more batteries of Rapier."[114] Rapier, the air defense system made by British Aerospace, was already operational in Qatar, and the British were anxious to sell more equipment to the sheikh. The Qatari air force now also included fourteen French Mirage F-1 fighters, delivered in 1984 and waiting at Doha's international airport for a new airbase.

Doha had stopped making payments to Iraq to help Baghdad in its war effort against Iran three years earlier, pleading economic difficulties. There were other reasons. One was defensive. "The Qataris are conscious of their exposed position in the Gulf and have tried to maintain as low a profile as possible, to the extent of ceasing financial support for Iraq," Britain's Foreign Office reported.[115] The economic slowdown begun in 1983 had also given the government an excuse to reduce the number of resident expatriates, particularly those of Iranian origin. By contrast, the Palestinians mainly remained, despite the desire of some senior Qatari officials to oust them from influential government posts. Outnumbered in their own country at least three to one by foreigners, many older Qataris were worried about the threat the influx of expatriates posed to their society and traditional way of life. Younger Qataris who were returning home with foreign university degrees also coveted the positions occupied by expatriate advisers.

By 1985 the slowdown in the local economy threatened to turn into a recession. Al Thani family expenses, heavy arms spending in the wake of the Iran-Iraq war, and the costs related to the North field all put increasing pressure on the exchequer. The published budget for that fiscal year envisaged revenue of QR 9,737 million and total expenditure of QR 17,050 million, implying a record deficit of QR 7,310 million ($2 billion) after two previous years of projected deficits. Qatar's last budgeted surplus was in 1982, when revenues exceeded expenditures by QR 2,733 billion.[116] There was no effort to rein in the bloated Al Thani civil list, and development spending essentially remained the same for 1985. The Council of Ministers also approved a 25 percent hike in QGPC's capital base, from QR 4,000 million to QR 5,000 million ($1.37 billion).[117] This represented the firm's fourth capital infusion since its establishment in 1974.

In the end, sufficient major works were canceled or postponed and contractors unpaid to reduce actual government expenditure for 1985 to QR 10,374 million ($2.85 billion), against total revenue from all sources of QR 10,393 million.[118] This habit of publishing budget deficits and then slashing spending during the year to balance the books was well established, and budget allocations were routinely dispersed at only half their original amounts. In 1984, for example, the state ended up with a surplus of nearly QR 1,437 million despite initially projecting a sizable deficit of QR 3,680 million. After months of squabbling among ministries, a much-trimmed draft budget for 1986 was unveiled putting revenues of QR 5,320 million against expenditures of QR 11,700 million. This implied a budget deficit of QR 6,380 million ($1.75 billion). The actual deficit for 1986 ended up being QR 2,753 million ($755 million).[119] It was the first such deficit to be recorded.

The Al Thani royal family by this time numbered between five thousand and six thousand.[120] At least eight hundred were high enough in the hierarchy to enjoy the status of sheikh. All male members of the family were still entitled to a state salary, paid irrespective of other income earned as government employees or from private sources. Infant boys in the ruling branch of the family, the A category, received a stipend of QR 4,000 per month ($1,100). Male offspring in the lower-ranking B and C categories got less, but all salaries were raised every four years by differing amounts until the male child reached the age of about twenty-four. Payments generally topped out at QR 36,000 ($9,900) per month for A category recipients, QR 30,000 for B category family members, and QR 24,000 for males in the C category.[121]

Ranking sheikhs and officials of the government received additional stipends. These included up to QR 100,000 ($27,500) for meat during the holy month of Ramadan and between QR 150,000 and QR 200,000 for coffee and cardamom.[122] Additional gifts and payments were paid on special occasions such as marriage, childbirth, foreign university attendance, or vacations abroad, including extended medical treatment outside the country. Female Al Thani children were excluded from the allowance system but often benefited indirectly via gifts from their families or from the amir and his sons.

With its oil revenues, the government remained the prime source of wealth and continued to be treated as a cash cow. Criticism of the government was not unwarranted. Ministers routinely flouted the clause in the provisional constitution banning them from carrying out professional work or having commercial dealings with the state while holding office. The local paper, for example, reported that Minister of Public Works Khaled Ibn Abdullah Al Attiyah awarded a tender for a new road underpass to his own construction company, signing the contract simultaneously on behalf of the ministry and the winning bidder.[123] "In such a climate it is not strange that complaints of governmental corruption and the use of undue influence should circulate, and that the Ruling Al Thani family, who are prodigal in their expenditure on hunting, jewelry and palaces, should not come in for a large share of the criticism," Ambassador Walker wrote in early 1985.[124]

Senior civil servants liked to keep control and influence firmly in their own hands and often failed to delegate responsibility to junior staff. This tendency did not necessarily apply to the ministers, who were mainly appointed in 1972 because of their family or tribal affiliations. Most of these posts had been static in the thirteen years since Sheikh Khalifa's bloodless coup, to the extent of remaining unfilled for years after the deaths of their previous occupants in the cases of the minister of justice and the minister of municipal affairs. Other ministers, notably those heading up economy and commerce, electricity and water, industry and agriculture, and communications and transport, were widely viewed as ineffectual.[125]

Despite the demise and incompetence of several ministers from the ruling family, Al Thani family members still retained over half of the sixteen ministerial posts and continued to dominate all the major sources of power in the state. Weak or absent ministers were often supported by competent undersecretaries who ensured that the machinery of government continued to operate, if not always smoothly. Sheikh Khalifa himself delegated very little authority to his Council of Ministers, preferring to run the state from his Diwan through the undersecretaries.

Unlike his predecessors, Sheikh Khalifa had largely resisted Al Thani family pressure for more and more largesse and had never spent beyond his means. As he grew older, the amir started spending more time at his villa in Geneva, leaving his son and heir apparent, Hamad Ibn Khalifa, in charge. "The Crown Prince continues to grow in stature (metaphorically as well as physically) and should in time prove a worthy successor to his father," the British Foreign Office opined in early 1985.[126] Sheikh Hamad was well liked by the Qataris, especially the country's youth, and had the support of many of the Al Thani. These included his uncle Sheikh Khalid, the powerful minister of the interior—who was also his father-in-law after Hamad married one of Khalid's daughters.

The amir now seemed to trust his sons more than his brothers, and his brothers more than his distant Al Thani relatives and other important Qataris. Sheikh Hamad was also the minister of defense and commander-in-chief of the armed forces, while Abdul Aziz Ibn Khalifa continued to run the important Ministry of Finance and Petroleum under his father's tutelage. Abdullah Ibn Khalifa, the amir's other prominent son, was playing an increasingly central role in the military.

OPEC GIVES UP DEFENDING OIL PRICES THROUGH OUTPUT REDUCTIONS

Qatar was continuing to honor its 280,000 barrels per day OPEC quota, even producing under this ceiling in December 1984 and January 1985. There was no question that OPEC itself was facing an existential problem following years of declining demand for its oil. The organization's production in early 1985 averaged below 16 million barrels per day, down nearly 50 percent from a daily rate of 31 million barrels in 1979. This was due to the combination of lower world energy consumption and a rapid rise in oil supplies from the North Sea, Mexico, West Africa, Southeast Asia, and other non-OPEC producers in the Middle East. OPEC had taken on the role of the world's residual oil supplier, responding to every oil price crisis since 1982 with production cuts that allowed other producers to maximize output in a period of declining oil demand.

Qatari officials like Ali Jaidah weren't at all happy with this role. "In the 1980s OPEC finds itself producing well below the levels consistent with the immediate revenue needs of its members," the QGPC head and former OPEC secretary general said in a speech to a petroleum conference held in Bahrain in early 1985. "The burden carried by OPEC members would have been just tolerable if non-OPEC output had remained broadly constant. But the growth in non-OPEC supplies has made this burden intolerable."[127] Ali Jaidah also warned that OPEC production was now so low that members were no longer able to make further cuts voluntarily. Indeed, the organization's production discipline—and Qatar's own quota adherence—was starting to unravel. Many OPEC members were also openly flouting the official price system.

Saudi Arabia was the notable exception, and soon began warning of market chaos. King Fahd put his fellow OPEC members on notice that the kingdom, which had reduced its own production to its lowest level in twenty years by mid-1985, would turn the taps back on unless the rest of OPEC stopped pushing discounted oil into the market.[128] Qatar's production, which had risen to 300,000 barrels per day, fell back to a daily average of 250,000 barrels in June 1985. The more serious transgressors in OPEC followed suit after dire warnings from Saudi Arabia that it was no longer prepared to act as a swing producer.

Oil ministers failed to agree on a redistribution of output at an extraordinary OPEC meeting held in Austria in early October 1985.[129] Qatar was one of several members to request quota increases, along with war-torn Iraq, Ecuador, and Gabon. Libya announced it would produce more if the others were given higher quotas, while Nigeria said its present allocation was only a temporary concession and that it intended to revert to its previous, considerably higher quota. The Iranians declared they would produce two extra barrels for every additional one produced by Iraq. Saudi Arabia made good on its pledge to forswear its role as swing producer, increasing its production from a self-imposed low of 2.25 million barrels per day in June to 4.1 million barrels per day in November. OPEC production hit 18.075 million barrels per day that same month, including 350,000 barrels per day from Qatar.[130]

At its next meeting, held in Geneva in December 1985, OPEC formally declared that it would henceforth be concerned with securing market share rather than defending oil prices through output reductions. The statement issued at the end of the conference said the market share goal should be "consistent with necessary income of member countries," suggesting a revenue objective rather than a specific output target.[131] Oil markets plunged, and OPEC's system of fixed prices totally collapsed, replaced by a chaotic patchwork of netback and other market-related pricing arrangements. Within a few months, Europe's Brent crude oil benchmark sank below $10 per barrel, while OPEC production surpassed 20 million barrels per day by mid-1986.[132]

Qatar's own production reached 400,000 barrels per day in the summer of 1986, while the average price of its two crude oil grades fell to a low of $7 per barrel.[133] Prices subsequently recovered to around $12 per barrel by the end of 1986, but they were still far off the 1981 peak of $35. The resulting income slump, together with serious but unforeseen expenditures linked to a border clash with Bahrain over the Dibal shoal in April, forced the government to withdraw about $800 million from its financial reserves in 1986. This was up from 1985, when Qatar withdrew just $200 million.[134] The country also sharply increased its debt load, hiking borrowing from foreign banks by over 44 percent to $532 million in 1986 according to the Basel-based Bank for International Settlements.[135] Qatar's financial reserves were estimated at $12 billion at the end of 1986, while the amir and his close relatives were reckoned to have private investments amounting to a further $12 billion abroad.[136]

On November 26, 1985, only days before the OPEC meeting in Geneva, Sheikh Khalifa unceremoniously removed Ali Jaidah as managing director of QGPC and appointed Jaidah's deputy, Rashid Ibn Awaidah Al Thani, as the new head of the state-owned oil company. Ali Jaidah's close associate Ahmad Hassan Bilal was also removed from his post as deputy executive manager of QGPC Offshore and replaced with Ajlan Al Kawari, who had previously led the reservoir engineering group. Press reports at the time of the shakeup at QGPC said that Ali Jaidah was expected to join the teaching faculty at Britain's Oxford University, where he had graduated with a degree in economics. There was also speculation that he was in line for an ambassadorial appointment.[137]

A little over a year later, in December 1986, Dr. Jabir Al Marri was appointed as deputy general manager of QGPC under Sheikh Rashid. He was also made a member of the company's board of directors. Al Marri's name had first surfaced publicly in late 1984 with his appointment to the gas steering committee overseeing the North field development, and he assumed the role of project head following Sheikh Rashid's appointment as QGPC's managing director. The decree appointing Al Marri to his new post at QGPC and his seat on the board was issued not by the amir, but by Crown Prince Sheikh Hamad Ibn Khalifa. He and Al Marri had a long working relationship.

QATAR'S NEW EXPLORATION ROUND ATTRACTS U.S. OIL COMPANIES

With OPEC abandoning production restraint to recapture market share, efforts were under way to reinvigorate Qatar's moribund exploration sector. In mid-1985 QGPC entered into its first exploration- and production-sharing agreement since the ill-fated Holcar deal in 1976. The deal was signed with Standard Oil Company of Ohio, or Sohio, on June 13, 1985. It covered 12,000 square kilometers offshore from just south of Khor on the peninsula's east coast to the border with Abu Dhabi and out to the west of the Hawar Islands. Sohio, which at the time was majority-owned by BP, agreed to shoot a 4,000 line-kilometer seismic survey and drill five exploratory wells in the first four-year period, followed by another three wells with a total depth of 30,000 feet in a second two-year exploration phase.[138] If Sohio found oil in commercial quantities and a subsequent field development program was approved by the government, production of up to 15,000 barrels per day would be split 80–20 in favor of QGPC after cost recovery. This would rise to 90–10, also in Qatar's favor, on output over 60,000 barrels per day.

Qatar opened three other oil and gas exploration areas, Block 2 onshore and Blocks 5 and 6 offshore, to international bidding the same month the deal with Sohio was signed.[139] Located off Qatar's northeast coast, Block 5 extended into the boundaries of the North field. Block 6 adjoined it to the east, above Qatar's already-producing offshore oil fields. Block 2 was onshore, covering 8,000 square kilometers in the southern part of the peninsula. The existing Khuff gas-bearing structure in the North field, and any extension of this formation that might be discovered, was excluded from the three blocks. There had been indications that some of the open territory overlapping and adjoining the North field was also rich in oil, and the local press reported that forty-six mainly American companies had shown interest in tendering bids.[140]

Amoco (the former Standard Oil of Indiana) won the bidding for Block 2. On February 17, 1986, it signed a twenty-five-year exploration- and production-sharing agreement that essentially spanned the whole of the Qatar peninsula except for the Dukhan field in the west and another block in the northeast.[141] Amoco agreed to acquire 4,000 line-kilometers of seismic data, drill seven exploratory wells, and, if necessary, sink three more appraisal wells in the first six-year exploration period. Two more exploration phases—a second period lasting two years and a third three-year period—would follow. Production-sharing terms mirrored the Sohio deal, although they reportedly contained more gradations over the output spectrum in the percentage share allocated between QGPC and Amoco.[142]

Qatar's oil production averaged 306,000 barrels per day in 1985, down nearly 24 percent from 1984. Output from the onshore Dukhan field surpassed offshore production, reversing the recent trend that had seen slightly higher flows from Qatar's marine fields. Onshore output averaged 166,000 barrels per day in 1985 while the three offshore fields accounted for 140,000 barrels per day. No exploration wells were drilled by QGPC in the offshore sector in 1985, although the state company drilled and tested three appraisal wells, two at the North gas field and a third at the Bul Hanine oil field.[143] QGPC also drilled six test wells into pre-Khuff zones at the onshore Dukhan field, drilling down to a depth of about eighteen thousand feet. No commercial gas was encountered. Drilling activity fell, with QGPC's four rigs drilling just eleven exploration and development wells in 1985 compared to twenty-five the previous year. These included four development wells in the Uwainat reservoir at the Bul Hanine field.

Associated gas output fell in line with crude oil, dropping from an average of nearly 315 million cubic feet per day in 1984 to 246 million cubic feet daily in 1985. Non-associated gas output increased to 342 million cubic feet per day, up from 277 million cubic feet per day in 1984. This was mostly gas from the Dukhan field's deep Khuff formation, augmented by 8 million cubic feet per day of Dukhan cap gas.[144] Capacity at the Dukhan gas cap, which was first produced in 1984, was rated at a much higher 150 million cubic feet per day, but this gas was only produced on an emergency basis to meet peak requirements. Cap gas accumulates in the upper portions of a reservoir where the pressure, temperature, and fluid characteristics are conducive to free gas not dissolved in reservoir liquids.

Electricity generators, water desalination plants, and local industrial users consumed an average of 360 million cubic feet per day of natural gas in 1985, an increase of 4 percent.[145] The natural gas liquids plants at Umm Said received less associated gas with the decline in crude oil production, with inflows falling from 109 million cubic feet per day in 1984 to 86 million cubic feet in 1985. Ethane and other NGL production dropped as a result, decreasing to 1.1 million tons in 1985 from 1.4 million tons in 1984.[146] The figures included the equivalent of 381,000 tons of ethane-rich gas as well as 329,000 tons of propane, 220,000 tons of butane, and 173,000 tons of plant condensate. Oil producers used another 67 million cubic feet of gas daily in their own field operations during 1985, down from 87 million cubic feet in 1984.

WINTERSHALL CONSORTIUM REFERS DISPUTE
TO ARBITRATION

In late 1985, apparently at the invitation of the Ministry of Finance and Petroleum, Wintershall and its partners offered to develop the North field at their own expense.[147] The five-member group proposed to supply 600 million cubic feet of gas per day to the domestic sector free of charge and recover its $500 million investment through the export sale of about 35,000 barrels per day of condensates. In considering the proposal, the Ministry of Finance and Petroleum laid down several conditions.[148] Two of these—that the consortium carry out its work in accordance with detailed engineering specifications supplied by QGPC and that it operate under the supervision of the managing consultant appointed by the Qatari oil company—were anodyne, if not entirely welcome.

More controversially, the Wintershall-led group would have to surrender gas rights in its adjoining acreage if the government accepted the North field proposal. The consortium had never discovered oil in commercial quantities in its block primarily because it wasn't allowed to drill in the western part of its contract area near the border with Bahrain. Seismic investigation had identified a potentially oil-bearing structure called Structure A at the disputed Dibal shoal some forty miles north of the Hawar Islands. Sheikh Khalifa had promised in 1978 to give the group more time to examine this structure, presumably as compensation for holding off on drilling in the sensitive border area. That same year, the consortium relinquished 50 percent of its contract area in accordance with the terms of its exploration- and production-sharing agreement. There were no further relinquishments, and the group was never asked to give up its rights to Structure A or the area around Dibal.

The consortium had more luck finding gas. In April 1980 Wintershall and its partners informed the government of Qatar they had discovered non-associated gas in substantial quantities and that in their view these reserves could be economically developed. This followed tests of the consortium's Qatar Marine Dia exploration well, which had found gas in the Khuff formation. After it became apparent that its July 1981 proposal to the government for a joint LNG project in the North field based on an 80-20 production split with QGPC wouldn't be acceptable, the consortium proposed a second project in May 1982: to produce 400 million cubic feet per day of gas for domestic use based solely on wells in its contract area. This was rejected on technical grounds by QGPC, who came back in 1983 with plans for a joint development of the same size drawing exclusively on wells in its adjacent North field contract area. QGPC later expanded this proposal further to 600 million cubic feet per day.

An integral part of the government's proposals involved the surrender by the consortium of any further rights to develop gas reserves in its adjacent concession. QGPC had never agreed with the Wintershall-led group that these reserves could be developed economically. As a result, the two sides had yet to negotiate a utilization plan for this non-associated gas. Frustrated with the lack of progress and unwilling to give up its own concession, the consortium referred the dispute to international arbitration in April 1986.[149] Wintershall and its four partners alleged that Qatar had breached the exploration- and production-sharing agreement and denied the consortium's contractual rights by withholding exploration permission for the Structure A area and by failing to agree on further arrangements for the non-associated gas discovered in 1980.[150]

Within days of the arbitration notice, Dibal became the focus of renewed hostility with Bahrain when four Qatari helicopters landed on the tiny shoal and forcibly removed twenty-nine workers employed by the Bahrain Defence Force. They had been engaged by the Dutch firm Ballast Nedam to construct a coast guard station for Bahrain on Dibal. Saudi Arabia immediately dispatched Minister of Defense Prince Sultan Ibn Abdul Aziz to Qatar and Bahrain for talks. Qatar soon withdrew its troops, and the construction workers were returned unharmed after seventeen days, but the Qatari government still declared the area around the shoal a restricted zone and warned other vessels to stay away.[151]

Saudi Arabia had been trying to mediate the territorial dispute between Bahrain and Qatar for some time without success. Dr. Hassan Kamel, the amir's influential Egyptian adviser, suggested taking the case to international arbitration. In late 1984 the Qatari ruler had written King Fahd suggesting that the Saudi ruler put the case for arbitration to the Bahrainis. This was done, but Bahrain took nearly three years to consider the matter. Finally, in December 1987 Saudi Arabia revealed that Qatar and Bahrain had agreed to settle their border dispute through international arbitration. Two months later Sheikh Khalifa announced that his government and the government of Bahrain had submitted their dispute over the sovereignty of Dibal and the Hawar Islands to the International Court of Justice at The Hague.

Bahrain subsequently objected to the idea of international arbitration, arguing that it would prefer a friendly out-of-court settlement arranged by its Gulf neighbors. More foot-dragging followed, and it wasn't until the end of 1988 that the Gulf Cooperation Council announced at a summit held in Bahrain that its member states would arbitrate the territorial dispute between the two countries. By late December both Bahrain and Qatar had agreed to GCC mediation over a period of six months, ending in mid-1989.[152] The GCC agreed to Qatar's request that if the council's mediation was unsuccessful, the dispute would ultimately be referred to the International Court of Justice.

CHAPTER 12

Qatar Embarks on First Stage of North Field Gas Project

Amid controversies with international oil companies, border disputes with neighbors, turmoil in OPEC, and confusion over development of the North gas field, Qatar continued to explore potential markets for the LNG it hoped eventually to produce. Shortly after his appointment as managing director of QGPC in late-1985, Sheikh Rashid led a mission to Seoul to discuss potential LNG sales opportunities in South Korea. The delegation, which also included representatives from BP, CFP, and Marubeni, met with officials from the Ministry of Energy & Resources and Korea's state-owned electric power and gas companies. The high-level visit to Seoul coincided with more negative news from Japan. Marubeni's Isao Hiroe reported the Japanese government had told both Qatar and the *sogo shoshas* (trading houses) that there was "no space for importation of LNG until 1995."[1] The Marubeni executive also warned Qatar it would have to compete on price with Indonesia and Malaysia in the 1990s. "We may be able to market Qatar gas in Korea, Taiwan and other Far East countries, besides Japan, if we could create confidence among ultimate consumers about the economic viability of gas usage and its stable supply," Hiroe said in early 1986.[2]

India was also mentioned as a potential market for LNG. Indian government officials grandiosely predicted in late 1986 that the South Asian country could consume nearly all the 6 million tons per year forecast to come from Qatargas when its cross-country Hajira-Bijapur-Jagdishpur gas pipeline was complete.[3] The pipeline project was started in 1986 following the incorporation of the Gas Authority of India Limited (now known as GAIL India Limited) to supply gas to fertilizer plants in the northern state of Uttar Pradesh. Sheikh Rashid visited New Delhi in January 1987 for further talks with senior Indian officials on the LNG offer. These efforts to market Qatari gas had yet to yield concrete results, and pressure was growing on the government to proceed independently with the first stage of North field development for the domestic sector. Frustrated with Marubeni's marketing efforts, QGPC engaged the New York–based consultancy firm Poten & Partners to explore all options for potential LNG sales.

QGPC was making headway on appointing a management consultant who would also perform detailed engineering for stage one. It had negotiated Bechtel down on price following the opening of bids the previous September. Bechtel had teamed up with Technip, and QGPC initially refused to even look at the U.S.-French duo's offer because it wasn't consulted on the decision to bid together. Just as this difficulty was resolved and negotiations were in full swing, the Qataris leaked that they were also considering an offer from Amoco to produce 400–600 million cubic feet per day of North field gas for domestic use. Like Wintershall's earlier proposal, Amoco would supply this gas to QGPC free of charge and recover its estimated $300 million investment from the sale of condensates. Amoco also offered QGPC at least 57.5 percent of the income from these exports under a new production-sharing agreement.[4] Yet another proposal was floated by Marubeni, who was willing to finance the first stage of work and market the condensates and other gas liquids for a percentage of the profits.

Bechtel was asked to study a scaled-down development that would reduce the production capacity in the first stage to 600 million cubic feet per day and that, like Amoco's proposal, would eliminate costly infrastructure to reinject surplus gas into the onshore Dukhan Khuff reservoir.[5] QGPC ultimately decided to proceed with its initial plans, however, reconfiguring the project to lower the cost estimate to $950 million from $1.5 billion. A contract for the management consultancy, detailed engineering design and procurement was signed with Bechtel and Technip on May 20, 1987, and the Qataris unveiled plans for a production cluster at the North field with nominal capacity of 800 million cubic feet daily. It included two wellhead platforms, a production platform with two 400 million cubic feet per day treatment trains, a riser platform, a utilities platform, an accommodation platform, and a flare.[6] These six platforms would be installed in about 50 meters of water and connected by bridges.

The offshore production facilities were to be linked to the landfall point at Ras Laffan by two 80-kilometer subsea pipelines. One 36-inch subsea pipeline would transport dry gas to shore while a second 22-inch line would be used for liquids. From Ras Laffan, the two lines would run 130 kilometers alongside the route to Umm Said, where the NGL-1 plant would be modified to produce 700 million cubic feet per day of lean gas together with 1.6 million tons per year of propane, butane, naphtha, and condensates. Much of the savings achieved from scaling down the project's costs had come from full utilization of this existing onshore infrastructure. Another 70-kilometer pipeline would be constructed to reach the Dukhan field, where surplus lean gas after liquids removal would be reinjected into the Khuff reservoir. QGPC estimated that 400–450 million cubic feet per day would be needed in the domestic sector, leaving 250 to 300 million cubic feet per day for reinjection.[7]

Gas liquids, including 500,000 tons per year of liquid petroleum gas and 1.2 million tons per year of condensate, were expected to generate enough revenue to pay for the project within five to six years.[8] This first development stage would be fully owned and financed by QGPC, who planned to fund the project mainly through international borrowing guaranteed by the state-owned firm. Shortly after the contract with Bechtel and Technip was signed, Bechtel's managing director said the two firms expected to complete the detailed engineering design within four to six months, followed by the commencement of construction work by mid-1988.[9] Construction would take two and a half years to complete, implying a commissioning date for the domestic phase of the North field project at the end of 1990 or early 1991.

QATAR'S FINANCIAL DIFFICULTIES MOUNT AS OIL INCOME DROPS

Even this scaled-down version of the North field's first development stage was beginning to look like a financial stretch. The government's total monthly income was estimated at approximately QR 547 million ($150 million) in late 1986.[10] Nondiscretionary spending on salaries for government workers and the armed forces, running costs, and minor capital expenditures cost the country about QR 406 million per month.[11] The surplus of QR 141 million was not sufficient to cover commitments for arms deals, outside aid obligations, contributions to international organizations, and payments on outstanding debts to contractors. Unless the price of oil recovered or the government was prepared to draw down its financial reserves significantly, it would have no capital available for major projects.

Many big-spending projects had already been delayed or abandoned, and general expenditures were reduced. The government had stopped providing building loans for real estate in 1984, saving it about QR 1,500 million ($412 million) per annum.[12] Payment of compensation for land acquired by the government, amounting to an estimated QR 400 million annually, was suspended temporarily in November 1986. The government was considering the imposition of charges for electricity and water, which were free for Qataris and considerably below the cost of production for expatriates. This was politically sensitive, however, and the amir was loath to impose fees at a time when government salaries were being cut back and efforts were under way to reduce the number of civil servants. Medical services, including dentistry, were still free for Qataris, but fees were being considered in this sector as well. In 1986 health care cost the government about QR 644 million ($177 million).[13]

The government employed 33,035 people, over half of them Qatari, in 1984. This represented slightly less than a third of the entire labor force. Government workers did not include those employed in what the Central Statistical Organization referred to as "mixed sector" institutions, which encompassed the Qatar General Petroleum Corporation and other partially state-owned industrial firms operating in Umm Said. Among the government institutions, the Ministry of Education was the largest employer, with 9,062 workers, while another 6,421 were employed at the Ministry of Electricity and Water. The third-largest government employer was the Hammad General Hospital, with 3,245 employees. Over a third of all government employees were illiterate or only functionally literate without any secondary education.[14] QGPC was the largest employer in the mixed sector, with 1,617 employees. A large majority were foreign non-Arab hires.

On December 20, 1986, with OPEC's strategy of increasing market share in tatters, the organization reached a new accord on production and prices after much gnashing of teeth. A ceiling of 15.8 million barrels per day for the first half of 1987 was introduced, including a quota of 285,000 barrels per day for Qatar. War-torn Iraq refused to accept any limit on its production level and was only allocated a nominal quota. The former system of fixed pricing was resurrected despite having collapsed in ruins the previous year. OPEC members pledged to eliminate netback and other market-related pricing with the aim of boosting the organization's reference price to $18 per barrel. Qatar had already followed Abu Dhabi in abandoning netback pricing in favor of linking its prices to Oman's system of retroactive monthly prices based on spot market values. It subsequently notified its crude oil lifters that the new OPEC-set official price for Dukhan would be $17.82 per barrel and $17.67 per barrel for Qatar Marine.[15]

Qatar's two main Japanese customers Mitsubishi and Marubeni agreed to pay official prices but refused to lift their full contract quantities.[16] Other buyers melted away when QGPC resisted pressure to discount official prices. Sales for February 1987 plummeted to 180,000 barrels per day, and firm nominations by lifters for March were even lower.[17] Qatar was not alone in facing fierce resistance to its official pricing. In Saudi Arabia the four international oil companies in Aramco lifted only 700,000 barrels per day in February, not the 1.3 million they originally nominated.[18] With its nominations for March dependent on a price flexibility it was not prepared to give, Qatar decided to contract oceangoing tankers to store its unsold crude oil rather than shut in production, chartering three or four large tankers for use as floating storage.[19]

The country also picked up a new contract for 20,000 barrels per day in early 1987 with the U.S. major Mobil—at official selling prices. Another deal was negotiated with Eni's Agip, who agreed to lift 20,000 barrels per day. Pressure was brought to bear on other contract customers, who were told by QGPC that they faced potential blacklisting and penalties of $4 per barrel for volumes underlifted in March.[20] Despite this arm-twisting, production cratered with the reintroduction of official prices. Qatar produced just 180,000 barrels per day in February and March, nearly 40 percent below its OPEC quota.

During this uncertainty, Abdul Aziz Ibn Khalifa unveiled deep spending cuts in the budget for the fiscal year beginning March 1, 1987. Spending was slashed nearly 22 percent, and reductions in current expenditures were adopted for the first time.[21] Revenue, estimated based on OPEC's December agreement to control prices, was put at QR 6,750 million ($1.85 billion). Total spending was budgeted at QR 12,229 million, including current spending of QR 9,450 million and QR 2,770 million on major projects, leaving a deficit of QR 5,470 million ($1.5 billion).[22] As in past years, the actual deficit was expected to end up substantially lower as government ministries responded to pressure to reduce their expenditures below budgeted levels. This deficit was also likely to be financed, as it had been in 1986, by drawing down the country's monetary reserves.

Qatar's oil output fell even further in April 1987 to 150,000 barrels per day, only slightly more than half of its OPEC quota, as QGPC struggled to place volumes at official prices. After three months of exceptionally low liftings, the state-owned oil company finally started granting discounts. Production soon jumped to 320,000 barrels per day, and Qatar was reported to be virtually sold out for June and July.[23] The December 1986 OPEC accord had included graduated production increases for the organization through 1987, with output rising from 15.8 million barrels per day in the first half to 16.6 million barrels per day in the third quarter and 18.3 million barrels per day in the fourth quarter. Amid concerns about Iraq's unbridled expansion and other cheating within the thirteen-member organization, however, this was revised in June to 16.6 million for the second half of 1987. Qatar's quota was set at 299,000 barrels per day for the entire six-month period.

Within weeks it was widely acknowledged that OPEC was producing over its 16.6 million barrels per day ceiling. Both the UAE and Qatar had stopped submitting data to the OPEC secretariat—the UAE as far back as the beginning of 1987 and Qatar from June onward. This had created a wide gap between OPEC's own production figures and those from secondary sources. The confusion was compounded in August when Iraq also stopped submitting data to the secretariat.[24] Rough estimates had OPEC output averaging 19 million barrels per day in the third quarter of 1987, reaching a peak of 19.7 million barrels per day in August before retreating to 18.7 million barrels per day in September.[25] Production was back up again to 19 million barrels per day by December 1987, when OPEC met in Vienna to go over its existing production accord, although this time it didn't bother assigning even a nominal quota to freewheeling Iraq.

Oil prices deteriorated further after Vienna, falling several dollars below the eighteen-dollars-per-barrel reference price. This put renewed pressure on individual OPEC members to protect their customer base by switching to market-related pricing. Qatar, whose relatively weak slate of lifters always left it vulnerable to market downswings, had already notified buyers that from October 1987 it would apply a price formula linked to spot prices for Oman crude.[26] Iran, Kuwait, and Iraq followed with discounts of their own, while the UAE was soon openly repudiating its quota. Even Saudi Arabia wavered. Reports surfaced that the U.S. companies in Aramco were receiving rebates on their oil purchases. Although invoiced at official prices, the Aramco partners were making provisional payments on a market price basis and deferring final settlement until a later date.[27] Within months, the price concessions were extended to all Saudi Arabia's customers.

Just two years after he was appointed as managing director of QGPC, Rashid Ibn Awaidah Al Thani was replaced by his deputy, Jabir Al Marri, who was appointed as acting managing director of QGPC on December 23, 1987.[28] Al Marri was already heading up the North field gas project, having assumed this role after Sheikh Rashid took over the helm at QGPC from Ali Jaidah in November 1985. Eight months after his appointment as acting managing director, Al Marri was officially confirmed as QGPC's managing director by Amiri decree on July 12, 1988. This coincided with a new law transferring responsibility for all negotiations and contracts involving the exploration and development of oil and gas to QGPC, further empowering the state-owned firm.[29] These had previously been handled by the Department of Petroleum Affairs at the Ministry of Finance and Petroleum.

Sheikh Rashid owed his position in large part to Abdul Aziz Ibn Khalifa. The decision to replace him at QGPC with Dr. Al Marri reflected the crown prince's plans to neutralize his brother, widely viewed as a potential rival for the throne, by putting his own loyalists in positions of both political and economic power. Wresting responsibility for all contract negotiations with foreign firms away from the Ministry of Finance and Petroleum, which Sheikh Abdul Aziz had long headed, and giving it to QGPC under Al Marri can also be seen in this context. Hamad Ibn Khalifa was deliberately moving into position nearly a decade before he would act to remove his father in another bloodless coup echoing Amir Khalifa's own overthrow of his cousin Ahmad in 1972.

FINANCIAL ADVISER SELECTED FOR NORTH FIELD GAS PROJECT

Meanwhile, Qatar General Petroleum Corporation had been narrowing its search for a financial adviser for its North field project. Still in contention were Morgan Grenfell & Company, the venerable British investment bank (acquired by Deutsche Bank in 1990); the French investment bank Banque Paribas (known today as BNP Paribas); and First Boston Corporation (acquired by Credit Suisse in 1990). QGPC appointed First Boston as its financial adviser in October 1987. Reports suggested the state-owned firm would fund 60 percent of the project via international borrowing and export credit facilities, 20 percent via its own resources, and 20 percent via the sale of crude oil to contractors.[30]

A project task force was set up by QGPC to work with Bechtel and Technip on the detailed engineering designs. QGPC awarded the contract for the iron and steel for the wellhead platforms to the UK's Kurvers International Supply

Services Limited in late 1987. The platforms were built by Abu Dhabi's National Petroleum Construction Company. Brown and Root of the United Kingdom won the installation contract for the offshore structures. More minor tenders related to the offshore pipe route survey, drilling equipment, heat exchangers, and a nitrogen unit went to U.S., West German, Japanese, French, UK, and Italian firms. Onshore, a temporary camp for two hundred workers was being built and site preparation for the natural gas liquids unit at Umm Said was under way. Italy's Nuovo Pignone (part of the Eni group) had agreed to supply three compressors for the NGL unit and two for the Dukhan gas injection station.

Nearly seventeen years after Shell's first discovery well in November 1971, actual development drilling at the North field was finally ready to begin. The two wellhead platforms, each of which would be used to drill eight wells over two years, were loaded from the fabrication yard in Abu Dhabi on June 20, 1988, and towed the short distance to drilling sites some eighty kilometers off the Qatari coast.[31] By the end of July they had been installed in fifty-two meters of water. On August 22 the Danish-owned rig *Maersk Victory*, under contract to QGPC, started drilling the first development well, targeting a depth of eleven thousand feet.[32] Another rig, the *Harurya-9*, was hired from the Japan Drilling Company. It arrived off the Qatari coast to begin drilling work in October 1988.

QGPC was financing this initial work from oil sales, the proceeds from which had been set aside for the project since mid-1987. The amount of crude oil allocated to the project had started out at twenty thousand barrels per day, but it quickly rose to thirty thousand barrels per day and by late 1988 had reached forty thousand barrels per day. Overall costs for the first stage of the North field development were trending up, partly because of the weak U.S. dollar. Dr. Al Marri told the trade press in August 1988 that QGPC hoped to complete the project within a revised budget of $1.3 billion, possibly less depending on the competition among bidders. Further funds would be necessary as development spending geared up, and Al Marri suggested that Qatar might enter the international capital market within a few months to borrow as much as $600 million.[33]

Qatar was already relying heavily on non-associated gas to meet local demand, and consumption was expected to increase sharply with completion of the North field project in late 1990. Output of Khuff gas from the Dukhan field had averaged 400 million cubic feet per day in 1987, its highest level ever. This compared to just 223 million cubic feet per day of associated gas, which fell along with crude oil.[34] The fertilizer company QAFCO was finalizing plans for a third ammonia unit with capacity of 1,500 tons per day, while petrochemical producer QAPCO dusted off a long-delayed project for a second low-density polyethylene plant to utilize the surplus ethylene it had been making since the start-up of its ethane recovery unit in 1986. Other gas-based industrial projects, including an energy-intensive aluminum smelter and methanol plant, were under discussion with companies from China, India, South Korea, Japan, and the United States.

Oil production averaged 293,000 barrels per day in 1987, of which 254,000 was exported and the balance refined domestically at the two Umm Said refineries.[35] This represented a drop of over 12 percent from Qatar's 1986 output, which had come in at 334,000 barrels per day. The onshore Dukhan field contributed 140,000 barrels per day of the 1987 total, while production of the offshore fields of Idd el-Shargi, Maydan Mahzam, and Bul Hanine averaged 153,000 barrels per day.

ARBITRATION TRIBUNAL ISSUES AWARD IN WINTERSHALL DISPUTE

Two years after Wintershall and its partners referred their contract dispute with the government of Qatar for arbitration, the three-man tribunal in The Hague issued a final award on May 31, 1988. The tribunal determined that QGPC had no obligation to enter a joint venture involving gas reserves outside the Wintershall consortium's contract area, nor was the state-owned firm required to guarantee a domestic market for natural gas as the proposals by Wintershall and its partners had in effect entailed. It rejected claims by the consortium that QGPC had reneged on an agreement involving the 600-million-cubic-feet-per-day gas-condensate proposal first floated by the government in 1983 and subsequently revived by the consortium in late 1985, or that the failure to agree to a domestic utilization plan for this gas was a breach of QGPC's duty to negotiate in good faith.

However, the tribunal also concluded that Wintershall and its partners had reasonably assumed negotiations with QGPC on a joint agreement relating to North field reserves beyond the consortium's contract area would achieve a positive outcome. This presumption—and the failure of the government to terminate these negotiations—had prevented the consortium from independently developing the gas reserves in its own area, the so-called go-it-alone option allowed under its exploration- and production-sharing agreement. The tribunal therefore extended the duration for gas exploitation in the consortium's concession by eight years from the date of the final award, until June 1, 1996. If the consortium was producing gas by this time, then the production-sharing terms agreed with QGPC would run until 2011. As for the potentially oil-bearing Structure A near the border with Bahrain, the tribunal ruled that relinquishment provisions would only begin once the consortium was permitted to begin exploration activities in this politically sensitive area.

The tribunal said that one potential go-it-alone option open to the consortium was a condensate stripping project, where the gas liquids are stripped out of the raw gas stream and the residual dry gas reinjected into the reservoir. It consequently expanded the definition of recoverable petroleum costs to expressly include reinjection costs at a maximum annual rate of 40 percent of the net production. But the tribunal allowed the parties involved to decide how they complied with their legal duty to offtake the remaining 60 percent of the net production, and it refused to legally oblige the government to enter into a joint marketing agreement with the consortium. "It is entirely a matter of the Government's discretion to decide in what manner it will comply with its legal duty to off-take the Natural Gas to which it is entitled, e.g., by agreeing with the Claimants on joint marketing, by re-injecting this Natural Gas, by separately marketing this gas, or otherwise," the tribunal explained in its award.[36]

Despite the time extensions given to Wintershall and its partners, the award was a victory for Qatar in that the tribunal confirmed the consortium's exploration- and production-sharing agreement did not give it any participatory rights in the main development of the North field.[37] The arbitrators also rejected claims by the consortium of breach of contract and wrongful termination of the exploration- and production-sharing agreement by the government, and they refused to grant damages, including reimbursement for the nearly $60 million the Wintershall group had spent on exploration. The consortium still had the option of developing its find, which the Ministry of Finance and Petroleum acknowledged covered "a part of the southern fringes of the North gas field," on its own, and the arbitration award now gave it more time to do so.[38]

ILLICIT PURCHASE OF STINGER MISSILES
STRAINS RELATIONS WITH THE UNITED STATES

In an apparent rebuke to the United States, Qatar established formal ties with China on July 9, 1988. The move followed what was described as an "uneasy meeting" between Hamad Ibn Khalifa and U.S. assistant secretary of state Richard Murphy the previous month.[39] At that meeting Murphy insisted that Doha disclose how it clandestinely acquired about a dozen U.S.-made antiaircraft Stinger missiles, prized because they could be carried easily, could be fired from the shoulder, and could bring down an aircraft.[40] These had been on display in an official military parade broadcast on television; the parade's announcer even identified the missiles as Stingers. Sheikh Hamad refused to divulge the source, and the meeting ended abruptly after Murphy warned the crown prince of a deterioration in relations unless the Stingers were returned to the United States. Speculation at the time was that Qatar purchased the Stingers from Iran, who had in turn obtained them from Afghan rebels. The Afghanis had themselves been covertly supplied with the weapons by the Reagan administration to fight the Soviets.[41]

The United States had refused to sell the weapons to Qatar. But it had recently approved a request from Bahrain, with whom Qatar was still embroiled in a bitter territorial dispute over the Hawar Islands, for seventy Stinger missiles to help defend Manama against a potential Iranian attack. Murphy told Sheikh Hamad that Washington considered Bahrain, where the U.S. Navy had a small logistical base for its Persian Gulf operations, more vulnerable to Iranian threats than any other Gulf state except Kuwait. Worried about the spread of weapons through the volatile region, the 100th U.S. Congress banned any American arms sales or defense assistance to Qatar until it returned all Stinger antiaircraft missiles that had been "illegally acquired or purchased."[42] This ban was tacked on to an appropriations bill approving funding for international institutions, including the World Bank and the Asian Development Fund, for the fiscal year ending September 30, 1989. Its impact was negligible though. Qatar wasn't buying other weapons from the United States at the time, nor was it receiving any military or economic aid from Washington.

Following the establishment of formal ties with Beijing, government sources indicated that Qatar was considering buying Chinese Silkworm missiles to seek arms parity with Bahrain.[43] Three weeks after its overture to China, Doha announced that it had established full diplomatic relations with the Soviet Union. This made Qatar the fourth Arab Gulf state after Kuwait, Oman, and the UAE to have diplomatic relations with the two great communist powers. Bahrain and Saudi Arabia were the lone holdouts. The moves toward China and the Soviet Union, as well as the break with Washington over the Stinger purchases, reflected the growing independence of Qatar's foreign policy from that of Saudi Arabia.

This shift away from Riyadh had been apparent for a few years. It was most clearly illustrated by Doha's efforts to ensure cooperation with Iran as development of the critically important North gas field progressed.

Iran was publicly laying claim to a portion of the North field. Its oil minister, Gholam-Reza Aghazadeh, told Tehran radio in early 1989 that, based on the results of a recent seismic survey carried out for the National Iranian Oil Company by the Dutch firm Delft Geophysical, the gas field extended at least twenty kilometers into Iranian waters.[44] This was much further than the Qataris had acknowledged in 1985, when Crown Prince Hamad told the British ambassador that the field stretched "a few miles" beyond the maritime border. Tehran estimated that 30 percent of the whole structure, which it said contained wet gas with a high liquids content, lay on the Iranian side of the demarcation line with Qatar. Iran claimed that several oil fields in the UAE, including the Fateh and Fallah oil fields off the emirate of Dubai and two other fields offshore Sharjah and Ras Al Khaimah, stretched into its waters as well.[45]

The Iranian oil minister said gas from the Iranian side of the North field structure—which Iran would eventually name South Pars to differentiate it from the portion of the field that lay in Qatari waters—could be piped directly to the 1,200-million-cubic-feet-per-day Kangan-Nar gas processing plant under construction on the Iranian coast about one hundred kilometers to the north.[46] Several months later Iran's newly elected president, Hashemi Rafsanjani, pointedly announced that permission would be given to the Oil Ministry to seek out foreign firms interested in developing its offshore gas reserves, including Iran's share of the North field.[47] This was part of a broader emphasis on foreign investment in Iran's oil and gas industries as the government's shaky finances prevented it from making the appropriate investment to expand production without help. It also represented a significant ideological shift for the Iranian government.

Iran was preoccupied with reconstructing war-ravaged infrastructure at its main oil export terminal on Kharg Island, and with repairing over half a dozen severely damaged offshore oil fields following its bloody eight-year conflict with Iraq. The Iran–Iraq war had ended on August 20, 1988, without a clear winner when Tehran formally accepted a cease-fire brokered by the United Nations. War damage to Iran's offshore oil platforms was assessed at $1.5 billion, while the government thought it would cost another $300 million to repair damaged onshore facilities. Iran could use local expertise to repair its onshore infrastructure, but the offshore oil field rehabilitation work would require the involvement of foreign contractors.

The Iranian claims reportedly took Doha by surprise, with Qatari officials insisting publicly that there had been no formal communication from Tehran on the North field.[48] They were keen to assure the Iranians that the sixteen wells being drilled as part of the first stage of the North field development were located some forty kilometers away from the median line between the two countries. Oil industry sources in Qatar also explained that these wells would be drilled entirely into the Khuff 4 zone.[49] Located at a depth of around 11,000 feet, the Khuff 4 was the most prolific and easiest to develop of the four zones from a technical perspective. Doha claimed, although not entirely accurately as it turned out, that the Khuff 4 lay entirely in Qatari waters.[50]

In an official estimate of total gas reserves—proven, probable, and possible—in the 6,000-square-kilometer North field presented publicly in late 1989, QGPC put the field's total gas reserves at 380 trillion cubic feet, or the equivalent of almost 65 billion barrels of oil.[51] The Khuff 4 zone alone contained an estimated 210 trillion cubic feet of this total. The Qataris would eventually divide the North field into a series of blocks, each about 10 × 10 kilometers in size, or the equivalent of 24,700 acres. These would be positioned over the structural accumulation of the Khuff 4 zone and oriented parallel to Qatar's maritime boundary with Iran. A buffer zone of 2 kilometers was positioned around each of these 100-square-kilometer blocks.

QATAR TAPS EUROMARKET FOR NORTH FIELD LOAN

Nine banks won the mandate to syndicate a $400 million loan for QGPC to partly finance work on the North field. The loan was divided equally between these nine lead managers at $44 million each, and syndication commenced on January 11, 1989.[52] Guaranteed by the state of Qatar, the three-year loan carried a 22.5 basis point spread over LIBOR. An estimated fifty thousand barrels per day of gas liquids and condensates from the project provided the cash flow for repayment. While the new loan represented the country's first Eurocredit since early 1984, Qatar's overall foreign debt was trending up—increasing over 15 percent from $628 million in 1986 to $724 million in 1987.[53] Because ongoing work was funded by the $400 million Eurocredit and the proceeds from the sale of forty thousand barrels per day of crude oil allocated to the project, the North field development was excluded from the government's capital spending allocations in the state budget for the fiscal year beginning April 1, 1989.[54]

While these loans were being arranged, two of the sixteen development wells at the North field had been completed and successfully tested. Several large contracts had also been awarded at the end of 1988. These included a $100 million contract with Italy's Saipem for the construction of the gas and liquids pipelines from the North field to the onshore gas treatment and separation facilities at Umm Said as well as another line to the Dukhan field for gas injection. The contract covered some 500 kilometers of pipeline in total, 160 kilometers of which would be laid offshore. Another $55 million contract was awarded to Belleli Saudi Heavy Industries Company for fourteen giant offshore modules to be manufactured at its fabrication yard in Saudi Arabia's Jubail industrial area. Weighing approximately 15,000 tons in total, these modules included the process plant as well as the necessary equipment for the gas treatment platform.

In early 1989 QGPC was on target with the North field project development. The design and engineering work was 70 percent complete and twenty-three out of twenty-four contracts representing nearly all the cost of the project were already committed. The state-owned firm announced in August that it planned to extend the project to include a $70 million gas sweeting plant at Umm Said and a $20 million sulfur processing unit to be constructed at QAPCO's petrochemical complex, and the management consultancy contract with Bechtel and Technip was revised to include consultancy and design services for these new units. The additions weren't expected to impact the timing of the field's first development stage or its completion schedule.[55] Work on the forty-one-month phase was still set to end on November 30, 1990, with commercial gas production for domestic use following at the beginning of 1991.[56]

Addressing a meeting of local business leaders in early 1989, QGPC's head, Jabir Al Marri, noted that North field gas would come online just as Khuff gas from the Dukhan field ceased completely. Non-associated gas—entirely composed of Khuff and cap gas from Dukhan—now accounted for nearly 70 percent of the gas supplied to Qatar's industrial consumers as well as its electricity and water desalination plants.[57] More gas was needed for the new electric power and water desalination complex at Wusail, where 250 megawatts of electricity and 10 million gallons per day of desalinated water was finally supposed to begin production in 1991 and 1992. Power consumption was growing annually at

5-7 percent, and officials warned that demand, particularly in the peak summer air conditioning season, was threatening to overwhelm an installed capacity of 1,095 megawatts.

Surplus gas from the North field's first stage would also fuel Qatar's industrial ambitions. QAFCO announced it was going ahead with plans to produce an additional 1,500 tons per day of ammonia and another 2,000 tons per day of urea by mid-1993. Italy's Enimont, the joint venture between state-owned Eni and Montedison, signed a memorandum of understanding with QGPC in early 1990 to carry out a feasibility study on a new methanol plant. Preliminary studies were also under way to produce the gasoline additive methyl tertiary-butyl ether, or MTBE. The British firm Davy McKee was tapped to build a $1.25 billion aluminum smelter, signing a letter of intent for the project with the Ministry of Industry and Public Works in October 1989. It would have an initial capacity of 193,000 tons per year as well as a 500-megawatt power station and desalination plant. These projects were all predicated on 250 to 300 million cubic feet per day of surplus gas becoming available.

Any project using gas from the North field's first stage would be established at the industrial city of Umm Said. But future industrial projects based on gas from the field's second or third phases were to be constructed at Ras Laffan, where the offshore pipelines came ashore. Bechtel was working on an optimization plan for Umm Said in preparation for the first-phase industry, and the U.S. firm was also expected to complete a similar plan for Ras Laffan by the end of 1990. Once flows from the North field started up, the government planned to increase the price of domestic gas for existing local industry from thirty-five cents to around fifty cents per million British thermal unit, or Btu, while new industrial users would pay one dollar per million Btu.[58] The government was also looking to its foreign partners in these joint ventures to contribute the lion's share of the project financing, leaving Qatar to supply the gas, infrastructure, and maybe some limited amount of equity capital.

GLIMMER OF HOPE ON THE LNG MARKETING FRONT

Fresh interest in the proposed export phase of the North field was starting to come from Japan. Marubeni had mounted a determined campaign to sell liquefied natural gas to Japanese utilities, telling them shipments would begin in the second half of the 1990s when a shortfall in LNG supplies was expected to emerge. The end of the Iran-Iraq war had been a big relief to the market, although the Qataris were quick to point out that Abu Dhabi's neighboring Das Island LNG plant did not cancel or delay a single cargo throughout the eight-year conflict despite frequent attacks on Gulf shipping by both combatants. A Qatari delegation led by Dr. Al Marri visited Japan in November 1988 to promote LNG sales, while the Japanese responded with a reciprocal fact-finding mission to Qatar in February 1989. This last delegation included a representative from the Japan's powerful Ministry of International Trade and Industry as well as officials from major electric power utilities and gas companies in the Asian country.

Mitsui's long-anticipated entry into the LNG phase of the North field project a few months later also bolstered the revitalized marketing effort, as the company committed to arranging a twenty-year sales contract with Japanese end-users as part of the transaction. The agreement gave Mitsui a 7.5 percent shareholding in Qatargas and was signed with QGPC on May 16, 1989. But there was no trace of either Mitsubishi or C. Itoh, Mitsui's original partners, who had bowed out of the consortium. Mitsubishi was probably concerned about offending Shell—its partner in other LNG supply projects. Mitsui's equity share came from QGPC's interest in the joint venture company, and as a result the state-owned firm's shareholding in Qatargas dropped to 70 percent. There was no change to the 7.5 percent equity allocated to BP, CFP-Total, and Marubeni. The five partners began convening in Doha to prepare detailed presentations for potential buyers in advance of a new marketing drive scheduled to kick off with another visit to Japan in December 1989.

Regional inter-Gulf sales were less promising. After a long hiatus, Qatar had resumed discussions with Kuwait regarding gas deliveries from the North field. But price remained a major stumbling block. Kuwait had been getting associated gas from Iraq since 1986, when a pipeline was completed between the two countries. Iraq was delivering that gas at just one dollar per million Btu, and Kuwait wanted to pay the same price for non-associated gas piped in from Qatar's North field. Kuwait was in a good position to negotiate: it was the only regional market for significant volumes of North field gas, with demand estimates ranging from 500 million to 1 billion cubic feet per day. Saudi Arabia had made it clear it didn't need imported gas from Qatar because of its own recent gas discoveries. Bahrain only wanted small amounts of imported gas on a peak-shaving basis.

A study by Bechtel had put the cost of a staged development of the North field for these regional Gulf Cooperation Council markets at $1.6 billion. This was to be funded entirely by QGPC. But Al Marri insisted the cost of building a pipeline from Qatar to Kuwait via Bahrain and Saudi Arabia would have to be shared with these gas buyers.[59] Qatar wanted at least one dollar per million Btu for supplies introduced into the pipeline at the point of origin, not delivered all the way to Kuwait, as the Kuwaitis hoped. Experts estimated that the cost of transporting this gas by pipeline would be around thirty to thirty-five cents per million Btu, adding significantly to Kuwait's final delivered price.[60]

Dubai also showed interest in gas for its Jebel Ali industrial zone, and there was talk of piping some excess gas from the first stage of the North field development to the UAE emirate rather than injecting it into the Dukhan's Khuff reservoir—at least initially, until the 250 million cubic feet per day surplus would be needed in Qatar's own industrial development.[61] Whether quantities would be sufficient to justify the expense of an underwater pipeline was questionable, and Dubai had not yet determined how much gas it would need to attract industries to Jebel Ali. There was also competition from Abu Dhabi, the neighboring emirate, which had large reserves of non-associated gas that could potentially supply Dubai.

OIL EXPLORATION EFFORTS PROVE DISAPPOINTING

While the search intensified for markets for Qatari natural gas, exploration for new oil reserves was disappointing. Sustainable production capacity at Qatar's onshore and offshore oil fields had fallen to just 350,000 barrels per day, with occasional bursts to 450,000. Falling capacity underscored the importance of finding more oil, but both Sohio and Amoco had failed in their exploration efforts so far. Sohio had drilled three dry holes on its 12,000-square-kilometer offshore block by early 1989. A fourth exploratory well struck oil, and the discovery was dubbed al-Karkara. However, it was ultimately declared uncommercial, leading Sohio to relinquish the block in mid-1989. Amoco had also drilled three dry holes in the south of its 8,000-square-kilometer onshore block. The one bright spot was the conclusion of an exploration- and production-sharing agreement in early 1989 with Elf Aquitaine of France on Block 6 located offshore near Qatar's already producing fields.

Qatar produced an average 340,000 barrels per day in 1988, up 16 percent over 1987 and uncomfortably close to the country's sustainable capacity. Associated gas output rose a similar percentage, to 257 million cubic feet per day.[62] The country's OPEC quota for the first six months of 1989 had been set at 312,000 barrels per day following the organization's latest production accord. This was agreed in Vienna in late November 1988 after twelve days of marathon negotiations to avert another market crash. OPEC produced nearly 23 million barrels per day that month, notching up a new peak for its thirteen members and causing oil prices in the Gulf area to dip below $10 per barrel once again. The Vienna accord specified a total OPEC ceiling of 18.5 million barrels per day for the first half of 1989, and it enshrined the principle of quota parity between Iran and Iraq that Baghdad and its Arab allies in the Gulf had long sought.

In January and February, the first two months of OPEC's new agreement, Qatar's oil output averaged 350,000 barrels per day—180,000 barrels of Qatar Marine and 170,000 barrels from Dukhan. Maintenance at the three offshore fields cut production at Idd el-Shargi, Maydan Mahzam, and Bul Hanine to an estimated 80,000 barrels per day in March, reducing total output and bringing in a first quarter average more or less in line with Qatar's first half 1989 OPEC quota of 312,000 barrels per day.[63] This quota was increased to 329,000 barrels per day in the second half of the year following OPEC's June accord, which specified a total ceiling of 19.5 million barrels per day for the organization as a whole.

By this time QGPC had terminated crude oil contracts with small trading companies and streamlined its customer base to mainly include big companies. Term contracts totaling 270,000 barrels per day were in place with lifters from Japan, the United States, France, and Brazil. The National Oil Distribution Company was exporting about 46,500 barrels per day of petroleum products from its two Umm Said refineries with another 15,000 barrels per day consumed locally.[64] Shipments now included super gasoline and jet fuel following completion of a petroleum products pipeline running from the new 50,000-barrels-per-day refinery to the pier at the Umm Said port. In addition, the state-owned company was refining some 20,000 barrels per day of crude oil in Singapore under processing deals with local refiners.

The government's 1989 budget forecast a revenue of QR 5,835 million ($1.6 billion) that was strictly consistent with the country's first half OPEC quota of 312,000 barrels per day at official prices.[65] It included a projected government deficit of about $500 million based on total government expenditures of $2.1 billion.

Several months after this budget was announced the state of Qatar returned to the Euromarket to borrow another $200 million from Chase Manhattan in an apparent coup for the U.S. bank. Like the earlier $400 million loan to QGPC to finance the first stage of the North field development, this second facility carried a 22.5-basis-point spread over LIBOR.[66] However, the new loan was for five years instead of three and included a grace period of two and a half years.

LONG-AWAITED CABINET RESHUFFLE STRENGTHENS HEIR APPARENT

In an obvious move to fortify his succession plan, Sheikh Khalifa announced a major cabinet reshuffle on July 18, 1989—the first in the nearly two decades since Qatar's independence. Eleven new ministers were brought in, many of whom were closely allied with Crown Prince Hamad Ibn Khalifa.[67] Seven ministers were dismissed, including the ruler's powerful brother Khalid Ibn Hamad, who had been minister of the interior since the 1972 coup. Sheikh Khalid was replaced by the amir's younger son Abdullah Ibn Khalifa, who had assumed an increasingly important role in the military and would now oversee the police. The heir apparent retained his posts of minister of defense and commander-in-chief of the armed forces while Abdul Aziz Ibn Khalifa was reconfirmed as the minister of finance and petroleum. Sheikh Khalifa retained the post of prime minister in addition to his role as ruler of Qatar.

Abdullah Ibn Khalifa Al Attiyah was appointed minister of foreign affairs, a position vacant since the death of the ruler's half brother Suhaym Ibn Hamad Al Thani in 1985. The new minister stayed in his post just one year, however, and in 1990 was succeeded by Mubarak Ali Al Khatir. The parallel Ministry of State for Foreign Affairs, created in 1977 so that the amir could avoid firing the recalcitrant Suhaym, was abolished in the 1989 reshuffle. Hamad Ibn Suhaym Al Thani, the former undersecretary at the Ministry of Foreign Affairs and Suhaym's son, replaced Issa Al Kawari as minister of information and culture. Al Kawari stayed on as the ruler's chef de cabinet and remained at Sheikh Khalifa's side as his most trusted aide and confidant.

The Ministry of Industry and Agriculture was abolished and its duties reassigned to two ministries: the Ministry of Municipal Affairs and Agriculture and the Ministry of Industry and Public Works. Hamad Ibn Jassim Ibn Jabir Al Thani was appointed minister of municipal affairs and agriculture. While a newcomer to the cabinet lineup, Hamad Ibn Jassim Ibn Jabir would eventually become so well known that he was referred to simply as HBJ. The Ministry of Economy and Commerce was renamed the Ministry of Economy and Trade and put under Hamad Ibn Jassim Ibn Hamad Al Thani, the former commandant of the police and the amir's nephew. Of the sixteen ministers in the reshuffled cabinet, nine were members of the ruling family. The shakeup extended down to the next tier of public officials. Several months after the cabinet reshuffle, Mohammed Ibn Khalifa, another of the amir's younger sons, was appointed undersecretary of the Ministry of Finance and Petroleum. A recent graduate from George Washington University, Sheikh Mohammed would work under his older brother Abdul Aziz Ibn Khalifa, the minister of finance and petroleum. The appointment of Sheikh Mohammed coincided with the departure of Sayyid Abdullah Sallat, the oil industry veteran who had been running the Department of Petroleum Affairs since 1979. Sallat was moved to the Ministry of Communications & Transport where he was appointed undersecretary.

Sheikh Khalifa had earlier established the Supreme Council for Planning under the crown prince's chairmanship to oversee the state's economic and social policies. It would set long-, medium-, and short-term development targets, coordinating responsibility among the various ministries for meeting these targets and ensuring implementation. The new body's recommendations would be submitted to the cabinet for approval and the amir for endorsement, but it had legal independent status and its own special budget within the government's. In addition to Hamad Ibn Khalifa, the Supreme Council for Planning included the ministers for education; economy and trade; industry and agriculture; finance and petroleum; and labor and social affairs, as well as the head of the Qatari monetary agency and private sector representatives nominated by Qatar's Chamber of Commerce.

JAPAN'S CHUBU ELECTRIC SHOWS LNG-BUYING PROMISE

Several Japanese power companies had expressed interest in LNG from Qatargas by the time Dr. Al Marri and his team left for Tokyo in December 1989. Chief among the prospective buyers was Chubu Electric Power Company, the local utility servicing the central region on the main island of Honshu and one of nine regional electric companies formed in 1951 as part of the restructuring of Japan's energy industry in the aftermath of World War II. Mainly coal-oriented, Chubu was looking for a cleaner-burning alternative for its power stations and was considering buying 4 million tons per year of LNG from Qatargas over twenty years beginning in the second half of the 1990s.[68] The Qatari team was hoping to convert Chubu's interest into a letter of intent while also seeking commitments for another 2 million tons per year from Tokyo Electric Power Company and Kansai Electric. This would give Qatargas annual sales of 6 million tons, enough to launch the LNG project.

Japan imported about 30 million tons of LNG in 1989, and forecasts saw demand rising to 50 million annually by 2000. Even with the expansion of existing LNG plants in Indonesia, Australia, Malaysia, and Abu Dhabi, there was thought to be room for large volumes from Qatar. Pricing remained a sticking point. The average cost of LNG imported into Japan was running about $3.45 per million Btu at the time, which would net Qatar less than $1.00 per million Btu after the high costs of liquefaction and tanker transportation were subtracted. But Japan's LNG imports were linked to crude oil prices. Conventional wisdom had the oil market—and, by extension, gas prices—improving considerably by the late 1990s when the Qatargas project was expected to start up.

QGPC had indicated it might be willing to charge Qatargas as little as 50 cents per million Btu for gas from the North field.[69] The foreign partners in the joint venture were holding out for an even lower price of 30 cents per million Btu. QGPC argued that this price—equivalent to $1.80 per barrel oil—was below what it cost to produce the offshore gas and that it would mean losing money on its upstream operations. However, this approach failed to account for the high-value gas liquids produced as part of the LNG development phase, which would more than offset any loss from gas sales. QGPC eventually compromised, agreeing with its foreign partners to price gas into the liquefaction plant at a base rate of 50 cents per million Btu, although with a caveat that a large portion of this fee could be deferred if LNG prices were too low for Qatargas to make a profit.

Work on the first phase of the North field development was running on schedule in early 1990. The sixteen development wells were almost complete, while the offshore installations had been transferred to the production site from Abu Dhabi and were being installed. A total of 570 kilometers of pipe had been laid, including the twin pipelines extending from the offshore production area to Ras Laffan and the two overland pipelines linking Ras Laffan to Umm Said. Onshore at

Umm Said, the gas treatment and fractionation facilities were on track for completion by the end of 1990. The work was being financed from the sale of 50,000 barrels per day of crude oil, up from a daily quantity of 40,000 barrels in early 1989.[70] This represented about 14 percent of Qatar's oil production at the time.

Just when everything seemed to be going smoothly, gas seepages were detected in fourteen out of the sixteen development wells in May 1990. "The leaks, which apparently have sprung from underwater cementing problems, could pose an extreme hazard for the producing platforms and other offshore facilities," the *Middle East Economic Survey* reported.[71] While the leaks were quickly plugged, the faulty cement, which held pipe called casing in place in the wells, raised questions about whether significant rises in wellhead pressures might cause dangerous blowouts in the future. The Qataris insisted that the problems had caused no delays and that the formal inauguration of the North field's first phase would go ahead as scheduled in early 1991. Every month mattered. As predicted, non-associated gas output from the onshore Dukhan field had fallen from its 1987 peak to around 374 million cubic feet per day. Associated gas from Qatar's onshore and offshore fields varied with crude oil but mainly ran above 250 million cubic feet per day.

AGING OFFSHORE OIL FIELDS GET MAJOR OVERHAUL

Spending cuts during the 1980s oil glut and years of concentrating on the North field had come home to roost. Long maintenance programs, particularly at Qatar's aging offshore fields, were constraining production. QGPC reportedly set a target for offshore oil production of 180,000 barrels per day in 1990, against theoretical daily capacity of 205,000 barrels.[72] This was widely seen as optimistic, given technical constraints at the three fields. Sources suggested Qatar would have to spend $2 to $3 billion over the next decade to maintain and expand its existing oil fields after years of neglect and underwhelming exploration by foreign operators.[73] The press reported that the long-delayed but inevitable investment program reflected a recognition that the government had so far failed to launch locally based, cash-generating industries using gas from the first stage of the North field and would be dependent on income from oil for longer than anticipated.

QGPC awarded a contract to Ewbank International of the United Kingdom to supervise upgrading work at the Idd elShargi, Maydan Mahzam, and Bul Hanine fields.[74] This major overhaul would be implemented in two phases between 1991 and 1992. Phase one involved replacing pipelines and modernizing equipment on two platforms while the second phase entailed shutting down platforms for major maintenance and upgrading work. A separate enhanced oil recovery project to boost capacity at Idd el-Shargi by forty thousand barrels per day through fifty gas injection wells, platform expansion work, and power generation was launched in mid-1990.[75] QGPC also announced plans to develop the onshore Diyab structure on Dukhan's southern flank, discovered in the late 1970s, to produce fifty thousand barrels per day by mid-1992. A new twenty-kilometer pipeline to Dukhan's Jaleha separation station, where handling capacity would be raised to one hundred thousand barrels per day, would accommodate the additional output.

Despite plans for major infrastructural development, including new desalination plants and upgrades to the electricity network, the government budget for the financial year beginning April 1, 1990, only projected a small increase in capital spending.[76] But it also allocated QR 865 million ($240 million) to the oil and minerals sector that was not included in the capital account. The extra commitment boosted the projected budget deficit for the financial year to QR 4,868 million (about $1.34 billion). Qatar's state reserves had declined in recent years as the government funded budget deficits, although the actual shortfall continued to remain below published figures as the government routinely delayed payments due. Revenues had increased in 1989, and this had also caused a slight improvement in the payments situation.[77]

Exploration efforts by foreign operators were still disappointing, although Amoco planned to drill three or four more wells on its onshore Block 2 in 1990 after completing a fourth well in late 1989. Discussions were under way with other companies on open acreage, and these led to the signature of a second exploration- and production-sharing agreement with Elf Aquitaine on June 14, 1990. This covered the 8,300-square-kilometer Block 1, which was mostly located off Qatar's east coast but extended onshore in the area around Ras Laffan in the northern part of the peninsula. The French company had completed a seismic survey of its offshore Block 6 in 1989 and was preparing to drill its first exploration well in late 1990. Elf was required to drill three exploration wells on Block 6 in the contract's first three-year exploration phase.

The new deal with Elf was signed by Mohammed Ibn Khalifa Al Thani, the undersecretary of the Ministry of Finance and Petroleum, rather than Sheikh Mohammed's older brother Abdul Aziz Ibn Khalifa. The long-standing minister had already missed a meeting of OPEC's eight-member Ministerial Monitoring Committee in Vienna in March 1990, with the minister of economy and trade heading up the Qatari delegation instead.[78] Sheikh Abdul Aziz had attended an important OPEC conference held in the Austrian capital the previous November, however, during which Qatar's OPEC quota was increased to 371,000 barrels per day for the first half of 1990 as part of an overall rise. (Qatar wasn't expected to benefit from this rise since it was already producing above its OPEC quota and had been for most of 1989.)

Crude oil output averaged 382,000 barrels per day in 1989, of which exports accounted for 320,000. Qatar's two refineries operated at their full capacity of 62,000 barrels per day during the year.[79] With domestic petroleum consumption of only 16,000 barrels per day, these refined products were mostly exported. QGPC entered 1990 with term lifting commitments for crude oil of 314,000 barrels per day.[80] These sales commitments rose to a daily rate of 348,000 barrels from the second quarter after two Japanese lifters and one South Korean customer hiked contractual volumes for 1990. The higher contract liftings coincided with a price collapse in April, leading OPEC to cobble together a three-month cutback deal in which Qatar was one of five members who voluntarily agreed to reduce production. But the cutbacks proved ineffectual, primarily because of quota busting by Kuwait and the UAE. The OPEC basket was still below fourteen dollars a barrel in June.

IRAQ LAUNCHES HARD-HITTING OPEC PRESSURE CAMPAIGN

Iraq now took the lead, with a hard-hitting campaign pressuring Kuwait and the UAE to cut output to quota levels. Its deputy prime minister, Dr. Saadoun Hammadi, described the loss of revenue from the oil price drop as intolerable, publicly castigating the two OPEC renegades for bringing about the situation through overproduction.[81] Saudi Arabia and Iraq orchestrated a deal to bring Kuwait and the UAE back into the quota fold at OPEC's next meeting, held in Geneva in late July 1990. At Iraq's insistence, the organization's ceiling was left unchanged at 22.5 million barrels per day, and a higher reference price was set for the OPEC basket of twenty-one dollars a barrel. Prices had already improved to nearly eighteen dollars per barrel on the expectation of output cutbacks and because of Iraq's verbal pressure. This had kicked off on July 17, when Iraqi president Saddam Hussein shattered the normal summer torpor with an impassioned speech accusing Kuwait and the UAE of conspiring with the United States to drive down oil prices, depriving Iraq of $14 billion annually.

Hopes that Saddam Hussein's speech was mainly intended to frighten the two producers into quota observance were dashed the following day, when Iraqi foreign minister Tariq Aziz delivered a letter to the Arab League accusing Kuwait of border violations.[82] Baghdad had earlier accused Kuwait of stealing oil from its Rumaila field, which straddled the border with Kuwait, and demanded $2.4 billion in compensation. Still, few observers expected Baghdad to take military action. Those who did believed Iraq would limit itself to seizing disputed border areas and possibly the strategically important islands of Bubiyan and Warbah at the head of the Gulf.[83] No one anticipated the blitzkrieg of August 2, 1990, when an Iraqi force of 150,000 troops overran Kuwait in a twenty-four-hour operation.

After failing to set up a puppet regime in Kuwait, Iraq formally annexed its neighbor a week later. Most of Kuwait was declared Iraq's nineteenth province, although parts of northern Kuwait including the Rumaila field and the islands of Bubiyan and Warbah were added to Iraq's Basra Province.[84] The U.S.-led international response was swift. On August 16 Washington initiated a naval blockade, and a multinational force began intercepting ocean commerce to and from Iraq and Kuwait. Under Operation Desert Shield, the United States also sent troops, ships, and aircraft into the region to protect the Saudi peninsula. Turkey shut down the Iraqi oil pipeline to the Mediterranean port of Ceyhan and cut off all shipments of goods to Iraq via Turkish land and sea routes. By mid-September the head of the U.S. Central Intelligence Agency, William Webster, claimed the embargo had shut off 95 percent of Iraq's oil exports.[85]

With some 4 million barrels per day of combined Iraqi and Kuwaiti production suddenly removed from the market, crude oil prices surged to thirty-two dollars per barrel. But they subsequently fell below twenty-six dollars after OPEC convened an emergency meeting in Vienna on August 29, 1990, to endorse a production rise. The organization increased output temporarily "according to need" without specifying any volume limitation either in terms of individual quotas or the overall OPEC ceiling. In September, the first month of quota free output, a large part of the lost production from Iraq and Kuwait was replaced and OPEC was back up to 22.5 million barrels per day. While Saudi Arabia contributed the lion's share of the incremental supply, other volume increases came from the UAE, Venezuela, Iran, Nigeria, and Libya. Qatar boosted output to 430,000 barrels per day in September, up from 370,000 barrels per day in July immediately before Iraq's invasion of Kuwait.[86]

QGPC deferred a six-week maintenance program at its three offshore fields that would have cut output to 280,000 barrels per day. Development work planned at the same time as this maintenance was also delayed.[87] Instead, QGPC staggered work at the fields over a three-month period to minimize production loss. Idd el-Shargi, now the smallest field with capacity of just 10,000 barrels per day, was shut down for one month on November 3, followed by the 60,000-barrels-per-day Maydan Mahzam field in early December and the 135,000-barrels-per-day Bul Hanine field on January 2, 1991.[88] Bul Hanine's closure reduced Qatar's total output to 350,000 barrels per day in January, down from a daily rate of 360,000 barrels in December, 400,000 barrels in November, and 430,000 barrels in October.[89] The onshore Dukhan field continued to operate normally at around 240,000 barrels per day throughout the offshore maintenance program.

The oil market remained on a knife-edge. Prices hit forty dollars a barrel in late September after Saddam Hussain threatened to attack oil fields in Saudi Arabia and the UN Security Council passed a resolution implementing an air embargo on Iraq. Then prices fell back as other OPEC countries turned up the taps, with the organization's output peaking at nearly 23.9 million barrels per day in December. By the end of November, Washington had obtained UN authorization for the use of force should Saddam Hussain refuse to withdraw his troops from Kuwait by January 15, 1991. Two days after this deadline, the United States launched F-117 stealth fighters and cruise missiles against Iraq and its military. With this air war, Operation Desert Shield had become Operation Desert Storm.

Oil prices lost more than one-third of their value on January 17, the first day of Operation Desert Storm. Within twenty-four hours, the price of Brent crude oil for prompt delivery fell ten dollars to around nineteen dollars per barrel on expectations of a quick end to the war without significant damage to oil production facilities and the worldwide oversupply.[90] An isolated incident did see an Iraqi artillery shell set fire to a crude oil storage tank at the Khafji refinery, and the Japanese-owned Arabian Oil Company shut down the offshore Khafji oil field shared between Saudi Arabia and Kuwait on January 17 because of its proximity to the potential combat zone. But all other production and export installations in Saudi Arabia continued to function normally. There seemed no reason why the kingdom wouldn't continue to produce the 8.3 million barrels per day that it had in December.

Exports from Iran, Qatar, and the UAE also continued with only short-term disruptions. Both Iran and Qatar announced plans to offer shuttle services to crude oil customers affected by injunctions on tanker movements due to vessel congestion and the operational requirements of the coalition forces.[91] Qatar's Umm Said export terminal was initially declared out-of-bounds to Japanese-flagged ships, who were banned from loading at ports west of longitude 52°E under an agreement with the seamen's union. This restriction was relaxed to allow Japanese tankers to load crude oil and liquid petroleum gas from Umm Said after QGPC said it would charge lifters an exorbitantly high $1.50 per barrel to transport onshore Dukhan crude to the offshore terminal at Halul island for transshipment.[92]

The Japanese ban extended to ports in Saudi Arabia, Bahrain, and Iran's Kharg Island. Kharg was also impacted by another ruling from the U.S. and British naval authorities restricting tankers from proceeding north of latitude 27.5°N, prompting the Iranians to arrange for ship-to-ship loadings off Lavan Island. The Saudis followed with a shuttle service allowing Japanese and other customers unwilling or unable to send tankers to Ras Tanura or Saudi Arabia's other Persian Gulf ports to load crude off Khor Fakkan on Sharjah's Indian Ocean coast outside the sensitive Strait of Hormuz. While Iran charged customers only 45 cents per barrel to switch to Lavan Island, the Saudis imposed a hefty fee of $1.20 per barrel to ensure that lifters taking advantage of its transshipment services did not gain financially from loading outside of the Persian Gulf.[93]

QATAR PARTICIPATES IN THE GULF WAR COALITION

Qatar joined the U.S.-led Gulf War coalition, contributing troops, tanks, coastal vessels, and combat aircraft to a thirty-nine-country effort that ultimately included an armed force of 737,000 troops as well as 190 ships and 1,700 combat aircraft.[94] In a reversal of previous policy, the government also permitted coalition forces from the United States, Canada, and France to operate out of Qatari territory.[95] Qatar's Mirage F-1 fighters flew strike missions against Iraqi targets in the Gulf War, although they reportedly always flew in direct contact with U.S. Air Force F-16s to avoid misidentification with Iraqi F-1s. Even so, there were several instances when coalition aircraft almost fired on the Qatari planes accidentally.

A Qatari mechanized battalion of 1,600 men, twenty-five tanks, sixty armored vehicles, and three to five artillery weapons participated in the Saudi-led battle to retake Al Khafji, a Saudi town on the shore of the Persian Gulf some eight miles below the Kuwaiti border. Al Khafji had been evacuated by the Saudis on the first day of Operation Desert Storm and was subsequently occupied by Iraqi forces on January 29. In a nighttime assault on January 30, a platoon of Iraqi T-55 tanks engaged a Qatari tank company south of the town. Qatar's AMX-30 main tanks destroyed three T-55s and captured a fourth while losing one AMX-30. This initial assault still failed, but within forty-eight hours Saudi and Qatari troops supported by massive U.S. air power retook Al Khafji in a second attack.

The Battle of Khafji was the Iraqi army's only major offensive in this war, and it was a devastating defeat. A majority of two mechanized divisions and one armored division were destroyed. Saddam Hussein also failed to lure coalition forces into a larger ground engagement or to create dissention among the coalition forces, while the untested Saudi–Qatari force performed much better than anticipated. Eighteen Saudi and Qatari soldiers were killed and fifty wounded at Al Khafji, while two Qatari AMX-30 tanks and ten Saudi V-150 armored vehicles were destroyed. Another twenty-five U.S. servicemen lost their lives—eleven from friendly fire. Two Saudis were also killed accidentally when they were bombed by U.S. and Qatari fighter-bombers. With Kuwait liberated and the Iraqi army in retreat, coalition forces suspended their operations just one hundred hours after the ground campaign began.

Pakistani contract soldiers or Qataris of Pakistani origin were heavily represented in Qatar's combat units at the time, and they dominated the tank corps which participated with considerable distinction in the Battle of Khafji. Indeed, in the early 1990s Qatari citizens constituted less than one-third of their country's army. While many officers came from the royal family or leading tribes, most enlisted personnel were recruited from Pakistan or other Arab countries.

GULF WAR DELAYS NORTH FIELD START-UP PLANS

The exodus of contractors from the Persian Gulf following Iraq's invasion of Kuwait slowed down work on the North field. In mid-February 1991 Dr. Al Marri announced that production from the gas field would be "slightly deferred" on account of skilled manpower issues and the delayed return to Qatar of contractors working at the site.[96] QGPC's managing director also denied that the company was still dealing with gas leaks at the offshore wells. This followed media reports that QGPC had hired Neal Adams Firefighters, who had advised the use of a special cement to plug the side casings of the fourteen leaking North field wells.[97]

QGPC now planned to begin producing gas from the North field in June, followed by an official inauguration of phase one in early September designed to coincide with the twentieth anniversary of Qatar's Independence Day on September 3, 1991. Expansion plans at Umm Said's existing petrochemical and fertilizer plants were finally coming together as well. At QAPCO, Italy's Enimont and the petrochemical subsidiary of France's Elf Aquitaine had edged out their rivals to acquire a combined 20 percent in the company. This left QGPC with an 80 percent interest in QAPCO, followed by Enimont and Elf Aquitaine's Atochem subsidiary at 10 percent each. The partners had agreed to a $400 million program to boost annual ethylene capacity to 470,000 tons and low-density polyethylene capacity to 380,000 tons per year. Ethane-rich feedstock for the new ethylene plant would come from the North field.

QAFCO was proceeding with a third fertilizer plant. This followed the completion of a commercial feasibility study on the $400 million expansion project, which envisaged the construction of two new units producing 1,500 tons per day of ammonia and 2,000 tons daily of urea. Norway's Norsk Hydro had relinquished managerial control of QAFCO at the end of 1990, although the 25 percent partner continued to provide technical services and expertise. The government had decided in 1988 to assume full managerial and marketing responsibilities for all industrial joint ventures with foreign firms, with the first application of this policy occurring on January 1, 1989, when QASCO took over management of the steel plant from Kobe Steel and Tokyo Boeki. The steel producer's two Japanese partners were, however, engaged as consultants.

Canada's International Octane Ltd., or IOL, teamed up with France's Total to build a MTBE complex with QGPC. The resulting Qatar Fuel Additives Company was incorporated in 1992 with QGPC as 50 percent partner and Total and IOL each holding 25 percent. There were synergies to combining the two products. The 660,000-ton-per-year methanol plant—which had earlier garnered interest from Enimont, among other contenders—would use around 75 million cubic feet per day of dry methane gas from the North field as feedstock. Some of the methanol would be used along with butane to make up to 500,000 tons per year of MTBE, leaving about 475,000 tons per year of methanol for export by Total and IOL. The two foreign shareholders would contribute cash toward the estimated $600 million complex, with QGPC's equity contribution coming in the form of infrastructure as well as the supply of methane gas and butane.

The United Kingdom's Penspen also joined QGPC in a second methanol and MTBE venture dubbed the Qatar Clean Energy Company. Plans called for a methanol plant making 825,000 tons per year and an MTBE facility of 500,000 tons per year. Methane gas feedstock of 90 million cubic feet daily would be provided from the first phase of the North field, but the butane needed to produce MTBE would be imported until the field's second development phase. The National Oil Distribution Company planned to modify existing units at the Umm Said refinery to process condensates from the North field. Total, which had a strong interest in condensates through what would become its dominant role in upstream field development at Qatargas, was pushing for a stand-alone refinery for processing these low-density, high-gravity liquid hydrocarbons into even higher-value refined products.

SHELL EXITS QATAR'S OFFSHORE OIL SECTOR

Nearly forty years after it first entered Qatar's offshore oil sector—and six years after its bitter arbitration dispute with QGPC over the destruction of the first natural gas liquids plant at Umm Said—Shell announced its local subsidiary would quit the country when its oil field service contract expired on December 31, 1991. Shell had been trying for years to find a way to restore its equity position in the three offshore fields of Idd el-Shargi, Maydan Mahzam, and Bul Hanine, offering to help QGPC Offshore develop its more difficult and expensive oil reserves in return for some production sharing rather than on a service fee basis.[98] But its efforts proved unsuccessful.

Several months later QGPC said it also planned to let its contract with the Dukhan Service Company for the onshore Dukhan field lapse when it expired on January 31, 1992. Shell subsequently signed a limited material services agreement with QGPC that allowed three of its twenty-five skilled secondees to remain in Qatar through 1992, while the BP-dominated Dukhan Service Company agreed to temporarily provide technical services on the old fee basis after expiration of its contract. Limited extension of these longstanding arrangements gave QGPC more time to negotiate new management-service contracts for the operation of its onshore and offshore oil fields with other interested oil companies. However, by mid-1992 both Qatar Shell Service Company and the Dukhan Service Company had pulled most of their staff from the country. Only ten people remained seconded to QGPC from the two firms.[99]

Their potential replacements were just as anxious to ensure that any new operating agreement would give them a share in crude oil production.[100] QGPC strenuously resisted any form of production-sharing deal initially. It also expressed a preference for a unified contract covering all its fields. This reflected QGPC's decision to finally merge its onshore and offshore divisions into a single organization effective October 1, 1991. The merger, which essentially converted QGPC from a holding company into a single integrated oil company, was forced on QGPC by its board of directors.[101] Its purpose was to eliminate the old rivalry between QGPC Onshore and QGPC Offshore and improve coordination in Qatar's oil industry. Abdul Aziz Al Dulaimi was made executive manager for Oil and Gas Operations, a new post responsible for all the country's producing oil fields as well as the Umm Said gas processing facilities and the North field.[102]

Recognizing it needed both cash and know-how to reverse falling output at its oil fields, QGPC eventually relented on the terms of the operating agreement. But it wanted production-sharing confined to incremental oil output from the northern dome of the Idd el-Shargi field, which QGPC said could be expanded from 12,000 to 60,000 barrels daily through enhanced oil recovery from the Arab C and D (formerly known as the Arab III and IV) reservoirs as well as the Shuaiba via a pilot program of horizontal drilling and either gas or water injection. Qatar's oil output, which peaked at 506,000 barrels per day in 1979 and fell to a post-1950s nadir of just 270,000 barrels per day in 1983, was averaging about 380,000 barrels per day in early 1992. This was well off QGPC's self-declared production capacity of 470,000 barrels.[103] It was in line with the 1991 actual daily average of 387,000 barrels. Production in 1990 had come in at 382,000 barrels per day despite a temporary boost to 430,000 following Iraq's invasion of Kuwait.

New output was due onstream in late 1992 to compensate for declines at Qatar's existing fields. One of these new sources was the onshore Diyab structure on Dukhan's southern edge. QGPC turned to Occidental Petroleum for help bringing Diyab online, signing a short-term service contract with the U.S. firm to install the necessary production facilities and link the field to Dukhan's Jaleha separation station between June and October 1992.[104] By the end of this five-month period, QGPC was able to begin production at a rate of 20,000 barrels per day. This rose to 30,000 barrels daily by December, and Diyab was expected to hit its ultimate level of 50,000 barrels per day in the first half of 1993. The boost from Diyab allowed QGPC to increase Qatar's overall crude oil production to about 420,000 barrels per day by the end of 1992.[105] Output for 1992, however, averaged 397,000 barrels daily.

Elsewhere on the peninsula, onshore exploration was disappointing. After drilling nine dry holes, Amoco was preparing to relinquish its 8,000-square-kilometer Block 2 in southern Qatar. Wildcatters had more luck offshore. Elf Aquitaine had encountered an oil show at its first well at Block 6 in the eastern part of Qatar's continental shelf. The French firm's second discovery well in a different structure on the block in mid-1991 caused even more excitement. Al Khalij No. 1 was followed by two more appraisal wells, leading to an initial estimate of probable reserves of 80 million barrels for the reservoir, which was located at a depth of 1,200 meters in the Mishrif formation of the Upper Cretaceous.

Al Khalij represented the most important oil discovery in Qatar in nearly two decades. Elf announced plans to start production from the oil field at a rate of twenty thousand barrels per day in the first half of 1993, rising to thirty-five thousand barrels in 1994.[106] The company said it would start delineation drilling in May 1992 to determine the field's extent and negotiated a farm-in deal with Agip under which the Italian oil firm took a 45 percent interest in Block 6. This reduced Elf's share in the block to 55 percent. QGPC also rebid Block 5 off Qatar's northeast coast in mid-1991. After its failed efforts elsewhere, Amoco tried to secure priority to drill this block. Its efforts were unsuccessful, and it seemed the U.S. company did not have the right local support for its bid. Instead, one year later a more flexible Maersk Oil and Gas of Denmark signed an exploration- and production-sharing agreement on the four-thousand-square-kilometer tract.

Maersk's agreement on Block 5 specifically limited the company's exploration and production operations to crude oil and other hydrocarbons located "only in structures lying above the Khuff formation."[107] Since Block 5 extended into the boundaries of the North field, there was a distinct possibility that the Khuff formation did as well, so the stipulation restricted the Danish firm to shallower strata. The dispute with the five-member Wintershall consortium at its adjacent concession had of course ended up in international arbitration, and QGPC wanted to avoid any further clashes with offshore operators over the development of contiguous or even non-contiguous Khuff reserves outside its main North field contract area.

As part of its agreement on Block 5, Maersk committed to spend $49 million over the first three-year exploration period. This included drilling horizontal wells and using water injection techniques in an area where previous wells drilled by other operators had produced oil shows. The firm already had extensive experience with horizontal drilling and water injection at similar geological formations through its activities in Denmark's North Sea sector, particularly the Dan field first developed in the early 1970s.

CHAPTER 13

Rocky Road for Qatar's First LNG Project

The first sales breakthrough for the Qatargas project came during the height of the Gulf War in early 1991 when Japan's Chubu Electric tentatively agreed to buy 4 million tons per year of LNG over twenty-five years. This letter of intent was signed on February 22, two days before coalition forces launched the land offensive to oust Iraq from Kuwait. It was a major coup for Mitsui, who had overcome competition from Marubeni to deliver a buyer less than two years after joining Qatargas. Although it already had long-term purchase deals in place with LNG ventures in Australia and Indonesia, Chubu had been working with Mitsui to find a new project where it could be the lead buyer. Chubu reckoned this role as an anchor customer in Qatargas, together with the company's established relationship with Mitsui, would give it more control over pricing and transportation, especially in the early years of the project.[1]

Chubu's decision to invest in Qatar came only after it evaluated other liquefaction projects proposed in western Canada, Alaska, Russia's Sakhalin Island, Thailand, Burma (now Myanmar), Papua New Guinea, and Iran.[2] It had already invested in Indonesia; its first LNG contract was signed with that country's state-owned oil and gas company, Pertamina, in 1973 during the oil crisis. This was followed in 1985 by a second purchase agreement from Australia's North West Shelf LNG project. In both cases, the electric utility had been part of a group of Japanese buyers acting in consortium. By the time North West Shelf commenced operations in 1989, a third of Chubu's power generation was fueled by LNG and the company was looking for a new project where it could strike out on its own.

The letter of intent with Chubu was soon overshadowed by the announcement that QGPC had awarded a development- and production-sharing contract for the upstream portion of the LNG project solely to the French partner in Qatargas. This was signed on May 29, 1991, with Total, which had only months earlier dropped CFP from its name when it listed on the New York Stock Exchange. The deal represented a firm contract for the development of a section of the North field to produce 800 million cubic feet daily of gas and 30,000 to 50,000 barrels per day of condensates. Total agreed to provide all the financing to develop the assigned area and assumed responsibility for the technical and operational aspects of the upstream project. Field development was initially put at $600 million between 1994 and 1996. This would pay for new gas wells, production platforms with the necessary separation units, and the pipelines to transport gas and liquids to landfall at Ras Laffan.[3]

QGPC issued a press release saying it was continuing "discussions with the remaining shareholders in Qatargas on joining this agreement with Total and working jointly with it to develop and produce North field gas accordingly."[4] But it was clear Total, with the right political support, had outmaneuvered its foreign partners. The agreement stipulated that Total would get a percentage of the condensates from the project, with its return on investment achieved solely from the sale of these liquids. The production-sharing terms allocated 65 percent of the net output of field condensates to Total for cost recovery in the first seven years of operation, falling to 25 percent thereafter. Production after cost recovery, the so-called profit oil, was split 65-35 in favor of the contractor on condensate output up to 38,000 barrels per day. This dropped to just 16.5 percent between 38,001 and 60,000 barrels per day, however.

Qatar would retain sole ownership of all the lean gas produced and delivered by Total, which would be for QGPC's account and ultimately delivered to Qatargas for a fee. Total guaranteed the quantity and quality of the feed gas from the commencement of LNG exports to Chubu in January 1997. Qatargas itself—which included QGPC and Total as well as BP, Marubeni, and Mitsui—would build and operate two LNG trains at Ras Laffan initially, each sized to produce 2 million tons per year, plus all the necessary export facilities. It would also acquire the tankers to transport this LNG to Japan. The government would charge Qatargas a base price of fifty-eight cents per million Btu for its feed gas. However, all but ten cents per million Btu of this gas price could be deferred if the liquefaction plant did not achieve certain profitability thresholds. The deferred amount would be treated as a loan to be repaid with interest as LNG prices—and profitability—improved.

Other companies were now clamoring to turn North field gas into LNG. Several weeks after the Qatargas sale to Chubu was announced, QGPC said it would form a 6-million-tons-per-year project with Italy's Snam; the Italian power generator Ente nazionale per l'energia elettrica, or Enel; and the U.S. firm Bunker Hunt. Field development was to be Bunker Hunt's responsibility, while Snam would handle the liquefaction facilities and, together with Enel, purchase the output. Elf Aquitaine then scored what amounted to an option on yet another area of the North field, given what it called the "possibility" to build an integrated gas project supplying 4 million tons per year of LNG over twenty-five years. In both cases QGPC insisted that its partners take the LNG themselves. This contrasted with Qatargas, where shareholders weren't interested in buying the LNG and the third-party marketing effort had proven tortuous. Having the buyers as part of the project selling the LNG also raised conflict-of-interest issues between QGPC and its partners. Snam's chair, for example, signaled early on that his company wanted a price linked less tightly to oil than traditional LNG formulas.

There was no mention of the North field in the government's budget for the financial year beginning April 1, 1991.[5] This was a startling omission, given the recent letter of intent with Chubu and the imminent launch of the Qatargas project. QGPC was actively seeking a financial adviser for this second stage of the North field development. Citibank was poised to win this advisory contract, although QGPC's board of directors had still not met to approve the appointment by the end of 1991. Engineering firms were bidding on a contract covering the front-end engineering and design for the LNG plant at Ras Laffan, including the preparation of tender documents. QGPC ended up awarding this contract to the U.S. firm M. W. Kellogg International in early 1992.

The government also signaled its commitment with the award of a major $780 million contract to Societa italiana per condotte d'acqua to build a port at Ras Laffan. This followed the completion of Bechtel's optimization plan for the port and an industrial area for the treatment, storage, and processing of gas piped in from the North field. Extending over an area of about 8 square kilometers, the port was designed to handle 360 vessels and 13 million tons of cargo annually in its first phase. It would have a protected basin 13.5 meters deep, two massive breakwaters, an approach channel dredged to 15 meters, four berths for LNG tankers and six for gas liquids carriers as well as berths for container ships and solid cargo vessels. The total cost for the port infrastructure was put at $1 billion. About half would be covered by export credits from the Italian export-credit agency SACE, but the rest was supposed to be funded from QGPC's own resources.

QGPC STARTS UP NORTH FIELD PHASE 1 DEVELOPMENT

QGPC missed its target for the North field start-up by two months, beginning gas production from well No. 1 on August 3, 1991. In its press release announcing this milestone, the Qatari firm said gas output was scheduled to rise to 800 million cubic feet per day by the end of September with the commissioning of all sixteen of the first-phase wells.[6] But technical snags arose almost immediately, and actual gas production was well below the forecasted rate. Although unconfirmed, there were reports that potentially dangerous chemicals had leaked into one of the onshore pipelines running to Umm Said. Other unnamed oil and gas sources told the industry press that the well casings at the North field were still leaking gas, requiring relief wells to be drilled.[7]

These technical issues were eventually resolved, and the North field hit its design capacity of 800 million cubic feet per day by the middle of 1992. This followed completion of the compressor station in the Fahahil area, allowing about half of this daily output to be injected into the Dukhan field's Khuff gas reservoir. The first cargo of condensate was loaded for Japan on January 30, 1992; lifters included Caltex and Nippon Mining.[8] Condensate exports were quickly followed by an inaugural shipment of 40,000 tons of liquid petroleum gas in March 1992. This was purchased by Mitsui and C. Itoh, who split the LPG cargo equally. QGPC had already lined up buyers in Japan for the LPG output from the North field development project, signing five-year contracts totaling half a million tons per year with Japanese buyers Marubeni, Mitsui, C. Itoh, and Cosmo as well as South Korea's Yosu Energy.

Some 142,000 tons of natural gas liquids, including 68,300 tons of propane and 50,260 tons of butane, were produced from North field phase 1 in the first half of 1992. Condensate output equated to another 500,000 tons, about 11,417 barrels per day.[9] This was less than the project's design capacity, which envisaged the production of 450,000 tons per year of LPG and 32,000 barrels per day of condensates. The shortfall was attributed to "normal teething problems" and, indeed, production soon improved.[10] QGPC was able to conclude an annual

contract with Nippon and Caltex for approximately 30,000 barrels per day of condensates from the North field at the end of 1992.

BP WITHDRAWS FROM QATARGAS

In a major blow to Qatargas, founding partner BP announced in early 1992 that
it was withdrawing from the joint venture company formed with QGPC and Total
in 1984 after so many years of effort. Citing inadequate economics returns from
the LNG project, where the estimated price tag was trending upward, the British major said Qatargas just did not stack up against other projects in BP's worldwide portfolio that offered better returns. "After looking at our financial and
investment priorities, we believe that the project does not give us a suitable return
given the stiff competition for funds within BP," the company told the industry
press on January 14, 1992.[11] Its spokesman in London subsequently stressed that
the decision to exit Qatargas was entirely related to factors internal to BP.[12]

The departure had been brewing since Total's development- and production-
sharing contract with QGPC six months previously. This closed-door negotiation and subsequent agreement had shattered any hope of creating an integrated
project where the shareholders in the LNG plant shared equally in the upstream
side of the project—particularly the lucrative natural gas liquids and condensate
sales. BP itself alluded to this dissatisfaction publicly, saying that the structure of
the project had contributed to its decision.[13] Total had offered to bring BP as
well as the two Japanese partners in Qatargas into the production-sharing contract, but BP balked at its asking terms. "I think the straw that broke the camel's
back was when BP found out that Total had cut a deal in the upstream," an oil
company executive who was working in the region at the time explained. "It gave
Total a bigger share in the gas liquids and thus a greater return from the LNG
project overall."[14]

It was also true that BP was undergoing changes at the corporate level and
suffering from a cash crunch when it withdrew from Qatargas. With the first
major cash calls for front-end engineering and design imminent, it was time to
either "fish or cut bait." BP chose the latter. Its decision immediately set alarm
bells ringing in Japan. Chubu Electric, whose president, Kamesaburo Matsunaga,
had been poised to fly to Doha to convert the firm's letter of intent for 4 million
tons per year of LNG into a firm twenty-five-year sale and purchase agreement,

immediately postponed the signing ceremony scheduled for February 22, 1992. There were frantic calls to Britannic House, BP's London headquarters, and senior executives had to fly out to Japan to explain the company's decision to a shaken Chubu and other prospective buyers. These included a group of electric and gas utilities that Mitsui was trying to corral for a potential third train at Qatargas.

Their concern was hardly surprising. Here was a company that had been selling LNG into Japan through its shareholding in Abu Dhabi's Adgas since 1977 abruptly exiting a second multibillion-dollar project located virtually next door in Qatar. "BP were leading the project, and all of a sudden they were pulling out from a place that had the largest gas field in the world eligible for LNG," the oil executive noted. "BP did not think it through before they pulled the plug at Qatargas, which is further evidence that they left because they were upset at what Total had done in the upstream."[15] Chubu assured the press that it still planned to sign the 4 million tons per year purchase contact with Qatargas in April or May, but the Japanese company was visibly unnerved by BP's exit, and there were concerns it was getting cold feet.[16]

The three remaining foreign partners in Qatargas agreed to divide BP's stake among themselves, leaving Total, Marubeni, and Mitsui with 10 percent each against QGPC's 70 percent. But the search was on to find a player with top-notch LNG credentials to replace BP. Total did not have the technical expertise to match BP, raising serious concern that the international banks would not finance the Qatargas project. For their part, Marubeni and Mitsui had been brought on board to help market output from the project. They had much less technical and engineering experience than Total. "The Japanese got very, very nervous and that made the Qataris nervous," another official whose firm was vying to replace BP remembers. "They had to get someone else in there fast, and they wanted an international oil company, a major that had LNG experience."[17] The list was a limited one: Shell, Exxon, and Mobil.

Shell was an obvious candidate. It had discovered the North field in 1971 and was involved in the original plans for developing the huge gas resource, both for LNG and domestic gas use. Shell hadn't made the final cut at Qatargas, of course. But that had more to do with the fallout from the 1977 explosion that destroyed the first natural gas liquids plant at Umm Said. The Qataris were still smarting over the subsequent arbitration battle with Shell, which Qatar essentially lost in 1986. Shell had just wound down its activities in Qatar's oil sector after nearly four decades, and local emotions were running high. It was widely felt that the

Anglo-Dutch firm hadn't always been totally candid with QGPC on technical issues related to its offshore oil fields, "Shell had treated the Qataris like mushrooms: they fed them manure and kept them in the dark," quipped an industry executive.[18]

No one could dispute Shell's LNG credentials, however. It had provided the technology for the world's first commercial liquefaction plant in Algeria back in 1964, before going on to lead large-scale export projects in Brunei, Malaysia, and Australia during the 1970s and 1980s. When BP dropped out of Qatargas in early 1992, Shell was putting together two more LNG ventures in Nigeria and Oman. These would cross the finish line in 1999 and 2000, in no small part due to Shell's leadership role. But this very experience—and the potential for conflicts of interest that went with it—also gave the Qataris pause. "They took a hard look at Shell, who fit the bill because it was a major and had extensive LNG experience," explained the official with the rival firm. "But Shell was in Australia, in Brunei, in Malaysia, and in Oman. Shell just had too many conflicts, and they weren't exactly popular in Qatar."[19]

Exxon's involvement in LNG dated from 1965, when it began building what became the world's second commercial liquefaction project in Libya. The Marsa El Brega plant was dogged by delays and did not start production until early 1970, followed by first exports in 1971. Exxon withdrew from Libya just ten years later amid heightened tensions between the Reagan administration and Libyan leader Col. Muammar Al Gaddafi, as well as clashes over oil production and prices. Marsa El Brega was taken over by Libya's state-owned Sirte Oil Company, which absorbed the assets of Exxon's local subsidiary Esso Standard Libya Inc. Shipments to Italy had already ceased in August 1980 over a price dispute, and the LNG plant all but shut down after Exxon's exit. When it did restart, Marsa El Brega's inability to extract natural gas liquids from the feed stream left Spain as the only import country able to handle the plant's very high Btu output.[20]

MOBIL RIDES TO THE RESCUE . . . EVENTUALLY

It was little wonder that the Qataris weren't particularly eager to team up with either Shell or Exxon in early 1992. That left Mobil, which, as the world's fourth-largest oil company (the second biggest in the United States), certainly classified as a "major." It also had LNG experience through its Arun project in Indonesia.

Initially, however, Mobil insisted it wasn't interested in replacing BP in the Qatar-gas project. "In response to press queries and rumors, Mobil advises that it has no interest in the 7.5% share in the Qatar LNG plant that was relinquished by British Petroleum," the U.S. company said in a one-sentence press release on January 31, 1992. This statement was released just seventeen days after BP's shock announcement that it was leaving Qatargas.

Together with Pertamina, Indonesia's state-owned oil and gas company, Mobil had built a highly successful LNG complex on the coast of northern Sumatra after Mobil's huge gas discovery near the village of Arun in 1971. Initially a three-train plant when it shipped its first LNG cargo to Japan in late 1978, Arun was expanded several times in the 1980s and had six trains totaling 11.6 million tons per year of capacity in 1986. By then Arun accounted for a large chunk of Mobil's gas production and, more importantly, around one-third of its corporate profits. "We were basically a $3 billion a year company at that point, and $1 billion was coming from Indonesia," explains a manager based in Jakarta during the late 1980s.[21] Mobil had done reservoir simulation studies on Arun, and senior management knew as far back as 1986 or 1987 that the gas field would go into decline in the late 1990s. By the time the Qatargas opportunity arose, the search to replace Arun was already in its sixth year.

Mobil was a crude oil marketer first and foremost, and it wasn't seeking another massive gas discovery to turn into LNG. It had been exploring for oil when it found gas with its Arun A-1 well on October 24, 1971, and at first the find had been a huge disappointment. It is much harder to monetize gas than oil, and company officials in New York, where Mobil was then based, questioned the practical value of a major gas resource in a remote part of Sumatra with no local demand. Distant markets like Japan, assuming they could be found, also posed giant-sized challenges.[22] Mobil would have preferred another Minas, Asia's largest oil field discovered in central Sumatra. But Pertamina got its keen interest in LNG from Japan's Nissho Iwai, the firm that in 1972 initiated a joint feasibility study. Pertamina then teamed up with Mobil and the Huffco Group led by Roy M. Huffington, who had found a huge accumulation of gas at Badak in East Kalimantan, to develop the Indonesian LNG trade.

Within two years Pertamina had formed an Indonesian company at Arun with Mobil and another at Badak with Huffco to build, own, and operate two large LNG plants. Pertamina took a majority 55 percent stake in each of these companies, leaving Mobil with 30 percent in the PT Arun Natural Gas Liquefaction

Company and Huffco with 30 percent in the PT Badak Natural Gas Liquefaction Company. The Japan Indonesia LNG Co., representing the five buyers who signed the first Indonesia–Japan sales contract in December 1973, held the remaining 15 percent in the companies. Both were established on a cost basis, with operating costs recovered out of LNG revenues. Pertamina was the only seller of LNG. Through supplemental agreements, Mobil and Huffco agreed to sell their share of LNG to Pertamina, which simultaneously sold these volumes to the Japanese buyers along with its own share. Pertamina divided the sales quantities between the two producing ventures. Chubu Electric's contract with Pertamina, for example, was sourced 70 percent from the Arun project and 30 percent from Badak.

There would be no rate of return on the billions of dollars invested in the infrastructure to turn the gas into LNG or to move output to market. Pertamina chose a common transporter for both plants, signing a transportation agreement with Burmah Gas Transport Limited to ship the refrigerated product to Japan. Neither Mobil nor Huffco participated in the transportation arrangements, although their representatives assisted in the negotiations. The profits from the sale of LNG in Japan were netted back to the wellhead and to the production-sharing contracts with Mobil Oil Indonesia at Arun and the Huffco Group at Badak, where they were split with Pertamina.[23]

The exploration effort to replace Arun, launched after Mobil had determined how much gas was ultimately in the reservoir and when it would go into terminal decline, was focused almost exclusively on oil. It can take years to identify potential prospects for exploitation, run geological studies, shoot and interpret seismic data, and drill an exploration well. If you're lucky enough to find oil after all that, you must then drill appraisal wells to define the extent of the reservoir and, once the geologists have determined whether the discovery is commercially viable, figure out how to develop the resource. The whole process can take seven to ten years, even longer in some cases. Mobil had started elephant hunting (oil industry language for very big exploration prospects) in the mid-1980s. At the time the average success rate was one discovery for every ten exploration wells drilled. The odds of finding an elephant were more like one in a thousand.

At first Mobil concentrated its efforts in countries where it already had a presence—Indonesia, Nigeria, the United States, Canada, Norway, and the United Kingdom. When those searches came up empty, the company formed an upstream outfit called New Exploration Ventures to work in countries where it did not already have a production affiliate. It spent $35 million—a huge amount of money at the time—drilling a wildcat in Peru's remote Huallaga River valley, where the guerrillas of the Shining Path were active and security was a big challenge. The seismic at the prospect was massive, and Mobil had high hopes of finding oil. But the well was dry, and it was plugged and abandoned in early 1992. By then the clock was ticking. The company turned its attention, still without luck, to so-called frontier areas in Vietnam, China, Kazakhstan, and particularly Russia. Altogether, the company spent $800 million over five years drilling wildcats in remote locations around the world.

Even with these disappointments, the focus remained squarely on exploration. No real thought had been given to joining existing ventures where the resource was already discovered and ready for development—particularly not if the resource was gas. As a result, when the Qataris first approached Mobil's senior management, it wasn't exactly receptive. Paul J. Hoenmans, then president of Mobil's exploration and production division under which LNG activities fell, was especially pessimistic about the Qatargas opportunity. The company moved to shut down the speculation by publicly denying any interest in BP's share. It wouldn't be long before Mobil changed its mind.

AMIR RESHUFFLES CABINET, APPOINTING NEW OIL MINISTER

By this time, Sheikh Abdul Aziz, the long-standing minister of finance and petroleum, had been noticeably absent from his functions for several years because of unspecified health problems, spending more and more time in his luxurious residences in Paris and Cannes. Abdullah Ibn Khalifa, the minister of the interior, had assumed the role of acting minister of finance and petroleum in his older brother's absence. Important milestones, including the signature of the 1991 letter of intent with Chubu Electric for the sale and purchase of LNG from Qatargas and the 1990 exploration- and production-sharing agreement with Elf Aquitaine, had fallen to Abdul Aziz's deputy, Mohammad Ibn Khalifa, another of the amir's sons and since 1989 the undersecretary of the Ministry of Finance and Petroleum.

On September 1, 1992, the amir replaced Abdul Aziz in a surprise cabinet reshuffle. Sheikh Khalifa abolished the Ministry of Finance and Petroleum and divided its functions between two new mega-ministries: The Ministry of Finance,

Economy, and Trade and the Ministry of Energy and Industry. Sheikh Moham-mad became the first minister of finance, economy, and trade. Abdullah Ibn Hamad Al Attiyah, a cabinet newcomer who had headed up the office of the Minister of the Interior since the late 1980s, was appointed as the minister of energy and industry. Al Attiyah had been attending OPEC ministerial meetings regularly for the past two decades as a member of Qatar's delegation, since his tenure as director of information at the Ministry of Finance and Petroleum in the early 1970s.

Al Attiyah's new position and the cabinet reshuffle reflected the growing influence of Crown Prince Hamad Ibn Khalifa. The two men were cousins raised in the same household; Sheikh Hamad's mother, Sheikha Aisha, the amir's first wife, was an Al Attiyah. Another close ally of the heir apparent, Hamad Ibn Jassim Ibn Jabir Al Thani, replaced Mubarak Ali Al Khatir as minister of foreign affairs. HBJ, as Hamad Ibn Jassim was now known, had been the minister of municipal affairs and agriculture as well as the acting minister of electricity and water in the outgoing cabinet. At times he had also assumed a very decisive role at the Ministry of Finance and Petroleum when important decisions were made. HBJ's sister Sheikha Rawhda was the amir's third wife and the mother of both Sheikh Abdullah, the minister of the interior, and Sheikh Mohammad, the newly appointed minister of finance, economy, and trade.

HBJ was replaced as minister of municipal affairs by his deputy, Ahmad Ibn Hamad Al Thani. Ahmad Mohammad Ali Al Subai, who had headed the Minis-try of Public Works in the outgoing cabinet, took over as minister of electricity and water. The amir's nephew Hamad Ibn Suhaym Al Thani became the new minister of public health. His place as the minister of information and culture was taken by Hamad Ibn Abdul Aziz Al Kawari. Reflecting a concern over rising Islamist sentiment in the country, a new Ministry of Endowments and Islamic Affairs was created. Abdullah Ibn Khalid Al Thani, who had previously com-manded the army's armored division, was appointed as its first minister.

Nine of the fifteen ministries, including the post of prime minister, which the amir retained, were headed by members of the ruling Al Thani family. There were three ministers of state in the cabinet as well, one of whom was Hamad Ibn Abdullah Al Thani, appointed minister of state for defense affairs as well as deputy commander-in-chief of the armed forces under the crown prince. Issa Al Kawari, Sheikh Khalifa's longtime aide, was reappointed as minister of state for Amiri Diwan. Mubarak Ali Al Khatir, the outgoing minister of foreign affairs, stayed on as minister of state and member of the Council of Ministers without a specific portfolio.

The cabinet reshuffle was quickly followed by a shake-up at the Qatar General Petroleum Corporation. On September 15 the crown prince issued an amiri decree appointing a new board of directors: Abdullah Ibn Hamad Al Attiyah became QGPC's chair and executive managing director while Dr. Al Marri was made deputy chair. Al Marri also retained his post as managing director of QGPC. Others appointed to the QGPC board included Abdul Aziz Al Dulaimi, the head of oil and gas operations at the state-owned firm; Yousef Hussain Kamal, an undersecretary at the Ministry of Finance, Economy and Trade; Faisal Al Suwaidi, the chair of the Qatar Fertilizer Company; Ibrahim Nuh Al Mutawa, QGPC's director of marketing; and Dr. Ibrahim Al Ibrahim, an adviser to the crown prince.

The crown prince had successfully maneuvered his own loyalists into key positions in government and throughout the tightly controlled economy, including the crucially important state-owned oil company. However, not everyone was happy with the decision to sideline the amir's son Abdul Aziz Ibn Khalifa. A letter drafted for Sheikh Khalifa's signature several months after the cabinet reshuffle pointed to this dissatisfaction. In the letter, which was apparently never signed but was made public, Sheikh Khalifa stated that in the event of his death and the ascension of Hamad Ibn Khalifa as ruler, Abdul Aziz was to automatically become the new crown prince. Sheikh Hamad suspected that Issa Al Kawari, the amir's right-hand man and the minister of state for Amiri Diwan, was behind the letter. While this was never confirmed, foreign observers noted that Al Kawari was absent from his office at the amir's administrative headquarters for several months after the letter came to light.

PROMINENT QATARIS PUSH FOR LIBERALIZATION

During this period Qatar was caught up in the liberalization movements then sweeping the Gulf region. In early 1992 a group of fifty-four prominent Qatari citizens presented Sheikh Khalifa with a petition demanding free parliamentary elections, a written constitution, and more civil and political rights. "The petitioners, who included university professors as well as senior officials, cited the spread of corruption, the deterioration of education and the lack of participation by common citizens in reaching decisions as the reasons for making their demand for a freely elected parliament," the *New York Times* reported.[24] Pressure from pro-democracy liberals had forced Kuwait's amir to call for free parliamentary elections, which were scheduled for October. Saudi Arabia had rejected similar demands, although King Fahd authorized the creation of a Consultative Assembly with power to overrule decisions by the Council of Ministers. The king would appoint the assembly's sixty members, however.

In their petition, the fifty-four Qataris said the Parliament would be responsible for creating a permanent constitution that guaranteed the establishment of democracy. "Such demands, while reflecting promises made in the past by the authorities themselves to hold free elections as long as two decades ago, constitutes a recognition of the right of citizens to run the affairs of their nation, and is in accordance with our Islamic faith, which directs us to adopt consultations and to abide by them," the petition read.[25] The liberalization effort was quickly extinguished with the arrest and detention of some of the petitioners. Others had their passports confiscated. The telephone lines of the signatories were tapped, and the foreign press reported that nearly all the petitioners were under government pressure to withdraw their signatures and apologize to Sheikh Khalifa.[26]

BORDER DISPUTES FLARE WITH NEIGHBORING STATES

There were also tensions with neighboring countries. After the failure of the Gulf Cooperation Council's Saudi-led mediation efforts, Qatar finally submitted an appeal to the International Court of Justice (ICJ) in The Hague in July 1991 to settle its long-standing dispute with Bahrain over the Hawar Islands and the Dibal and Jaradeh shoals. The ICJ subsequently announced that it would decide by June 1992 whether it was competent to judge the case. In its appeal, Qatar asked the court to affirm its sovereignty over the islands and shoals. While it expressed support for the 1947 British demarcation of the median line between the two states, Qatar objected to the exclusion of the Hawar Islands from the demarcation. It considered the previous British decision of 1939 (that Qatar should relinquish sovereignty over the Hawar Islands) null and void.

Sheikh Khalifa wasn't inclined to wait for the international court's decision to act. In April 1992, two months before the ICJ was expected deliberate on the matter, he issued an amiri decree defining the width of Qatar's territorial waters at twelve nautical miles while also adding an adjacent area of another twelve miles in which his country would exercise "all the rights and authorities provided in the provisions of international law."[27] This essentially asserted Qatari control over most of the disputed area. Unsurprisingly, the move was immediately and vociferously rejected by Bahrain. A spokesman for Bahrain's Foreign Ministry said his government totally rejected "what is implied in the decree about extending the territorial waters of the State of Qatar."[28] The spokesman also said Sheikh Issa Ibn Salman Al Khalifa, the amir of Bahrain, reserved the right to take any legal measures necessary to preserve Bahrain's rights.

When Bahrain appealed to U.S. president George H. W. Bush for help, the U.S. State Department cautioned both parties against the use of force and described the dispute as one of the most persistent obstacles to harmony within the GCC. Washington had to tread carefully in the imbroglio. It had already signed defense cooperation agreements with Bahrain and Kuwait and entered a similar pact with Qatar on June 23, 1992. As in the case of Bahrain and Kuwait, the defense agreement with Doha involved joint exercises, military training, the use of local naval facilities, and the stockpiling of U.S. military supplies in Qatar but stopped short of establishing a permanent U.S. military presence in the country. The Americans immediately began surveying sites in northern Qatar for equipment warehousing and started building these facilities in 1993.

Bahrain and Qatar subsequently agreed to abide by ICJ arbitration of their conflict, although Bahrain contended the two countries should file a new joint petition with the ICJ to settle their dispute over Hawar and the two shoals. This delaying tactic was immediately rejected by Qatar. To make matters worse, simmering tensions between Qatar and Saudi Arabia over their ill-defined border flared into a full-blown row following a violent clash on September 30, 1992. Qatar claimed Saudi soldiers had attacked one of its border posts, killing two Qatari border guards as well as one Saudi. Riyadh insisted there had merely been an exchange of gunfire between rival Saudi and Qatari Bedouin. The following day the Qatari News Agency reported that Saudi troops had surrounded the frontier post and forced the remaining Qatari border guards to abandon it. After an emergency session on October 1, Qatar's Council of Ministers said it was breaking off participation in the 1965 border agreement, although it stopped short of abrogating the accord.

Doha also called for immediate bilateral talks to draw an unambiguous border between the two countries, as the 1965 agreement contained no final demarcation and had essentially functioned for twenty-seven years as an ad hoc arrangement. The Saudis were unhappy with what they saw as creeping Qatari encroachment in the area around the border post. This had been ceded to Saudi Arabia by the United Arab Emirates in 1974, leaving Qatar with no land access to the UAE. For their part, the Qataris accused the Saudis of ignoring repeated requests for a negotiated border and of acting unilaterally to take military control of the frontier. Such action would close a key access route at the base of the peninsula from Khor al Odaid westward to Dohat al Salwa.

Western diplomats pointed to the recent cabinet reshuffle in Qatar and the appointment of HBJ as minister of foreign affairs as hardening Doha's stance on the border dispute. The amir was away on one of his extended absences during the initial confrontation and its immediate aftermath. Crown Prince Hamad Ibn Khalifa was running Qatar in his absence, and reports suggested the dispute had turned personal. Sheikh Hamad was said to have visited the contentious border post on October 1, the day it was overrun by Saudi forces. Upon his arrival, the crown prince reportedly spoke by telephone to the Saudi defense minister, Prince Sultan Ibn Abdul Aziz Al Saud, who cheekily welcomed Sheikh Hamad to Saudi Arabia. After the crown prince replied that he was on Qatari territory, the Saudis gave him just one hour to leave.[29]

Qatar recalled its ambassador from Saudi Arabia and added further tension by becoming the first member of the anti-Iraq Gulf War coalition to normalize relations with Baghdad. Qatar had already alarmed its GCC allies by openly soliciting and receiving support from Iran in its border dispute with Saudi Arabia. The decision to resume relations with Iraq, including reopening its embassy in Baghdad, was still a surprise, given the bellicose comments emanating from Saddam Hussein's regime. Barzan al-Tikriti, Saddam Hussein's half brother, had even suggested that Iraq, Saudi Arabia, and Oman should partition the other Gulf states among themselves. Kuwait would of course go to Iraq, Saudi Arabia would get Bahrain and Qatar, while Oman would absorb the UAE. The result, al-Tikriti claimed, would be a more stable region from which the United States could withdraw.[30]

Until the September 30, 1992, border post incident, the text of the 1965 treaty between Saudi Arabia and Qatar had not been publicly released. Sections of it were subsequently published in the *Saudi Gazette* in early October 1992. The border was thought to approximate the territorial limit claimed by Britain on Qatar's behalf at the February 1952 Anglo-Saudi Damman Conference but had never been formally demarcated. Neither side had seemed particularly bothered by the lack of land markers. Indeed, atlases and maps published by both Qatar and Saudi Arabia continued to show this same border, as did contemporary British navigation and pilotage charts.[31]

Saudi Arabia and Qatar announced they had resolved their rancorous border dispute on December 20, 1992. This rapprochement followed energetic mediation by Egypt's president, Hosni Mubarak. In a joint statement the foreign ministers of Qatar, Saudi Arabia, and Egypt announced the formation of a Saudi-Qatari committee to determine the final border within one year. The map signed in 1965 would be appended to show this finalized line, which was to be marked with physical demarcations installed by third-party international specialists hired specifically for the job. It took another four years to appoint a French survey firm to carry out this demarcation, and it wasn't until early 2001 that the two countries signed fifteen maps and documents finalizing their sixty-one-kilometer border from Saudi Arabia's Salwa frontier crossing point to Qatar's Odaid border post.

As part of the overall agreement ending the 1992 hostilities, Saudi Arabia vacated the border post it had occupied on October 1, and King Fahd publicly announced the "retirement" of the head of his country's border security police. The dispute also claimed the job of a Qatari minister. Mubarak Ali Al Khatir, the former minister of foreign affairs who had remained on as minister of state without portfolio after the September 1 cabinet reshuffle, was fired by the amir in dramatic fashion on December 14. The minister's dismissal came one day after he predicted in an Egyptian radio interview that the border confrontation between Qatar and Saudi Arabia would soon be resolved, presumably angering the amir by preempting government plans for announcing the resolution.[32]

INDUSTRIAL PROJECTS COMPETE FOR LIMITED GOVERNMENT FUNDS

Once again, there was no mention of Qatar's development plans for the North field in the government budget for the fiscal year beginning April 1, 1992. Nor did the budget refer to any of the other major industrialization projects under consideration.[33] While QGPC planned to inject equity into these ventures, this was likely to be in the form of infrastructure, natural gas, or other feedstock supplies rather than cash. The guiding principle behind the country's industrialization plans was that projects should be self-financing. The non-equity finance needed to support Qatar's ambitious industrialization program was estimated at about $5 billion, an enormous amount for a small country with a gross domestic product of $7.4 billion in 1990.[34]

Qatar's state budget did include QR 400 million (about $110 million) to cover new port infrastructure and associated dredging at Ras Laffan in northern Qatar, where the LNG project would be built under the second phase of the North field gas development. QGPC had followed up the award of the massive port construction contract to Societa italiana per condotte d'acqua with the appointment of the United Kingdom's L. G. Mouchel and Partners as consultants. Mouchel Middle East, the firm's local subsidiary, was responsible for project and design management and for construction supervision. The $10 million contract was awarded in February 1992, just a few weeks after BP's abrupt departure from the Qatargas joint venture.

Unlike Saudi Arabia, where local banks had substantial overseas deposits that could easily be deployed in financing industrial expansion, Qatari banks held just $1.7 billion in net foreign assets at the end of 1990.[35] The government depended on local banks to cover its short-term borrowing needs, and it didn't want them to divert funds into project lending. "In Qatar the domestic banks are even being prevented from involving themselves in the country's huge industrialization plans, so that their resources will continue to be available to the government," the *Middle East Economic Survey* reported.[36] Straight government guarantees for commercial finance, like the one given to QGPC for its $400 million syndicated loan back in 1989, were now out of the question as well. This applied even to the much-needed Wusail power plant and desalination complex, whose price tag had risen to QR 4,000 million ($1.1 billion). Deemed too expensive at a time of fierce competition for limited funds, Wusail was shelved again in late 1992.

Qatargas was preparing an information memorandum, including a time schedule and other project details, with a view to approaching international banks for funds at the beginning of 1993. This date proved overly optimistic, as the financing process was far more complex than the 1989 loan to QGPC for the first phase of the North field development. The onshore facilities for Qatargas were expected to cost $2.2 billion, of which $1.4 billion was to come from external finance. Total was responsible for arranging the financing for the offshore infrastructure under the controversial development- and production-sharing agreement it had signed with QGPC in 1991. The French firm had estimated the cost of field development at $600 million, but the tab was likely to be closer to $800 million. Dr. Al Marri said an additional $2 billion would be needed to build tankers to transport the LNG, putting the final project tally at about $5 billion.[37]

Qatar had already mortgaged a large chunk of its crude oil production, both to help fund the $1.6 billion first development phase of the North field and to pay other government obligations. Its three largest sales contracts, with Marubeni, Mitsubishi, and C. Itoh for a combined 150,000 barrels per day over three years beginning in 1990, were subject to prepayment arrangements (also known as pre-export financing deals). These arrangements involve upfront cash payment in return for future oil deliveries and give producers another source of liquidity while lessening their reliance on external capital markets.[38] Qatar's other oil contracts were negotiated on an evergreen basis and subject to annual renewal. Altogether, QGPC's contract sales amounted to 337,000 barrels per day in 1992.[39] This compared to total annual average production of 397,000 barrels per day.

The financial strains became evident in late 1992, when QGPC tried unsuccessfully to roll over its $400 million North field loan. With the date for repayment looming on December 15, the underwriting banks were asked to replace the facility with a new, higher-interest loan of equal amount and duration as it matured. Gulf Riyadh Bank and National Westminster, two of the underwriters, quickly declined to participate in the new facility. QGPC was eventually persuaded that rolling over the first loan it had ever raised on the international capital markets would send the wrong signal at a time when it was preparing to raise hundreds of millions of dollars—if not billions—in commercial finance for the second phase of the North field.[40] The original loan agreement had provided for bullet repayment, where the entirety of the loan amount is paid at maturity, after three years. Fortunately for QGPC, it had only drawn down $248 million of the $400 million facility.

Depressed oil prices were taking their toll. The government had stopped paying its bills on time, and payments to local businesses were running five to six months behind schedule. Ministries started laying off staff; nine hundred jobs were eliminated at the Ministry of Municipal Affairs and Agriculture alone. Most of the layoffs were confined to non-Qataris. Expatriates outnumbered Qataris by a ratio of three to one, with three hundred thousand foreign workers overwhelming the local population of one hundred thousand.[41] The country's per capita income was still among the highest in the world, at $28,000 for Qatari citizens. And the generous welfare system remained very much intact. Qataris paid no income or consumer taxes; benefited from free education, healthcare, and electricity as well as heavily subsidized housing; and were guaranteed employment in the government or at a state-owned firm after graduation.[42]

MOBIL NEGOTIATES ENTRY INTO QATARGAS

After his exploratory discussions with Mobil's point man about taking a position in Qatargas following BP's departure, QGPC head Dr. Al Marri tried to move up the food chain to entice senior management into serious talks. "I remember I got a phone call from Jabir Al Marri," says Michael Tusiani (the principal author of this book), then chair and chief executive of ship and commodities brokerage and consulting firm Poten & Partners. Poten had been involved with QGPC as an LNG adviser and on the trading side in Qatar's liquid petroleum gas and petroleum products sectors since 1977, and Tusiani knew the country well. Poten also enjoyed a long history with Mobil. "BP had just pulled out of Qatargas, and Mobil had issued the press release that it wasn't interested in the project," he recalls. Al Marri wanted Tusiani to talk to his friend Lucio (Lou) Noto, who was then Mobil's chief financial officer but would soon become its chair and chief executive officer. Noto and Tusiani had struck up a friendship in the early 1980s after being introduced by mutual Saudi friends. Tusiani had long been talking up the virtues of gas, especially in Qatar, to his friend and he made the call.

"There was a lot of institutional resistance to gas when the Qatargas opportunity came up," Noto recalled in an interview for this book.[43] "But there was also a growing realization that we had been completely unsuccessful in replenishing Arun, and we needed to do something quickly before all that revenue disappeared." Even Mobil's head of exploration and production, Paul Hoenmans, was coming around to the idea of gas. By early 1992 all of Mobil's exploration ventures had failed. It had become crystal clear that Arun was going to go into rapid decline within the decade, exactly as the company's geologists had predicted in the mid-1980s. Noto says the immediacy of Arun's revenue fall-off opened a lot of eyes in the company, including his own. "I didn't fully understand how important Arun was to the company until I got to be CFO," Mobil's former chief admits.

But Mobil still saw two major problems with the project structure at Qatargas. One was Total's dominant position in the upstream and the big slice of the profitable condensate stream it had secured through its North field development- and production-sharing agreement with QGPC. This was of course the same concern that had led BP to exit Qatargas earlier that year. The other hurdle was the relatively small amount of equity participation on offer in the LNG plant, which at 10 percent really wasn't enough to entice the Americans.

Mobil was not above appealing personally to the amir to get Total out of Qatargas. A senior Mobil executive told Sheikh Khalifa during a face-to-face meeting in the Amiri Diwan that the best way to realize the ruler's dream of seeing an LNG tanker leave the port of Ras Laffan for Asia by 1997 was to get rid of the French firm, presumably replacing it with Mobil. In the end, however, the amir wouldn't budge on Total's upstream role. The shareholdings in the upstream— which covered gas extraction, separation, and the marketing of condensates— and the downstream liquefaction plant infrastructure would remain unaligned. These two facets of the project also had different fiscal terms, setting the stage for future partnership disputes.

The U.S. major had better luck on the equity issue with Dr. Al Marri. Mobil told him frankly that a 10 percent interest was simply not enough to attract the company. From a resource perspective, Mobil found it devoted the same amount of human and technical capital to a project in which it had a 10 percent stake as it did to one in which had a 50 percent shareholding. It told Al Marri that it needed a minimum of 20 percent to make participation in Qatargas worth its while. This was a nonstarter for the other partners: Total, Marubeni, Mitsui, and QGPC. While the latter signaled it would give up some of its majority stake in the project to accommodate Mobil, the amount QGPC was willing to relinquish was not enough to meet the U.S. company's insistence on 20 percent.

Al Marri, however, had a plan to appease Mobil and put his country on track to become a major exporter—perhaps even the world's largest—of LNG by the end of the decade. As one former Mobil manager remembers it:

> Dr. Jabir came to us and said: "OK, I tell you what we will do. You come into Qatargas for 10 percent and we will form a new and separate LNG joint venture called Ras Laffan LNG in which you can have a 30 percent stake. And after the first 6 million tons in Qatargas, the next 10 million tons sold from Qatar will be exclusively dedicated to Ras Laffan. You will have 10 percent of 6 million tons per year and 30 percent of 10 million tons per year, and that exceeds your 20 percent minimum."[44]

The U.S. major almost immediately accepted Al Marri's proposal.

On August 27, 1992, Mobil signed an agreement with QGPC for the acquisition of equity in the two LNG ventures—10 percent in Qatargas and 30 percent in Ras Laffan LNG, which would later be known as RasGas. The deal was announced by Issa Al Kawari, the minister of state for Amiri Diwan and the acting chair of Qatargas.[45] While Marubeni and Mitsui each ceded the additional equity in Qatargas they had absorbed after BP's withdrawal, Total insisted on maintaining the same shareholding in the LNG plant as Mobil. QGPC was forced to make up the difference from its majority 70 percent share. The state-owned firm's interest in the downstream infrastructure fell to 65 percent, with Total and Mobil each taking 10 percent and Marubeni and Mitsui both reducing their stakes to the original 7.5 percent. A different breakdown would apply to the upstream, with the other three partners eventually joining QGPC and Total in this portion of the project. But there was a great deal of bargaining, and much gnashing of teeth, before the shareholding in the development- and production-sharing agreement was finalized.

In a statement following signature of the initial agreement, Mobil touted its experience and technical expertise in gas development and LNG processing as well as its marketing strength. The firm put the amount of North field reserves required for Qatargas at 9 trillion cubic feet of gas and 375 million barrels of condensate.[46] It estimated project costs of $3.5 billion to cover field development and the construction of two liquefaction trains to support the 4 million tons per year sale to Chubu Electric. Another $2.8 billion would be needed to build seven 135,000-cubic-meter LNG tankers. Qatargas had signed the final twenty-five-year sale and purchase agreement with Chubu for the base volume on May 14, four months to the day from BP's departure. The Japanese utility also secured an option for another 2 million tons annually, potentially boosting deliveries to 6 million tons per year and necessitating a third LNG train at Qatargas.

The second project, Ras Laffan LNG, would be roughly twice the size of Qatargas and require reserves of 15 trillion feet of gas and 625 million barrels of condensate.[47] Mobil took pains to ensure alignment throughout the upstream and downstream parts of Ras Laffan LNG to avoid the conflicts of interest inherent at Qatargas. "We did not like the structure of Qatargas, and we structured Ras Laffan LNG very differently," explains one retired Mobil executive. "It was a 70–30 split between QGPC and Mobil from the upstream resource through to the LNG sale. It was the same shareholding in the gas, in the condensate, in the LPG, and in the LNG. We made it clean and integrated, so that we could avoid these conflicts."[48] In its statement announcing the August 27 agreement, Mobil cited a preliminary estimate of $8.75 billion for field development and the five liquefaction trains to produce 10 million tons per year of LNG.[49]

Almost immediately questions arose about Chubu's optional quantity of 2 million tons per year and whether it would stay with Qatargas or go to Ras Laffan LNG. Chubu had until May 1994 to decide whether it wanted this extra volume. It was widely assumed that, if Chubu did exercise this option, it would assign the additional LNG to other users in Japan rather than retain it for itself; Chubu's base quantity of 4 million tons per year already represented the largest purchase ever made by a Japanese company from a single project. Indeed, Mitsui was already working hard to cobble together a group of six other Japanese utilities to buy the additional 2 million tons reserved by Chubu. The trading house had even dangled this volume in front of Mobil, indicating it might bring any deal it brokered with the Japanese group to Ras Laffan LNG in exchange for a stake of around 5 percent in this second liquefaction venture.

Mobil readily agreed to Mitsui's overture. An early sale to blue-chip companies in Japan would launch the first train at Ras Laffan LNG and ease marketing efforts with potential buyers in South Korea and Taiwan for subsequent liquefaction trains. It would mean giving up some of its shareholding in Ras Laffan LNG, as Mobil had agreed with QGPC that the assumption of equity by new partners would derive from its 30 percent interest rather than the Qatari firm's 70 percent.[50] At the time, this was viewed as a small price to pay for a project potentially as large as 10 million tons per year.

This concept that Mobil would have to make room for all comers in order to facilitate deals ended up being sorely tested. QGPC would eventually pressure the American company to relinquish part of its stake in Ras Laffan LNG to other Japanese trading houses in what essentially resulted in a financing arrangement that allowed the cash-strapped Qataris to avoid putting in any equity capital. But that was still several years away.

QATARIS JUGGLE OTHER PROSPECTIVE LNG PROJECTS

QGPC had not forgotten its other prospective LNG projects. Less than a week after the initial accord with Mobil was announced, the Qataris signed a joint venture agreement with Snam, the gas distribution arm of Italy's Eni group, and the U.S. company Bunker Hunt. This deal was signed by Abdullah Ibn Hamad Al Attiyah, Qatar's minister of energy and industry; Pio Pigorni, the chair of Snam; and Nelson Bunker Hunt. It called for the formation of the Qatar Europe LNG Company to produce 6 million tons per year for the Italian market. Dubbed Qatar Eurogas by its three partners, 65 percent of the joint venture was owned by QGPC, 30 percent by Snam, and 5 percent by Hunt. It was to be fully integrated from the wellhead to the sale of the LNG in Italy and (after possible expansion to 10 million tons per year) other European markets.[51]

Enel, who had earlier planned to join Qatar Eurogas, was notably absent from the partnership lineup. The state-owned power generator did acknowledge that it was still "interested" in the Qatari project at the time the venture agreement was signed. Snam stressed that if Enel eventually joined Qatar Eurogas, its acquisition would have to come out of Snam's own equity stake. According to Snam, its 30 percent shareholding in Qatar Eurogas represented the total Italian participation in the joint venture.[52] But Enel was in the process of being privatized by the Italian government, and it formally opted out of the project two months after Qatar Eurogas was formed.

The Italian electricity company had already contracted to buy about half of the output from the first two trains at Nigeria LNG. This twenty-year sale was one of the main reasons Shell and the other shareholders in Nigeria LNG had decided to proceed with the project, which at the time the deal with Enel was signed in 1992 was due online in 1997. Enel would end up canceling the contract after stiff environmental opposition forced it to bow out of plans to build a receiving terminal on the Tuscan coast. The cancelation, which Nigeria LNG described as totally unprecedented in the international gas industry, contributed to the project's two-year delay. A complicated LNG-for-pipeline gas swap arrangement was eventually negotiated with Gaz de France, but not before Nigeria LNG sued Enel for breach of contract.

Elf Aquitaine was also working to turn the option negotiated with QGPC in mid-1991 into a concrete project. QGPC had attributed a part of the North field to the French firm, potentially allowing Elf to build an integrated project to provide LNG from two liquefaction trains over a period of twenty-five years. Elf had subsequently teamed up with Sumitomo Corporation, signing an agreement with the Japanese trader to promote the sale of LNG into Japan on July 8, 1992. Elf stressed that it would continue to be responsible for all feasibility studies and operations required to implement the 4-million-tons-per-year project. Sumitomo, which was labeled a "potential helper" in the announcement of the agreement, would take charge of "part of the work" related to the marketing of LNG in Japan as well as project financing and maritime transport.[53]

NEW QATARGAS PARTNERS SIGN JOINT
VENTURE AGREEMENTS

Competition between Mobil and Total made for some hard bargaining in the months leading up to signature of the official Qatargas joint venture agreements on January 31, 1993. As the sole remaining oil major in Qatargas after BP's departure, Total demanded the highest equity interest among the foreign partners in all phases of the project while also holding out for a stake in the new venture between QGPC and Mobil. For its part, Mobil refused to let Total enter Ras Laffan LNG and had tried to secure the general management of Qatargas for itself. In the end, neither company got everything it wanted. Total beat back Mobil to secure a 20 percent stake in the upstream development- and production-sharing agreement at Qatargas, leaving the U.S. major with 10 percent followed by Marubeni and Mitsui with 2.5 percent each. But the French company had to accept the same equity shareholding in the downstream infrastructure as Mobil, and it was not able to participate in Ras Laffan LNG. QGPC retained a 65 percent interest across the spectrum at Qatargas.

Despite the different upstream and downstream alignments, the partners agreed to manage and operate Qatargas as an integrated venture, with QGPC responsible for general management, Total assuming a lead role in upstream operations, and Mobil taking the same position downstream. Dr. Al Marri was appointed acting general manager. Michel Naylies of Total was named deputy general manager for fields, while Mobil's Ronny Parker became deputy general manager for plants. QGPC's Ajlan Al Kawari took over as deputy manager for administration and finance.[54]

The official signing ceremony at the Doha Sheraton almost didn't come off after Mobil's auditors raised red flags over a $20 million commission Total had already paid and wanted the new partner to split. "We had to pay our share of the sunk costs, so we sent in people to audit the books to make sure we were paying legitimate costs," remembers one Mobil manager. "There was a commission that Total had paid that we deemed inappropriate, and we made it known to everyone that we were not going to pay our share of it."[55] The day the joint venture agreements were to be signed, the partners began gathering at the Doha

Sheraton. QGPC's delegation was headed by Abdullah Ibn Hamad Al Attiyah, the minister of energy and industry, who was to sign the joint venture agreements in his capacity as chair of the board and executive managing director of the state-owned company. Paul Hoenmans, the president of Mobil Exploration and Production, had flown in to represent his company, while Total had sent Alain Brion, the managing director of Total Trading and Middle East. Marubeni and Mitsui also had senior executives in attendance.

Total was not happy with what it saw as Mobil's obstinacy over the commission, which had apparently been paid to a senior government official. With the signing ceremony about to begin, the French company seized on the opportunity for a little Gallic-style brinkmanship. Brion sent one of his aides to the hotel conference hall where the dignitaries had gathered with a message: he would not come down from his room on the eighth floor until Mobil agreed to pay its share of the disputed commission. The Qataris, no strangers to eleventh-hour negotiating ploys, would have none of it. As one attendee later recalled, the energy minister sent Total's messenger back up to the eighth floor with a message of his own. "Al Attiyah told him to tell Alain Brion to get down here in the next two minutes or Total would be out of the project."[56] Total's managing director acquiesced, and the ceremony proceeded as planned with all parties signing the joint venture agreements. The French company continued to seek payment from Mobil for years but was never successful.

Qatargas had already selected J. P. Morgan as its financial adviser, while Citibank provided informal advisory services. Financing had been delayed pending final agreement on the structure of the joint venture, and the information memorandum had still not been released to potential lenders. The foreign partners would now have to put up the initial cash required to start work as the timeline for first exports was tight and the financial package wouldn't be in place until the end of 1993 at the earliest. Because of the large Japanese component, banks in Japan were expected to be the main providers of loan finance to Qatargas. The Industrial Bank of Japan, Chubu's in-house bank and a major arranger of energy finance for Japanese firms, was maneuvering to take the lead in putting together an underwriting syndicate for the project. However, the Bank of Tokyo, another big player in energy finance with close ties to Mitsui and Marubeni, was also interested in taking the role of agent bank in coordinating and leading the banks in their dealings with Qatargas.[57]

M. W. Kellogg had already completed the front-end engineering and design for the liquefaction plant, and the bidding process to find a contractor for the main construction contract was under way with an award scheduled for the end of April. Preparatory work, including a camp for workers, had already commenced at the Qatargas plant site in the Ras Laffan Industrial City. Total had started the basic engineering for the offshore development in its Paris headquarters, and it was preparing to drill a confirmation well in its specific North field block. A total of sixteen wells, including this pilot well and fifteen development wells, would be drilled into the Khuff 4 zone to produce 800 million cubic feet per day of non-associated gas. The French firm said it expected to award the main contracts for the two wellhead platforms, a production and utilities platform, an accommodation platform, and connecting bridges by the end of 1993. Plans also called for the construction of an eighty-two-kilometer pipeline with a diameter of thirty-two inches linking these offshore facilities to the liquefaction plant.

In a separate announcement the day after the Qatargas joint venture agreements were signed, Mobil put the total cost of the project including field development at over $5.5 billion—at least $3 billion for the two liquefaction trains dedicated to Chubu and more than $2.5 billion for LNG tankers.[58] Mobil said an optional third train at Qatargas would increase this cost estimate. But the U.S. company clearly hoped Mitsui would be able to deliver the additional 2 million tons per year reserved by Chubu to Ras Laffan LNG, and it referred to "other utilities and gas companies in Japan" as potential customers for this competing project. QGPC had assigned a letter of intent with Korea Gas Corporation for 2.4 million tons per year to Ras Laffan LNG, while Taiwan's China Petroleum Corporation had also expressed interest in LNG from the project. These companies were far less credit-worthy than the buyers in Japan, however. The 2 million tons per year being held back for Chubu would be in play once its option at Qatargas expired, and Mobil needed the demand to kick start Ras Laffan LNG.

QATAR IMPROVES TERMS TO ENTICE
UPSTREAM INVESTMENT

Qatar's oil production averaged 430,000 barrels per day in early 1993, the boost ascribed in part to incremental output from the recently commissioned Diyab structure on Dukhan's south end. This level was substantially over the country's OPEC quota of 380,000 barrels per day. Qatar was assigned an even more restrictive quota of 364,000 barrels per day under a cutback deal reached by the twelve-member cartel on February 16, forcing QGPC to inform contract lifters of cuts to their March nominations of up to 15 percent for onshore crude and as much as 5 percent for Qatar Marine.[59] Flows dropped to 380,000 barrels per day that month, still higher than Qatar's new quota. Production creeped back above 400,000 barrels per day by June, however, and remained at this level for the rest of 1993. The average for the year was 403,000 barrels per day, up from 397,000 barrels daily in 1992.[60]

OPEC's membership had fallen to twelve following Ecuador's withdrawal from the organization in December 1992. Ecuador had joined the cartel in 1973 and was the first member to leave. Its energy minister, Andrés Barreiro Vivas, pointed to the annual $2 million membership fee and OPEC's refusal to increase the South American country's 320,000-barrel-per-day quota as the major reasons for the withdrawal.[61] Smaller producers like Ecuador, Qatar, and Gabon argued that larger contributors such as Saudi Arabia and Iran should cut their production to bolster sliding prices. Two years later Gabon also suspended its membership, citing similar concerns. Both countries would eventually rejoin the organization many years later—Ecuador in 2007 and Gabon in 2016. Ecuador withdrew its OPEC membership again at the start of 2020. This followed Qatar's departure in 2019.

Qatar's sustainable production capacity in late 1993 was around 430,000 barrels per day. QGPC knew it needed to develop additional reserves either through new discoveries or enhanced oil recovery to maintain this rate. Recoverable oil reserves stood at 3.74 billion barrels at the end of 1993.[62] This was considerably less than the 4.5 billion barrels Qatar had reported to OPEC every year since 1984, but it was marginally better than the 3.3 billion barrels reported in 1983. The reserves figure for 1993 included 2.27 billion barrels in the onshore Dukhan area and 1.47 billion barrels in the offshore fields, excluding the Bunduq structure shared equally with Abu Dhabi.[63] In contrast, Qatar's recoverable gas reserves of 227 trillion cubic feet (equivalent to 44 billion barrels of oil) had only just begun to be tapped.

Economic pressure and depleting crude oil reserves had already forced Qatar to soften its go-it-alone approach and offer production-sharing terms for the incremental output of the northern dome of the Idd el-Shargi field. This deal, still under negotiation with three foreign oil companies, was linked to a system-wide technical service agreement covering all exploration and production activities at QGPC's producing fields—the onshore structures formerly managed by the Dukhan Service Company as well as the offshore fields Shell's local subsidiary had previously handled. No other existing fields were yet put forward to foreign investors on production-sharing terms, although this was under consideration.

Elf Aquitaine and Maersk continued to carry out drilling and evaluation work at their respective offshore exploration blocks, but Amoco relinquished its onshore acreage after disappointing results from nine wildcats. Four onshore and offshore blocks remained open to international firms on exploration- and production-sharing terms, and the dozen or so companies studying data on these tracts had yet to make a commitment. QGPC itself was not conducting any exploration drilling in its areas of operation, although it was doing some development work at Idd el-Shargi North Dome targeting the Shuaiba and Arab D reservoirs. The state-owned company's severely stretched resources—human, technical, and capital—were squarely focused on getting Qatar's huge offshore gas reserves onstream.

Elf's promising al-Khalij discovery on Block 6 was proving expensive because of reservoir complexity. The French company and its Italian partner, Agip, had still not submitted a development plan for the offshore field, despite earlier plans to begin production in the first half of 1993. Instead, the time had been spent renegotiating the terms of their upstream accord. QGPC finally agreed to raise the cost recovery allowance to 50 percent in mid-1993. Cost recovery allows contractors, or concessionaires, to recoup the cost of exploration, development, and operations out of gross revenue and is a standard feature of production-sharing contracts. The amount of oil allocated for cost recovery typically ranges from 30 percent to 60 percent, with unrecovered costs carried forward to succeeding years.

A development plan for al-Khalij, where proven recoverable reserves were eventually put at 200 million barrels of 28° API gravity crude oil, was due for submission to QGPC in the first half of 1994.[64] Elf still envisaged a production rate of 35,000 barrels per day for the field, although the firm acknowledged that it could take time to reach this level. Hoping to make other small and technically challenging oil discoveries attractive for development, QGPC signaled it would extend the improved cost recovery terms secured by Elf and Agip at al-Khalij to other foreign investors. QGPC also held out the prospect of enhanced production splits to operators who applied new technologies such as 3D seismic and horizontal drilling to improve recovery factors at known fields.

Elf had drilled two wells at Block 1, which was located mostly offshore but extended onshore near Ras Laffan. One land-based wildcat was dry, but a second well drilled into the Shuaiba formation at what would eventually be called

Idd el-Shargi South Dome flowed at 2,400 barrels per day. Elf was considering the possibility of linking this small discovery to Idd el-Shargi North Dome,
as the French firm was among the three companies negotiating with QGPC for
the technical service agreement at its producing fields. The winner would provide
support to QGPC via specialized experts and access to its research facilities.
Atlantic Richfield and Occidental Petroleum of the United States were also
competing for this work, which was coupled with a production-sharing agreement to expand Idd el-Shargi North Dome through enhanced recovery of the
Arab C and D and Shuaiba formations.

Maersk had drilled one appraisal well in its offshore Block 5, targeting the
Shuaiba formation at 7,200 feet to appraise an old QGPC discovery. While this
block contained a large portion of the North field, the gas-bearing Khuff zone
underlying the oil formations was off limits to the Danish firm. Maersk planned
to drill two more wells to further assess known oil accumulations.[65] Amoco's relinquished Block 2 had been divided into two equal areas called Block 2N and Block
2S to appeal to smaller firms, while two additional tracts known as Block 7 and
Block 8 were available offshore. Block 8 straddled the Maydan Mahzam, Bul
Hanine, and Idd el-Shargi fields as well as the Halul island terminal, but QGPC
retained a belt equivalent to three square kilometers around each of these structures. Blocks 3 and 4 were listed as "awaiting management approval" on QGPC's
situational map.[66]

Elsewhere offshore, Canada's Gulfstream Resources completed the purchase
of Veba Oel's stake in the Wintershall-led exploration- and production-sharing
agreement. Shareholdings in the two offshore blocks now covered under this
accord had shifted several times since the 1988 arbitration award, with Koch
Industries and Deutsche Schachtbau leaving the consortium and Deilmann Erdoel &
Erdgas (a subsidiary of the German company Preussag) joining the lineup. Wintershall was now the largest partner, with a 50 percent interest, while Gulfstream
was next, with 33.85 percent. Deilmann Erdoel & Erdgas held the remaining
16.15 percent. The original block was broken up into so-called east and west blocks,
and its acreage was no longer contiguous following mandatory relinquishments.

Gulfstream put recoverable reserves at the gas-prone east block, which contained a southern extension of the North field, at 32 trillion cubic feet of dry gas,
576 million barrels of condensate, and 538 million barrels of liquid petroleum
gas.[67] These estimates were based on the 1980 study by DeGolyer & MacNaughton. The Canadian firm also revealed that its consortium planned to sell the gas

it extracted from this block by pipeline to Gulf Cooperation Council countries, particularly to Bahrain and the UAE emirate of Dubai and possibly also to Kuwait. This project involved the production of 800 million cubic feet of gas and up to 50,000 barrels per day of condensate and liquids and entailed the construction of two offshore platforms and a new onshore processing and treatment facility at Ras Laffan.[68]

No start date for east block production was given, but time was getting tight for Wintershall and its partners. According to the terms of the 1988 arbitration, they had to begin producing gas from the contract area by June 1, 1996. If the consortium met this deadline, its production-sharing rights would extend to 2011. Otherwise, it would have to relinquish the east block unless QGPC agreed to an extension. No such restrictions applied to the west block, where Wintershall had still not been allowed to commence exploration activities at the potentially oil-bearing Structure A. Located near the Dibal shoal north of the Hawar Islands, the area was claimed by both Qatar and Bahrain and was subject to ongoing proceedings at the International Court of Justice in The Hague.

Following Qatar's earlier move to impose a twenty-four-mile limit, Bahrain issued its own decree setting the width of the country's territorial waters at twelve nautical miles and claiming sovereignty over a further twelve. This tit-for-tat declaration was issued by Bahrain's deputy ruler, Hamad Ibn Issa Al Khalifa, on April 20, 1993, and came almost one year to the day after Sheikh Khalifa's nearly identical amiri decree. Like Qatar's decree, the Bahraini claim covered the Hawar Islands and the Dibal and Jaradeh shoals. The ICJ had still not weighed in on whether it was competent to judge the territorial dispute between Qatar and Bahrain. After a year's delay, the court finally announced it would hold preliminary hearings on February 24, 1994, to determine its authority to settle the dispute.

QATARGAS LAUNCHES ARDUOUS FINANCING EFFORT

Qatargas and its financial adviser, J. P. Morgan, had delayed approaching international banks for the downstream financing even after the joint venture agreements were finally signed in early 1993. They now hoped to raise all the funds required in Japan, and in late 1993 four Japanese banks were asked to assemble an underwriting group for that purpose. The Bank of Tokyo was selected to lead this effort with participation from the Industrial Bank of Japan, Fuji Bank, and

Sakura Bank. One complicating factor was the lack of an LNG market price in the sale and purchase agreement with Chubu Electric, on which the cash flows from the liquefaction project were entirely dependent. It was a glaring omission, but in refusing to agree pricing in advance, the electric utility gained considerable leverage. "Chubu knew how desperate the Qataris were to get Qatargas off the ground," a retired Mobil executive explains. "And it is much easier, from a buyer's perspective, to negotiate a price once the seller has invested in a project."[69]

The vague language in the Chubu contract about keeping its Qatargas price competitive with other LNG imports into Japan wasn't enough to appease the bankers. After some arm-twisting, Hajime Okada, Chubu's vice-president for fuel purchases and its point man on Qatargas, was convinced to sign a letter tightening up the contract's pricing clause. Herb Gammons, a Mobil executive who had worked in Indonesia and was now assigned to the Qatargas project, was involved in the process. "I remember Gammons waving the letter from Okada in the air, saying it was only one page, but it was worth $4 billion," recalls the former Mobil official.[70] Ultimately, the banks demanded more price protection from Chubu before financing was agreed.

The final tally for the first two trains at Qatargas ended up remarkably close to that $4 billion figure: $3.75 billion, including $2.85 billion for downstream infrastructure and $903 million in upstream field development. This commitment for a single project represented an enormous amount of capital, exceeding half of Qatar's total gross domestic product of $7.2 billion in 1993. It certainly was not a stretch to claim, as one Japanese financier did in early 1995, that Qatar's economy hinged on the project's success.[71] Qatargas also represented the first essentially all Japanese LNG project financing since the Indonesian plants at Arun and Badak, which were launched in 1973 during the height of the first oil shock and formed a major plank in the Japanese government's urgent initiative to secure alternative energy sources for the oil-dependent country.

Qatargas and the original group of four arranging banks finally initialed the $1.995 billion financing package with the Bank of Tokyo, the Industrial Bank of Japan, Fuji Bank, and Sakura Bank on April 29, 1995. Finalization of the loan agreement was delayed another five months by the subsequent entry of two European banks whose identity the minister of energy and industry declined to disclose. After returning to Doha from the signing ceremony in London, Abdullah Ibn Hamad Al Attiyah announced on October 3, 1995, that a final agreement with the four Japanese banks as well as these two newcomers had been signed.[72] Qatargas was able to start withdrawing funds in late October.

After much handwringing, the banks accepted nonrecourse financing—meaning cash flow from the project would provide the primary security on loan repayment, not guarantees from the government of Qatar or individual Qatargas shareholders. This was only obtained after Chubu Electric agreed to pay a floor price that, regardless of what long-term pricing formula was eventually negotiated, ensured Qatargas would be able to meet its operational costs, repay its bank loans and return a reasonable profit to its shareholders. A memorandum set this minimum price at $3.60 per million Btu in 1994 dollars, subject to annual escalation in line with the U.S. Consumer Price Index. Prices for LNG imported into Japan were running significantly below this critical threshold when the memorandum was signed, and they ended up averaging just $3.45 per million Btu in 1995.[73]

Mobil pushed particularly hard for a minimum price at both Qatargas and Ras Laffan LNG. Its treasury group had warned that the level of financing for the two projects, but especially Ras Laffan LNG, would be very low without a minimum price. "Taking a sales contract with a minimum price in it to the banks would get us about $2 billion worth of financing," recalls a Mobil official. "If we did not have the minimum price, we could only get $1 billion, so the minimum price was worth about $1 billion in financing to the project."[74] The minimum price concept originated in the 1970s when the commercial LNG industry was in its infancy and the banks viewed big grassroots projects as inherently risky investments. A standard feature in Indonesia's sales contracts as well as those from other Far East suppliers, minimum prices were still considered crucial when the Qatargas financing was being arranged. However, it would not be long before market forces made them a relic of the past.

The complex web of cross guarantees among banks, export-credit agencies, and other state sponsors in Japan that was eventually negotiated for the Qatargas downstream financing meant it was not always clear which entity was taking the financial risk. Ultimately, it was the Japanese government that stepped in, with an array of support mechanisms designed to promote the participation of Japan's commercial banks. "Putting together the financial package for Qatargas was a difficult task and in the end required GOJ [Government of Japan] financial guarantees before it could be finalized," the American Embassy in Tokyo reported to Washington in early 1995, as the four Japanese banks prepared to initial the nearly $2 billion loan agreement.[75]

This loan package included $1.6 billion in export facilities guaranteed by the Export-Import Bank of Japan, whose own risk was guaranteed by the commercial banks. Japan's Ministry of International Trade and Industry then insured part of this bank risk. Another $400 million in commercial bank loans was guaranteed by the Japan National Oil Corporation, a government institution. This amount represented the full commercial finance component—70 percent of the total cost of the downstream infrastructure. While the shareholders in Qatargas provided the guarantees during the construction phase, the lenders and their guarantors assumed the liability for this debt once Qatargas started generating cash flow. At that point, to prevent government raids, all the revenue from the sale to Chubu would be deposited in an offshore account managed by an agent bank.

With the tortuous process of arranging finance still under way, civil engineering work at the Qatargas plant site in Ras Laffan and the procurement of equipment was being funded by shareholder contributions. Chiyoda Chemical Engineering and Construction Company emerged in mid-1993 as the lowest bidder for the liquefaction plant, squeezing out two other contractors. The Japanese contractor's bid of ¥160 billion ($1.395 billion) covered the engineering, procurement, construction, and commissioning of two LNG trains with a capacity of 2 million tons per year each. France's Technigaz and two local contractors were awarded a $115 million contract to build three 85,000-cubic-meter cryogenic storage tanks.

Total did not allow parallel efforts to arrange financing for the upstream facilities at Qatargas to derail the project's schedule, and the major field development contracts were awarded in December 1993. The contract for two wellhead platforms, an accommodation platform, and connecting bridges went to the Franco-American joint venture McDermott-ETPM. Abu Dhabi's National Petroleum Construction Company and Technip Geoproduction of France won another contract for the production and utilities platform. Both deals covered everything from the engineering, procurement, and construction of the platforms to their transportation and installation. Japan's Toyo Engineering was also retained to build receiving facilities for gas and condensate piped in from the North field as well as installations for treating, storing, and loading condensates.

Bankers complained early in the upstream financing process that Qatargas refused to specifically pledge the revenue from the sale of around thirty thousand barrels per day of condensates from the field as security, which was expected to equate to about $200 million a year. At least one international bank withdrew for this reason and because there was no provision for excess cash flow from the liquefaction plant to be transferred to the upstream phase to repay debt if required.[76] The $570 million financing package ended up being partly guaranteed by condensate sales as well as some Western credit agencies. But the actual loan agreement would not be signed until December 1996—the same month that Qatargas exported its first condensate cargo. Nine international and regional banks participated in the financing, as did credit agencies from France, the United Kingdom, Germany, Italy, and the United States.

The nearly $2.7 billion debt financing for Qatargas was in many respects unprecedented. It was the largest project finance scheme thus far in the Middle East. It was also the longest, with repayment terms after project completion of up to twelve years depending on the specific debt tranche. Additionally, it was the first grassroots LNG project where the upstream and downstream financing were pursued separately yet simultaneously with different banking consortia. As successful as these efforts were, the debt portion of the project still represented just 70 percent of the funds needed to pay for Qatargas. The shareholders still had to come up with the remaining 30 percent in the form of equity capital. This wasn't going to be easy for cash-strapped QGPC, the majority partner in both segments of the project.

QGPC STRUGGLES TO LINE UP EQUITY CAPITAL FOR QATARGAS

Oil prices at the end of 1993 had fallen to their lowest level since 1986, causing Qatar's gross domestic product to drop to $7.2 billion. There was no way QGPC could raise its equity commitment of over $700 million for Qatargas without borrowing money. Qatar's own small banking sector wasn't an option. The total assets of local banks, around $8 billion, were already mostly lent to the state. Indeed, the Qatar National Bank still functioned essentially as a state treasury despite the recent conversion of the Qatar Monetary Agency into a central bank.

Three-quarters of Qatar National Bank's assets of $4.1 billion were extended to the government, even as it reduced its deposits with the bank. Although the state tended to borrow relatively small amounts to cover spending shortfalls, the sheer number of loans started to affect liquidity. Several other Qatari banks also reported unusually high loans to deposits ratios.

Regional banks led by the Gulf International Bank raised a $250 million general-purpose loan for the State of Qatar in early 1994, some of which went to clear delayed contractor payments.[77] Within months Sumitomo Bank was putting together a second $250 million loan for the government targeted specifically at European and Japanese banks.[78] Another $300 million sovereign loan followed in late 1995, arranged by a mix of regional and international banks.[79] When the Qataris had trouble paying for port development work at Ras Laffan, including the berths for the LNG vessels and other related infrastructure crucial to Qatargas, the Export-Import Bank of Japan stepped in with an unsecured $200 million loan to the government. This covered QGPC's direct financial contribution to the $1 billion port project, the majority of which was financed through commercial facilities backed by Italy's credit agency, SACE, because of the dominance of Italian contractors.

None of this sovereign borrowing was specifically tied to the government's equity commitments at Qatargas, but the loans were clearly used to fund QGPC's cash calls at the LNG venture. The government was raising funds for other crucial projects as well, including a second power and water desalination complex next to the existing Ras Abu Fontas plant. Meant as a replacement for the recently canceled Wusail project, the $1.1 billion Ras Abu Fontas B project was designed to generate 625 megawatts of electricity and 33 million gallons per day of water. It was financed in part through promissory notes issued by the Ministry of Finance, Economy, and Trade and syndicated by Chemical Bank. These notes required a special amiri decree before they could be issued.

The government had hoped its focus on all-Japanese financing at Qatargas would leave non-Japanese banking markets available for other industrial projects. Despite this, a telex sent out in early 1993 by Morgan Stanley to invite expressions of interest from international banks in a $300 million loan to finance QAPCO's petrochemical expansion received a decidedly lukewarm response.[80] A second attempt one year later was more successful, raising $200 million partly from domestic banks. Elsewhere, Morgan Grenfell was unable to win enough support for a package of export credits and commercial loans totaling around $400 million for the Qatar Fuel Additives Company, the joint venture between QGPC, Total, and International Octane Ltd. formed to build a grassroots plant to produce methanol and the gasoline additive MTBE. Total subsequently threatened to drop out of QAFAC, and the remaining Canadian partner was given until the end of 1993 to advance the project.

After initially appointing Chase Manhattan as its financial adviser, the fertilizer company QAFCO had abandoned efforts to raise separate commercial finance to effectively double its capacity. Instead, the three construction contractors competing for the project were asked to bring their own financing. A consortium comprising Germany's Uhde GmbH and Belleli of Italy ended up winning the contract in 1994 after securing an eight-year commercial loan led by Germany's government-owned development bank, Kreditanstalt fur Wiederaufbau; Dresdner Bank; and Paribas as well as export credit finance provided by German and Italian state agencies.[81] QAFCO also put up funds from accumulated profits that had been set aside from previous years. Involving a third fertilizer plant called QAFCO-3, the $540 million expansion project was designed to boost the production of ammonia by 1,500 tons per day and granulated urea by 2,000 tons per day.

Qatar's financial situation remained precarious. The government forecast a 19 percent drop in revenues because of lower oil prices in the fiscal year beginning April 1, 1994. While it slashed expenditures by nearly 10 percent, primarily from current account spending, this wasn't enough to compensate for the revenue decline, and the projected budget deficit jumped nearly 30 percent to QR 3,470 million (just under $1 billion).[82] A similar deficit scenario appeared in the next budget cycle, with a modest rise in projected revenues offset by even higher expenditures. Priority was given to funding further development of the North gas field, specifically Qatargas, as well as major projects like the Ras Abu Fontas B electricity and water desalination plant. The government also promised to fulfill the basic needs of its citizens. Tight controls were imposed on internal expenditures, including limiting ministries from hiring new workers and restricting government spending to "necessary items."[83]

CHAPTER 14

Tough Launch for Mobil's RasGas LNG Project

Financing Qatar's second liquefaction project was even tougher than the first. At least Qatargas had a guaranteed market in Japan that could be used to bankroll the project, even if the tortuous financing effort highlighted the deficiencies in the sale to Chubu Electric and necessitated the adoption of a floor price. Ras Laffan LNG, or RasGas as it was now known, had only preliminary letters of intent, none with a top-notch Japanese buyer. When the amiri decree formally incorporating the joint venture was issued by Crown Prince Hamad Ibn Khalifa in July 1993, it still seemed possible Mitsui might be able to bring the 2 million tons per year it was aggregating in Japan to RasGas in return for an equity slice in the project for itself. It was not meant to be. Chubu Electric transferred its option to seven other Japanese utilities just before it expired in May 1994. The following month those buyers initialed an agreement with Qatargas to purchase 2 million tons per year from a third LNG train.

In the end, the banks and the Japanese government rejected Mitsui's plans. Reports suggested the Export-Import Bank of Japan and the other government agencies made their loan guarantees contingent on all the LNG from Qatargas being dedicated to Japan.[1] Other buyers from the Far East were interested in the third train, and the Japanese government wasn't keen on sharing LNG from Qatargas with other countries whose own banks and export credit agencies hadn't taken any financial risk. Mitsui may not have had much choice in the matter, but the trading company's defection was still a huge blow for RasGas. "Everyone at Mobil just went ballistic when Mitsui took the 2 million tons per year to Qatargas," explains a Mobil retiree. "We really felt we had a deal with Mitsui. The 2 million from the Japanese essentially represented one train. When RasGas lost that deal, it threw a monkey wrench into all the planning, and it threw a monkey wrench into the financing, big time."[2]

RasGas still had the letter of intent for 2.4 million tons per year with Korea Gas Corporation that QGPC had assigned to it in late 1992, which included an option for another 1.6 million tons per year. Mobil announced a second letter of intent with Taiwan's state oil and gas company China Petroleum Corporation, or CPC, for 2 million tons per year on September 22, 1993. QGPC had earlier said it planned to supply another letter of intent for 2.5 million tons per year signed with two affiliates of the U.S. company Enron on April 11, 1993, to RasGas as well.[3] But this deal, which was linked to an LNG-fueled second phase of a 2,550-megawatt power plant Enron Development Corporation planned to build at Dabhol in the western Indian state of Maharashtra, was never formally assigned to RasGas.

Instead, Enron lobbied for its own LNG project based on the demands of the Indian power plant and a more controversial sale to Israel. The first indication that the Qataris were talking to Israel about natural gas, or anything else for that matter, came shortly after the Oslo 1 accord introducing Palestinian self-rule to the occupied West Bank and Gaza Strip signed in September 1993. Israel's foreign minister, Shimon Peres, traveled to New York after the signing ceremony to meet secretly with his Qatari counterpart, Hamad Ibn Jassim Ibn Jabir Al Thani.[4] Several weeks later an Israeli foreign ministry official visited Qatar to discuss economic and political relations. When Energy Minister Moshe Shahal announced in late October that Israel was poised to sign a twenty-five-year gas supply contract with an unnamed Gulf emirate, it was obvious he was referring to Qatar.

The Israeli minister's claim of an impending agreement finally prompted a public response from Abdullah Ibn Hamad Al Attiyah on October 28, 1993. In his statement, the minister of energy and industry denied that a gas supply deal with Israel was imminent but did not explicitly dispute that Qatar was in discussions with Israel. It had emerged that the deal was being actively promoted by a multinational company (later identified as Enron) and that it involved the supply of LNG from Qatar to a regasification terminal that would be built at the southern Israeli port of Eilat on the Gulf of Aqaba. From Eilat, a gas pipeline network would be constructed to serve the domestic market where Israeli electric power stations would be converted from heavy fuel oil to natural gas. Any excess gas could be potentially piped northward to Turkey and Europe.

By early 1994 Enron's chair, Kenneth Lay, was meeting privately in Doha with Crown Prince Hamad Ibn Khalifa about a new LNG project with its own block in the North field. The company's introduction to Qatar had supposedly come through the Mannai Group, closely aligned with Foreign Minister Hamad Ibn Jassim Ibn Jabir. Press reports suggested Qatar was attracted to Enron because, unlike the major oil companies, it did not have long-standing ties to other Middle Eastern countries. "Even now, the major oil companies wouldn't want to be in the middle of the project because of sensitivities that still exist in the Arab world about doing business in Israel," the *Wall Street Journal* quoted one source at the time.[5] It didn't hurt that Enron had a bevy of political high-fliers on its payroll, including former U.S. secretary of state James A. Baker III and former U.S. commerce secretary Robert A. Mosbacher. The company hired the two men in early 1993 to advise its executives on international opportunities and visit foreign countries promoting natural gas projects.[6] Other former high-ranking U.S. military officers were also brought into Enron.

Enron was either blissfully unaware of the exclusive marketing clause in the development and fiscal agreement at RasGas or had decided to ignore this potential impediment until the Qataris chose to formally notify it of the provision. This clause granted Mobil and QGPC the right to produce, sell, and supply all LNG from Qatar up to 10 million tons per year. While the clause wasn't open-ended, the partners had until 1997 to sell the first half of this volume and until 2002 to place the full amount. Only deals that existed before August 20, 1992, the date the RasGas agreement had been signed, were excluded. These had been further spelled out in a supporting document titled "Existing Qatar LNG Projects" and were limited to Chubu Electric's contract with Qatargas as well as preliminary sales from the Qatar Eurogas joint venture between QGPC, Snam, and Nelson Bunker Hunt. Also exempted was the separate project covered under Elf Aquitaine's 1991 memorandum of understanding with QGPC. This now included Sumitomo as Elf's marketing partner.

More ominously for RasGas, sources at the Amiri Diwan signaled after the crown prince's meeting with Ken Lay that he supported the Enron project "in principle." Dr. Jabir Al Marri, the head of QGPC, reminded the crown prince that Qatar was effectively prevented from pursuing any new LNG venture until RasGas sold the 10 million tons per year covered under its exclusivity clause. Timely implementation of the Enron project, which involved sales to both India and Israel, would require Mobil to waive this exclusivity. Sheikh Hamad, who saw the project as a way to advance the Middle East peace process and burnish Qatar's international standing, demurred. The crown prince ordered QGPC to continue its discussions with Enron on the 5-million-tons-per-year project. "QGPC has made the decision not to disclose the relevant Ras Laffan documentation to Enron until after the Letter of Intent is signed," an internal Mobil memo reads. "They are also not willing to officially approve Mobil contacting Enron until after the Letter of Intent is signed."[7]

Given the high-level royal support for Enron, Al Attiyah clearly did not want the crown prince or others at the Amiri Diwan to view the Ministry of Energy and Industry or QGPC as obstructionist. Instead, the energy minister and QGPC head Jabir Al Marri planned to get Mobil to resist the Enron project for them once the letter of intent was signed.

PRICE DISPUTE SHELVES QATAR EUROGAS LNG PROJECT

Qatar Eurogas was in its death throes by the time Enron appeared. Snam wanted to pay an oil-linked price in line with its LNG imports from Algeria and pipeline gas supplies from Russia, which were delivered into Italy at around $2.50 per million Btu.[8] That price was only acceptable to QGPC if it applied to LNG at Ras Laffan, not at the delivery point in Italy. Transportation, including fees for transiting the Suez Canal in Egypt, added another $1.25 per million Btu to Snam's final price. The stakes were too high for QGPC to budge; the 6-million-tons-per-year project's price tag had already ballooned to at least $7 billion. Accepting a lower price from the Italians would also undermine Qatar's now sacrosanct floor price provisions at Qatargas and RasGas.

Dramatic political events in Italy, including revelations of high-level corruption, the assassination of a senior anti-Mafia prosecutor, and the resignation of the leader of the Socialist Party in a bribery scandal, also contributed to the slow pace of negotiations. On February 9, 1994, after nearly eighteen months of protracted and ultimately unsuccessful efforts to agree on a supply contract with Snam, the three shareholders in Qatar Eurogas met to decide the project's fate.[9] Snam and Nelson Bunker Hunt both elected to exit the joint venture and transfer their shares to QGPC. The Qatar Europe LNG Company was dissolved in all but name, with QGPC retaining the legal entity. A similar fate befell Elf

Aquitaine and Sumitomo, whose memorandum of understanding was allowed to lapse in May 1994 after they failed to find customers.

Other prospective Mediterranean buyers who had expressed interest in joining Qatar Eurogas and purchasing output from the project now transferred their attention to RasGas. This included Turkey, whose prime minister, Suleyman Demirel, had raised the prospect of Turkish entry into Qatar Eurogas during a state visit to Qatar in early 1993.[10] Turkey's state-owned pipeline and distribution company Botas wanted to take a 5 percent equity stake in the project and buy 2 million tons per year of LNG. Elf Aquitaine and Sumitomo would also try to join RasGas following the demise of their own venture, with the Japanese trader making the furthest headway before ultimately backing out.

RASGAS SALES EFFORT HITS ROADBLOCKS

RasGas was concentrating on turning the letters of intent with Korea Gas Corporation and Taiwan's CPC into definitive sale and purchase agreements. Talks did not always go smoothly with the South Koreans, and the Qataris ruffled feathers in Seoul when Foreign Minister Hamad Ibn Jassim Ibn Jabir visited Pyongyang in late 1993 to establish diplomatic ties with North Korea. Al Attiyah happened to be in Seoul at the same time holding commercial discussions with Korea Gas Corporation, and it became clear that the two ministers had not coordinated their calendars to avoid the unfortunate optics. Qatar was only the second Gulf Cooperation Council member to establish diplomatic relations with North Korea, following Oman in 1992. (Kuwait and Bahrain would follow suit in 2001 and the United Arab Emirates in 2007. Saudi Arabia, the sixth GCC member, still does not have diplomatic relations with Pyongyang.)

Another setback came in 1994 when RasGas lost the 2 million tons per year sales prospect to Taiwan. Instead, CPC purchased this LNG from Indonesia's Pertamina. Negotiated by Total, a major gas supplier into PT Badak's LNG plant in East Kalimantan, deliveries under the Indonesian sale to CPC were set to begin in 1998. Both the volume and the commencement date were identical to those in CPC's letter of intent with RasGas. Losing this supply tranche meant RasGas could not count on the Taiwanese market to help launch the project. CPC would eventually sign up for expansion volumes from RasGas, but these would not commence until 2008. With both Japan and Taiwan out of contention for the time being, Mobil and QGPC were left with just one potential import market in the Far East: South Korea. The project's fate now essentially hinged on converting the letter of intent with Korea Gas Corporation into a firm sale. And the Korean company knew it held most of the bargaining chips.

Several of South Korea's prominent family-owned conglomerates, or *chaebols*, were jockeying to join RasGas on the coattails of the planned 2.4-million-tons-per year sale. Hamad Ibn Jassim Ibn Jabir aggressively championed Daewoo, which at its peak was South Korea's fourth-largest *chaebol* with interests in trading, motor vehicles, shipbuilding, heavy industry, aerospace, electronics, telecommunications, and financial services. When a representative from Samsung, another of South Korea's top five *chaebols*, called on the foreign minister in Doha to pitch his company's participation in RasGas, he was told by HBJ that Samsung would first need to reach agreement "internally" with Daewoo. Samsung claimed it could get Korea Gas Corporation to exercise its option for the additional 1.6 million tons per year covered under the letter of intent at RasGas but wanted its own stake in exchange.

Mobil was not averse to giving Daewoo and Samsung an equity position in RasGas if the two chaebols could get Korea Gas Corporation to sign on the dotted line. But the U.S. major didn't want to appear as if it was working with HBJ, who had already locked horns with Al Attiyah. Indeed, the two ministers were in near-constant conflict as Al Attiyah fought an uphill battle to keep HBJ out of the petroleum sector. The crown prince not only knew about this rivalry but appeared to endorse it. Rumors swirled that the foreign minister, who had been instrumental in getting Ali Jaidah appointed as Qatar's ambassador to the United Kingdom, was hoping to bring the former head of QGPC back home to replace Al Attiyah as energy minister. Mobil decreed that company business was to be conducted only through the Ministry of Energy and Industry or QGPC. Senior executives were told not to have any direct or indirect commercial dealings with the foreign minister unless the crown prince authorized them in writing.

The foreign minister openly conducted private business from his government office, often to the surprise of visiting businessmen. He was behind many of the foreign companies in Qatar through sometimes murky partnerships and agent connections, often via alliances with leading Qatari families. These included the Swedish–Swiss engineering firm ASEA Brown Boveri, which in early 1994 won a contract for the Ras Abu Fontas B power and water plant. The $1.1 billion award prompted a critical and widely circulated letter from Mohammad Ibn Hamad, the amir's elder brother and the former minister of education, culture, and youth. The older Al Thani criticized the wide scale of corruption in Qatar, pointedly singling out HBJ's private business dealings. This letter was sent to all the foreign ambassadors in Doha and created quite a buzz, but it may also have been linked to an internal Al Thani family feud. Rumors suggested the writer's son had recently tried to plant an explosive device on the foreign minister's plane. The son and several of Sheikh Mohammad's staff had been jailed and were still in custody when the letter was being circulated.

There was speculation the amir was planning to bring his son Abdul Aziz back from exile in France and install him as prime minister or as crown prince after Hamad took over as ruler from Sheikh Khalifa. Hamad opposed the move, as did the amir's two other cabinet-level sons, Abdullah Ibn Khalifa, the minister of the interior, and Mohammad Ibn Khalifa, the minister of finance, economy, and trade. HBJ was also firmly in Sheikh Hamad's camp. The crown prince returned the foreign minister's loyalty by buying him a $32 million house in London and a $14 million yacht in Italy. Sheikh Hamad's eldest son, Mishal Ibn Hamad, worked for HBJ and often traveled with the foreign minister. The government also paid for a QR 150 million ($40 million) extension to HBJ's Doha offices as well as his new home in the capital city. All this came as anonymous circulars about Qatar's shaky economy and poor leadership spread in Doha.

Mobil itself was being criticized for not lining up firm customers, and it was keen to place some "brick and mortar" on the designated plant pad to demonstrate that RasGas was a real project and possibly to shift market psychology. The company had made its entry into Qatargas contingent on the establishment of this second liquefaction venture and the opportunity to market the next 10 million tons per year of LNG from Qatar. It had yet to deliver a single customer, and Mobil's commercial rivals smelled blood. "Total, Mitsui, Marubeni, Elf, Sumitomo, Enron, etc. are all saying that Mobil is no better marketer of LNG than they are, or else the product would have been sold," an adviser informed senior management in early 1994.[11] Knowing it would take time to bring Korea Gas Corporation across the finish line at RasGas, the U.S. major tried to find other ways to shore up its position in Qatar.

Following a request from the crown prince, Mobil offered to work with QGPC to draw up a master plan for Ras Laffan that would include an orderly roadmap for further monetizing the North field. While the LNG projects were still viewed as the backbone of the North field development, the master plan would extend these gas reserves to petrochemicals, derivatives, condensate refining, and other related projects. Mobil hoped to invest in some of these spin-off industries. It also saw the master plan as an avenue for high-level access to the crown prince, potentially allowing Mobil's new chair and chief executive officer, Lou Noto, to forge a personal bond with the future amir.

Noto had made a name for himself in Saudi Arabia during the 1980s heading Mobil's Jeddah-based subsidiary Mobil Saudi Arabia. There he had helped create a similar master plan for Yanbu Industrial City on the kingdom's Red Sea coast about 350 kilometers northwest of Jeddah. The Saudi government had poured $15 billion into Yanbu and a larger sister city across the country in Jubail that became the world's largest new industrial city when it opened in 1987. Saudi private and state-owned companies and foreign firms such as Mobil, Exxon, Shell, and Mitsubishi had invested another $30 billion in petrochemical partnerships and petroleum refining ventures.[12] Sheikh Hamad dreamed of recreating this success at Ras Laffan, and the crown prince formally endorsed the master plan in a meeting with the Mobil chief on November 22, 1994. The two men agreed to meet again in six months to review its progress.

MOBIL TRIES TO DERAIL ENRON PROJECT

The primary reason for Noto's visit was to derail the Enron project, or at least get concessions for Mobil if Qatar went ahead with it despite the exclusivity clause at RasGas. Noto had planned to put Mobil's case to the amir, but Sheikh Khalifa came down with the flu and canceled all his appointments for several days. Meeting instead with Issa Al Kawari, the minister of state for Amiri Diwan, Noto and his team came away with the impression that Sheikh Khalifa's right-hand man was not altogether up to date on the Enron project and the issues it posed for RasGas and Mobil's continued involvement in the country. This raised the question as to how much the amir himself was aware of the finer details of the Enron project, reinforcing the perception that it was driven by the foreign minister and the crown prince. "The timeliness of Mr. Noto's visit to update Dr. Issa on the situation could prove meaningful in how the Enron situation plays out," one Mobil executive wrote hopefully.[13]

The crown prince tried to dispel Mobil's concerns in a meeting later that day, although Sheikh Hamad also emphasized that Qatar saw the possible gas sale to Israel brokered by Enron as an opportunity to help the Middle East peace process.[14] Confirming that a letter of intent with Enron for a third grassroots LNG project was imminent, he assured Noto that Enron would be limited to specific secondary markets. These would presumably include Israel and power plants in India where Enron had an equity stake. The crown prince also said he'd instructed QGPC not to give Enron better commercial terms than Mobil had received at RasGas. In response Noto argued bluntly that a business project should not be driven by politics. This was particularly true of the Middle East peace process, which Mobil's CEO pointed out rather presciently might not be sustained in the long-term.[15]

Noto urged Sheikh Hamad to reconsider the Enron project. If Qatar nonetheless decided to proceed, he told the crown prince that he needed to bring something back for Mobil's board of directors or it would question the country's commitment to RasGas. This could include increasing the marketing rights at RasGas beyond 10 million tons per year and dedicating additional gas reserves within the North field to support this increase. In addition, Mobil wanted to secure "most favored nations" treatment for RasGas. QGPC's Al Marri had earlier told Noto that QGPC had already reserved a second block for RasGas.[16] Dubbed the Northeast block, this second 24,700-acre tract was located immediately east and adjacent to the project's current block. RasGas had spudded its first delineation well in this North contract location in early 1994, drilling down to 9,900 feet to test the Khuff formations.

Senior Qatari officials promised to give Mobil the QGPC-Enron letter of intent once it was signed, after which the U.S. major would have thirty days to comment on Enron's proposal. "The Letter of Intent permits this disclosure by giving QGPC the right to disclose the document to parties who have existing agreements with QGPC," an internal Mobil memo reads.[17] QGPC did not plan to ask Mobil to officially waive the exclusivity clause at RasGas until it had signed the preliminary agreement with Enron. Similarly, it had decided not to formally disclose the documentation related to the RasGas project's marketing rights to Enron until Mobil had commented on the letter of intent. "Once this response is received, it is QGPC['s] intention to have Mobil, Enron and QGPC discuss the effect of Ras Laffan's marketing rights on the Enron project," the memo concludes.[18]

QATAR SIGNS LETTER OF INTENT WITH ENRON

The letter of intent with Enron was signed in Doha on January 18, 1995, by Al Attiyah and Enron's Ken Lay. Press reports suggested Enron had agreed to arrange and provide all the financing for the project, including QGPC's equity share.[19] Shareholding was 60-40 in favor of QGPC until the loan to QGPC to fund its equity stake was paid off, after which it would revert to 65-35 with advance agreement on the price the Qatari firm would pay Enron to purchase back this 5 percent.[20] Enron itself revealed few details of the agreement, other than to confirm the LNG was destined for Israeli and Indian markets. Its spokeswoman also pointed out that the nonbinding letter of intent was subject to numerous conditions.[21]

These conditions became apparent once Mobil was given a chance to comment on Enron's proposal. In exchange for agreeing "in principle" to waive its marketing rights at RasGas in order to allow the Enron project to proceed, Mobil convinced QGPC to amend its letter of intent with Enron to include two main conditions. The first related to the designated markets to which Enron would export LNG from the project. These were defined as the Eastern Mediterranean (specifically excluding Italy, Greece, Turkey, and Egypt) and power generation projects or regasification facilities in India where Enron or its affiliates had an equity or participation interest. A side letter to the letter of intent with Enron capped the volume of LNG for regasification in India—excluding its Dabhol power plant in Maharashtra—to 1.3 million tons per year. Dabhol itself was now expected to need 1.7 million tons per year in its second 1,350-megawatt phase.

By excluding all the major regional markets except Israel, Jordan, and the Palestinian Authority from the Eastern Mediterranean, the Qataris avoided specifying Israel as the intended output destination for the Enron project. The letter of intent with Enron also limited the maximum capacity of its project to 5 million tons annually. Any expansion would require QGPC's written consent, and it promised to take the marketing situation at RasGas into consideration should Enron request an increase in capacity. Al Attiyah assured Mobil that "in deciding whether to accede to any subsequent request for expansion of this capacity, QGPC will naturally give full regard to the legal rights and interests of Ras Laffan Project that may subsist at the time."[22] Should Enron seek LNG sales outside of its designated markets, QGPC said it would take swift action.

The second condition absolved Mobil from responsibility for funding any expansion of the Ras Laffan port, facilities, or infrastructure needed to accommodate Enron. QGPC also acceded to Mobil's request to defer publicizing the venture until its negotiations with Korea Gas Corporation at RasGas were concluded. While Enron was already prohibited from disclosing the letter of intent to third parties, Al Attiyah agreed to maintain this blackout until the sale and purchase agreement with the Koreans was executed. Nor would Enron be allowed to disclose related transactions, including its sales negotiations with third parties in Israel and India. The minister did prod Mobil to accelerate its sales efforts. "QGPC and Enron will be fully occupied, for the coming months, with the negotiations in private of several definitive agreements, by which time you will have concluded your negotiations with KGC which you anticipate occurring in the near future," Al Attiyah wrote to Mobil's Paul Hoenmans in reference to Korea Gas Corporation.[23]

Mobil viewed the Enron project as a threat to RasGas and more generally to its plans to become the dominant player in Qatar's gas sector. The project also raised embarrassing issues with other Arab partners, particularly in Saudi Arabia, where Mobil was one of the kingdom's largest investors. Riyadh objected to economic relations with Israel in the absence of an Israeli–Syrian peace treaty. Mobil believed much of Enron's success in Israel was due to the assistance of former U.S. secretary of state James Baker. Baker was now on its rival's payroll. "Jim Baker's relationship with the Israelis was such that no one other than Enron could do that deal," recalls Lou Noto. "Obviously, Mobil could not supply Israel from RasGas because the Saudis would be upset."[24]

Qatar's Sheikh Hamad Ibn Khalifa attended the signing of the Oslo II Accord between Israel and the Palestine Liberation Organization in the Egyptian town of Taba on September 24, 1995. Four days later a second signing ceremony in Washington, D.C., was witnessed by U.S. president Bill Clinton and other world leaders. Although the Clinton administration played a limited role in negotiating the two Oslo accords, it spent vast amounts of time and resources trying to get the Israelis and Palestinians to implement the agreements. The administration also had invested a considerable amount of political capital in the Enron project and its potential gas sale to Israel. It wanted both the Enron and Mobil projects to succeed, preferably at the same time. Commerce Secretary Ron Brown, who became the first secretary to visit Qatar in 1995, made the administration's position abundantly clear. Brown's trip to Qatar came just one month after a trade mission to India during which the secretary was accompanied by Ken Lay of Enron.

To ease Mobil's concerns about RasGas—and to underscore Enron's greatly proscribed marketing options—the Qataris orchestrated a flurry of preliminary agreements with buyers in Turkey and India in the days immediately preceding and following the letter of intent with Enron. The first was an initial accord between RasGas and Botas covering the sale of 2 million tons per year to the state-owned Turkish firm starting in mid-1999. Signature of this letter of intent coincided with an official visit to Qatar by Turkey's energy minister, Veysel Atasoy, in early January. Later that same month India's private Essar Group signed a memorandum of understanding with RasGas for a similar amount of LNG. Both deals were signed by Dr. Al Marri in his capacity as the chair of RasGas.

ENERGY MINISTER ABRUPTLY FIRES, THEN REINSTATES, QGPC HEAD

The award of the eagerly awaited production-sharing agreement on the offshore Idd el-Shargi North Dome, together with the technical service arrangement on QGPC's other producing fields, to Occidental Petroleum precipitated a short-lived internal crisis. Reports suggested Al Marri had objected to the decision to go with Oxy over competing offers from Elf Aquitaine and Atlantic Richfield. Al Marri argued that Oxy had not performed well at the onshore Diyab structure in southern Dukhan, where the U.S. firm had installed production facilities and pipeline infrastructure under a service contract in 1992.[25] The QGPC head also considered the contract terms at Idd el-Shargi North Dome, particularly the production-sharing split during cost recovery, far too favorable to Oxy. This opinion was obviously not shared by the minister of energy and industry, who regularly clashed with Al Marri and viewed him as a rival, although both men were close to the crown prince.

Using his opposition to Oxy as a pretext, Al Attiyah summarily fired Al Marri as well as Abdul Aziz Al Dulaimi, QGPC's head of oil and gas operations, via fax from London on August 27, 1994. Al Marri appealed directly to the amir, who, on September 1, 1994, ordered the minister to reinstate him as managing director of QGPC. The episode was just one more example of the Al Thani "divide and conquer" strategy, where no one but the ruler was allowed to become too powerful. However, the reversal did not include Al Dulaimi, who was still replaced in an acting capacity by his deputy, Mubarak Al Muhannadi. The production-sharing agreement with Oxy at Idd el-Shargi North Dome signed with QGPC on July 24 was formally approved by the Council of Ministers on September 21, 1994. So was the five-year technical assistance program at QGPC's other producing fields, for which Oxy was to be paid $1.9 million annually.[26] Also approved at the same cabinet meeting was a deal with Pennzoil covering an exploration- and production-sharing agreement for Block 8, one of six blocks available for bidding in QGPC's ongoing licensing round.

Oxy was contractually obligated to invest over $700 million in the first seven years to develop the Arab C, Arab D, and Shuaiba reservoirs at Idd el-Shargi North Dome via enhanced oil recovery techniques. But it started getting oil—and, crucially, generating cash flow—from the field immediately. QGPC had nearly completed development of the Arab D reservoir as well as a pilot gas injection project at the Shuaiba when Oxy assumed operatorship of the field in September 1994. Output had risen to twenty thousand barrels per day as a result, and analysts put Oxy's net share at eleven thousand barrels per day virtually from the beginning.[27] The firm planned to hike flows to ninety thousand barrels per day by the end of the decade, ultimately giving it fifty-three thousand barrels per day from Idd el-Shargi North Dome during the cost recovery period.

Under its exploration- and production-sharing agreement with QGPC on Block 8, Pennzoil agreed to an extensive seismic acquisition program, including a 3D seismic survey. The U.S. company also committed to drilling four test wells in the Jurassic and Cretaceous intervals by the end of 1998. Pennzoil had high hopes for the acreage, describing Block 8 as a salt basin with similar geological characteristics to the Gulf of Mexico (where the firm had been active for many years).[28] Stretching over 2,800 square kilometers, Block 8 overlapped and surrounded Bul Hanine, Maydan Mahzam, and Idd el-Shargi North Dome. However, QGPC maintained a belt of 3 kilometers around each of these fields, within which Pennzoil was not allowed.

MAERSK LAUNCHES FIRST FOREIGN-OPERATED OIL FIELD IN DECADES

Maersk started commercial production of ten thousand barrels per day from the Al Shaheen field in its offshore Block 5 on October 22, 1994. Its commencement was accompanied by remarkably little fanfare, given what Al Shaheen portended for the reintroduction of foreign oil companies to Qatar's upstream sector. The field represented the first oil reserves fully financed and developed by an outside operator since the Bunduq field shared with Abu Dhabi was brought online by Japan's United Petroleum Development in 1976. It was the first foreign-operated structure to commence production in strictly Qatari waters since the Bul Hanine field in 1972. Al Shaheen became the first of many fields developed by foreign companies under production-sharing terms. These reserves would contribute to a huge rise in Qatar's oil output by the end of the century and would ultimately account for over half of its production capacity in the early 2000s.

Test production at Al Shaheen from oil horizons overlaying the Khuff gas zones had commenced the previous July after Maersk drilled one vertical and two horizontal wells known as Al Shaheen 1, 2, and 3. Initial output went by tanker to the Halul island terminal, where it was commingled with other offshore flows for export as Qatar Marine. By the end of 1995, however, Al Shaheen was being marketed as a separate crude oil stream. Output had doubled to around twenty thousand barrels per day by then, and plans called for further increases to thirty thousand barrels per day by 1996 and sixty thousand barrels per day by 1999.[29] Maersk also drilled and abandoned two unsuccessful vertical exploration wells on the four-thousand-square-kilometer block in 1994.

Elsewhere, Elf Aquitaine finally submitted a development plan for its Al Khalij field in Block 6 in early 1995, four and a half years after announcing Qatar's first commercial discovery in nearly twenty years. This followed seven exploration and appraisal wells and two years of talks with QGPC to renegotiate the terms of the production-sharing agreement on the block. Elf's initial plan, involving four development wells, an unmanned production platform, and a pipeline link to export facilities on Halul island, envisaged initial production of thirty thousand barrels per day by early 1997. The French firm was still in discussions with QGPC regarding Al Khalij's ultimate potential, with the Qataris favoring a more accelerated development plan than the one Elf had proposed.[30]

In the meantime, Elf had relinquished Block 1, where it had made the Idd el-Shargi South Dome discovery in 1994. Elf's unsuccessful bid for Idd el-Shargi North Dome had included linking this southern dome discovery to existing infrastructure at the field, and the release may have been related to the decision to award Idd el-Shargi North Dome to Oxy. QGPC subsequently divided Block 1 into two separate blocks. Block 1NW went northwest, mostly offshore but extending onshore around Ras Laffan. The southeasterly Block 1SE included Idd el-Shargi South Dome as well as two other undeveloped finds known as the A-Structure and Al Karkara, which had been discovered in 1971 and 1989. While Block 1NW was considered a pure exploration play, QGPC described Block 1SE as an appraisal and development area. Oil companies already operating in Qatar were invited to evaluate this block for an appraisal-, development-, and production-sharing agreement.[31]

The application of new technologies boosted total expected recoverable oil reserves at Qatar's four producing fields to 4.2 billion barrels at the beginning of 1995.[32] This included 700 million barrels of enhanced oil recovery prospects. Provisional estimates put reserves at newly discovered fields like Al Khalij and Al Shaheen at an additional 1 billion barrels. Qatar's oil output, which had averaged 399,000 barrels per day in 1994, was running at around 420,000 barrels per day in early 1995.[33] The onshore Dukhan field contributed about 270,000 barrels daily to this total, while the offshore sector, where new drilling by Oxy had already pushed flows at Idd el-Shargi North Dome above 30,000 barrels per day, was supplying the remaining 160,000 barrels per day. Plans called for increasing sustainable production capacity to 500,000 barrels per day by 2000 and potentially even higher if optimistic forecasts for the various upstream projects were realized.[34]

QGPC had already launched a 3D seismic campaign at Maydan Mahzam and Bul Hanine using two seismic vessels owned by the U.S. company Western Geophysical and planned to drill one hundred more wells at the two offshore fields, depending on the results of these surveys. Maydan Mahzam dropped to 38,000 barrels per day in 1995, and QGPC hoped to boost production to 47,000 barrels per day in 1997 with new drilling. Output at Bul Hanine, which held steady at 80,000 barrels per day in 1995, was expected to decline to 70,000 barrels per day by 2000, even with the development of additional reserves. But QGPC was also considering a major gas cap recycling project at the field's Arab C reservoir, which could result in a 100-million-barrel gain in field condensate reserves.

Onshore at the Dukhan field, QGPC planned a mainly horizontal drilling program of both producer and injection wells using three rigs to boost output as high as 335,000 barrels per day in three to five years. These would be drilled into the Arab C and Arab D reservoirs, where most of Dukhan's output was already sourced. QGPC also launched a gas recycling project at Dukhan's Khatiya area, where about 800 million cubic feet per day of so-called wet gas from the Arab D gas cap would be produced in order to extract about 38,000 barrels per day of condensates and around 750 barrels per day of other natural gas liquids. Residue gas, around 600 million cubic feet per day, would be reinjected into the Arab D to maintain reservoir pressure. QGPC introduced a new type of contract for this $300 million project under which contractors and equipment suppliers would provide and install the necessary facilities at their own expense in return for a share in the accruing revenues.

Downstream, the National Oil Distribution Company finally unveiled plans for upgrading and expanding its Umm Said refinery on July 3, 1994.[35] These included boosting the capacity of the newer Unit No. 2 from 50,000 to 62,500 barrels per day, installing a 20,000-barrel-per-day fluid catalytic cracker to turn heavy fuel oil into higher value petroleum products, and constructing a 30,000-barrel-per-day unit to process condensate from the North field's first development phase operated by QGPC. Total costs for the Umm Said project were estimated to be between $400 and $500 million. Contractors would finance 100 percent of the work program and be repaid in refined products after completion.

ARCO TAKES OVER AS OPERATOR AT WINTERSHALL'S TWO BLOCKS

In early 1994 Wintershall notified Gulfstream Resources and Deilmann Erdoel & Erdgas that it had reached agreement to sell a 35 percent stake in the consortium's two offshore blocks to British Gas. Gulfstream immediately exercised its rights of first refusal over the Wintershall sale, eventually announcing a convoluted deal of its own on November 29, 1994, that brought both British Gas and Atlantic Richfield, or Arco, into the group while reducing the stakes held by Wintershall and Deilmann Erdoel & Erdgas, its two existing partners.[36] In exchange, Gulfstream received an undisclosed amount of cash from Arco as well as a 25 percent participating interest in Arco's producing Margham gas-condensate field in Dubai. Arco assumed operatorship of the consortium from Wintershall, who had operated the Qatari acreage since 1973. Gulfstream retained a 27.5 percent interest in the two blocks, as did Arco. British Gas received 25 percent, followed by Wintershall at 15 percent and Deilmann Erdoel & Erdgas with 5 percent.

Gulfstream and Arco had formed a 50-50 joint venture to develop, market, and transport some 800 million cubic feet per day of gas by pipeline from the consortium's east block. Dubai was considered the principal market for this gas, but the pipeline network could also serve other short-haul markets like Bahrain and possibly Kuwait. The consortium decided to implement an appraisal program based on the oil shows Wintershall had encountered during gas drilling. Toward the end of 1995 Arco drilled a horizontal well in the Arab B structure down to 2,200 feet. QMB-4 was the twelfth well drilled at the offshore block but the first to exclusively target the oil pay. It tested at 9,655 barrels per day with this flow rate limited by pump and flare capacities. Gulfstream estimated that the discovery, dubbed the Al Rayyan field, could produce over 25,000 barrels per day. It put the amount of oil in place in the Arab B at 1.3 billion barrels, including 700 million of proved reserves.[37]

The consortium had still not begun exploration activities at the potentially oil-bearing A-Structure in its separate west block near the Dibal shoal claimed by both Qatar and Bahrain. After hearing legal representations from both states, in July 1994 the International Court of Justice finally decided that it had jurisdiction to rule on the long-standing border dispute involving the Hawar Islands and the Dibal and Jaradeh shoals. The ICJ asked Qatar and Bahrain to resubmit their claims. Both sides did so toward the end of 1994, although Bahrain argued that the ICJ had no jurisdiction to arbitrate the dispute. Instead it continued to push for an out-of-court settlement mediated by King Fahd of Saudi Arabia.

CROWN PRINCE DEPOSES FATHER IN PALACE COUP

Long-simmering tensions between Sheikh Khalifa and the crown prince came to a head in the early hours of June 27, 1995, when Sheikh Hamad ousted his father and declared himself amir in a palace coup. Khalifa had left the country on June 18 on official visits to Egypt and Tunisia, with a short private stopover in Switzerland and a subsequent official trip to Germany. The sixty-three-year-old amir was in Switzerland when the forty-three-year-old crown prince made his move back home, famously refusing to take Hamad's call when he telephoned his father at a Zurich hotel to inform him of the regime change.[38] The new amir put Qatar's army on high alert and sent troops to his father's private Rayyan Palace and the Doha airport as a precautionary measure. He also briefly closed the border with Saudi Arabia. Hamad easily won over the ruling family council, particularly his two brothers, Abdullah Ibn Khalifa, the minister of the interior, and Mohammad Ibn Khalifa, the minister of finance, economy, and trade. The brothers had been siding with Sheikh Hamad against their father for some time, and both carried messages from the new ruler to Gulf Cooperation Council leaders in the days following the coup.[39]

It is not clear if Sheikh Hamad staged his power grab simply because the amir was out of the country or if the timing was related to other behind-the-scenes machinations. Reports suggested that Sheikh Khalifa had actually gone to Cairo to ask President Hosni Mubarak for Egypt's help in securing the support of other GCC countries in clawing back power ceded to the crown prince after the 1992 cabinet reshuffle. QGPC's managing director, Dr. Al Marri, was added to the list of officials accompanying Sheikh Khalifa at the last minute, ostensibly in order to discuss gas issues with the Egyptians and Germans. Issa Al Kawari, the minister of state for Amiri Diwan and the ruler's right-hand man, had been scheduled to accompany Sheikh Khalifa as well but was removed from the list at the eleventh hour by Sheikh Hamad. This prompted considerable speculation in Doha about the next moves in the father–son feud even before the amir's departure for Cairo.[40] Al Marri was back at his post in Doha within days of the coup, while Al Kawari left Qatar to join Khalifa in exile in France soon after Hamad took power.

In an emergency cabinet meeting following the coup, Sheikh Hamad tactfully did not elaborate on the "difficult circumstances" that had forced him "to take the reins of power in the country, thus replacing my father, who will remain the respected and beloved father of everyone."[41] Sheikh Khalifa, on the other hand, refused to go quietly. In a statement issued from Geneva on the day of the coup, the deposed ruler called his son an "ignorant man" and pledged to return to Qatar. "I am still their legitimate emir, whether it is for the royal family, for the people or for the army and I will return home whatever it costs," he vowed.[42] Khalifa also claimed to have contacted the rulers of the five other Gulf Cooperation Council states, saying they and other Arab leaders had all expressed their support for his legitimate rule and denounced the coup.[43] He then decamped to his villa in the South of France.

It was too late. Sheikh Hamad had already dispatched the ministers of the interior and foreign affairs to Saudi Arabia to seek King Fahd's recognition. This was forthcoming the following day. The other four members of the GCC quickly fell in line too. King Fahd's swift and decisive recognition of the new amir was surprising, given the maverick foreign policy Hamad and his allies had charted since the 1992 cabinet reshuffle. Qatar's moves to restore ties with Iraq, its

14.1 Sheikh Hamad Ibn Khalifa Al Thani, r. 1995–2013.

Source: Image in Lizzie Dearden, "Former Qatar Ruler Sheikh Hamad bin Khalifa Al Thani Flies to Switzerland for Treatment After Breaking Leg on Holiday," *Independent* (U.K.), December 29, 2015 (AFP/Getty Images), https://static.independent.co.uk/s3fs-public/thumbnails/image/2015/12/29/10/Sheikh-Hamad.jpg.

maintenance of "friendly and good neighborly" relations with radical Iran, and its nascent but increasing political and economic contacts with Israel were all opposed by Saudi Arabia. Riyadh's own relations with Doha had been frosty since their violent border skirmish three years earlier, which the Saudis had privately blamed on the crown prince and the minister of foreign affairs, Hamad Ibn Jassim Ibn Jabir Al Thani.

Washington also immediately recognized Hamad; the State Department described the takeover as a "private decision" made by the ruling Al Thani family. This may have been because the United States was building a base near Dukhan to preposition equipment for a U.S. armored brigade as part of a strategy to meet regional emergencies like Iraq's invasion of Kuwait. Qatar was funding this new infrastructure itself, and the United States obviously did not want to rock the boat, although State Department spokesman Nicholas Burns said Washington had received unspecified assurances from the new amir regarding Iran and Iraq.[44] This burgeoning military relationship with Qatar, widely attributed to Sheikh Hamad, would lead to the construction of the 262-acre Camp As Sayliyah army base outside Doha in 2000 and the transfer of the U.S. Central Command's air operations from Saudi Arabia to Qatar's Al Udeid Air Base in 2003.

On July 7, ten days after the coup, Sheikh Hamad appointed a new seventeen-man cabinet. Like his father before him, the new amir assumed the post of prime minister while retaining the positions of minister of defense and commander-in-chief of the armed forces. His brother Abdullah Ibn Khalifa was made deputy prime minister as well as minister of the interior. But speculation that Hamad would name Abdullah crown prince in return for his critical role during the coup proved unfounded when the ruler issued an amiri decree amending Article 21 of Qatar's provisional constitution and establishing the line of succession as passing from father to son, rather than simply within the Al Thani family.[45]

The amendment did specify that the selected crown prince must be approved by most of the ruling family's members. Foreign Minister Hamad Ibn Jassim Ibn Jabir had already announced that the amir's eldest son, Mishal Ibn Hamad, had been selected by the Al Thani family as crown prince. HBJ himself was reappointed to his post in the new cabinet, as were most of the other ministers. One exception was Issa Al Kawari, who was replaced as minister of state for Amiri Diwan by former minister of public health Hamad Ibn Suhaym Al Thani. Ali Said Al Khayarin was appointed minister of public health. Dr. Najib Mohammad Al Nuaimi became the minister of justice, replacing the new minister of state,

Ahmad Ibn Saif Al Thani. Ahmad Ibn Abdullah Al Mahmud was given the resurrected post of minister of state for foreign affairs, and Mohammad Ibn Khalid Al Thani became the new minister of state for cabinet affairs and joined the Council of Ministers.

Sheikh Hamad lifted formal press censorship three months after assuming power and considered abolishing the Ministry of Information and Culture, which was responsible for providing radio and television programming in the country.[46] Journalists were warned to be gentle in criticizing government officials, however. The following year Hamad acquired the British Broadcasting Corporation's Arabic-language news channel lock, stock, and barrel. This came after BBC Arabic Television's Saudi backers, who had established the service with the BBC in 1994, pulled the plug following a Panorama documentary on Islamic law in Saudi Arabia that showed the beheading of a convicted criminal. The core news team—about 150 Arab reporters, editors, presenters, producers, and technicians—moved to Doha and the channel was relaunched as Al Jazeera with a loan of QR 500 million ($137 million) from the amir underwriting its first five years.

KOREA GAS CORPORATION ACCEPTS RASGAS FLOOR PRICE

Early in 1995 RasGas scored a breakthrough in its crucial quest to secure LNG sales agreements. Kogas, as Korea Gas Corporation was now known, finally accepted the floor price principle and agreed to pay a minimum of $2.50 per million Btu if its market price fell below this threshold.[47] This minimum price was in 1993 dollars and escalated at 3 percent per annum rather than rising with the U.S. Consumer Price Index, as was the case with Chubu Electric's sales contract at Qatargas. Escalation would only apply until RasGas paid off its debt or twelve years from the first LNG cargo, whichever came first. After this milestone the minimum price would remain fixed and no longer escalate.

Unlike Qatargas, where the minimum price with Chubu Electric applied to LNG delivered into Japan, both the market price and the minimum price in the Kogas deal were free-on-board, or FOB. This meant Kogas bought the LNG from RasGas at the load port, arranging its own transportation to Korea and paying all shipping costs. The market price formula was tied to a basket of crude oils imported into Japan, but it also included a small, fixed component that escalated at an agreed level every year. It equated to $3.09 per million Btu at an oil price of $18 a barrel, although slight adjustments were included because of gas boil-off enroute and the comparatively high shipping costs from Qatar versus other potential LNG suppliers.

After accepting the minimum price, Kogas sent RasGas a letter in April 1995 confirming plans to sign the sale and purchase agreement for 2.4 million tons per year by the end of July. The letter allowed Mobil to release the tender package for the main engineering, procurement, and construction contract to short-listed bidders. This covered two liquefaction trains with individual annual capacities of 2.6 million tons—larger than any LNG trains then in operation worldwide—with an option for a third train of equal size. Japan's Chiyoda Corporation had already completed the front-end engineering and design for this onshore infrastructure, and contractors had been prequalified. A subsidiary of the U.S. company McDermott Inc. was still designing the offshore gas facilities.

RasGas desperately needed Kogas to buy enough LNG to support two trains; the project was not particularly attractive based on a single train whose projected return on investment was just 6 or 7 percent. A second train sale would nearly triple this return thanks to economies of scale. "Getting the second 2.4 million tons per year from Kogas jumped the rate of return up to around 18 percent. It was a substantial increase because the additional cost for the second train was so small," explains one former Mobil executive.[48] The total installed cost excluding financing fees and interest during construction for a single train was estimated at $2.207 billion, while the figure for two trains was put at $2.754 billion.

The sale and purchase agreement with Kogas was finalized in July 1995, and the contract was formally signed by RasGas chair Dr. Jabir Al Marri and Kogas president Han Gap-Soo on October 16 of that year. The optional quantity had risen from 1.6 to 2.4 million tons per year, and RasGas offered Kogas a 5 percent equity stake in the project if it exercised this option by the end of 1995. But the Koreans were in no hurry to commit to more volume from RasGas. Immediately after the signing ceremony in Doha, President Han left for Muscat to hold supply discussions with the rival Oman LNG project, where Royal Dutch Shell was the largest foreign shareholder and marketer. Kogas already had a letter of intent for 3 million tons per year with Oman LNG, and the Korean firm hoped to squeeze better terms out of Shell and its partners.

If RasGas was keen to proceed simultaneously with two trains, Oman LNG was just as eager to launch its project on the same basis. The venture had been set up in mid-1993 by the Omani government, Shell, Total, and Partex—the four

shareholders in Petroleum Development Oman, the country's dominant oil producer—as well as the Japanese trading companies Mitsubishi, Mitsui, and Itochu.
Oman LNG planned to build two trains with a total capacity of 6.2 million tons
per year at Al Ghalilah near Sur on the northeast coast, and the government had
dedicated 7 trillion cubic feet of non-associated gas from three fields in north-
central Oman to the project. In addition to the revenue stream from LNG, the
Barik, Saih Rawl, and Saih Nihayda fields were expected to yield about eighty
barrels of high-value field condensates for every million cubic feet of gas produced,
as opposed to about sixty barrels in Qatar.

After Kogas formally committed to the first 2.4 million tons per year, Ras-
Gas reworked the engineering, procurement, and construction package so that it
could proceed with the first train upon contract award while securing another
twelve months for the second train. (The third train option was eliminated.) A
joint venture consisting of Japan's JGC Corporation and the U.S. firm M. W.
Kellogg won the competition to build the LNG plant and associated onshore
infrastructure in March 1996. Important long-lead items, including the LNG
storage tanks, main cryogenic heat exchanger, refrigerant compressors, and turbines, had already been awarded in late 1995. Offshore facilities quickly followed.
Chiyoda and McDermott-ETPM won the contract for the process utilities and
platforms, and Italy's Saipem was retained to build the eighty-five-kilometer
pipeline system to Ras Laffan.[49]

KOREANS BREAK OFF NEGOTIATIONS FOR ADDITIONAL
RASGAS LNG

Kogas failed to exercise its option for more volume by the end of 1995, and within
a few months the negotiations had all but broken down. This followed Shell's
shock decision to waive the minimum price at Oman LNG in return for a commitment from Kogas to buy 4.1 million tons per year. Kogas made no secret of its
dissatisfaction with the floor price provision at RasGas in the wake of its achievement in Oman, and it made revision of the minimum price in the first contract
a condition for discussing the second 2.4-million-tons-per-year tranche. Working-
level meetings resumed in late April after RasGas lowered the minimum price,
but the two sides were still far apart. RasGas was now demanding a floor price
of $2.25 per million Btu on the full 4.8 million tons per year, against an offer from

Kogas of $1.95 per million Btu on 3.6 million tons annually with an option for another 1.2 million tons per year.[50] They also differed on escalation, with RasGas sticking to 3 percent per year from 1993 and Kogas holding out for 2.5 percent starting in 2000.

Several factors influenced the elimination of a minimum price at Oman LNG. One was lower overall capital costs; the liquefaction venture was not responsible for upstream field development or the 360-kilometer pipeline to the LNG plant site at Al Ghalilah. Another was the feed gas pricing structure, which provided higher downstream margins during the critical peak debt service period. Upstream development costs at the three onshore gas fields (handled for the government by Petroleum Development Oman) dedicated to Oman LNG were expected to be higher than Qatar's offshore North field, but these were offset by the more generous condensate yields.

President Han informed his board and the Korean government that negotiations had been called off after RasGas rejected a minimum price offer of $2.00 per million Btu from Kogas in June 1996. Attempts to restart the official dialog failed. Kogas refused to even hear the seller's counterproposal, trotting out the well-worn excuse that it preferred not to buy more LNG from inside the Strait of Hormuz for security reasons. Many saw this as a smoke screen. The Qataris were convinced the Koreans would come back to the table eventually. Yousef Kamal, the undersecretary of the ministry of finance, economy, and trade, had just taken over as chair of RasGas. He did not want to show weakness by trying to reestablish official contact with Kogas. Mobil maintained informal links with Kogas through its Korean representative, John Lee, whose office also helped Indonesia's Pertamina manage its supply contract out of PT Arun. In the meantime, formal negotiations on the second train volumes at RasGas ground to a halt.

Mobil's chair and chief executive officer, Lou Noto, was soon on his way back to Doha to prod the Qataris into accepting the Korean firm's last offer if it could not be improved. It wasn't going to be easy to change minds in Qatar, where Mobil itself had been selling QGPC on the absolute necessity of minimum prices in securing bank financing and ensuring project viability for years. The concept had already been adopted at Qatargas as well as with Kogas on the first RasGas train. QGPC did not want to jeopardize deals with Chubu Electric and the other Qatargas buyers, who would surely demand equal treatment if the Koreans got more favorable terms at RasGas. Qatargas was on track to begin shipping out LNG at the end of 1996, just six months away. There was still no market price agreed with the Japanese. QGPC was worried it would lose revenue initially if these customers didn't honor their minimum price commitments.

Shell had changed the rules of the game at Oman LNG, market forces had shifted in the buyer's favor, and the lower engineering, procurement, and construction bids at RasGas had reduced the need for a robust floor price to guarantee the project's economic viability. Volume was now more important to Mobil than minimum price, and it needed to convince its Qatari partners that Korea represented the only viable market for the second train. "We need to find a way to reopen discussions with Korea Gas Corporation to see if a compromise solution is possible," Paul Hoenmans advised his boss. "If we are not able to improve [the] current offer, we recommend that Ras Laffan accept it."[51] If QGPC continued to resist, he suggested that Mobil offer a $400 million loan to "bridge the burden" if the Kogas market price fell below the agreed minimum level.

Noto and his team laid out their case in a meeting with the amir, the minister of energy and industry, and the new RasGas chair in Doha on July 20, 1996. The Qataris agreed to quietly reopen negotiations with the Koreans. Mobil would use the services of Robert Strauss, the former U.S. ambassador to Russia and President Jimmy Carter's chief Middle East trouble-shooter after the 1978 Camp David Accords. Akin Gump Strauss Hauer & Feld, the Washington law firm founded by Strauss in 1945, was one of the most prestigious U.S. lobbying firms. It was also the legal counsel to the Blue House, the executive office and official residence of Korea's head of state. For their part, the Qataris retained Ambassador Philip Kaplan of Patton, Boggs & Blow, another Washington lobbying powerhouse. In addition to investigating the situation in Korea, Ambassador Kaplan agreed to lobby for U.S. government support in Seoul for the RasGas sale to Kogas.

DEPOSED RULER CONTINUES TO ASSERT CLAIM TO THRONE

Sheikh Khalifa continued to agitate from exile in France, reasserting his claim to the throne in a letter to the Gulf Cooperation Council summit held in Muscat in early December 1995. Sheikh Hamad himself refused to attend the final summit session on December 6, when Qatar's nominee to take the rotating post of GCC secretary, Gen. Abdurrahman Ibn Hamad Al Attiyah, was passed over in favor of the Saudi Jamil Al Hujailan. The amir skipped the session and headed for the airport after Abu Dhabi's Sheikh Zayid Ibn Sultan Al Nahyan, the seventy-eight-year-old president of the UAE, urged the much younger Sheikh Hamad to avoid an open breach within the six-member GCC. Qatar's relations with its neighbors deteriorated further after Khalifa began a tour of the Gulf later that month, visiting Bahrain, the UAE, Kuwait, and Saudi Arabia to affirm, as one of his aides put it, that "he has not and will not relinquish power under any circumstances and that he is returning to rule his dear country Qatar soon."[52] The deposed ruler was received in every country with full honors by the head of state (or, in the case of Saudi Arabia, by the acting head of state).

The new leadership in Doha claimed to be unfazed by the former amir's shuttle diplomacy. "I assure you the situation in Qatar is more than stable and we are not harmed by Sheikh Khalifah's tours. We wish him well and hope he will consider rest during his trip and that he thinks of the possibility of returning to his country Qatar," Minister of Foreign Affairs Hamad Ibn Jassim Ibn Jabir declared on December 27, 1995.[53] But Qatar nonetheless responded to Bahrain's decision to receive the ousted amir as a ruling head of state by broadcasting a TV interview with a Bahraini opposition leader the following month, just as antigovernment Shiite protesters demonstrated in Manama.

In early 1996 Sheikh Zayid turned over the top floors of the government-owned Abu Dhabi Intercontinental, the emirate's most luxurious hotel, to Sheikh Khalifa, his staff, and a contingent of French and Moroccan bodyguards.[54] The deposed amir issued a statement from exile that he still considered himself the legal ruler of Qatar and that his return home would take place soon. This suggested that his UAE hosts tacitly supported Sheikh Khalifa's efforts to reclaim the throne. As the *Middle East Economic Survey* wrote presciently on February 5, 1996, "in a region where discretion is the political norm, that is close to open support from Abu Dhabi (and presumably Saudi Arabia) for his campaign to return to power."[55]

Just two weeks later, Qatar said it had thwarted a coup against Sheikh Hamad that had received "outside support and assistance."[56] The U.S. Embassy in Doha immediately faxed a fairly anodyne alert to all U.S. companies operating in Qatar. "This morning [February 20] the government of Qatar announced that there was a foiled attempt to overthrow the ruler. The government has further assured the Embassy that the situation is peaceful and well in hand," it wrote, although the embassy still cautioned members of the American community to exercise prudence.[57] The coup attempt unfolded during the Eid al-Fitr holiday marking the end of the Muslim holy month of Ramadan. "Several of us have been visiting

Qatari ministers and dignitaries in their homes as part of the Eid al-Fitr holiday, and other than a noticeable increase in police car presence, there are no signs of unrest within the community," one Mobil executive reported to headquarters in the United States.[58]

The government soon named Sheikh Khalifa's nephew Hamad Ibn Jassim Ibn Hamad Al Thani, the former commandant of police, as the plot's mastermind.[59] While the alleged leader eluded arrest for three years, over one hundred other co-conspirators were quickly apprehended. They comprised prominent members of the Al Marri tribe with close links to Saudi Arabia as well as several Saudi nationals, including a passport official at the Salwa border crossing who helped the plotters enter Qatar. All the GCC states except Oman pointedly refrained from expressing shock and horror at the abortive operation and rebuffed Qatar's efforts to convene an emergency meeting to discuss it. Washington, which intervened on Doha's behalf to persuade the other GCC members to attend, was told by Saudi Arabia, Bahrain, and the UAE that Qatar had to apologize for hinting at their implication in the coup attempt before they would agree to meet.

France was quick to condemn the incident, possibly to dispel Qatari suspicions of official support for the attempted overthrow following the participation of a former French security official and longtime aide to Sheikh Khalifa. It sent a senior government official and a military general to Doha to discuss the situation and also directed two small navy ships to Qatar to participate in joint exercises with the Qatari and U.S. navies. A senior Qatari official told the London-based Arabic daily *Al Hayat* that his country would seek the help of additional French troops to protect it against foreign risks, noting that Doha had tactfully refused an offer from Tehran to send thirty thousand Iranian soldiers.[60]

It wasn't until July 1999 that the Qatari authorities finally apprehended Hamad Ibn Jassim Ibn Hamad, the prime suspect in the coup attempt. The circumstances of his capture were unclear; either his private plane was intercepted by Qatari security forces midflight from Beirut or he was effectively snatched from the Beirut airport and forcibly returned to Qatar with or without Interpol's help. Six months later a lower court sentenced the alleged leader and thirty-two co-conspirators to life in prison.[61] Eighty-five other defendants were acquitted on charges ranging from conspiracy to treason and armed rebellion. Nine of those found guilty were tried in absentia, as were twenty of the acquitted.

Hamad Ibn Jassim Ibn Hamad and the other men sentenced to life appealed their convictions. The appeals court sided with prosecutors, who were now asking for the death penalty. Nineteen of the thirty-two defendants, including the coup's leader, were sentenced to death on May 21, 2001.[62] The amir subsequently pardoned his royal cousin and Amnesty International reported that Hamad Ibn Jassim Ibn Hamad was released from prison in September 2005. Other important participants in the coup attempt were also set free; it is not clear if Qatar ever carried out any of the death sentences. Wabram Ali al-Yami, the only Saudi in the conspiracy given the death penalty, was pardoned by the amir in July 2008 after twelve years in prison. A group of other Saudis imprisoned for their role in the failed coup were also released in May 2010 after Saudi Arabia's king, Abdullah, appealed personally to the Qatari ruler.

QATAR SEEKS BILLIONS HELD ABROAD BY DEPOSED AMIR

Sheikh Hamad's government was also busy tracking down billions of dollars held in overseas bank deposits, equities, and bonds controlled by Sheikh Khalifa and the former amir's right-hand man Issa Al Kawari. Before he deposed his father in 1995, Sheikh Hamad retained the Washington law firm Patton, Boggs & Blow, reportedly on the advice of Oman's Sultan Qaboos Ibn Said Al Said. This gave the new amir a small army of lawyers who could be deployed to recover what his government publicly described as "misappropriated assets of the State of Qatar."[63] The Qatari authorities initiated action in the local civil courts in April 1996, two months after the squashed takeover attempt, and subsequently approached judicial institutions in eight different countries. By August, the *Guardian* in Britain reported that cash deposits in Sheikh Khalifa's name had been frozen in Luxembourg, the Channel Islands, France, the United States, and Switzerland.[64]

France was the first country to accede to Qatar's request to freeze accounts held by Sheikh Khalifa and Issa Al Kawari. This decision came on the eve of a five-hour stopover in Qatar on July 8, 1996, by French president Jacques Chirac. Announcing the asset freeze, Chirac's spokesperson, Catherine Colonna, stressed France's close political, economic, and military cooperation with Qatar.[65] She also noted that a full 80 percent of the equipment used by the Gulf state's armed forces was supplied by France. The French decision was closely followed by successful legal action at London's High Court in late July, freezing up to $300 million in assets and restricting the former amir's access to a Boeing 747 presumably owned by the Qatari state.

Qatar's official news agency issued a statement from the Ministry of Justice on October 20, 1996, that an out-of-court settlement had been reached with the former amir and his aide. According to the ministry, the government agreed to drop all lawsuits against Sheikh Khalifa and Issa Al Kawari "in return for the payment of accounts that were the subject of the dispute."[66] No details of the agreement were disclosed, but the *New York Times* subsequently reported that the deposed ruler had promised to return $2 billion to the Qatari treasury while keeping another $1.2 billion or so for himself.[67] Qatari officials said the settlement paved the way for Sheikh Khalifa to return home, indicating that the former amir might finally have relinquished his claim to the throne. It was also agreed that Sheikh Khalifa would assume the title of father-amir while Sheikh Hamad retained executive power as amir.

The message that Qatar's new ruler was indisputably in charge was reinforced just two days later when Sheikh Hamad appointed his seventeen-year-old third son, Jassim Ibn Hamad, as crown prince. In doing so, the amir passed over two older sons from his first wife, Sheikha Mariam, in favor of the first-born son of his second wife, Sheikha Mozah. "One played too much, the other prayed too much," was the refrain often used to explain Sheikh Hamad's decision to rule out these elder sons as candidates to succeed him. It was true that the ruler's first-born son, Mishal Ibn Hamad, who had been tipped as heir apparent only the previous year, was well known as an avid sportsman, equestrian, and racing enthusiast. His second son, Fahd Ibn Hamad, was reportedly deemed unsuitable because of his ultraconservative religious views and fondness for the Afghan Taliban.[68]

Sheikh Hamad's appointment of his third-born son as the new crown prince was followed in late October by an extraordinary decree separating the prime minister's office from those of the royal court. Cabinet ministers would henceforth be appointed by the prime minister rather than the amir, although the ruler remained the ultimate authority, and the cabinet was collectively responsible to him. Sheikh Hamad continued to endorse and issue laws and decrees and retained supreme supervision over their execution.

The amir appointed Minister of Interior Abdullah Ibn Khalifa, his younger half brother, as the new prime minister. This represented the first time since before Qatar's independence in 1971 that the reigning amir had not acted as his own prime minister, appointing or dismissing cabinet ministers at his sole discretion. The new twenty-man cabinet was dominated by Al Thanis, and prominent members of the ruling family retained key ministries. Sheikh Hamad himself held on to the posts of minister of defense and commander-in-chief of the armed forces, while other Al Thanis retained ministries responsible for the interior, foreign affairs, finance, economy and trade, and communications and transport.

Abdullah Ibn Hamad Al Attiyah was reappointed as minister of energy and industry, putting paid to long-running speculation that Sheikh Hamad would replace this ministry with a Supreme Energy Council headed by himself and chaired by the powerful minister of foreign affairs. An earlier version of the proposed energy council floated in late 1995 originally envisaged Dr. Jabir Al Marri as its secretary general, perhaps even with ministerial rank. Al Marri's star had waned considerably since the coup attempt, however, as several prominent members of his extended tribe were implicated in the operation. He was still deputy chair and managing director of QGPC when Sheikh Hamad announced his new cabinet on October 30, 1996. But Al Marri had been fired by Al Attiyah the previous June from the chairmanships of both RasGas and Qatargas, ostensibly because he objected to personnel changes imposed by his boss.

As he had in 1994 when Al Attiyah first fired him, Al Marri appealed directly to the amir to reverse his dismissal from the two LNG companies. Unlike his father, Sheikh Hamad refused to overrule the energy minister, although he did say Al Marri could remain as head of QGPC or become an adviser in the Amiri Diwan. It is not clear what happened next, but Sheikh Hamad issued an amiri decree on November 20, 1996, appointing a new board of directors at QGPC that did not include Al Marri. Al Attiyah himself became managing director of the state-owned firm in addition to its chair, while Yousef Kamal, the undersecretary of the Ministry of Finance, Economy and Trade, was named deputy chair of QGPC. Kamal, a rising star and close ally of Al Attiyah, had already replaced Al Marri as the chair of RasGas in June. Dr. Ibrahim Al Ibrahim, the amir's longtime economic adviser, became its deputy chair. Al Attiyah took Al Marri's place as chair of Qatargas, and Faisal Al Suwaidi, the managing director of the Qatar Fertilizer Company, was appointed its deputy chair and effective head. Al Suwaidi was also named to the QGPC board in the November 20 reshuffle.

CHAPTER 15

Financial Difficulties Mount After 1995 Coup

With billions of dollars in overseas assets still under Shaikh Khalifa's control, low international oil prices, and no let-up in funding requirements for Qatar's ambitious development plan, the new amir publicly alluded to financial problems during the opening of the twenty-fourth session of the Advisory Council on November 14, 1995. "The overall development plan has encountered difficulties which are due to unusual financial circumstances," Sheikh Hamad announced, although he also noted that these problems should ease at the beginning of 1997 with the startup of LNG production from Qatargas. "Qatar has no choice but to continue with the development plan. . . . Without the various and abundant additional resources which the development plan offers we will find ourselves in a difficult economic position which we may not be able to confront."[1] While vowing to continue with the country's industrial objectives, the amir also exhorted his new cabinet to limit public expenditures to necessities.

Renewed emphasis was put on gas development, and shortly after assuming power Sheikh Hamad listed obtaining the necessary financial credits for this sector as a top priority.[2] Expansions at Qatar's long-standing petrochemical and fertilizer companies were already well on their way. Other projects were on more shaky ground. The Qatar Clean Energy Company suffered a fatal blow in early 1996 when Malaysia's Petronas, which had joined QGPC and the UK's Penspen in Qatar Clean Energy the previous year, withdrew from the methanol-MTBE project. Following years of internal strife, Total finally quit the rival Qatar Fuel Additives Company after failing to convince its partners to focus solely on methanol. International Octane Ltd., the Canadian partner who had founded QAFAC in 1992 with Total and QGPC, took a portion of the French firm's stake, as did later Taiwanese entrants CPC and Lee Chang Yung Chemicals Industry Company. The project now envisaged 610,000 tons per year of methanol output and 825,000 tons per year of MTBE.

Sheikh Hamad moved forward with plans to introduce financial instruments such as treasury bills to fund budget deficits rather than relying on loans from the Qatar National Bank, or QNB, and other local banks. While monetary authorities had introduced some long-awaited measures to liberalize the banking system in 1995, including allowing commercial banks to determine interest rates and commissions on credit facilities, the Central Bank retained control of interest rates on time deposits. It wouldn't be until early 1998 that legislation was passed allowing the Central Bank to issue treasury bills and bonds denominated in Qatari riyals, and it took another year after that before the first local bonds were issued. QNB would remain the government's principal banker for the time being, playing a front-line role in extending overdraft and loan facilities to finance Qatar's large public sector deficits. Liquidity in the banking sector remained tight, with the ratio of loans to deposits exceeding 95 percent.[3]

The International Monetary Fund, or IMF, warned of serious short-term consequences, including delays in Qatar's oil and gas projects, if fiscal reform was not implemented. In a report published in early 1996, the IMF called on the government to eliminate restrictions on deposit rates, start issuing government bonds, and set up a working stock market as soon as possible.[4] (Sheikh Hamad had issued a decree approving the establishment of an official stock exchange within days of assuming power, but the Doha Securities Market wouldn't begin floor trading until May 1997.) It also urged the authorities to hike utility charges for commercial users, increase gasoline prices, and raise the price of natural gas used for domestic consumption from 50 cents per million Btu to a market rate of $2.50 per million Btu. The IMF nonetheless admitted that Qatar's financial circumstances would improve significantly within three or four years without these reforms due to the projected growth in Qatar's crude oil production and the completion of its two LNG projects.[5]

Amid the cash crunch, QGPC sought creative ways to fund its equity capital commitments at RasGas. Lining up another sovereign loan to give the state-owned firm some money was a possibility, although not a particularly favorable one following the sub-investment-grade rating given to Qatar by Moody's in early 1996.[6] The U.S. ratings firm had specifically cited the government's high current account deficits in assigning its "Not Prime" rating. Qatar National Bank was already in the process of arranging a $250 million loan for the state, the fourth sovereign borrowing since early 1994. This facility was co-arranged with J. P. Morgan, the government's main financial adviser, and would be Qatar's only sovereign loan in 1996. It was presumably needed to meet QGPC's ongoing obligations at Qatargas.

QGPC WEIGHS OFFER FROM JAPANESE TRADERS AT RASGAS

At this point three Japanese trading companies eager to get a piece of the action at RasGas approached QGPC with a tempting offer. Sumitomo, Nissho Iwai, and Itochu would lend QGPC up to $1.08 billion under a subordinated financing—meaning this debt would be ranked behind the project's other loans in terms of the order of repayment—in return for a 10 percent stake in RasGas. From the outset, the trading companies made it abundantly clear their offer was not conditional on bringing in additional sales. Even so, QGPC expected Mobil to give up a 5 percent share in the project to the prospective partners. Mobil resisted strenuously: RasGas still only had the 2.4 million tons per year sale to Kogas in hand, and the *sogo shoshas* brought nothing to the table in terms of additional market demand in Japan.

In the end, Mobil had no choice in the matter. Unable or unwilling to underwrite QGPC's equity capital obligations itself, the cash-tight U.S. major reluctantly agreed to reduce its stake in RasGas so that the Qatari firm could get its much-needed loan. Mobil did extract some concessions in return. Sumitomo, Nissho Iwai, and Itochu would get an equity position in the first two trains at Ras-Gas only up to 5 million tons per year. If these firms wanted to participate in future trains, they would have to bring in sales volume. The three trading companies also said they would try to deliver customers for the second train, and Sumitomo promised to start marketing LNG in Japan as soon as the agreement was signed. Abdullah Al Attiyah personally assured Mobil that its equity interest in RasGas would not fall below 25 percent. If additional divestment were required to accommodate Kogas or other Korean companies, the minister promised, QGPC would provide this equity from its own share of the project.

Just as the three Japanese firms were preparing to sign the preliminary agreement with QGPC, Sumitomo was hit with a very big and very public scandal. In June 1996 its star copper trader, Yasuo Hamanaka, lost $1.8 billion in unauthorized copper trades. At the time this represented the largest loss ever by a single rogue trader. It certainly eclipsed the $1.4 billion lost the previous year by Nick Leeson of Barings Bank, which had caused the collapse of Britain's oldest investment firm and its sale to the Dutch group ING for the nominal sum of one British pound. Sumitomo's losses were later adjusted to $2.6 billion, fourteen times its 1996 profits, after the firm had to close out Hamanaka's complex trading positions in a plunging copper market.[7]

Sumitomo had originally planned to take a 4 percent stake in RasGas. It was instead forced to back out of the deal because of the scandal. This delayed matters by several months as Itochu and Nissho Iwai renegotiated the details of their so-called soft loan. Itochu ultimately decided to take a 4 percent stake in RasGas while Nissho Iwai signed on for 3 percent. The project's two founding shareholders each relinquished 3.5 percent to accommodate the new partners. In exchange for their equity participation in RasGas, the Japanese trading companies agreed to loan QGPC $864 million in two tranches and provide marketing assistance for the project in Japan. This debt was secured by the royalties RasGas owed the state of Qatar on gas and condensates under the 1992 development and fiscal agreement and eliminated a previous loan commitment of $300 million that Mobil had extended to QGPC back in October 1995.

Since QGPC needed to begin drawing down the loan from Itochu and Nissho Iwai immediately, it was agreed that funds would be made available to the borrower within thirty days after signature of the preliminary agreement in Tokyo on December 9, 1996.[8] This was necessary because it would take several months to formally bring the new partners into the joint venture. The two tranches of $540 million and $324 million were repayable in twenty semiannual installments beginning six months after project completion, with interest accruing on both tranches at LIBOR plus 95 basis points until project completion and LIBOR plus 13 basis points thereafter. Mobil was still prepared to loan QGPC another $160 million if this proved necessary, although alternate security would need to be pledged as collateral.

Qatar's financial situation had begun to improve by the end of 1996, however. Crude prices and production increased, adding about $500 million to revenue for the year. The financial settlement reached with the exiled former amir in October was expected to result in the return of several billion dollars of offshore funds to the state treasury in 1997. Sheikh Hamad traveled to Europe in mid-December, where he met with his father for the first time since the June 1995 coup. Liquidity in the economy grew in 1996, particularly toward the end of the year, with money supply increasing over 5 percent. Citing "improved economic and financial prospects" following the imminent completion of Qatar's first LNG project, Moody's upgraded the country's sovereign ratings to investment grade on November 4, 1996.[9] Just two weeks later the U.S. ratings service raised the long- and short-term deposit ratings on three local banks, including Qatar National Bank, to investment grade as well.

QATARGAS BEGINS OPERATIONS

The country's inaugural shipment of LNG was due to set sail for Chubu Electric's Nagoya receiving terminal on December 23, 1996. Field startup had begun the previous June, allowing Qatargas to export its first shipment of condensate earlier on September 26. It was now well past the market price cutoff date in Chubu's sale and purchase agreement, which specified that the two sides should conclude their pricing negotiations ninety days before the first LNG cargo. The deadlock lay in the issue of escalation. Chubu and the other Japanese buyers were holding out for a price based primarily on crude oil equivalence that would also have a fixed element subject to periodic renegotiation, potentially exposing Qatargas to downward price pressure every four or five years. Keen to avoid such price review, the seller pressed for a fixed element that would escalate at an agreed level over the twenty-five-year contract.

With the first LNG cargo imminent, Qatargas was considering all its options. Mobil wanted to bill Chubu at the minimum price after adjusting for inflation. Total, Mitsui, and Marubeni supported a proposal from the buyer for a provisional price. This second stance was eventually endorsed by QGPC. In early January, with the first LNG cargo still steaming toward Japan, the two sides agreed to a three-month interim fixed price of $4.10 per million Btu, the energy equivalent of $24 per barrel crude.[10] Interim pricing remained in effect in one form or other for another four years, with Qatargas only throwing in the towel in early 2001 when it acquiesced to buyer demands for a market price that included a fixed element subject to periodic adjustment. It did get one concession: a longer gap of six years before this portion of the price was up for review. The seller also formally dropped the minimum price agreed with Chubu in 1995 at this time. It was never activated, although Chubu had come under withering criticism from the other Japanese buyers in Qatargas for agreeing to it.

QGPC was not happy with the low prices Total and Mobil, who were taking turns marketing the condensate from Qatargas, were securing for this new production stream. Since field condensates resemble lighter grades of crude oil, they typically sell in the crude oil market. But the high mercaptan content and volatility of the Qatargas condensate meant initial cargoes were priced at a discount of up to $2 per barrel under Qatar Land, as Dukhan crude was now known.[11] A naturally occurring sulfurous compound, mercaptans create problems for refiners due to their high toxicity, corrosivity, and foul-smelling odor. Qatargas had rejected a proposal to install condensate treatment facilities to remove mercaptans. Instead, it wanted to build its own large-scale refinery at Ras Laffan to process condensates from Qatargas and RasGas. It invited Total, Mobil, and the other LNG partners to participate in this refinery, which was seen as the first step toward establishing a petrochemical industry at Ras Laffan including a possible aromatics plant using naphtha from the refinery as feedstock.

The second train at Qatargas was on track to start making LNG in January 1997, and QGPC and Total were already marketing excess cargoes in Europe. Contractually, Chubu was only committed to buy 2 million tons in 1997 under a four-year ramp up schedule to its annual plateau volume of 4 million tons. This was expected to leave up to fifteen excess cargoes, roughly 500,000 tons, available for sale during 1997. There would be more spare volume in 1998 with the commencement of the project's third train, as the seven other Japanese electricity and gas utility customers who had committed to buy 2 million tons per year were not due to begin taking LNG until the beginning of 1999. In early 1997 Qatargas secured its first European customer with a multicargo sale totaling 420,000 tons to Spain's Enagas.[12] This was soon followed by a similar short-term deal with Turkey's Botas.

The first two trains at Qatargas were running so well by early 1997 that plant operator Mobil was already predicting the three-train project would be able to produce 20 percent above its nameplate production capacity of 6 million tons per year. There had been some issues offshore with corrosion in heat exchangers used to cool the high-pressure, high-temperature Khuff gas before it is sent ashore. These were ultimately traced to acid gas components like hydrogen sulfide and carbon dioxide. Similar corrosion problems were found in the acid gas removal section of the liquefaction plant. One of the three heat exchangers was repaired on site, while a second was brought ashore for repairs and the third sent back to France for a complete workover by Technip. This hadn't hurt LNG production, as the two working heat exchangers were functioning normally.

Chiyoda Corporation, the onshore contractor at Qatargas, was running ahead of schedule on the third train. It was now due for commissioning in May 1998 rather than early 1999. The Japanese contractor had won the $600 million contract to build this expansion train in August 1995. McDermott-ETPM was awarded the $130 million field development contract twelve months later, with these upstream supply facilities designed boost gas production across the three trains at Qatargas to 1,200 million cubic feet per day at full capacity.

QGPC obtained a loan facility to finance the equity and debt contribution to Qatargas for the third train. This was arranged in two tranches. The first tranche was a $440 million limited recourse loan from the Export-Import Bank of Japan that carried an interest rate of LIBOR plus 125 basis points and was payable in seventeen semiannual installments beginning on August 20, 2001. A second $110 million loan from the Bank of Tokyo, Fuji Bank, Industrial Bank of Japan, and Sakura Bank was priced at LIBOR plus 50 basis points and repayable in three semiannual installments beginning on August 20, 2000.[13] This $550 million package was finalized in July 1996 and the funds released when the first two trains at Qatargas were formally inaugurated by the Amir on February 24, 1997. The ceremony, which also marked the official opening of Ras Laffan port, was attended by France's minister of industry; the oil ministers of Iran, the UAE, and Oman; and over five hundred senior foreign company officials.[14]

In parallel with the inauguration ceremonies at Qatargas and the port of Ras Laffan came a blockbuster of an announcement from RasGas: it had signed a memorandum of understanding with the Korea Gas Corporation to double its LNG purchases by 2.4 million tons per year to an annual rate of 4.8 million tons.

KOREANS RESUME SUPPLY NEGOTIATIONS WITH RASGAS

It had taken over six months of intensive lobbying to get the Koreans back to the table after they abruptly broke off talks with RasGas in June 1996. The negotiating sessions had only resumed in January 1997, just one month before the Qataris announced the memorandum of understanding with Kogas during the formal inauguration ceremonies for Qatargas and the port of Ras Laffan. This followed a visit to Seoul by a RasGas delegation led by its chair, Yousef Kamal, in December 1996, which included a meeting with Kogas president Han Gap-Soo and a private dinner hosted by the Korean firm. Han played hardball, telling his visitors that Kogas would only buy additional volumes from RasGas if the seller dropped the minimum price provision entirely. It was a significant hardening of the buyer's position.

President Han told the delegation that Kogas planned to sign a heads of agreement with a competing venture in western Canada. Proposed by a developer group called Pac-Rim LNG, the project at Kitimat on the coast of British Columbia had attracted Phillips Petroleum, Daewoo, and Bechtel as partners. Phillips saw Pac-Rim as an avenue for its patented Cascade liquefaction technology, which it was also trying to get the Qataris to use in expansion trains at RasGas. Kogas planned to take a stake in Pac-Rim in addition to buying all its output of 3.5 million tons per year. QGPC and Mobil viewed its interest in Pac-Rim as a ploy to put pressure on RasGas, and indeed the project soon died when the sponsors were unable to negotiate supply arrangements with Canadian gas producers. (It would be resurrected on a much bigger scale by Shell over twenty years later as LNG Canada.)

Still loath to give up the minimum price, the RasGas team informally floated two alternatives during the December 1996 meeting with Han. Its first proposal was to sell the second 2.4 million tons per year without a minimum price but to keep the terms under the existing sale and purchase agreement signed in October 1995 unchanged at $2.50 per million Btu in 1993 dollars escalating thereafter at 3 percent per annum.[15] Alternatively, RasGas said it was willing to negotiate a reduced common minimum price covering both trains. No number was put forward by the seller, although the six months of virtual silence from Kogas had convinced RasGas it needed to be more accommodating.

When the two sides resumed formal negotiations the next month, RasGas lowered its expectations still further. Its written offer on January 28, 1997, included two options on minimum price.[16] One was to sell the second train at no minimum and the first train at a significantly lower number than the existing $2.50 per million Btu. The second option was a single minimum price for both trains at a level slightly higher than the last Kogas offer of $2.00 per million Btu made the previous June. It was soon clear that neither of these options would be acceptable to Kogas. Nothing short of full elimination of the minimum price would do, and the Koreans insisted that they would only resume discussions with RasGas on that basis. RasGas explained that it needed a minimum price to support the project's financing, but this fell on deaf ears.

Kogas was well aware that RasGas had only one month to finalize the sale of the second train volumes before the option with JGC and M. W. Kellogg, the contractors building the onshore plant, expired. All the upstream contracts were in place, the jacket structures for two of the three wellhead platforms had been installed, and RasGas was on schedule to spud the first of fifteen wells at its North field block at the end of March. Two drilling rigs were already on their way from Sharjah in the UAE. RasGas could allow the second train option to expire and then rebid the construction contract for the second train. This would give it more time to negotiate with Kogas. But such rebidding would probably cost RasGas an additional $300 million, increasing the final tally for train two from around $600 to $900 million. Alternatively, JGC and M. W. Kellogg might be willing to extend the second train option by a few months. At an estimated $10 to $15 million a month for an extension, this would be costly as well. Building the second train on speculation wasn't being seriously considered.

The Koreans held all the cards, and they weren't budging on the minimum price. "There was enormous pressure to get this done," recalls a member of the RasGas marketing team.[17] Yousef Kamal was now convinced Kogas would not purchase additional volumes without elimination of the minimum price on the first 2.4 million tons per year, but he was in a bind. As Dr. Jabir Al Marri's replacement as RasGas chair, it was politically untenable for Kamal to cut a deal with Kogas that resulted in less financing and potentially a less attractive return than his predecessor had secured. He reached out to Mobil through Dr. Hussein Al Abdullah, the head of the RasGas finance team: Would Mobil guarantee the minimum price to support the financing in return for some type of quid pro quo? Nothing concrete was offered in exchange, but Mobil hoped it could use Kamal's request to get the Qataris to increase the sales exclusivity at RasGas from 10 million tons per year to 15 or possibly even 20 million tons per year.

In order to achieve 70 percent financing on a two-train project with 4.8 million tons per year sold to Kogas, Mobil's treasury department estimated that the company would have to guarantee a minimum price of approximately $1.70 per million Btu with no escalation on the first 2.4 million tons per year until 2014 when the debt was repaid.[18] That translated into a Brent crude oil price of $13 to $14 per barrel. The concept was really quite simple. If the market price fell below this threshold and RasGas did not have sufficient cash on hand to cover its obligations, then Mobil would loan RasGas the money it needed to close the gap. This would be repaid with interest once cash flows improved.

It was a "no-brainer" for Mobil. The second train sale to Kogas would hike the company's rate of return from the project to over 20 percent, double what it would be for a single train. Mobil bowed to the inevitable and agreed to provide a minimum price guarantee, provided that RasGas concluded the second train sale with Kogas. With this pledge in hand, RasGas accepted the buyer's counteroffer, formally dropping the minimum price on the full 4.8 million tons per year. In the meantime, Qatar's minister of foreign affairs was pulling strings behind the scenes in Korea. Through well-connected intermediaries with influence extending into the Blue House and the family of South Korean president Kim Young-sam, Hamad Ibn Jassim Ibn Jabir Al Thani kept up steady pressure on Kogas to close the deal.

Kogas finally signed the memorandum of understanding with RasGas on February 23, 1997. This paved the way for the announcement of the expanded sale during the Qatargas inauguration ceremonies the following day—just four days before the train two option with JGC and M. W. Kellogg was due to expire.

ELIMINATION OF MINIMUM PRICE UPSETS RASGAS FINANCING

RasGas hadn't let its marketing travails get in the way of financing. It had broken new ground in December 1996 with the first capital markets issue for an LNG project anywhere in the world as well as the first ever for a Qatari issuer and the first in the Middle East with a maturity beyond seven years. Members of Mobil's finance team later wrote that the project's two sponsors essentially had to educate the credit-rating agencies about the state of Qatar, the LNG business, and RasGas itself in the lead up to the debt issue.[19] It was worth the effort to secure a cheaper source of capital with a repayment schedule that better matched the project's cash flow profile. The longer maturities offered by the public debt markets, where the repayment of principal could be stretched out well beyond the first six to eight years of operation, simply weren't available through syndicated loans from traditional banks.

The hard work paid off when Moody's and Standard and Poor's rated QGPC and the pending RasGas debt issue—representing the first corporate and corporate debt ratings ever carried out by the agencies in the Arab world.[20] Ras-Gas received investment-grade ratings from both agencies, while Standard and Poor's gave QGPC the same rating as the state of Qatar. This was slightly lower than its RasGas rating, but still investment grade. Originally, the sponsors hoped to raise $400 million from the capital markets. The final offering raised $1.2 billion in two tranches, accounting for a full one-quarter of the total amount of project bonds issued globally in 1996.[21] The RasGas bonds sold out within two hours on the first day and were oversubscribed, mainly by U.S. financial institutions, by a factor of three. With a face value of $800 million, the long bond due in 2014 was priced at an issue yield of 8.294 percent, or 187.5 basis points over U.S. Treasuries. The smaller bond maturing in 2006 raised $400 million and was priced at 7.628 percent, yielding 135 basis points.[22]

The bonds had been sold down on the basis of one train, with bankers saying they had not been advised by RasGas or its partners that the terms of the original sale and purchase agreement with Kogas were being renegotiated.[23] The first train was initially equity and bond financed, but a bond covenant gave RasGas the option of funding a larger two-train project with private debt provided that customers with credit ratings of "A" or better purchased the LNG volumes. Commercial banks and export credit agencies agreed to accept additional LNG sales without minimum prices subject to higher financial ratio tests, although this did not extend to the first 2.4 million tons per year sale to Kogas. The full financing package of $2.55 billion was finalized on December 19, 1996. In addition to the $1.2 billion in bonds, it included a $450 million commercial bank loan as well as three loans totaling $900 million, guaranteed by export credit agencies in the United States, Britain, and Italy.[24]

Once the expanded deal with Kogas was made public, Mobil moved to placate jittery creditors concerned about the removal of the minimum price. The U.S. major announced it would offer RasGas lenders limited credit support, although it clarified that the form and substance of this support was subject to future negotiations. This assurance did not stop Moody's from immediately putting its A3 bond rating—its highest ever for a project financed bond offering—under review for possible downgrade.[25]

By the end of March, however, Moody's had taken the RasGas bonds off credit watch and confirmed its A3 investment-grade rating. Standard and Poor's, which had not put the bonds under review, also reconfirmed its BBB+ rating. This followed an agreement in principle between Mobil and the project's lead banks and export credit agencies under which the company effectively gave all senior debt-holders a minimum price guarantee for debt service purposes.[26] While only half of the twenty-five or so banks involved in the financing had approved the terms of Mobil's credit support, getting these additional institutions on board was not seen as an issue. Documenting the changes to the loan agreements would also take a few months, probably taking finalization up to May 1997 at the earliest. This wasn't considered a problem either.

The guarantee took the form of an unsecured subordinated line of credit of up to $200 million that Mobil would make available to RasGas for debt repayment if the market price under the sale to Kogas fell below a certain threshold. This ended up being slightly different than Mobil had initially estimated. The *Middle East Economic Survey* reported that it had been set at $1.90 per million Btu from 2002 through 2009 and $1.65 per million Btu from 2010 through 2014.[27] Both figures were in 1996 dollars and fixed over their allotted time period. This was much lower than the minimum price of $2.50 per million Btu stipulated in the first 2.4 million tons per year contact with Kogas, which had been subject to 3 percent annual escalation after 1993. Given the Kogas market price formula, Mobil estimated that Brent crude oil would have to fall below $12.90 per barrel on a flat basis in the first period and below $11.30 per barrel during the second period to trigger the loan provisions.[28]

Since all the RasGas debt was pari passu—meaning that the banks, export credit agencies, and bondholders shared the same seniority in terms of repayment—the senior debt-holders benefited equally from Mobil's guarantee during the life of their respective instruments.[29] Nor did it create risks for bondholders in the form of additional claims on the project's collateral because Mobil's price guarantee loan was subordinated to all senior debt. If the loan was disbursed in any amount, the U.S. major would be last in line for repayment. But it would be repaid at an interest rate of 12 percent per annum before any dividend distributions to shareholders. In the end, prices never dropped low enough to trigger the loan provisions. Mobil did not have to capitalize the line of credit through 2014, at which point all the debt for the first two trains was paid off. But its offer calmed nervous debt-holders and kept the multibillion-dollar financing in place.

Mobil couldn't convince QGPC to increase the sales exclusivity at RasGas as a quid pro quo for extending this financial safety net to the joint venture. Even the 10 million tons per year was routinely criticized by certain factions in the Amiri Diwan who felt it gave RasGas (and, hence, Mobil) a virtual monopoly over future LNG production in the country. Mobil did manage to tighten up the language on the royalty that RasGas would pay the government for all gas delivered to the two trains and related onshore facilities. There was no change in the fixed portion of this gas royalty, already set at 50 cents per million Btu. But the indexation was modified to remove any reference to a minimum sales price with Kogas, and it was agreed that the 50 cents per million Btu would escalate from 1995 with the ratio of the Kogas market price to a fixed reference price of $2.50 per million Btu. The 9 percent royalty on condensates was left unchanged. While the integrated venture was subject to government income taxes at the normal 35 percent rate, a tax holiday applied until the twelfth anniversary of the first shipment of LNG.

EQUITY ISSUE COMPLICATES FINAL NEGOTIATIONS WITH KOGAS

There were still some loose ends to tie up before the amended sale and purchase agreement could be signed, not least of which was the amount of equity in Ras-Gas that would be made available to Kogas or its designees. Oman LNG had not only broken the mold by eliminating the minimum price in its own supply deal with Kogas. It had also set a precedent by giving the firm and four other Korean companies a combined 5 percent stake in the liquefaction plant. Most of this equity had come out of Shell's interest in the Omani venture. Once formal negotiations with RasGas resumed in January 1997, Kogas insisted on an even bigger percentage of the Qatari project. But it eventually settled for 5 percent, and the memorandum of understanding signed in February had expressly limited its participation to the first two trains at RasGas. This put the Korean partner on a par with Itochu and Nissho Iwai, whose shareholdings were also limited to the first two trains.

When the two sides met again in March to finalize terms, Kogas tried to expand this participation to the entire project, including any future trains. "Kogas initial position was that limited participation was 1) infeasible, and 2) unfair since it would not share economies of scale," the seller's team reported. "They commented that in Korea an offer of equity was assumed to include full participation in the company. They did not deny that the MOU stated otherwise and blamed their misinterpretation on poor understanding of English."[30] RasGas reiterated that the buyer's equity participation was limited to the first two trains, although it suggested Kogas could participate in additional capacity if it made further purchases beyond 4.8 million tons per year. Kogas did not agree. It argued forcefully that it had made the RasGas project possible and was therefore entitled to the same rights as QGPC and Mobil.

A face-saving compromise on the equity issue was finally reached on May 25, 1997. The two parties agreed that the Kogas equity of 5 percent would apply to a set sales volume of 6.4 million tons per year from RasGas rather than the first two trains. While this amount was more than the design capacity of 5.2 million tons per year, LNG trains almost always produced above design, and RasGas was confident that it could deliver 6.4 million tons per year from the base project. If RasGas could not satisfy this volume from the first two trains, it would make up the difference from a third. Kogas would pay its 5 percent of the project costs associated with the third train proportional to whatever volume was still outstanding but would not get any equity in the additional train per se, as its participation was limited to 6.4 million tons per year of sales. This equity also entitled Kogas to a seat on the RasGas board of directors.

The 5 percent equity assigned to Kogas or its designees would come mostly from QGPC's shareholding in the first two trains at RasGas. Its equity would fall to 63 percent from 66.5 percent. Mobil would give up a further 1.5 percent to Kogas, reducing its stake in the project to 25 percent from 26.5 percent. Between the 3.5 percent it had already transferred to the Japanese trading companies and the 1.5 percent relinquished to Kogas or its assignees, Mobil agreed to divest 5 percent in order to kick off the first two RasGas trains. QGPC gave up 7 percent, including a combined 3.5 percent to Itochu and Nissho Iwai and another 3.5 percent to Kogas. It was well worth it. The increase in contracted sales and the construction of a second train effectively doubled the projected returns, and the two-train sale to Kogas enabled Mobil to add 154 million barrels of oil equivalent to its proved reserves.

Once a solution to the equity impasse was found, a cover letter was drafted for the amended sale and purchase agreement. This was signed by Sheikh Mohammad Ibn Ahmad Ibn Jassim Al Thani, QGPC's manager for refined petroleum products and a member of the six-man RasGas marketing committee, and by Yong-Soo Kang, the Kogas director of LNG purchase. Kogas would start lifting LNG from RasGas in July 1999, rising to the contract plateau of 4.8 million tons per year from 2002. RasGas also agreed to give the Korean firm two free cargoes annually (up from one initially), and the contract was extended by one year, to

December 31, 2024. There was no change in the market price agreed in the original deal signed in 1995, and the "most favored nations" clause was eliminated.

BUMPY ROAD FOR ENRON'S LNG MARKETING EFFORTS

While RasGas was clearing the final hurdles, Enron's LNG project was running into problems in its two crucial markets, starting with India. In early 1995 Enron announced it had completed financing for the first phase of its $2.8 billion Dabhol power plant in India's Maharashtra state. This 695-megawatt phase was expected to be fueled by naphtha produced from local refineries and to cost $920 million. The second 1,320-megawatt phase would run on imported LNG. It would cost effectively twice as much because of the construction of a regasification terminal at the Dabhol receiving end. Enron's majority-owned Dabhol Power Company had signed a twenty-year power purchasing agreement with the Maharashtra State Electricity Board in late 1993 which essentially authorized construction of the first phase but left the second phase optional. This contract was amended in early 1995 following counter-guarantees from the state government as well as the central authorities in New Delhi, both of which were controlled by the ruling Congress Party of Prime Minister P. V. Narasimha Rao.

The controversial Dabhol project quickly became a lightning rod in the Maharashtra state elections, with the national opposition Bharatiya Janata Party and its regional allies in the Shiv Sena party threatening to "throw Enron into the Arabian sea." When this coalition finally wrested control of the state government from the Congress Party in March 1995, it immediately ordered a review of the Enron transaction. The power purchasing agreement had been awarded without competitive bidding, and Congress Party officials were accused of accepting kickbacks during the award process.[31] A committee appointed to investigate the allegations concluded in July 1995 that Enron had obtained unduly favorable terms from the previous government. The following month the Dabhol Power Company was ordered by the Maharashtra State Electricity Board to stop work on the power plant's first phase.

Enron offered to lower its electricity tariff and switch to other fuels, including naphtha, in Dabhol's second phase in order to revive the project. But it also initiated arbitration proceedings in London against the government of Maharashtra for breach of contract. The state immediately challenged the jurisdiction of the arbitration tribunal to decide the dispute, while the Maharashtra State Electricity Board filed suit in Bombay to void the power purchasing agreement based on fraud and misrepresentation. Negotiations between the state and Enron resumed just before the arbitration tribunal ruled that it had exclusive authority to decide the dispute. This followed a meeting on November 3, 1995, between Rebecca Mark, the chair and CEO of Enron Development Corporation, and Bal Thackeray, the leader of the Shiv Sena party and the self-proclaimed power behind the throne in Maharashtra.

Within days Maharashtra accepted a revised power purchasing agreement at Dabhol. This committed the state to a bigger version of the first phase, rising to 740 megawatts. In addition, the second regasified LNG phase was no longer optional. Dabhol's total capacity was hiked to 2,450 megawatts, 2,184 megawatts of which was now binding on the Maharashtra State Electricity Board. While the state claimed it had received a lower tariff on the first phase, the expanded power plant now involved payments of $1.4 billion a year for twenty years from 2002, when phase two was expected to be fully online.

Enron received plenty of support from the Clinton administration during this cancellation and revival process. Clinton's chief of staff, Mack McLarty, worked with the U.S. ambassador to India, Frank Wisner, to closely watch Enron's efforts, while Energy Secretary Hazel O'Leary and Treasury Secretary Robert Rubin both waded into the dispute as well.[32] Interestingly, Wisner eventually joined the board of Enron Oil and Gas upon his retirement from the U.S. Foreign Service in 1997.

While all this was evolving, Israel's minister of energy and infrastructure, Gonen Segev, said publicly that cancellation of the Dabhol contract would not affect his country's own negotiations to buy LNG from Enron.[33] These talks resulted in a memorandum of intent between Enron Qatar LNG Marketing Ltd. and the Israeli ministry for at least 2 million tons of year of LNG, signed with much fanfare on October 31, 1995, during the Middle East and North Africa Economic Summit in Amman, Jordan. The initial accord with Israel was preceded earlier that same month by the finalization of Mobil's waiver conditions at RasGas, which were spelled out in a so-called harmonization agreement with the government of Qatar, QGPC, and Enron. This addressed potentially conflicting marketing efforts and rights between the two projects by capping the capacity of Enron's LNG project at 5 million tons per year and limited its export markets to Israel, Jordon, and the Palestinian Authority as well as Enron-owned power plants or regasification terminals in India.

Prospects for sales into Israel were soon bolstered by an economic cooperation agreement between Qatar and the Jewish state on April 2, 1996. This was signed in Qatar by Israel's prime minister, Shimon Peres. The two countries agreed to exchange trade missions, and Israel immediately set up a commercial representative office in Doha. But it all started to unravel in May 1996 when Benjamin Netanyahu of the right-wing Likud party unseated Peres in Israel's general election. Within days of Netanyahu's upset victory, Qatar postponed plans to open its own trade office in Tel Aviv pending confirmation that the new Israeli government would continue the peace process. No such assurance was forthcoming, although the Israeli trade office in Doha remained open for nearly five more years. Qatar finally bowed to pressure from its Gulf allies and forced the closure of the office in November 2000.

Several months after Netanyahu's election, Israel declined to extend Enron's negotiating exclusivity. This had been limited to 180 days in the initial accord signed at the Amman economic summit in late 1995. "A letter to this effect was sent to Enron in late September informing the company of our decision," a spokesman for the Ministry of National Infrastructure (as the Ministry of Energy and Infrastructure had been renamed) told Reuters on October 10, 1996.[34] Enron responded to this letter with a request to extend its exclusivity period with the ministry by another 90 days. Recently appointed minister of national infrastructure Ariel Sharon pointedly ignored the request because it also included a demand that the Israelis reach a definitive supply agreement within the three-month period.[35]

By this time Enron had all but given up on Israel as a market for LNG and was squarely focused on India as a recipient for the 5 million tons per year project it planned to build in Qatar.

ENRON FLIRTS WITH JOINING RASGAS PROJECT

With its political and legal disputes at Dabhol finally settled, Enron resumed construction on the Indian power plant's first phase. It signed letters of intent for LNG supplies with GAIL and the Gujarat Gas Company Ltd. while also pursuing other power plants in northern and southern India that could be fueled by regasified LNG. This renewed emphasis on India worried Mobil officials in Qatar, who were concerned RasGas would have to cede even more of its marketing rights to Enron. The rival company was indeed pressing the Qataris to throw their support behind Enron's marketing effort in India. A high-level delegation from Maharashtra state was confused by the contradictory signals it had received from QGPC and other government officials during a visit to Doha, some of whom had said they would prefer to supply Dabhol from RasGas rather than a third LNG project sponsored by Enron.

Enron's Rebecca Mark appealed directly to Minister of Energy and Industry Abdullah Ibn Hamad Al Attiyah to put an end to this confusion during a meeting in early January 1997 that was also attended by RasGas chair Yousef Kamal and Dr. Ibrahim Al Ibrahim, the amir's economic adviser and the vice-chair of RasGas. Al Attiyah suggested that Enron merge its project with RasGas, which at that point had yet to resume formal negotiations with the Koreans and was facing the looming expiry of its second train option with its contractor. Mark told the minister she had heard that RasGas was having difficulty selling these volumes to Kogas and offered to help place the second train into Dabhol.

Within weeks of this meeting, Enron tabled an ambitious proposal for a single expanded joint venture at RasGas with capacity of 15 million tons per year or more. The company wanted a 5 percent equity share in the first two trains at RasGas if the Dabhol power plant was supplied from the second train as well as 15 percent participation in the third train and any additional trains built to supply the next 10 million tons per year of nominal plant capacity. In return Enron would "by February 15, 1997 deliver to QGPC and Mobil a contract for the CIF purchase by Dabhol Power Company of approximately 2 mmt/y of LNG to be supplied by the JV with deliveries commencing in 2001," Enron vice-president Jim Noles promised RasGas chair Yousef Kamal on January 26, 1997.[36] A CIF sale means the price includes the cost of the commodity as well as all costs including insurance and transportation to its destination (in this case Dabhol).

Enron said it was prepared to invest heavily in India over and above its commitments at Dabhol. This included building LNG import and regasification terminals in other locations around the country as well as new gas transmission pipelines to get the regasified LNG from these facilities to other power plants and industrial users. But the company wanted a free hand in the marketing of this LNG within India, and it wanted to be given the lead role on behalf of the joint venture in all sales into this market.[37] In addition to the 2 million tons per year of regasified LNG needed by the Dabhol Power Company, Enron had identified target buyers in Maharashtra, in the neighboring state of Gujarat, along the 1,750-kilometer Hajira-Bijapur-Jagdishpur pipeline operated by GAIL, and in southern India.

These terms of reference were a nonstarter for Mobil. It hit back with its own letter to the RasGas chair three days later. "Enron has proposed participation in Ras Laffan on the same basis as QGPC and Mobil. This would entail participation in the whole Ras Laffan project as opposed to participation in specific sales," wrote Mobil Qatar president and general manager Ken Hull.[38] He also noted the proposal included no obligation on Enron's part to finance the RasGas venture or QGPC's equity capital requirements, and no commitment to procure additional sales in exchange for participation in capacity beyond the first and second trains. The U.S. major also strongly objected to Enron taking a lead marketing role in India, saying this should be left to the joint marketing committee established by QGPC and Mobil at the end of 1995.

Mobil did say it would consider equity participation for the Dabhol Power Company in specific sales from RasGas.[39] Enron, which had much grander plans, was not interested. In the end, the question was academic. The very next month RasGas finally clinched the deal with Kogas on the second train volumes, and its interest in bringing Enron into the project immediately waned. Enron would later claim it had only pursued the idea of joining RasGas at the request of Yousef Kamal, who had wanted Dabhol as a backup market for the second train in the event the Korean sale did not materialize.

MINISTER DELAYS SIGNING PROJECT AGREEMENT WITH ENRON

Enron completed its negotiations with QGPC for Qatar's third grassroots LNG project in early April 1997. However, Enron's twenty-five-member team left Doha without any fanfare. This was because Al Attiyah put off signing the project agreements until Enron delivered firm sales contracts covering the entire capacity of the 5-million-tons-per-year plant. Unlike either Qatargas or RasGas, where the joint venture itself sold the LNG directly to the end users, the structure of the QGPC–Enron project involved FOB sales to Enron's marketing affiliate at the load port in Qatar. This entity would purchase the LNG from the joint venture on take-or-pay terms and contract with a shipping company to provide transportation to the delivery point. Follow-on sale and purchase agreements between Enron's marketing affiliate and the Dabhol Power Company as well as other Indian buyers would be negotiated on delivered terms. The minister, never an enthusiastic supporter of Enron, wanted to wait until this contract chain was secured before signing the joint venture agreement and the related development and fiscal agreement.

A joint study had already identified the North field's D block as the best potential offshore site. Block selection had been influenced by several factors unique to the QGPC–Enron project, not least of which was that Enron carried all the financial risk. Since Enron was limited to specific, nonconventional markets for the LNG, it had to minimize third-country political risks as much as possible to attract project financing. This meant staying away from Qatar's maritime border with Iran. Block D was located just thirty-nine miles offshore in 150 to 200 feet of water. Although there had been no drilling in this part of the North field, well log correlations on either side of the block were nearly identical and encouraging. Enron would have to confirm the geology with an appraisal well of its own, but its technical team was confident the block could produce at a plateau rate of 1,000 million cubic feet per day for twenty-five years without the need for costly compression.[40]

Enron was required to submit turnkey bids prior to the signature of definitive project agreements. It had kicked off negotiations with engineering, procurement, and construction contractors at the end of 1996. A site west of the existing Qatargas project was identified for the LNG plant, which would have two trains each with a capacity of 2.5 million tons per year.[41] Offshore, Enron decided to drill from four remote well platforms. These would each have nine well slots with five producing wells. Exploitation of the Khuff 4 zone would be at subsea depths ranging from 8,100 to 9,800 feet, and the individual wells were expected to flow at a minimum of 60 million cubic feet per day.[42] The well platforms would connect to a single production platform with dual 600-million-cubic-feet-per-day process facilities to separate the well fluids, dehydrate the gas and liquids, and meter each stream. The dehydrated gas and condensate would then be recombined and directed to shore via a single multiphase pipeline thirty-two inches in diameter.

QATAR WAITS IN VAIN FOR ENRON TO DELIVER FIRM SALES CONTRACTS

At the end of 1997 QGPC was still waiting for Enron to line up definitive markets for the project's full capacity of 5 million tons per year. But the Qataris didn't seem to be in any hurry. One former QGPC official who was responsible for nego-tiating with Enron's marketing affiliate says his team spent three years on just one clause of the sale and purchase agreement—that related to take-or-pay.[43] Al Attiyah himself encouraged this go-slow approach. "The foreign minister sup-ported the Enron project, and that was good enough reason for Al Attiyah not to let it happen," says the former official, commenting on the ongoing rivalry between the two ministers.[44] Commercial negotiations with Enron were always focused exclusively on markets in India, particularly the Dabhol power plant. Israel never came up in the discussions.

Enron's plans for a coastal pipeline link from its LNG import and regasifica-tion terminal near Dabhol to serve gas users in both Maharashtra and Gujarat had run into resistance from Gujarati officials. That state's maritime board wanted to build its own LNG import infrastructure at Hazira, and it was holding talks with a litany of potential partners. One of these was India's Essar Group, which in mid-1997 formed a joint venture with Amoco to supply its power plants in Gujarat. The U.S. company had offered to buy up to 2.5 million tons per year of LNG on take-or-pay terms and sell it on to Essar, potentially overcoming the credit risk issues that had complicated earlier discussions between RasGas and the Indian firm. Despite its earlier disappointments, Amoco had not given up on Qatar. Indeed, it hoped to use its relationship with Essar to gain entry into RasGas.

The biggest threat to Enron's marketing ambitions in India turned out to be a new holding company called Petronet LNG Ltd. Formed in 1997 and incorpo-rated in 1998, Petronet grouped four of India's largest public sector oil and gas companies: GAIL, Indian Oil Corporation, Oil and Natural Gas Corporation, and Bharat Petroleum Corporation Ltd. The company planned to build no fewer than four LNG import and regasification terminals in India, three on its west-ern seaboard in the states of Gujarat, Karnataka, and Kerala and one in Tamil Nadu on the east coast. It had already prequalified seven bidders, including Ras-Gas, to participate in a tender to supply its first two import sites at Dahej in Guja-rat and Kochi in Kerala. Petronet planned to tap into the Hajira-Bijapur-Jagdishpur pipeline from Dahej. This was the same cross-country pipeline that Enron was eyeing for its Dabhol terminal—and one that just happened to be owned and operated by one of Petronet's four founding partners.

Competition into the Petronet tender was fierce, and it took some time to fully play out after final commercial proposals were submitted in June 1998. RasGas eventually emerged as the winner, however. On December 14, 1998, the two sides signed a heads of agreement covering 7.5 million tons per year for Dahej and Kochi. The following year this was converted into a twenty-five-year sale and purchase agreement signed by Petronet's Suresh Mathur and Yousef Kamal of Ras-Gas on July 31, 1999.

By this point QGPC had completely given up on a third project with Enron. Al Attiyah announced publicly on March 18, 1999, that he did not see any scope for new grassroots LNG projects in Qatar beyond Qatargas and RasGas.[45] This prompted an enthusiastic response from Enron's principal rival in Qatar. "I was pleased to read of your recent statement that Qatar does not plan any new grass roots LNG projects and that the expansion of RasGas and Qatargas will be the foundation of Qatar's LNG industry," Mobil's Lou Noto immediately wrote to the minister.[46]

Qatari officials insisted Enron could remain as a buyer of LNG.[47] This didn't interest Enron, although the company had briefly resumed talks with RasGas in mid-1998 before the two sides once again parted ways—this time permanently. Publicly, at least, Enron shrugged off the cancellation of the project it had been working on since at least 1993. Its spokesperson, John Ambler, insisted Enron had only ever been in the early stages of planning with the Qataris. "We never progressed far enough to proceed with a formal contract," he told the press two days after Al Attiyah revealed the cancellation publicly.[48]

Ambler also insisted that Enron itself had allowed the letter of intent with QGPC to lapse when it opted not to exercise the annual renewal clause in mid-1998. Since then Enron had concluded sale and purchase agreements with alternative LNG producers in the Middle East for the full 2.1 million tons per year it needed to fuel the Dabhol power plant's second phase. The first contract, covering 1.6 million tons per year beginning at the end of 2001, was signed with Oman LNG on December 8, 1998, while a second deal for 0.5 million tons annually was finalized with Abu Dhabi's Adgas on February 24, 1999. Another confirmation of intent for up to 2.6 million tons per year was signed in mid-1999 with Malaysia LNG to meet demand from other users in Maharashtra and potentially Gujarat.

Not a drop of LNG was ever delivered under these contracts. While the Dabhol power plant started producing electricity from its first phase in May 1999, the Maharashtra State Electricity Board soon defaulted on its payments to the Dabhol Power Company. Operations at the plant were halted two years later. The second phase was mothballed, as was the nearly completed LNG import and regasification terminal. Enron's subsequent bankruptcy complicated efforts to restart the plant, and it sat idle for five years. Dabhol finally came back online in May 2006 as Ratnagiri Gas and Power, an all-Indian affair led by GAIL and the country's largest power producer, NTPC Limited.

Dabhol's restored capacity of 1,967 megawatts now runs primarily on domestic gas. The power plant has also received regasified LNG from Petronet's Dahej import terminal since completion of GAIL's 577-kilometer Dahej-Panvel-Dabhol pipeline in 2007. Gujarat's second LNG import terminal at Hazira, which the state's maritime board ultimately awarded to Shell, is linked into this pipeline system as well. Dabhol's own terminal was only commissioned in late 2012 and still operates at reduced capacity as a result of continuing technical issues.

Mobil had worked tirelessly to fight off Enron in Qatar ever since Rebecca Mark and her team showed up in Doha in early 1993. It was relieved, if not exactly surprised, when the rival project finally collapsed six years later. Enron's loss was Mobil's—or at least Lou Noto's—gain, in more ways than one. Noto had four boxes of rare Davidoff Dom Perignon Cuban-made cigars on the line with Sheikh Abdulrahman Ibn Saud Al Thani, Qatar's ambassador to the United States. "I bet him four boxes against four boxes that Enron would let him down," remembers Mobil's former CEO. "And I still have five of those eight boxes."[49]

OIL CAPACITY RISES DESPITE EMPHASIS ON GAS DEVELOPMENT

Qatar was now firmly focused on developing its gas reserves, which vastly exceeded its oil deposits. In 1997 Minister of Energy and Industry Abdullah Ibn Hamad Al Attiyah put the country's gas reserves at fifty times its recoverable oil reserves.[50] Crude oil production capacity was nonetheless expected to rise to 707,000 barrels per day by the end of the decade, following a $7.6 billion oil sector investment program funded almost entirely by foreign oil companies. Offshore fields operated by these players on production-sharing terms had already started to make a real difference, and QGPC predicted they would soon add nearly 300,000 barrels per day to Qatar's total oil output.[51]

Oxy's enhanced oil recovery project at Idd el-Shargi North Dome was the first to pay dividends, with output topping 75,000 barrels per day in mid-1996. Daily flows reached 95,000 barrels in early 1997—the highest yield since startup in 1964. Maersk's Al Shaheen field on Block 5 was also doing well despite the lack of permanent production facilities, hitting 45,000 barrels per day in early 1996 and rising steeply to 100,000 barrels per day in mid-1997. Elf Aquitaine finally started development work at Al Khalij on Block 6, although a pipeline leak delayed first production until March 8, 1997. The field averaged 23,000 barrels per day in 1998 with plans to reach 45,000 barrels per day by 2000. Mandatory relinquishments had reduced Block 6 to a small area around Al Khalij. The relinquished 3,174 square kilometers was renamed Block 10 and offered out to bidders. The acreage was ultimately secured by Canada's Talisman in late 2002.

QGPC approved the installation of temporary production facilities at Arco's Al Rayyan discovery in early 1996, allowing the five-member consortium to bring the field online by August. By the end of 1996 Al Rayyan was producing around 30,000 barrels per day. The east block that contained Al Rayyan was split in two: Block 12, the producing oil field, and Block 11, a larger block to the south. There was no change to the consortium's renamed western Block 13 near the Dibal shoal in waters claimed by both Qatar and Bahrain. The partners signed a new exploration and production agreement on Block 11 the following year. This was limited specifically to crude oil and other hydrocarbons located in structures above the deep Khuff formation. The consortium agreed to drill at least two wells on Block 11 during the first four-year exploration period as well as shooting a minimum of 2,000 kilometers of 2-D seismic data and reprocessing another 500 kilometers of existing seismic data.

The Arco-led consortium simultaneously signed an amending agreement to Wintershall's 1976 production-sharing agreement covering the portion of the North field that extended into Block 11. As part of this agreement QGPC delayed the deadline for Arco and its partners to begin producing Khuff gas from its assigned North field area by three years. But the Qataris also reduced the size of this section to just 8–10 trillion cubic feet of proven gas reserves rather than the 32 trillion cubic feet previously cited. Arco was still trying to secure a deal with Dubai for 800 million cubic feet per day of pipeline gas. The extension gave Arco until July 16, 1999, to get the project off the ground. This deadline was later extended for another year, but Arco's talks with Dubai were ultimately suspended after the UAE Offsets Group appeared on the scene with its own plan to supply Qatari gas to Abu Dhabi, Dubai, and Oman through what would eventually become the Dolphin export pipeline.

Block 1NW went to Chevron and Hungary's Magyar Olaj Gazipari, which signed an exploration deal with QGPC on the 7,500-square-kilometer tract in early 1996. Four years and three dry holes later, the partners relinquished the block. Block 1SE, the other tract formed from Block 1 after it was relinquished by Elf Aquitaine, was rezoned again so that it essentially included only the Idd el-Shargi South Dome discovery. The block's two other discoveries—the A-Structure discovered in 1971 by the Fuji Oil-led Qatar Oil Company and Sohio's 1988 Al Karkara find—were hived off and awarded to a Japanese consortium grouping Bunduq operator United Petroleum Development, Cosmo Oil, and Nissho Iwai. This consortium, which became the Qatar Petroleum Development Company when it was incorporated in 1997, began pilot production of 6,500 barrels per day from Al Karkara in late 1998 with output transported to the Halul island terminal.

Oxy won the bidding for Idd el-Shargi South Dome, signing a development- and production-sharing agreement with QGPC on Block 1SE on December 10, 1997. The U.S. company planned to develop the field initially as a satellite of Idd el-Shargi North Dome, temporarily eliminating the need for costly on-site production facilities. Shortly afterward Oxy announced that by 2000 it would hike combined production from the two fields to 210,000 barrels per day. After failing to attract interest from smaller exploration players, the two onshore blocks known as Block 2N and Block 2S were merged back into Block 2. An exploration- and production-sharing agreement on this recombined 10,900-square-kilometer tract was signed with Chevron in early 1998.

Enhanced oil recovery and gas lift projects in the southern part of Dukhan were expected to boost flows from the onshore field to 335,000 barrels per day by mid-1998. QGPC originally invited foreign oil companies to participate in this expansion, with Mobil, Oxy, and Chevron all putting in bids, but ultimately it decided to keep the country's largest oil field in Qatari hands. Qatar's crude oil production capacity reached 714,000 barrels per day in mid-1998, well ahead of Al Attiyah's earlier estimate. In announcing a revised production capacity target of 854,000 barrels per day for the end of the decade, the minister of energy and industry cited newly developed fields like Idd el-Shargi South Dome and Al Karkara as well as expectations for enhanced flows from Dukhan, Idd el-Shargi North Dome, Maydan Mahzam, Al Rayyan, and Al Khalij.[52]

Output of field condensates was expected to hit nearly 150,000 barrels per day by the end of the century, adding a significant revenue stream exempt from OPEC's quota restrictions.[53] In addition to the 27,000 barrels per day of condensates from the North field's first development stage, Qatargas contributed 40,000 barrels per day from 1998 when its third train was commissioned. The Dukhan Arab D gas cap recycling project added another 40,000 barrels per day after it was brought online that same year, while condensate output from RasGas was expected to reach 35,000 barrels per day in 2000 once its first two trains were fully operational. In 1998 plans to build a 100,000-barrel-per-day refinery at Ras Laffan to process a large portion of this condensate stream were put on hold pending higher oil prices and a more conducive investment climate. The refinery project would be resurrected on an even larger scale nearly ten years later by QGPC and its foreign partners in the two LNG ventures.

FOREIGN OPERATORS REDUCE OIL OUTPUT AFTER 1998 PRICE CRISIS

Qatar produced 479,000 barrels per day of crude oil in 1996, up 13.5 percent over 1995. Output rose even more sharply to 619,000 barrels per day in 1997 and averaged 662,000 barrels per day in 1998, including an all-time high of 720,000 barrels per day early in the year. But already weak oil prices collapsed at the end of 1998 in the face of continued OPEC overproduction. Prices slipped to just $10 per barrel, with some of OPEC's heavier crude oil grades selling as low as $6. Qatar agreed to cut production to 593,000 barrels per day in early 1999 as part of an OPEC effort to remove nearly 2 million barrels a day from the market and announced an austerity budget based on an oil price assumption of just $10 per barrel.[54] Yousef Kamal, who had taken over from Sheikh Mohammad Ibn Khalifa Al Thani as the minister of finance, economy, and trade in a cabinet reshuffle at the beginning of 1998, blamed "the worst financial crisis witnessed in over the past quarter of a century."[55]

Foreign operators in Qatar's offshore sector were forced to shoulder the burden equally with QGPC, despite having invested heavily to expand output. The reductions extended to Maersk's Al Shaheen field, where production capacity had just risen to 150,000 barrels per day following the inauguration of permanent production facilities. Output cuts and low oil prices led Oxy to postpone the installation of another permanent production facility at Idd el-Shargi South Dome, where an initial pilot phase was brought onstream in late 1999 at 2,500 barrels per day, with plans to reach 15,000 barrels per day in 2001. A full field development plan to boost production at the Al Rayyan field to 60,000 barrels per day was also delayed, first by low oil prices and later by BP's 1999 takeover of Arco. Following this acquisition, BP became operator of Al Rayyan's Block 12 as well as Block 13 off western Qatar, where exploration activities were still on hold pending a settlement in the territorial dispute with Bahrain.

Total output averaged 625,000 barrels per day for 1999 following a rise in oil prices and a relaxation in production constraints. The purse strings loosened, and QGPC awarded a major contract for a so-called gas lift project to sustain Dukhan's production capacity at 335,000 barrels per day to Italy's Snamprogetti. It also resumed talks with foreign companies on expanding operations, with Elf Aquitaine announcing a full field development plan at Al Khalij to double output by late 2001. Maersk was moving forward with plans to boost output at Al Shaheen to 200,000 barrels per day by 2004 through enhanced water injection facilities while also installing facilities to gather associated gas, which would be piped to QGPC's Alpha platform in the North field and from there to natural gas liquids plants on the mainland. BP completed a detailed assessment of Al Rayyan, revising its expansion plans to 35,000 barrels per day following a sharp dip in production capacity at the field to just 13,000 barrels per day.

QATAR AND BAHRAIN BOTH HAIL SETTLEMENT IN TERRITORIAL DISPUTE

Twenty-six years after gaining independence, Qatar and Bahrain finally agreed in early 1997 to put aside their long-standing border dispute—still pending before the International Court of Justice—and establish diplomatic ties. The two sides exchanged ambassadors at the end of 1999, at which time they also formed a joint committee to "explore the possibility" of reaching an amicable settlement of their competing territorial claims. There was, however, no move to delay the ICJ hearings scheduled to start in 2000. Bahrain subsequently suspended the bilateral effort just as the ICJ proceedings were getting under way in The Hague. Public hearings were held in May before a seventeen-judge panel. When the ICJ finally handed down a judgment in the case—the longest in its history—nearly a year later, both Qatar and Bahrain immediately accepted it.

In their March 16, 2001, ruling the judges found unanimously that Zubara on the peninsula's northwest coast belonged Qatar. Sovereignty over the Hawar

Islands was awarded to Bahrain by a vote of twelve to five. The Jaradeh and Dibal shoals were divided between the two countries, with Jaradeh going to Bahrain by a vote of twelve to five and Qatar taking Dibal by unanimous opinion. In a vote of thirteen to four, the panel also awarded the island of Janan to Qatar. The maritime boundary was set, and Qatar's right of free passage in the territorial sea of Bahrain separating the Hawar Islands from the other Bahraini islands confirmed. With the territorial dispute now resolved, both countries opened the formerly contested acreage to international bidding. Bahrain created three new blocks in its zone, and exploration deals on these were signed with the Malaysian state oil company Petronas and the U.S. firm Texaco in late 2001.

With the status of Dibal finally settled in Qatar's favor, Doha was able to lift the decades-long ban on exploration activities in its zone. The partners at Block 13, where seismic shot back in the 1960s had identified a potentially oil-bearing structure that Wintershall claimed was on trend with the onshore Dukhan field, could now begin the drilling work denied to them since the original concession was signed in 1973. Wintershall itself was no longer in the block, having sold its stake in both Block 13 and the producing Block 12 to Gulfstream Resources in September 2000. Gulfstream had then bought out British Gas, before selling itself lock, stock, and barrel to Anadarko Petroleum in mid-2001. Operator BP was also actively trying to sell its stake in the two blocks, as its return to Qatar via the Arco acquisition had not been well received. The Qataris had not forgotten the British firm's abrupt departure from Qatargas in 1992 or the challenges that followed it. The resentment toward BP for its perceived betrayal ran deep.

Exploration at Block 13 only started after Anadarko purchased all of BP's interests in Qatar in mid-2002. This boosted Anadarko's stake in Blocks 12 and 13 to 92.5 percent. Preussag Energie continued to hold the remaining 7.5 percent, although the German company sold its entire international exploration and production portfolio to Austria's OMV the following year. Anadarko's earlier acquisition of Gulfstream had also given it a 49 percent interest in Block 11, the exploration tract that adjoined Al Rayyan's Block 12. Wintershall had assumed operatorship of Block 11 in 2000, and it still held a 51 percent stake in this acreage. Anadarko started work on Block 13 soon after taking over from BP, drilling an exploration well near Dibal. The results were disappointing. After reaching a total depth of 8,784 feet, the well found only water and had to be plugged and abandoned. Anadarko sold its interests in Blocks 12 and 13 to Occidental Petroleum in 2007 for $350 million. While Oxy relinquished Block 13 in 2009, it held on to Al Rayyan until May 31, 2017, when the production-sharing agreement on Block 12 expired and operatorship reverted to the government.

Qatar split Block 4 into two blocks: one 3,132-square-kilometer area in the far northwest that remained Block 4 and another 1,900 square kilometers closer to shore that was named Block 3. Anadarko signed an exploration- and production-sharing agreement on the new Block 4 in 2004 while a group led by Wintershall concluded a similar deal on Block 3 in 2007. Anadarko's rights only extended to the geological horizons located above and below the Khuff, and it was forced to relinquish a portion of Block 4 when it identified a prospect in the Khuff reservoir through 3D seismic. This 544-square-kilometer area was put out to bid as Block 4N and then snatched up by Wintershall in late 2008. Anadarko sold off Block 4 to France's GDF Suez the following year, discouraged by the incident and the fact that the Qataris had forced it to hand over its seismic data on the Khuff prospect to its competitors without compensation.[56]

Wintershall would go on to make the Al Radeef discovery on Block 4N in 2013. This relatively small, 2.5-trillion-cubic-foot find in the Khuff reservoir was hailed as Qatar's first offshore gas discovery since the North field in 1971. Despite high hopes for Al Radeef, Wintershall turned its stake in Block 4N back to the government just two years later after failing to secure access to the local infrastructure needed to develop its find. Block 4N was Wintershall's only exploration activity in Qatar by this time. It had relinquished Block 11 in 2010 after drilling five unsuccessful wells and had abandoned Block 3 in 2013. Wintershall, which had been present in Qatar since 1973, ceased its exploration activities and closed its Doha office in 2015. It was a bitter pill to swallow. Wintershall had sunk hundreds of millions of dollars over more than four decades into exploring for oil and gas in Qatari waters with nothing to show for it other than its short-lived participation in the Al Rayyan field.

After taking over at Block 4 from Anadarko in 2009, GDF Suez made a gas discovery beneath the Khuff at a depth of around 15,000 feet with its second well. Reports in early 2013 put the size of this pre-Khuff accumulation at 2–4 trillion cubic feet of gas in place.[57] Not only was the find small, but the lack of high-value liquids in the pre-Khuff gas ruled out commercializing these reserves and GDF Suez relinquished Block 4 in 2015. A similar fate befell two other pre-Khuff plays—a 5,649-square-kilometer block off Qatar's east coast called Block BC and Block D, which covered 8,089 square kilometers of onshore and offshore acreage near Ras

Laffan. The China National Offshore Oil Corporation, or CNOOC, signed an exploration- and production-sharing agreement on Block BC in 2009, and Total farmed into the license two years later. Block D attracted a winning bid from Shell and PetroChina in 2010. Shell was the first to sink a pre-Khuff well, drilling QSD-1 in 2013. CNOOC followed in early 2014 with its CQBH-1 test well. Both were dry, and the two blocks were abandoned in 2015.

Nothing materialized on a third pre-Khuff opportunity, the 6,173-square-kilometer Block A off the northeast coast held by JX Nippon Oil since 2011. The Japanese firm drilled an initial test well, JXQA-1, on the block in 2014, and the Qataris subsequently reported it as a pre-Khuff discovery. JX Nippon spudded a second well on Block A in December 2016, the results of which weren't revealed publicly. Unlike the pre-Khuff, which was offered out to foreign companies on production-sharing terms, Qatar has conducted exploration and appraisal drilling into the Khuff formation underlying its Maydan Mahzam and Bul Hanine fields itself. In 2009 and 2010 its state-owned firm drilled two wells—BH-116 and BH-147—to appraise the original 1974 Khuff discovery at Bul Hanine. The Qataris also discovered the Khuff formation at Maydan Mahzam in 2012 with their MM-93 exploration well.

PETROCHEMICAL PROJECTS TAKE OFF DESPITE
ASIAN DEMAND WOES

QGPC unveiled plans in 1997 for a second phase of its Dukhan Arab D gas cap recycling project, under which high ethane content stripped gas would be piped to a major new natural gas liquids plant at the Mesaieed industrial area (as Umm Said had been renamed). Called NGL-4, this plant would produce 3,200 tons of ethane; 5,100 tons of propane and butane; and 780 tons of plant condensate daily. NGL-1 and NGL-2, Mesaieed's two operating natural gas liquids plants, were also expanded, while a revamp of QGPC's North field gas treatment and separation plants at Mesaieed was included in the overall NGL-4 project. These plants, now known collectively as NGL-3, had processed Khuff gas and condensate from the North field Alpha platform since 1990 and were expanded in 1997 to process additional gas from Qatargas. The revamp would allow raw liquids from NGL-3 to be sent to NGL-4 for fractionation. Surplus gas from NGL-3 would be reinjected into Dukhan's Arab D reservoir as well as the field's Khuff reservoir.

Ethane from NGL-4 was to be used at a new, $1.12 billion ethylene-based petrochemical complex planned by QGPC and Phillips Petroleum at Mesaieed. The two firms formed Qatar Chemical Company, or Q-Chem, in late 1997 to build a 500,00-tons-per-year ethylene plant as well as facilities for producing 453,000 tons per year of high-density polyethylene and linear low-density polyethylene and 47,000 tons per year of hexene-1. Phillips, which took a 49 percent stake in Q-Chem against QGPC's 51 percent share, had been trying for nearly ten years to break into Qatar. In 1990 it had lost out to the French and Italians in the bid to join the country's existing petrochemical company, QAPCO. More recently, Phillips had fought off Dow Chemical, whose rival offer for Q-Chem had been championed by the minister of foreign affairs. The minister of energy and Industry threw his support behind Phillips, and QGPC's project committee ultimately recommended it.

Financing for NGL-4 and Q-Chem was pursued simultaneously, raising nearly $2 billion despite tough market conditions. Of the $1.2 billion raised for NGL-4, only $500 million was needed to build the plant. The remainder went to QGPC for general corporate purposes. Because it wasn't possible to link the financing specifically to NGL-4, the decision was made to borrow against QGPC's entire NGL operation and maximize the borrowing based on this cash flow. The money was raised in three tranches, including two syndicated bank loans of $400 million each and a third capital market component comprising $400 million worth of eleven-year notes issued to two commercial paper conduits and guaranteed by monoline insurers in the United States.[58] The insurance guarantees allowed Standard and Poor's to give the notes—the first of their kind in the Middle East—its highest possible rating, higher than Qatar's own sovereign rating.[59] Q-Chem raised a further $750 million through a syndicated loan in late 1999. This was launched after the first tranche at NGL-4, as QGPC had to ensure sufficient funds for NGL-4 before it could seek financing for Q-Chem. Both projects were brought online in early 2003.

QAPCO's expansion was inaugurated in June 1996, boosting ethylene capacity at its petrochemical complex in Mesaieed to 525,000 tons per year and low-density polyethylene to 360,000 tons per year. Some of this ethylene production was earmarked for a new $680 million chlorochemicals complex at Mesaieed called the Qatar Vinyl Company, or QVC. Established in January 1997, QVC grouped

QGPC at 25.2 percent, QAPCO with 31.9 percent, Norway's Norsk Hydro at 29.7 percent, and Elf Atochem with 12.9 percent. A contract for QVC's main ethylene dichloride unit as well as other facilities for the production of vinyl chloride monomer and caustic soda was awarded to Technip and Germany's Krupp Uhde at the end of 1998. Financing proved challenging, and a $475 million syndicated loan signed in early 1999 set a new benchmark in regional lending after it had to be repriced. But it also demonstrated that Qatar was prepared to move ahead with its petrochemical projects rather than haggle over basis points. QVC was inaugurated in June 2001 and by the end of 2003 had refinanced the plant on much better terms.

The $690 million methanol-MTBE project planned by the Qatar Fuel Additives Company at Mesaieed finally got off the ground in early 1997 with the award of a construction contract to Japan's Chiyoda Corporation. A $350 million limited recourse loan on the project, signed with a consortium of international and regional banks in late 1997, was divided into two tranches and required QGPC to supply methane and butane feedstock on favorable terms. QAFAC's Taiwanese and Canadian partners also agreed to purchase all the output at market prices for the life of the loans. This project was brought online in 1999. Another methanol venture with Canada's Methanex planned for Ras Laffan remained under discussion with QGPC for years after it was first announced in late 1997. Methanex ultimately dropped the Qatari project and turned its attention to Egypt.

QAFCO completed its third fertilizer plant in early 1997, increasing capacity to 3,800 tons per day of ammonia and 4,500 tons per day of urea. Preliminary studies were under way on a fourth QAFCO plant, but this next expansion wouldn't get the green light until late 2000 following a revival in Asian demand and a big economic turnaround. Qatar Steel Company became completely government owned in early 1997, with the state purchasing the 30 percent owned by Kobe Steel and Tokyo Boeki for $165 million. QGPC and Norsk Hydro, which had set up a joint venture to build a 200,000-tons-per-year aluminum smelter in Ras Laffan in late 1997, abandoned the $1 billion project a year later. But the two partners would go on to form Qatar Aluminum, or Qatalum, in 2006 and would resurrect the smelter on a much grander scale at Mesaieed. This $5.8 billion project, the largest primary aluminum plant built in one phase, includes a smelter with capacity of 585,000 tons per year and a dedicated 1,350-megawatt power plant.

QATAR EXPANDS REFINING CAPACITY AND LAUNCHES GAS-TO-LIQUIDS SECTOR

The National Oil Distribution Company (NODCO) also finally moved forward with plans to expand and revamp its refinery at Mesaieed after much delay. Central to this effort was a five-year petroleum product offtake contract signed with Japan's Mitsui in late 1998. This would be used to pay off a $510 million loan with thirteen banks guaranteed by QGPC, agreed after a larger financing package failed to attract underwriting interest. Participants included several German banks brought in by Germany's Lurgi Oel, Gas, Chemie GmBH, which, together with South Korea's LG International Corp. and LG Engineering Co., had won contracts for the expansion project.

Plans now called for boosting capacity at the 50,000-barrels-per-day Unit No 2 to 70,000 barrels per day and adding a fluid catalytic cracker to convert 28,000 of heavy fuel oil into lighter products. The new condensate unit, originally intended for the 27,000 barrels per day from QGPC's North field Alpha platform, was now sized at 57,000 barrels per day in order to process another 30,000 barrels per day of condensates from the Dukhan Arab D gas cap recycling project. This refinery expansion was commissioned in late 2001 at a total cost of $850 million.[60] It also included new utilities and tank farms and a plant information system as well as instrumentation and control system upgrades.

These projects addressed changing local consumption patterns that called for more gasoline, diesel oil, and kerosene at the expense of heavy fuel oil. "The expansion will not only meet domestic needs for various oil products in the coming two decades, but will also make available significant volumes of high quality products for export to international markets," Al Attiyah announced at the inauguration ceremony held in early 2002.[61] Local fuel consumption was running around 22,000 barrels per day by this time, up from 14,000 barrels per day in 1984 when Unit No 2 was inaugurated, while another 37,000 barrels per day of petroleum products were exported. The expansion tripled export capacity.

Formed in 1969 after the government bought the tiny 680-barrels-per-day topping plant from Qatar's foreign-owned onshore operator, NODCO had ceased to function as QGPC's separate oil distribution arm on December 30, 2000, when it was merged into Qatar Petroleum, as QGPC had been renamed. QP also took over QGPC's controlling interests in the country's fertilizer, petrochemical, and LNG companies as well as its stakes in other hydrocarbon-related ventures. With the change, the Qataris essentially took back the name adopted by the international partners in the Iraq Petroleum Company nearly half a century earlier when they formed the Qatar Petroleum Company in 1954.

Qatar also sought to bring gas-to-liquids, or GTL, technology to the Middle East, signing an accord with Phillips Petroleum and South Africa's Sasol Synfuels in 1997 to study a GTL plant at Ras Laffan to produce low-sulfur diesel and naphtha from North field gas. The process, a variation of a technology pioneered by German scientists during the 1920s, uses methane and oxygen to make a gaseous feedstock for giant reactors, where it is heated and reacted with a catalyst. After Phillips dropped out, Sasol pursued GTL on its own with QP. They formed Oryx GTL in mid-2001, with Sasol taking 49 percent in the 34,000-barrels-per-day plant against QP's 51 percent. The $1 billion project started producing in 2007, but technical problems kept it from reaching full capacity until 2014. With no upstream component, Oryx GTL still purchases 330 million cubic feet per day of methane gas from AKG-1—the first phase of the 2-billion-cubic-feet-per-day Al Khaleej Gas project implemented in conjunction with expansion trains at RasGas.

Exxon had completed a study on a much larger GTL plant in late 1996, determining that a gas royalty of thirty cents per million Btu was needed to make the project viable. Nothing materialized until 2001, when the company, now Exxon-Mobil following a $81 billion merger between the two companies in 1998, signed a letter of intent with QP to conduct a detailed feasibility study for a 110,000-barrels-per-day GTL plant. When ExxonMobil finally abandoned the project in early 2007, citing ballooning costs, capacity had risen to 154,000 barrels per day and the price tag to $18 billion. Similar blow outs dogged Shell's 140,000-barrel-per-day Pearl GTL plant in Ras Laffan, where costs nearly quadrupled to $18.5 billion by the time the project started up in 2011. Pearl GTL is a fully integrated project, unlike Oryx GTL. It was funded entirely by Shell under a twenty-five-year development- and production-sharing agreement signed with QP in 2004. Shell pumps 1.6 billion cubic feet per day of gas from an assigned block in the North field, which is stripped to remove the equivalent of 120,000 barrels per day of condensate, LPG, and ethane. After liquids removal, the dry methane gas is sent to the GTL plant.

GOVERNMENT TURNS TO BOND MARKETS TO RAISE FUNDS

Refinery expansion and the first step toward GTL occurred during a period of financial strain for Qatar. Low oil prices, which saw Qatar Land fall sharply from $23 per barrel in early 1997 to just $12 a barrel by mid-1998, forced the Ministry of Finance, Economy, and Trade to slash both revenues and expenditures in the government's annual budget for the fiscal year beginning April 1, 1998. The spending cuts extended to the ministries, some of which even faced redundancies, while QGPC froze recruitment and laid off hundreds of expatriate workers. A projected 11 percent rise in the budget deficit to QR 3,306 million ($908 million) soon had Moody's Investors Service warning of unsustainably high public sector deficits, while the head of the Qatar Central Bank predicted more appetite for government borrowing.[62] A law allowing the Central Bank to start issuing treasury bills and bonds denominated in Qatari riyals had finally been approved earlier in the year, but the first local debt instruments weren't introduced for another eighteen months. The government turned again to the domestic banks to meet its short-term borrowing needs.

Government officials mused publicly that they were considering both a debut sovereign Eurobond issue and more project-specific bonds like the one pioneered by RasGas in late 1996.[63] A law authorizing the government to issue global securities was approved in June 1998, and within days Qatar's first foray into the sovereign bond market was unveiled at a road show in Doha. The issue was expected to raise at least $1 billion and potentially as much as $1.5 billion. It was postponed just two months later after Russia declared a moratorium on repayments to foreign creditors and the economic crisis in Asia worsened. Asia's market meltdown also affected RasGas, whose bonds were downgraded several times due to the LNG project's exposure to Kogas and the uncertain outlook in Korea. Qatar's fiscal position continued to deteriorate on further oil price declines and a rising debt load.

A circular published at the relaunch of the sovereign bond the next year put the country's external debt at nearly $9.8 billion, up from just $910 million in 1993.[64] The $1 billion offering on May 12, 1999, was nonetheless oversubscribed by institutional investors in Europe and the United States because of its generous price spread of 395 basis points over U.S. Treasuries. This set an expensive precedent for other borrowers in the region and led Oman to cancel its own sovereign Eurobond several months later.[65] Plans by petrochemical projects to raise funds through bonds were also abandoned, including one at QVC that was intended to build on the success at RasGas. Bonds would remain largely absent from project finance in Qatar until early 2004, when RasGas again tapped the capital markets with a $665 million offering. The government raised $1.4 billion in a second sovereign bond in 2000 and followed this up in 2003 with its first-ever Islamic bond, raising $700 million for a new medical city in Doha.

The austerity budget for the 1999 fiscal year included even more dramatic spending cuts. When the minister of interior, the amir's younger brother Abdullah Ibn Khalifa, objected to the proposed reductions at a cabinet meeting, Sheikh Hamad responded that he would just have to learn to manage with less. Despite slashing expenditures, the government still projected a 9 percent rise in the deficit to QR 3,600 million ($989 million) for the fiscal year as the revenue projection was based on a conservative oil price assumption of only $10 per barrel.[66] Some of the budget shortfall was financed through the first riyal-denominated government bonds, valued at QR 2,000 million ($549 million) and on June 20, 1999, sold by the Central Bank on behalf of the Ministry of Finance, Economy and Trade. The first treasury bills were launched in 1999 as well. Within a year, short- and medium-term debt securities issued by the Central Bank had reduced the amount of short-term loans from Qatar's commercial banks by nearly 40 percent.

There was talk of raising money via privatization, including by floating the steel company QASCO on the Doha Securities Market. This was put off after an initial public offering of the state-owned telecommunications company Q-Tel in early 1999, which initially wasn't considered a success. Four years later, the government transferred full ownership of QASCO to Qatar Petroleum, which formed a new holding company called Industries Qatar to manage its interests in the steel firm as well as its stakes in the fertilizer producer QAFCO and the two petrochemical companies, QAPCO and QAFAC. Industries Qatar was listed on the Doha Securities Market, with 15 percent of its total share capital of QR 5,000 million offered to the Qatari public through a network of local banks beginning in May 2003. Industries Qatar, which is still 51 percent owned by QP, is now the largest publicly traded company in Qatar.

FINANCIAL FORTUNES IMPROVE AS QATAR ENTERS NEW MILLENNIUM

In early 1999 oil prices recovered significantly after a large OPEC cut in output engineered by Saudi Arabia. Qatar's two main crude grades averaged seventeen dollars per barrel for the fiscal year ending March 31, 2000, rather than the ten dollars assumed in the government's austerity budget. Higher oil revenue coupled with fairly good adherence to the spending cuts imposed at the beginning of the fiscal year virtually eliminated the budget deficit, which ended up at only QR 255 million ($70 million). New revenue streams were also added. RasGas exported its first condensate cargo in April 1999, followed two months later by its maiden LNG shipment. Qatar produced 6.2 million tons of LNG in 1999, comprising 5.5 million tons from the three Qatargas trains and 0.7 million tons from the first RasGas train. The RasGas deliveries included all ten cargoes booked by Korea's Kogas in 1999 plus another three spot cargoes sold into the United States. QAFAC also exported its first methanol cargo in August, formally launching the country's first petrochemical venture since 1982, when QAPCO started operating. QAPCO itself saw profits spike 30 percent in 1999 due to rising production and higher prices.

The economic situation in Qatar continued to improve in 2000 on a sharp rise in oil and gas revenues. Prices for the country's two crude oil grades averaged twenty-seven dollars per barrel for the year, against a conservative assumption of fifteen dollars per barrel in the government's budget. In 2000 total oil output rose more than 11 percent, to 696,000 barrels per day. There was a big jump in LNG and condensate revenue as well. The country's trade surplus rose by nearly 27 percent in 2000, to just under QR 23 billion ($6.3 billion). According to the head of the Central Bank, the country's gross domestic product increased 19 percent in nominal terms, to QR 53 billion ($14.6 billion). This followed a similar 18.9 percent rise in 1999.[67]

Most of Qatar's Gulf Cooperation Council neighbors used the revenue boost from higher oil prices to pay down debt. Not Qatar. Its total external debt increased to $13.1 billion in 2000, nearly 90 percent of gross domestic product, as the government intensified its North field industrialization drive.[68] Managing this rising debt load was not seen as a problem. New revenue streams from its gas reserves meant Qatar entered the millennium with its cash flow woes largely in the rearview mirror. Just a few years earlier, export credit agency support and comfort letters from the government had been necessary to get projects off the ground. Now bankers were queuing up to lend money to Qatar. As Moody's Investors Service observed, solid oil prices in 1999 and 2000 together with new gas-related energy projects had "markedly improved Qatar's economic and financial situation."[69]

Epilogue

North Field Gas Transforms Qatar into Energy Superpower

Abdullah Ibn Hamad Al Attiyah kept his 1999 pledge to limit the expansion of the LNG industry to Qatargas and RasGas. Over a decade later, the minister of energy and industry presided over a lavish ceremony as the two flagship projects hit a combined production capacity goal of 78 million tons per year across fourteen trains, including six megatrains of 7.8 million tons each. By this time Qatar had already been the world's largest LNG producer for five years. Since the last train began producing in early 2011, the capacity figure has been closer to 79 million tons per year. Qatar held onto its production crown through 2019, although it lost out to Australia for one month in November 2018.[1] It fell slightly behind its closest competitor again in 2020 and 2021, while the United States surpassed both Qatar and Australia in the first half of 2022.[2] But Qatar is unlikely to lag these rivals for long: six new megatrains that will boost production capacity to 126 million tons per year are being built, and the first of these additions will be ready in 2025.

Qatar has made certain that ExxonMobil and Total aren't the only major oil companies participating in its LNG expansion. ConocoPhillips and Shell were brought in as shareholders in separate megatrains in 2005, partnering with Qatar Petroleum in two of the seven joint ventures formed to own the fourteen trains. The Qataris used the rivalry among their partners to get the best fiscal terms for the state, including increasingly higher royalty rates on gas, condensates, and, eventually, liquid petroleum gas at each successive joint venture. In 2018 the two foundation projects were merged into a single entity to further capitalize on economies of scale and save costs, combining the distinct management, marketing, and back-office functions to improve efficiency. However, the revenue from the sale of LNG and other products still flowed back to the seven joint ventures that split ownership of the various trains. The merger is expected to save QR 2 billion ($550 million) in costs annually. Qatargas, as the merged entity is called, is headed by Khalid Ibn Khalifa Ibn Jassim Al Thani, who also led the former company of the same name.

The integration effort, which also extends to petrochemicals, is driven by Saad Sherida Al Kaabi, QP's hard-charging CEO since September 2014. Al Kaabi was also appointed the minister of state for energy affairs in a government reshuffle announced by Amir Tamim Ibn Hamad Al Thani on November 4, 2018. Sheikh Tamim had replaced his elder brother Sheikh Jassim as crown prince in 2003, and became ruler on June 24, 2013, upon his father's voluntary abdication. Sheikh Tamim disbanded the Ministry of Energy and Industry in the 2018 reshuffle, giving the energy portfolio to Al Kaabi and creating a new Ministry of Commerce and Industry under Ali Al Kawari. The two men replaced Mohammad Ibn Saleh Al Sada, the minister of energy and industry, who took over from Al Attiyah in 2011.

ExxonMobil is still the dominate foreign player in Qatar's LNG sector, with stakes in twelve of its fourteen trains (including four of its six megatrains). The U.S. major has also invested in two other North field projects that supply domestic users. This includes the 2 billion cubic feet per day Al Khaleej Gas project, which began operating in 2005, as well as the Barzan venture, which has a first phase capacity of 1.4 billion cubic feet per day. Barzan effectively replaced ExxonMobil's gas-to-liquids plant when that project was canceled in 2007. The Barzan project was originally supposed to start up in 2012, but it suffered a series of setbacks. These included a 2015 pipeline explosion caused by poor welding and a gas leak in 2016. While ExxonMobil reported in its 2020 Annual Report that Barzan had started up that year, the project was only officially inaugurated by the amir on March 15, 2022.

Total (now TotalEnergies) also maintains a large presence on the gas side, partnering in four LNG trains, one of which is a megatrain, and in the Dolphin pipeline project that since 2007 has exported 2 billion cubic feet per day of gas to the UAE and Oman. Dolphin Energy was created in 1999 by the UAE Offsets Group, a branch of the UAE Ministry of Defense, and now groups Abu Dhabi's state-owned Mabadala Development Company, Total, and Occidental Petroleum. It is supplied from a dedicated block in the North field, where 2.45 billion cubic feet per day of wellhead gas is produced and then piped ashore to processing facilities at Ras Laffan. In addition to the 2 billion cubic feet daily of lean gas exported by pipeline to the UAE and Oman, the project produces 100,000 barrels per day of condensate and significant volumes of liquid petroleum gas, ethane, and sulfur under a development- and production-sharing agreement. The export pipeline has about 1.2 billion cubic feet per day of spare capacity.

Both Total and ExxonMobil invested in the 146,000-barrel-per-day Laffan 1 condensate refinery that began operating in 2009. Total also took a stake in the adjacent 146,000-barrel-per-day Laffan 2 refinery completed in 2016. Unlike ExxonMobil, the French major is a shareholder in two producing oil fields as well as four petrochemical ventures. Shell bought its way back into Qatar through hefty investments in Pearl GTL and Qatargas 4, a joint venture with QP formed to own the country's fourteenth train. This megatrain was developed in conjunction with Qatargas 3, another 7.8-million-tons-per-year train in which ConocoPhillips is the largest foreign investor. Shell has poured a massive amount of money into Qatar's gas development since its return, even more than ExxonMobil. This is due to the hefty price tag on its gas-to-liquids plant, whose $18.5-billion-cost Shell footed entirely on its own under a 2004 agreement with QP. Altogether, QP and its foreign partners had invested around $80 billion to commercialize the North field reserves by 2020, when Barzan finally started up.

The four-pronged strategy for monetizing the massive North field—whose proven recoverable reserves were officially put at 900 trillion cubic feet of gas and 23 billion barrels of condensate in 2002—has been to develop the resource for export as LNG, GTL, or pipeline gas, and for domestic use. Once Barzan production reaches its rated capacity, North field gas production will top 24 billion cubic feet per day, supplying fourteen LNG trains, two GTL projects, one pipeline export project, and three separate ventures targeting the local market, including the original North field Alpha development. Gas is used domestically as a fuel for power generation, water desalination, and in the production of value-added petrochemicals as well as other industrial applications. Qatar's total gas production will rise further to a daily rate of around 32 billion cubic feet when its six new LNG megatrains are fully online toward the end of the 2020s.

IRAN DEVELOPS SHARED STRUCTURE DURING NORTH FIELD MORATORIUM

Qatar Petroleum said this next North field expansion, the first since a decade-long development ban was lifted in early 2017, will be confined to sections of the field located away from the country's maritime border with Iran. When it was imposed in 2005, officials cited technical reasons for the North field moratorium, including the need to assess the performance of the reservoir after the last gas project had been in production for several years.[3] At the time, the North field plan envisaged increasing production to 24 billion cubic feet per day by 2010. The Qataris wanted to ensure this level of output was sustainable for over a century, and a series of multiyear studies and appraisal drillings were needed to evaluate the field's potential following unexpected pressure drops and wide variations in liquid gas content between wells.[4] Barzan's delay kept the field from reaching the 2010 target, although production was steady at around 22 billion cubic feet per day from 2013 and will presumably reach 24 billion cubic feet per day once Barzan reaches full production capacity in 2022.

The moratorium was supposed to last just four years but was repeatedly extended. There were other reasons besides reservoir concerns for keeping it in place, not least of which was giving Iran time to catch up at South Pars on its side of the maritime border. Tehran complained that rapid field development was causing pressure differentials and the resulting migration of gas and condensate into Qatar, compounded by the fact that the North field's best drilling sites were right up against the median line. The 1969 boundary agreement between Qatar and Iran banned drilling within 125 meters on either side of this line, and this no-drill zone was extended to 1 kilometer in the late 1980s to help prevent migration. The South Pars development started up in 2002, a full eleven years behind the North field, and production capacity on the Iranian side had purportedly reached 5 billion cubic feet per day from five development phases when Qatar imposed its moratorium in early 2005.

Iran made further gains at South Pars during Qatar's twelve-year North field development hiatus, bringing thirteen more phases with total gas output capability of 16.7 billion cubic feet per day online on its side of the maritime border by April 2017 when Doha finally lifted its self-imposed ban. The vigor with which the Iranians developed their portion of the shared field was undoubtedly a factor in Doha's decision to lift the moratorium, despite Qatari denials. "The reality is that two giant gas producers are dipping into the same reservoir, one silently determined not to be outdone by the other," the *Petroleum Economist* reported soon after the ban was formally rescinded.[5]

Iran's oil minister, Bijan Zanganeh, announced on state TV in early 2019 that production had hit 21.5 billion cubic feet per day at South Pars following the completion of the nineteenth development phase at the structure.[6] Output has risen subsequently to about 24 billion cubic feet per day, and South Pars accounted for about 90 percent of Iran's total gas output in 2021.[7] All the gas from South Pars is used internally, and Iran does not yet have the infrastructure to export LNG. The National Iranian Gas Company started work on a liquefaction project at the port of Tombak in Iran's southern Bushehr Province in 2009, but progress has been stymied by U.S. sanctions and a lack of foreign backers. Gas for this facility was to be sourced from South Pars, where in-place Iranian reserves are put at nearly 500 trillion cubic feet of gas and 18 billion barrels of condensate.

When QP finally lifted the North field moratorium, the state-owned firm said it anticipated boosting daily output by just 2 billion cubic feet, about 10 percent. CEO Saad Al Kaabi pointedly avoided saying what the company planned to do with this expansion volume when he announced the decision to end the moratorium at a press conference on April 3, 2017. Outside observers immediately assumed the additional gas would be used to build new LNG capacity, in anticipation of an expected worldwide supply shortage in the early part of the next decade. Increased volume could also help Qatar maintain its competitive edge against rival producers in Australia, the United States, and Russia.

Al Kaabi later said that he had been negotiating with the UAE for more gas through the Dolphin pipeline just before the North field moratorium was lifted and had held off on what to do with the extra gas pending those discussions.[8] He made no mention of Bahrain, which had put the final touches on a pipeline gas deal just as the moratorium went into effect in 2005. Bahrain had originally been promised top priority by then-minister of energy and industry Al Attiyah via a spur line from a much longer pipeline linking the North field to Kuwait through Saudi waters. The pipeline to Kuwait was shelved when Riyadh refused to give Doha transit rights following a diplomatic row over a 2002 Al Jazeera television program critical of the kingdom and the Saudi royal family. Kuwait has since built LNG import infrastructure, first offshore through a floating storage and regasification unit and then through a massive onshore terminal capable of regasifying close to 1.5 billion cubic feet per day that was inaugurated in 2021. Bahrain's first LNG regasification terminal was commissioned in 2020 but has seen limited imports as the country's own gas production has covered its needs.

Saudi Arabia originally objected to the Dolphin pipeline, sending a letter of complaint to the project's lenders and two of its oil company partners in 2006. In this it claimed the pipeline's 364-kilometer route crossed through Saudi waters and demanded that Dolphin Energy cease all activity in its maritime area. Dolphin did not receive the Saudi letter directly, however, nor was it sent to the Qatari government. Occidental's regional manager also said no one had raised the issue with his company.[9] So work on the undersea pipeline continued on schedule. Part of the problem was that the 1974 border agreement between the UAE and Saudi Arabia had not resolved the issue of maritime boundaries. It merely stated that "both parties shall as soon as possible delimit the offshore boundaries between the territory of the Kingdom of Saudi Arabia and the territory of the United Arab Emirates."[10]

"As soon as possible" never came. After Abu Dhabi's Sheikh Zayid Ibn Sultan Al Nahyan died in 2004, his son Sheikh Khalifa tried to link delineation of its offshore border with Saudi Arabia to the amendment of other provisions in the 1974 agreement. This included a proposed revenue-sharing scheme on a huge onshore oil field known as Shaybah or Zararah that crossed the land boundary between the two counties but had been ceded to Saudi Arabia, which was given all hydrocarbon rights. The Dolphin letter was therefore viewed as a warning that the kingdom could cause trouble for Abu Dhabi offshore if it continued to push for changes to other aspects of the original accord. Certainly, the U.S. government believed that the proposed path of the Dolphin pipeline took it well outside any Saudi territorial claims.[11]

In 2015 Dolphin upgraded its gas compression facilities and flare system so that it could purchase additional North field gas from third parties to fill the spare capacity on its export pipeline. QP also built a five-kilometer link, the Third Party Gas Pipeline, from its station 4 near the Barzan gas project to the Dolphin plant at Ras Laffan, and in late 2016 the Qatari firm signed a new gas sale and purchase agreement with Dolphin Energy. No details on the additional volume for the UAE were given, although the new pipeline link can transport up to 1 billion cubic feet per day.

QATAR RIDES OUT EMBARGO BY ARAB QUARTET

Any hope the Emiratis had of pushing more North field gas through the Dolphin pipeline was shattered on June 5, 2017, when the UAE, Saudi Arabia, Bahrain, and Egypt severed diplomatic ties with Qatar and imposed a land, sea, and air embargo on the country. This was supposedly for financing terrorism and supporting Islamist groups such as Egypt's Muslim Brotherhood, Al Qaeda, the Islamic State, and Lebanon's Hezbollah—claims Doha vehemently denies. Qatar was also criticized for its cordial relations with Tehran, its independent foreign policy, and its sponsorship of Al Jazeera, which has been a thorn in the side of Qatar's Arab neighbors for years. The quartet gave Doha a list of thirteen sweeping demands that included curbing diplomatic and economic relations with Iran, severing ties to "terrorist organizations," shutting down Al Jazeera and four other news outlets, closing a Turkish military base in Qatar, stopping all contact with the political opposition in the blockading countries, and paying reparations for the loss of life, property, and income stemming from Doha's maverick policies.

Qatar never considered agreeing to these demands. With Doha refusing to budge and the Trump administration in the United States only belatedly pushing the Saudis and Emiratis to relent, the blockade remained in place until January 2021. It also proved largely ineffectual. While Qatar initially dipped into its $340 billion sovereign wealth fund to airlift in supplies and shore up the financial sector after banks from the blockading countries withdrew their deposits, the hemorrhaging eventually stopped. It wasn't the first time the state had bailed out the financial sector. During the economic downturn of late 2008 and early 2009, the Qatar Investment Authority made direct capital injections into the country's commercial banks through a plan to purchase as much as 20 percent of the equity in all domestic banks listed on the Doha Stock Exchange. In mid-2009 the state even announced it would buy the investment portfolios of seven of these nine local banks at the net book value and would purchase their real estate holdings.

Before the embargo Qatar relied heavily on the UAE and Saudi Arabia for its imports, including about a third of its food. When the embargo was imposed, it quickly secured alternative supply routes through Turkey, Oman, Kuwait, and Iran. This was aided by the inauguration of a new deep-water port forty kilometers south of Doha, which allows large cargo ships to dock directly in Qatar without having to break bulk into smaller vessels at Dubai's Jebel Ali re-export hub.[12] Hamad port opened just three months after the embargo was imposed and continues to receive large quantities of food as well as building materials for high-profile projects such as the construction of stadiums ahead of the 2022 FIFA World Cup. The embargo also drove a new degree of self-sufficiency. One state entity even airlifted in thousands of American dairy cows to ensure a continued supply of fresh milk for the country's 2.7 million residents.[13]

Hydrocarbon shipments continued unabated. The only hiccup was a ban initially imposed by the UAE and Saudi Arabia on co-loadings of their crude oil grades with those from Qatar. This sparked a customer revolt and was soon dropped. Qatar's export revenues surged 25 percent to $84.3 billion in 2018, the first full year of the embargo, in the best economic performance since 2014 when the country realized $130.7 billion on much higher oil and gas prices. Government finances also swung back into surplus for the first time in five years in 2018 as oil prices improved, hitting $4.15 billion.[14] A smaller surplus of $1.2 billion was recorded in 2019 and then fell to a $2.1 billion deficit in 2020 amid the global COVID-19 pandemic and low oil prices. The budget for 2021 anticipated a $9.5 billion deficit based on an oil price projection of just $40 per barrel and high government spending ahead of the 2022 FIFA World Cup.[15] However, a revival in oil prices allowed Qatar to run a surplus through the first three quarters of 2021, and it is thought to have finished off the year with a final budget surplus in excess of $2 billion.[16]

Within a month of the blockade QP announced it was more than doubling its North field expansion to 4.6 billion cubic feet per day. Its CEO specified that the gas would be used at three new megatrains, boosting annual LNG production capacity to 100 million tons.[17] Nine months later the company added a fourth megatrain.[18] These new trains, comprising the first phase of the North Field Expansion Project and known as North Field East, will lift total LNG capacity to 110 million tons per year and require an additional 6 billion cubic feet per day of gas. The decision to liquefy this gas left the UAE without any extra pipeline volumes, although Qatar was scrupulous in maintaining flows through Dolphin at pre-embargo levels to burnish its reputation as a reliable supplier—and to avoid antagonizing Oman, who imports Dolphin gas via an overland route from the UAE and stayed neutral in the row among its Gulf neighbors.

Two additional megatrains were announced in late 2019 as part of a second phase of the North Field Expansion Project dubbed North Field South. These trains will boost Qatar's total LNG production capacity to 126 million tons per year. Gas for the North Field South phase could come from producing layers that have recently been revealed to extend well into Qatari land in Ras Laffan. QP made a final investment decision on the four LNG trains in North Field East in early 2021, and this first phase is expected to cost $28.75 billion. Qatar's main oil company partners immediately began queuing up to invest in the new infrastructure, with TotalEnergies, ExxonMobil, Shell, ConocoPhillips, and Eni eventually awarded small stakes in North Field East. While the expansion will be implemented in separate joint ventures with these five firms, TotalEnergies, ExxonMobil, and Shell will each own stakes equivalent to 6.25 percent in North Field East followed by ConocoPhillips and Italy's Eni at 3.12 percent. QatarEnergy, as Qatar Petroleum was renamed in late 2021, will hold the remaining 75 percent.[19] This interest may appear one-sided, but it must be kept in mind that QatarEnergy no longer needs foreign partners or even debt financing to fund its new trains. Nor does it need outside technical expertise to develop them, except for experienced engineering, procurement, and construction firms.

The main construction contract for the four megatrains comprising North Field East was awarded in early 2021 to Japan's Chiyoda Corp. and the French firm Technip Energies, well before QatarEnergy completed the selection process for its five oil company partners in the four-train expansion project. Both contractors have deep ties in Qatar and history developing upstream and liquefaction projects in the county. The award of this engineering, procurement, and construction contract followed separate contracts for the offshore wellhead platform jackets and site preparation at Ras Laffan in 2019. Production from the first train at North Field East is scheduled to begin by the end of 2025, and all four trains should be fully completed in 2027. QatarEnergy also plans to complete North Field South in 2027, and the company said in April 2022 that it expected to award the main construction contract covering these two megatrains by the end of 2022.[20]

The choice of partners for these new megatrains was based as much on geopolitics as commercial factors, since the forty-three-month blockade by Qatar's Arab neighbors underscored the importance of expanding investment ties with countries outside the region. Unlike QatarEnergy's other partners in the expansion project, Eni's participation in North Field East represents its first foray into Qatar's LNG sector. This is not for want of trying, as Eni tried unsuccessfully to get its Qatar Eurogas LNG venture with Bunker Hunt off the ground in the early 1990s. Eni's success at North Field East follows recent partnerships with Qatar's state oil firm in offshore exploration in Kenya, Mozambique, Mexico, Morocco, and Oman. Italy is among the most exposed economies in Europe to Russian pipeline gas, and Eni is one of many European companies scrambling to line up other fuel sources in the wake of Russia's invasion of Ukraine.

There will be opportunities for further foreign oil company participation in North Field South, the second phase of Qatar's LNG expansion for which initial engineering and design work is now under way. First in the queue are China's large energy players, who are seeking more LNG under long-term contracts as the country's economy recovers from the COVID-19 pandemic and diversifies away from an overreliance on coal.[21] China is on an aggressive growth trajectory, and it overtook Japan as the world's largest LNG importer in 2021.[22] Chevron may also be a contender at North Field South, having lost out on the bidding for a stake in North Field East. The one major oil company that will not be given a seat at the table is BP, still *firma non grata* following its 1992 departure from Qatargas.

OPEC EXIT WIDENS POLITICAL RIFT WITH NEIGHBORS

Qatar's announcement some eighteen months into the embargo that it was leaving OPEC after nearly six decades deepened the political rift with its neighbors. Its exit made Qatar the first Middle East country to leave the group; the departure was dubbed Qatexit in a nod toward Britain's Brexit withdrawal from the European Union. The decision was unveiled on December 3, 2018, by Saad Al Kaabi, who had just been appointed as the minister of state for energy affairs, and it became effective on January 1, 2019. Qatar attended OPEC's inaugural meeting in Baghdad in 1960 as an observer and formally joined its five founding members—Iraq, Kuwait, Saudi Arabia, Iran, and Venezuela—at the organization's second meeting the following year. Its exit was therefore highly symbolic, although without much market impact as Qatar's 610,000 barrels per day represented a mere 2 percent of OPEC's total flows at the time. The country's crude oil flows have declined further since then, to 550,000 barrels annually in 2021.[23]

Production is closer to 1.31 million barrels per day when condensates are included. Condensates are natural gas liquids and therefore aren't included in OPEC quotas, incentivizing certain members to classify light crude grades as condensate in order to circumvent production restrictions. Qatar's condensate output overtook oil in 2012 and averaged about 760,000 barrels per day in 2021. Unlike oil, where the emphasis is on stemming declines at mature fields, further condensate gains are on the horizon as natural gas production increases. Barzan eventually will boost flows by 30,000 barrels per day, while the North Field East LNG expansion phase will contribute another 260,000. This will lift daily condensate production over 1 million barrels for the first time. The extra output is destined for the export market as there are no plans to increase condensate refining capacity.

Al Kaabi dismissed speculation that Qatar's OPEC exit was related to politics, particularly its toxic relationship with OPEC kingpin Saudi Arabia.[24] The energy minister said the decision to leave the organization would allow Qatar to focus on its gas industry, including its aggressive LNG expansion plans. But he also hinted that Saudi Arabia, whose oil production was running about eighteen times higher than Qatar's at the time, was at least partly to blame for the departure. "We are not saying we are going to get out of the oil business, but it is controlled by an organization managed by a country," Al Kaabi said, without citing Saudi Arabia by name.[25]

REDUCED OIL-SECTOR PARTICIPATION
BY FOREIGNERS AT HOME . . .

No foreign companies have explored for oil in Qatar since Wintershall and its partners relinquished offshore Block 3 in 2013. The last significant oil discovery was the Al Rayyan field in 1995, although QP reported that it had found oil in a southern extension of the Al Khalij field in 2016 and planned a 3D seismic survey in the area.[26] This lack of success extended to gas exploration by outside firms, and all the international players who had been hoping to discover additional Khuff and pre-Khuff reserves outside the North field subsequently pulled out. While several of these companies found gas on their exploration blocks, these discoveries were either too small, too dry, or too far away from existing infrastructure to be commercially viable. Japan's JX Nippon was the last to leave, giving up its Block A in 2017 after drilling two pre-Khuff wells.

Qatar Petroleum itself has enjoyed significant exploration success recently at the North field, announcing in November 2019 that new studies had revealed that the field's producing zones extended well into Qatari land in Ras Laffan. The company said the NF-12 appraisal well drilled onshore in the Ras Laffan Industrial City had confirmed that gas reserves in the North field were over 1,760 trillion cubic feet together with 70 billion barrels of condensate and "massive" quantities of liquid petroleum gas, ethane, and helium.[27] It is not clear how much of these reserves are recoverable, and the new estimate represents a huge increase on Qatar's official recoverable reserve figure of 900 trillion cubic feet of gas and 23 billion barrels of condensate for the North field. But there is no question the find is exciting—and a long time coming, as the Qataris have been trying to find an onshore extension of the North field for decades. "Studies and well tests have also confirmed the ability to produce large quantities of gas from this new sector of the North field," energy minister Saad Al Kaabi said at a press conference announcing the discovery.[28]

Oil production in Qatar peaked at 860,000 barrels per day in early 2008. Focus is now on redevelopment projects to stabilize and extend the life of the aging Dukhan, Bul Hanine, and Maydan Mahzam fields. The onshore Dukhan field contributes around 175,000 barrels per day, while the offshore Bul Hanine and Maydan Mahzam structures produce a combined 50,000 barrels, down from 85,000 a decade ago. QP has also been steadily regaining control of maritime fields operated by foreign oil companies. It negotiated a more advantageous joint venture arrangement with Total at the Al Khalij field when its production-sharing agreement expired in early 2014 and then took over completely from Occidental Petroleum at Al Rayyan in mid-2017 upon expiry of its contract. Al Khalij produces 11,000 barrels per day, while daily output at Al Rayyan has fallen to just 4,000 barrels.[29]

Maersk was ousted from Al Shaheen when its production-sharing agreement expired, and the field has been operated by a joint venture called the North Oil Company since mid-2017. Total won the bidding to join QP in this new entity as a minority partner. Now Qatar's largest oil field, Al Shaheen produces about 243,000 barrels per day. Maersk had originally hoped to increase the daily rate to 525,000 barrels, but QP capped the field at 300,000 barrels due to geological concerns. Work was geared toward returning to this optimum level following apparent maintenance lapses by the Danish firm at the end of its contract.[30] A similar joint venture arrangement was ruled out at the Idd el-Shargi North Dome, and QP assumed operatorship of the 56,000-barrels-per-day field when the agreement with Oxy expired on October 6, 2019. QP simultaneously took over Idd el-Shargi South Dome, an 8,000-barrel-per-day satellite, from Oxy.

The contract held by the Qatar Petroleum Development Company—now owned by Cosmo Oil and Nissho Iwai's successor, Sojitz Corporation—at Al Karkara and A-Structure is due to expire at the end of 2022. At 4,000 barrels per day, the structures now produce about the same as Al Rayyan. Operations at the nearby Bunduq field shared with Abu Dhabi continued throughout the embargo, with output running around 13,000 barrels per day. The feuding neighbors even extended the concession agreement held by Japan's United Petroleum Development at Bunduq after it expired on March 8, 2018. No details were given, and QP stated only that the new deal would ensure the field's development and operation for many years to come. Lest anyone think the two states had cooperated on Bunduq's extension, the UAE's official news agency issued a statement saying the concession was extended by each respective government with no direct communication or engagement between Abu Dhabi and Qatar.[31]

This go-it-alone mentality has extended to LNG and the expiration of the joint venture at Qatargas 1, the country's first LNG project, which was established in 1984 and operates the original three trains. In early 2021 QP announced that it would not be renewing the arrangement with affiliates of Total, Exxon-Mobil, Marubeni, and Mitsui upon its expiry at the end of that year. As a result, Qatar's state energy company became the sole owner of these assets and facilities on January 1, 2022. The decision reflects the firm's growing confidence in its technical and commercial abilities as it moves largely on its own toward global LNG dominance.

. . . BEING REPLACED WITH EXPANDED PARTNERSHIPS ABROAD

If Qatar is assiduously reducing the role of foreign companies in its domestic oil and gas sector, the same cannot be said for its expanding footprint abroad. QP has been on a buying spree, acquiring exploration and production assets with oil company partners in Argentina, Brazil, Canada, Congo, Cyprus, Egypt, Guyana, Ivory Coast, Kenya, Mexico, Morocco, Mozambique, Namibia, Oman, and South Africa. After shedding its first acquisition in Canada, where QP teamed up with the UK's Centrica in 2013 to buy the bulk of Suncor Energy's conventional gas and crude oil resources in Alberta, British Columbia, and southern Saskatchewan, the Qataris are now partnered with ExxonMobil on an exploration license offshore Newfoundland and Labrador. QP also switched horses in Morocco, relinquishing three deep-water blocks acquired in 2016 with Chevron and farming into Eni's Tarfaya Shallow exploration permit, a series of twelve blocks off Morocco's Atlantic coast, in early 2019. The two companies are exploring for oil off the coast of Oman and partnering in three oil fields and one exploration block in

Mexico's Campeche Bay. First output from the three fields—Amoca, Mizton, and Tecoalli—commenced in June 2019.

Deep-water fields shared with Shell in Brazil and Total in Congo are also in production. Shell's Parque das Conchas project in Brazil's Campos basin netted QP 10,100 barrels of oil per day in 2020, while QP has a 15 percent stake in Total's Moho-Nord venture in Congo, which started up in 2017 and is expected to reach peak production of 140,000 barrels per day.[32] It has partnered with Shell in two offshore exploration blocks in Egypt, four in Mexico's Perdido basin, and a deep pre-salt block in Brazil's Santos basin. In early 2018 ExxonMobil and QP were awarded two blocks in the Santos basin, plus two in the Campos basin together with Brazil's Petrobras, and later that year won the bidding for the pre-salt Tita block in the Santos basin. In 2019 QP secured stakes in three more blocks in the Campos basin with Shell and Total, while in 2021 it won a stake in the producing Sepia pre-salt oil field in the Santos basin operated by Petrobras. Billions of barrels of oil are thought to be trapped in the Santos and Campos basins under a thick layer of salt, and Sepia alone is expected to have a production capacity of over 350,000 barrels per day.[33]

The Qatari firm won exploration rights at five blocks off Argentina in April 2019. These include three blocks with ExxonMobil in the Malvinas West basin and two with Shell in the North Argentina basin. The successful bids followed an earlier deal in mid-2018 under which QP bought into two ExxonMobil affiliates in Argentina with interests in hydrocarbon licenses on seven blocks in the Vaca Muerta shale oil and gas play in the onshore Neuquén basin. This acquisition represented the Qatari firm's first international investment in unconventional oil and gas resources and is unlikely to be its last. The Argentine licenses include exploration licenses with active drilling plans as well as exploitation licenses with pilot drilling and production. Elsewhere in South America, QP bought a stake in the Orinduik and Kanuku blocks in Guyana from Total in 2019. Guyana is considered an exploration hot spot, and the acreage is located very close to a string of discoveries made by ExxonMobil. These include the Hammerhead-1 find, which could extend into the Orinduik block.

QP and ExxonMobil also joined forces in Mozambique, partnering in 2018 with the east African country's state-owned oil firm Empresa Nacional de Hidrocarbonetos and Russia's Rosneft in three offshore exploration blocks in the relatively unexplored Angoche and Zambezi basins. The following year QP joined Eni in an adjacent block in the Angoche basin. QP farmed into three deep-water blocks in Kenya's largely unexplored Lamu basin in 2019. The deal with Eni and Total gave the Qatari firm a relatively large position in blocks L11A, L11B, and L12. In South Africa, QP bought a stake in Total's Brulpadda find off the country's southern coast in early 2019. Total has said the discovery could hold up to 1 billion barrels of oil equivalent, mostly gas but also some condensate.

Namibia's offshore Orange basin, where QatarEnergy has interests in four blocks, is shaping up to be another hot play in Southern Africa. Back-to-back discoveries on the deep-water PEL-39 license operated by Shell and the Venus-1X prospect in Block 2913B led by TotalEnergies were announced in February 2022. The Graff-1 well on PEL-39 contains "a working petroleum system with light oil," although QatarEnergy said more exploration is necessary to determine its resource potential.[34] Also located in deep water, Venus-1X is a significant light-oil and associated gas discovery. QatarEnergy is cooperating with Namibia's national oil company to support and develop a sustainable upstream oil and gas sector in the African country under an agreement signed in March 2022. In West Africa, the Qatari firm farmed into two blocks operated by TotalEnergies in Ivory Coast's offshore Ivorian-Tano basin in 2020.

In the Mediterranean, ExxonMobil and QP announced a substantial gas discovery off Cyprus with their Glaucus-1 well on Block 10 on February 28, 2019. ExxonMobil has said the find, in water depths of over two kilometers about 180 kilometers offshore, could hold up to 8 trillion cubic feet of in-place gas reserves—minuscule in comparison to Qatar's North field but still encouraging. A second appraisal well on Glaucus completed in early 2022 also confirmed the presence of high-quality gas. The two partners joined forces on another exploration block in Cypriot waters in late 2021, while QatarEnergy acquired an interest in ExxonMobil's North Marakia exploration block off Egypt's Mediterranean coast in early 2022. The farm-in at North Marakia represented QatarEnergy's second foray into Egypt's upstream sector, following the acquisition in 2021 of interests in two offshore blocks operated by Shell in the Egyptian side of the Red Sea.

QatarEnergy CEO Al Kaabi has been the driving force behind the company's overseas expansion, with all but the now unwound Canadian acquisition with Centrica signed since he took the helm in 2014. The firm insists it has no special geographic focus. The Qataris have instead tried to balance the acquisition of large proven reserves with exploration acreage. "This is a huge growth strategy on which we are going to spend billions of dollars," Al Kaabi said in late 2017. "It's really

[the] size of reserves that we are looking at, along with the partners that we go in with. And it is aimed at increasing the reserves and production of [QatarEnergy] worldwide on the long term."[35]

QATAR TO EXPORT LNG FROM UNITED STATES IN FIRST OVERSEAS GAS PROJECT

The firm's most important investment abroad could be in the United States, where QatarEnergy and ExxonMobil are spending over $10 billion in repurposing their Golden Pass LNG import terminal near Port Arthur, Texas, to liquefy about 2 billion cubic feet of gas per day, or 16 million tons per year of LNG, for export beginning in 2024. Golden Pass, located in the middle of North America's most developed gas pipeline network with easy access to major markets in the northeastern and eastern United States, was supposed to receive and regasify LNG from three of Qatar's megatrains. At the time Golden Pass was conceived, onshore and offshore fields in the Gulf of Mexico which accounted for half of all domestic U.S. production were expected to decline. Some 6.4 billion cubic feet per day of LNG regasification capacity was in operation or under construction in the area, while import terminals totaling another 8.8 billion cubic feet per day had either been granted permits by U.S. regulators or had applications pending.

By the time Golden Pass received its first import cargo in late 2010, the narrative of declining production had been turned on its head by the development of shale gas deposits in Texas, Louisiana, and the Appalachia region. Shale gas was running about 20 billion cubic feet per day, or one-third of the country's total dry gas production of 60 billion cubic feet per day. Eight years later, as QP and ExxonMobil were making a final decision on converting Golden Pass into an LNG export facility, those players and a host of others had boosted shale gas output to 72 billion cubic feet per day. This represented 70 percent of total dry gas production in the United States, which hit a daily high of 97 billion cubic feet in December 2019.[36]

The United States became a net gas exporter for the first time in nearly six decades in 2017. By the end of 2018 exports had risen to 11.7 billion cubic feet per day, including 4 billion cubic feet exported in the form of LNG from four plants in Louisiana, Maryland, and Texas. Of these, two were import terminals repurposed to liquefy gas for export, while a third was originally permitted to receive LNG but switched its orientation as the domestic gas surplus emerged. LNG exports from the United States have continued to grow substantially, coinciding with large increases in export capacity, and 2021 marked the first year that LNG shipments exceeded gas exports by pipeline. The United States became the world's largest LNG exporter during the first half of 2022, averaging 11.2 billion cubic feet per day, or about 78 million tons of LNG.[37]

QP and ExxonMobil applied for regulatory approval to convert Golden Pass in 2014, three years after it received its last import cargo.[38] The two partners initially expected to reach an investment decision on the project in 2015, followed by first exports in 2019. But Golden Pass Products LLC did not receive final regulatory approval until late 2016. The project was finally approved internally by its partners more than two years later, on February 5, 2019. In the meantime, Golden Pass has remained virtually dormant.

ExxonMobil says this trajectory will put Golden Pass at the forefront of the second wave of lower-48 LNG export projects, although it has not said why it opted to avoid the first wave that began in 2016. Baseload LNG export capacity in Louisiana, Maryland, Georgia, and Texas reached 77 million tons per year at the end of 2021.[39] The U.S. Energy Information Agency expects this to increase to over 114 million tons per year in 2024 as export facilities currently in the commissioning stage or under construction are brought into service.[40]

While ExxonMobil has invested heavily in the shale gas industry, QatarEnergy has yet to acquire an upstream position in the United States. CEO Saad Al Kaabi told Reuters in late 2018 that the company plans to invest at least $20 billion in the United States and is looking at buying both conventional and unconventional oil and gas assets.[41] Earlier reports suggested the Qataris were in talks with ExxonMobil about joining forces with the oil major's XTO Energy subsidiary to invest in future shale gas wells.[42] ExxonMobil acquired 45 trillion cubic feet of unconventional gas resources, including a foothold in most major shale basins in the United States, in 2010 when it purchased XTO in a stock-and-debt deal valued at $41 billion. The company has since extended XTO's reach significantly, including its 2017 purchase for $6.6 billion of 3.4 billion barrels of oil equivalent in the Permian basin, widely considered the nation's hottest shale play.

All the output from Golden Pass will be purchased by Ocean LNG Limited, a joint venture set up in 2016 to market LNG supplies sourced outside of Qatar. Both Ocean LNG and Golden Pass Products LLC are 70 percent owned by

QatarEnergy and 30 percent by ExxonMobil. ConocoPhillips, which originally invested in the import terminal as part of its megatrain in Qatar, opted not to participate in the export project. QP has said Ocean LNG will focus on selling its U.S. volumes worldwide with focus on the Atlantic basin markets, but the decision to go ahead with Golden Pass was made without contracts with buyers—both short- and long-term ones. This marked a big departure for the Qataris, who until recently have always ensured their LNG had a home before committing to large-scale projects. However, it fits a recent trend that has seen buyers turning more and more to companies with global supply pools.

QatarEnergy's overseas expansion is transforming the firm into a truly global player. Al Kaabi has already put his competitors on notice that he has big plans for his company. "[QatarEnergy]; in 10 years from now you will not recognize it, because it is going to be so much bigger than it is today," Al Kaabi said in a 2017 interview with the *Middle East Economic Survey*. "My ambition is for [QatarEnergy] to be seen as an international oil company and be talked about at the same level as ExxonMobil, Shell, ConocoPhillips, Total."[43] The firm's foreign partners—both those who already have stakes in projects on its home turf and others with whom it has linked up abroad—are still being given opportunities to invest in Qatar as minority shareholders with severely restricted control. These include the six new LNG trains planned as part of the two-phase North Field Expansion Project as well as a major petrochemical complex QatarEnergy hopes to build. But it will be commercial or geopolitical reasons that drive the choice of partners for these projects, not economic necessity or the need to secure finance.

As Qatar's footprint has expanded abroad, its geopolitical standing with its regional neighbors has greatly improved with the lifting in early 2021 of the air, land, and sea blockade imposed by Saudi Arabia, the UAE, Bahrain, and Egypt in mid-2017. This was announced at the Gulf Cooperation Council summit held in Saudi Arabia on January 5, 2021, and included a historic "hug" between Qatari amir Tamim Ibn Hamad Al Thani and Saudi crown prince Mohammad Ibn Salman Al Saud, the de facto ruler. The lifting of the embargo came with full restoration of diplomatic and commercial ties—and, crucially for Doha, no meaningful concessions from Qatar. Within six months of their rapprochement with Qatar, Saudi Arabia and the UAE had turned on each other in a public feud over the UAE's oil production within OPEC—suggesting the squabbles among Gulf states will continue with or without Qatar.

Regional alliances may be constantly shifting, but one thing is certain: Qatar will continue to forge its own identity apart from its neighbors, employing its almost limitless financial resources to punch well above its weight both politically and economically. As this book attests, the journey from black gold to frozen gas ultimately transformed this tiny country into an energy superpower, one that will almost certainly continue to flex its muscles on the world stage for decades to come.

Acknowledgments

There are so many people to thank for assisting me with this book—first and foremost, Anne-Marie Johnson, who has been a colleague and friend for nearly thirty years. Prior to joining Poten & Partners in 1999, she worked in various capacities for two major oil companies and was a key reporter and editor at the *Middle East Economic Survey*, the archives of which were essential in our research. Without Anne-Marie's involvement, this book would not have been possible.

Many others provided their expertise and guidance (in no special order): Steve Garten, Steve Morley, Gordon Shearer, Jason Feer, and Peggy Kastner. Special thanks to Majed Liman, Priscilla Hermann Gray, Nicholas Buttacavoli, Christine Ahn, Kai Ng, Alex Shneyder, and Maisie Zhang for their extraordinary efforts. They were always there to support me. Also, a word of thanks to Bob Tippee who provided much-needed editorial advice. I am most grateful to Abdullah Al Attiyah for sharing his perspective. I want to express my appreciation to Lisa Anderson, dean emerita at Columbia's School of International and Public Affairs (SIPA), and to Jason Bordoff, the cofounding dean of the Columbia Climate School and the founding director of the Center on Global Energy Policy at SIPA, for their support of this book. I am also grateful to Caelyn Cobb, editor of global history and politics at Columbia University Press, for her valuable editorial advice and overall guidance.

I would be remiss not to mention my life-long friend and mentor, Lucio Noto. As Mobil's CEO, he made the first and most important step to put Qatar on the world energy map.

I thank my wife of fifty-one years, Beatrice, and our children, Paula and Michael, and their beautiful families for their support and encouragement.

—Michael D. Tusiani

I am honored to have worked on this book with Michael, who I have always referred to as a "prince among men" for his unique capacity to combine business acumen and deep understanding of the energy industry with compassion, empathy, and the ability to earn the unwavering loyalty of his colleagues and associates, including myself.

I thank my husband, Martin, for his unwavering patience and support.

—Anne-Marie Johnson

Notes

ABBREVIATIONS IN THE NOTES

FCO	Foreign and Commonwealth Office (UK)
FO	Foreign Office (UK)
MEED	*Middle East Economic Digest*
MEES	*Middle East Economic Survey*
NARA	National Archives and Records Administration (U.S.)
NA-UK	National Archives, United Kingdom
POWE	Ministry of Power, Petroleum Division (UK)

INTRODUCTION

1. Tamin Ibn Hamad Al Thani, quoted in Declan Walsh, "Tiny, Wealthy Qatar Goes Its Way and Pays for It," *New York Times*, January 22, 2018.
2. The Victorian adventurer was William Gifford Palgrave; see his *Personal Narrative of a Year's Journey Through Central and Eastern Arabia (1862–63)* (London: Macmillan, 1908).
3. Ben Hodges and Sam Mundy, "The West Has a Crucial Ally in Qatar," *Wall Street Journal*, May 2, 2022.
4. Hodges and Mundy, "Crucial Ally."
5. Ben Hubbard, "West's Vying for Gas to Be Qatar's Boon," *New York Times*, May 17, 2022.

1. QATAR BEFORE OIL

1. Jill Crystal, *Oil and Politics in the Gulf: Rulers and Merchants in Kuwait and Qatar* (Cambridge: Cambridge University Press, 1990), 113.
2. William Gifford Palgrave, *Personal Narrative of a Year's Journey Through Central and Eastern Arabia (1863–63)* (London: Macmillan, 1908), 387.
3. Palgrave, *Personal Narrative*, 387.
4. Rosemarie Said Zahlan, *The Creation of Qatar* (London: Croom Helm, 1979), 42.

5.   Zahlan, *Creation of Qatar*, 42.

6.   Zahlan, *Creation of Qatar*, 47.

7.   Frederick F. Anscombe, *The Ottoman Gulf: The Creation Of Kuwait, Saudi Arabia and Qatar* (New York: Columbia University Press, 1997), 144–149.

8.   Zahlan, *Creation of Qatar*, 54–55.

9.   Zahlan, *Creation of Qatar*, 54–55.

10.   Aileen Keating, *Mirage: Power, Politics and the Hidden History of Arabian Oil* (Amherst, N.Y.: Prometheus, 2005), 25.

11.   Bahman Oskoui, comp., "Oil in Persia and the Bakhtiaris: A Summary," http://www.bakhtiarifamily.com/oil.php.

12.   Keating, *Mirage*, 26.

13.   Keating, *Mirage*, 110.

14.   The political resident in the Persian Gulf was a very powerful figure, administering British policy in the region for over two centuries. Dubbed the "uncrowned king of the Persian Gulf," he and his subordinate officers exerted huge influence in the British-protected states—Qatar, Bahrain, the Trucial states, and Kuwait.

15.   Keating, *Mirage*, 110.

16.   Keating, *Mirage*, 110.

17.   The Persian Gulf political residency was a subdivision of the British Raj from 1763 to 1947, after which control passed to the Foreign Office in London.

18.   Keating, *Mirage*, 95.

19.   Keating, *Mirage*, 178.

20.   Keating, *Mirage*, 215.

21.   "File 10/3 I Qatar Oil Concession," fol. 153r, image 322/468, British Library: India Office Records and Private Papers, IOR/R/15/2/410, Qatar Digital Library, https://www.qdl.qa/archive/81055/vdc_100023493207.0x00007b.

22.   "File 10/3 I Qatar Oil Concession," fol. 168r, image 354/468, https://www.qdl.qa/archive/81055/vdc_100023493207.0x00009b.

23.   "File 10/3 I Qatar Oil Concession," fol. 153r, image 322/468.

24.   "F-82 82/27 I: QATAR OIL," fol. 4r, image 22/730, British Library: India Office Records and Private Papers, IOR/R/15/1/626, Qatar Digital Library, https://www.qdl.qa/archive/81055/vdc_100023609687.0x000017.

25.   "F-82 82/27 I: QATAR OIL," fol. 4r, image 22/730.

26.   "F-82 82/27 I: QATAR OIL," fol. 9r, image 32/730, https://www.qdl.qa/archive/81055/vdc_100023609687.0x000021.

27.   "F-82 82/27 I: QATAR OIL," fol. 11r, image 36/730, https://www.qdl.qa/archive/81055/vdc_100023609687.0x000025.

28.   Crystal, *Oil and Politics*, 116. Article V of the Treaty, signed on November 3, 1916, and ratified on March 28, 1918, reads: "I [Sheikh Abdullah Ibn Jassim Al Thani] also declare that, without the consent of the High British Government, I will not grant pearl-fishery concessions, or any other monopolies, concessions, or cable landing rights to anyone whomsoever."

29.   "F-82 82/27 I: QATAR OIL," fol. 30r, image 74/730, https://www.qdl.qa/archive/81055/vdc_100023609687.0x00004b.

30. "F-82 82/27 I: QATAR OIL," fol. 31r, image 76/730, https://www.qdl.qa/archive/81055/vdc_100023609687.0x00004d.

31. "F-82 82/27 I: QATAR OIL," fol. 39r, image 92/730, https://www.qdl.qa/archive/81055/vdc_100023609687.0x00005d.

32. "File 10/3 I Qatar Oil Concession," fol. 2r, 18/468, https://www.qdl.qa/archive/81055/vdc_100023493206.0x000013. This equated to £113, or the equivalent of £7,822 in 2019. The Indian rupee was the standard currency in Qatar and the neighboring sheikhdoms. It was tied to the pound sterling at a statutory value of 1 shilling, 6 pence under the Indian Currency Act of 1927. One pound was worth 13.33 Indian rupees from 1927 until 1966, when the Indian rupee was devalued and Qatar and Dubai established the Qatar-Dubai riyal (QDR).

33. "File 10/3 I Qatar Oil Concession," fol. 44r, image 102/468, https://www.qdl.qa/archive/81055/vdc_100023493206.0x000067.

34. Jacques, LeBlanc, *A Historical Account of the Stratigraphy of Qatar, Middle East (1816 to 2015)*, December 1, 2015, https://sites.google.com/site/leblancjacques/fossilhome, p. 45.

2. QATAR'S FIRST OIL CONCESSION

1. "File 10/3 I Qatar Oil Concession," fol. 159r, image 336/468, British Library: India Office Records and Private Papers, IOR/R/15/2/410, Qatar Digital Library, https://www.qdl.qa/archive/81055/vdc_100023493207.0x000089.

2. "File 10/3 I Qatar Oil Concession," fol. 97r, image 208/468, https://www.qdl.qa/archive/81055/vdc_100023493207.0x000009.

3. "Oil Concessions," fol. 189r, image 396/480, British Library: India Office Records and Private Papers, IOR/R/15/2/98, Qatar Digital Library, https://www.qdl.qa/archive/81055/vdc_100023943531.0x0000c5.

4. Aileen Keating, *Mirage: Power, Politics and the Hidden History of Arabian Oil* (Amherst, N.Y.: Prometheus, 2005), 382.

5. "File 10/3 I Qatar Oil Concession," fol. 177, image 372/468, https://www.qdl.qa/archive/81055/vdc_100023493207.0x0000ad.

6. "File 10/3 I Qatar Oil Concession," fol. 198r, image 414/468, https://www.qdl.qa/archive/81055/vdc_100023493208.0x00000f.

7. "File 10/3 I Qatar Oil Concession," fol. 205r, image 430/468, https://www.qdl.qa/archive/81055/vdc_100023493208.0x00001f.

8. "File 10/3 III Qatar Oil Concession," fol. 43r, image 99/470, British Library: India Office Records and Private Papers, IOR/R/15/2/412, in Qatar Digital Library, https://www.qdl.qa/archive/81055/vdc_100023550519.0x000064. "His Majesty's Government" refers to the British government, here and in other quotes.

9. Keating, *Mirage*, 462.

10. "File 10/3 II Qatar Oil Concession," fol. 52r, image 118/520, British Library: India Office Records and Private Papers, IOR/R/15/2/411, in Qatar Digital Library, https://www.qdl.qa/archive/81055/vdc_100023464530.0x000077.

11. Jill Crystal, *Oil and Politics in the Gulf: Rulers and Merchants in Kuwait and Qatar* (Cambridge: Cambridge University Press, 1990), 115.

12. Crystal, *Oil and Politics*, 115.

13. Rosemarie Said Zahlan, *The Creation of Qatar* (London: Croom Helm, 1979), 64.

14. "File 10/3 II Qatar Oil Concession," fol. 128r, image 270/520, https://www.qdl.qa/archive/81055/vdc_100023464531.0x000047.

15. "File 10/3 II Qatar Oil Concession," fol. 175r, image 364/520, https://www.qdl.qa/archive/81055/vdc_100023464531.0x0000a5.

16. "File 10/3 II Qatar Oil Concession," fol. 232r, image 480/520, https://www.qdl.qa/archive/81055/vdc_100023464532.0x000051.

17. "File 10/3 II Qatar Oil Concession," fol. 224r, image 464/520, https://www.qdl.qa/archive/81055/vdc_100023464532.0x000041.

18. "File 10/3 II Qatar Oil Concession," fol. 227r, image 470/520, https://www.qdl.qa/archive/81055/vdc_100023464532.0x000047.

19. "File 10/3 II Qatar Oil Concession," fol. 232r, image 480/520.

20. "File 10/3 III Qatar Oil Concession," fol. 66r, image 147/470, https://www.qdl.qa/archive/81055/vdc_100023550519.0x000094.

21. Zahlan, *Creation of Qatar*, 72.

22. "File 10/3 III Qatar Oil Concession," fol. 107r, image 230/470, https://www.qdl.qa/archive/81055/vdc_100023550520.0x00001f.

23. "File 10/3 III Qatar Oil Concession," fol. 90r, image 196/470, https://www.qdl.qa/archive/81055/vdc_100023550519.0x0000c5.

24. "File 10/3 III Qatar Oil Concession," fol. 102r, image 220/470, https://www.qdl.qa/archive/81055/vdc_100023550520.0x000015.

25. Richard Schofield, *Territorial Foundations of the Gulf States* (London: UCL Press, 1994), 17.

26. Schofield, *Territorial Foundations*, 17.

27. Schofield, *Territorial Foundations*, 18.

28. Schofield, *Territorial Foundations*, 53.

29. "File 10/3 III Qatar Oil Concession," fol. 134r, image 289/470, https://www.qdl.qa/archive/81055/vdc_100023550520.0x00005a.

30. "File 10/3 III Qatar Oil Concession," fol. 138r, image 297/470, https://www.qdl.qa/archive/81055/vdc_100023550520.0x000062.

31. Zahlan, *Creation of Qatar*, 82.

32. "File 82/27 III (F 84) APOC: Qatar Oil," fol. 227r, image 459/638, British Library: India Office Records and Private Papers, IOR/R/15/1/628, in Qatar Digital Library, https://www.qdl.qa/archive/81055/vdc_100023873573.0x00003c.

33. "File 82/27 III (F 84) APOC: Qatar Oil," fol. 252r, image 509/638, https://www.qdl.qa/archive/81055/vdc_100023873573.0x00006e.

34. "File 82/27 III (F 84) APOC: Qatar Oil," fol. 281r, image 569/638, https://www.qdl.qa/archive/81055/vdc_100023873573.0x0000aa.

35. "File 10/3 IV Qatar Oil Concession," fol. 218r, image 468/534, British Library: India Office Records and Private Papers, IOR/R/15/2/413, in Qatar Digital Library, https://www.qdl.qa/archive/81055/vdc_100023509763.0x000045.

36. "File 10/3 V Qatar Oil Concession," fol. 28r, image 70/527, British Library: India Office Records and Private Papers, IOR/R/15/2/414, in *Qatar Digital Library*, https://www.qdl.qa/archive/81055/vdc_100031220648.0x000047.

37.   "File 10/3 V Qatar Oil Concession," fol. 83r, image 180/527, https://www.qdl.qa/archive /81055/vdc_100031220648.0x0000b5.

38.   "File 10/3 V Qatar Oil Concession," fol. 83r, image 180/527.

39.   "File 10/3 V Qatar Oil Concession," fol. 174r, image 364/527, https://www.qdl.qa/archive /81055/vdc_100031220649.0x000025.

40.   "File 10/3 VI Qatar Oil Concession," fol. 11r, image 36/481, British Library: India Office Records and Private Papers, IOR/R/15/2/415, in Qatar Digital Library, https://www.qdl .qa/archive/81055/vdc_100023727831.0x000025.

41.   "File 10/3 V Qatar Oil Concession," fol. 240r, image 499/527, https://www.qdl.qa/archive /81055/vdc_100031220650.0x000064.

42.   "File 10/3 VI Qatar Oil Concession," fol. 125r, image 263/481, https://www.qdl.qa/archive /81055/vdc_100023727832.0x00003f.

43.   "File 10/3 VI Qatar Oil Concession," fol. 157r, image 327/481, https://www.qdl.qa/archive /81055/vdc_100023727832.0x00007f.

44.   "File 10/3 VI Qatar Oil Concession," fol. 178r, image 369/481, https://www.qdl.qa/archive /81055/vdc_100023727832.0x0000a9.

45.   "File 10/3 VI Qatar Oil Concession," fol. 219r, image 453/481, https://www.qdl.qa/archive /81055/vdc_100023727833.0x000035.

46.   "File 10/3 VII Qatar Oil Concession," fol. 29r, image 72/536, British Library: India Office Records and Private Papers, IOR/R/15/2/416, Qatar Digital Library, https://www.qdl.qa /archive/81055/vdc_100024084949.0x000049.

47.   "File 10/3 VII Qatar Oil Concession," fol. 69r, image 152/536, https://www.qdl.qa/archive /81055/vdc_100024084949.0x000099.

48.   "File 10/3 VII Qatar Oil Concession," fol. 101r, image 216/536, https://www.qdl.qa/archive /81055/vdc_100024084950.0x000011.

49.   "File 10/3 VII Qatar Oil Concession," fol. 177r, image 368/536, https://www.qdl.qa /archive/81055/vdc_100024084950.0x0000a9.

50.   "File 10/3 VII Qatar Oil Concession," fol. 230r, image 474/536, https://www.qdl.qa/archive /81055/vdc_100024084951.0x000049.

51.   "Coll 30/83 QATAR OIL CONCESSION, POLICY AND PROTECTION," fol. 13r, image 36/1018, British Library: India Office Records and Private Papers, IOR/L/PS/12 /3800, Qatar Digital Library, https://www.qdl.qa/archive/81055/vdc_100057526956 .0x000025.

52.   "File 10/3 VIII Qatar Oil Concession," fol. 26r, image 55/456, British Library: India Office Records and Private Papers, IOR/R/15/2/417, Qatar Digital Library, https://www.qdl.qa /archive/81055/vdc_100023947940.0x000038.

3. EUREKA!

1.   "File 82/27 VIII F 91 QATAR OIL," fol. 19r, image 46/468, British Library: India Office Records and Private Papers, IOR/R/15/1/633, Qatar Digital Library, https://www.qdl.qa /archive/81055/vdc_100023800656.0x000030.

2.   "File 82/27 VIII F 91 QATAR OIL," fol. 23r, image 54/468, https://www.qdl.qa/archive /81055/vdc_100023800656.0x000038.

3. "File 82/27 VIII F 91 QATAR OIL," fol. 23r, image 54/468.

4. "File 82/27 VIII F 91 QATAR OIL," fol. 172v, image 358/468, https://www.qdl.qa/archive/81055/vdc_100023800657.0x00009f.

5. "Memorandum and Articles of Association of Petroleum Development (Qatar) Limited," fol. 196r, image 51/80, British Library: India Office Records and Private Papers, IOR/R/15/1/749/3, Qatar Digital Library, https://www.qdl.qa/archive/81055/vdc_100035849170.0x0000c7.

6. "File 82/27 VIII F 91 QATAR OIL," fol. 174r, image 360/468, https://www.qdl.qa/archive/81055/vdc_100023800657.0x0000a2.

7. T. E. Williamson wrote: "A geological reconnaissance had already been made and a small area of [Jebel] Dukhan had been mapped in detail to aid in siting the first test well on that easily recognizable structure and it was now considered necessary to map the whole country. I was joined by R. Pomeyrol, a French geologist. N. E. Baker, the Chief Geologist, followed us soon after our arrival to fix the location of the first well." Quoted in Jacques LeBlanc, *A Historical Account of the Stratigraphy of Qatar, Middle East (1816 to 2015)*, December 1, 2015, https://sites.google.com/site/leblancjacques/fossilhome, p. 58.

8. "File 10/3 XI Qatar Oil Concession," fol. 83r, image 180/594, British Library: India Office Records and Private Papers, IOR/R/15/2/418, Qatar Digital Library, https://www.qdl.qa/archive/81055/vdc_100024164772.0x0000b5.

9. "File 10/3 XI Qatar Oil Concession," fol. 151r, image 316/594, https://www.qdl.qa/archive/81055/vdc_100024164773.0x000075.

10. "File 10/3 XI Qatar Oil Concession," fol. 185r, image 384/594, https://www.qdl.qa/archive/81055/vdc_100024164773.0x0000b9.

11. "File 10/3 XI Qatar Oil Concession," fol. 214r, image 442/594, https://www.qdl.qa/archive/81055/vdc_100024164774.0x00002b.

12. "File 10/3 XI Qatar Oil Concession," fol. 243r, image 500/594, https://www.qdl.qa/archive/81055/vdc_100024164774.0x000065.

13. "File 38/3 I, P. C. L. Qatar Concession," fol. 44r, image 92/484, British Library: India Office Records and Private Papers, IOR/R/15/2/864, Qatar Digital Library, https://www.qdl.qa/archive/81055/vdc_100025664363.0x00005d.

14. Michael Field, *The Merchants: The Big Business Families of Arabia* (London: John Murray, 1984), 251.

15. "File 38/3 I, P. C. L. Qatar Concession," fol. 44r, image 92/484.

16. Ministry of Power, Petroleum Division (POWE), "QATAR: Temporary Suspension of Operations. Agreement Between Ruler of Qatar & the Political Agent," November 26, 1943, file 33/459, National Archives, United Kingdom (NA-UK).

17. Jill Crystal, *Oil and Politics in the Gulf: Rulers and Merchants in Kuwait and Qatar* (Cambridge: Cambridge University Press, 1990), 117.

18. Crystal, *Oil and Politics*, 118.

19. Daniel Yergin, *The Prize: The Epic Quest for Oil, Money, and Power* (New York, Simon & Schuster, 1991), 398.

20. "File 38/3 I, P. C. L. Qatar Concession," 91r, image 186/484, https://www.qdl.qa/archive/81055/vdc_100025664363.0x0000bb.

21. POWE, "Qatar Development," June 13, 1946, file 33/459, NA-UK.

22. Stephen Hemsley Longrigg, *Oil in The Middle East: Its Discovery and Development*, Royal Institute of International Affairs (Oxford: Oxford University Press, 1954), 137-38.

23. POWE, "Qatar Development."

24. "File 38/3 I, P. C. L. Qatar Concession," fol. 205r, image 414/484, https://www.qdl.qa/archive/81055/vdc_100025664365.0x00000f.

25. POWE, Commonwealth Relations Office to Political Resident, telegram, February 28, 1948, file 33/459, NA-UK.

26. POWE, S. H. Longrigg (PCL) to Bernard Burrows (Foreign Office), letter, April 19, 1948, file 33/459, NA-UK.

27. Nasser Al-Othman, *With Their Bare Hands: The Story of the Oil Industry in Qatar* (Essex: Longman, 1984), 35.

28. "File 38/3 II P. C. L. Qatar Concession," fol. 109r, image 217/336, British Library: India Office Records and Private Papers, IOR/R/15/2/865, Qatar Digital Library, https://www.qdl.qa/archive/81055/vdc_100025667477.0x000012.

29. "File 4/13 IV Zubara," fol. 72r, image 148/412, British Library: India Office Records and Private Papers, IOR/R/15/2/205, Qatar Digital Library, https://www.qdl.qa/archive/81055/vdc_100025602521.0x000095.

30. Foreign Office (FO), the Political Resident, Sir Rupert Hay, to the Foreign Office, letter, December 30, 1948, ref. 371/75040, NA-UK.

31. FO, Hay to the Foreign Office, letter December 30, 1948.

32. FO, the Political Resident, Sir Rupert Hay, to the Foreign Office, letter, September 13, 1949, ref. 371/74944, NA-UK.

33. "File 38/3 II P. C. L. Qatar Concession," fol. 144r, image 287/336, https://www.qdl.qa/archive/81055/vdc_100025667477.0x000058.

34. "File 38/3 II P. C. L. Qatar Concession," fol. 144r, image 287/336.

35. "File 3/21 Political Officer, Qatar and Political Affairs, Qatar," fol. 30r, image 59/94, British Library: India Office Records and Private Papers, IOR/R/15/2/2000, Qatar Digital Library, https://www.qdl.qa/archive/81055/vdc_100026682295.0x00003c.

36. POWE, the Foreign Office to the Political Resident, memo, January 10, 1950, file 33/459, NA-UK.

37. POWE, "Administration Report of the British Agency, Doha from August to December, 1949 as Reported by Mr. A. J. Wilton, Political Officer, Qatar," file 33/459, NA-UK.

38. POWE, *Qatar: Extract from Summary of Events in Persian Gulf During Jan 1950*, file 33/459, NA-UK.

4. CHOPPY WATERS

1. "ECONOMIC DEVELOPMENTS IN SAUDI ARABIA," fol. 7r, image 13/24, British Library: India Office Records and Private Papers, IOR/R/15/2/483, Qatar Digital Library, https://www.qdl.qa/archive/81055/vdc_100025643231.0x00000e.

2. FO, *Superior Oil Company and Central Mining Investment Corporation Operations in Qatar, Abu Dhabi, Kuwait and Dubai*, 1950, ref. 371/82084, EA file 1273, papers 1-32, NA-UK.

3.   FO, *Superior Oil Company and Central Mining Investment Corporation.*

4.   FO, Foreign Office to Treasury, letter, January 19, 1950, ref. 371/82084, NA-UK.

5.   FO, *Arbitration Between the Sheikh of Qatar and Petroleum Development (Qatar) Ltd Regarding the Extent of the Oil Concession in the Agreement of 17 May 1935,* 1950, ref. 371/82082, NA-UK.

6.   FO, Petroleum Concessions Limited to Foreign Office, letter, April 13, 1950, ref. 371/82082, NA-UK.

7.   FO, Petroleum Concessions Limited to Foreign Office, letter, June 27, 1950, ref. 371/82082, NA-UK.

8.   FO, *Seabed Concessions (Qatar), January 10–May 18, 1951,* January 6, 1951, ref. 1016/50, NA-UK.

9.   FO, *Superior Oil Company and Central Mining Investment Corporation,* papers 54 to end.

10.   FO, *Superior Oil Company's Withdrawal from Oil Operations in the Persian Gulf,* 1952, ref. 371/98431, EA file 15311, NA-UK.

11.   FO, *Superior Oil Company's Withdrawal from Oil Operations in the Persian Gulf.*

12.   POWE, Foreign Office Memo, *Continental Shelf: Shell Company Interest, 1952–1958,* May 13, 1952, ref. 33/1976, NA-UK.

13.   POWE, Qatar-Shell memo to file, May 21, 1952; draft of letter from Foreign Office to Anglo-Iranian, NA-UK.

14.   Compagnie française des pétroles, the French oil company and IPC member, ended up joining Anglo-Iranian in the Abu Dhabi and Dubai seabed concessions.

15.   POWE, Foreign Office, memo, May 13, 1952.

16.   POWE, Sir Donald Fergusson (POWE) to Sir Francis Hopwood (Shell), letter, May 23, 1952, ref. 33/1976, NA-UK.

17.   POWE, Political Resident to Foreign Office, telegram, May 28, 1952, ref. 33/1976, NA-UK.

18.   POWE, Political Officer (Qatar), M. S. Weir, to Political Agent (Bahrain), letter, May 22, 1952, ref. 33/1976, NA-UK.

19.   POWE, Foreign Office to Shell Petroleum Company Limited, letter, September 2, 1952, ref. 33/1976, NA-UK.

20.   POWE, agreement between Sheikh Ali Bin Qasim El Thani, Ruler of Qatar, and George Ormsby Higgins on behalf of Shell Overseas Exploration Company, November 29, 1952, ref. 33/1976, NA-UK.

5. QATAR'S RULER PRESSES FOR BETTER OIL TERMS

1.   POWE, PCL, letter, February 8, 1951, *Persian Gulf, Qatar: Oil Concession Agreements, 1935–1952,* ref. 33/459, NA-UK.

2.   POWE, Foreign Office, memo, December 6, 1952, *Qatar: Oil Concessions, 1952–1961,* ref. 33/2094, NA-UK.

3.   POWE, Foreign Office, memo.

4.   POWE, PCL to the Ruler of Qatar, letter, June 1951, *Persian Gulf, Qatar: Oil Concession Agreement, 1935-1952,* NA-UK.

5. POWE, Foreign Office to Treasury, letter, January 1, 1952, *Persian Gulf, Qatar: oil concession agreement*, 1935–1952, NA-UK.

6. Jill Crystal, *Oil and Politics in the Gulf: Rulers and Merchants in Kuwait and Qatar* (Cambridge: Cambridge University Press, 1990), 123.

7. Stephen Hemsley Longrigg, *Oil in the Middle East: Its Discovery and Development, Royal Institute of International Affairs* (Oxford: Oxford University Press, 1954), 231.

8. Crystal, *Oil and Politics*, 143.

9. Crystal, *Oil and Politics*, 143.

10. FO, British Resident Sir Bernard Burrows to Foreign Office, letter, June 21, 1954, *Activities of the Oil Companies in the Oil-Bearing Persian Gulf States*, ref. 371/98420, EA file 1533, NA-UK.

11. POWE, Political Officer J. S. R. Duncan, Doha, memo, July 31, 1958, *Qatar: Oil Concessions, 1952–1961*, NA-UK.

12. POWE, Duncan, memo.

13. POWE, Political Resident Sir Bernard Burrows to the Foreign Office, letter, August 6, 1958, NA-UK.

14. "Underwater Oil Search, Shell Vessel for Persian Gulf," *Financial Times*, April 9, 1953.

15. FO, Political Office, Doha to Political Agency, Bahrain, letter, April 9, 1953, *Treasury Agreement to Raising of One Million Pounds of Capital in Shares by the Shell Company of Qatar*, ref. 371/104403, EA file 15313, NA-UK.

16. FO, Shell Overseas Exploration Company Limited to Treasury Chambers, letter, March 17, 1953, NA-UK.

17. *Glasgow Herald*, October 19, 1954.

18. POWE, Foreign Office to British Residency, letter, December 2, 1955, *Continental Shelf: Shell Company Interest*, 1952–1958, NA-UK.

19. POWE, F. B. Richards, British Residency to Foreign Office, letter, July 3, 1956, NA-UK.

20. POWE, British Resident Bahrain to Kuwait, extract of letter, September 11, 1956, NA-UK.

21. POWE, British Resident Bahrain to Kuwait.

22. POWE, R. P. R. McGlashan, Political Agency, Doha to Political Resident in the Persian Gulf, Bahrain, letter, December 30, 1956, NA-UK.

23. POWE, Sheikh Ahmed bin Ali from Shell Company of Qatar, letter, January 28, 1957, NA-UK.

24. "Search for Oil to Be Resumed Under Persian Gulf," *Manchester Herald*, June 21, 1957.

25. FO, Dubai Political Agent to Foreign Office, telegram, December 15, 1959, NA-UK.

26. FO, J. C. Moberly, Political Officer (Doha) to British Residency (Bahrain), letter, December 17, 1959, NA-UK.

27. Richard Schofield, *Territorial Foundations of the Gulf States* (London: UCL Press, 1994), 17.

28. FO, Political Agency, Doha, to Political Residency, Bahrain, letter, August 31, 1964, ref. 371/174662 Oil, NA-UK.

29. FO, Political Agency, Doha, to Political Residency, 52.

6. LABOR STRIKES, ANOTHER ABDICATION, AND AN INDUSTRIAL PROJECT

1. FO, agreement between QPC and Ruler of Qatar, August 17, 1955, Qatar Petroleum Company, 1955, ref. 1016/433, NA-UK.

2. Jill Crystal, *Oil and Politics in the Gulf: Rulers and Merchants in Kuwait and Qatar* (Cambridge: Cambridge University Press, 1990), 145.

3. FO, British Residency, Bahrain to Foreign Office, letter, August 15, 1955, Labour Situation in Qatar: Strike at Qatar Petroleum, 1955, ref. 371/114774, NA-UK.

4. Crystal, *Oil and Politics*, 145.

5. FO, extract from a minute prepared by QPC covering discussions held with the Ruler in Doha, October 13, 1953, Qatar Petroleum Company Ltd.: Relations with Ruler of Qatar, 1956, ref. 1016/524, NA-UK.

6. FO, extract from a minute prepared by QPC.

7. FO, the British Residency, Bahrain to Political Agency, Kuwait, letter, September 11, 1956, Qatar Petroleum Company Ltd: Relations with Ruler of Qatar, 1956, ref. 1016/525, NA-UK.

8. FO, Representative to the Ruler of Qatar from Qatar Petroleum Company Limited, letter, May 30, 1956, ref. 1016/525, NA-UK.

9. Michael Field, *The Merchants: The Big Business Families of Arabia* (London: John Murray, 1984), 260.

10. Crystal, *Oil and Politics*, 152.

11. Crystal, *Oil and Politics*, 151.

12. "Sheik Escapes Bullets: Attempt on Ruler of Qatar in Lebanese Resort Fails," *New York Times*, May 31, 1960.

13. Rosemarie Said Zahlan, *Creation of Qatar* (London: Croom Helm, 1979), 102.

14. FO, "A Report on the Dukhan Oil Field and the Possibility of Increasing Its Production Capacity," *Oil*, 1961, ref. 371/156988, NA-UK.

15. Qatar Section, *Middle East Economic Survey* (hereafter, *MEES*) 12, no. 11 (January 10, 1969).

16. "Secretary General Parra Outlines OPEC's Plans and Policies at Rome Energy Symposium," *MEES* 11, no. 19 (March 15, 1968).

17. "Joukhdar Outlines OPEC Views on Current Middle East Oil Issues," *MEES* 10, no. 27 (May 5, 1967).

18. FO, Political Agency, Doha to Political Resident, Bahrain, letter, June 12, 1961, Oil, 1961, ref. 371/156988, NA-UK.

19. FO, Political Agency, Doha to Foreign Office, letter, January 10, 1962, Oil, 1962, ref. 371/162998, NA-UK.

20. FO, Political Agency, Doha to Foreign Office, letter.

21. FO, D. I. Morphet of Foreign Office, minutes, September 24, 1964, ref. 371/174662, NA-UK.

22. "Qatar Could Net over One Dollar per Barrel Under New Japanese Agreement," *MEES* 12, no. 23 (April 4, 1969).

23. "Japan Group Wins Qatar Offshore Acreage," *MEES* 12, no. 22 (March 28, 1969).

24. "Qatar Could Net."

25. "Oil Developments in Qatar," *MEES* 13, no. 13 (January 23, 1970).

26. "Oil Developments in Qatar."

27. Foreign and Commonwealth Office (FCO), Political Agent, Doha, to Political Resident, Bahrain, letter, January 11, 1970, *Oil Affairs in Qatar*, 1970 Jan 1–1970 Dec 31, ref. 8/1478, NA-UK.

28. FCO, FCO to Political Agent, Doha, letter, June 22, 1970, ref. 8/1478, NA-UK.

29. FCO, Political Agency, Doha to Political Residency, Bahrain, letter, February 1, 1970, ref. 8/1478, NA-UK.

30. "New Award in Qatar," *Petroleum Press Service* 37, no. 5 (May 1970).

31. FCO, Shell Company of Qatar, "Press Release—Bul Hanine," June 6, 1970, in *Oil Affairs in Qatar*, 1970 Jan 1–1970 Dec 31, ref. 8/1478, NA-UK.

32. FCO, Political Agency, Doha to British Residency, Bahrain, letter, June 7, 1970, ref. 8/1478, NA-UK.

33. FCO, Oil Department to FCO's Arabian Department, memo, dated February 11, 1970, ref. 8/1478, NA-UK.

34. FCO, Arabian Department at Foreign and Commonwealth Office to Political Agency, Doha to dated, letter, July 13, 1970, ref. 8/1478, NA-UK.

35. FCO, British Embassy, Washington, D.C., and Oil Department at FCO, correspondence, July 29, 1970, ref. 8/1478, NA-UK.

36. FCO, Political Agency, Doha, to British Residency, Bahrain, letter, September 14, 1970, ref. 8/1478, NA-UK.

37. FO, Political Agency, Doha, to British Residency, Bahrain, letter, May 18, 1964, ref. 371-174662, NA-UK.

38. Crystal, *Oil and Politics*, 153.

39. Crystal, *Oil and Politics*, 155.

40. Daniel Yergin, *The Prize: The Epic Quest for Oil, Money, and Power* (New York: Simon & Schuster, 1991), 566.

41. The Gulf rupee, also known as the Persian Gulf rupee, was Qatar's official currency from 1959 to 1966. It was equivalent to the Indian rupee until June 6, 1966, when the Indian government devalued the Gulf rupee against the Indian rupee. After this devaluation, Qatar replaced the Gulf rupee with the Saudi riyal as an interim measure for several months until the QDR was issued on September 18, 1966. The Qatar and Dubai Currency Board was established to administer the QDR. Qatar and Dubai each appointed two directors to this board, while a fifth director was appointed by the Bank of England.

42. Department of State to the Consulate General in Dharan, telegram, February 20, 1970, no. 79, in *Foreign Relations of the United States, 1969–1976*, vol. 24, *Middle East Region and Arabian Peninsula, 1969–1972; Jordan, September 1970*, ed. by Linda W. Qaimmaqami, Adam M. Howard, and Edward C. Keefer (Washington, D.C.: U.S. Government Printing Office, 2008).

7. INDEPENDENCE, FIRST GAS LIQUIDS PROJECT, AND A BLOODLESS COUP

1. Jill Crystal, *Oil and Politics in the Gulf: Rulers and Merchants in Kuwait and Qatar* (Cambridge: Cambridge University Press, 1990), 155.

2.   Rosemarie Said Zahlan, *Creation of Qatar* (London: Croom Helm, 1979), 111.

3.   FCO, Department of Trade and Industry, Petroleum Division, "The Oil Industry in Qatar" (report), *Oil Affairs in Qatar*, 1973 Jan 1–1973 Dec 31, ref. 8/2086, NA-UK.

4.   FCO, British Agency, Doha to British Residency, Bahrain, letter, March 13, 1971, *Production of Oil in Qatar*, 1971 Jan 01–1971 Dec 31, ref. 67/615, NA-UK.

5.   FCO, "The Oil Industry in Qatar."

6.   "QPC Payments for 1971 Rise by 57 Percent," *MEES* 15, no. 40 (July 28, 1972).

7.   In 1970, QPC was owned 23.75 percent by BP, 23.75 percent by CFP, 23.75 percent by Shell, 11.875 percent by Mobil, 11.875 percent by Jersey Standard (Exxon) and 5 percent by Partex (Gulbenkian interests).

8.   FCO, FCO Oil Department, internal memo, July 1, 1970, ref. 8/1478, NA-UK.

9.   FCO, British Political Agency, Doha, to Oil Department at FCO, letter, July 13, 1970, ref. 8/1478, NA-UK.

10.   FCO, British Political Agency, Doha to FCO, telegram, October 25, 1970, ref. 8/1478, NA-UK.

11.   "QPC to Construct a £25-Million Gas Liquefaction Project," *MEES* 14, no. 19 (March 19, 1970).

12.   Plant condensate is one of the natural gas liquids along with ethane, propane, and butane. It consists mostly of pentanes and heavier hydrocarbons and is also referred to as natural gasoline. It is not the same as field or lease condensate, which is typically separated out of the natural gas stream at the point of production and is generally treated as a very light crude oil.

13.   "Shell Taking Over Plan for Qatar Gas Exports to Japan," *Petroleum Intelligence Weekly* 11, no. 40 (October 2, 1972).

14.   "Japanese Group Hits Oil with Second Well in Offshore Qatar," *MEES* 14, no. 51 (October 15, 1971).

15.   FCO, copy of Agreement for Area No. One (1) between the Government of Qatar and Belgian Oil Corporation, August 12, 1971, ref. 67/615, NA-UK.

16.   FCO, British Embassy, Doha, to FCO Oil Department, letter, March 22, 1972, Oil Affairs in Qatar, 1972 Jan 1–1972, ref. 67/798, NA-UK.

17.   "Qatar Awards Contract for 6,000-b/d Refinery," *MEES* 15, no. 14 (January 28, 1972).

18.   "Qatar Awards Contract."

19.   Zahlan, *Creation of Qatar*, 112.

20.   FCO, Edward Henderson, British Ambassador, Doha, to FCO Arabian Department, letter, February 21, 1972, Change of Government in Qatar: Coup of Sheikh Khalifa, 22 February 1972, 1972 Jan 1–1972 Dec 31, ref. 8/1891, NA-UK.

21.   Qatar Government English-language telex, February 22, 1972, Change of Government in Qatar: Coup ofSheikh Khalifa, 22 February 1972, 1972 Jan 1–1972 Dec 31, ref. 8/1891, NA-UK.

22.   FCO, British Embassy to FCO, telegram, February 28, 1972, Change of Government in Qatar: Coup of Sheikh Khalifa, 22 February 1972, 1972 Jan 1–1972 Dec 31, ref. 8/1891, NA-UK.

23.   FCO, British Embassy to FCO, telegram, February 28, 1972.

24.   FCO, British Embassy to FCO, telegram, February 22, 1972, ref. 8/1891NA-UK.

25. FCO, FCO response to Doha telegram number 71, February 23, 1972, ref. 8/1891, NA-UK.

26. FCO, British Embassy, Jeddah, to FCO, telegram, February 26, 1972, ref. 8/1891, NA-UK.

27. FCO, Edward Henderson, British Ambassador, Doha, to FCO, telegram, February 25, 1972, ref. 8/1891, NA-UK.

28. FCO, British Embassy, Doha, to UK Department of Trade & Industry, letter, February 29, 1972, ref. 8/1891, NA-UK.

29. Paul Martin, "Why Sheikh Khalifa Ousted His Cousin," *Times* [London], February 28, 1972.

30. Zahlan, *Creation of Qatar*, 116.

31. FCO, Edward Henderson, British Ambassador, Doha, to FCO Oil Department, letter, January 16, 1972, ref. 67/798, NA-UK.

32. Mohammed E. Ahrari, *OPEC: The Failing Giant* (Lexington: University Press of Kentucky, 1986), 103.

33. FCO, Henderson to FCO Oil Department, letter, January 16, 1972.

34. FCO, British Embassy, Doha, to FCO Oil Department, letter, April 28, 1972, ref. 67/798, NA-UK.

35. Ahrari, *Failing Giant*, 104.

36. "Qatar's Support for Saudi Position on Oil Negotiations," Kuwait, July 12, 1972, 17:00 GMT, in Arabic; English translation available in FCO, ref. 67/798, NA-UK.

37. Updated book value is a type of replacement cost basis without compensation for remaining oil reserves or loss of future profits. In this concept the book value of the net fixed assets is adjusted for past inflation in accordance with an index of oil plant and equipment in the Middle East. Updated book value was a hard-negotiated compromise between the desire of the Gulf states for historical net book value and the oil companies' stand for the net present worth of future earnings from recoverable reserves.

38. Ahrari, *Failing Giant*, 104.

39. Ahrari, *Failing Giant*, 104.

40. FCO, Henderson to FCO Oil Department, letter, January 16, 1972.

41. FCO, "The Oil Industry in Qatar."

42. Quoted in FCO, Abu Dhabi Marine Areas Ltd to British Embassy, Abu Dhabi, letter, November 20, 1972, ref. 67/798, NA-UK.

43. Mohammed Ali M. Al-Kubaisi, "Industrial Development in Qatar: A Geographical Assessment" (Ph.D. dissertation, Durham University, UK, 1984), 130. Based on data from the Ministry of Economy and Commerce, Ministry of Finance and Petroleum, and QGPC.

44. "Qatar: Q.P.C.'s Annual Review," *Middle East Economic Digest (MEED)* 14, no. 49 (December 4, 1970).

45. Al-Kubaisi, "Industrial Development in Qatar," 130.

46. Al-Kubaisi, "Industrial Development in Qatar," 130.

47. FCO, British Embassy to FCO Middle East Department, letter, July 3, 1973, ref. 8/2086, NA-UK.

48. FCO, British Embassy to FCO Middle East Department, letter.

49. FCO, British Embassy to FCO Middle East Department, letter.
50. Zuhair Ahmed Nafi, *Economic and Social Development in Qatar* (London: Frances Pinter, 1983), 68.
51. "QPC Payments for 1971."

8. THE EARLY KHALIFA YEARS

1. Shareholding in QPC after January 1, 1973 (the effective date of the first participation agreement), comprised Shell, BP, CFP, and Near East Development Co. (Exxon, Mobil) each 17.8125 percent; Partex 3.75 percent; and QNPC 25 percent. Shareholding in Shell Company of Qatar was Shell 75 percent and QNPC 25 percent.
2. FCO, British Embassy, Doha to FCO Middle East Department, January 16, 1973, ref. 8/2086, NA-UK.
3. FCO, British Embassy, Doha to FCO, telegram, July 2, 1973, ref. 8/2086, NA-UK; and "Price of Qatar Participation Crude Reported to be $3.15/Barrel," *MEES*, June 29, 1973.
4. Qatar section, *MEES*, October 26, 1973.
5. "Qatar Decrees 25 Percent Production Cut," *MEES*, November 9, 1973.
6. Ian Skeet, *OPEC: Twenty-Five Years of Prices and Politics* (Cambridge: Cambridge University Press, 1988), 100.
7. "Qatar Offering 68,000 b/d of Participation Crude," *MEES*, February 15, 1974.
8. Shareholding in QPC after January 1, 1974 (the effective date of the second participation agreement), comprised Shell, BP, CFP, and Near East Development Co. (Exxon, Mobil) each 9.5 percent; Partex 2 percent; and QNPC 60 percent. Shareholding in Shell Company of Qatar was Shell 40 percent and QNPC 60 percent.
9. FCO, British Embassy, Doha to FCO, telegram, February 20, 1974, Oil Affairs in Qatar, 1974 Jan 1-1974 Dec 31, ref. 8/2300, NA-UK.
10. FCO, copy of Agreement between the Government of Qatar and Qatar Petroleum Company Limited, February 20, 1974, ref. 8/2300, NA-UK; and FCO, FCO to British Embassy, Washington, letter, April 29, 1974, ref. 8/2300, NA-UK.
11. The 60 percent of Qatar government participation oil that the companies agreed to lift in the two-year period January 1, 1974, through December 31, 1975, comprised (1) For 10 percent of the buy-back oil (about 20,000 barrels per day), the full posted price, and (2) for the remainder (about 183,000 barrels per day), a price of $11.04 per barrel for Dukhan and $11.17 per barrel for Qatar Marine over the first six months (January 1-June 30, 1974) subject to renegotiation on June 30, 1974, and every three months thereafter during the two-year agreement. This worked out to an average price per barrel of 93 percent of postings for the first six months of 1974.
12. Qatar section, *MEES* 17, no. 26, April 19, 1974.
13. FCO, British Embassy, Doha, to FCO, telegram, April 8, 1974, ref. 8/2300, NA-UK.
14. FCO, British Embassy, Doha, to FCO Energy Department, letter, November 19, 1974, NA-UK.
15. FCO, British Embassy, Doha, to FCO Energy Department, letter.
16. FCO, English translation of statement by Minister of Finance and Petroleum Sheikh Abdul Aziz Ibn Khalifa Al Thani, December 22, 1974, ref. 8/2300, NA-UK.

17. FCO, David Crawford, British Ambassador, Doha, to FCO Energy Department, letter, December 17, 1974, ref. 8/2300, NA-UK.

18. U.S. Embassy, Manama, "Government of Qatar and Shell Sign Agreement Establishing Qatar Gas Company," Wikileaks Cable, dated September 9, 1974, https://wikileaks.org/plusd/cables/1974MANAMA00717_b.html.

19. "Ruler of Qatar Says Decision to Reduce Oil Production Is Not Related to Fall in World Demand," *MEES* 18, April 4, 1975.

20. "Qatar Concludes New Buy-Back Arrangements," *MEES* 19, no. 7 (December 5, 1975).

21. "Qatar Allocates $376 Million to Industry in 1976 Budget," *MEES* 19, February 27, 1976.

22. FCO, British Embassy, Doha, to FCO Energy Department, letter, January 7, 1975, Oil and Finance in Qatar, 1975 Jan 1–1975 Dec 31, ref. 8/2532, NA-UK.

23. Eric Pace, "Qatar Perturbed By Cutback in Oil," *New York Times*, March 4, 1975.

24. FCO, British Embassy, Doha, to FCO Middle East Department, letter, June 23, 1975, ref. 8/2532, NA-UK.

25. FCO, British Embassy, Doha, to FCO Middle East Department, letter.

26. FCO, British Embassy, Doha, to FCO Energy Department, letter, September 1, 1975, ref 8/2532, NA-UK.

27. FCO, British Embassy, Doha, to FCO Middle East Department, letter, October 20, 1975, ref. 8/2532, NA-UK.

28. FCO, British Embassy, Doha, to FCO Middle East Department, letter, March 25, 1975, ref. 8/2532, NA-UK.

29. FCO, British Embassy, Doha, to FCO Economists Department, letter, May 11, 1975, ref. 8/2532, NA-UK.

30. FCO, David Crawford, British Ambassador, Doha, to FCO, telegram, May 21, 1975, ref. 8/2532, NA-UK.

31. FCO, Department of Energy, "Oil Industry in Qatar" (report), June 1975, ref. 8/2532, NA-UK.

32. "Qatar and Shell Weigh Major LNG Venture from Big New Offshore Gasfield," *MEES* 19, no. 30 (May 17, 1976).

33. "Deep Gas Well Drilled to Assess Reserves," *MEED* 18, no. 20 (May 17, 1974).

34. FCO, David Crawford, British Ambassador, Doha, to FCO Energy Department, letter, January 20, 1975, ref. 8/2532, NA-UK.

35. "Qatar opts for 100% Takeover Combined with Management Contract," *MEES* 19, no. 3 (May 17, 1976).

36. "Qatar Demands Retroactivity for 100% Takeover to December 1974," *MEES* 19 (July 5, 1976).

37. "Qatar Demands Retroactivity."

38. "Qatar Takeover Negotiations Resumed; Gap on Financial Terms Still Wide," *MEES* 19, no. 44 (August 23, 1976).

39. "Qatar Takeover Deal Ready For Signature," *MEES* 19, no. 48 (September 20, 1976).

40. "Qatar Service Fee to Escalate in Line with Oil Prices," *MEES* 20 (October 25, 1976).

41. "Qatar Service Fee to Escalate."

42. "Qatar Takeover Agreement Signed," *MEES* 19, no. 48 (September 27, 1976).

43.   "Negotiations on Shell Takeover Continue; Disagreement Persists on Size of Service Fee,"
       MEES 20, no. 4 (November 15, 1976).

44.   "Shell Relinquishes 30 Percent Share of NGL Project In Qatar," declassified/released U.S.
       Department of State cable, October 19, 1976, National Archives, Washington, D.C.,
       https://aad.archives.gov/aad/createpdf?rid=311174&dt=2082&d1=1345.

45.   "Negotiations on Shell Takeover Continue."

46.   "Terms of Qatar-Shell Takeover Deal," *MEES* 20, February 21, 1977.

47.   "Terms of Qatar-Shell Takeover Deal," *MEES*.

48.   "Terms of Qatar-Shell Takeover Deal," *MEES*.

49.   International Monetary Foundation, *Survey*, August 15, 1977.

50.   "Gulfstream Reports Offshore Findings," *MEED* 20, no. 29 (July 16, 1976).

51.   "Qatar Raises $350 million on Euromarket," *MEES* 20 (May 1, 1977).

9. EXPLOSION DESTROYS QATAR'S FIRST NGL PLANT

1.   "Qatari Economy to Suffer From Loss of NGL Plant," declassified/released U.S. Depart-
       ment of State cable, April 9, 1977, National Archives and Records Administration
       (NARA), Washington, D.C., https://aad.archives.gov/aad/createpdf?rid=79849&dt=2532
       &dl=1629.

2.   "Qatar Development Expenditure to Rise by 44% in 1977 Budget," *MEES* 20 (April 17,
       1977).

3.   "Qatar's Liquidity Crisis," declassified/released U.S. Department of State cable, Octo-
       ber 5, 1977, NARA, Washington, D.C., https://aad.archives.gov/aad/createpdf?rid
       =230576&dt=2532&dl=1629.

4.   "Qatar Reassesses Spending—No New Projects in 1978," declassified/released U.S.
       Department of State cable, October 11, 1977, NARA, Washington, D.C., https://aad
       .archives.gov/aad/createpdf?rid=235175&dt=2532&dl=1629.

5.   "Special Report Series: Qatar," *MEED*, August 1981.

6.   "Update of Qatar Investment Climate," declassified/released U.S. Department of State
       cable, January 29, 1978, NARA, Washington, D.C., https://aad.archives.gov/aad/create
       pdf?rid=26001&dt=2694&dl=2009.

7.   "Tariff Imposed on Imported Steel," *MEED* 23, no. 9 (March 2, 1979).

8.   "QASCO Sets New Record," *MEED* 26, no. 2 (January 14, 1982).

9.   "U.S. Firm Negotiates for Construction of NGL Facility," declassified/released U.S.
       Department of State cable, September 16, 1977, NARA, Washington, D.C., https://aad
       .archives.gov/aad/createpdf?rid=214245&dt=2532&dl=1629.

10.   Jill Crystal, *Oil and Politics in the Gulf: Rulers and Merchants in Kuwait and Qatar* (Cambridge:
       Cambridge University Press, 1990), 157.

11.   "Saudi Crown Prince Fahd Remarks on Qatari Succession Question," declassified/
       released U.S. Department of State cable, April 17, 1977, NARA, Washington, D.C.,
       https://aad.archives.gov/aad/createpdf?rid=86402&dt=2532&dl=1629.

12.   "Visit of Qatari Foreign Minister and Party to the U.S," declassified/released U.S.
       Department of State cables, October 11, 1978, NARA, Washington, D.C., https://aad
       .archives.gov/aad/createpdf?rid=248435&dt=2694&dl=1629.

13. "Unfounded Reports of Coup D'Etat Attempt in Qatar," declassified/released U.S. Department of State cable, August 6, 1979, NARA, Washington, D.C., https://aad .archives.gov/aad/createpdf?rid=49611&dt=2776&dl=2169.

14. FCO, David Crawford, British Ambassador to FCO Middle East Department, letter, November 16, 1977, Oil Affairs in Qatar: Production Output and International Obligations, 1977 Jan 01–1977 Dec 31, ref. 8/3005, NA-UK.

15. "Reflections on Qatar's Ruling Family and Prospects for Future Stability," declassified/ released U.S. Department of State cable, February 12, 1979, NARA, Washington, D.C., https://aad.archives.gov/aad/createpdf?rid=87719&dt=2776&d1=2169.

16. FCO, "Qatar: Basic Facts," prepared for 4 January 1978 call on the Minister of State by HE Shaikh Abdul Aziz, ref. 8/3005, NA-UK.

17. "Sumitomo Buys 25,000 B/D of Qatar Crude," *MEES* 20 (June 20, 1977).

18. "U.S. Shell Buys 25,000 B/D of Dukhan Crude," *MEES* 21 (November 21, 1977).

19. "Qatar Crude Sales for 1978," *MEES* 21 (February 20, 1978).

20. "Strike of Qatari Members of Intermediate and Junior Staff at Qatar Petroleum Producing Authority Offshore Division," declassified/released U.S. Department of State cable, January 29, 1978, NARA, Washington, D.C., https://aad.archives.gov/aad/create pdf?rid=26004&dt=2694&dl=1629.

21. "Strike of Qatari Members of Intermediate and Junior Staff."

22. FCO, British Embassy, Doha, to FCO Middle East Department, letter, November 23, 1977, ref. 8/3005, NA-UK.

23. FCO, Ambassador Colin Brant, British Embassy, Doha, to FCO Middle East Department, letter, June 5, 1978, Oil Affairs in Qatar, 1978 Jan 1–1978 Dec 31, ref. 8/3225, NA-UK.

24. FCO, Ambassador Colin Brant, British Embassy, Doha, to FCO Middle East Department, letter, June 5, 1978.

25. FCO, "Qatar: Proposed Integration of Off and Onshore QPPA," note for the record, August 30, 1978, ref. 8/3225, NA-UK.

26. FCO, Colin Brant, British Ambassador, Doha, to FCO Energy, Science and Space Department, letter, September 7, 1978, ref. 8/3225, NA-UK.

27. "Trade Opportunity," declassified/released U.S. Department of State cable, April 29, 1979, NARA, Washington, D.C., https://aad.archives.gov/aad/createpdf?rid=7266&dt =2776&dl=2169.

28. "Holcar Oil Concession In Qatar," declassified/released U.S. Department of State cable, March 7, 1978, NARA, Washington, D.C., https://aad.archives.gov/aad/createpdf?rid =52625&dt=2694&dl=2009.

29. "Production Resumed from Bunduq Field After Three-Month Shutdown on Government Orders," *MEES* 21 (August 21, 1978).

30. "Production Resumed from Bunduq Field."

31. FCO, Colin Brant, British Ambassador, Doha, to FCO Middle East Department, letter, August 1, 1978, ref. 8/3225, NA-UK.

32. "Bul Hanine Output to Increase by 30,000 B/D," *MEES* 22, no. 8 (December 4, 1978).

33. "Qatar's Development Expenditure Up 15% in 1979 Budget," *MEES* 22, no. 11 (December 25, 1978).

34.   "Capital of QGPC Raised to $782 Million," *MEES* 22, no. 14 (January 22, 1979).

35.   FCO, British Embassy, Doha, to FCO Middle East Department, letter, November 23, 1977.

36.   FCO, British Embassy, Doha to FCO Middle East Department, letter, December 7, 1977, ref. 8/3005, NA-UK.

37.   FCO, Ambassador David Crawford, British Embassy, Doha to FCO Middle East Department, letter, December 7, 1977.

38.   U.S. Ambassador Andrew Killgore, "New On-Shore Gas Discovery in Qatar," declassified/released U.S. Department of State cable, March 21, 1978, NARA, Washington, D.C., https://aad.archives.gov/aad/createpdf?rid=67428&dt=2694&dl=2009.

39.   "Wintershall Draws Up Exploration Program for 1978," *MEED* 22, no. 4 (November 13, 1978).

40.   U.S. Ambassador Andrew Killgore, "Drilling Operations to Prove Out Size Of Qatar's Unassociated Gas Field," declassified/released U.S. Department of State cable, November 8, 1978, NARA, Washington, D.C., https://aad.archives.gov/aad/createpdf?rid=277375&dt=2694&dl=2009.

41.   FCO, British Embassy, Doha, to FCO Energy, Science and Space Department, letter, December 9, 1978, ref. 8/3225, NA-UK.

42.   "Qatar's Development of Offshore Gas Field Depends on Future Gas Prices," *MEES* 22, no. 32 (May 28, 1979).

43.   "Shell Joins Gas Field Study," *MEED* 23, no. 19 (May 11, 1979).

44.   "Production Resumed from Bul Hanine Field After 7-Week Shutdown," *MEES* 22, no. 31 (May 21, 1979).

45.   "Three Japanese Firms Sign Five-Year Contracts for 460,000 T/Year of Qatar LPG," *MEES* 23, no. 28 (April 21, 1980).

46.   U.S. Ambassador Andrew Killgore, "Amir of Qatar Reacts Favorably To President's Letter," declassified/released U.S. Department of State cable, June 24, 1979, NARA, Washington, D.C., https://aad.archives.gov/aad/createpdf?rid=174372&dt=2776&d1=2169.

47.   "New Government Sales Price," *MEES* 23, no. 9 (December 17, 1979).

48.   "Qatar Oil Production For November 1979," declassified/released U.S. Department of State cable, December 17, 1979, NARA, Washington, D.C., https://aad.archives.gov/aad/createpdf?rid=66805&dt=2776&d1=2169.

49.   U.S. Ambassador Andrew Killgore, "Unfounded Rumors That Qatar Minister of Foreign Affairs Will Become Prime Minister," declassified/released U.S. Department of State cable, September 6, 1979, NARA, Washington, D.C., https://aad.archives.gov/aad/createpdf?rid=321676&dt=2776&dl=2169.

50.   Killgore, "Unfounded Rumors."

51.   U.S. Ambassador Andrew Killgore, "Additional Reflections on Amir of Qatar and Al-Thani Family: More Money, Less Tranquility," declassified/released U.S. Department of State cable, November 7, 1979, NARA, Washington, D.C., https://aad.archives.gov/aad/createpdf?rid=243852&dt=2776&dl=2169.

52.   "The Earnings of Iraq, Iran, Kuwait, Libya, Qatar, Saudi Arabia and the UAE from Their Foreign Assets for the Period 1972–1979," *MEES* Special Report, May 1980.

53. U.S. Ambassador Andrew Killgore, "Qatar Arms Sales Request Received," declassified/ released U.S. Department of State cable, October 28, 1979, NARA, Washington, D.C., https://aad.archives.gov/aad/createpdf?rid=288972&dt=2776&dl=2169.

54. Killgore, "Qatar Arms Sales."

55. FCO, "Qatar: Annual Review for 1980," Diplomatic Report no. 37/81, January 8, 1981, *Qatar: gas,* 1981 Jan 01–1981 Dec 1981, ref. 96/1309, NA-UK.

56. "Special Report Series: Qatar."

57. "Special Report Series: Qatar."

58. Qatar Section, "In Brief," *MEED* 26, no. 13 (March 26, 1982).

10. CRUNCH TIME LOOMS FOR NORTH WEST DOME GAS FIELD

1. American Embassy, Doha, "North West Dome Non-Associated Offshore Gas Field," declassified/released U.S. Department of State cable, December 13, 1979, NARA, Washington, D.C., https://aad.archives.gov/aad/createpdf?rid=63381&dt=2776&dl%20=%20 2169.

2. In early 1978 Sheikh Khalifa asked David Rockefeller, the chairman of Chase Manhattan Bank, about the potential for Qatari-American ventures in the United States using LNG from the North West Dome. The amir discussed the possibility of establishing U.S. joint ventures owned 40 percent by Qatar using Qatar LNG to make fertilizers, plastics, and petrochemicals. Rockefeller and his team, who met with Sheikh Khalifa for an hour and a half on February 27, expressed polite interest but there was no follow up. See Ambassador Andrew Killgore, "Visit to Qatar of Chase Manhattan Chairman David Rockefeller," declassified/released U.S. Department of State cable, March 1, 1978, NARA, Washington, D.C., https://aad.archives.gov/aad/createpdf?rid=76754&dt =2694&dl=2009.

3. Killgore, "Visit to Qatar."

4. Ambassador Andrew Killgore, "Qatar Decision to Exploit Huge Natural Gas Reserves," declassified/released U.S. Department of State cable, December 18, 1979, NARA, Washington, D.C., https://aad.archives.gov/aad/createpdf?rid=68560&dt=2776&dl=2169.

5. "Major Gas Find Announced," *MEED* 24, no, 13 (March 21, 1980).

6. "West Germans Suggest LNG scheme," *MEED* 24, no. 36 (September 5, 1980).

7. "Qatar Has No Plans for Development of Northwest Dome," *MEES* 23, no. 28 (April 21, 1980).

8. FCO, "Qatar: Annual Review for 1980," Diplomatic Report no. 37/81, ref. 96/1309, NA-UK.

9. "Qatar Offers Foreign Partners in Dome Gas Project 20%," *Platts Oilgram News* 59, no. 7 (January 13, 1981).

10. FCO, British Embassy, Doha, to Department of Trade, letter, March 8, 1981, ref. 96/1309, NA-UK.

11. FCO, British Embassy, Doha, to Department of Trade, letter, March 8, 1981.

12. FCO, British Ambassador, Doha, to FCO, telegram, March 23, 1981, ref. 96/1309, NA-UK.

13. FCO, British Embassy, Washington, to Prime Minister's Private Secretary, letter, May 15, 1981, ref. 96/1309, NA-UK.

14. FCO, discussion between the Prime Minister and the Amir of Qatar, Sheikh Khalifa Bin Hamad Al Thani, Qatar, April 25, 1981, 1000 Hours, record, ref. 96/1309, NA-UK.

15. FCO, Department of Trade, Supplementary Briefing on the North-West Dome Gas-Field, April 10, 1981, ref. 96/1309, NA-UK.

16. The steering committee comprised Sheikh Rashid Awaidah Al Thani (the committee's chairman and QGPC's deputy managing director), Dr. Taher Al Hadidi (the committee's deputy chairman and senior petroleum expert at the Ministry of Finance and Petroleum), Dr. Mohamed Orabi (QGPC's manager for refining, gas processing, and petrochemicals), Dr. Helmi Samara (oil and gas adviser to the minister of finance and petroleum), Nasir Al Ali (deputy director of the Department of Petroleum Affairs), and Fouad Mahmoud (assistant director in the Office of the Minister of Finance and Petroleum).

17. "Ras Laffan Gets New Town," *MEED* 25, no. 32 (August 7, 1981).

18. FCO, British Embassy, Doha, "North Field" (file note), June 22, 1981, Qatar: Gas, 1981 Jan 1–Dec 31 1981, ref. 96/1310, NA-UK.

19. FCO, British Ambassador to FCO, telegram, June 15, 1981, ref. 96/1310, NA-UK.

20. Ambassador Colin Brant, FCO, British Embassy, Doha, to FCO Energy, Science and Space Department, letter, January 4, 1981, ref. 96/1309, NA-UK.

21. FCO, British Ambassador, Doha, "Shell and the Natural Gas Liquids Pipeline from the Offshore Fields to Umm Said," note to file, December 29, 1980, ref. 96/1309, NA-UK.

22. FCO, brief status report on the 24″, 12″, and 18″ Gas and Gas Liquids Lines, attached to letter from QGPC (Onshore Operations) to the British Ambassador, Doha, April 28, 1981, ref. 96/1309, NA-UK.

23. FCO, the Prime Minister's Private Secretary to Department of Energy, letter summarizing results of meeting between Shell and Prime Minister, June 12, 1981, ref. 96/1310, NA-UK.

24. FCO, QGPC (Onshore Operations) to British Ambassador, Doha, letter, April 29, 1981, ref. 96/1310, NA-UK.

25. FCO, British Ambassador, Doha, "Shell and the Natural Gas Liquids Pipeline."

26. FCO, Shell's Sir P. B. Baxendell to Prime Minister Margaret Thatcher, letter, May 7, 1981, ref. 96/1310, NA-UK.

27. FCO, Baxendell to Thatcher, letter.

28. FCO, Prime Minister Margaret Thatcher to Shell's Sir P. B. Baxendell, letter, May 13, 1981, ref. 96/1310, NA-UK.

29. FCO, British Ambassador, Doha, to FCO Energy, Science and Space Department, letter, June 2, 1981, ref. 96/1309, NA-UK.

30. FCO, FCO to FCO Middle East Department, letter, May 18, 1981, ref. 96/1309, NA-UK.

31. "Qatar Plans 150,000 B/D Export Refinery," *MEES* 23, no. 33 (May 26, 1980).

32. "Capital of QGPC Raised to \$1,099 Million," *MEES* 23, no. 39 (July 7, 1980).

33. "QGPC to Renegotiate Service Contracts," *MEES* 24 (May 18, 1981).

34. FCO, British Ambassador, Doha, to Department of Trade, letter, December 15, 1981, ref. 96/1310, NA-UK.

35.　FCO, Department of Trade, "Qatar: North Field Gas Project: Shell," note for the record, October 19, 1981, ref. 96/1310, NA-UK.

36.　FCO, Stephen Day, British Ambassador, Doha, to Department of Trade, letter, October 24, 1981, ref. 96/1310, NA-UK.

37.　"Qatar's Crude Oil Production Down by 14.4% in 1981," *MEES* 25 (February 8, 1982).

38.　"Rising Oil Price Boosts State Revenue" *MEED* 25, no. 34 (August 21, 1981).

39.　FCO, British Ambassador, Doha, "North Field," file note, April 28, 1982, *Qatar: Gas*, 1982 Jan 1–1982 Dec 31, ref. 96/1651, NA-UK.

40.　FCO, British Embassy, Doha, to Department of Trade, letter, June 15, 1981, ref. 96/1310, NA-UK.

41.　"Cost Estimate of Qatar's LNG Project Rises to $5–6 Billion," *MEES* 24 (September 14, 1981).

42.　FCO, British Embassy, Doha, "North Field," file note, June 22, 1981.

43.　"Japanese Interested in LNG Scheme," *MEED* 25, no. 30 (July 24, 1981).

44.　FCO, copy of notification sent to bidders by the Chairman, Executive Committee for the Development of the North Field, July 1981, ref. 96/1310, NA-UK.

45.　"Special Report Series: Qatar," *MEED*, August 1981.

46.　FCO, British Ambassador, Doha, to British Petroleum, London, letter, April 12, 1981, ref. 96/1309, NA-UK.

47.　FCO, "Leading Personalities Report: Qatar 1985," *Leading Personalities in Qatar*, 1985 Jan 1–1985 Dec 31, ref. 8/5960, NA-UK.

48.　FCO, British Ambassador, Doha, to FCO, telegram, June 15, 1981, ref. 96/1309, NA-UK.

49.　FCO, British Ambassador, Doha, "North Field and the Germans," file note, October 5, 1981, ref. 96/1310, NA-UK.

50.　FCO, British Ambassador, Doha, "Qatar: North Field Gas Project," note for the record, December 5, 1981, ref. 96/1310, NA-UK.

51.　FCO, Department of Trade, "Qatar: North Field Gas Project: Shell."

52.　FCO, Stephen Day, British Ambassador, Doha, "Qatar: North Field Gas Project: Shell," note for the file, November 5, 1981, ref. 96/1310, NA-UK.

53.　FCO, Stephen Day, British Ambassador, Doha, to FCO, telegram, November 17, 1981, Ref. 96/1310, NA-UK.

54.　Paul Lewis, "A Soviet Project Tempts Europe," *New York Times*, May 30, 1982.

55.　"Special Report: Japan & the Middle East," *MEED* 25, no. 5 (December 17, 1981).

56.　FCO, notes of interdepartmental meeting held on January 19, 1982, to discuss North Field development project, Qatar, January 28, 1982, Qatar: Natural Gas; North Field Development Project and Royal Dutch Shell Dispute with Qatar, 1982 Jan 1–1982 Dec 31, ref. 8/4690, NA-UK.

57.　FCO, notes of interdepartmental meeting held on January 19, 1982.

58.　FCO, British Ambassador, Doha, to FCO, telegram, December 1, 1981, ref. 96/1310, NA-UK.

59.　FCO, Department of Trade, interdepartmental letter, January 14, 1982, ref. 8/4690, NA-UK.

60.　FCO, notes of interdepartmental meeting held on January 19, 1982.

61. FCO, British Ambassador, Doha, to Department of Trade, letter, February 10, 1982, ref. 8/4690, NA-UK.

62. FCO, FCO Energy, Science and Space Department, meeting between Sir J. Leahy and senior Shell officials, record, December 16, 1982, ref. 8/4690, NA-UK.

63. FCO, British Ambassador, Doha, to FCO Energy, Science and Space Department, letter, June 2, 1981.

64. FCO, internal FCO memo, December 31, 1982, ref. 8/4690, NA-UK.

65. "Shell Agrees to Replace Gas Pipeline," *MEED* 26, no. 34 (August 20, 1982).

66. FCO, Stephen Day, British Ambassador, Doha, "Shell in Qatar," note for the file, December 17, 1981, ref. 96/1310, NA-UK.

67. "Qatar: A MEED Special Report," *MEED* 26, no. 35 (August 27, 1982).

68. MEED, *Qatar: A MEED Practical Guide* (London: MEED, 1983), 105.

69. MEED, *Qatar: A MEED Practical Guide*, 105.

70. MEED, *Qatar: A MEED Practical Guide*, 102.

71. MEED, *Qatar: A MEED Practical Guide*, 102.

72. "Qatar: A MEED Special Report."

73. "Qatar: A MEED Special Report."

74. "Qatar: A MEED Special Report."

75. FCO, Stephen Day, British Ambassador, Doha, to FCO, letter August 24, 1982, ref. 8/4690, NA-UK.

76. FCO, Day, British Ambassador, Doha, to FCO, letter August 24.

77. "New Gas Discovery in Qatar," *MEES* 25, (August 30, 1982).

78. "Qatar North Dome Talks After Ramadan," *World Gas Report* 3, no. 14 (July 19, 1982).

79. FCO, Stephen Day, British Ambassador, Doha, to FCO, telegram, November 25, 1982, ref. 8/4690, NA-UK.

80. "Exxon Joins North Field Talks," *World Gas Report* 26, no. 13 (March 26, 1982).

81. "Qatar North Dome Talks."

82. "Qatar North Dome Talks."

83. FCO, British Embassy, Doha, to FCO Middle East Department, letter, August 22, 1982, ref. 8/4690, NA-UK.

84. Jill Crystal, *Oil and Politics in the Gulf: Rulers and Merchants in Kuwait and Qatar* (Cambridge: Cambridge University Press, 1990), 160.

85. FCO, "Country Assessment Paper: Qatar," December 1982, *Qatar: Gas,* 1982 Jan 1–1982 Dec 31, ref. 8/4690, NA-UK.

86. FCO, "Country Assessment Paper: Qatar," December 1982.

87. FCO, Day, British Ambassador, Doha, to FCO, telegram, November 25, 1982.

88. FCO, Day, British Ambassador, Doha, to FCO, telegram, November 25, 1982.

89. FCO, British Embassy, Doha, to Department of Trade, letter, November 11, 1982, ref. 96/1651, NA-UK.

90. "Onshore Gas Option Proves Not Feasible," *MEED* 26, no. 42 (October 15, 1982).

91. FCO, British Embassy, Doha, to Department of Trade, letter, November 11, 1982.

92. FCO, Day, British Ambassador, Doha, to FCO, telegram, November 25, 1982.

93. FCO, Day, British Ambassador, Doha, to FCO, telegram, November 25, 1982.

94. FCO, British Embassy, Doha to FCO, letter, November 5, 1982, ref. 96/1651, NA-UK.

95. FCO, British Embassy, Doha, to FCO, letter, November 5, 1982.
96. FCO, British Embassy, Doha, to FCO, letter, November 5, 1982.
97. FCO, British Embassy, Doha, to FCO, letter, November 5, 1982.
98. FCO, British Ambassador, Doha, to FCO, telegram, December 9, 1982, ref. 8/4690, NA-UK.
99. FCO, British Ambassador, Doha to FCO, telegram, December 9, 1982.
100. FCO, British Ambassador, Doha to FCO, telegram, December 9, 1982.
101. FCO, British Ambassador, Doha, "Qatari Claims Against Shell," note, December 22, 1982, ref. 8/4690, NA-UK.
102. FCO, British Ambassador, Doha, "Qatari Claims Against Shell."
103. "Qatar Pursues Local Court Suit Against Shell, While Arbitration Goes on in Paris," *Platts Oilgram News* 62, no. 105 (May 31, 1984).
104. FCO, Stephen Day, British Ambassador, Doha, to FCO, telegram, December 9, 1982.
105. FCO, Day, British Ambassador, Doha, to FCO, telegram, December 9, 1982.
106. FCO, British Ambassador, Doha, "Qatari Claims Against Shell,"
107. FCO, FCO Energy, Science and Space Department, internal memo, December 13, 1982, ref. 8/4690, NA-UK.
108. FCO, FCO to British Embassy, Doha, telegram no. 136, December 17, 1982, ref. 8/4690, NA-UK.
109. FCO, FCO to British Embassy, Doha, telegram no. 136, December 17, 1982.
110. FCO, FCO to British Embassy, Doha, telegram no. 137, December 17, 1982, ref. 8/4690, NA-UK.
111. FCO, FCO to British Embassy, Doha, telegram no. 137, December 17, 1982.
112. FCO, FCO to British Embassy, Doha, telegram no. 137, December 17, 1982.
113. FCO, British Ambassador, Doha, to FCO, telegram, December 19, 1982, ref. 8/4690, NA-UK.
114. FCO, British Ambassador, Doha, to FCO, telegram, December 19, 1982.
115. FCO, British Ambassador, Doha, "Qatari Claims Against Shell,"
116. FCO, British Ambassador, Doha, "Qatari Claims Against Shell,"
117. FCO, British Ambassador, Doha, "Qatari Claims Against Shell,"
118. FCO, British Ambassador, Doha, to FCO Energy, Science and Space Department, telegram, January 17, 1983, *Qatar: Natural Gas; North Field Development Project and Royal Dutch Shell Dispute with Qatar*, 1983 Jan 1–1983 Dec 31, ref. 8/5229, NA-UK.
119. FCO, British Ambassador, Doha, "Qatari Claims Against Shell."
120. FCO, FCO Energy, Science and Space Department, "BP Services Agreement in Qatar," note, June 4, 1982, ref. 96/1651, NA-UK.
121. FCO, British Embassy, Doha, to FCO Energy, Science and Space and Middle East Departments, telegram, July 16, 1982, ref. 96/1651, NA-UK.
122. FCO, BP to QGPC, letter (copy), June 23, 1982, ref. 96/1651, NA-UK.
123. FCO, British Embassy, Doha, to Department of Trade, letter, July 6, 1982, ref. 96/1651, NA-UK.
124. FCO, British Embassy, Doha to Department of Trade, letter, July 6, 1982.
125. FCO, British Embassy, Doha to Department of Trade, letter, November 11, 1982.
126. FCO, "Country Assessment Paper: Qatar," December 1982.

127.   FCO, British Embassy, Doha, to FCO, telegram, January 26, 1981, ref. 8/5229, NA-UK.

128.   FCO, British Ambassador, Doha, to FCO, letter, February 9, 1983, ref. 8/5229, NA-UK.

129.   FCO, British Ambassador, Doha to FCO, telegram, January 26, 1983, ref. 8/5229, NA-UK.

130.   Robert D. McFadden, "Major Damage Feared in Persian Gulf Oil Spill," *New York Times*, April 3, 1983.

131.   "Qatar: Capital Spending Curbs Put Contractors at Risk," *MEED* 27, no. 32 (August 12, 1983).

132.   "Qatar Cuts Down," *MEED* 27, no. 45 (November 11, 1983).

133.   "Qatar Raises Prices of Oil Products on Local Market," *MEES* 26, no. 31 (May 16, 1983).

134.   Qatar Section "In Brief," *MEES* 28, no. 41 (October 12, 1984).

135.   "Qatar Cuts Down."

136.   Crystal, *Oil and Politics*, 157.

137.   FCO, "Report on a Security Visit to the British Embassy at Doha by FCO Security Department," February 1984, British Embassy in Qatar, 1984 Jan 1–1984 Dec 31, ref. 8/5641, NA-UK.

138.   "Payments Made in Oil for Desalination Project," *Straits Times* (Singapore), June 15, 1983.

139.   "Qatari Local Firm Accepts Crude Oil in Payment for $56mn Construction Contract," *MEES* 27, no. 5 (November 14, 1983).

140.   "Qatari Local Firm Accepts Crude Oil."

141.   "Qatar Inaugurates New 50,000 b/d Refinery," *MEES* 27, no. 20 (February 27, 1984).

142.   *Khaleej Times* (Dubai), February 23, 1984.

143.   "Brazil Lines Up Mideast Crude," *Platts Oilgram News* 61, no. 163 (August 23, 1983).

11. PARTNERS SELECTED FOR MAJOR NORTH FIELD GAS PROJECT

1.   FCO, Stephen Day, British Ambassador, Doha, to FCO, telegram, December 5, 1982, ref. 8/4690, NA-UK.

2.   FCO, Day to FCO, telegram, December 5, 1982.

3.   FCO, Stephen Day, British Ambassador, Doha, to FCO, telegram, December 19, 1982, ref. 8/4690, NA-UK.

4.   FCO, Stephen Day, British Ambassador, Doha, to FCO, telegram, February 7, 1982, ref. 8/5229, NA-UK.

5.   "Qatar Selects BP and CFP as Partners for Huge Gas Venture," *MEES* 26, no. 20 (February 28, 1983).

6.   FCO, Stephen Day, British Ambassador, Doha, "BGC Interest in Qatar Gas," file note, March 22, 1983, ref. 8/5229, NA-UK.

7.   FCO, British Embassy, Doha, to Department of Trade, letter, August 22, 1983, ref. 8/5229, NA-UK.

8.   FCO, Stephen Day, British Ambassador, Doha, to Department of Trade, telegram, August 30, 1983, ref. 8/5229, NA-UK.

9.   FCO, Stephen Day, British Ambassador, Doha, to FCO, telegram, January 25, 1983, ref. 8/5229, NA-UK.

10. FCO, Stephen Day, British Ambassador, Doha, to FCO Middle East Department, teleletter, January 26, 1983, ref. 8/5229, NA-UK.

11. FCO, Day to FCO Middle East Department, teleletter, January 26, 1983.

12. FCO, Day to FCO Middle East Department, teleletter, January 26, 1983.

13. FCO, Day to FCO Middle East Department, teleletter, January 26, 1983.

14. FCO, Day to FCO Middle East Department, teleletter, January 26, 1983.

15. FCO, Stephen Day, British Ambassador, Doha, meeting between Ambassador at Doha and Shaikh Khalifah Bin Hamad Al Thani, Amir of Qatar, February 6, 1983, record, February 9, 1983, ref. 8/5229, NA-UK.

16. FCO, meeting between Ambassador at Doha and Shaikh Khalifah Bin Hamad Al Thani, Amir of Qatar, record, February 9, 1983.

17. FCO, Stephen Day, British Ambassador, Doha, to FCO, teleletter, May 19, 1983, ref. 8/5229, NA-UK.

18. FCO, British Embassy, Doha, to FCO Energy, Science and Space Department, letter, June 6, 1983, ref. 8/5229, NA-UK.

19. FCO, British Embassy, Doha, to FCO Energy, Science and Space Department, letter, June 6, 1983.

20. FCO, British Embassy, Doha, to FCO Energy, Science and Space Department, letter, June 6, 1983.

21. FCO, British Embassy, Doha, to FCO Energy, Science and Space Department and FCO Middle East Department, teleletter, July 18, 1983, ref. 8/5229, NA-UK.

22. FCO, British Embassy, Doha, to FCO Energy, Science and Space Department, letter, October 25, 1983, Qatar: Natural Gas; North Field Development Project and Royal Dutch Shell Dispute with Qatar, 1983 Jan 1–1983 Dec 31, ref. 8/5230, NA-UK.

23. FCO, Stephen Day, British Ambassador, Doha, to FCO, teleletter, October 4, 1983, ref. 8/5229, NA-UK.

24. FCO, Stephen Day, British Ambassador, Doha, to FCO, telegram, October 8, 1983, ref. 8/5229, NA-UK.

25. FCO, Day to FCO, telegram, October 8, 1983.

26. FCO, Stephen Day, FCO to British Ambassador, Doha, teleletter, November 3, 1983, ref. 8/5229, NA-UK.

27. FCO, British Embassy, Doha, to FCO Energy, Science and Space Department, letter, December 11, 1983, ref. 8/5230, NA-UK.

28. FCO, Stephen Day, British Ambassador, Doha, "Shell Dispute: Hearing in the Qatar 'Justice' Courts on 27 November 1983," note for the file, December 11, 1983, ref. 8/5230, NA-UK.

29. FCO, Stephen Day, British Ambassador, Doha, to FCO Energy, Science and Space Department, teleletter, December 12, 1983, ref. 8/5230, NA-UK.

30. FCO, Day to FCO Energy, Science and Space Department, teleletter, December 12, 1983.

31. FCO, Stephen Day, British Ambassador, Doha, to FCO, telegram, October 4, 1983, ref. 8/5230, NA-UK.

32. FCO, Day to FCO, telegram, October 4, 1983.

33.   FCO, Stephen Day, British Ambassador, Doha, to FCO Energy, Science and Space Department, Department of Trade, and British Embassy, Tokyo, teleletter, December 12, 1983, ref. 8/5230, NA-UK.

34.   FCO, Stephen Day, British Ambassador, Doha, to FCO Middle East Department, teleletter, February 27, 1984, Qatar: Gas, 1984 Jan 1–1984 Dec 31, ref. 8/5639, NA-UK.

35.   "Jaidah Estimates Qatar's Proved Gas Reserves at 150 TCF with Probable Rated at 300 TCF," *MEES* 27, no. 20 (February 27, 1984).

36.   "Results of QGPC's Deep Test Well Prove Southeastern Extension of North Gas Field," *MEES* 27, no. 39 (July 9, 1984).

37.   "Results of QGPC's Deep Test Well."

38.   FCO, Stephen Day, British Ambassador, Doha, to FCO, Department of Energy and Department of Trade, letter, March 27, 1984, ref. 8/5639, NA-UK.

39.   "Proved Gas Reserves at 150 TCF."

40.   "Proved Gas Reserves at 150 TCF."

41.   "CDF-Chimie Awarded $55mn Contract for QAPCO's Ethane Recovery Plant," *MEES* 27, no. 21 (March 5, 1984).

42.   FCO, background note to claim by Qatar General Petroleum Corporation against Shell internationale petroleum maatschappij [SIPM], in respect of the NGL/1 Gas Liquids Plant, March 20, 1984, ref. 8/5639, NA-UK.

43.   FCO, Stephen Day, British Ambassador, Doha, to FCO, teleletter, February 13, 1984, ref. 8/5639, NA-UK.

44.   FCO, Day to FCO, teleletter, February 13, 1984.

45.   FCO, Stephen Day, British Ambassador, Doha, "Shell Dispute: 'Projectile Theory,'" note for the file, February 14, 1984, ref. 8/5639, NA-UK.

46.   FCO, "Shell Dispute: 'Projectile Theory,'" note for the file.

47.   FCO, background note to claim by Qatar General Petroleum Corporation against SIPM.

48.   FCO, Day to FCO, teleletter, February 13, 1984.

49.   FCO, background note to claim by Qatar General Petroleum Corporation against SIPM.

50.   FCO, Day to FCO Middle East Department, teleletter, February 27, 1984.

51.   FCO, Day to FCO Middle East Department, teleletter, February 27, 1984.

52.   FCO, Day to FCO, teleletter, February 13, 1984.

53.   FCO, Julian Walker, British Ambassador, Doha, from FCO Middle East Department, letter, January 24, 1985, Qatar: Annual Review for 1984: First Impressions Dispatch by Julian Walker, HM Ambassador, Doha, 1985 Jan 1–1985 Dec 31, ref. 8/5962, NA-UK.

54.   FCO, Walker from FCO Middle East Department, letter, January 24, 1985.

55.   FCO, FCO Middle East Department to British Ambassador, Doha, teleletter, March 25, 1985, ref. 8/5960, NA-UK.

56.   FCO, FCO Middle East Department to British Ambassador, Doha, teleletter, March 25, 1985.

57.   FCO, Day to FCO, Department of Energy and Department of Trade, letter, March 27, 1984.

58.   FCO, Day to FCO, Department of Energy and Department of Trade, letter, March 27, 1984.

59.   "Qatar Output Rises in Wake of Gulf Crisis," *MEES* 27, no. 36 (June 18, 1984).

60. "Qapco Reduces Losses," *MEED* 28, no. 26 (June 29, 1984).

61. "Qatar Boosts Crude Output in November," *MEES* 27, no. 5 (November 14, 1983).

62. "Qatar Cuts Production to 280,000 b/d," *MEES* 28, no. 6 (November 19, 1984).

63. FCO, Julian Walker, British Ambassador, Doha, to FCO Middle East Department, letter, November 7, 1984, ref. 8/5639, NA-UK.

64. FCO, Julian Walker, British Ambassador, Doha, to FCO Middle East Department, letter, December 12, 1984, ref. 8/5639, NA-UK.

65. "Qatar's NGL Production Increases by 18% in 1984," *MEES* 28, no. 33 (May 27, 1985).

66. "1984 Petrochemical Output in Qatar," *MEES* 28, no. 30 (February 25, 1985).

67. "Qatar Initials Agreement with BP and CFP-Total for North Gas Field," *MEES* 27, no. 25 (April 2, 1984).

68. FCO, Stephen Day, British Ambassador, Doha, to FCO, teleletter, April 10, 1984, ref. 8/5639, NA-UK.

69. FCO, Day to FCO, teleletter, April 10, 1984.

70. FCO, Day to FCO, teleletter, April 10, 1984.

71. FCO, Day to FCO, teleletter, April 10, 1984.

72. FCO, Day to FCO, teleletter, April 10, 1984.

73. FCO, Day to FCO, teleletter, April 10, 1984.

74. FCO, Stephen Day, British Ambassador, Doha, to FCO Middle East Department, Department of Trade and commercials departments at the British Embassies in Tokyo and Seoul, letter, May 12, 1984, ref. 8/5639, NA-UK.

75. FCO, Stephen Day, British Ambassador, Doha, to FCO Middle East Department, letter, May 5, 1984, ref. 8/5639, NA-UK.

76. "Qatar Signs Agreements with BP and CFP for Development of North Gas Field," *MEES* 27, no. 38 (July 2, 1984).

77. "Qatar Signs Agreements with BP and CFP."

78. "Cashing in on Qatar Gas," *MEED* 29, no. 16 (April 19, 1985).

79. FCO, Stephen Day, British Ambassador, Doha, "North Field Development," note for the file, July 15, 1984, ref. 8/5639, NA-UK.

80. FCO, British Ambassador, Doha, "North Field Development."

81. FCO, British Ambassador, Doha, "North Field Development."

82. FCO, British Ambassador, Doha, "North Field Development."

83. FCO, British Ambassador, Doha, "North Field Development."

84. FCO, British Ambassador, Doha, "North Field Development."

85. FCO, FCO Middle East Department to British Ambassador Julian Walker, Doha, letter, May 3, 1985, ref. 8/5960, NA-UK.

86. FCO, FCO Middle East Department to Walker, letter, May 3, 1985.

87. "BP Signs Fuel Oil Supply Contract with Qatar," *MEES* 27, no. 42 (July 30, 1984).

88. "BP Signs Fuel Oil Supply Contract."

89. FCO, British Embassy, Doha, to FCO Middle East Department, letter, November 17, 1984, ref. 8/5639, NA-UK.

90. FCO, British Embassy, Doha, to FCO Middle East Department, letter, November 17, 1984.

91. FCO, Walker from FCO Middle East Department, letter, January 24, 1985.

92.   FCO, Julian Walker, British Ambassador, Doha, to FCO Export Credit Guarantee Department, telegram, November 18, 1984, ref. 8/5639, NA-UK.

93.   FCO, Walker to FCO Export Credit Guarantee Department, telegram, November 18, 1984.

94.   "Bechtel Gets Initial Qatar Gas Pact," *Platts Oilgram News* 63, no. 152 (August 8, 1985).

95.   "QAFCO to Construct Third Ammonia Plant," *MEES* 29, no. 13 (January 6, 1986).

96.   "QAPCO's $55mn Ethane Recovery Unit Commissioned," *MEES* 29, no. 21 (March 3, 1986).

97.   FCO, Julian Walker, British Ambassador, Doha, to FCO Middle East Department, teleletter, November 28, 1984, ref. 8/5630, NA-UK.

98.   FCO, British Embassy, Doha, to FCO Middle East Department, letter, November 21, 1984, ref. 8/5630, NA-UK.

99.   FCO, Walker to FCO Middle East Department, teleletter, November 28, 1984.

100. FCO, British Embassy, Doha, to FCO Middle East Department, letter, November 21, 1984.

101. "Japan's Marubeni Officially Joins Qatar LNG Project, Commits for Purchase," *Platts Oilgram News* 62, no. 172 (September 6, 1985).

102. "Qatargas to Open London Office; Mission to Far East Planned," *Platts Oilgram News* 63, no. 221 (November 15, 1985).

103. "Gulf States Must Agree on Price for Gas Before Engineering Work Can Begin on Projected Gas Grid," *MEES* 28, no. 5 (November 12, 1984).

104. FCO, British Embassy, Bahrain, to British Ambassador, Doha, teleletter, October 25, 1983, ref. 8/5229, NA-UK.

105. "Rome Gas Conference Hears of Qatar's Export Plans," *Platts Oilgram News* 62, no. 212 (November 1, 1984).

106. FCO, British Embassy, Doha, to British Embassy, Muscat, letter, September 16, 1984, ref. 8/5639, NA-UK.

107. FCO, British Embassy, Doha, to British Embassy, Muscat, letter, September 16, 1984.

108. FCO, Julian Walker, British Ambassador, Doha, to FCO Middle East Department, letter, March 27, 1985, ref. 8/5960, NA-UK.

109. "Qatar Conditions Gasline to Turkey On European Purchase Commitments," *Platts Oilgram News* 63, no. 113 (June 12, 1985).

110. Kieran Patton, "Qatar: Markets for New Gas Sought," *An-Nahar Arab Report & Memo*, June 7, 1985.

111. FCO, Julian Walker, British Ambassador, Doha, to FCO Middle East Department, letter, April 15, 1985, ref. 8/5960, NA-UK.

112. FCO, FCO Middle East Department to British Ambassador, Doha, letter, May 1, 1985, ref. 8/5960, NA-UK.

113. Richard Schofield, *Territorial Foundations of the Gulf States* (London: UCL Press, 1994), 209.

114. FCO, FCO Middle East Department to British Ambassador, Doha letter, May 1, 1985.

115. FCO, FCO Middle East Department, note on meeting with Mr. J. F. Walker, Ambassador-Designate to Qatar, September 5, 1984, ref. 8/5641, NA-UK.

116. "Qatari Budget Deficit Increases, Revenues Fall," *MEES* 28, no. 29 (April 29, 1985).

117.   "QGPC's Capital Raised by 25% to $1.37bn," *MEES* 28, no. 30 (May 6, 1985).

118.   "Qatar Records First Current Account Deficit," *MEES* 30, no. 48 (September 7, 1987).

119.   "Current Account Deficit."

120.   FCO, British Embassy, Doha, to FCO Middle East Department, letter, March 5, 1985, ref. 8/5960, NA-UK.

121.   FCO, British Embassy, Doha, Al Thani Allowances, November 4, 1985, ref. 8/5960, NA-UK.

122.   FCO, British Embassy, Doha, Al Thani Allowances, November 4, 1985.

123.   FCO, Julian Walker, British Ambassador, Doha, to the Secretary of State for Foreign and Commonwealth Affairs, letter, February 5, 1985, ref. 8/5962, NA-UK.

124.   FCO, Walker, to the Secretary of State for Foreign and Commonwealth Affairs, letter, February 5, 1985.

125.   FCO, Walker to the Secretary of State for Foreign and Commonwealth Affairs, letter, February 5, 1985.

126.   FCO, FCO Middle East Department, internal letter, March 20, 1985, NA-UK.

127.   Ali M. Jaidah, "OPEC, Non-OPEC and Cooperation in Pursuit of Price and Market Stability," *MEES* 28, no. 22 (March 11, 1985).

128.   "Saudi Arabia Warns OPEC Members on Consequences of Continued Production and Price Indiscipline," *MEES* 28, no. 35 (June 10, 1985).

129.   "OPEC Fails to Agree on New Quota Distribution," *MEES* 28, no. 52 (October 7, 1985).

130.   "OPEC Crude Output Tops 18mn B/D in November," *MEES* 29, no. 9 (December 9, 1985).

131.   Nordine Ait-Laoussine, "Oil Prices: What Next," *MEES* 29, no. 19 (February 17, 1986).

132.   "OPEC Production Tops 20mn B/D as Geneva Countdown Approaches," *MEES* 29, no. 42 (July 28, 1986).

133.   FCO, British Embassy, Doha, to FCO Middle East Department, letter, December 15, 1986, Economic Situation in Qatar, 1986 Jan 1–1986 Dec 31, ref. 8/6365, NA-UK.

134.   FCO, British Embassy, Doha, to FCO Middle East Department, letter, December 15, 1986.

135.   "Iraq, Jordan, Algeria Increase Foreign Bank Borrowing," *MEES* 30, no. 41 (July 20, 1987).

136.   FCO, British Embassy, Doha, to FCO Middle East Department, letter, December 15, 1986.

137.   "Qatar's Changes at Top of State Oil Company Linked to Inefficiency," *Platts Oilgram News* 63, no. 230 (December 2, 1985).

138.   "Details of Sohio's Production Sharing Agreement with Qatar," *MEES* 28, no. 39 (July 7, 1985).

139.   R. Mohan, "Qatar: Three Areas for Oil, Gas Exploration Opened," *Khaleej Times* (Dubai), July 2, 1985.

140.   Mohan, "Three Areas."

141.   "Qatar Signs Production Sharing Agreement with Amoco," *MEES* 29, no. 20 (February 24, 1987).

142.   "Production Sharing Agreement."

143.   "QGPC's Crude Oil Production Averages 306,186 B/D in 1985," *MEES* 30, no. 1 (October 13, 1986).

144.   "Crude Oil Production Averages 306,186 B/D."

145.   "Crude Oil Production Averages 306,186 B/D."
146.   "Crude Oil Production Averages 306,186 B/D."
147.   "Wintershall Offers to Finance, Develop Qatar's North Field Gas," *Platts Oilgram News* 63, no. 227 (November 25, 1985).
148.   Wintershall Offers to Finance."
149.   "Wintershall Consortium Seeks Arbitration over Dispute with Qatar," *MEES* 29, no. 31 (May 12, 1986).
150.   "Ad Hoc Arbitral Tribunal: Partial Award and Final Award in the Matter of an Arbitration Between Wintershall A.G., et al., and the Government of Qatar (Exploration and Production Sharing Agreement)," *International Legal Materials* 28, no. 4 (1989): 795–841.
151.   "Agreement Reached on Settling Bahrain-Qatar Reef Dispute," *MEES* 29, no. 33 (May 26, 1986).
152.   "GCC to Mediate in Bahrain-Qatar Territorial Dispute," *MEES* 32, no. 14 (January 9, 1989).

12. QATAR EMBARKS ON FIRST STAGE OF NORTH FIELD GAS PROJECT

1.   "Sakhalin LNG Has Top Priority over Other Import Plans, Japanese Tell Qatar," *Platts Oilgram News* 64, no. 61 (March 31, 1986).
2.   "Sakhalin LNG Has Top Priority."
3.   "India Offers to Buy Large Portion of Qatari LNG Output," *Platts Oilgram News* 64, no. 237 (December 9, 1986).
4.   "Amoco Offers to Produce Qatari Gas in Return for Share of Condensates," *Platts Oilgram News* 64, no. 143 (July 25, 1986).
5.   "QGPC Asks Bechtel to Do a New Study of First-Phase North Field Gas Project," *Platts Oilgram News* 64, no. 172 (September 5, 1986).
6.   "Qatar About to Embark on $950mn First Stage of North Field Gas Project," *MEES* 30, no. 29 (April 27, 1987). At that time, the author was the CEO of the firm.
7.   "Qatar Signs Agreement for First Stage North Field Gas Project," *MEES* 30, no. 33 (May 25, 1987).
8.   "Qatar About to Embark."
9.   "Bechtel Details Qatar Gas Work," *Platts Oilgram News* 65, no. 101 (May 27, 1987).
10.   FCO, British Embassy, Doha, to FCO Middle East Department, letter, December 15, 1986, Economic Situation in Qatar, 1986 Jan 1–1986 Dec 31, ref. 8/6365, NA-UK.
11.   FCO, British Embassy to FCO Middle East Department, letter.
12.   FCO, British Embassy to FCO Middle East Department, letter.
13.   FCO, British Embassy to FCO Middle East Department, letter.
14.   "Qatar," *Khaleej Times* (Dubai), September 12, 1985, 2.
15.   "Buyers Show Reluctance to Enter Into Term Volume Commitments at Fixed Prices," *MEES* 30, no. 14 (January 12, 1987).
16.   "Japanese Customers Agree to Pay Official Prices for Qatar Crude for February," *MEES* 30, no. 19 (February 16, 1987).

17. "Gulf Oil Ministers to Meet Again as Oil Market Deteriorates Still Further," *MEES* 30, no. 20 (February 23, 1987).

18. "OPEC Suppliers Face Tough Decisions on Prices" *MEES* 30, no. 21 (March 2, 1987).

19. "Buyer's Resistance Stiffens to Official Price Liftings," *MEES* 30, no. 22 (March 9, 1987).

20. "Buyer Acceptance of Official Prices Leads to Boost in Qatari Crude Output," *Platts Oilgram News* 65, no. 61 (March 30, 1987).

21. "Qatar Plans Deep Spending Cuts," *MEES* 30, no. 22 (March 9, 1987).

22. "Deep Spending Cuts."

23. "Increased Production in Oman and Qatar," *MEES* 30, no. 36 (June 15, 1987).

24. "OPEC Secretariat Report Highlights Confusion over Actual Production," *MEES* 30, no. 50 (September 21, 1987).

25. "OPEC 3Q Output Still High Despite Estimated 1mn B/D Drop in September," *MEES* 30, no. 52 (October 5, 1987).

26. "Qatar to Apply Market Price Formula for October," *MEES* 31, no. 3 (October 26, 1987).

27. "Japan's Miti Sets Quota Guidelines for Contract Purchases of Iranian Oil by Japanese Firms," *MEES* 31, no. 13 (January 4, 1988).

28. "QGPC Head Resigns Post," *MEES* 31, no. 15 (January 18, 1988).

29. "QGPC Entrusted with All Contracts for Oil and Gas Exploration and Development," *MEES* 31, no. 41 (July 18, 1988).

30. "QGPC Weighs Bids by 6 Investment Firms for Gas Project Advisory Role," *Platts Oilgram News* 65, no. 134 (July 14, 1987).

31. "Development Drilling for North Field Gas Project to Begin in August," *MEES* 31, no. 38 (June 27, 1988).

32. "QGPC Starts Drilling in North Gas Field," *MEES* 31, no. 47 (August 29, 1988).

33. "Qatar Set to Launch North Field Drilling," *Platts Oilgram News* 66, no. 156 (August 12, 1988).

34. "QGPC's Acting Managing Director Says Qatar's 1987 Production Averaged 293,000 B/D," *MEES* 31, no. 21 (February 29, 1988).

35. "Qatar's 1987 Production Averaged 293,000 B/D."

36. "Ad Hoc Arbitral Tribunal: Partial Award and Final Award in the Matter of an Arbitration Between Wintershall A.G., et al., and the Government of Qatar (Exploration and Production Sharing Agreement)," *International Legal Materials* 28, no. 4 (1989): 795–841.

37. "Ad Hoc Arbitral Tribunal."

38. "Qatar Government Issues Statement on Wintershall Group Arbitration Award," *MEES* 31, no. 38 (June 27, 1988).

39. "Qataris Explain Rebuff to U.S.," *Platts Oilgram News* 66, no.138 (July 19, 1988).

40. Elaine Sciolino, "Qatar Rejects U.S. Demand For Return of Illicit Stingers," *New York Times*, June 28, 1988.

41. John H. Cushman Jr., "U.S. Says Qatar Has Stinger, Raising Fear of Missile Spread," *New York Times*, April 1, 1988.

42. Foreign Operations, Export Financing, and Related Programs Appropriations Act of 1989, Pub. Law 100-461, 102 Stat. 2268 (1988), https://www.congress.gov/100/statute/STATUTE-102/STATUTE-102-Pg2268.pdf.

43.   "Qataris Explain Rebuff."

44.   "Aghazadeh Claims Qatar's North Gas Field and Other Gulf Offshore Fields Extend into Iranian Waters," *MEES* 32, no. 25 (March 27, 1989).

45.   "Aghazadeh Claims."

46.   "Aghazadeh Reaffirms Large Part of Qatar's North Gasfield Extends into Iranian Waters," *MEES* 32, no. 27 (April 10, 1989).

47.   "Rafsanjani Invokes Some Rightist Economics," *MEES* 33, no. 4 (October 30, 1989).

48.   "Prospects Improve for Future Qatar Gas Exports," *MEES* 32, no. 28 (April 17, 1989).

49.   "Prospects Improve."

50.   "Prospects Improve."

51.   "Japanese Customers Show Signs of Interest in Qatar LNG," *MEES* 33, no. 11 (December 18, 1989).

52.   "GB Syndicates Qatari Gas Deal," *MEES* 32, no. 15 (January 16, 1989).

53.   "Mid-East Foreign Debt Up 10% to $186bn in 1987," *MEES* 32, no. 18 (February 6, 1989).

54.   "Qatar Trims Spending and Budget Deficit," *MEES* 32, no. 26 (April 3, 1989).

55.   "QGPC Plans Gas Sweetening and Sulfur Process Units for North Field Gas Project," *MEES* 32, no. 44 (August 7, 1989).

56.   "North Field Gas Project Progress Cited," *Gulf Times* (Doha), January 23, 1989.

57.   "North Field Gas Project Progress Cited."

58.   "Qatar Plans for New Generation of Gas-Based Industries," *MEES* 33, no. 17 (January 29, 1990).

59.   "Qatar Weighs Options in Funding Gas PL," *Platts Oilgram News* 67, no. 243 (December 19, 1989).

60.   "Qatar Gas Supply Project was Main Topic for Discussion at GCC Oil Ministers' Meeting," *MEES* 33, no. 8 (November 27, 1989).

61.   "Prospects Improve for Future Qatar Gas Exports."

62.   "Qatar's Crude Oil Production Rises to 340,000 B/D in 1988," *MEES* 32, no. 27 (April 19, 1989).

63.   "QGPC Production, Term Contracts and February Prices," *MEES* 32, no. 19 (February 13, 1989).

64.   "Qatar's Products Exports Average 46,600 B/D," *MEES* 32, no. 37 (June 19, 1989).

65.   "Qatar Trims Spending and Budget Deficit."

66.   "GIB Misses Qatar Loan Mandate," *MEES* 32, no. 38 (June 12, 1989).

67.   Jill Crystal, *Oil and Politics in the Gulf: Rulers and Merchants in Kuwait and Qatar* (Cambridge: Cambridge University Press, 1990), 184.

68.   "Japanese Customers Show Signs of Interest in Qatar LNG."

69.   "Qatar Readies LNG Sales Pitch to Japan, but Development Issues Remain Unresolved," *Platts Oilgram News* 68, no. 6 (January 9, 1990).

70.   "Qatar Projects Higher Revenues and Reduced Deficit," *MEES* 33, no. 26 (April 2, 1990).

71.   "QGPC Invites Bids for Plugging Gas Leaks in North Gas Field Wells," *MEES* 33, no. 42 (July 23, 1990).

72.   "Qatar's New Offshore Oil Push Linked to Slow Start for North Dome Gas Project," *Platts Oilgram News* 68, no. 66 (April 4, 1990).

73.   "New Offshore Oil Push."

74. "QGPC Awards Design Contract for Expansion of Idd el-Shargi Oilfield," *MEES* 33, no. 42 (July 23, 1990).
75. "QGPC Awards Design Contract."
76. "Higher Revenues and Reduced Deficit."
77. "Higher Revenues and Reduced Deficit."
78. "OPEC," *Platts Oilgram News* 68, no. 53 (February 15, 1990).
79. "Review of QGPC's Operations in 1989," *MEES* 33, no. 23 (March 12, 1990).
80. "Qatar Contract Volumes for 1990," *MEES* 33, no. 12 (December 25, 1989).
81. "Iraq Targets $25/B Minimum Price for Crude," *MEES* 33, no. 39 (July 2, 1990).
82. "The Political Scene," *MEES* 33, no. 42 (July 23, 1990).
83. "The Political Scene."
84. Crystal, *Oil and Politics*, 174.
85. Lt. Col. Joseph P. Englehardt, "Desert Shield and Desert Storm: A Chronology and Troop List for the 1990–1991 Persian Gulf Crisis," SSI Special Report (Strategic Studies Institute, U.S. Army War College, March 25, 1991), 21.
86. "OPEC Crude Production Reaches Nearly 22.5MN B/D In September," *MEES* 34, no. 1 (October 8, 1990).
87. "Qatar Maintenance Said Deferred as Oil Prices Surge," *Platts Oilgram News* 68, no. 158 (August 15, 1990).
88. "Qatar to Begin Maintenance of Offshore Fields," *MEES* 34, no. 5 (November 5, 1990).
89. "OPEC Production Drops in January," *MEES* 34, no. 19 (February 11, 1991).
90. "Gulf War Leaves Oil Supplies Intact So Far," *MEES* 34, no. 16 (January 21, 1991).
91. "Oil Supplies Intact So Far."
92. "Saudi Arabia Maintains High Production Level; Plans Gulf Tanker Shuttle," *MEES* 34, no. 17 (January 28, 1991).
93. "Saudi Arabia Maintains High Production Level."
94. Englehardt, "Desert Shield and Desert Storm," 5–10.
95. Crystal, *Oil and Politics*, 184.
96. "QGPC Delays Start Up of North Field Gas Project," *MEES* 34, no. 20 (February 18, 1991).
97. "QGPC Delays Start Up."
98. "Shell Decides to Terminate Its Service Contract with QGPC at Year End," *MEES* 34, no. 24 (March 18, 1991).
99. "Qatar Plans Major Entry into World Gas Market," *MEES* 35, no. 40 (July 6, 1992).
100. "Bidders for New Qatar Oilfield Operating Contracts Are Pressing for Production Sharing," *MEES* 35, no. 17 (January 27, 1992).
101. "QGPC Merges Its Offshore and Onshore Divisions," *MEES* 35, no. 2 (October 14, 1991).
102. "QGPC Merges."
103. "Qatar Plans Major Entry."
104. "Occidental to Complete Diyab Production Facilities in October," *MEES* 35, no. 50 (September 14, 1992).
105. "Production from Diyab Field Averages 30,000 b/d," *MEES* 3, no. 50 (December 21, 1992).
106. "Elf Plans 20,000 b/d Production from Offshore Qatar by 1H 1993," *MEES* 35, no. 18 (February 3, 1992).

107. "Maersk Oil Signs Production Sharing Agreement for Offshore Block No. 5," *MEES* 35, no. 39 (June 29, 1992).

13. ROCKY ROAD FOR QATAR'S FIRST LNG PROJECT

1. Kohei Hashimoto, Jareer Elass, and Stacy Eller, "Liquefied Natural Gas From Qatar: The Qatargas Project," in *Geopolitics of Natural Gas Study*, Program on Energy and Sustainable Development, Stanford University and James A. Baker II Institute for Public Policy, Rice University (December 2004), http://www.bakerinstitute.org/research/liquefied-natural-gas-from-qatar-the-qatargas-project/.
2. Hashimoto, Elass, and Eller, "Liquefied Natural Gas From Qatar."
3. "Qatar Awards Development Contracts for North Gas Field to Total and Elf," *MEES* 34, no. 35 (June 3, 1991).
4. "Contracts for North Gas Field to Total and Elf."
5. "Qatari Budget Pegs Expenditure but Forecasts Rise in Revenues," *MEES* 34, no. 29 (April 22, 1991).
6. "QGPC Starts Production from North Gas Field," *MEES* 34, no. 45 (August 12, 1991).
7. "QGPC Severs Services Contract; Three Former Partners Eye New Bid," *Platts Oilgram News* 69, no. 157 (August 15, 1991).
8. "QGPC Begins NGL Exports from North Gas Field," *MEES* 35, no. 19 (February 10, 1992).
9. "LPG/Condensate Production from North Field Totals 640,650 Tons in 1H 1992," *MEES* 35, no. 42 July 20, 1992).
10. "640,650 Tons in 1H 1992."
11. "BP Relinquishes Share in Qatargas," *MEES* 35, no. 16 (January 20, 1992).
12. "Qatar," *Platts Oilgram News* 70, no. 12 (January 17, 1992).
13. "BP Relinquishes Share."
14. Former Total executive, interview by author, December 12, 2016.
15. Former Total executive, December 12, 2016.
16. "Qatar," *Platts Oilgram News* 70, no. 38 (February 25, 1992).
17. Former Mobil executive, interview by author, June 27, 2016.
18. Former Mobil executive, interview by author, June 3, 2015.
19. Former Mobil executive, June 27, 2016.
20. Michael D. Tusiani and Gordon Shearer, *LNG: A Nontechnical Guide* (Tulsa, Okla.: PennWell, 2007), 260.
21. Former Mobil executive, June 3, 2015.
22. Pertamina, *Hands Across the Sea: The Story of Indonesian LNG* (Jakarta, Indo.: Pertamina 1985).
23. Pertamina, *Hands Across the Sea.*
24. Youssef M. Ibrahim, "54 Qatar Citizens Petition Emir for Free Elections," *New York Times*, May 13, 1992.
25. Ibrahim, "54 Qatar Citizens."
26. Ibrahim, "54 Qatar Citizens."
27. "Qatar Issues Decree Defining Territorial Waters; Bahrain Rejects It," *MEES* 35, no. 30 (April 27, 1992).

28. "Qatar Issues Decree."

29. "GCC Meet Overshadowed by Qatar Spat," *Platts Oilgram News* 70, no. 246 (December 21, 1992).

30. Paul Lewis, "Immovable Object: Granite Regime of Saddam Hussein Seems Little Worn by Political Storm," *New York Times*, July 31, 1992.

31. Richard Schofield, *Territorial Foundations of the Gulf States* (London: UCL Press, 1994), 18.

32. "Qatar, Saudi Spat Flares Anew; GCC in Question," *Platts Oilgram News* 70, no. 242 (December 15, 1992).

33. "Qatari Budget Sees Big Rise in Capital Spending but Pegs Recurrent Costs," *MEES* 35, no. 30 (April 27, 1992).

34. "Qatari Budget Sees Big Rise."

35. "Chubu Signing Will Boost Qatargas Plans, But Many Questions Remain over Financing for Qatar's Industrialization Program," *MEES* 35, no. 30 (April 27, 1992).

36. "Gulf Banks Grow Healthily but Grow Apart," *MEES* 35, no. 52 (September 28, 1992).

37. "QGPC Appoints Management Consultants for Ras Laffan Port Project," *MEES* 35, no. 22 (March 2, 1992).

38. Neil Hume, "Oil Producers Seek Liquidity from Prepayment Deals," *Financial Times*, February 6, 2015.

39. "Qatar Contract Volumes for 1992," *MEES* 35, no. 16 (January 20, 1992).

40. "QGPC Abandons Request to Roll Over \$400mn Loan; Repayment Due December," *MEES* 36, no. 6 (November 9, 1992).

41. Youssef Azmeh, "Qatar Set to Prosper from Natural Gas," Reuters, July 29, 1993.

42. Azmeh, "Qatar Set to Prosper."

43. Lou Noto, interview by the author, February 25, 2019.

44. Former Mobil executive, June 27, 2016.

45. "Mobil Enters Qatar Gas Scene," *MEES* 35, no. 48 (August 31, 1992).

46. "Mobil, Qatar Sign LNG Agreements; Second Deal Twice Size of Qatargas Scheme," *Platts Oilgram News* 70, no. 168 (August 28, 1992).

47. "Mobil, Qatar Sign LNG Agreements."

48. Former Mobil executive, June 27, 2016.

49. "Mobil, Qatar Sign LNG Agreements."

50. "Qatar and Mobil Sign for 10mn T/Y LNG Joint Venture," *MEES* 36, no. 13 (December 28, 1992).

51. "Nelson Hunt Takes Stake in Qatar Plan," *Platts Oilgram News* 70, no. 173 (September 4, 1992).

52. "Nelson Hunt Takes Stake."

53. "Elf and Sumitomo Agree to Promote Qatari LNG in Japan and the Far East," *MEES* 35, no. 410 (July 13, 1992).

54. "Mobil Signs Qatargas Joint Venture Agreements," *MEES* 36, no. 19 (February 8, 1993).

55. Former Mobil executive, June 3, 2015.

56. Former Mobil executive, June 3, 2015.

57. "Four Banks Compete for Qatargas Financial Advisory Mandate," *MEES* 36, no. 2 (October 12, 1992).

58. "Joint Venture Agreements."

59. "OPEC's Vienna Agreement: So Far So Good," *MEES* 36, no. 22 (March 1, 1993).

60. "OPEC Crude Production Hits 24.8mn B/D in December," *MEES* 37, no. 15 (January 10, 1994).

61. Youssef M. Ibrahim, "OPEC Is Forced to Confront Life in Post-Cold-War Era," *New York Times*, September 19, 1992.

62. "Qatar Seeks Wider Upstream Involvement by International Companies," *MEES* 37, no. 9 (November 29, 1993).

63. "Wider Upstream Involvement."

64. "Wider Upstream Involvement."

65. "Wider Upstream Involvement."

66. "Wider Upstream Involvement."

67. "Gulfstream Resources Acquires Veba Oel's Stake in Qatar Offshore Blocks," *MEES* 36, no. 17 (January 25, 1993).

68. "Qatar Development Set," *Platts Oilgram News* 71, no. 138 (July 19, 1993).

69. Former Mobil executive, interview by author, July 1, 2016.

70. Former Mobil executive, July 1, 2016.

71. Wataru Aoki, "The Japanese Approach to Financing LNG Projects," Ltd Tokyo, Japan (presentation, first Doha Conference on Natural Gas, March 13–15, 1995).

72. "Qatargas Finalizes $2Bn Downstream Loan Agreement," *MEES* 39, no. 2 (October 9, 1995).

73. Annual Report, 1995, Commodity by Country, Import, Trade Statistics of Japan, Ministry of Finance, p. 28.

74. Former Mobil executive, interview by author, August 9, 2016.

75. U.S. Embassy, Tokyo, to U.S. Department of State, Washington, cable, March 16, 1995, in the author's possession.

76. "Financing for Qatar Proceeds on Four Fronts," *MEES* 37, no. 21 (February 21, 1994).

77. "Financings for Oman, Kuwait's PIC and Qatar Move Ahead," *MEES* 37, no. 16 (January 17, 1994).

78. "Qatar Seeks $250 Mn to Fund Equity Contributions to Major Projects," *MEES* 38, no. 4 (October 24, 1994).

79. "Qatar Loan Worth $300Mn Launched," *MEES* 38, no. 52 (September 25, 1995).

80. "Morgan Stanley Seeks Interest in Financing QAPCO," *MEES* 36, no. 31, May 3, 1993.

81. "QAFCO Signs Expansion Contract with Germany's Uhde and Italy's Belleli," *MEES* 37, no. 23 (March 7, 1994).

82. "Qatar to Maintain Project Spending Despite Budget Cutbacks," *MEES* 37, no. 37 (June 13, 1994).

83. "Qatar to Maintain Project Spending."

14. TOUGH LAUNCH FOR MOBIL'S RASGAS LNG PROJECT

1. "Seven Japanese Firms Agree to Purchase 2Mn T/Y of Qatargas LNG," *MEES* 37, no. 40 (July 4, 1994).

2. Former Mobil executive, interview by the author, July 1, 2016.

3. "Enron of the U.S. to Purchase Qatari LNG for India," *MEES* 36, no. 29 (April 19, 1993).
4. Clyde Haberman, "Israel Seeks Deal with Qatar on Gas," *New York Times*, October 29, 1993.
5. Amy Docker Marcus and Caleb Soloman, "Growing Mideast Peace Is Opening New World for Energy industry," *Wall Street Journal*, January 16, 1993.
6. Bloomberg Business News, "Baker and Mosbacher Are Hired by Enron," *New York Times*, February 23, 1993.
7. Mobil, memorandum, "Ras Laffan's Right to Market the Next 10 Million Tons of Qatar LNG," undated (circa 1994), in the author's possession.
8. "Price Differences End Eurogas LNG Venture," *MEES* 37, no. 20 (February 14, 1994).
9. "Price Differences End Eurogas LNG Venture."
10. "Turkey's Botas Expresses Interest in Qatar's Eurogas LNG Project," *MEES* 36, no. 22 (March 1, 1993).
11. Michael D. Tusiani, "Preliminary Report on Qatar," April 4, 1994, in the author's possession.
12. Peter T. Kilborn, "For Saudis, a $45 Billion City," *New York Times*, February 17, 1987.
13. Meeting notes, visit to Qatar, November 22, 1994, in the author's possession.
14. Meeting notes, Qatar.
15. Meeting notes, Qatar.
16. L. A. Noto to Dr. Jabir Al Marri, letter, November 22, 1994, in the author's possession.
17. Mobil, memorandum, "Ras Laffan's Right to Market."
18. Mobil, memorandum, "Ras Laffan's Right to Market."
19. "QGPC and Enron Sign Letter of Intent for Grassroots LNG Venture," *MEES* 38, no. 17 (January 23, 1995).
20. "QGPC and Enron Sign Letter of Intent."
21. Bloomberg News, "Deal by Enron with Qatar," *New York Times*, January 20, 1995.
22. Abdullah Ibn Hamad Al Attiyah, Minister of Energy and Industry to Mobil Oil Corporation, letter, April 15, 1995, in the author's possession.
23. Al Attiyah, to Mobil Oil Corporation, letter April 15, 1995. Korea Gas Corporation was initially widely known in Qatar by its initials, KGC, which later became Kogas. Documents from key government ministries and agencies were frequently available during this time, often leaked by secretaries and other low-level functionaries.
24. Lou Noto, former CEO of Mobil Oil Corporation, interview by author, February 25, 2019.
25. "QGPC General Manager Dismissed, Then Reinstated," *MEES* 37, no. 49 (September 5, 1994).
26. "Qatar Approves Production Sharing Deals With Oxy and Pennzoil," *MEES* 37, no. 52 (September 26, 1994).
27. "Oxy's Qatar Deal to Open Mideast Door," *Platts Oilgram News* 72, no. 187 (September 27, 1994).
28. "QGPC Awards Production Sharing Contract to Pennzoil," *MEES* 37, no. 42 (July 18, 1994).
29. "Yukong Lifts First Shipment from Maersk's Al-Shaheen Crude," *MEES* 39, no. 8 (November 20, 1995).

30.   "Qatar Plans to Raise Production Capacity to over 500,000 B/D by Year 2000," *MEES* 38, no. 33 (May 15, 1995).

31.   "Qatar Plans to Raise Production Capacity."

32.   "Qatar Plans to Raise Production Capacity."

33.   "Qatar Plans to Raise Production Capacity."

34.   "Qatar Plans to Increase Sustainable Production Capacity to 500,000 B/D," *MEES* 38, no. 41 (July 10, 1995).

35.   "Qatar Plans Major Upgrading and Expansion of Umm Said Refinery," *MEES* 37, no. 41 (July 11, 1994).

36.   "Arco/British Gas Acquire Interests in Gulfstream's Qatar Offshore Gas Field," *MEES* 38, no. 10 (December 5, 1994).

37.   "Arco Completes Appraisal of Arab B Structure in Qatari Offshore Block," *MEES* 39, no. 22 (February 26, 1996).

38.   Danna Harman, "Backstory: The Royal Couple who put Qatar on the Map," *Christian Science Monitor*, March 5, 2007.

39.   "Qatar's New Ruler Consolidates His Power with Prompt Regional and International Support," *MEES* 38, no. 40 (July 3, 1995).

40.   "Qatar's New Ruler Consolidates His Power."

41.   Patrick Cockburn, "Emir of Qatar Deposed by His Son," *Independent*, June 28, 1994.

42.   "Prince Deposes Father in Qatar Palace Coup," Reuters, June 27, 1995.

43.   "Prince Deposes Father."

44.   Cockburn, "Emir of Qatar Deposed."

45.   "Qatar's New Emir Appoints a Cabinet," United Press International, July 11, 1995.

46.   Richard H. Curtiss, "Qatar's New Ruler Breaks the GCC Policy Mold," *Washington Report on Middle East Affairs*, May/June 1996, 78–79.

47.   "South Korean Acceptance of Qatari LNG Price Formula Opens Door to Sales Agreement," *MEES* 38, no. 28 (April 10, 1995).

48.   Former Mobil executive, July 1, 2016.

49.   "Qatar Awards 3 LNG-Related Deals Worth $200 mln," Reuters, December 11, 1995.

50.   Status of Ras Laffan LNG Sale Negotiations, May 6, 1996, in the author's possession.

51.   Paul Hoenmans, letter, July 15, 1996, in the author's possession.

52.   "The Political Scene," *MEES* 39, no. 15 (January 8, 1996).

53.   "The Political Scene."

54.   Richard H. Curtiss and Andrew I. Killgore, "Abrupt Change of Ruler in Qatar Has a Precedent," *Washington Report on Middle East Affairs*, May/June 1996, 74–76.

55.   "The Political Scene," *MEES* 39, no. 19 (February 5, 1996).

56.   "The Political Scene," *MEES* 39, no. 22 (February 26, 1996).

57.   U.S. Embassy Alert, February 20, 1996, in the author's possession.

58.   Fax to headquarters regarding U.S. Embassy alert, February 20, 1996, in the author's possession.

59.   In a confidential profile on Hamad Ibn Jassim Ibn Hamad Al Thani written in 1985, eleven years before the attempted countercoup, the British government wrote of the former commandant of police: "There is a 'Hitlerian' glint in his eye. If one were looking for a potential leader of a coup, he is the obvious choice." The profile also notes that, as

commandant, Hamad Ibn Jassim Ibn Hamad was particularly critical of his cousin Sheikh Hamad Ibn Khalifa, then the commander-in-chief of the armed forces. See FCO, "Leading Personalities Report: Qatar 1985," Leading Personalities in Qatar 1985 Jan 1–1985 Dec 31, ref. 8/5960, NA-UK.

60. "The Political Scene," *MEES* 39, no. 23, March 4, 1996.

61. "Life Sentences for Qatari Coup Plotters," *BBC News*, February 29, 2000.

62. "Death Sentences for Qatari Plotters," *BBC News*, May 21, 2001.

63. "Qatar Seeks Funds Held by Deposed Emir," United Press International, September 23, 1996.

64. "Former Emir of Qatar Has Assets of Over $8Bn," *MEES* 39, no. 48 (August 26, 1996).

65. "Chirac Hopes to Meet Saudi King," United Press International, July 5, 1996.

66. "Details of Qatari Financial Settlement Remain to Be Negotiated," *MEES* 39, no. 57 (October 28, 1996).

67. Douglas Jehl, "Young Turk of the Gulf: Emir of Qatar," *New York Times*, July 10, 1997.

68. Mehran Kamrava, "Royal Factionalism and Political Liberalization in Qatar," *Middle East Journal* 63, no. 3 (Summer 2009).

15. FINANCIAL DIFFICULTIES MOUNT AFTER 1995 COUP

1. "Ruler of Qatar Alludes to Financial Problems," *MEES* 39, no. 8 (November 20, 1995).

2. "Al Thani Puts New Emphasis on Qatar's Gas Development," *Platts Oilgram News* 73, no. 136 (July 18, 1995).

3. "IMF Urges Fiscal Reform in Qatar," *MEES* 39, no. 43 (July 22, 1996).

4. "IMF Urges Fiscal Reform in Qatar."

5. "IMF Urges Fiscal Reform in Qatar."

6. "Moody's Assigns Sovereign Ceilings for Six Gulf States," *MEES* 39, no. 19 (February 5, 1996).

7. "The Rise and Fall of Mr. Copper," *Treasury Today Group*, November 2015, https://treasurytoday.com/perspectives/profiles/the-rise-and-fall-of-mr-copper-ttbigp.

8. "New Japanese Partners in Ras Laffan LNG to Sign HOA on 9 December," *MEES* 39, no. 62 (December 2, 1996).

9. "Moody's Upgrades Qatar's Sovereign Ratings to Investment Grade," *MEES* 39, no. 59 (November 11, 1996).

10. "Qatargas Agrees Three-Month Interim Price with Japanese Buyers," *MEES* 40, no. 2 (January 13, 1997).

11. "ADNOC Benefits from Success of Initial Thamama Condensate Sales Campaign," *MEES* 40, no. 3 (January 20, 1997).

12. "Spain's Enagas to Purchase up to 13 Cargoes of LNG from Qatargas," *MEES* 40, no. 20 (May 19, 1997).

13. "Japanese Eximbank in $550 Million Loan to Qatargas," *MEES* 39, no. 45 (August 5, 1996).

14. "Qatar Launches LNG Industry with 10.8Mn Tons/Year Sales Contract to Japan and South Korea," *MEES* 40, no. 9 (March 3, 1997).

15. Meeting with KGC, memorandum to file, December 12, 1996, in the author's possession.

16. Notes, meetings with Kogas, January 29, 1997, in the author's possession.

17.   Former Mobil executive, interview by author, August 9, 2016.

18.   Mobil, letter to Michael Tusiani, January 29, 1997, in the author's possession.

19.   Robert J. Minyard and Michael O. Strode, "Project Financing Knits Parts of Costly LNG Supply Chain," *Oil and Gas Journal* 95, no. 22 (June 2, 1997).

20.   "Moody's and S&P Rate Ras Laffan and QGPC," *MEES* 39, no. 61 (December 2, 1996).

21.   "Ras Laffan LNG Bond Issue," *MEES* 39, no. 64 (December 16, 1996).

22.   Henry T. Azzam, *The Emerging Arab Capital Markets: Investment Opportunities in Relatively Underplayed Markets* (Oxon: Routledge, 2013), 76–77.

23.   "Ras Laffan LNG Bond Issue."

24.   "Ras Laffan Financing Finalized," *MEES* 40, no. 1 (January 6, 1997).

25.   "Moody's Puts Ras Laffan Bonds on Review for Possible Downgrade," *MEES* 40, no. 9 (March 3, 1997).

26.   "Foreign Partners Fill the Gas as Buyers Shun Floor Prices in Mideast LNG Sales Contracts," *MEES* 40, no. 15 (April 14, 1997).

27.   "Foreign Partners Fill the Gas."

28.   "Foreign Partners Fill the Gas."

29.   Mansoor Dailami and Robert Hauswald, "Credit-Spread Determinants and Interlocking Contracts: A Study of the RasGas Project," *Journal of Financial Economics* 86, no. 1 (October 2007).

30.   Korea Gas Corporation (Kogas), Negotiations Update, April 7, 1997, in the author's possession.

31.   Reuters News Service, "Enron Seeks Arbitration to Settle India Power Plant Conflict," *Los Angeles Times*, August 7, 1995.

32.   Minority Staff, Committee on Government Reform, "Background on Enron's Dabhol Power Project," U.S. House of Representatives, February 22, 2002.

33.   Gonen Segev was convicted of drug smuggling and credit card fraud in 2005, and in 2019 he was sentenced by the Jerusalem District Court to eleven years in prison for spying for Iran. See Yonah Jeremy Bob, "Gonen Segev, Ex-Minister, Gets 11 Years in Jail for Spying for Iran," *Jerusalem Post*, February 27, 2019.

34.   "Israel, Qatar Natural Gas Deal in Doubt," Reuters, October 10, 1996.

35.   "Qatari LNG Sales to Israel Will Depend on Success of Peace Talks: Otherwise Supplies Will Go to India," *MEES* 39, no. 56 (October 21, 1996).

36.   Enron Development Corporation, "Terms of Reference for Restructured QGPC/Ras Laffan/Enron Joint Venture," letter, January 26, 1997, in the author's possession.

37.   Enron Development Corporation, "Terms of Reference."

38.   Mobil Oil Qatar Inc., "Comments on Enron's Proposal for Participation in Ras Laffan," January 29, 1997, in the author's possession.

39.   Mobil Oil Qatar Inc, "Comments."

40.   *Enron Qatar LNG Project Technical Status Report*, 1996, in the author's possession.

41.   *Enron Qatar LNG Project.*

42.   *Enron Qatar LNG Project.*

43.   Former QGPC official, interview by author, January 15, 2019.

44.   Former QGPC official, interview.

45.   "Qatar Cancels LNG Deal with Enron," *MEES* 42, no. 12 (March 22, 1999).

46. Lou Noto to Abdullah Ibn Hamad Al Attiyah, letter, March 25, 1999, in the author's possession.

47. "RasGas to Gain Extension at Qatari Field," *Platts Oilgram News* 77, no. 125 (July 1, 1999).

48. Bloomberg News, "Enron and Qatar Cancel a Gas Project," *New York Times*, March 20, 1999.

49. Lou Noto, former CEO of Mobil Oil Corporation, interview by author, February 25, 2019.

50. Abdullah Al Attiyah, "Qatar's Energy Policy and Future Trends," *MEES* 40, no. 39 (September 29, 1997).

51. "Qatar's Crude Production Capacity Is Projected to Top 707,000 B/D by 2000," *MEES* 39, no. 35 (May 27, 1996).

52. "Qatar's Production Capacity to Ride to 854,000 B/D at End-1999," *MEES* 41, no. 24 (June 15, 1998).

53. Condensate Exports from RasGas LNG Venture Set to Start in April," *MEES* 42, no. 9 (March 1, 1999).

54. "Qatar Approves $10/B Based Austerity Budget," *MEES* 42, no. 14 (April 5, 1999).

55. "$10/B Based Austerity Budget."

56. U.S. Embassy Doha to Department of Commerce, "GOQ Solicits Massive Charitable Contributions from International Oil Companies: May Signal a Troubling Shift in Qatar's Energy Sector," Wikileaks Cable, dated April 9, 2008. https://wikileaks.org/plusd /cables/08DOHA286_a.html.

57. "QP Considers Next Step for North Field," *MEES* 56, no. 6 (February 8, 2013).

58. According to *Investopedia*, "a monoline insurance company is an insurance company that provides guarantees to issuers, often in the form of credit wraps that enhance the credit of the issuer. . . . Issuers . . . will often go to monoline insurance companies to either boost the rating one of their debt issues or to ensure that a debt issue does not become downgraded." For further information, see Julia Kagan, "Monoline Insurance Company," *Investopedia*, July 24, 2021, https://www.investopedia.com/terms/m/monolineinsurance .asp.

59. "QGPC Mandates Eight-Bank Consortium for $400Mn Tranche 2 of NGL-4," *MEES* 33, no. 14 (April 3, 2000).

60. "Qatar's Refinery Expansion Inaugurated as Oil/Gas/GTL Projects Proliferate," *MEES* 45, no. 3 (January 21, 2002).

61. "Qatar's Refinery Expansion Inaugurated."

62. "Qatari 1997 Banking Profits Up 16.5%," *MEES* 41, no. 38 (September 21, 1998); and "Oil Producers Face Up to Declining Oil Revenues," *MEES* 41, no. 13 (March 30, 1998).

63. "Qatar to Approach Bond Market," *MEES* 41, no. 10 (March 9, 1998).

64. "Qatari Government Debt Stands at $69.4% of GDP in 1999," *MEES* 42, no. 21 (May 24, 1999).

65. "Oman Pursues Diversification Strategy as Oil Prices Rebound," *MEES* 42, no. 46 (November 15, 1999).

66. "$10/B Based Austerity Budget."

67. "Qatar Approves FY2001–02 Budget with Surplus of $137Mn as Gas Sales Take Off," *MEES* 44, no. 15 (April 9, 2001).

68.   "ESCWA External Debt Trends Downwards in 2000," *MEES* 44, no. 52 (December 17, 2001).

69.   "Moody's Says Qatar's Stable Outlook Based on Vast Energy Resources and Diversification," *MEES* 45, no. 8 (February 25, 2002).

EPILOGUE

1.   Jessica Jaganathan, "Australia Grabs World's Biggest LNG Exporter Crown from Qatar in Nov," Reuters, December 9, 2018, https://www.reuters.com/article/us-australia-qatar-lng/australia-grabs-worlds-biggest-lng-exporter-crown-from-qatar-in-nov-idUSKBN1O907N.

2.   "U.S. Becomes Top LNG Exporter in First Half of 2022—EIA," Reuters, July 25, 2022, https://www.reuters.com/business/energy/us-becomes-top-lng-exporter-first-half-2022-eia-2022-07-25/.

3.   Gerald Butt, "Qatar's Foot off the Brake," *Petroleum Economist*, June 20, 2017, https://www.petroleum-economist.com/articles/upstream/exploration-production/2017/qatars-foot-off-the-brake.

4.   "Qatar Delays Start of Three Proposed GTL Projects," *MEES* 48, no. 18 (May 2, 2005); and "Qatar Restarts Gas Expansion Plans as Iranian Output of Shared Field Sours," *MEES* 60, no. 14 (April 7, 2017).

5.   Butt, "Qatar's Foot."

6.   "Iran Says Gas Production at South Pars Hits 610 mln Cubic Meters per Day," Reuters, February 6, 2019, https://www.reuters.com/article/idUSL5N2017FW.

7.   "Iran Unveils 10 Year Upstream Investment Plan," *MEES* 64, no. 48 (December 3, 2021).

8.   "Building on Resilience: QP Chief Talks Embargo & LNG Plans with MEES," *MEES* 60, no. 49 (December 8, 2017).

9.   Joint U.S. Embassy Riyadh–U.S. Embassy Abu Dhabi, "What's Behind the UAE-Saudi Border Dispute," Wikileaks Cable, dated September 10, 2005, https://wikileaks.org/plusd/cables/05ABUDHABI3851_a.html.

10.   Saudi Arabia and the United Arab Emirates, "Agreement on the Delimitation of Boundaries (with Exchange of Letters and Map)," signed on August 21, 1974 (Jeddah, Saudi Arabia), *Treaty Series: Treaties and International Agreements Registers or Filed and Recorded with the Secretariat of the United Nations* 1733, no. 30250 (1993): 23–41, https://treaties.un.org/doc/publication/unts/volume%201733/i-30250.pdf.

11.   Joint U.S. Embassy Riyadh–U.S. Embassy Abu Dhabi, "What's Behind the UAE-Saudi Border Dispute."

12.   Matt Smith, "How Is Qatar Coping with Its Economic Embargo?" *BBC News*, January 10, 2019, https://www.bbc.com/news/business-46795696.

13.   Smith, "How Is Qatar Coping."

14.   "Qatar Repeats with $1.2bn Bond Issuance," *MEES* 62, no. 10 (March 8, 2019).

15.   Davide Barbuscia, "Qatar Expects $9.5 Billion Deficit Next Year on Lower Revenues," Reuters, December 10, 2020, https://www.reuters.com/article/qatar-budget-int/qatar-expects-9-5-billion-deficit-next-year-on-lower-revenues-idUSKBN28K1DE.

16. "Qatar Unveils Overly Conservative 2022 Budget," *MEES* 64, no. 49 (December 10, 2021).

17. "Building on Resilience."

18. Qatar Petroleum, "Qatar Petroleum Increases LNG Production Capacity from 77 to 110 Million Tons Annually," press release, September 26, 2018.

19. "Qatar Brings Major Players Into LNG Expansion," *MEES* 65, no. 25 (June 24, 2022).

20. QatarEnergy, "QatarEnergy Awards Final Major North Field East Project EPC Contract," news release, April 28, 2022, https://www.qatarenergy.qa/en/MediaCenter/Pages/newsdetails.aspx?ItemId=3711.

21. "China in Talks with Qatar for Gas Stakes Worth Billions," *Bloomberg*, June 17, 2022, https://www.bloomberg.com/news/articles/2022-06-17/china-in-talks-with-qatar-for-gas-field-stakes-reuters-says.

22. U.S. Energy Information Administration, "As of 2021, China Imports More Liquefied Natural Gas Than Any Other Country," news release, May 2, 2022, https://www.eia.gov/todayinenergy/detail.php?id=52258#:~:text=In%202021%2C%20China%20imported%20more,according%20to%20data%20from%20Cedigaz.

23. *BP Statistical Review of World Energy 2022*, 71st edition, https://www.bp.com/content/dam/bp/business-sites/en/global/corporate/pdfs/energy-economics/statistical-review/bp-stats-review-2022-full-report.pdf.

24. "Building on Resilience."

25. Ben Hubbard and Stanley Reed, "Qatar Says It Will Leave OPEC and Focus on Natural Gas," *New York Times*, December 3, 2018.

26. Qatar Petroleum, *Annual Review 2016*, https://www.qatarenergy.qa/en/MediaCenter/Publications/QP%20Annual%20Review%202016%20-%20English.pdf.

27. QatarEnergy, *2020 Annual Review*, https://www.qatarenergy.qa/en/MediaCenter/Publications/QatarEnergy%20Annual%20Review%202020%20-%20English.pdf#search=annual%20report.

28. Pratap John, "Qatar to Raise LNG Production Capacity to 126mn Tonnes a Year by 2027," *Gulf Times*, November 25, 2019, https://www.gulf-times.com/story/648555/Qatar-to-raise-LNG-production-capacity-to-126mn-tonnes-a-year-by-2027.

29. QatarEnergy, *2020 Annual Review*.

30. "Building on Resilience."

31. Emirates News Agency, "No Concession Awarded to Qatar Petroleum," March 13, 2018, http://wam.ae/en/details/1395302674138.

32. QatarEnergy, *2020 Annual Review*.

33. QatarEnergy, "QatarEnergy Wins Working Interest In A Large Oil Field in Brazil," news release, December 17, 2021, https://www.qatarenergy.qa/en/MediaCenter/Pages/newsdetails.aspx?ItemId=3697.

34. QatarEnergy, "QatarEnergy and Partners Announce Oil Discovery Offshore Namibia," news release, February 4, 2022, https://www.qatarenergy.qa/en/MediaCenter/Pages/newsdetails.aspx?ItemId=3699.

35. "Building on Resilience."

36. U.S. Energy Information Administration, "U.S. Natural Gas Production Hit a New Record High in 2018," *Today in Energy* news release, March 14, 2019, https://www.eia.gov/todayinenergy/detail.php?id=38692.

37. U.S Energy Information Administration, "The United States Became the World's Largest LNG Exporter in the First Half of 2022," *Today in Energy* news release, July 25, 2022, https://www.eia.gov/todayinenergy/detail.php?id=53159#:~:text=The%20United%20States%20became%20the%20world's%20largest%20liquefied%20natural%20gas,day%20(Bcf%2Fd).

38. "Public Notice: Golden Pass Products LNG Export Project," notice of proposed construction and operation of liquefied natural gas export facilities and interstate natural gas pipeline facilities, http://goldenpassproducts.com/assets/docs/Filings.Orders/GPPFERCPublicNotice.pdf.

39. Federal Energy Regulatory Commission, Docket No. CP14-517-000, filed by Golden Pass Products LLC on July 7, 2014.

40. U.S. Energy Information Administration, U.S. Liquefaction Capacity.

41. Rania El Gamal, Eric Knecht, and Dmitry Zhdannikov, "Qatar Petroleum to Invest $20 Billion in U.S. in Major Expansion," Reuters, December 16, 2018, https://www.reuters.com/article/us-qatar-gas-qp/qatarpetroleum-to-invest-20-billion-in-us-in-major-expansion-idUSKBN1OF07X.

42. "Exxon, Qatar in Talks for Potential U.S. Shale Gas Deal: Report," Reuters, April 10, 2018, https://www.reuters.com/article/us-exxon-mobil-qatar/exxon-qatar-in-talks-for-potential-u-s-shale-gas-dealreport-idUSKBN1HH1R0.

43. "Building on Resilience."

Bibliography

Ahrari, Mohammed E. *OPEC: The Failing Giant.* Lexington: University Press of Kentucky, 1986.

Al Thani, Mohamed Ibn Ahmad Ibn Jabir. *The Arab Spring & the Gulf States: Time to Embrace Change.* London: Profile, 2012.

—. *Jassim the Leader: Founder of Qatar.* London: Profile, 2012.

Al-Othman, Nasser. *With Their Bare Hands: The Story of the Oil Industry in Qatar.* Essex: Longman, 1984.

Anscombe, Frederick F. *The Ottoman Gulf: The Creation of Kuwait, Saudi Arabia and Qatar.* New York: Columbia University Press, 1997.

Brewer, Lynn, with Matthew Scott Hansen, *Confessions of an Enron Executive: A Whistleblower's Story.* Bloomington, Ind.: AuthorHouse, 2004.

Bryce, Robert. *Pipe Dreams: Greed, Ego, and the Death of Enron.* New York: PublicAffairs, 2002.

Chisholm, Archibald H. T. *The First Kuwait Oil Concession Agreement: A Record of the Negotiations, 1911–1934.* London: Frank Cass, 1975.

Collins, R. Thomas, Jr. *White Monkey: A Journey Upstream.* Oakton, Va.: RavensYard, 2003.

Crystal, Jill. *Oil and Politics in the Gulf: Rulers and Merchants in Kuwait and Qatar.* Cambridge: Cambridge University Press, 1990.

El Mallakh, Ragaei. *Qatar: Development of an Oil Economy.* London: Croom Helm, 1979.

Field, Michael. *The Merchants: The Big Business Families of Arabia.* London: John Murray, 1984.

Fromherz, Allen J. *Qatar: A Modern History.* Washington, D.C.: Georgetown University Press, 2012.

Gray, Matthew. *Qatar: Politics and the Challenges of Development.* Boulder, Colo.: Lynne Rienner, 2013.

Hay, Sir Rupert. *The Persian Gulf States.* Washington, D.C.: Middle East Institute, 1959.

Joyce, Miriam. *Ruling Shaikhs and Her Majesty's Government 1960–1969.* Oxfordshire, UK: Routledge, 2012. First published 2003 by Frank Cass (London).

Kamrava, Mehran. *Qatar: Small State, Big Politics.* Ithaca, N.Y.: Cornell University Press, 2013.

Keating, Aileen. *Mirage: Power, Politics and the Hidden History of Arabian Oil.* Amhurst, N.Y.: Prometheus, 2005.

Longrigg, Stephen Hemsley. *Oil in The Middle East: Its Discovery and Development.* Royal Institute of International Affairs. Oxford: Oxford University Press, 1954.

Mehta, Abhay. *Power Play: A Study of the Enron Project.* New Delhi: Orient Longman, 2000.

Nafi, Zuhair Ahmed. *Economic and Social Development in Qatar.* London: Frances Pinter, 1983.

Pertamina. *Hands Across the Sea: The Story of Indonesian LNG.* Jakarta: Pertamina, 1985.

Schofield, Richard. *Foundations of the Territorial Gulf States.* London: UCL Press, 1994.

Skeet, Ian. *OPEC: Twenty-Five Years of Prices and Politics.* Cambridge: Cambridge University Press, 1988.

Tusiani, Michael D., and Gordon Shearer. *LNG: A Nontechnical Guide.* Tulsa, Okla.: PennWell, 2007.

Ulrichsen, Kristian Coates. *Qatar and the Arab Spring.* New York: Oxford University Press, 2014.

Ward, Thomas Edward. *Negotiations for Oil Concessions in Bahrain, El Hasa (Saudi Arabia), the Neutral Zone, Qatar and Kuwait.* New York: Ardlee Service, 1965.

Yergin, Daniel. *The Prize: The Epic Quest for Oil, Money, and Power.* New York: Simon & Schuster, 1991.

Zahlan, Rosemarie Said. *The Creation of Qatar.* London: Croom Helm, 1979.

Index

About the Authors

MICHAEL D. TUSIANI

Michael D. Tusiani joined Poten & Partners in 1973. From 1983 to 2016 he served as its chair and chief executive officer. He is currently chairman emeritus. During his career he has been active in all aspects of oil and gas trading and transportation. He has written numerous articles and five books on energy and shipping matters: *The Petroleum Shipping Industry: A Nontechnical Overview* (Penn Well, 1966); *The Petroleum Shipping Industry: Operations and Practices* (Penn Well, 1966); *LNG: A Nontechnical Guide* (Penn Well, 2007, coauthor); and *LNG Fuel for a Changing World: A Nontechnical Guide* (Penn Well, 2016, coauthor); and *LNG: After the Pandemic* (Penn Well, 2023, coauthor). He received a bachelor's degree from Long Island University and a master's degree in economics from Fordham University.

ANNE-MARIE JOHNSON

Anne-Marie Johnson has covered Middle East oil and gas for over thirty years, beginning in 1987 as an analyst in Mobil's Middle East Department. She switched to oil industry journalism in 1991 and never looked back. In 1993 Anne-Marie joined the *Middle East Economic Survey*, where she won the 1997 award for excellence in written journalism from the International Association for Energy Economics. At *MEES*, she covered Qatar's herculean efforts to monetize its expansive gas reserves through liquefied natural gas. It was during these years that she met Michael Tusiani, whose rolodex in the LNG industry was second to none. He convinced her to join Poten & Partners in 1999, where she edited the company's flagship LNG publication for fifteen years. Anne-Marie received a bachelor's degree from the University of California, Berkeley, and a master's degree from the Fletcher School of Law and Diplomacy at Tufts University.

Printed in the USA
CPSIA information can be obtained
at www.ICGtesting.com
LVHW072356260923
759391LV00014B/58/J